AMERICAN METHODIST PIONEER
THE LIFE AND JOURNALS
OF
THE REV. FREEBORN GARRETTSON
1752-1827

Freeborn Garrettson
1752-1827

AMERICAN METHODIST PIONEER

THE LIFE AND JOURNALS

OF

THE REV. FREEBORN GARRETTSON

1752-1827

Social and Religious Life in
the U. S. during the Revolutionary
and Federal Periods

INTRODUCTORY BIOGRAPHICAL ESSAY
AND NOTES

by

Robert Drew Simpson

Editor

Published under Sponsorship of
Drew University Library
Madison, New Jersey

by

ACADEMY BOOKS
Rutland, Vt.

ISBN 0-914960-49-0

Library of Congress Card No. 83-71532

Printed in United States of America

Copyright © 1984 by Drew University Library

Printed and bound by
Sharp Offset Printing Inc.
P.O. Box 757
Rutland, Vt. 05701

To My Family,
Source
of
Love and Encouragement

TABLE OF CONTENTS

ACKNOWLEDGMENTS

Any project of the magnitude of the Garrettson journals requires the support and assistance of many. I wish to acknowledge gratefully some of those who helped in its completion: my friends, Dorothy Simpson, Mary Wheat, Joy Bland, and Marion Schmitter, who helped with typing; JoAnne Simpson, who helped page the manuscript; the Commission on United Methodist Archives and History, which provided a grant which helped with some of the costs of typing; Ruth Schreiber, who compiled the index; the staff of the Drew University Library, especially Mrs. Louise Capron, and particularly the Rev. Dr. Kenneth Rowe, Drew University Methodist Librarian, and Dr. Arthur Jones, Director of the Drew University Library, whose arrangements, assistance, and continual support helped make the project possible. I wish to thank as well Dr. Megan Demarest Simpson, my wife, for her help in editing, as well as her unceasing encouragement. A special debt of gratitude is owed the publisher, Mr. E. Farley Sharp, a layman devoted to Methodist history, and by whose generosity this Garrettson material is being made available.

Robert D. Simpson, Ph.D.

Chatham, New Jersey
July 29, 1983

FOREWORD

Freeborn Garrettson was unquestionably the most competent native-born Methodist preacher in the American colonies in the founding period. Historians from Nathan Bangs in the 1840's to Frederick Norwood in the 1970's have acknowledged him to be, next to Asbury, one of the principal founding fathers of the Methodist Episcopal Church. Born in Maryland in 1752, Garrettson became a Methodist under Strawbridge and an itinerant preacher in 1776. In the Bicentennial Year of American Methodism we especially remember his Advent journey up and down the seaboard calling the preachers to a conference at Christmas in Baltimore where John Wesley's religious societies would be formed into an independent church. As sturdy as his given name suggested, there was much about the man to make his selection as messenger a happy and successful one. In some of his experiences he paralleled his fellows and in others he outstripped them. He had been converted under Methodist preaching after a frivolous and aimless youth. He had entered the ministry at the age of twenty-four, renouncing the world and obeying the edicts of a stringent conscience. Son of a prosperous planter, he inherited slaves, and after his conversion he had stood in the midst of his household at family prayer and declared the slaves belonging to Freeborn Garrettson to be free.

Nor was his conscience limited to the ethics of slavery. He was opposed to war. Although in sympathy with the Revolution, he refused military service and was often stoned, beaten and jailed. Yet from the time he entered the ministry of the Methodists in 1776 until eight years later when he was given his mission as messenger, Freeborn continued to preach without interruption, save those imposed by persecutions.

The esteem in which Garrettson had been held enhanced through the years and made his influence on the young church great. He had the prestige of piety and good connections besides, having married Catherine Livingston, sister of Robert Livingston who had administered the oath of office to George Washington. He had ably extended Methodism northward along the Hudson and Mohawk valleys in New York and beyond to Canada and Nova Scotia. Asbury made him a member of his famous Council and conferred with him often at his home in Rhinebeck, New York. When the governance controversy over how to balance the power of the Bishops with the power of the preachers in conference swept the church in the 1790's, Garrettson held back from any overt division of the church. But he was on O'Kelly's side in the debate of 1792. His clearly expressed views indicated that the reforms O'Kelly advocated were not the passing fancies of a lone agitator. Garrettson continued to advocate a "moderate Episcopacy" until his death in 1827.

Throughout most of his years in the Methodist saddle Garrettson kept a journal. Yet until now little of it has been available in print. Garrettson himself published a portion of it in Philadelphia in 1791 which contains an abbreviated account of his "experiences and travels" through June of 1790. Although three printings were issued in Philadelphia, two by John Dickins in 1791 and a third by Joseph Crukshank in 1792, copies of all three printings of the journal are very rare today. In 1828, shortly after his death, Freeborn's family requested the church's foremost historian, Nathan Bangs, to prepare a full-scale biography. Having access to Garrettson's journals, letters and other papers, Bangs sprinkled large extracts throughout his biography, which went through five editions from 1829 to 1872. In 1910 Ezra Squier Tipple used the papers, then housed in the library of Drew Theological Seminary of which he was President, as the basis for a fresh sketch of Garrettson's life and work. In the 1950's Robert Drew Simpson was the first to make full use of the extensive Garrettson collection at Drew University for his doctoral dissertation. But until now a full transcription of the journals has not been available to the scholarly community. With introduction, notes and commentary by Dr. Simpson, a leading authority on Garrettson, their publication together with a reprint of the 1791 "Experiences and Travels" is an important publishing event. Not since the journal and letters of Francis Asbury were issued in 1958 has so important a document of the founding period of American Methodism been published.

KENNETH E. ROWE
*Associate Professor of Church History
and Methodist Librarian
Drew University*

FREEBORN GARRETTSON—A BIOGRAPHICAL ESSAY

Scarcely more than a decade before Methodism was planted in Maryland, Sarah Garrettson gave birth to her fifth child on August 15, 1752. This son became one of Maryland's most celebrated contributions to the leadership of early American Methodism.

Freeborn Garrettson was born at a place called Bush River Neck. On current maps the place may be identified as a low, flat stretch of land extending into the northern end of the Chesapeake Bay. The Garrettson lands are now largely occupied by the Aberdeen Proving Grounds. Garrettson's parents, even in that early year, were third generation English settlers, rooted firmly in the traditions of the Church of England. His ancestors had been among the first to settle in the Province of Maryland, staking their claim on the west side of the Chesapeake Bay near the mouth of the Susquehanna River. The settlement came to be known by the family name, and as late as 1828 part of the family still lived there.

Though Garrettson's family made no claim to aristocratic lineage, they enjoyed above average economic circumstances. They owned considerable land, a farm, a store, a smithy, and a number of slaves. Their lives were comfortable, concerned with proper social, religious, and educational values appropriate to their status in the community. In 1773, when Freeborn Garrettson was twenty-one, his father died and he fell heir to all the family holdings.

As might be imagined, the Garrettson family actively supported the Church of England. Freeborn's mother, who died when he was ten, had been influenced by the preaching of the English evangelist, George Whitefield, as well as the Tennants. His father, John, was a churchman of considerable integrity. The combination of evangelistic piety and the established church traditions bore significant fruit in Garrettson's religious character and development. Even in early years he sensed a profound emptiness in his life. When his mother died, this feeling was sharpened. He later wrote, "I had none to take me by the hand and lead me into the narrow path."

Garrettson's education, although it hardly prepared him for his later ministry, was significantly above the average for his time. Since the family were farmers and landowners, he was trained not only in the usual elementary subjects but also in mathematics, bookkeeping, and surveying. At fourteen he was sent to a schoolmaster who introduced him to astronomy. His studies under this schoolmaster had important consequences, for the opportunity to contemplate the heavens and to be alone for hours stirred his philosophical and religious inclinations.

Garrettson left school at eighteen and by twenty was managing a farm ten miles from his father's home. Later, he looked back on this period as the time when he drifted the furtherest from any moral and religious influence. He remarked in his *Journal:* "I was as destitute of the power of religion as a hottentot. . . . I lived near a very wicked town. I kept company with the pleasure-takers about town . . . but . . . the Lord . . . began loudly to call me to repentance."

Such repentance and the religious conversion which inevitably followed became the watershed of Garrettson's life, the beginning of a veritable spiritual pilgrimage. How much this was so is uniquely revealed in his first manuscript journal for 1752-1777. Across the top of the Journal in very large letters he wrote: "a Journal of the Life of Freeborn Garrettson 'till his conversion." Like John Wesley's Aldersgate experience, Garrettson's conversion to the Christian faith became the focal point by which all that preceded could be interpreted and all that followed could be understood.

The journal kept in these earlier years opens numerous windows on some of Garrettson's more formative religious experiences. At the tender age of nine, while walking alone in a field, he became personally aware of the scriptural promise, "Ask, and it shall be given you." He ran to the house and told his elder brothers that he was to be very rich. Later, the same year, again while alone, he felt himself addressed: "Do you know what a saint is? . . . A saint is one who is wholly given up to God." He wrote, "Immediately I saw such a person, the most beautiful of any I had ever beheld, I . . . prayed to the Lord to make me a saint." This experience at such a young age seems incredibly precocious, and yet it suggests the tenor of his emotion and the sensitivity of his nature. His temperament seems akin to that of the mystic, for throughout his life he responded to dreams, visions, and strong impressions which suggested meaning and direction.

For this deep-feeling and impressionable child, the deaths of his mother, his sister Sally, and two family servants when he was ten were devastating events. As the bottom seemed to drop from his world, he showed increased signs of depression and melancholy. At this critical time he began his lifelong companionship with the Bible, being especially drawn to New Testament descriptions of the suffering of Christ. In addition, he turned to a deeper interest in the Established Church, attending faithfully. But this failed to satisfy him, and more normal adolescent interests diverted his attention. From the age of twelve to twenty he felt his life was superficial. In his opinion they were frivolous years spent in school and devoid of religious growth. In actuality those less serious years may have been significant factors in preserving his sanity.

Robert Strawbridge, the zealous Methodist local preacher from Ireland, must be credited with reviving Garrettson's dormant religious feelings. After one Methodist meeting near his home Garrettson and Strawbridge talked the night away. More and more Garrettson frequented the Methodist meetings, seeking a deeper religious experience. But before such an experience could be his, months of inner conflict and struggle lay ahead of him. Finally under the preaching of Joseph Pilmoor, one of Wesley's first missionaries to America, Garrettson experienced for the first time the moment of faith he had been seeking. When Francis Asbury arrived shortly after in 1771, he became Garrettson's true mentor and spiritual father. Asbury's influence and friendship were of profound effect. Garrettson's response after hearing him the first time was: "How does this stranger know me so well!"

Despite the faith experience and the nurturing presence of Asbury, Garrettson had not yet reached the climactic moment of conversion. In a continual state of emotional turmoil he cast about everywhere for help. He flirted with the Presbyterians and the Quakers. By June 1775, however, at age twenty-two, he had been prepared by an accumulation of influences for a decision. For the first time in his intense inner conflict he saw the possibility for peace. His description of his conversion struggle is classic: the call of the world and wealth was set over against a humble life of service. The closing words in that episode give the verdict: "Lord, I will part with all and become a humble follower of thine."

Once his decision was made, Garrettson vacillated concerning his loyalty to a particular religious group. After a period of profound inner searching, when he lived only on bread and water, he chose the Methodists. "Something told me," he wrote, "these are my people. I was so happy in the time of preaching, that I could conceal it no longer; so I determined to choose God's people for my people, and returned home rejoicing."

His first step as a Methodist was especially revealing: he freed his slaves. By this decision he seemed, in deliberate fashion, to repudiate his dependence upon his past life and means. In a sense when Garrettson freed his slaves, he freed himself. The actual record of Garrettson's Emancipation Proclamation describes the event. He writes that after leading his slaves in prayer, "it struck my mind, 'it is not right for you to keep your fellow creatures in bondage; you must let the oppressed go free!' . . . I paused a minute, and then replied, "Lord, the oppressed shall go free! And I was as clear of them in my mind, as if I had never owned one. . . .'"

The fight against slavery became one of Garrettson's primary crusades. He preached, wrote, and fought for abolition of slavery at great cost to himself. This issue provided a concrete means of expressing his spiritual conversion and pilgrimage. And his actions on behalf of the black people set the stage for a lifetime of practical, humanitarian service which reached ultimately into many areas of human concern.

Garrettson did not readily give himself up to the itinerant ministry. It was one thing to be a Methodist, but quite another to be a preacher. The Rev. Daniel Ruff, a Methodist preacher, threw down the gauntlet with an invitation to Garrettson to take his circuit while he was away on business. Garrettson accepted and his preaching experience strengthened his conviction. Doubts continued, but Ruff was obviously satisfied with

Garrettson's work, for he immediately dispatched him to open a new circuit. With these trial efforts over, Ruff insisted that he appear before the next session of the Methodist Conference for examination and proper licensing to preach. This was accomplished at the session in Baltimore in May, 1776. At the age of twenty-four Garrettson was for the first time officially listed with the Methodists. He arranged for a competent manager for his farm, and sold his store and blacksmith shop. The new Methodist preacher had cut the ties with the past, and a new career lay before him.

Garrettson's beginnings as a Methodist preacher were nearly coincidental with the beginnings of the American Revolution. The years of the Revolution, 1775-1784, were formative ones both for our nation and for American Methodism. But the war brought Methodism into conflict with national interests. In his person and his principles Garrettson objectified that conflict. His ministry in this period reflects the persecution Methodists experienced during the war.

The name "Methodist" in the colonies designated a set of newly-arrived British preachers who were propagating a British religious society. The Revolutionary mind naturally concluded that all Methodists were Loyalists. John Wesley's own anti-American attitude, as well as the behavior of some of his preachers, only served to justify such feelings. The British Methodist preacher, Martin Rodda, one of Garrettson's first traveling companions, was a case in point. Rodda on one occasion distributed the royal proclamation while traveling his circuit. The hostility resulting from this kind of behavior, together with the natural sympathies of several of the preachers for their own homeland, eventuated in the return of most Methodist missionaries to England. Only one remained, the incomparable Francis Asbury, who by 1778 was forced into retreat at the home of Judge White, an enthusiastic Methodist.

Freeborn Garrettson soon became Asbury's executive officer in the field. Since he was an American and thus free to travel, Asbury used him to oversee the Methodist work. But Garrettson's own position was soon in jeopardy on two counts: he refused to bear arms or take the oath of allegiance as a matter of conscience (this was true of most of the preachers), and he openly opposed slavery. Garrettson was threatened, beaten, and ultimately imprisoned. But as the Lord's Rebel, this defiant young preacher only drew more attention to his message and himself. More than once he was assaulted, even knocked from his horse. Once in Dover, Delaware in 1778, he fully expected to be hanged by a mob. He was saved by a local alderman who came to his defense. The alderman led him through the mob to a platform where Garrettson, undaunted, preached his sermon. Before he left Dover he had formed a Methodist society.

By 1779 when Garrettson finished his work in the Delmarva Peninsula territory, the Methodist membership in societies there numbered 1288, or about one-seventh of the total membership of the American Methodist Societies. This was remarkable considering the intense anti-Methodist sentiment prevalent in that area.

During 1779 the management of Methodist work rested chiefly upon Garrettson's shoulders, a fact usually overlooked by Methodist historians. Francis Asbury was still in self-imposed confinement at Judge White's home. It was simply not safe for him to travel. Garrettson remained in regular touch with Asbury, representing him in the general Methodist work. Asbury, for instance, asked him to visit Philadelphia. The work there was in confusion since the British army had just broken up winter quarters and withdrawn. Garrettson spent two months in Philadelphia attempting to strengthen the societies. Using Philadelphia as his base he pushed into other parts of Pennsylvania and New Jersey preaching ten or twelve sermons a week.

By the autumn and winter of 1779, Garrettson was back again in Maryland, especially working in Dorchester County. But by the early weeks of 1780 his conflicts with the patriots and the law had become more frequent. He faced regularly angry taunts of Toryism. Finally, on February 25, 1780, a company of men captured him and a magistrate sentenced him to jail in Cambridge, Maryland. No common court would try his case. Therefore he faced the prospect of a year in jail until the next general court would meet.

But assistance came from a rather unexpected source. An appeal was made to Thomas Sim Lee (1745-1819), the governor of Maryland. Under his direction a process was quickly developed for obtaining Garrettson's release. Although Garrettson was a Marylander by birth and property, he could likewise claim citizenship in the state of Delaware. Why this was true is not clear from his Journals, unless he owned property there. Since Delaware was more tolerant of Garrettson's behavior, he was taken before Governor Caesar Rodney (1728-1784) of Delaware, who was a friend of the Methodists. A letter from Rodney to Lee was all that was necessary to secure Garrettson's liberty. The incident represents a rather unusual use of the governor's power to deal with the process of justice.

Garrettson was released from jail only to face another major crisis. Threatened division among the Methodist societies loomed large. The dispute turned upon the question of administering the sacraments and rites of the church. John Wesley conceived of Methodism as a movement within the Church of England and insisted that his followers, whenever possible, receive the Sacraments and rites within the Established Church. He was not prepared for the American situation of revolution and the flight of clergy from the Established Churches. In response to the exigencies of actual circumstances, the Methodist preachers, especially in the South, began administering the Sacraments and rites among their followers. Increasing tension developed, for Asbury and most of the northern Methodist preachers opposed this innovation. Not only did it suggest an open break with the Established Church, but it also challenged the authority of both Wesley and Asbury.

The question of the administration of the Sacraments first emerged at the Deer Creek Conference, May 20, 1777. With no resolution, the issue was laid over to the next year. Even though the war prevented the northern preachers from attending, the southern men met anyway and decided among themselves to administer the sacraments until they met next in Conference in May, 1780.

All the elements of schism were present in this developing situation. On April 24, 1780, the preachers north of Virginia met in Conference at Baltimore. With firm resolution they decided not to continue in fellowship with the southern preachers unless they suspended all of their sacramental administrations for one year. At the end of this year, they would all meet in Baltimore to reach a final decision. Freeborn Garrettson, together with William Watters and Francis Asbury, was appointed the task of relaying this decision to the Southern Conference which was held the next month in Manakintown, Virginia.

The northern delegation had hardly reached the Southern Conference session before it became evident that the southern group was resolute in its views. Although Asbury himself presented the case and the conditions set forth by the northern men, the conditions were rejected and schism appeared inevitable. During the night, however, minds were changed, and the next morning the southern position was reversed. The southern men now agreed to suspend their administration of the Sacraments for one year and to meet in General Conference in Baltimore the next spring. In the meantime the problem would be laid before John Wesley, and his judgment would be obeyed. Wesley did rule, as expected, against the southern practice, and in April 1781 the General Conference unanimously agreed to follow his counsel. Methodism was saved a damaging division. In fact if this division had occurred, it is probable that the organization of Methodist societies in America into a church would have been delayed for many years.

Garrettson's more democratic and conciliatory manner was no doubt prominent in saving this difficult situation, for Asbury was noted for his more autocratic rule. Garrettson's key role in the critical deliberations spotlighted his persuasive talents. As soon as the Baltimore Conference ended, he was assigned the task of traveling the circuits in Virginia and North Carolina to help convince preachers and people of the Wesleyan viewpoint. But in moving south Garrettson moved into the vortex of the final battles of the Revolution. As he traveled down the dusty roads of Virginia, he traveled in the very midst of war. Cornwallis was harassing the people with his forces while the American army was in constant movement and counter-movement to meet the enemy. At one point Garrettson preached and lectured day and night within sound of the thundering cannon in the seige of Yorktown. Garrettson was in peril not only from military fighting but also from civilian animosity, for he was distressed both by the war and by the practice of slaveholding. His sermonic blasts against war and slavery kept him in constant danger and open to persecution.

During 1781 Garrettson traveled about five thousand miles visiting most of the circuits in Virginia and North Carolina, and he preached five hundred sermons. He represented Asbury in stationing the preachers and holding their quarterly meetings. Obviously his task of pacifying the Methodists regarding the sacraments and rites was successfully accomplished for it never had to be repeated.

In 1782-1784 Garrettson happily shifted his attention to home territory, the Peninsula country. As the black people drew his increasing attention, he preached to large congregations and formed numerous classes. In general as the war ended Methodism enjoyed considerable success among both blacks and whites. Time and again Garrettson preached to thousands. By May 1784 the total membership of the American Methodist societies had reached 14,988 with 89% residing in the South.

On November 3, 1784 Thomas Coke (1747-1814), together with Whatcoat and Vasey, arrived from England on a mission that would change the character of Methodism. Acting under the pressure and restlessness of the American Methodists, Wesley had dispatched his emissaries with plans to organize the American Methodist societies into a church.

Freeborn Garrettson was involved very early in the presentation of this plan. He met Coke on November 14 at Judge Richard Bassett's home in Dover, Delaware. After hearing Wesley's plan for ordination, he and the other representatives met with Asbury at Barratt's Chapel, Sussex County, Delaware. A general meeting to discuss the plan was scheduled for Baltimore on Christmas Day. Garrettson postponed his planned expedition to Charleston, South Carolina and, instead, set out immediately for Virginia and North Carolina. In the process of summoning the preachers to the historic Christmas Conference in Baltimore, this "Paul Revere" of American Methodism rode twelve hundred miles in six weeks. If he had been able to resist preaching, he would have traveled even farther. It was fitting that this man, who had entered the itinerancy as the war began, and had suffered persecution and imprisonment, should be chosen to herald the news of the Conference which would organize the Methodist societies in America into a united and independent Methodist Episcopal Church. In the formation of an American church, he saw his labor bear abundant fruit.

With the formation of the Methodist Episcopal Church, Thomas Coke promptly pushed other interests which proved a challenge for the new church. Nova Scotia, a harbor for American loyalists as well as English settlers, had become a fertile ground for Methodism. Thomas Coke laid that urgent concern on the Americans, and they responded with enthusiasm. Before it adjourned the Christmas Conference of 1784 commissioned Freeborn Garrettson and James O. Cromwell as the first foreign missionaries of new world Protestantism. Garrettson, along with eleven others, had just been set apart as an elder in the infant church. His first assignment sent him beyond the borders of his newly established country to Nova

Scotia. John Wesley called Garrettson's missionary efforts a "labour of love."

The voyage from Boston to Halifax in February, 1785 was a stormy and dangerous passage of thirteen days. The general setting and plan for the work in Nova Scotia is carefully described in a letter Garrettson wrote to Bishop Thomas Coke shortly after arrival.

"Halifax, 1785.

"*Rev. and dear sir*,—After a stormy and dangerous passage of thirteen days, we arrived safely, at Halifax, where we met with a kind reception from Mr. Marchington, and a few other poor sheep in the wilderness. As yet I do not know as much of the country, or the state of affairs, as I shortly shall, God being my helper.

"A few days ago brother Cromwell set sail for Shelburn. Brother Marchington has hired a house at ten dollars a month, that will contain about three hundred souls. I have preached five sermons. The number has increased so that we now have our little apartment filled. I cannot speak of any visible good, more than that they seem to hear with attention and solemnity, and I have joined a society of seven or eight members. Shortly after I came to town, I waited on the old rector. 'Sir,' said he, 'you are on a blessed errand; I will do what I can in assisting you. I desire to see the gospel spread.'

"The next day I waited on his excellency, the governor, accompanied by Mr. Marchington. I found him very accessible. After telling him my business, from whence I was, and by whom I was sent: 'Mr. Wesley,' said he, 'is a good man—a very good man. How long do you purpose to stay?' I told him twelve months, or two years. 'I am glad you called upon me: you have my approbation, and whenever you call for my assistance, if I can help you I will.' I could but humbly thank him.

"God willing, on Monday next I purpose to take a tour through the country, to collect, if possible, the sheep so widely scattered. I believe there are many precious souls who desire to hear us. I am well assured we shall have hard work this year; but who would not labour, and suffer in so good a cause. I bless God for health, and as great a desire as ever to do his blessed will, and spend and be spent in the best of causes. We shall, as the people are poor, do little in the sale of books. Indeed I expect we shall be under a necessity of giving some of the small tracts away. The travelling here is extremely expensive. The packet has no less than four or five dollars for carrying a person from Halifax to Shelburn, and as much to Annapolis or St. John's Town: besides long journeys by land to the different towns and settlements. I am fully persuaded that our voyage to this part of the world is of God; the very time when preachers of our order ought to have come. But if possible we must be assisted, for our preachers are left without horses, and but four pounds a piece. Next year I trust the people will be able to support the gospel. When I am more acquainted with the country, I shall send on another letter to conference. By the grace of God I shall do all that lies in my power to promote the Redeemer's kingdom.

"Dear sir, I remain your affectionate friend and brother,

"F. GARRETTSON.

"To the Rev. Dr. Coke."

Garrettson and Cromwell met with continued success, although heckling and persecution were also a part of their daily experience. The Methodist movement grew, churches were organized, and chapels were built. No social group escaped Garrettson's appeal. Whether in drawing room or dockyard, jail or poorhouse, he sought the people out. The work grew so extensively that a Conference was planned for Halifax in the autumn of 1786. Bishop Coke promised reinforcements from England. Coke's ship, however, was driven by storms to Antigua, and Garrettson was left with the chief responsibility for the mission.

In the spring of 1787, Thomas Coke requested Garrettson's return to the United States to attend the General Conference of the Methodist Episcopal Church in Baltimore. A plan was in the making to ordain Freeborn Garrettson bishop or General Superintendent of Methodism for the British North American provinces and the West Indies. Bishops Asbury and Coke both wrote urging him to accept. John Wesley apparently had devised the plan, and the Conference at Baltimore was expected to approve.

Here begins one of the first political mysteries of the new church. Even though Garrettson was not happy with the whole idea at the outset, he was persuaded over the next few months to accept. When the Conference opened May 1, 1789, the plan to ordain Garrettson a bishop was unanimously adopted. But then, without serious explanation, the plan was shelved. What happened cannot be determined. Garrettson himself was astonished. Two factors may have affected the situation: (1) Garrettson didn't really have a deep desire to sever ties with his homeland, and (2) the strong hands of Wesley and Coke, who were the instigators, may have generated antagonism. In any event the plan was abandoned.

Although Garrettson never did return to Nova Scotia, his interest in the work there continued across the years. His influence was far reaching. One historian observed that Garrettson's impact upon Nova Scotia was almost equal to that of Wesley in Great Britain and Asbury in the United States.

After the Nova Scotian plan aborted, Garrettson was asked to return to old familiar territory, the Peninsula. He did so for a year. It was a congenial time; the war was over, and Methodism was growing rapidly. As Garrettson traveled those fourteen counties in Virginia, Delaware, and Maryland, he was clearly at home. The contrast between this period and his earlier visits was marked, however, for now he was received warmly and enthusiastically where less than ten years before he had been beaten scorned, and jailed.

But Bishop Asbury had other work in mind for this pioneer preacher, missionary, and builder of churches—New England. Methodism had enjoyed little success in the strongholds of New England Calvinism. Asbury felt Garrettson's skills were needed. Since he had already visited Boston twice in his Nova Scotian journey, he was acquainted with the territory.

On his way to New England, however, Garrettson visited New York City and found Methodist work a shambles. In addition to the deplorable state of Methodist work in New York City and on Long Island, an almost untouched territory lay north of the city, up the Hudson River Valley. The plan to enter New England was shelved, at least for the time being. When the Conference of 1788 met in John Street Methodist Episcopal Church, it allowed Garrettson to marshal a corps of twelve young preachers. Garrettson was directed to enlist men who were "pious, zealous, and laborious." With Garrettson at their head, this group looked to the vast northern district bordering on the Hudson River Valley. The territory they were to evangelize reached to the Canadian border, and from the Berkshires to the headwaters of the Mohawk River.

Garrettson set out from John Street Church, New York, in 1788 for his first tour through this huge territory. Visiting the Dutch villages and hamlets as he went, he reached Rhinebeck, New York, where he was received by Thomas Tillotson, Esq., a prominent citizen. Garrettson preached the first Methodist sermon there in Tillotson's barn. Tillotson was an important contact for he provided an indication of a cordial reception for Methodism. But as important as this reception was for the encouragement of Methodism, it opened other doors which had far reaching significance not only for Garrettson himself, but also for Methodism in general. Tillotson's wife was the daughter of the wealthy and influential Judge Robert R. Livingston. During Garrettson's first visit, he met Mrs. Tillotson's sister, Catherine Livingston, and a romance developed which would culminate in their marriage five years later. As might be imagined, the complications and obstacles to such a marriage were many. The very thought of a member of one of the leading colonial aristocracy marrying a Methodist itinerant preacher brought opposition from every quarter of the family.

Catherine, born October 14, 1752, was the sixth child of Judge Robert R. Livingston and Margaret Beekman Livingston and was surrounded everywhere by wealth and prominence. Two of her brothers were men of national and international prestige. Robert R. was a leading statesman of the Revolutionary period, having helped draft the Declaration of Independence. He administered the oath of office to President George Washington, and was Thomas Jefferson's Minister to France. Another brother, Edward, among other offices of political leadership became Andrew Jackson's Secretary of State. Catherine was close to her family and especially her brothers. Their dismay in those early years of her courtship with Garrettson led one brother to say: "Catherine, enjoy your religion here at home all you please, but for heaven's sake don't join those Methodists; why, down at the ferry, nobody belongs to them only three fishermen and a negro." His sister replied, "Well, what if, as you say, now nobody belongs to the Methodists; I will join them and then you will say somebody does." Only the Tillotsons were encouraging, allowing their home to be a place of rendevous.

Through the Livingston connection Garrettson had access to several of the leading families in the Hudson River Valley aristocracy. To name a few is to appreciate the local as well as the larger acceptability afforded Garrettson and Methodism: brother Robert R. Livingston, first Chancellor of the State of New York; "Lord" Livingston, resident proprietor of the original family manor; the Van Ness Family at Kinderhook; Van Rensselaer, brother of the patron; John Jay, first Chief Justice of the U.S. Supreme Court whom Garrettson later converted to Methodism; Pierre Van Courtlandt, first Lieut. Governor of New York State, among others. Because these people eventually were very sympathetic to Methodism, the work went rather well. Up and down the valley, many houses, large and small, were gradually opened and several large circuits were formed before the first winter set in.

The entrenched Dutch clergy, of course, offered considerable resistance. Their brand of Calvinsim, which for most of them was a theoretical theological system, came into explosive conflict with the free-will, experiential religious faith taught by the Methodists. Prejudice against the Methodists spoke chiefly through rumor. The Dutch clergy suggested these Methodists were British agents come to incite another war, or with an eye to those less politically inclined, the story was planted that the Methodists threw blue spiders on their intended victims. Therefore they need be feared.

Garrettson kept careful watch on the work being developed by the twelve young preachers under his leadership. Among them were: Peter Moriarty, Albert Van Nostrand, Andrew Harpending, Lemuel Smith, Cornelius Cook, Samuel J. Talbot, Darius Dunham, David Kendall, and Samuel Wigton. Every three months he traveled the vast district. Practically living in the saddle as he journeyed about his territory from New York City northward, he covered on each trip about a thousand miles and preached a hundred sermons. One year's work, therefore, totaled approximately four thousand miles by horseback and four hundred sermons. But statistics cannot picture the nature of his travel experiences. Although there were comfortable homes opened, there were hundreds of untracked miles through virgin forests and high mountains. The rains, the snows, the heat, and the cold left them often scurrying for any shelter available, and often there was none. The lot of Garrettson and his associates was a rugged one. Nor can statistics record the unexpected and unusual experiences, such as the one that developed during Garrettson's first visit to Albany, New York, in June 1789. When he arrived in Albany, the legislature was in session. He sent a petition to the Speaker for permission to preach in the Assembly Room that evening. The subject was laid before the Assembly and after a debate that lasted throughout the day, permission was finally granted. That evening, Garrettson appeared in full canonical robes and preached his sermon. This is the only recorded instance of Garrettson wearing clerical attire. It may be that he felt this garb on this occasion gave validity to his clerical credentials as an acceptable representative of the faith.

This tour of the circuit closed with his return to New York City, his home base. Upon his arrival he found a summons from Bishop Asbury

to come immediately to Baltimore to attend the first session of the ill-fated
Methodist Council. Leaving New York late in November 1789, Garrettson
arrived in time for the opening session on December 11.

This Methodist Council was a brief unique administrative episode
in American Methodist history. Prompted by a rapidly growing church,
and the need for overall planning and supervision, the Council was intended to serve a four-fold purpose. Asbury envisioned it as a device (1)
to maintain general union in the church; (2) to maintain continuity and
pattern in the worship services of the church; (3) to correct abuses and
disorders; (4) to provide for anything and everything the Council might
see necessary for the good of the church. The Council's membership consisted of the Bishop and Presiding Elders of the church. This was the first
official use of the term "Presiding Elder," a term which in recent years
has fallen into disuse in favor of District Superintendent.

The plan for such a Council was uneasily received even from the beginning. It faced continuous opposition on the grounds that rather than
preserving unity, it threatened unity by strengthening the power of the
episcopacy. But both Asbury and Garrettson counted the first Council
session a success. Strong opposition, however, arose in other quarters of
the church. After the Council met a second and last time in 1790, the
whole plan was dropped from Methodist procedure.

Returning to his district, Garrettson planned a summer mission through
some of his territory, but this time his plans included a trip through Connecticut and Massachusetts, ending in Boston. Boston had been his original
target in 1788 when the opportunities in New York State captured his
imagination. When Garrettson's plans had changed, Jesse Lee had gone
to Boston in his place. This trip, therefore, appears to have been both
exploratory and supervisory in scope.

On July 1, 1790, Garrettson reached Boston. Although much impressed
with the elegance of the public and private buildings, he decried the ir-
religious spirit of the people. Their worldliness shocked Garrettson's Methodist sensitivities. Despite impassioned preaching, his attempts to move
the Bostonians were frustrated.

Garrettson's only trip out of Boston proved to be an historic one. Making
a junket to Providence, Rhode Island, he met Jesse Lee whom he charged
with the difficult mission to Boston and much of New England. At this
meeting Lee clearly agreed to become the Apostle to New England. Such
a strategy may, in fact, have been the purpose of Garrettson's visit to New
England in the first place.

By the time the New York Conference met in New York City in 1791,
the growth of the northern districts of the Conference required a division
in the work. The growth in the area which Garrettson and his young preachers had pioneered was nothing short of amazing. When Garrettson had
entered this area in 1788, four Methodist circuits had been named: New
York, Long Island, New Rochelle, and Dutchess. As this Conference as-

sembled in 1791, preachers rode in from twelve circuits. The additional ones were Columbia, New Britain, Cambridge, Albany, Saratoga, Otsego, Newburgh, and Wyoming. With the division of the Methodist work at this Conference, Garrettson assumed leadership for the northern-most nine circuits.

After 1791, the records for Garrettson's work are not complete. The journals Garrettson had kept for many years were published in 1791. John Wesley had urged him in 1789 to publish his Journals, but, unfortunately Wesley did not live to receive the published edition. The ship carrying Wesley's copy was lost at sea, and before another could be sent, Wesley was dead. After the Journals were published in 1791, Garrettson continued to keep a Journal describing his work, but there are significant gaps. Some of the gaps have been filled by materials supplied by the family, others have gained information from the history of the church. But from whatever sources, Garrettson's story after 1791 is able to be told and represents a significant and mature part of his ministry.

Although Garrettson's methods of church supervision continued much the same as they had been, his Journals evidence a growing concern with problems a church faces in the process of being established. For example, they record church building concerns and the discipline of wayward members who were being enticed by groups like the Shakers in Massachusetts. But the Journals reflect the larger, national concerns of a growing denomination as well. One significant concern, church polity, reached a crux in 1792. In the fall of 1792, Garrettson met Bishop Asbury, and together they continued to Baltimore to attend the first quadrennial General Conference of the Methodist Episcopal Church. The Conference, which opened on October 31, 1792, included all the clergy of the church. Garrettson's Journal offers one of the few known sources for this historic meeting.

The temper which gripped this General Conference was apparently in the making long before it assembled. Garrettson mentions that he and Asbury on their trip to Baltimore had numerous conversations about church polity. Evidently Garrettson was aware of the unrest created by Asbury's autocratic rule, for he wrote in his Journal: "We had some close conversation on church government. On this subject there is not a perfect unanimity of sentiment."

Apparently Garrettson was at odds with Asbury concerning certain matters of church rule, for on the second day of the Conference when James O'Kelly, the distinguished Presiding Elder from Virginia, recommended a radical change in church organization, Garrettson was firmly on O'Kelly's side. O'Kelly's resolution reflected the tension within the young church. It radically modified the appointive powers of the Bishop and gave each preacher the right to appeal his appointment to the Conference. The Conference, according to this resolution, would have the power to overrule the Bishop.

The first great General Conference debate lasted two or three days.

Garrettson helped lead the debate in favor of O'Kelly's resolution, and, for a time, it appeared that the resolution would carry the majority. But "the Appeal," as the resolution is known historically, was finally lost. As a result O'Kelly abandoned his seat in the Conference and his place among the Methodists.

Garrettson, willing to abide by the Conference decision, joined a committee to affect a reconciliation with O'Kelly and other recalcitrants, including William McKendree, a future bishop. Their efforts to pacify O'Kelly failed. O'Kelly returned to Virginia to found the Republican Methodist Church. For a time his group prospered and posed a genuine threat to the unity of the Methodist body.

Despite the schism provoked at this first General Conference, Garrettson, a veteran preacher-missionary at the age of forty, was able to view the church with affectionate warmth. Indeed, his appraisal seems almost too idealistic in the light of the discord and strife. Ignoring the harsh feelings, he wrote: "What a wonder to see so large a body of preachers gathered from all parts of the continent, and, like little children sitting at each other's feet, united as the heart of one man . . . all engaged in one common cause . . ."

The General Conference over, Garrettson returned to his own district and managed to press the Methodist work to its most westerly point at Whitesboro beyond Utica, New York. But as he returned home from his tour, his mind was filled with plans for marriage. Since their meeting in 1788, the relationship between Freeborn Garrettson and Catherine Livingston had grown steadily. The Livingston family maintained their strong opposition to this relationship, but Catherine never left Garrettson in doubt concerning her intentions regarding him. In open defiance of her family, she joined the Methodist church in Rhinebeck, New York.

Catherine's mother, sensing that her wishes were going unheeded, took desperate measures. She threatened her daughter with disinheritance, loss of property and loss of family position if she persisted in her relationship with Garrettson. But Catherine was not to be denied. The family finally relented, and Freeborn and Catherine were married on June 30, 1793 in the Methodist Episcopal Church in Rhinebeck.

The new Mrs. Garrettson was a woman of considerable stature in her own right. At the age of forty she brought to this marriage considerable potential wealth and acknowledged social position. As was indicated earlier, her brothers were all men of prominence in the early government of the United States. Like herself, her sisters married men of importance, two of whom, Montgomery and Armstrong, were generals in Washington's army.

Catherine's religious convictions were profound. Later in life she wrote an extensive religious diary, never published, which mirrors her religious emotion and expressions. Like her husband, her convictions led her to reach out in concern for others. The doors of her home were open to religious people of all classes. Among more prominent friends who followed her into the Methodist Church were the Robert Sands, Miss Rusten, and Mrs. Schuyler. She never ceased in her correspondence to attempt to convert non-Methodist friends and relatives. A striking illustration may be found in her letters to brother Edward Livingston, who was at the time Secretary of State in the Jackson administration. Her letters by-pass all matters of national or political interest, and go directly to the state of Edward's spiritual health and the matter of his conversion. Brother Robert equally was the focus of her evangelistic letters to the point that on his death bed he relented and professed a deep faith in the Gospel.

After their marriage, Freeborn Garrettson spared no time introducing his bride to his way of life. Very early in July 1793, they were off on a new assignment. Garrettson had been appointed Presiding Elder of the Philadelphia Conference. Bishop Asbury preceded them to the city and was preaching there when they arrived. Even before they arrived, however, news reached them that an epidemic of yellow fever had broken out. Despite the great risk involved, the Garrettsons continued their journey. Mrs. Garrettson pictured the situation: "How solemn is this place. The bell no longer tolls nor do the friends of the deceased follow to the grave except sometimes a few with timid steps at a distance from the hearse, holding handkerchiefs to their faces steeped in vinegar."

The Garrettsons fled the city, and remained some distance from the city for several months. Finally they returned when the epidemic subsided, continuing there until the spring of 1794. Their return to Rhinebeck was prompted by Catherine's pregnancy. Hastily they set about the task of purchasing a home—a new experience for an itinerant preacher. It was in a modest Dutch farmhouse in Rhinebeck that their only child was born in 1794. Eight days after her birth she was christened, Mary Rutherford. From the beginning she was handicapped by illness and as she reached adolescence was an obvious victim of scoliosis, a crippling curvature of the spine. Her physical handicap may well have been attributable to the age of her parents at the time of her conception.

But 1794 brought more than family interests and concerns. Garrettson was appointed Presiding Elder of the New York District, and for five years he traveled a familiar territory, including Pittsfield, Cambridge, Dutchess, Columbia, New Rochelle, Long Island, New York City, and Brooklyn circuits.

By 1799 the Garrettson family fortunes had risen sharply. Relinquishing the modest Dutch farm house, Garrettson built a substantial mansion on a magnificent property overlooking the Hudson River at Rhinecliffe, New York. The estate took the local name it had carried for generations—Wildercliffe, a name derived from the Dutch meaning "wild Indian's rock." Situated on the east bank of the Hudson River, the mansion's architecture reflects the Dutch influence. It commands a magnificent view down the river and also of the distant hills on the western shore.

But the Garrettson home became more than a family residence. It became a center of Methodist interest and activity, both locally and internationally. (Bishop Asbury, a frequent visitor, gave it the name, Traveler's Rest.) Still standing on spacious lawns that slope down to the river's edge, it remains a little known shrine of American Methodism.

With his family comfortably settled in their new home, Garrettson quickly returned to the very different life of the itinerant preacher. For this one year, 1799, he traveled throughout the Philadelphia Conference. The name Philadelphia is misleading, for the Conference reached well beyond the city. In fact Garrettson's District reached from Cape May, New Jersey to Newburgh, New York. The circuits in his charge were Salem, Burlington, Bethel, Trenton, Freehold, Elizabethtown, and Flanders in New Jersey, and Newburgh in New York. His visit to the church in New Providence, New Jersey prompted a description of him as "dignified, impartial, and firm; his preaching, acceptable, exemplory, and useful."

The New York Conference minutes indicate that in the following year, 1800, Garrettson returned to the New York District, where he worked for the ensuing years. In 1805 he was appointed the Conference missionary, an appointment which relieved him of supervisory responsibilities and allowed him freedom of movement within the entire New York Conference. He continued in this role until 1810.

In 1808 Garrettson represented his Conference at the General Conference meeting in Baltimore. It was an historic meeting for the church for at this session William McKendree (1757-1835), leader of Methodism in the West, was elected the first native-born American Methodist bishop. Freeborn Garrettson, who had nearly been granted this honor several years before, joined Bishop Asbury in the consecration of McKendree.

But this General Conference was historic for another reason. Garrettson's New York delegation proposed a memorial urging a delegated General Conference. This resolution, designed to create a more representative government for Methodism, made the session the most important conference since the Christmas Conference of 1784 founding the Methodist Episcopal Church. In place of a General Conference made up only of the clergy, the resolution recommended that each Annual Conference be allowed to elect one delegate for every five members to attend the General Conference. Garrettson, solidly behind the resolution, moved its adoption. Even though the original memorial was defeated after considerable debate, a reconsideration, restricting the power of the General Conference, did carry. Therefore, by compromise, Methodism took an important step toward more democratic procedure. It was not until 1812, however, that a delegated General Conference became a reality. Lay delegates were not admitted to General Conference until 1872.

In 1811 Garrettson returned from Baltimore to serve one final term as Presiding Elder of the New York District. For four years he traveled the territory which for so many years had been his primary interest. His Annual Conference in 1812 gave him the signal honor of being chief delegate to the first delegated General Conference of the Methodist Episcopal Church. He was elected to every such General Conference for the remainder of his life.

The 1812 session of the General Conference opened on Friday, May 1, in John Street Methodist Episcopal Church, New York City. Although Garrettson kept no Journal for that period, the minutes of that session reveal that he reported for the Committee on Administration of Doctrine, Discipline, and Practice. The report was evidently based on a section of Bishop McKendree's address which dealt with these matters, but the report has not been located. Garrettson was forever pressing for more democratic church practices. Nathan Bangs, Garrettson's contemporary, may have been hinting at this, as well as the major thrust of the report, when he mentioned that "though he [Garrettson] often differed with some of his brethren on certain points of church government, he always manifested the most stern and inflexible opposition to any innovation upon the established doctrines of the church; at the same time cheerfully bowing to the will of the majority on matters of indifference."

Garrettson was no doubt concerned with one other issue before this General Conference. There was considerable support for the proposal that Presiding Elders should be elected by their Conference rather than serve by Episcopal appointment. On this issue, which long divided the Conference, Garrettson remained clearly in favor of election. But his position never prevailed, and the appointment of Presiding Elders, or District Superintendents, persists as the order of the Methodist Church. It is evidence of Garrettson's personality and character that this man of wealth and authority always sided against Asbury and others in favor of a more democratic spirit and process. Quite the opposite might have been expected to be the case.

In the absence of any regularly kept Journals, the chief source of information for 1811-16 is the correspondence Garrettson carried on with his wife. The letters are of informal nature and represent the normal, personal concerns of a man for his family and affairs. One letter from Mrs. Garrettson dated July 25, 1812 reads in part: "Our people have been very diligent in the hay and are now mowing the orchard. The north meadow is only half cut and has already yielded twenty-two loads." In October 1813, Mrs. Garrettson wrote: "The sloop went last Saturday. I know nothing we want at the store but some coffee, a cheese, 2 pounds salt peter, 2 pounds pepper . . . Mary wants a small work trunk and four sheets of drawing paper."

Another letter recently discovered mentions Garrettson's interesting encounter with three American army officers, and reflects his attitude toward his own preaching as well as response to some of the social conditions of the time. Dated 1814 from Croton, New York, it reads in part: "I preached at Poughkeepsie last evening and started this morning at 4 oc and came to this place about 12 oc. Last evening after preaching

I was very poorly; but at present I am very well. It will not do for me to nurse myself much—labour is best for me. . . . Three officers from the lines came in the stage. Two of them were wicked in the extreme. I talked very seriously with [them], and they promised to refrain, and not hurt my feelings. One of them said, 'Mr. Garrettson, I read your Journal in England twenty years ago; my mother was a Methodist, and at that time I a serious lad, but I have lost it all, and now I can not reform all at once, but I will try, and not hurt your feelings . . . I was once,' said he, 'at a camp-meeting in your woods. I was courting a Methodist girl in the Jersey, and Lorenzo Dow happened to be in the place, and told her I was too wicked for her, and I don't know but he was very right.' I awfully fear our armies have very little of the fear of God . . . P.S. You know next Saturday and Sunday Quarterly Meeting will be at Bedford. I think I shall go by Mr. Jay's [Chief Justice Jay] and spend one night with him."

The New York Conference of 1815 left Garrettson without appointment at his own request so that he might remain closer to home. Why this was true is not stated, but his health seemed to be a concern in this period, and some physical problem may well have been the reason.

Years later Mary Rutherford Garrettson reflected that all that was dearest in life to her father in these later years lay at Wildercliffe. The life there was comfortable. His nephew, Freeborn Garrettson, Jr., managed his holdings so that temporal concerns were no burden. Actually it appears that the rugged itinerant was gradually accepting his position as an elder statesman of the church. This is not to suggest that he assumed a sedentary posture; on the contrary, Garrettson was by nature a restless, intense individual who saw his itinerancy as his "way to heaven." If he remained inactive too long, his guilt overwhelmed him. So by 1816 his pattern of life changed because of lessening strength, not because of determination. Semi-retirement was settling upon him.

At the age of sixty-four, with forty-one years of circuit riding behind him, Garrettson took seriously and vigorously his role as an elder statesman of American Methodism. In 1816 the Rev. Lyman Beecher (1775-1863), a prominent minister of the Presbyterian church and later President of Lane Theological Seminary, made a stern attack upon a large segment of American Protestantism. In a pamphlet entitled, *An Address of the Charitable Society for the Education of Pious Young Men for the Ministry of the Gospel*, Beecher attacked all denominations not connected with his charitable society. Only the Congregational, Dutch Reformed, and Presbyterian orders were pure according to Beecher. Actually in his efforts to gain financial support for the work of the charitable society, Beecher became over-enthusiastic in his description of the nation's spiritual desolation. The chief blame, he claimed, lay in the dearth of a competent, educated clergy. On these grounds he based his appeal for funds for clergy education.

Beecher made a serious mistake, for he argued from facts which were incomplete. For example, he declared there were "only 3000 competent religious instructors" at that time. In reality Beecher was only considering those ministers who were Calvinists. On that assumption, he portrayed the United States as a vast religious wilderness. He urged that his *Address* "be communicated on the Sabbaths to all our worshipping assemblies" alerting the nation to this grave danger.

Beecher's pamphlet drew immediate fire from every quarter. No one protested more loudly than Freeborn Garrettson. Not only had Beecher included Methodism in his general attack, but also he had singled out Maryland, Garrettson's native state and the cradle of American Methodism, as an area devoid of spiritual knowledge and ministry.

Garrettson's response to Beecher's attack was a twenty-eight page pamphlet entitled: *A Letter to the Rev. Lyman Beecher containing Strictures and Animadversions on a Pamphlet entitled An Address of the Charitable Society for the Education of Indigent Pious Young Men for the Ministry of the Gospel.* The material deserves summary for it reflects Garrettson's point of view concerning the state of religion in the nation and the relationship of the clergy to current conditions.

The pamphlet opens with a reminder to Beecher that Garrettson himself had served for more than forty years in the ministry and had witnessed the spread of the work "from end to end of our country." Garrettson accused Beecher of being grossly unfair in his assumptions, and as a leader of a charitable society, of being most uncharitable in the representation of the religious state of the nation. As evidence Garrettson noted: "In that section of the Episcopal Church called Methodists, [an unusual manner of defining Methodism] there are more than 214,000 in close church membership, who are spread from the Province of Maine to the Natchez and have the word and sacraments duly and piously administered to them. . . . Our regularly organized ministry alone, preach in at least 7000 places statedly. . . ."

Typical of Garrettson's method in this material is the outburst he directs toward Beecher himself: "Oh! Lyman, where has a prejudiced heart led you? I am an old man, and I trust I love the cause of God; but it grieves me to see the insinuating form of your address, and the thirst for preeminence which it seems to exhibit."

Garrettson compares the work of the church in Maryland with the work in Beecher's Connecticut, and concludes that the state of religion in the South ranks as well as, if not better than, that in New England. He sums up: "Persons of intelligence think that your pamphlet would have been better received had you come out boldly and said, 'There are about 3000 ministers of our sentiment in the United States; we do not believe it possible to have ministerial qualifications without seeing as we see. Of course, all others are ignorant and unqualified for the ministry. . . . We want 5000 more of our own sentiments, and as our seminaries are insufficient, let us stir ourselves, raise an immense fund . . . then we shall have fine times.' "

Garrettson reacted with a flash of sarcasm to Beecher's reference to Westchester, Putnam, and Dutchess Counties. Beecher called this Hudson River Valley a moral wilderness. Garrettson's response admitted there had been hindrances, but, he concluded: "Should you send one or two of your indigent young men, they may find a home, especially if they are pious and can be satisfied with a small salary."

Through the years Garrettson had seen his share of so-called settled clergy, and this pamphlet allowed him opportunity to pour out his feelings. Rhetorically he asked Beecher what he would answer, "were they to say you are a set of unregenerated men, who make a trade of the gospel, and want to crush every other denomination. That your collegians, undetermined what profession to take till a little before commencement, and then being told (or conscious themselves) that they have not talents for the bar, were divided for a time between physicians and divines till at length they preponderate in favor of the later—come out under a glimmering profession of religion and say that they are called to the ministry. After studying for a few months a theology which will no more hold together than a rope of sand, they take their saddle bags and go in search of a call; when they find a salary to their inclination, they settle down and read their sermons on the Lord's Day. . . . After years are elapsed, not a soul by their means has been brought to the knowledge of Christ; and if awakenings should take place in their vicinity, they are sure to raise disputations, throw cold water on the work, and if possible, put out the fire. . . . Though they profess to be learned, they are only smatterers, and have no spiritual qualifications for the ministry."

Into this scathing attack, Garrettson threw for good measure the accusation that the Beecherites sought to establish a state church. Beecher's reaction to all of this was swift. He immediately withdrew his pamphlet, but he insisted upon the principles he had stated.

But the Beecher episode occupied only part of Garrettson's attention in 1816. On March 29 one of his oldest and closest friends, Bishop Francis Asbury, died at Spottsylvania, Virginia. There are no Garrettson records, (extant for this year) either Journals or letters, which refer to Asbury's death. Therefore, the deep, personal impact Asbury's death made upon Garrettson and his family cannot be measured. Miss Mary Garrettson has written of the intimate friendship that existed between Asbury and her father and of the frankness and sincerity characterizing their relationship. She related how once when Asbury was visiting Traveler's Rest, Garrettson questioned Asbury's attitude relating to the church. He told Asbury, frankly, that he must give up the idea that he was an American John Wesley. Further he cautioned Asbury that his belief that all his Conference appointments were made by Divine inspiration was not only erroneous, but also harmful. In spite of such frankness, Miss Garrettson pointed out, they remained true friends.

Miss Garrettson's remembrance of Asbury's last visit to their home provides further evidence of his close relationship with the Garrettson family. She wrote:

> How well I remember his last visit here. The infirmities of age were coming upon him; and we felt that we should see his face no more. Before he left, he requested all the household to be called in. He spoke to each of them fervently and earnestly. I hoped for some precious words of counsel; but when he came to me, he was so exhausted by the efforts he made, that he merely pressed my hand affectionately as he bade me farewell. I stood on the piazza looking after the carriage . . . and that was the last time I saw him. . . .

A little more than a month after Asbury's death, the General Conference of 1816 met in Baltimore. Bishop William McKendree presided. As usual Freeborn Garrettson led the New York Conference delegation. The opening session of the Conference was dominated by concerns about Asbury's death, the loss of his leadership, and the proper disposition of his body. But by the time of adjournment at the end of May, the Conference had managed to wrangle over every issue—slavery, free pews, election of the Presiding Elders—that had concerned the church in recent years. Now that Asbury's firm, autocratic hand was gone, the winds of reform were blowing more steadily.

The Conference over, it was a tired and aging itinerant who made his way back by stage and steamboat to Traveler's Rest. Family, home, and Conference missionary work occupied his time until the New York Conference met in Middlebury, Vermont, in the session of 1817.

The adjournment of the New York Conference left Garrettson for the first time, except by his own request, without assignment. Although it was done for his own sake, he could not understand why. He had reached those years when men of great energy and purpose find it difficult to recognize the ebb of their own strength and faculties. His friends tried to make him understand that in these later years the world was to be his parish, that freedom from a specific assignment would make it possible for him to preach and travel wherever and whenever he chose.

Garrettson, however, did not find retirement satisfying. A week or two at home only exacerbated his deep restlessness and his unrelenting desire to preach and travel. Horse and saddle had to give way to horse and carriage, but travel he must. Thus he soon set off in the company of his daughter, on a trip to Schenectady to visit a friend of long standing, Eliphalet Nott (1773-1866), the President of Union College.

One suspects, however, that Garrettson's visit to Schenectady had another motive than a social visit with Nott. With no Conference assignment, he gave himself his own assignment; the trip was extended to include a visit to Troy, New York. His survey of the Methodist work there brought back memories of his first mission to Troy nearly thirty years before. At that time he had found only a few scattered dwellings and no Methodist society; now Troy had become a small, thriving city with four prosperous churches. The Methodist Church had three hundred members.

The interdenominational spirit in Troy gave Garrettson great satisfaction. This cooperativeness, he felt, was one of the prime reasons for the general success of religion there. All, however, was not serene among the Methodists. There were some in the group who were opposed to efforts toward reformation. He refers to those in opposition as "the great ones," and reflects that his efforts "to do them good" were to no avail.

Returning to Wildercliffe on June 30, Garrettson took the remainder of the summer and the autumn to relax and enjoy his home and family. He occupied his time by writing, and by preaching in nearby churches, none farther away than Connecticut and New York City. He recorded in his journal, "From the 20th of June to the 9th of December, I have travelled about 1,000 miles and preached whenever and wherever I could find an opening." This was the best Garrettson could do with retirement.

Although his periods of retirement at Wildercliffe were obviously periods of constant activity, Garrettson looked upon them as a selfish and a useless waste of his call to the ministry. His feeling of unfaithfulness and restlessness would not let him remain at home. The Puritan work ethic was engrained in him and was compounded in effect by a constant sense of religious guilt. The following entry in his journal illustrates the agony of self questioning he faced regularly:

> Being pressed in spirit, though a great cross for me to leave my precious wife and daughter, I entered into an examination in regard to my motives in leaving home—whether duty called me in my sixty-sixth year to leave a quiet, plentiful habitation . . . to encounter the cold and storms of winter, at my own expense;— but having made up my mind, a little before sunset, I bade adieu to my family. . . . went on board the steamboat. . . .

Within five days he had preached in New York, Trenton, Burlington, and had reached Philadelphia, where he preached regularly until January 6, 1818.

Between January 6 and 10 Garrettson made his way to Abingdon, Maryland on his way south. He was much concerned about the state of religion in Abingdon. Noting that the younger generation was too little interested in the church, he asked:

> What can be done? Our plan seems incomplete. Circuit preaching only comes around once in two weeks in which case there can be but a small part of ministerial duties performed, especially as it respects the youth, and rising generation. We baptize the infants, and I fear too little care is taken of them afterwards.

This analysis of the circuit preaching problem remains valid today in areas where one minister must serve several churches. Garrettson offers the analysis, but unfortunately, no solution. As a matter of fact the only solution possible is a settled ministry. Of course, Garrettson and the Methodists of his day were unwilling to accept such an arrangement.

Part of Garrettson's reason for going south was to visit his old home near Aberdeen, Maryland. In middle January he spent several days visiting old friends and relatives. Again he was disturbed by the attitude and circumstances of the younger people. They seemed to be indolent. The land he had farmed and seen farmed was now exhausted. He visited Bush Chapel (Garrettson claimed this to be the second oldest Methodist Church in America) not far from Aberdeen and found it sinking into ruin. He was greatly discouraged by all he saw. After preaching in the old court house at Bel Air, Maryland, the county seat of Harford County, he continued his journey to Baltimore. Here his spirits brightened. The depression he had felt while visiting his old friends and relatives gave way to a new confidence, for the Methodist work in Baltimore was indeed prospering. The churches could not contain all who wanted to hear.

In Garrettson's first two weeks in Baltimore, he preached fourteen times. Yet despite the satisfactions of being in active service once again, he longed for home and family. Consequently, he soon set out for Rhinebeck. A journey for Garrettson, however, meant meeting people and overnight stops. These all provided opportunity for preaching and religious conversation. Whether it be to three or four, or to three or four hundred, he was never too busy or too tired to speak of his religious convictions. Asbury once remarked, "Brother Garrettson will let no person escape a religious lecture. . . ."

Because of preaching stops along the way, his trip lasted nearly four months. The next year he traveled no farther than New York. Instead of teaching, he turned his attention to founding a seminary. In a letter to his wife on October 1, 1818 he wrote about the search for a site. "We seem engaged about the seminary, determined if possible to push the business. I suppose I walked more than four miles last Tuesday in search of a suitable site. The trustees are to meet again next Thursday. . . ." The seminary was established April, 1819 to educate Methodist children. Temporarily it occupied a building on the corner of Pump and Eldridge Streets. The next year a brick building, forty by sixty-five feet, was erected between Howard and Grand Streets.

The first report for this long-forgotten Wesleyan Seminary indicates the scope and nature of the school.

> The Seminary is divided into two departments, a Male and Female . . . The whole number . . . about one hundred and sixty. Mr. N. Morris . . . is the Principal . . . The general routine of study comprises the ordinary branches of a useful and polite education. The lower classes are taught Reading, Writing, Arithmetic, etc., the higher . . . Mathematics, Geography, English, Grammar, and the Greek and Latin Classics.
>
> In order to encourage industry and excite a laudable emulation, premiums of books, etc. were bestowed upon the most deserving.
>
> It is now only six months since the Seminary was opened. It's progress . . . has been rapid.
>
> —New York City, July 22, 1819

The institution lasted only ten years.

During this period, Freeborn Garrettson was also involved in another project. At the same time the New York Methodists were founding a school to educate their young people, they also took the action necessary to establish the Missionary and Bible Society of the Methodist Episcopal Church. The Missionary and Bible Society of the Methodist Episcopal Church was no unique venture at the time of its inception. Other denominations had already formed such societies. This was partly the reason for Gabriel P. Disosway's plea to Nathan Bangs that a Methodist missionary society should be formed. The first definite action came when the ministers of the New York Circuit held their regular meeting. The ministers present were Freeborn Garrettson, Nathan Bangs, Samuel Merwin, Joshua Soule, Thomas Mason, Laban Clark, Seth Crowell, Samuel Howe, and Thomas Thorpe. Clark, Bangs, and Garrettson were appointed a committee of three to draft a constitution for the society. The action was consummated April 5, 1819 at a general meeting held in the Bowery Methodist Church. Nathan Bangs presided. The historic moment came when Freeborn Garrettson asked permission to speak. He arose and read the resolution: "Resolved, That it is expedient for this meeting to form a Missionary and Bible Society of the Methodist Episcopal Church in America." When Garrettson moved the resolution he set going the missionary organization of the Methodist Church.

Garrettson could not remain at home for long, however. After attending the meeting of the New York Conference in Troy, New York, he was disturbed by the discord which marked the session. He blamed a few aspiring men who took advantage of the young presiding officer, Bishop George. "We sensibly felt," Garrettson commented, "the need of the wise decisive hand of an Asbury in the exercise of our episcopacy." From Troy he set off for a two-week tour of the northern regions. In these two weeks, he traveled two-hundred miles visiting the places where he had established Methodism.

Hardly had he returned home before word came of serious trouble among the New York Methodists. The trouble arose from the General Conference requirement that all Methodist Churches must remain open to duly appointed Conference ministers. This was interpreted as a clergy attempt to gain control of all church property. Garrettson quickly made his way to the city and used all his wisdom and skill to try to heal the breach. Yet his advice went largely unheeded. He left his friends in New York with the word: "My prayer is that all things may be overruled for good." A large number of members obviously did not see the "good" as Garrettson did, for they seceded from the New York City Methodist Churches under the leadership of one Samuel Stilwell.

The trip to New York had interrupted Garrettson's plan to tour New England. As soon as he was free to travel, he set out, with John Luckey as traveling companion, on an itinerary which took him as far as Boston and Providence. Alert to the drift of popular sentiment, he expressed genuine alarm over New England religious trends. "Many are convinced," he said, "of the impropriety of Calvin's horrid decrees, and not knowing where to fix the line of demarcation, have run wild into universalism. . . . The Deists are rather ashamed of open infidelity and are smothering down to Unitarianism." The need for authentic preaching was glaringly apparent, and before Garrettson reached home six weeks later, he traveled six hundred miles and preached more than sixty sermons.

The next spring, May 1820 he led the New York delegation to the General Conference at Baltimore. The question of the election of Presiding Elders, in which Garrettson was vitally interested, was before the Conference. On May 9 Garrettson wrote his wife:

> There is business of vast importance in Conference and I do not wish to be absent a minute. I am in good health. I have about half a mile to walk, and our session is 5 or 6 hours, and the time really seems short. We progress in business slowly owing to the multiplicity of speeches. This is the ninth day of our sitting, and the third part of our business is not done. We know not whom will be chosen bishop or whether there will be another chosen.

But the Conference dealt with a more pressing question—slavery. Garrettson was a keen opponent of slavery, and was a member of the all-important Committee on Slavery in the General Conference. A book he published in 1820, *A Dialogue Between Do-Justice and Professing Christian*, gives insight into his attitude towards the slavery issue. He dedicated it to "the Respective and Collective Abolition Societies, and to all other Benevolent, Humane Philanthropists in America." The setting for the dialogue is in the South. Do-Justice is guest in the home of Professing Christian, a typical Southern slave holder. In this dialogue, Garrettson develops a closely knit argument proving in Christian terms the wrongness of slavery. One statement typifies his views: "I compare a person in perpetual slavery to a very thirsty person going to a deep well to quench his thirst, who can raise but a single drop at a time: I am, says the slave, not only a slave for life, but my children after me. What stimulus can they have?"

Garrettson effectively argued that slavery was out of keeping with the principles upon which our nation was founded. Since freeing slaves was legally forbidden in certain states, he urged that in these areas a master should make every effort to satisfy the slaves' physical needs; teach them to read the Scriptures; and pray for their release. However, those masters who were able to free their slaves and did not do so stood without excuse. A Christian should only purchase slaves at the slave's own solicitation, and even then the slave should be paid wages and have some agreement as to length of bondage.

Garrettson suggested colonization and gradual emancipation as the solution to slavery. Although he recommended that some of the newly acquired territories, particularly the Louisiana Purchase, be used for colonization of emancipated slaves, he believed that most blacks would ultimately prefer remaining with the white population. In this event he urged legislation that would provide for gradual emancipation. Such an emancipation would open a door of hope and expectation for the slaves, and provide an example for the rest of the world.

Obviously Garrettson in his opinion was aligned with others of his day who, opposed to slavery, sought solutions in colonization and abolition. How far the Methodist Church as a whole agreed with this position, beyond official condemnation of slavery, is a difficult question to answer. The 1820 General Conference at Baltimore instructed the Committee on Slavery "to inquire into the expediency of expressing our approbation of the "American Society for Colonizing the Free People of Colour of the United States,' and of recommending the same." The period from 1800-1824 has generally been looked upon as a period of growing toleration of slavery in the Methodist Church. Strong resistance from the Southern quarter of the Methodist Church continued concerning slavery.

Garrettson returned home after the General Conference, but his innate restlessness and sense of mission would not let him remain inactive. On December 28 he took the steamboat to New York on his way South. While stopping over in the city, he slipped on some ice and suffered a painful injury to his leg. His fall on the ice, however, was not sufficient cause for him to interrupt his proposed journey, and he continued on by stage to Philadelphia. By the time he arrived his leg injury had worsened. For three weeks he was confined to his room. Greatly depressed in mind and spirit, he questioned why an old man such as he would leave his family and a comfortable home at such a treacherous time of year. He rationalized by telling himself that it was God's will. Nathan Bangs testified to Garrettson's restless temperament. "Often when I have been favored with a visit to his . . . mansion, have I witnessed, even in the midst of everything calculated to make life desirable, the anxiety of his mind to be in the field."

When the physician finally released him, Garrettson wasted no time in continuing his journey. Stopping in Harford County, Maryland, he spent several days among his old friends and relatives. From there he traveled to Baltimore in time to attend the Baltimore Conference in March 1821. It was an occasion for reunion. Many of the older men he had not seen for years. He found one of his acquaintances suffering from mental illness, and Garrettson's explanation of the disturbance is rather amusing. "He was a man of strong reasoning powers," he said, "and . . . his exercising of those powers on obtuse subjects was the cause of his derangement, particularly in labouring to reconcile the infinite mercy and goodness of God with the eternal tourments of the damned." Garrettson added that he, personally, solved the dilemma long ago by leaving "all to God, in full confidence, that he will do right. . . ."

From Baltimore Garrettson traveled to the Peninsula where he revisited the scenes of his early ministry. A visit to Cambridge brought back vivid memories of his imprisonment there in the town jail during the American Revolution. In May he attended the Peninsula Conference session in Milford, Delaware.

By May 29 the four-month tour had ended. Returning home once again to Wildercliffe, Garrettson remained only long enough to prepare for his journey to Troy for the meeting of the New York Conference of 1821. The Methodist work in Rhinebeck had grown rapidly in Garrettson's absence. He was delighted. His last entry for 1821 reflects the energy which characterized this man. Speaking of Rhinebeck, he wrote: "If the work continues, we shall have to enlarge it."

By 1822 Garrettson was convinced that the Methodist work in Rhinebeck did require larger facilities, and he devoted his energies to the building of a new church. As early as March a letter from Mrs. Garrettson to a friend indicated that the project was under way. "Our dear Freeborn is actively engaged about building a church. His whole soul is in the business, and this morning he took his breakfast before we were up, to go with the carpenter in the woods and mark the trees that were to be felled. . . ."

The Rhinebeck congregation, meeting in March, had directed Freeborn Garrettson as their chairman to go forward with the building of the church if funds could be secured. Mrs. Janet Montgomery, sister of Mrs. Garrettson and widow of Gen. Montgomery, gave the building site. On May 1, 1822, Garrettson laid the cornerstone and by October the building was finished. Evidently all were not pleased with the new church for some scornfully called it the "Lord's barn." Garrettson, however, was probably more enthusiastic. The total debt on the church was $300 and this Garrettson himself assumed. Not one accident occurred during the construction, a blessing laid to the fact that none of the workmen were allowed to drink liquor while working on the building.

Despite his increasing years, Garrettson persisted in traveling. His Journal of 1824 records that in March the Garrettsons came into the city as apparently was their custom. Mrs. Garrettson and Mary had many friends with whom they spent their time, while Garrettson himself preached in the churches in New York and Brooklyn. The first of April he left the city bound for the General Conference due to open in Baltimore on May 1. He left a month early in order to have time for one more visit to his childhood home in Harford County, Maryland. His seventy-two years were weighing heavily upon him. The persons he had known were all dead. Led by his nephew, he moved from place to place like a visitor in the land of memories. He was frequently reminded of childhood days sixty years before, especially when he visited the old Spesutia Church, St. George's Parish, The church in which he was baptized.

The General Conference, meeting in Baltimore, was, according to Garrettson, the largest Conference of its kind that had been held. Delegates came from north, south, east, west, from Canada and England. Garrettson looked forward to debate on the vital issues of slavery and lay representation which were the chief business of the Conference. He was much

perturbed by that fact that the Conference spent four days fixing the govern-
ing rules for the session. Such a set of congressional rules he felt only served
to perplex and retard the business of the meeting. "I am," he remarked,
"and hope always shall be, an old-fashioned Methodist." Plainly his attitude was that of an old man whose church was growing beyond him.

For four weeks and one day the Conference continued. There was
such a diversity of opinion on all questions that Garrettson remarked,
"I was ready sometimes almost to conclude that we had better amicably
divide the work from the Atlantic by Washington, leaving the Genesee
and the Canadas in the northern session." He observed that there seemed
little ground for compromise. "The southern Brethren seem as much opposed to Pewed Churches in New England, as the Eastern Brethren are
against slavery."

Matters of church policy also divided the churches. Since the days
of Asbury's leadership, Garrettson had stood with those in favor of the
election rather than the Episcopal appointment of Presiding Elders. In
every issue he had favored a more democratic spirit. Although Garrettson
never wavered in his loyalty to the Methodist system, his Journal for this
period carefully outlines a compromise scheme of government calculated
to satisfy the various challenges to the Methodist system.

Two points in his plan are especially important: (1) He urged that
the office of Presiding Elder be eliminated and that each Annual Conference have a Bishop presiding. The Bishop or Superintendent would
be amenable to his own Conference. (2) He urged that since the church
at large had no lay delegation sitting in legislation with clergy, any law
that "touches the terms of communion, or the property of the people"
would not be binding until it received a majority vote of all the Conferences
and the membership. This latter proposal raises an interesting question.
Would the church have divided in 1830 creating the Methodist Protestant
Church and would the church have divided over slavery had there been
adopted such a democratic program as Garrettson formulated?

The meeting of the New York Conference followed immediately after
the close of the General Conference in Baltimore. Late in May, Garrettson
made the arduous journey back to New York City where the Conference
met, no mean task for a man of his years. But the long road was the only
road the old prophet knew. For the Conference session had hardly adjourned
before the entire Garrettson family began a tour of the northwest sections
of the New York Conference. After preaching in Schenectady on July 4,
they set out by canal boat for Utica. This tour, like Garrettson's recent
visit to Maryland, constantly suggested experiences long past, and invited
comparisons of the old with the new. Typical is this reflection:

> What an astonishing alteration in this country! More than thirty years since,
> when I was traveling through these parts, preaching and forming circuits,
> I could find here and there only a log hut to screen me from the blasts of winter,
> or the scorchings of a summer's sun. But now the country is thickly populated,

farms highly cultivated, villages multiplied, and churches erected in every direction, splendid coaches rolling through the streets. . . .

In such prosperity Garrettson saw danger. "I awfully fear," he said, "for the inhabitants of this fertile country."

After personal conferences on the way with Bishops George and Hedding, Garrettson and his family returned to Rhinebeck. August, however, was camp meeting time and Garrettson's evangelistic message was much in demand. Thus by the end of July he had boarded the steamboat bound for the camp meeting on Long Island. By his own admission he was now "bending over eternity." On August 11 he preached to six thousand people. "I often think," he wrote, "of my dear old friend Bishop Asbury, who spent the last shred of his . . . life in the service of his great Master . . . I endeavor in every sermon I preach to deliver it as if it were my last." It was this devotion which held him on his way.

Garrettson's restless nature made it more and more difficult for him to remain at home. After the camp meeting on Long Island, the inactivity at home depressed him. Retirement was a thorn in his side. "A dismal gloom hangs over the mind," he wrote, "and the sensations are painful. It vanishes as a shadow. . . . We form resolutions to guard against another attack but unawares the enemy approaches from another quarter."

The camp meeting at Newburgh, New York, helped to stir Garrettson from his doldrums. The opportunity to preach to six thousand people gave him the feeling that there was yet some use in his ministry. Garrettson, however, regarded camp meetings with a critical eye, for he despised extremes and disorder. Even though Garrettson appreciated the preaching opportunity at the Newburgh Camp Meeting, he lamented the disruptive behavior of some of the participants. "The young lads who were charged with keeping order," he commented, "themselves became the reasons for disorder."

Autumn was the time for social visits. The Garrettsons made their rounds as was expected. Garrettson mentions with particular delight their visit to the Jay home. He found the eminent old statesman, John Jay, in his eightieth year devoting himself more and more to religious pursuits as President of the American Bible Society.

Kingston, New York had always been a difficult place to preach Methodism. Garrettson made one more effort near the end of 1824. Years before he had planted the seeds there, but there was little growth. "This is poor soil for Methodism," he wrote. "This is an ancient village first settled by emigrants from Holland, whose descendants seem to hold fast the religious profession of their ancestors, and think it borders on a crime to depart from it."

Garrettson's habit of grasping any and all opportunities to exhort an unrepentant sinner was sometimes touched with humor. In the 1825 Journal there is a typical incident. His old German gardener fell seriously ill. Garrettson's efforts to convert him had failed. But when the old man recovered, Garrettson gave him a shirt as a New Year's gift. Not to miss even this opportunity to alarm the unconverted, Garrettson reminded him, "Perhaps you will be buried in it!"

Despite Garrettson's efforts to continue his ministry, he could not deceive himself about his advancing years. The deaths of several old friends and associates in 1825 pressed home the fact that his life energies were waning. The deepest loss in the circle of friends came with Mrs. George Suckley's death. This prominent New York Methodist woman and her wealthy merchant husband had long been friends of the Garrettsons. Garrettson conducted her funeral service on November 28 in Rhinebeck. She was buried behind the Rhinebeck Methodist Church in a tomb which eventually held the bodies of her husband and the Garrettsons.

Now Garrettson's journeys were motivated not only by his unflogging concern for the work of the church, but also by his need to enjoy the company of past associates. The urge to see old friends in Philadelphia led him in April, 1826 to make the twenty-five hour, two-hundred mile journey to attend the session of the Philadelphia Conference. The visit was filled with hours of reminiscence. To be in the company of his fellow ministers was the most this old soldier of the Cross could ask of life. Characteristic of his continuing wide-ranging interests is this amusing note: "I had a long conversation with Bishop Soule concerning the Western Indians. He seems confirmed that they are descendants of the twelve tribes of Israel."

The crowning hour of Garrettson's long career came at the New York Conference, May 10, 1826. The memorable session convened in the Forsyth Street Church with Bishop William McKendree in the chair. Bishops George and Hedding were both present. The Conference had invited Garrettson to preach a semi-centennial sermon, and Garrettson's words, spoken as he entered his fifty-first year of ministry, stand as a unique contribution to the history of American Methodism. His address articulates the perspective of one looking down the long hall of history. It is at once autobiographical, historical, and philosophical. In broad outline the address presents the history of Methodism, and suggests Garrettson's own part as an itinerant preacher in the making of that history. Here and there the veteran preacher sounds warning and admonition to his younger associates.

The address, however, represents not only a long look backward. Garrettson's remarks also reveal his keen prescience of what possibly lay in Methodism's future. For example, he stated:

> I fully believe that the doctrines taught by Mr. John Wesley are Scriptural, and will stand the test; but what his people will be a hundred years hence we cannot say. They may be a numerous and a learned people; but it is possible that by slow degrees they may retrograde, until they have very little of the spirit of old Methodism; and this certainly will be the case, without a steady and conscientious perseverance in the good old paths . . . We must look well to our doctrines and discipline, and guard the sacred ministry. 'Lay hands

suddenly on no man:'—look more to genuine piety, and to real call from God, than to any literary qualification without it. Keep a pure membership. The fall of the primitive Church began with the clergy; and should we fall, our declension will begin here. It is better to have a pious, laborious, successful ministry, than to have wealth and ease without such a ministry.

The last entries in Garrettson's Journal for 1826 find him again in the company of old friends. Bishops McKendree and Hedding, after the New York Conference, returned with him to Wildercliffe to rest before the opening of the Genesee Conference. In these months Garrettson traveled when and as his health permitted, preaching in the churches near his home (Rhinebeck, Hillside, and Rhinecliff) and frequently in New York City. A letter written to his wife on one such mission to New York states succinctly his life philosophy: "I have heard people talk of laying up a stock of grace; but . . . happy is that person who has a sufficiency from moment to moment, to keep him humble, innocent, and pure. We are every moment dependent upon God."

For several years Garrettson had been free from the managerial cares and problems connected with his Wildercliffe estate. His nephew, Freeborn Garrettson, Jr., lived with the family and acted as overseer, becoming a prominent member of the community. It was left for him to carry on the distinguished family name in the Hudson River Valley, for Mary Garrettson, Garrettson's only child, never married.

Although his life was nearing its close, Garrettson persisted in attending conferences and preaching. In May, 1827, at the age of seventy-five Garrettson attended his last New York Conference. At this Conference, held in Troy, Garrettson was elected to be one of the New York Conference delegation to the General Conference scheduled to meet at Pittsburgh, Pennsylvania, in May, 1828. It was a fitting tribute to Methodism's elder statesman.

On August 17, two days after his seventy-sixth birthday, he left Rhinebeck to preach in the Duane Street Methodist Church, New York City. After the sermon and the service of Holy Communion he was stricken with an attack of strangury, a painful condition of the urinary system. Hourly the attack increased in severity. For nearly five weeks he lay in unremitting agony in the home of George Suckley. His wife, daughter and friends remained at his bedside. At two o'clock, on the morning of September 26, he died.

Garrettson's body was returned to Rhinebeck for burial at the Methodist Church. The Rev. Thomas Birch and the Rev. Nathan Bangs officiated at the services. In the seventy-sixth year of his life and the fifty-second of his ministry, this grand old pioneer of American Methodism, was forced into unqualified retirement.

The Man, Freeborn Garrettson, is now visible for what he was; not only a pioneer in the saddle, pushing back the spiritual wilderness, but also a pioneer in thought. In the great General Conferences of his church, his was an acknowledged voice of authority. It was not, however, always a voice of agreement. Insistence upon democratic rule and action marked his thought on church government. His brilliant organizational ability born of common sense and human understanding often led him beyond the thinking of his colleagues. His high ideal for the Christian ministry and its necessary educational requirements made him an advocate of more rigid training and selection of ministerial candidates. A deep hatred of slavery kept him as a ready voice of reform urging definitive action.

Garrettson's strong mind and will which made him a dynamic leader also led him to errors in judgment of men and things. A perfectionist in many respects he gave little quarter to the man who sought less than the highest. An intense emotional temperament made him direct and outspoken in his dealing with those who disagreed with him.

But more than the portrait of a pioneer churchman acquainted with hardship and conflict, Garrettson's life is also the portrait of a thoroughly delightful personality, deeply sensitive, deeply religious, restless enough to be intriguing, humorous enough to be attractive. It is the picture of a man who was able to bear wealth and family position humbly; whose devotion to the Church could only be equalled by his devotion to family and home; whose integrity and strength of character made him an inspiration to friend and foe alike.

In all the movements of Garrettson's dramatic life, there is one note clearly struck. It is the note of dedication. In all matters temporal and spiritual he strove after perfection. This and this alone brought him satisfaction, peace. The verse of the Psalm chisled on his gravestone bears mute testimony to this his dominant desire. "Mark the perfect man, and behold the upright, for the end of that man is peace." Psalm 36:37

Mrs. Garrettson never fully recovered from the shock of her husband's death. She wrote publicly in 1828, "O what a loss is ours!" Several years later she would express her deep sorrow more fully. "What a sad blank is left in this once cheerful dwelling . . . God alone can heal the wound this death hath made. . . . It will soon be five years since this deep, deep affliction befell me . . . the most trying, the most afflicting scene of our lives. The winter that followed was the most sorrowful one I had ever seen."

Mrs. Catherine Garrettson, however, lived for twenty-two years after her husband's death. She continued to make Wildercliffe a comfortable retreat for the leaders of the Methodist Episcopal Church. Until her death in 1849 at the age of ninety-six, she remained a generous benefactor of innumerable Methodist institutions and causes. Her interest in the missionary program of the church was unceasing. In this cause she offered a lasting memorial to her husband. The legacy to the New York Conference carried this inscription:

> I have more than once heard my dear friend say it would be his wish to leave a Legacy behind when he was taken away, which would be enough to have a Missionary in his place till the Millennium.

We feel gratified in complying with the request of one so justly dear to us, and one to whom the cause of God was precious to the last moment of his mortal life . . ."

Mary Rutherford Garrettson, the Garrettson's only child, continued the Garrettson family traditions at Wildercliffe for thirty years beyond her mother's death. She was a prominent figure in the church of her day, generous to all needful causes. Her correspondence, like that of her mother, was voluminous. Several of her religious publications are particularly valuable for the glimpses they give of her father and his work. Mary Garrettson died in 1879.

With the death of his daughter, the story of Freeborn Garrettson closes. But his thoughts, words, and deeds live on after him.

PART ONE

The Experiences and Travels of
Mr. Freeborn Garrettson, Minister of the
Methodist Episcopal Church in North America
Philadelphia: Printed by Parry Hall,

1791

NOTES
AND
MANUSCRIPT MATERIAL

EXCERPT FROM THE PREFACE

PREFACE

Some time ago I was solicited by Mr. Wesley, to send him an account of my experience and travels. I was at a loss to know what was best to be done in this case; but after some consideration, I informed him that I would comply with his request. After I began to write, I found some scruples in my mind which I communicated to him. But some time after, I received a second, and then a third letter, in which he intreated me to lay aside my scruples and comply with his request.

Having at length prepared the piece, I sent it from New-York in a vessel which I understood was cast away, so that he did not receive it; of which I had no *certain* account, till he informed me in another letter; and that if it did not come to hand soon, it would not be in time for him to see it: which was, in fact, the case; for whilst I was sitting in my room in Albany, finishing a letter to be enclosed with it, a friend came in, and presented me with a news-paper, in which I read the account of the death of that eminent servant of God.

I have since consented to have it printed in America, with very little alteration, except an enlargement. I trust in this my eye hath been single, and my intention pure. In keeping my regular journal, it was not uncommon for me to write the exercises of the day before I closed my eyes in sleep. But should there be any misrepresentations, or any circumstances exaggerated, (which I think is not the case) I hope my reader will have charity enough to impute it either to mistake, or wrong information. I can appeal to the Searcher of hearts when I say, in the relation of any subject I had rather be under than over the truth.

SECTION I

In this opening section Garrettson sketches his life from his birth in 1752 until his conversion in 1775, a period of roughly twenty-three years. Characteristic of religious journals his spiritual heritage and inclinations are vigorously documented. The influence of George Whitefield as well as the Tennants upon Garrettson's area of Maryland surely sensitized the people to a more evangelical fervor than the typical English churches offered. But the air of cosmopolitanism springing up in the vicinity of Baltimore in 1752 also must be noted. The element of dissent was growing as Lutheran, Reformed, Quaker and Presbyterian groups became more vocal preparing a seedbed for yet another dissenting religious group—the Methodists.

SECTION I.

From my Childhood till my Conversion.

I was born in the year of our Lord 1752.[1] My parents were of the church of England; and brought up their children in that way. My father was a very moral man, and thought by his neighbours to be a very good Christian: and my mother was a woman that feared the Lord. I was (as my parents informed me) from my infancy prone to pride, self-will and stubbornness: which I afterwards sensibly felt, to the sorrow of my heart. My father's grandfather was an emigrant from Great Britain; and numbered among the first settlers in the province of Maryland.[2]

I was very early taught the Lord's prayer, creed, and ten commandments, together with the catechism of the church of England;[3] and was in early life restrained by my tender parents from open sin. It pleased the Lord to remove my dear mother into an awful eternity when I was young. But I shall never forget the admonitions which she gave me. One Lord's day when I was about seven years of age, my mother was retired, (I was sitting by her side) and whilst she was reading the two last chapters of the Revelations, when she came to the place where it speaks of the tree and water of life; she made a full stop, and with eyes uplifted to heaven, and tears flowing down; "O!" said she, "that I may be happy enough to eat of that fruit, and drink of that water, in my heavenly Father's kingdom!" I believe the blessed Spirit was with her, and I felt the divine operations: but I knew him not; for we lived in a dark time. One day when I was about nine years of age, as I was walking alone in the field, it was as strongly imprest on my mind, as if I had heard a voice, "Ask and it shall be given you." I was immediately desirous to know what it meant, and it occurred to my mind, that this was a scriptural promise. But I, having no ideas of spiritual things, immediately ran to the house and told my elder brother, it was revealed to me, that I should be very rich: shortly after this, I was by myself and there was a question asked me, "Do you know what a saint is?" I paused a while in my mind, and answered, there are no saints in this our day on earth. The same voice replied, "a saint is one that is wholly given up to God." And immediately in idea, I saw such a person who appeared the most beautiful of all I ever beheld. I was affected, and prayed to the Lord to make me a saint, and it was strongly imprest upon my mind that I should be one; and a spirit of joy sprung up within me; but I had no one to open to me the way of salvation.

Some time after this, a great affliction befel my father's family: first a sister, then my mother, and then two servants were removed into an awful eternity. The ninth day of my sister's illness, she asked for nourishment, and eat heartily for one in her low state. After she had done she desired to be raised in the bed; I am, said she, about to leave the world. The family were called together, and were in a flood of tears: "Weep not for me," said she, "for I am not afraid to die. I am going to my Jesus; who will do

more for me than any of you can do." I believe her soul was happy. And
the affecting exhortation which she gave will never be forgotton by me.
When almost spent, she desired to be laid down, bidding all fare-well.
And within a few minutes, with a smiling countenance, bid the world
adieu. From her infancy her conscientiousness, and uprightness, were
noticed by all who knew her. It was not common to find her on the Lord's-
day without a Bible; her old uncle, who was a communicant in the church,
used to say, "Sally lives as she would wish to die." From this time a melancholy gloom hung over me, and I frequently went alone to weep. I knew
I wanted something, but what it was I knew not; for I had none to take
me by the hand, and lead me into the narrow path. I know the blessed
Spirit often strove with me, so that I have been melted into tenderness;
but I knew not the way of salvation. About this time it was I bought myself
a pocket Testament, and frequently withdrew and read; and was much
affected with the sufferings of our dear Lord. Our unhappy minister was
a stranger to God, and the most of his flock, I fear, were in the way to ruin.

When I was about twelve years of age, I was removed to another school,
where after a time I threw off all seriousness; and became as wild as the
rest of my young playmates. The most of my school-hours, after I turned
fourteen, were taken up in branches of the mathematics and book-keeping,
and the intervals of my time, in the study of astronomy.[4] I have often continued alone in the study of this till after midnight without a serious thought
of God, or my eternal welfare. Between the seventeenth and eighteenth
years of my age I left school, and began to think of living in the world.
But alas! I was careless, and carnal; though what the world calls a moral
youth. I was fond of pleasure, and loved this world more than God. Oh!
what reason have I to praise God for his goodness, in pursuing me with
the overtures of mercy. About this time it was, that there began to be much
said of the people called Methodists in Baltimore county where I lived.
Many went out to hear them,[5] and I among the rest, but the place was so
crouded I could not get into the house: but from what I could understand,
I thought they preached the truth, and did by no means dare to join with
the multitude in persecuting them: but thought I would let them alone,
and keep close to my own church. Oh! those soul damning sins, pride
and unbelief, which kept me from God and his people!

Blessed be God, it was not long after, that his holy Spirit began again
to work powerfully with me. One day as I was riding home, I met a young
man who had been hearing the Methodists, and had got his heart touched
under the word. He stopt me in the road, and began to talk so sweetly
about Jesus and his people, and recommended him to me in such a win-
ning manner, that I was deeply convinced there was a reality in that religion, and that it was time for me to think seriously on the matter.

Not many days had passed, before a little book fell into my hands,
called Russel's seven sermons.[6] By this book I was advised to make as exact
an estimate of all my sins as possible; I did so, and found they were numerous,

for I began to see myself in the gospel glass; and many were the tears I
shed over this book. And I promised an amendment of life; but my repentance was too much like the early dew, or morning rain. Still the way
of salvation was not open to me, and there was an unwillingness in me
to submit. But as my dear Lord was not willing that I should perish, his
good Spirit still strove with me. One day as I was passing over a rapid
stream, a log on which I had frequently gone, gave way, and I was near
being swept down the stream; after struggling a while, I got out, though
much wounded among the sharp rocks. This query struck my mind with
great weight, "What would have become of your soul, had you been drowned?" I wept bitterly, and prayed to the Lord under a sense of my guilt.
Still my stubborn heart was not willing to submit, though I began to carry
a little hell in my bosom.

In May 1772, as I was riding out one afternoon, I went down a descent
over a large broad rock; my horse stumbled and threw me; and with the
fall on the rock, and the horse blundering over me, I was beaten out of
my senses. I was alone, and how long I laid I know not; but when I recovered, in some measure, I found myself on my knees, with my hands
and eyes raised to heaven, crying to God for mercy. It came strongly into
my mind that had I then been taken, I should have dropt into hell. I felt
my misery, and praised God, as well as I knew how, for my deliverance;
and before I moved from the place, I promised to serve him all the days
of my life. But before I arose from my knees, all my pain of body was removed, and I felt nearly as well as ever I did in my life. I also felt the drawing of God's Spirit, and in a measure saw a beauty in Jesus: but I did not
know that my sins were forgiven; neither was the plan of salvation clearly
open to me; but I went on my way determined, by grace, to be a follower
of Christ. All the Antinomians in the world, could not make me believe,
that a man cannot feel sweet drawings before he experiences justification.

I now procured a collection of the best religious books that I could;[7]
amongst which were, the writings of Mr. Hervey, the travels of true godliness, and Allein's alarm to the unconverted: for as yet I had not seen
any of Mr. Wesley's publications, nor conversed on religious subjects
with any of the Methodists.

As I lived a retired life, I frequently read, prayed, and wept till after
midnight: and often withdrew to the woods, and other private places for
prayer. In some measure my name was already cast out as evil, though
I was ashamed to let any one know the exercises of my mind, or that I
used secret prayer: and in order to conceal it when in company, I have
frequently grieved the blessed Spirit, by joining in trifling conversation.
For I was much afraid of being thought a hypocrite. But the Holy Spirit
still pursued me, and I attended strictly to the duties of the family, over
which I was placed. I had as yet heard very few Methodist sermons; and
the devil strove very hard to keep me from going among those people.
Some time after, my late well-tried friend and brother Mr. F. A.[8] came

to our country: I went to hear him one evening at R. W's.[9] The place was crouded, however I got to the door and sat down, but he had not preached long, before I sensibly felt the word: and his doctrine seemed as salve to a festering wound. I heard him with delight, and bathed in tears could have remained there till the rising of the sun, the time passed so sweetly away: I was delightfully drawn, and greatly astonished to find a person go on so fluently, without his sermon before him. I suppose hundreds of thoughts passed through my mind. But I returned home with gladness, fully persuaded that he was a servant of God, and that he preached in a way I had not heard before, I followed him to another preaching place; and fixing my attentive eye upon him, I found him to be a workman that need not be ashamed, rightly dividing the word. He began to wind about me in such a manner that I found my sins in clusters, as it were, around me: and the law in its purity, probing to the very bottom, and discovering the defects of my heart. I was ready to cry out, "How does this stranger know me so well!" After sermon was ended, I wished not to speak to any one, but returned home in a very solemn manner.

My father began to be troubled about me, and came to see me. We sat up talking till near midnight. "I have no objection," said he "to your being religious; but why would you turn from the church?" I replied, I have no intention to leave the church, but whenever persons become serious, they are called Methodists, and their names are cast out as evil. After we parted I found great tenderness of heart, and shed many tears in private, and many promises occurred to my mind; I loved the Methodists, and yet the enemy of my soul kept me at a distance from them. Unbelief and pride kept me from the comforts of assurance.

In April 1773, my brother John was taken dangerously ill, so that his life was despaired of. One Lord's day, many of our relations and others came to see him, expecting every minute he would breathe his last. I was greatly concerned on account of his soul, which to appearance was just launching into eternity, and my fear was that he was unprepared. I went round to the back part of the bed, and kneeling down, I prayed earnestly to the Lord to have mercy on his soul. After I had done praying, I perceived his lips were moving, but could not hear a word that he spoke, till I put my ear close to his mouth, (to appearance he was just going) and heard him say, "Lord thou knowest I am unprepared to die, have mercy on me, and raise me up, and give me a longer space, and I will serve thee; thy Spirit has often strove with me, but I have rejected thee," &c. Thus did he plead with the Lord for a considerable time. He knew and so did I, the moment of time when the Lord answered prayer, and granted him a longer space. Immediately I rose from my knees, and told the waiting company they need not be uneasy, for the Lord would raise him again; instantly the disorder turned, he fell into a dose, and within a few days was able to walk about his room. After his recovery, I conversed with him on the subject, and he told me that he saw death, that he was summoned to appear in the world of spirits, and that hell was his doom. I know, said he, when a reprieve in answer to prayer was sent, the blow averted, and the tender thread lengthened, on condition that I would give the remainder of my days to the Lord. A few years after he was really changed in heart, and lived two years and eight months happy in the service of God, died a witness of perfect love.

About this time my dear Lord laid me under his hand, and I was brought nigh unto death. During the time of my illness, I was in a very strange way; I lay on my bed singing praises to God without any dread of death; I felt my mind easy; I thought if I was removed I should go to Heaven; I was willing to die; I did not know my sins were forgiven; but I felt a strong hope, yet I was not fully acquainted with the plan of salvation. Who can tell what state my soul was in? I was a good church-man, but a poor Methodist. Blessed be the name of the Lord! He delights not in the death of a sinner, for he raised me up again; but still the enemy of my soul strove to keep me from amongst God's dear despised children.

The August following, it pleased the Lord to take my father into eternity —Surely it was painful to lose the tenderest of parents. From my earliest knowledge of his family, consisting of about twenty in number, I do not remember ever to have heard an oath sworn either by black or white; and it was a rare thing for him to correct either children or servants, though still there was a trembling at his word. I frequently visited him in the time of his illness, (for he had a long and tedious sickness) and he seemed very fond of my company;[10] and I have reason to believe he went happy out of this dangerous world. Being now left in the entire charge of a family, and the settlement of my father's business mostly devolving on me; I was surrounded with many cares and troubles, which were no help to the affairs of my salvation. The devil strove hard to drive away all my good desires, but still I attended constantly to my secret devotions, though at times cold enough. It was not long after the death of my father, that I had a particular interview with the new parish minister,[11] who was a very clever man, of a moral character, and much respected in the place: I was a constant attendant on his ministry, and frequently conversed with him on divine subjects. He told me the Methodists carried matters too far, that a man could not know his sins were forgiven: and all we might expect in this life was a hope springing from an upright life. This doctrine exactly tallied with my experience, and was food for my fallen nature. I soon fully agreed with him in sentiment, and plead that no man could know his sins forgiven in this world. The grand enemy began now to exercise my mind in another way; namely, to seek a literary qualification for the ministry in the church. This hung upon me for a considerable time; and I applied myself to reading and study for that purpose, often consulting my new counsellor. The Spirit of the Lord at times strove very powerfully, and I was frequently afraid that all was not well with me, especially when I was under Methodist preaching. To these people I was drawn; but it was like death to me; for I thought I had rather serve God in any way than among them; at the same time something within would tell me they were right. Being amazingly agitated in mind, I at length came to this conclusion, to give up my former pursuits and bend my mind to the improvement of my worldly property, and serve God in a private manner. I now sat out as it were in full pursuit of business, with an expectation of accumulating the riches of the world.

During the time of my self-secure state, I had the form of godliness, attended the church constantly, and sometimes went to hear the Methodists: I fasted once a week, prayed frequently every day in secret places, endeavoured to attend strictly to the Sabbath, often reproved open sin, and denied myself of what the world calls pleasure. I was so fast set in my way, that I thought I should certainly go to Heaven. And if at any time I was overtaken, I would endeavour to mend my pace and pray more frequently. I cannot say I was always without doubts; for often, under Methodist preaching, my poor foundation would shake, especially under the preaching of dear brother G. S.[12] and I would scarcely recover my hope for many days; then I would be tempted to think they were a deluded people, and I would go among them no more: but still I was drawn again and again. I stood in a manner between the children of God and the world. When I was with the people of God I would endeavour to confute them; and when I was among their enemies, I plead their cause.

One day being at a distance from home, I met with a zealous Methodist exhorter. He asked me if I was born again? I told him I had a hope that I was. Do you know, said he, that your sins are forgiven? No, replied I, neither do I expect that knowledge in this world. I perceive, said he, that you are in the broad road to hell, and if you die in this state you will be damned. The Scripture, said I, tells us that the tree is known by its fruit; and our Lord likewise condemns rash judgment. What have you seen or known of my life that induced you to judge me in such a manner—I pity you, said I, and turned my back on him. But I could not easily forget the words of that pious young man, for they were as spears running through me.

In this state I continued till June 1775. The blessed morning I shall never forget! In the night I went to bed as usual; and slept till day break—Just as I awoke, I was alarmed by an awful voice, "Awake, sinner, for you are not prepared to die." This was as strongly impressed on my mind, as if it had been a human voice as loud as thunder. I was instantly smitten with conviction in a manner I had not been before. I started from my pillow, and cried out, Lord have mercy on my soul! As it was about the commencement of the late unhappy war, and there was to be a general review that day near my house, I had promised myself much satisfaction; for I was a professed friend to the American cause: however, instead of giving my attendance, I passed the morning away in solitude; and in the afternoon went out and heard a Methodist sermon. In sorrow I went, and in sorrow returned; and in sorrow the night passed away. None but those that have experienced the like exercises, can form an idea of what I underwent for several days.

The devil, and the enmity of my heart seemed to rise higher and higher. On the Tuesday following, in the afternoon I heard Mr. D. R.[13] preach; and was so opprest that I was scarce able to support under my burden. After preaching I called in with D. R. at Mrs. G—'s, and staid till about nine o'clock. On my way home being much distressed, I alighted from my horse in a lonely wood, and bowed my knees before the Lord; I sensibly felt two spirits, one on each hand. The good spirit set forth to my inmost mind, the beauties of religion; and I seemed almost ready to lay hold on my Saviour. Oh! unbelief! soul damning sin! it kept me from my Jesus. Then would the enemy rise up on the other hand, and dress religion in as odious a garb as possible; yea, he seemed in a moment of time, to set the world and the things of it in the most brilliant colours before me; telling me, all those things should be mine, if I would give up my false notions, and serve him. His temptations of a truth might be compared to a sweeping rain. I continued on my knees a considerable time, and at last began to give way to the reasoning of the enemy. My tender feelings abated, and my tears were gone; my heart was hard, but I continued on my knees in a kind of meditation; and at length addressed my Maker thus: Lord spare me one year more, and by that time I can put my worldly affairs in such a train, that I can serve thee. (I seemed as if I felt the two spirits with me.) The answer was, "Now is the accepted time." I then plead for six months, but was denied—one month, no—I then asked for one week, the answer was, "This is the time." For sometime the devil was silent, till I was denied one week in his service; then it was he shot a powerful dart. "The God," said he, "you are attempting to serve, is a hard Master; and I would have you to desist from your endeavour." Carnal people know very little of this kind of exercise: but it was as perceptible to me, as if I had been conversing with two persons face to face. As soon as this powerful temptation came, I felt my heart rise sensibly (I do not say with enmity) against my Maker, and immediately I arose from my knees with these words. "I will take my own time, and then I will serve thee. I mounted my horse with a hard unbelieving heart, unwilling to submit to Jesus. Oh! what a good God had I to deal with! I might in justice have been sent to hell.

I had not rode a quarter of a mile, before the Lord met me powerfully with these words, "These three years have I come seeking fruit on this fig tree; and find none." And then the following words were added, "I have come once more to offer you life and salvation, and it is the last time: chuse, or refuse." I was instantly surrounded with a divine power: heaven and hell were disclosed to view, and life and death were set before me. I do believe if I had rejected this call, mercy would have been forever taken from me. Man hath power to chuse, or refuse in religious matters; otherwise God would have no reasonable service from his creatures. I knew the very instant, when I submitted to the Lord; and was willing that Christ should reign over me: I likewise knew the two sins which I parted with last, pride, and unbelief. I threw the reins of my bridle on my horse's neck, and putting my hands together, cried out, Lord I submit. I was less than nothing in my own sight; and was now, for the first time, reconciled to the justice of God. The enmity of my heart was slain—The plan of salvation was open to me—I saw a beauty in the perfections of the Deity. and felt that power of faith and love that I had ever been a stranger to before.

SECTION II

Garrettson graphically describes his struggles leading to his conversion. The experience of conversion for Garrettson was the watershed from which flowed his entire source of life. The struggle clearly drawn rages in his mind between the forces of establishment and new life direction represented by the Methodists.

Garrettson's emancipation of his slaves and the beginnings of the American revolution, both discussed in this section, represent two major concerns which affected both his ministry, and that of Methodism in this early period.

SECTION II.

*From my Conversion till I entered the Connection as a
Travelling Preacher.*

After I found this pearl of great price, my soul was so exceedingly happy that I seemed as if I wanted to take wing and fly away to heaven. Although alone in an unfrequented wood, I was constrained to sound forth the praises of my dear Redeemer. I thought I should not be ashamed to publish it to the ends of the earth. As I drew near to the house, the servants heard me, and came to meet me at the gate in great surprize. The stars seemed as so many seraphs going forth in their Maker's praise. I called the family together for prayer, but my prayer was turned into praise.

About midnight I laid down to rest; but my soul was so happy in God, I scarcely wished for sleep; however at length my eyes were closed; but behold! about day break I awoke, and was strongly tempted by the devil, "Oh!" said the adversary, "where is your religion now? It was only a dream." I started from my pillow—I remembered the time, and place where I received the blessing: and was enabled to repel that temptation. Again said he, "It is all a delusion." This assault pained me to the heart. Not feeling as I had done, I began to conclude perhaps it might be so; and betook myself to the fields and woods, under deep distress. I frequently bowed my knees before the Lord; and blessed be his dear name, about nine in the morning my beloved Master visited my heart with his love. And I think I received as great a manifestation as at the first. This visit was attended with an impression to go to such a place, and declare to all who might be there, what great things the Lord had done for me. I went to the house, got my horse, and set out. When I arrived at the place, I found a Methodist preacher, and several of my acquaintance. And it was strongly impressed on my mind, to deliver my message. I sat down among them, but the cross was too heavy. I sat hours, and grieved the blessed Spirit, till I was brought under heavy trials; yea, deep distress of soul; and in that way I returned home.

For the good of others, I shall speak of a few days exercise on this occasion. The dear Redeemer left me, or rather hid his face from me: and I had to wade through deep waters. I fasted and prayed, till I was almost reduced to a skeleton; but did not open my mouth to any one. I was sinking into desperation.—O! how powerfully was I harassed by the devil, day and night! The Saturday following I was walking through the fields; all nature was clothed with beauty and verdure; but I could discover no charms in aught around me: but was under the deepest exercises of mind, and severely tempted of the devil. "Ah," suggested he, "where is your God now?" He thrust atheism, and deism against me; and thus suggested to my mind, "You see you have been deluded; and if you will now take my advice, you will deny every pretension to this religion. The Methodists are a set of enthusiasts, and you have now a proof of this." Then with what splendor was the world exhibited to my imagination: "All these things," suggested he, "will I give you if you will deny that God you have been attempting to serve, and pray to him no more." I was sunk as low as I could possibly be; for my mind was encompassed with darkness, and the most severe distress. I was afraid my lips would be forced open to deny the God who made me. Glory, glory to my Lord! who again gave me a view of an opening eternity, and a sense of his dread Majesty; the sight of which brought me into the dust, prostrate with my face to the ground, where I lay for a considerable time with language similar to this, if I perish, it shall be at thy feet, crying for mercy. Thus I lay, till I recovered a gleam of hope that I should be saved at last.

I arose from the earth and advancing towards the house in deep thought, I came to this conclusion, that I would exclude myself from the society of men, and live in a cell upon bread and water, mourning out my days for having grieved my Lord. I went into my room and sat in one position till nine o'clock. I then threw myself on the bed, and slept till morning. Although it was the Lord's day, I did not intend to go to any place of worship; neither did I desire to see any person, but wished to pass my time in total solitude. I continued reading the Bible till eight, and then under a sense of duty, called the family together for prayer. As I stood with a book in my hand, in the act of giving out a hymn, this thought powerfully struck my mind. "It is not right for you to keep your fellow creatures in bondage; you must let the oppressed go free."[14] I knew it to be that same blessed voice which had spoken to me before—till then I had never suspected that the practice of slave-keeping was wrong; I had not read a book on the subject, nor been told so by any—I paused a minute and then replied, "Lord, the oppressed shall go free." And I was as clear of them in my mind, as if I had never owned one. I told them they did not belong to me, and that I did not desire their services without making them a compensation; and I was now at liberty to proceed in worship. After singing, I kneeled to pray. Had I the tongue of an angel, I could not fully describe what I felt: all my dejection and that melancholy gloom, which preyed upon me, vanished in a moment: a divine sweetness ran through my whole frame—O! in what a wonderful manner was my poor soul set into the depths of my Redeemer's love! Praise and glory to his name forever!

I had now no desire to confine myself to a cell, but wished to spread my Redeemer's glory to the ends of the world. I bless the Lord for leading me safe through such fiery trials! My late affliction of mind was for my good. It was God, not man, that taught me the impropriety of holding slaves: and I shall never be able to praise him enough for it. My very heart has bled, since that, for slave-holders, especially those who make a profession of religion; for I believe it to be a crying sin. In the forenoon I attended church, but I could not find what I wanted.[15] In the afternoon I went to hear the Methodists;[16] and something told me, "these are the people." I was so happy in the time of preaching, that I could conceal it no longer; so I determined to chuse God's people for my people, and returned home rejoicing.

A few days after, I attended a class-meeting on Deer creek,[17] for the first time, and was convinced it was a prudential institution; and my heart was more than ever united to this community. I told Br. H. a pious man, what the Lord had done for me. I now began again to be pressed in spirit to visit my friends and neighbours; and especially some particular families which laid with weight on my mind. The first visit I made, the man of the house was much enraged against me; but my dear Lord gave me one or two of his children. Shortly after I visited another family; and the master was brought to cry for mercy, on his knees, before the Lord. The third was near twenty miles off: I seemed to go with confidence, and got there a little before night: I told him what God had done for me, and desired he would send out and call in the neighbours, and I would pray with and for them. The person did so, and after prayer I was obliged, for the first time, to open my mouth by way of exhortation; and the Lord filled it, and sent his arrows to the hearts of three sinners, one of whom slept very little that night; and another followed me near sixteen miles the next day.

I again attended class for the second time at Mr. D's; and as they had not heard what had happened to me, some of them were fearful that I had come in to spy out their liberties. I arose from my seat, and, for the first time among the Methodists, publicly declared what the Lord had done for me.[18] A divine kindling ran through the whole house; and we had a blessed meeting. The leader offered to give up his paper to me; but I refused, saying, I would visit them as often as I could; and so returned home, praising God.

I felt an impression to go to that brother I have before mentioned, who was raised from the jaws of death: he was in a seeking way; but did not profess the faith of assurance. I begged of him to call a meeting in his own house, and I found great freedom to speak, and appointed another meeting; about forty people gathered;[19] and whilst I was speaking, the power of the Lord came down in a wonderful manner: near half the poor sinners that were present, were struck to the floor, and cryed for mercy,[20] to such a degree, that they were heard at a great distance. After the meeting was over, many continued crying for mercy.

The next morning a gentleman who lived not far off, came to the house to beat me: soon after he entered he began to swear, affirming I would spoil all his negroes. I told him if he did not leave off swearing, he would send his soul to hell. He replied, "If I said that again, he would level me to the floor." I assured him I would reprove him, whenever he took the Lord's name in vain. He then rose up and struck me on the side of the face, and followed his blows. There were five of us in the house, my brother, his overseer, myself and two enemies. I was afraid we should have had a general battle. My brother was only awakened; his overseer had no religion, beyond a zeal for the truth, and such a love for my brother and myself, that he would almost have lain down his life for us. My mind was perfectly calm and my soul so happy, that I scarce felt his blows. I saw the Lord's hand in my preservation; for though he was in so violent a rage, I had not been exhorting many minutes (with tears) before he was as quiet as a lamb: and he and his man, bidding us good morning, went away. Dear man! not long after, he was taken into an awful eternity.

I now began to hold evening meetings in different places, several times in a week: and united those who were awakened into a kind of society; and several, I trust, were happily united to Jesus. O! what sweet times I used to have. Frequently we have continued singing, praying and praising God till after midnight. Many of my relations were sorry for, and pitied me; but glory to God! I delighted in the cross of my dear Saviour. I was assaulted by many inward conflicts from the devil and the corruptions of my own heart; but Jesus was precious to me.

I had an appointment, one Lord's-day,[21] but before I got there a company of Belial's children gathered to prevent the meeting; but blessed be God, I was enabled to speak boldly; and although some raged and threatened me, my faith was so strong, I did not believe they could hurt me. I shall never forget that day; it was a time of rejoicing to my poor soul! O that I may always give glory to my dear Lord!

I was determined I would have nothing to do with the unhappy war;[22] it was contrary to my mind, and grievous to my conscience, to have any hand in shedding human blood. On this account I was taken, at the general meeting, before the rulers.[23] But my dear Lord was with me, and gave me words, that my opposers could not resist. While surrounded by my enemies, my soul was happy, and with tears flowing from my eyes, I told them their danger, and entreated them to turn to the Lord: they laid a fine upon me, but the Lord would not permit them to take a farthing of my property. On being dismissed, I withdrew and found great freedom to pray for them; and returned home with a glad heart.[24]

It was pressed on my mind to have some conversation with Mr. W—.[25] He had been the means of keeping me from God and his people for a long time. We had a long discourse in the vestry chamber, before the vestry: where I told him what God had done for me. He desired to know who gave me authority to hold meetings in his parish? I told him I did not do it either for money or honour; that while there were sinners in his parish, and the Lord pressed it on my mind, I should call them to repentance. "You have no right to do it," said he, "unless you were ordained."[26] The love of God constraineth me, said I, and I must open my mouth in his cause. Having tasted his goodness, I have a longing desire that my neighbours should be made happy too. After a conversation of near two hours on the new birth, finding his mind disturbed, I told him in a plain manner, what I thought of his doctrine, and what effect it formerly had on me, and so our meeting ended. After I withdrew to my home, being young in the way, very few to strengthen and many to weaken my hands, I was sorely tempted of Satan to give up my confidence in my dear Lord. And under heavy affliction of mind I withdrew, and wrestled in prayer till the Lord visited me, and dispersed every doubt and every fear; giving me these words for my comfort, "Fear not, I am with you, and will support you under all your trials." O what consolatory streams flowed into my heart! and how was I strengthened and enabled to rejoice in the Lord!

Mr. T. R.[27] understanding that my mind was exercised respecting the ministry, sent to me to meet him at Mr. D—'s; I did so, and although he was a stranger to me, I found in him a father, who gave me most salutary advice, which I stood much in need of: for I had been wading through deep waters, and under very severe exercises. I left him, much strengthened and encouraged to go on in the blessed work. Some time after my brother requested to have preaching at his house, and it was there I became acquainted with Mr. R—a, who applied to me to travel with him. I complied, and found myself very happy; and at times had freedom to speak, though the cross was very heavy; and I was often ready to start back. I had not been with him long before I returned home, and was so powerfully exercised, that I concluded it would not do to become a travelling preacher. Here my enemy stepped in, and told me there was one way to prevent it, which was to alter my condition. The object was soon determined on, and I made her a visit, told my errand, and set a time when I should expect to have her answer. Many pleasing prospects now opened upon me; all this time I was willing to do any thing about home to promote the cause of religion: but it was like death to me to travel. The time arrived, and I went to know the person's mind respecting my late proposal; but behold! the hand of the Lord was against it: during the night it was as if some person was telling me, "You are about to do your own will; I have a greater work for you: you must go out and preach the gospel." My mind was so disquieted, I scarcely closed my eyes throughout the night; till being fully convinced I was entering on a work the Lord had not called me to, I determined to give the matter up. In the morning early, I met the person in the hall, I told her my difficulty; and that I believed the Lord had a greater work for me to do.[28] I have written on this subject for the benefit of young preachers, into whose hands this may fall: being persuaded the enemy of souls exercises many of them in the same way. O that they may be wise and break the snare of the devil! Mr. Martin Rodda desired me to meet him in Baltimore town at a certain time: I went, and he forced me into the pulpit, but the cross was so heavy, and my temptations so great, I could scarcely support under them; but blessed be God, after I opened my mouth, I felt my dear Saviour, and it was a sweet time to me, and I expect to many more. I travelled a few days with him, after which, he sent me on a circuit alone. This was the fall after my conversion. I found great liberty of speech, and the word was blessed to many souls, for the Lord greatly assisted me, and I had sweet refreshing seasons. Oh! how happy might I have been, had I guarded against my powerful adversary! I had not been on the circuit more than fifteen days, before I gave way to the devil's suggestions; and concluded I was not called to this work. I left the circuit under deep dejection, and returned home; determined I would never attempt it again. The devil told me, the more I went among the Methodists, particularly the preachers, the more my mind would be distressed about travelling. I was still willing to speak occasionally about home; but to go through the world, I knew not where, was a burden too heavy for me to bear.

'Tis not in my power to give a full account of my exercises from the fall till the following spring. It may however be necessary to touch on a few particulars; for about four months I spent my time in prayer, reading, and such like exercises, except when I was from home, at preaching, or holding meetings myself. The idea of travelling, and preaching the gospel was constantly held up to my view. Frequently when riding, or walking, I was drawn out on divine subjects, and at times the Bible seemed all open to me: it was not uncommon for me to preach in my sleep. One night the whole world of sinners seemed to be exhibited as it were in the air, suspended by a slender thread, and the dismal pit beneath them. I saw them careless and unconcerned, in all kinds of ungodly practices, as secure as if in no sort of danger: in my sleep I began to cry aloud to convince them of their danger; till I awakened my brother, who then awoke me: I was sitting up in my bed, trembling, and as wet with sweat as if I had been dipped in a river. Although I lived so abstemiously, I had very little happiness; except at those times when I felt a degree of willingness to labour for my dear Lord. I have frequently stood astonished, wept and mourned in secret before the Lord, and entreated him to send some one else that was more sensible, and capable than myself: looking around in my mind and nominating such and such persons, who I conceived to be more fit for the office of the ministry; saying, how can it be, that such an unworthy ignorant being should be set apart for so great a work? When on my way to my occasional appointments, I would promise in my mind, that if the Lord attended his word with great power, I would consent to give up, and labour for him. And at such times I have had great displays of the goodness of God, and sinners weeping all around; and although my mind at the present would be resolved, unbelief would again assault and over-power me.

In the month of March my conflicts were so great, I almost sunk under them. The ungodly amongst my acquaintances knew not what was the matter with me: some would ask if I was sick (for I was much worn away.)

Others would say behind my back, he will come to nothing. I believe I had a more severe travail of soul before I submitted to be a travelling preacher, than I had gone through for justifying grace. One day being almost weary of life, and under deep dejection, I thought if the Lord would manifest his will, I would, through grace obey. I was next led to enquire how I was to expect this desired favour. I kneeled down by the bed and prayed to the Lord, by some means or other, to make a discovery to me, in the clearest manner, of what he would have me to do. I arose from my knees without any particular answer, much burdened and greatly distressed. I threw myself on the bed again, and in less than two minutes I was in a sound sleep. I dreamed I saw the devil come in at the door, and advance towards me; I thought a good angel came and spake to me saying, "Will you go and preach the gospel?" I replied, "I am unworthy, I cannot go:" Instantly the devil laid hold of my hand, and I began to struggle to get from him; I saw but one way that I could escape, and that was a very narrow one. The good angel said to me, "There is a dispensation of the gospel committed to you, and woe unto you, if you preach not the gospel." I struggled for some time to get from him, but in vain, at length I cried out, "Lord send by whom thou wilt, I am willing to go and preach thy gospel." No sooner had I thus submitted, than I saw the devil fly as it were through the end of the house in a flame of fire. I awoke, immediately every cloud was dispersed, and my soul was enraptured with the love of my dear Saviour. I wanted now to converse with some experienced person on the subject, my way now appeared so open, I thought I should never have any more doubts to contend with. I believe it was the next day, I received a letter from brother Daniel Ruff desiring me to come and take the circuit a few weeks while he went to Philadelphia. I had no doubt, but the Lord directed him to write thus. Before the day arrived that I was to set off, the enemy strove again to prevent me; telling me, I was deluded, that it was only my own fancy, or the vanity of my own heart. After I set out I was persecuted to that degree, I was ready to desire my horse might throw me, and put an end to my life; or maim me so that I might not be able to go on. In the evening I got to brother Daniel Ruff's, in Cecil, where he had an appointment for me; but my exercises were so severe, that I could say but little. The next day he left me, and I concluded to go on the circuit. Of all creatures in the world, I have the greatest reason to be thankful to the Lord, for his tender care of me, a poor weak rebel against him. At the first and second places to which I went, the Lord was powerfully present; and I believe good was done. I was now quite willing to be an exhorter; but thought I would not take a text: However I had not travelled far before I had a text suggested to me, and I refused, till my gift of exhortation was almost taken away; and my mind was amazingly distressed again.

One Sabbath I came to a place near Choptank bridge, where I again refused to give out a text, and it pleased the Lord to hide his face, so that

I was unable to speak with any degree of freedom. I went to my after-noon's appointment very low both in mind and body; having taken very little refreshment for several days. I determined if a text opened to me, I would give it out boldly, and trust in the Lord. It was so, and I gave out "Behold the man." I shall never forget the afternoon; it was a time of power to me and many others, the whole Bible seemed open to me. The next day I went to my appointment, with some willingness to be a preacher. I gave out this text, "The great day of his wrath is come, and who shall be able to stand." I endeavoured to shew, as I could, how awful that day would be; and who would; and who would not be enabled to stand, with the dreadful consequence. The power of God in a very remarkable manner came down among the people, and hardened sinners were brought to cry for mercy. When almost spent, I stopt; but the people continued pray-ing; O! it was a memorable season! my soul was happy, and my heart humbled. I was now willing to be a preacher, and thought surely I shall never doubt again.

When brother Daniel Ruff returned, he took the circuit, and I went out to open a new one. As I passed along through Tuckeyhoe Neck, I called at a house and asked the woman, if she wanted to hear the word of the Lord preached, if she did, to send and call in her neighbours; she did so, and I found great freedom. I gave out, that I would preach again the next day. The man of the house was an officer of rank, and it being a day of general mustering, he marched up all the company, and I spoke to hundreds with freedom; many tears were shed, and several convicted, one of whom has since become a preacher.[29] I continued several days in the Neck, and my labours were attended with success.

I again met brother D. R.[30] in Cecil county, where we had a quarterly-meeting, and from thence we set out for Hartford. He solicited me not to fail attending the Baltimore conference. On the Lord's-day following, an appointment was made for me to preach in my native place; and a multitude gathered: amongst whom many of my old friends and relations were there, which made the cross very heavy. I gave out my old text, "The great day of his wrath is come, and who shall be able to stand." Just as I had entered on the subject, I fainted under the cross, and fell to the ground, (I was preaching under the trees) where I laid till water was brought and thrown on me, when I immediately recovered, and was enabled to rise. I then proceeded, the subject opened to me, and we had a solemn season. On Monday I had a severe conflict about attending the conference. The exercise of my mind was too great for my emaciated frame. I betook myself to my bed and lay till twelve o'clock, and then rose up, and set off. I got into Baltimore about sun-set. The conference was to begin the next day: I attended, passed through an examination, and was admitted on trial: and my name was, for the first time, classed among the Methodists; and I received of Mr. T. R.[31] a written license. My mind continued so agitated (for I still felt an unwillingness to be a traveling preacher) that after I went from the preaching-house to dinner, I again fainted under my burden, and sunk to the floor.[32] When I recovered, I found myself in an upper chamber on the bed, surrounded by several preachers; I asked, "where I had been," and seemed to be lost to all things below, appearing to have been in a place from whence I did not desire to return: the brethren joined in prayer, my soul was so happy, and every thing wore so pleasing an aspect, that the preachers appeared more like angels to me than men. And I have blessed my dear Lord ever since, that I was ever united to this happy family; though unworthy of a seat among them.[33]

SECTION III

This material is a fair representation of the kind of experiences Garrettson had in his first year, 1776. While still uncertain of his fittness for his work, he nonetheless plunged ahead like a young colt. His conflict with the Presbyterian minister, for instance, led him in later years to observe with some embarrassment that ". . . we were both beginners in the great work of the ministry, and probably a few years longer experience, and we should have been capable of handling the controversy more profitably."

SECTION III.

*A Short Account of my First year's Travels
in Maryland and Virginia.*

I was appointed to travel in the Frederick circuit with Mr. R.[34] and as the conference ended on Friday, I set out and got as far as Mr. W—n's,[35] and the next day got into my circuit. I preached on the Lord's-day with very little freedom or happiness to my own soul: the enemy still pursued me, throwing in his fiery darts. At times I had sweet communion with my dear Lord; but a consciousness of my weakness and inability for the great work in which I had engaged, caused my hands to hang down. I was a young soldier, and knew but little about exercising the Christian armour. The goodness of God was great to me, in opening the hearts of the people to receive and bear with my weaknesses.

One day on my way to my appointment, the difficulties appeared so great, that I turned my horse, three different times, homeward. I was in a solitary wood, entirely alone; I wept, and mourned, and prayed at the feet of my Lord, and was encouraged to go forward: I did, and a sweet and powerful meeting we had. Sometimes when I have been at the appointed place, and the people assembling, I have been tempted to hide myself, or wish that I was sick; at other times I have envied the happiness of crawling insects on the face of the earth; and I have constantly found, that the greater cross it was to speak for God, the greater was the blessing, both to myself and the people. In similar cases, I seldom opened my mouth to speak in public, but what the power of the Lord was sensibly felt. My Bible, at particular times, would appear so small that I could not find a text. I remember one day, a congregation was gathered, and I was alone, under deep exercise; and it appeared as if there was not one verse in the Bible that I could speak upon: but all on a sudden, whilst I was on my knees before the Lord, the following text was powerfully applied: *The Spirit of the Lord God is upon me, because he hath anointed me to preach glad tidings to the meek, to bind up the broken hearted, to proclaim liberty to the captives, and the opening of the prison to them that are bound.* Isaiah lxi. 1. I immediately met the assembly, and after singing and prayer, gave out the text, and the power of God descended in an extraordinary manner. Before this, the people were so hardened, that we had no more than four members; but before I left the house, twenty, who seemed to be that day broken in heart, were added to the society: and we continued singing and praying till near sunset, and there appeared to be very few in the congregation whose hearts were not touched; my voice being almost lost in the cries of the distressed. O! blessed be God! this was a day of marrow and fat things to my poor heart.

Some time after I was requested to appoint a watch-night, and I consented. Mr. R.[36] was displeased that I had not consulted him; but I was innocent, knowing very little of the discipline. Many people came together, and many of the children of the devil were angry and stoned the house; but our dear Lord was powerfully present. God's people had a little paradise; and I trust there were several new-born souls, and some poor sinners brought to tremble. I can truly say it was a great time with me.

I continued six months in this circuit: and blessed be God! many were added to the society; his children much quickened; and many happily brought into the kingdom of grace. My heart was closely united to the people, and they were remarkably kind to me, all around the circuit. I thought it a great favour to be received as a preacher: and I verily believe the Lord inclined the hearts of the people to overlook my many weaknesses and want of knowledge; and for the sake of his dear Son, he in a small measure owned my efforts. To his honour be it spoken.

I think it was in November I was sent to Fairfax circuit,[37] where I staid three months. I had many happy moments, and preached the gospel with freedom. I cannot say I met with much success, neither was I so powerfully harrassed by the devil. I was now better acquainted with his devices; and I trust, had a more steady confidence in my dear Saviour. I began to preach the word more freely, and was not so easily shaken with respect to my call to the ministry: and I was now entirely willing to be a travelling preacher: and blessed be God! he gave me favour in the sight of the people.

As there were many doors open for us in New Virginia, and several small societies formed, Mr. R. thought it expedient to send me into those parts of the country; and blessed be my God! I found a willingness to go any where, and to do any thing that would bring most honour and service to the church of God. I bless and praise the Lord for his goodness to me during my stay in that part of his vineyard, for he wonderfully enlarged my desires after him; and increased my gifts, and opened the hearts and houses of the people to receive his servant and his word. And many were added to the society.

I visited Shepherd's town,[38] lying high up on the Patowmack river. On the Lord's-day I attended the church, and heard their minister preach on *Keep holy the Sabbath-day*. He was a slow spoken man, and I think his discourse took up fifteen minutes. He said there was no harm in civil amusements on a week day; but they ought to refrain from them on the Sabbath. I had no doubt but his discourse was his own composition. I do not remember a word about the fall of man, faith, or repentance. I asked liberty, and went up into the pulpit after him, and gave out, *How shall we escape, if we neglect so great salvation?* Heb. ii. 3. After I had done, one of his hearers asked him what he thought of the doctrine the stranger had delivered? Why, said he, he seems to bring scripture to prove it; it may be so, but if it is, I know nothing of it.

I preached every other Sunday in church, during my stay in this new circuit; and the fourth sermon there were as many people as could croud into the building. There was a great agitation among the congregation, and the word took such effect on the heart of a woman, that she cried so loud for mercy as to make the church ring: the people being unacquainted with such things, strove to get out; but the ailes, and every place were so crouded, that they could not, unless they had first given way at the doors. In a few minutes the Lord set her soul at liberty. She clapped her hands in an ecstacy of joy, praised the Lord, and then sat down quietly. The whole congregation seemed to be lost in amazement, and the divine presence appeared to run through the whole house: most of the people were melted into tears. The presbyterian minister was among the croud and most of his congregation came to hear what the babler had to say. This man with his deacon I met on the road a few days after. "I was hearing you preach," said he, "and I did not like your doctrine." What was your objection, said I. "Why it was a volley of stuff." Well, said I, if the Lord makes use of it to bring souls to himself, I wish to be thankful and satisfied. "You preach perfection," said he, "and that I do not believe to be attainable in this life." Then, said I, you do not hold with the doctrine of our Lord and his apostles; our Lord says, *be ye perfect as your Father in heaven is perfect*, and the apostle says, *the blood of Christ cleanseth from all sin*. When are we to be made perfect? "Not till death," said he. Our Lord, said I, *came to destroy the works of the devil;* and do you suppose he will call death to his assistance? Death in scripture is called the last enemy, and we learn, that as death leaves us, judgment will find us; and that there is no knowledge or work in the grave. *And if we die in our sins, where the Lord is, we cannot come:* I want to know how death is to bring this work about. "Why," said he, "at the article of death, sin is done away, and not till then." Then first, you must hold with a death purgatory, or secondly, a purgatory after death, or thirdly, a salvation from all sin in this world. The Papists say, we must be refined by the fire of purgatory: The Universalians say, that the last farthing will be paid in hell; and you say, nay, death will do it: but we witness to the doctrine of the holy scriptures, and say, that *his name shall be called Jesus, for he shall save his people from their sins*. Do you not, said I, believe that the Lord is able to wash and cleanse the soul from all sin one minute before death? He agreed at last that it might be a minute before death. And if a minute, why not a day, a month, yea, why not seven years? The apostle faith, *behold, now is the accepted time! behold, now is the day of salvation!* How dare any man limit the holy one of Israel. "I have done with you," cried he and his deacon, and so saying turned their backs upon me.

A few evenings after, I preached near his house, and he and his deacon were present again; a precious sweet season we had; a great shaking among sinners, and I expect the heart of the minister was also softened. He came to me after sermon and asked my pardon if he had said any thing amiss.

Glory to God, he enabled me to travel largely through that country during my stay there; and preach one, two, three, and sometimes four sermons a day. The last sermon I preached was from *Finally, brethren farewell, &c.* This was a time not soon to be forgotten. A large congregation seemed to drink in every word; such attention was given, and so much of the divine presence felt, that I continued near three hours, and then the people hung around me in such a manner that I could scarcely get from them, begging me with tears not to leave them.

I rode about ten miles and preached to a number of people in a meadow surrounded by mountains; and I do believe good was done.

Having an invitation, I went to the house of an old Quaker; and in the morning before my departure had family prayer; the Lord touched the hearts of both the old people and their children; for they were in tears and entreated me to return that way again.

I attended a quarterly meeting in Fairfax, and met Mr. T. R.[39] with several others, who were on their way to the conference, which was held at Deer-Creek. During this year I had many sweet moments, though severely buffetted by the enemy of my soul; but I bless God, I was enabled to go on in his work.

SECTION IV

The material in this section covers a period of one year, 1777 to 1778. Garrettson's travels took him into Virginia and North Carolina. The growing intensity of feeling about the war and the hostility expressed toward Garrettson as a Methodist preacher are clearly evident. No doubt his preaching to blacks contributed to his disfavor among some of the people.

SECTION IV.

A short Account of my first Journey through
Old Virginia and Carolina, including one year.

Conference began at Deer-Creek the 20th of May, 1777, and continued till the Friday following. I was greatly refreshed among the servants of God; some of whom I have never seen since, nor shall again on this side of eternity.

My appointment was in Virginia, in what was called Brunswick circuit, with brother W. and brother T.[40] After spending a few days among my relations and old friends, on Monday I set out for my circuit, and on Tuesday met the preachers at brother M—r's[41] in Fairfax: and the next morning we set out in company on our way. My appointment was much to my mind, and I had a lively hope that my dear Lord would be with me, and bless my weak endeavours to promote his cause.

We travelled several days before we met any Methodists; but my dear Lord befriended us, for we had happy times together; and had an opportunity of preaching several sermons before we reached our circuit: we had a sweet season at the house of a good old man; and I think we were providentially sent thither, not only for the benefit of the family; but likewise of many others.

June the 4th I parted with my company, and thanks be to God, my soul was refreshed as with new wine. The same day I was brought to the house of a kind widow, who sent out and called a company together. There was a young growing society in this neighbourhood. I preached from, *Fear not little flock*, &c. Luke. xii. 32. From what I could understand they had seldom had such a time of refreshing. I could say, it is good for me to be here. My confidence still grew stronger, with respect to my call to the ministry.

On the fifth of June I got into my circuit, and on Saturday the 7th, began my ministry among a lively people.[42] I was attacked by an officer who wanted to know my mind respecting fighting. I told him God had taught me better than to use carnal weapons against the lives of human creatures. He intimated something about stopping me. I told him I was not afraid of man—that if he did not learn to fight with other weapons he would go to hell.

On Sunday the eighth of June, I preached at brother I—'s to many serious people. While I was pointing out the gospel-salvation, there was a shout in the camp of Israel; and after the meeting ended there was a rejoicing among the people. I met the society, and was more than ever confirmed in my belief, that the Lord had sent me into that part of his vineyard. I there met with a black boy that was happy in the Lord; and I thought he exceeded all the youths that ever I saw for a gift and power in prayer.

Monday June the 9th, I preached a few miles off, from those words, *Loose him and let him go.* There were as many people as the house could contain. And after preaching near two hours, the cries of the assembly were so great that I gave over. The people continued together a long time after, and I doubt not but several were set at liberty. O Jesus! thou still increasest my faith; thou givest me lively sensations of thy pardoning love; and that thou hast called me to the ministry of thy blessed word. At this meeting we were so wonderfully drawn out that we knew not when to part, having seldom felt the like. The next day I had great freedom to preach, and one soul was born to God.[43]

Thursday June 12, I found much ease in preaching at Dr. C—r's to an attentive, solemn congregation; but not very lively. I rode to Col. T—r's[44] and met brother F. P.[45] We held a watch-night, and I think I never had more freedom to speak. The word was blessed to the colonel and his family, and they treated me ever after, more like a son than a stranger; yea, I may say, more like an angel than a poor clod of earth. And I, on my part, shall ever respect them for their kindness to me.

The next day I again crossed the Roanoak river, and had great liberty to preach from these words, *For lo, the winter is past, the rain is over and gone, the flowers appear on the earth, the time of the singing of birds is come, and the voice of the turtle is heard in the land, &c.* After this, we had a love-feast, and many spake freely of the goodness of God. In this place the people wanted to gain me with their kindness,[46] but I refused their obliging offers, being convinced I should do more good in wandering up and down the earth without any incumbrances; and as for riches, I had enough to serve my purposes. The temptation was considerable, and pleasing to nature. Vain world, away with your flattery! I could rejoice in my God, with the testimony of a good conscience, knowing that the oblation was made for the good of Christ's church which he purchased with his own blood. It was no time to think of houses and land, &c. I passed on, rejoicing in God my Saviour, and was greatly encouraged in the blessed work. But halcyon days did not always attend me. For again I experienced the severe buffettings of Satan; but my exercises proved a blessing to me, for my soul was humbled, and I was made in a measure sensible of the need of a deeper work of grace on my heart, before I could be compleatly happy.

Sunday June 22d, in Roan-oak chapel I preached to about five hundred whites, and almost as many blacks who stood without; I found freedom of mind, and tears trickled down the faces of many, both white and black. And the next day while I was preaching a funeral sermon, we had much of the divine presence. In this way, I continued around the circuit, till the quarterly meeting, which was held in August, at Maberry's chapel.[47] The Lord was with me, blest my endeavours, and increased my love to him and his people. In this circuit I conversed with some deeply experienced Christians, and by their humble walk, and heavenly conversation, I was much stirred up to seek a deeper work of grace; especially by the experience of sister B.—I believed there was such a thing as perfect love to be attained in this world; and I likewise knew I was not in possession of it: I saw a beauty in the doctrine, and preached it, but it was at a distance.

About this time the state-oath began to be administered, and was universally complied with, both by preachers and people where I was; but I could by no means be subject to my rulers in this respect, as it touched my conscience towards God: so I was informed I must either leave the state, take the oath, or go to gaol. I told those who came to tender the oath to me, that I professed myself a friend to my country: that I would do nothing willingly or knowingly to the prejudice of it: that if they required it, I would give them good security of my friendly behaviour during my stay in the state. "But why," said they, "will you not take the oath?" "I think," said I, "the oath is too binding on my conscience: moreover, I never swore an oath in my life: and ministers of the gospel have enough to do in their sphere. I want, in all things, to keep a conscience void of offence, to walk in the safest way, and to do all the good I can in bringing sinners to God."[48]

Many of my friends endeavoured to pursuade me to comply; alledging, that I might be more useful among the people: but it was to no purpose. The rulers said, "You must leave the state." This I cannot do, for first, the conference appointed me to labour in this state: and in the second place, I am confident that my appointment is approved of by my heavenly Father; and therefore, I dare not leave the state. "Then," said they, "you must away to prison." That matter, I replied, I leave to the God of Daniel; assured he is able to defend my cause; whether in, or out of gaol.

The many trials I had on this occasion drove me nearer to God, and as many thought that every sermon would be my last, many more attended than otherwise would; and I found much freedom to preach the word; and good was done: I also found a great degree of sweetness in my dear Saviour, for great was his goodness to me.

At a certain place several of the rulers bound themselves to put me to gaol, when I came that way again: my friends persuaded me to decline going *there;* but I told them I could not be clear if I distrusted so good a God. Before I came round to that place, the Lord laid his afflicting hand on some of those ruling men who had threatened to imprison me; so that when I went there, several of them had already made their exit off the stage of human action: and another was lying at the point of death. I preached with much freedom, but there was none to lay the hand of violence upon me; though I had been chased for several months before: and the persecution from this quarter entirely subsided during my stay in the state. In this circuit I met with a number of inward, and outward trials; but I bless God, that ever he sent me into this part of his vineyard: for I can truly say, that the life and conversation of many of my worthy friends, (some of whom were older in the grace of God than myself,) were made a great blessing to me. O! how shall I make suitable returns to my God for the thousands of his favours.

In September I went to North-Carolina, to travel Roan-oak circuit,[49] and was sweetly drawn out in the glorious work, though my exercises were very great, particularly respecting the slavery, and hard usage of the poor afflicted negroes. Many times did my heart ache on their account, and many tears run down my cheeks, both in Virginia and Carolina, while exhibiting a crucified Jesus to their view; and I bless God that my labours were not in vain among them. I endeavoured frequently to inculcate the doctrine of freedom in a private way, and this procured me the ill will of some, who were in that unmerciful practice. I would often set apart times to preach to the blacks, and adapt my discourse to them alone; and precious moments have I had. While many of their sable faces were bedewed with tears, their withered hands of faith were stretched out, and their precious souls made white in the blood of the Lamb. The suffering of those poor out-casts of men, through the blessing of God, drove them near to the Lord, and many of them were amazingly happy.

Respecting Christian perfection, I believed such a thing to be attainable in this life, and in public and private contended for it, and had often felt the need of it in my own soul: but I never had such a view of it in my life as in this circuit. My dear Lord, in a very powerful and sudden manner, gave me to see and feel the need of this blessed work. Every heart-corruption was discovered to me by the blessed Spirit, at the house of that dear afflicted mother in Israel Mrs. [Yansey]. I have had many sweet moments with that precious family; but she has since gone to Abraham's bosom. This discovery was made to me while I was alone in the preachers' room. I expected in a few moments to be in eternity; and the cry of my heart was, Lord save me from inbred sin. The purity of God, heaven, and the law, with the impurity of my heart, were so disclosed to my view, that I was humbled in the very dust; and expected never to enter into the kingdom of heaven without a greater likeness to my dear Lord. I rejoiced that the cold hand of death was not upon me; for I saw with my bodily eyes a ghostly appearance, which in a few moments vanished away. And for more than a week, an earnest struggle continued in my heart for all the mind which was in Christ. My appointments were made, or I am apprehensive I should have declined preaching so pure a gospel, till the heart-corruptions which I felt were washed away. The enemy strove very hard to rob me of my confidence; but although I was at times brought very low, yet I did not let go my hold of the dear Redeemer, the witness of my justification, &c.

One day, I went to my appointment, and whilst the people were gathering, I withdrew about a quarter of a mile from the house, and wrestled with the Lord in prayer; and thought I could not meet the congregation, unless I was delivered from my inbred chains. However, after the people had waited about an hour, I went to the house, but my struggle seemed to be at the height. I thought I would pray with the people and dismiss them. After prayer my Lord gave me this text, *Blessed are the pure in heart; for they shall see God.* Never had I such freedom before that time, to describe 1st. the impurity of the heart: 2dly. how it is to be purified: and 3dly. the blessing consequent thereon—That they shall see God. While I was speaking of the travail of a soul for purity, all my inward distress vanished; and I felt a little heaven on earth. I know that the Lord deepened his work; but I did not claim the witness; yet my soul was happy from day to day.

From this time I began to preach the doctrine of Christian perfection more than ever; the plan seemed as clear to me as the noon-day sun. And many were convinced of the need of it; and some were brought into the perfect liberty of God's children. The word of our dear Lord prospered in the circuit; and some of the children of Belial were stirred up to persecute. One day a very wicked man came into the house while I was preaching; he supposed my discourse pointed at him; and stood for a considerable time, swelling, and threatening in his heart that he would haul me down and beat me. But before the sermon was ended, he gave heed to the things delivered, and a spirit of conviction took hold of his heart; so that before he left the house he prosessed justifying faith; and I trust became a changed man.

I then went to the house of a Christian man, whose brother was a violent persecutor, and lived next door. Whilst I was at family prayer in the evening, he ran over with a loaded gun, and stood with it presented for a considerable time; but had not power to draw the trigger. A few days after, he was in a rage with his brother on account of his receiving the preaching; shot at him, and slightly wounded his body. I was very thankful I escaped him.

In this circuit there was a blessed gathering for good; during my stay sinners were convinced and converted, and at the spring quarterly meeting we had some lively witnesses of perfect love; and others greatly moved to seek after that deep work of grace. Glory to God! I can say I had many blessed, happy moments while traversing the Virginia, and Carolina forests, endeavouring to gather poor lost souls to my dear Redeemer's fold. And it did rejoice my heart to see them flocking after him.

I have often thought, that the consolations afforded me were an ample compensation, for all the difficulties and trials I met with, in wandering up and down through an ill-natured world. And I often reflect and bewail my backwardness, when I first entered so unwillingly as a labourer into my Lord's vineyard. But now, thanks to his dear name, I go willingly; and desire cheerfully to obey all his commandments, and do all the little good I can to promote his honour and glory.

In May, I left the people to whom I found myself closely united, and in whose sight the Lord gave me great favour; and set out for the Leesburgh conference.

SECTION V

*The Journal for this period-May 1778 to July 1779 finds Garrettson
leaving the Conference in Leesburg, Virginia to spend more than a year
and a half in the Peninsula. The occasions of persecution and harrass-
ment are numerous, and the material largely illustrates the nature of
those incidents.*

SECTION V.

*My first regular Travels through the Peninsula,
including the Delaware and part of Maryland.*

We had a comfortable conference in Leesburgh, and May 20, 1778,
I set out for my destined place. After preaching a few sermons, and visiting
my old friends and relations, on the 30th of May I crossed the Chesapeak;
and in the evening had a delightful opportunity of pressing the necessity
of holiness on the minds of many. Blessed be God! there was a shout in the
camp among our blessed Saviour's despised followers. And I have no doubt
but that my Lord directed my lot into this part of the work.

On Sunday I spoke in Kent preaching-house with much liberty; and
we had a sweet refreshing season. This was the first Methodist preaching-
house that was built on this shore. In the evening I was much drawn out
in prayer and self-examination; and felt the sweet beams of the blessed
Spirit, and experienced the bliss of prayer, with a comfortable hope that
my dear Lord had deepened his work of grace in my heart. Four preachers
were appointed by conference for the Peninsula—Brothers H. L. C. and
myself.[50] The enemy of souls had stirred up a great persecution against
the Methodists. Brother H. was taken by the rulers, and put in confinement.[51] Brother L. thought it his duty to return to Virginia. And poor
brother C. was too unwell to travel much: so that for a considerable time
I was left almost alone.

To human appearance our prospects were gloomy. In this place what
was called a tory company embodied themselves, and a backsliding Methodist was at the head of them.[52] It was soon circulated through the country
that the Methodists were enemies to the American cause: and were em-
bodying themselves to meet the English army. A short time before this,
the English preachers had embarked for Europe; and the conduct of Mr.
R. had been very injurious to the persecuted flock: so that the cloud which
arose in the East, grew very dark. During this time, dear Mr. F. A. found
an asylum at the house of good old judge W.[53] and I believe none but the
Lord and himself knew what he suffered for near twelve months. And
we have since seen the hand of the Lord in his preservation, and continu-
ation among us. I am sure if the Lord had not been on our side, we should
have been torn to pieces by our enemies.

My exercises of mind were very great, and my friends in Kent, on
every side, entreated me to stay among them; and not to travel at large
at the hazard of my life. I was ready at first to consent, but had not staid
more than a week among them, when my spirit was stirred within me,
and I cried earnestly to the Lord to know his will. I felt an impulse to go;
that he would stand by me, and defend my cause. And I received such
a deep sense of God on my heart, and such precious promises of his parental
care over me, that I took leave of my Kent friends, and set out without
any dread of my worst enemies. I then travelled largely through the country,

preaching once, twice, three, and sometimes four times a day, to listening multitudes bathed in tears.[54]

I shall not soon forget the 24th of June 1778. O what a wringing of hands among sinners, and crying for mercy! God's people praising him from a sense of his divine presence powerfully felt. O how did my heart rejoice in my dear Saviour! I went through Cecil, and part of the Delaware state. A precious flame was kindled in many hearts, and many were brought to enquire, what they should do to be saved. I visited Mr. F. A. at Mr. W's, and found him very unwell. I had a sweet opportunity of preaching at Mr. W's. After some agreeable conversation with Mr. F. A. I went on to Maryland, and had much liberty in preaching to our persecuted friends in Queen Ann.

In this place they threatened to imprison me; but as they did not take me in the public congregation, I concluded they did not intend to lay hands on me: however, the next day, as I was going to Kent, John B.[55] met me on the road (he was formerly judge in that county). When I came near him, he made a full stop as if he wanted something; apprehending nothing, I stopped and enquired the distance to Newtown: his reply was, You must go to gaol: and instantly took hold of my horse's bridle. I desired him in the Lord's name, to take care what he was about to do: assuring him I was on the Lord's errand, and requesting him to shew his authority for his proceedings. With that, he alighted from his horse, and taking a large stick that lay in the way, for some time beat me with it over the head and shoulders. Not being far from his quarter, he called aloud for help. I saw several persons as I thought, with a rope, running to his assistance. Providentially, at this moment he let go my bridle; had not this been the case, it is probable they would have put an end to my life: for the beasts of the field seemed to be in the utmost rage. I thought the way was now open for my escape; and being on an excellent horse, I gave him the whip, and got a considerable distance before he could mount; but he, knowing the way better than myself, took a nearer rout, and came in upon me with a full strain; and as he passed, struck at me with all his might; my horse immediately made a full stop, my saddle turned, and I fell with force upon the ground, with my face within an inch of a sharp log. The blows I had received, together with my fall and bruises, deprived me of my senses. Providentially, at this time, a woman passed by with a lancet. I was taken into a house not far distant, and bled; by which I was restored to my senses, but it was not expected I had many minutes to live. My affliction was good for me; and I can confidently say, nothing induced me to wish to stay any longer in this world, but the thirst I had for the salvation of my fellow-creatures. The heavens, in a very glorious manner, seemed to be open; and by faith, I saw my dear Redeemer standing at the right-hand of the Father, pleading my cause; and the Father smiling, as reconciled to my poor soul.

I was so happy I could scarce contain myself. My enemy was walking to and fro, in great agitation, wishing he had not molested me. I had a heart to pray for him, and desired him to sit down by me and to read such and such chapters. He did so; I told him if he did not experience that blessed work, he would surely go to hell. I said, if the Lord should take me away, I had a witness within me that I should go to heaven; and that I had suffered purely for the sake of our Lord's blessed gospel; and that I freely forgave him; and entreated him to seek the salvation of his soul, and never again persecute the followers of our Lord. The poor unhappy man did not know which way to look. "I will take you in my carriage," said he, "wherever you want to go." When he perceived I was likely to recover, he went to a magistrate who was nearly as bitter against us as himself, and brought him to me.

They both appeared as if the enemy was in them. With a stern look the magistrate demanded my name: I told him; and he took out his pen and ink, and began to write a mittimus to commit me to gaol. Pray sir, said I, are you a justice of the peace? He replied he was: why then, said I, do you suffer men to behave in this manner? If such persons are not taken notice of, a stranger can with no degree of safety travel the road. "You have," said he, "broken the law." How do you know that? answered I; but suppose I have, was this the way to put the law in force against me? I am an inhabitant of, and have property in this state; and if I mistake not, the law says, for the first offence the fine is five pounds, and double for every offence after. The grand crime was preaching the gospel of our dear Lord and Saviour, Jesus Christ, in which I greatly rejoice. My enemy, said I, conducted himself more like a highway-man, than a person enforcing a law in a Christian country. Be well assured, this matter will be brought to light, said I, in an awful eternity. He dropped his pen, and made no further attempt to send me to prison. By this time the woman who bled me, came with a carriage; and I found myself able to rise from my bed and give an exhortation to the magistrate and my persecutor, and the others who were present.[56]

I rode to the house of old brother D. and preached my dear Master's gospel, with much delight, in the evening, to a few despised disciples, as I sat in the bed, from these words, *In me ye shall have peace, in the world ye shall have tribulation; but be of good cheer, for I have overcome the world*, John xvi. 33.

I can truly say, what I suffered was for my good, and I think it was rendered a blessing to the people around: for the work of the Lord was carried on in a blessed manner, and I met with very little persecution in that country afterwards. (Some time after I preached the funeral sermon of the wife of the above magistrate, and he was very much moved.) In the morning I awoke about four, and desired the friend of the house, if possible, to prepare a carriage for me by six; as I had a long way to go and to preach twice. But being disappointed in getting a conveyance; though scarce able to turn in my bed, my body being so bruised, I looked to the Lord for help, which was granted with sweet consolation. I mounted my horse about seven o'clock and rode about fifteen miles, and preached at eleven o'clock.[57] O! what a nearness I had to my dear Lord, while I held up a crucified Jesus to upwards of five hundred persons! My face bruised, scarred, and bedewed with tears! the people were for the most part much affected. I rode afterwards ten miles further, and preached to hundreds with great freedom. O! how sweet my dear Saviour was to me! I seemed as if I could have died for him.

After a few days respite, I went to the place where I was beaten, and found that the persecuting spirit had in a measure subsided; and that my way was surprisingly opened. I had many hearers, and the word was much blessed to many souls. The language of the hearts of many was, Surely this must be the right way.

The Lord was very kind to me in making a discovery, in a vision of the night, of the things I was to pass through; and they came to pass just as they were made known to me.

From Queen Ann's, I again travelled through the Delaware state, and had many blessed opportunities of inforcing the truth on the attentive multitudes that flocked together from various quarters.[58] In the neighbourhood of Mr. S. the people had been deprived of the privilege of hearing for some time, and when I went among them, I found them hungering for the word. I preached from, *Who is she that looketh forth as the morning, fair as the moon, clear as the sun, and terrible as an army with banners?* Solomon's songs vi. 10. I was so wonderfully drawn out, and my spirit so taken up with divine things, that I almost thought myself in heaven; and many of the persecuted children of God seemed as if they would take wings and fly away. O! it was a great day for an awakening power! and the love-feast was remarkable for the sanctifying operations of the blessed Spirit. Many of our happy friends came from afar, and returned with their hearts all on fire for God. Many happy moments have I had among those loving followers of our dear Lord.

Sunday July 19, I visited and preached to the people of Mashey Hope. I was sorely tempted of the devil all the morning before preaching; he strove to destroy or weaken my faith. I was afraid I should not be a means of doing any good. I wept and mourned in secret at my dear Lord's feet, and sensibly felt the powers of darkness; and as if I never had a commission to preach the everlasting gospel. There was an unexpected congregation. And shortly after I stood up before the people, the devil and unbelief fled; and I gave out, *How shall we escape, if we neglect so great salvation?* Heb. ii. 3. The word run through all the congregation, and there was a great shaking among the people. Among the rest, a woman was struck, and cried aloud for mercy, till she fell to the ground. Her husband was much offended, and I was informed that he threatened me, as he said, for killing his wife. After sermon I spent sometime in praying for, and comforting the distressed.

In the afternoon, accompanied by many, I rode four miles, and preached from *Cut it down, why cumbereth it the ground?* and I found myself greatly at liberty. In this place a few months ago, the people were fast asleep, but now many are awaking up, and several united to Jesus.

After travelling and preaching with great freedom and success in the Delaware state, I was brought on my way in the heat of July to Talbot county, in Maryland, where I laboured for about two weeks night and day with tears. Many souls were refreshed, and I thought it good for me to be there.[59] Many sweet refreshing seasons had I among those dear *loving* people: I shall not soon forget those mothers in Israel, sister P. and sister B. who are now lodged in Abraham's bosom.[60] They, I trust, lived and died witnesses of perfect love.

In this place the people, especially the society, were much alarmed, and stirred up by an uncommon voice, which was heard three evenings successively; and the last time several reputable persons were present. While they were at prayer, it exhorted them to pray mightily; and when one asked who it was, it replied, "I am a good spirit." The last time of its appearance, it seemed to be ascending. At the next quarterly-meeting, a man who was awakened by it, arose and spoke powerfully, and said, "Curiosity that day brought me out, but I was cut to the heart, and rested not till I found peace to my soul:" of this fact I entertain no doubts.

In August I left Talbot, and accompanied by several friends went to Kent Island.[61] I preached frequently to a very gay, high-minded people, with freedom. An admirable change for the better has since taken place in that island. From thence I attended the August quarterly meeting in Kent, but had none to assist me except a few local speakers; but the Lord was powerfully present, both in public worship and at the love-feast. The hearts of many were glad, and I spake freely and feelingly of the goodness of God.

I cannot help thinking the circumstance I am going to relate very remarkable. One day after meeting, my brother John came up to me and shook hands; and looking me very wishfully in the face, without any caution said, "I shall never see you again in this world." And it was even so; for by the time I got round as far as Cecil, he was taken very ill; and a few hours before I got to his house, he was interred on the East side of the preaching-house; where he bid me his last farewell, not more than two weeks before. He was my second spiritual son; and there was an uncommon intimacy between us. His dissolution was revealed to him a long time before he died. An eminent physician was with him the evening before his death, and his wife speaking low to the doctor, enquired how soon he supposed he would die; he told her he apprehended he would not stay till the morning. He over hearing them, said, "Doctor, I shall not go till eight o'clock in the morning." He was a leader of three classes, and beloved by all the people of God; and spent much of his time in the public and private exercises of religion. He had his senses perfectly in his last moments, and his exhortation which he gave was striking. After exhorting his wife and a brother who lived with him, to stand fast in the faith; and entreating the servant to love the Lord; in a very affecting manner he said, "Now there is but one thing which lies heavy on my mind, and that is, the case of two unconverted brothers. Tell them," continued he, "from me, I never expect to see them in heaven," (they lived on the Western shore) "unless they repent, and turn to the Lord." This he said to my brother Richard. Not long after they heard the message, they sought and found the Lord. Thus were his prayers answered. At eight o'clock, as he said, he resigned his spirit to his God, a witness of perfect love.

In September 1778, I again returned to Delaware; and on the 5th for the first time, preached at Mr. W's in Muskmelon, a kind man who had been a Quaker.[62] I had for several days suffered deep exercises of mind, especially while on my way to this place. The devil wanted to persuade me, the Lord was a hard master: and the whole Sabbath morning I was sorely tempted. This appointment was made for Mr. F. A. which caused my trial to be greater. At the meeting there were between five hundred and a thousand people; many of whom came out of curiosity. I preached under a large spreading tree;[63] but the wind being high. I concluded to preach the 2d sermon in the house; but the house could not contain near half the people. I gave out, *One thing I know, whereas I was blind now I see*. Glory to God! Jesus makes use of clay, in this our day to open the eyes of the blind. While I was in the first place describing the blindness of the human mind, my dear Lord displayed his almighty power. There was a great weeping and mourning among poor sinners: I likewise felt much happiness, while describing the Lord's method in bringing sinners to himself, and in shewing the blessed privileges they enjoy. How many were convinced at this meeting, and how many converted, I will not undertake to say; but I believe the number of both was great. I shall take notice of one instance of the power of God at this meeting. A man noted for wickedness, came cursing and swearing (as he has since told me.) But under the first head of the discourse, his sins fell, as it were, with the weight of a millstone on him, and stared him in the face. "I would," said he, "have ran out; but I was afraid to put one foot before the other, lest I should drop into hell, for the pit was disclosed to my view; and I saw no way to escape it: I thought every minute I should fall; but I held myself up by the chair. Oh! said he, under the second head of your discourse, while you were holding up Christ, I saw a beauty in him; and without any dependance on myself, I cast my soul on Jesus; and in a moment the burden fell, and my soul was happy; and I went home rejoicing in my Saviour." I knew him six years after, and had no cause to doubt the soundness of his conversion. Among the rest an officer was cut to the heart, and soon after threw up his commission; and became a pious follower of Christ. I do not think I ever saw a more powerful day in a new place. After meeting, the people all around were begging to have preaching at their houses. Among other places, I appointed to speak at Mr. L's.[64] whose heart the Lord had touched, he lived in Mother Kill; a place famed for wickedness. Previous to my entering this place, the Lord awakened a woman of distinction, by an earthquake; and she found peace to her soul shortly after I came to the place. And about a year after, she died a witness of perfect love. I preached at a variety of places all around, and the work of the Lord went on prosperously: many being brought into newness of life; we began to have a little heaven on earth.

When first I preached at Mr. Lewis's, few came to hear; but the numbers gradually increased; souls were awakened, and I joined many to the society. In the second sermon, among others, a youth by the name of C. B.[65] was awakened, and after a time became a light in the church of God. I preached at his father's, and the work of the Lord prospering, a large society was raised in that neighbourhood, which did honour to the cause of God!

I bless God for it, I had many hearts, hands, and houses, opened around me; and many enquired, "What shall I do to be saved?" The people about Mother Kill, were brought up Presbyterians,[66] and their pastor strove by every means to keep them from the Methodists; but all in vain; they were convinced there was more in religion than a mere form. Multitudes gathered to hear the word, and many large societies were formed in different places.[67]

September 12th, 1778, was the first day of my entering the town of Dover; a proverb for wickedness. I had desired for some time to attack this place, but had no opening, till an old gentleman came one day and heard me preach at Mr. S's:[68] his heart was touched, and he gave me an invitation to preach in the academy.[69] Scarcely had I alighted from my horse before I was surrounded by hundreds; some cried one thing, some another; some said, he is a good man, others said nay, he deceiveth the people—and I was also accused of being a friend to King George. They cried, "He is one of Clowe's men—hang him—hang him." I know not what the event would have been, had not the Lord interposed. There were so many tongues going, and voices heard, that I had no possible chance to speak for myself; and to all human appearance, I was in a fair way to be torn in pieces every moment: I was, however, rescued by several gentlemen of the town, who hearing the uproar, ran to my assistance.

The chief of these were Mr. P. a merchant, who was formerly awakened under Mr. Whitefield, Mr. L. and the alderman of the town.[70] The little Squire pressed through the croud, Zaccheus like, and taking me by the hand, led me through the mob, desiring me to preach and he would stand by me. I mounted the stage at the door of the academy; the people flocked round, both within and without. And after singing and prayer, I gave out, *If it bear fruit well, and if not, then after that, thou shalt cut it down.* My dear Lord was with me of a truth. It was not difficult for me to speak, to be heard a quarter of a mile. Many who did not come to the place, heard me from their gardens and windows. We had much of the presence of the Lord with us. We rarely see such a weeping company in a new place. One woman was powerfully wrought upon, who sat in her window more than a quarter of a mile off. She knew no rest day nor night, till she found a resting place in her heart for the God of Jacob. It was thought by some of my Christian friends, who accompanied me, that very few of the extensive congregation were left without a witness on their hearts, of the truth of what was delivered: More than twenty got the word of truth so fastened, that they did not desire to lose it, and it terminated, I trust, in a found conversion to the souls of many.

The mob hung their heads; many of them were affected, and their ringleader said, he would come and ask my pardon (so I was informed) if he thought I would forgive him; and I understood he betook himself from that day to reading the Bible; and never again persecuted the children of God—at least to my knowledge.

In the evening I lectured at Mr. S's,[71] the old gentleman who had first given me an invitation to the town; many of the chief people of the place came to hear, and we had a very solemn time. When I withdrew to my room, I was severely buffetted by satan. I felt as miserable as Jonah under his withered gourd: It was as though I had given all to the people, and had nothing left for myself. Ah! said the enemy, the Lord will make use of you for the good of others, and then cast you away, as a parent does a rod after correcting the child. I was in such deep exercise, that I could scarcely close my eyes throughout the night, but passed the greater part of it away in sighs and groans, and silence before the Lord. I believe I was permitted to be thus tried in order to keep me at the feet of my dear Lord, and hope I shall be always thankful for his dealings with me.

Monday, September 13th, I preached a few miles out of town, accompanied by many, and the Lord was with us. In the afternoon I returned and found many mourning after Christ; but the devil, and some of his adherents were striving to make them believe, that what I had told them was a delusion; but they were not successful. I joined those who were deeply awakened into a society; and the Lord was with them, spreading his work and converting the souls of many: among the rest there was an old lady stripped of her own righteousness, who had been a communicant in the church for many years; also ten of her children with their husbands and wives were brought under concern for their souls. I preached at her house, and sixteen or eighteen of her children, and children in law were present. The old lady was mourning; but several of them the Lord had set at liberty; and before many months he visited the old lady with his forgiving love, as well as the most of her children. Such a family as this I have seldom seen in any part of America.

The fields appeared white for harvest; but the labourers were very few; and I was engaged in strong cries to the Lord, to open the way and send out more; and blessed be his name, it was so; for he raised up several young men, and sent others from the Western shore. I wrote to brother F. A. who was at Mr. W's, informing him how matters were, and that his way was open into any part of the state, and I requested him to make a visit to Dover: which he did, and brought in many whom I could not reach. The Lord gave us great favour in the sight of Dr. M. minister of the church,[72] and he proved a great blessing to the cause of Methodism. The prejudices of the people began to fall astonishingly; and there was a great gathering to the connection from all quarters, and hundreds enabled to rejoice in the Kingdom of Grace.

The 19th of September, 1778, I attended the funeral of my brother, and a solemn season it was; my youngest brother[73] was there from Baltimore, a wild youth, but the Lord laid his convincing hand upon him, and he returned a penitent mourner: he could stay but a few weeks till he returned to see me, and continued with me till the Lord set his soul at liberty.[74]

Monday September 20th, as I was walking, and meditating through the fields, I heard the cries of one on the top of a tree: and lifting up my eyes, I saw a man about taking his own life; a rope was tied to a limb with a noose in it, and the poor wretch bemoaning himself thus—"O what a wretch I am; once I had a day of grace, but now it is a gone case with me!—I may as well put an end to my wretched life!" He then made a motion to put the rope over his head, bidding the world farewell. I instantly called out to him, and told him to stop a few minutes while I conversed with him. He did; and after some time I persuaded him to give over his wicked intention, and come down from the tree. In the course of our conversation, I found the good Spirit had from time to time strove with him, and he had rejected the offers of mercy: till at length the arch fiend persuaded him, his day of grace was past; and that he had better know his doom as quick as possible. My being an instrument (to human appearance) of saving the life of a human being, as well as, perhaps, an immortal soul, was no small comfort to me.

Tuesday I rode as far as Queen Ann's, and found a very prosperous work going on. I was very comfortable in my dear Lord; and experienced it was sweet to wait on him in secret. I found many hungering for the word, and had liberty in preaching.

Wednesday, September 22d, I awoke and arose early from my pillow, and felt a great nearness to the Lord, and had a sweet time in secret. I visited poor John W.[75] a brother of the Dr. and found him near death, in his sins. In his health he was a great persecutor; but now a penitent, begging the prayers of those he once despised.—O! how did he warn his old companions to flee from their sins; and to take example by him. I was greatly affected with his situation, and did not find freedom to leave him in the arms of the devil. "O! cried he, I am sleeping over hell!" I prayed with him frequently, and still it bore upon my mind; you must not leave him. I seemed as if I had a travail of soul for this young man: I retired into a secret place, and wrestled with the Lord for him, a long time; and I thought the Lord would surely grant him favour. I came to the house and called the family together again for prayer; several of them were happy in the Lord. And in time of prayer the Lord set his soul at liberty; and I do not seem to entertain a doubt, but he went to rest.—O! what a blessed thing it is in such a case, to have Christian friends!—He spake freely of the love of God which he felt in his soul, and his willingness to die. Numbers attended his funeral; and I preached a sermon, with much liberty, on *I heard a voice from heaven, saying unto me, Write, Blessed are the dead which die in the Lord, from henceforth: yea, saith the Spirit, for they rest from their labours, and their works do follow them*, Rev. xiv. 13. Our dear Lord was present, and I trust measurably accompanied his word.

Individuals thought me an enthusiast, because I talked so much about feelings; and impressions to go to particular places. I know the Spirit of God is the guide, and his word is the rule, and by it we are to try all our dreams and feelings. I also know, that both sleeping and waking, things of a divine nature have been revealed to me. One night the state of the people in Somerset and Sussex county, seemed to be revealed to me. In idea I thought I had a large circuit formed; and the people gathering to the banner of our Lord. On Friday October 22d, I set out to go to that place in order to form a circuit; and on Sunday 24th arrived, and had an opportunity of preaching in a forest, to hundreds who gathered, both morning and afternoon, to hear the new doctrine: and suppose many of them expected to be greatly diverted: for they were a people who had neither the form, nor power of Godliness. My text was, *Behold the Lamb of God, which taketh away the sins of the world*, John i. 29. The first sermon was only preparatory to the second, which I preached, after a few minutes intermission, from, *And I saw the dead, both small and great, stand before God, and the books were opened, and another book was opened, which was the book of life, and the dead were judged out of those things written in the books, according to their works*, Rev. xx. 12. I was convinced my impressions in respect to this place, were not enthusiastical, for the power of God ran in a surprizing manner through the congregation; and there was weeping on every side. I suppose that more than thirty were powerfully wrought upon, and joined the society not long after. I had invitations to preach from various quarters, and the way prepared in the same manner in which the Lord had revealed it to me; and sinners flocked to Jesus. Some of the people among whom I went appeared as familiar to me, as if I had been there frequently before. It seemed as if the Lord opened the way before me, step by step.

Monday October 25th, I preached a funeral sermon in the same neighbourhood; and the devil sent out a woman with a pistol or two to shoot me: and while I was preaching from, *Acquaint now thyself with him, and be at peace, thereby good shall come unto thee*, Job. xxii. 21. she came in; and made so much noise that I stopped till they put her out and shut the door. O!

how precious this season was to me! And the divine power was sensibly felt among the people. After the sermon many hung around me in tears, begging of me to pray for them, and likewise to visit them, and not to let the disturbance prevent my coming among them again.

The wife of Mr. N.[76] a merchant in Salisbury, was powerfully awakened; and many others who came from a distance. This part of the world was famous for gambling and dancing; but as the word spread, these vices fell; until there was scarce a frolic heard of in Broad creek. About this place I joined many broken-hearted sinners in society, and many became acquainted with the power of religion.

Saturday Nov. 7th, on my way to Talbot quarterly-meeting, I preached at Mr. P's,[77] and two very dressy young women, who came on a visit to their relations, were wounded, and I left them crying for mercy.

On Sunday Nov. 8th, quarterly meeting began. Brother P.[78] preached a very useful sermon; and I found freedom to discourse on Solomon's chariot: the people were engaged and solemn.

Monday 9th, love-feast began in the morning, and it was a refreshing time. Many rejoiced in the Lord, and spoke freely and feelingly of what God had done for them. After the love-feast I found great freedom to preach from, *The Lord knows how to deliver the godly out of temptation,* 2 Peter ii. 9. and we had a time not soon to be forgotten among the children of God.

Tuesday Nov. 10th, I called again at Mr. P's, and found those young women dressed very plain, and under deep distress. In the evening I read and lectured on the 16th of John, and the Lord was with us of a truth. The power of the Lord was sensibly felt, and his presence filled the room, where about fifteen of us were met for prayer. Brother H.[79] my brother Richard (who had come from some distance to see me) and myself, continued in prayer, exclusive of the time we spent in singing and exhorting, from about eight o'clock till near two; and in that time five souls were set at liberty: the two young women of whom I have spoken, Dr. W.[80] and his two sisters, who came from a distance to quarterly-meeting. This was an extraordinary night to my poor heart, and to the souls of most present.

Wednesday Nov. 11th, greatly refreshed, and strengthened, I set out again on my way to Somerset, and found my young disciples growing in grace, and increasing in number. In my way round, having an invitation from Mr. N.[81] I preached in Salisbury, where the Lord began a blessed work; but the devil strove to stop it; for he raised up enemies against me, who sent the sheriff with a writ to take me to gaol. After he served it on me, he told me I must be confined. I told him, I was a servant of the Lord Jesus, and that if he laid a hand on me, it would be touching, as it were the apple of his eye. He was afraid to injure me: and friends and enemies followed me to the next preaching-place. Many assembled from all quarters, and I preached from, *Behold ye despisers, and wonder and perish; for I work a work in your days, a work which ye shall in no wise believe, though a man declare it unto you,* Acts x. 41. It appeared to me as if the place was shaken by the power of the Lord; many of my enemies trembled like a leaf; I had faith to believe they had no power to stop me; and so it proved, for I went on my way rejoicing in God my Saviour. This day one soul was set at liberty.

I preached at a place called Quantico, and the same flame broke out there. The Lord raised a society, and many souls were converted. Among others, old sister R.[82] who was formerly a hearer of Mr. Whitefield: but the Lord raised her up as a pillar in our society; and she became a mother indeed to the preachers. This society was mostly composed of young people, who were as tender as lambs.

In April 1779, I was led still farther in the wilderness, to enlarge the circuit; and though I met with a variety of trials, and was severely buffetted of Satan; yet my Lord was with me daily. And although in those new places, I had none to converse with, at first, who knew the Lord; yet Jesus was sweet company to me in my retirements. And often the wilderness was my closet, where I had many sweet hours converse with my dear Lord. Whose heart can help rejoicing to think of the kind condescensions of our blessed Lord!—to send his Son to die for man—to permit them to lean on his bosom—and to have such heavenly conversation with *him*! How blind must those deists be, who deny the second person in the ever blessed Trinity! O! that the eyes of all such may be opened, together with all that are enemies to their own souls!

Saturday April 3d, I preached at a place called the Sound, for the first time, near the sea-shore, to about two hundred people. They had been as sheep without a shepherd; but I preached not without hope. There were several who are under the appellation of Baptists in this place; and one of their preachers who spoke after me, cried *down Baby sprinkling*, as he called it. I requested the people to attend the next day at such a place, and I would preach on the subject.

Sunday April the 4th, a number of people assembled and I preached from, *Go ye unto all the world, and preach the gospel to every creature. He that believeth and is baptized shall be saved; but he that believeth not, shall be damned,* Mark xvi. 15, 16. Very great attention was paid. And as they were mostly Presbyterians and Church-men, a vindication of infant baptism was very agreeable to them. If it was of no other service, it prepared their minds for what was to follow; for they knew not who, or what I was. I told them that after a few minutes intermission, I would preach again; I did, from these words, *If the righteous scarcely be saved; where will the ungodly and the sinner appear?* 1 Peter iv. 18. This day will not soon be forgotten—The work of the Lord broke out. Though I continued more than three hours in the two sermons, the people, after I concluded, appeared as if nailed to their seats; for they did not seem as if they wished to move from the place; and weeping was on every side.

Monday April the 5th, I preached still nearer to the sea; and the same convincing power ran through the audience: some of them thought but little of walking ten or twelve miles to hear the word. I appointed a day to read, and explain the rules of our society; and many came together. I preached with great freedom; and then opened the nature and design of our society; and desired the weeping flock that wished to join, to draw near and open their minds. I examined and admitted about thirty. But being weary, I declined taking any more at that time. Weeping and mourning was heard on every side.

I went to a place some distance off, and preached to a gazing company: and while I was speaking, a man started from his seat, saying, "Sir, it is a shame for you to go on as you do; why, do you think you can make us believe your doctrine is true?" I stopt immediately, and desired him to point out wherein it was false. I conversed with him before the people, until he asked my pardon; and was sorry he had exposed his ignorance: and as he was a man of some note, it proved a blessing to the people.

I returned again to the Sound, and preached two, three, and frequently four times a day. And notwithstanding this, they were so hungry for the word, that many would follow me to the house where I was to stay, enquiring, "What they should do to be saved?" The devil in this, as well as other places, had his factors: one man of note set up a reading meeting in opposition to the society; but the power of God reached his heart, so that he gave it up and joined the society. Several hired a clergyman of the church to come and preach against us. He came once, and appointed to come again; but before the time, I met him on the road, and told him, I was the man against whom he preached in such a place. I asked him, if he had ever heard a Methodist? He told me he never had. And after explaining to him our doctrine, and conversing with him more than an hour, he promised that he would never do the like again, and confessed that he was led into it before by a few individuals: and his people could never after persuade him to preach against us, all the time he stayed among them.

In this neighbourhood I have preached to a thousand, or fifteen hundred souls assembled together under the trees; and many were brought to experience justification by faith.[83]

But my mind was amazingly exercised, and I believe the Lord permitted this affliction for the humiliation of my soul. I was frequently afraid, lest after preaching to others, I myself should be a cast-away; and many hours I have spent in secret, weeping before the Lord. Sometimes I was tempted to think, I did more harm than good, and that the people, after a while, would be worse than ever; or that they were hypocrites. At other times, the cross was so heavy a little before I had to preach, that I was constrained, as it were, to cry out, *The burden of the Lord!*—And at such particular times, I was sure to have a happy meeting.

"O! to grace how great a debtor,
Daily I am constrain'd to be:
Let that grace now like a fetter,
Bind my wandering soul to thee."
(Hymn 93 — Methodist Hymnal)

One day I was wandering through the wilderness in search of poor lost sheep, and called at several houses; but they did not want me. At length night came on; and I had been all day, at least from the morning, without any refreshment for myself or horse; and I got lost withal in a thick wilderness, called, the Cyprus Swamp. The night was dark and rainy; and after wandering about for a considerable time, I concluded to take up my lodging as well as I could; for this purpose I stopped my horse; but before I got down, I espied a light, by following which I was led to a house, where I was most kindly entertained. I sat down, and found my soul very happy and thankful. The man of the house fixed his eyes upon me, and at last said, "What are you, or who are you; for I am sure I never saw such a man as you appear to be?" I told him, I was a follower of our blessed Saviour; and asked him, if he would join me in prayer? I then read the 7th chapter of Matthew, and lectured from it; and found great sweetness in prayer. After I withdrew to bed; the wife said to the husband, "That is a man of God; one whom the Lord hath sent to reform the world." When I arose in the morning, he asked me, to what place I was bound, and offered his service and company. I perceived that the Lord had reached his heart: and I now saw for what purpose the crook was in my lot the day before. I asked the woman, if she had a love for the Lord? she said, "Yes." I asked if she ever prayed: she replied, "I pray always." I asked if she knew her sins forgiven, she said, "she did not; but she knew that she should go to heaven when she died. And," said she, "I know that you are a servant of God; but you cannot teach me, for I understand all the scriptures, and I know what kind of death I am to die." After breakfast we got on our way, and as we rode, the man asked me, "What I thought of his wife?" I told him, she was a mystery to me. "Why," said he, "some time ago, she was taken in a kind of melancholy way, and no one knew what was the matter; for thirteen days, she would neither eat nor drink, and frequently she would embrace the pitcher and kiss it, but would not taste a drop, till at length she became so weak, that she betook herself to her bed; and the thirteenth day of her fasting, a number of people waited around, expecting to see the last of her; but all on a sudden she raised up, and said, "You thought that mine was a bodily disorder; but it was not. Now," said she, "I know that my Maker loves me." They gave her food and she eat as heartily as ever: and she has been in that serious way ever since." She appeared to be a very solemn woman, and I had a hope that the Lord had taken her into his favour.

On my return I called on him again, and conversed more fully with the woman, who continued to believe that man could not teach her. I suppose the people in this part of the country had scarce heard any kind of preaching, and knew no more about the new birth than the Indians. I met a man one day, and asked him if he was acquainted with Jesus Christ? "Sir," said he, "I know not where the man lives." Lest he should have misunderstood me, I repeated it again; and he answered, "I know not the man."

Glory to God! I preached in a variety of places all through the wilderness; and many were convinced and brought to the knowledge of the truth. They built a church, and the Lord raised up several able speakers among them. There was an amazing change both in the disposition and manners of the people. The wilderness and the solitary places began to bud, and blossom as the rose; and many hearts did leap for joy. Hundreds who were asleep in the arms of the wicked one, awoke, and were enquiring the way to Zion with their faces thitherward.

As my brethren, in rotation, began to travel largely through this part of the work, I had an opportunity to visit the friends in various parts of Maryland; and found it good for me to be among old established Christians. I had great freedom to preach a full salvation from all sin; and many were on full stretch for all the mind which was in Christ; while others were brought into the perfect liberty of the children of God. I knew what it was to be severely buffetted by the enemy of my soul; but my dear Lord bore me up under all my trials.

On the 1st of June, I returned back to the Sussex circuit in Delaware; and June 6th I preached with great freedom at Thomas L's in the Fork, from *Friend, how camest thou in hither, not having on a wedding garment?* Matt. xxii. 12. I rode six miles and met brother M. We held a watch-night, and I had much satisfaction in hearing several of the exhorters, and gave them notes of permission to speak.

Sunday, June 7th. I spent the morning in retirement, sorely tempted by the devil; and after I went to my appointed place, my mind was so bewildered, I thought there was not a text in all the Bible that I could speak from. I felt myself less than the least. At eleven o'clock there was such a number collected, that I was obliged to preach under the trees. I had been before the people but a few minutes, till the Lord bless me with great light, and the Bible seemed all plain to me. I am sure if I had held the Quaker principle, I should not have attempted to speak; but glory to God! it proved a day of days to many others as well as myself.[84]

Whenever the Lord begins his work in any place, the devil and his children are sure to rise up against it. After preaching I set out for my afternoon's appointment, accompanied by about thirty, whose hearts the Lord had touched. I was pursued by a party of men who way-laid me, and the head of the company, with a gun presented, commanded me to stop.[85] Several of the women who were with us surprised me; they were in an instant off their horses, and seizing hold of his gun, held it until I passed by. That same man was a penitent some time after, and became a member of the society. I went on and preached at old Mr. T—'s, to a large attentive company, and united a prosperous society.

I am not surprised at the devil's rattling his chains, for his kingdom is coming down very fast. It appeared as if hundreds in the congregation were more or less wrought upon, and many appeared to be broken-hearted. We could never get a society in this place till now. I know the day when the Lord began his work in the Fork; I preached from these words, *And in hell he lift up his eyes, being in torment;* and intended, if I saw no fruit, to leave them: but blessed be God, he visited the place in mercy, and the devil's kingdom is like to receive a wonderful shock.

Monday June 8th, 1779. Why does the evil one harrass me in this manner? If possible, a legion of devils are around me: I am attacked on all sides—fighting within and persecution without. I rode about eight miles, and the devil followed me all the way, and frequently told me, "You are a fool, and may as well go back;" and after I got there, he told me, "my journey would be fruitless." I withdrew and mourned before the Lord, and entreated him to grant that the devil might be disappointed; and so it was, for a large number attended at eleven o'clock, and we had much of the divine presence. I spent a good portion of time, after sermon was over, in reading and explaining the rules of the society.

Tuesday June 9. I preached at I. T's. My mind was greatly disturbed all the morning by the enemy of souls: so that I could not keep it fixed upon one thing for a minute at a time; which was a great grief to me. It is surprising that the devil should have power to carry the mind, in the manner he does, to the ends of the earth; but though he has power to tempt, he cannot force us to give way to the temptation; this must be with the concurrence of the will. We had a large gathering of the people here, and a solemn time.[86]

Wednesday June 10th. What is the devil afraid of? why does he chase me in this manner? I do not know that I have given way to sin, either inwardly or outwardly; and yet he tells me frequently, "my commission is run out, and that my labours never will be blessed again." I have had great strugglings in my mind, to know my standing; not that I doubt my adoption into the family of heaven; but respecting my salvation from all inward sin. From this quarter have arose my greatest fears, for more than twelve months past. I know that my dear Lord has given me power to serve him, and that I love him supremely; but these are comprehensive words, *to love the Lord with all the heart.* My wishes have frequently gone up, desirous of a stronger assurance of this perfect love which casteth out fear. I have thought sometimes that I should doubt no more; but fearfulness hath kept me back.

This day I felt strangely: I was so burdened (not with guilt, blessed be God) that I could scarcely bear my own weight. None know what I mean, but such as have received a commission to deliver a message for the Lord.[87] The prophet knew when he cried out, *The burden of the Lord*— Jonah knew something of it when he was called to go to Nineveh—and Jeremiah was well acquainted with exercises of this kind. It is a sweet thing to preach the gospel, but the cross is to be borne. I remember the words of St. John, who eat the little book; in his mouth it was sweet, but it made his belly bitter.

I crossed the river and went to my appointment, which was at I. Mores on Broad creek. The people assembled from all quarters; and many came out who were enemies to the way, and some from afar. I had scarce opened my mouth when my burden dropped off: and in an uncommon manner I was let into the holy scriptures; and the flame ran from heart to heart. I felt as though I had almost faith enough to remove mountains. One thing was noticed, not only by my friends, but likewise by those who were enemies—There had been a great drought, so that the vegetable creation hung in mourning; and it was thought by many they would lose their crops, if it continued much longer. In a particular manner I was led to pray for rain; and a few minutes after the congregation was dismissed, the face of the sky was covered with blackness, and we had a plentiful shower; which greatly surprised and convinced the people. I was now happy enough to see the prosperity of the young converts. While the Lord was plentifully watering the earth, I collected the family for prayer; and we had a great time of refreshing from the presence of the Lord. My soul was so happy while the Lord was uttering his voice in thunder, that it seemed as if I saw, by an eye of faith, the blessed Jesus; and the glorified company around him, in exalted strains, singing and shouting his praise. And this flame continued with me till some time in the night; I then sweetly rested in the arms of my Lord.[88]

Thursday June 11th, I preached to a poor people. Some who came from a distance thought I pointed my discourse at them. Thursday was a very solemn day of fasting. I have noticed that the evil one is more spiteful on my fast-days than at other times. But I feel there is a necessity of keeping my body under, lest after preaching to others I should be a castaway. My public labours this day, as I was among a curious people, were to reconcile some seeming contradictions in scripture. After I had done, I was warmly opposed by an enemy to the cross of Christ. I visited one of the spiritual children of Mr. Whitefield, on her death-bed; and I trust her soul was happy in the Lord.

In the evening I met and examined a large society, and we had a comfortable time. I had a sweet night's rest, and awoke at my usual hour with a happy mind, and prayed earnestly to the Lord, to grant that every moment of my life might be given to him.

I rode to Quantico to visit the young lambs. I expected that the Lord intended to do something for them, for the devil pursued me all the way even till I got to the place. An unexpected congregation assembled in the afternoon, and the Lord was with us of a truth. Several were set at liberty; and the cries of the distressed were heard—Sweet Jesus, thou art lovely to my soul!—O Jesus! thou hast overcome me with thy looks, and the kisses of thy lips! I found great freedom in meeting the society, and in the morning I met them again, and a precious time we had.

Sunday June the 14th. I felt this morning as if my dear Lord intended to do great things for the people. I spent the morning in wrestling with the Lord for a blessing on my labours. I preached at old brother R's. at eleven o'clock: the old judge who came as a hearer, gave great attention; and we had a melting time. I rode ten miles to Salisbury;[89] when I came in, the man of the house took me into a room; and told me I had better leave the town immediately; for a mob was waiting and intended to send me to gaol; "They came to my house last night," said he, "expecting to find you here; but when they found you not, they laid hold on me, and dragging me down the chamberstairs, hauled me along the street till my arms were as black as ink from my wrists to my shoulders; and I know not what would have been the consequence, if I had not been rescued by a magistrate." This mob was made up of what they call the first people in the county. I told my informer that I had come to preach my dear Master's gospel, and that I was not afraid to trust him with body and soul.[90] Many came out to hear me; I understood the mob sent one of their company, to give information to the most convenient time to take me. While I was declaring. *The Lord knoweth how to deliver the godly out of temptation, and reserve the wicked to the day of judgment to be punished,* the heart of the spy, who sat close by me, was touched, and tears plentifully ran down his face. After service he returned to his company, and told them I had preached the truth, and if they laid a hand on me he would put the law in force against them. They withdrew to their homes, without making the slightest attempt upon me. O, who would not confide in so good a God! After our blessed meeting was over, I rode three miles and had a pleasant time with a few of my friends. Glory be to God! he is carrying on a gracious work about this place. All this week I spent in preaching and visiting the young societies.[91]

Sunday June 21, I was to preach at the Sound.[92] In the morning I intended meeting the society at eight o'clock; but such a croud gathered that I declined it; and preached a sermon. At twelve about 1500 gathered, and the Lord made bare his arm under the spreading trees. After a short intermission, I preached another sermon: and it seemed as if the whole country would turn to the Lord. While preaching I was so wonderfully drawn out, that it appeared to me as though I saw our blessed Saviour working prosperously through the assembly. Weeping was on every side.

I spent a week in the neighbourhood preaching several times a day, besides visiting and conversing with the distressed. I believe this work was greatly hindered by the Baptists, who came among the people and drew off a few; and set others to disputing about the decrees, and their method of baptizing.

Sunday June 28th, when I came to brother W's in Muskmelon, I found that a Nicolite preacher had been sowing his seed in the young society, and endeavouring to destroy the new-born children. He told them, "It was a sin to wear any kind of cloathing that was coloured; and that they ought never to pray but when they had an immediate impulse, and that it was wrong to sing." Many people came together, but I perceived a considerable alteration; for some would not sing at all, and others sat both in time of singing and prayer. Some had taken off the borders of their caps, and condemned those who would not do as they had done; in short, some of my own spiritual children would scarcely hear me, because I wore a black coat. I gave out my text, *The kingdom of God is not meat and drink, but righteousness, and peace, and joy in the Holy Ghost*, Rom. xiv. 17. My dear Lord made bare his arm and humbled me among them; and there was a shaking, convincing power. After sermon was ended, I met the society and excluded the leader and one or two more; those that remained took a fresh start, and grew more then ever. I spent the week in Mother Kill, and several other places, and was greatly comforted among the growing societies.

Sunday July 5th, I preached in Dover a little after sun-rise, then rode four miles and preached at brother B's at nine, to hundreds who stood and sat under the trees for want of room in the house, from *Behold a sower went forth to sow*, Matt. xiii. 3. I was in my element, and we had a great display of the power of the Lord. Many about this place are enquiring, *What shall I do to be saved?* I rode on six miles and preached at one o'clock to a listening multitude, under the trees in Mother Kill. O how good my dear Lord was to my soul! It was little trouble to me to preach, for the scripture seemed all open. I rode five miles and preached in Muskmelon again at brother W's, and had I think more freedom than at either of the other places. At the last sermon there was a Quaker preacher present, and after meeting was ended he told a person, that I "spake by the Spirit, if ever man did." The person said, it was my fourth sermon that day— he then altered his mind, and replied, "If that was the case, I was a deceiver; for it was nothing but will worship." This day I stood upwards of six hours in the four sermons, and concluded about sun-set. My spirit was so united to my Jesus, and so transported, that I scarcely felt the fatigues of the day; and the only sustenance I had taken was a little milk and water. I have seldom seen a greater day than this: I do not know but I may say thousands are flocking to Jesus. There is a childish fondness in these people, and I feel unwilling to leave them; but the will of the Lord be done

Monday July the 6th. Having it on my mind, I set out to make an inroad through the Delaware state, where I had never been: I had appointed a friend, who had given me an invitation to Lewis-Town, to meet me at such a time, and conduct me through the country; so that numbers had knowledge of my intention to pass that way. All along the road, many were standing at their doors and windows gazing, and I could hear some of them say, as I passed, "There he is;" "O," said another, "he is like another man." I rode about 30 miles and got to my appointment about three; about four o'clock I began, and shortly after I gave out the text, I. W. brother to the man at whose house I was to preach, came to the door with a gun and a drum, and several other utensils, and after beating his old drum a while, he took the gun, and was dodging about as though he was taking aim to shoot me: this greatly terrified the women, so that there was nothing but confusion. I then stopped, and withdrew to a private room. Soon after the townsquire and several other magistrates came, and among the rest the Presbyterian minister. The town-squire commanded him to depart immediately to his own house, or behave himself, otherwise he would send him to gaol. We now had peace, and I found great freedom to finish my sermon. I have no doubt but the Lord began his work. The minister told some of the people afterwards, that I held out nineteen errors. The town-squire told me the courthouse was at my service, and I should be welcome to his house. I was sensible of the anger of the devil, for his temptations were powerful; he strove to raise a party against me, and to banish me from the place. I preached in and about the town day and night, and the Lord owned his word.

Wednesday 8. My old enemy Wolf by nature and name, set on by a few others, came into the court-house while I was preaching, not with a gun and a drum, but with fire which he put in the chimney, and then began to heap on wood, though the day was exceeding warm—finding that this did not disturb me, he brought in a bell, and rung it loudly through the house. I stopped and enquired if any would open a large private room. Many were offered, and I withdrew and finished my sermon at the house of a kind widow woman. In spite of all the opposition, the word found the way to the hearts of the hearers, and many clave to me; and though severely tempted of the devil and persecuted by many of his votaries, my heart was with the Lord; and many were the sweet moments I had in secret.

Sunday July 12th, my appointments were at nine in the morning and three in the afternoon, that I might not interfere with the hours of the church. The court-house was crouded at nine, and a most pleasent time I had. In the morning it rained, so that Mr.—did not make his appearance, and as the people were waiting, the Squire said I had better begin my 2d sermon. Just as I began, he arrived, and waited till I was nearly done; and then the bell rung over my head for church; but the people would not move until I concluded; after which we all went into church; but his pulpit and that of Mr. W. rang against me; and all such runabout fellows. His having the bell rung over my head, much offended, not only those who were my friends, but many of his also. The more they preached and spoke against me, the more earnestly did the people search their Bibles to know, whether these things were so.

I had an appointment a few miles from the town, by the side of a river: and some declared, if I went there they would drown me. I went and found a large concourse of people; and preached with much freedom; but no man assaulted me. I had five miles to my afternoon's appointment; and when I had got two miles on my way I looked behind and saw a man, drest like a soldier, riding full speed, with a great club or stick in his hand. I now found it necessary to exercise my faith. When he came up to me, he reached out his hand, saying, "Mr. Garrettson, how do you do? I heard you preach at such a time; and believe your doctrine to be true; I heard you was to be abused at the river to-day, and I equipt myself as you see me, and have rode twenty miles in your defence, and will go with you if it is a thousand miles, and see who dare lay a hand upon you." Friend, said I, the scripture tells us, that vengeance belongs to God, and not to man. "Very true sir," said he, "but I think I should be justifiable in so glorious a cause." I travelled and preached all through the forest, and the Lord enlarged my heart, and gave me many precious souls; for numbers were brought to enquire after Religion.

Saturday July 18, I went to the Fork, accompanied by my dear old friends brother and sister W. And on July 19, I preached again in the open air to many hundreds; and found that the work of the Lord was still going on. In the afternoon I preached to almost as many at old Mr. Ts. His daughter Rebecca is a very happy young woman. A few months since she was in the height of the fashion, but now sees the evil and folly of these things.

Monday July 20, I went to preach at a house by the river, on the edge of Dorset county; here the Lord had greatly weakened Satan's kingdom. I preached at the door to abundantly more than could get into the house. I was so surprisingly drawn out, and the people so engaged, that I could not conclude under two or three hours. From the looks of the people, I should not have thought I had an enemy in the congregation. After sermon, being much spent, I withdrew. Shortly after a person came to me and said, "two men wanted to see me." I told him to desire them to walk up, thinking they were persons in distress, and wanted instruction; but when I saw them, I discovered wickedness in their very looks. One of them was a magistrate, and he was a Churchman; the other was a Presbyterian, and he was a disputant. The magistrate brought him out in order to confuse me in points of religion: and then his intention was to send me to prison. I desired them to sit down, and the disputant began; he said but a few words until I asked him if his soul was converted to God? I charge you, said I, in the presence of him before whom we shall shortly stand; tell me, is your soul converted to God? Do you know that your peace is made with God? He was struck, and knew not what to say; but at last he said, "I do not know that I am." Then, replied I, you are in the way to hell. And I began to exhort him to repent, and turn to the Lord. I think I never saw a man so confused in my life. He made attempts to quote scripture, but could get hold of none. The magistrate seeing in what a condition his disputant was, in a rage said, "Sir, do you know the laws of this state? You have not taken the oath, and you have broken the law by preaching; you must go to gaol." I bless God, said I, that I am not afraid of a gaol.— They withdrew, and after I had eaten dinner, I mounted my horse and set out to attend my afternoon's appointment; but a sheriff met me a few rods from the house, and commanded me to stop. Many of my friends gathered around me, and offered to be security for my appearance at court; but I told them I would give no security. I had faith to believe that he had not power, or at least would not be permitted, to stop me. I looked him in the face, and said, I am going on the Lord's errand, and if you have power, here I am, take me; but remember, that the God against whom you are fighting, who made yonder sun, is just now looking down upon you; and I know not but that he will crush you to the earth, if you persist in fighting so furiously against him. I am now on my way to Philadelphia to preach the glorious gospel of my Redeemer; and the consequence of your stopping me in this manner will be rueful. After conversing with him a few minutes, I perceived his countenance fall, and he said, "It is a pity to stop you;" and so turned his back upon me. I went rejoicing on my way, accompanied by many of my kind friends, some of whom were weary and heavy laden; and had an opportunity in the afternoon to inculcate precious truths on as many people as could croud into a large house standing by the river side.

After attending several quarterly meetings, where we had a very large number of people, and great displays of the power of convincing and converting grace, I pursued my journey to Philadelphia, accompanied by several of my friends from that city. In my way I preached at Mr. S's, in Queen Ann's: and after preaching, to get clear of a mob which they expected would surround the house, (for there were many violent opposers in this part of the county) I rode, accompanied by a tender friend, the best part of the night, and got into another county. The next day my friends met me: we then went on together and arrived safe in Philadelphia.

SECTION VI

The Journal offers only a brief summary of Garrettson's journey to Philadelphia and New Jersey. His manuscript journal, however, gives a much more detailed account of this period from September, 1779 to February 8, 1780. Much of the material is from the manuscript and has never been published.

SECTION VI.

An Account of a few months spent in Pennsylvania and the Jerseys.[93]

During my stay in the Peninsula, on this visit, which was about fifteen months, several new circuits were formed; hundreds entered in the society; a great reformation had taken place; great numbers were really and powerfully converted to God; and several preachers raised. I suppose in this time, I preached in more than a hundred new places, where my dear Lord began a glorious work. All manner of evil was said of me by the wicked; but blessed be God, for the answer of a good conscience, and a heart united to my dear Saviour; and for the friendship and good wishes of thousands, whose hearts were touched under the word.

I staid about two months in Philadelphia, and as it was shortly after the British troops left that city, there was much confusion in the society, as well as among the people at large: I met with a variety of trials, and saw very little fruit of my labours. But many of our dear friends were near, dear, and precious to me: and frequently since that time I have had a great desire to spend a few months in that city.

I bless and praise my dear Lord, for the prosperous journey he gave me through the Jerseys: several were awakened, and some brought to know Jesus. One day, after preaching, an old man came to me and said, all in tears, "This day I am an hundred and one years old, and this is my spiritual birth-day." The dear man's soul was so exceedingly happy, that he appeared to be ready to take his flight to heaven.

I preached at a new place, where the congregation consisted mostly of young people, from, *The Son of man is come to seek and to save that which was lost*, Luke xix. 10. We had a wonderful display of the power of the Lord. After I had finished, the young people hung around each other crying for mercy; and I believe many will praise the Lord eternally for that day. A remarkable circumstance happened respecting a young woman, who was brought up in the Quaker persuasion. It pleased the Lord to awaken her when very young, without preaching; she experienced the pardoning love of God, and continued happy for some time; still by degrees she got off her watch, having none to strengthen, but many to draw her away. She at length fell from God, and became as wild and trifling as ever. Soon after this she was entirely deprived of her speech; and the enemy of her soul persuaded her to believe, it was a sin for her to do any kind of work, or even to dress herself; and if they gave her a book to read she thought it sinful to turn over a leaf, and would read no more, unless some one would do this office for her. It was impressed on her mind that there was a people in such a place, that served the Lord; and if she could get among them, they would be a blessing to her; and she would be restored to her speech. She had never heard of a Methodist; and the place which was revealed to her was near twenty miles off, where there was a young, loving society. Though she knew nothing of the way, she set off to find that place and people. Her family missing her, pursued and brought her back. Not long after she made a more successful attempt, and found the society. The Lord revealed her case to them. There was a preacher present, Mr. Daniel Ruff who being agreed, they called a meeting, and cried to the Lord in her behalf that day and the next; she then went into a private room, kneeled down to prayer, and continued therein till the Lord blessed her soul. At the same time her tongue was loosened, and she could speak forth the praises of Israel's God. She had been dumb about two years. Sometimes after, I came into this neighbourhood and sent word to her mother, I would preach such a day at her house. When the day arrived, I took the young woman home, accompanied by many friends, and we were received like angels: some thought the Methodists could work miracles. Many of the friends and neighbours came, and could not but observe how angelic this young woman appeared to be; who was now able to speak and work as well as usual. I bless the Lord who gave me great freedom in preaching on this remarkable occasion. The people seemed to believe every word which was delivered: and a precious sweet season it was. The old lady was ready to take us in her arms, being so happy, and so well satisfied with respect to her daughter.

SECTION VII

Garrettson's imprisonment forms the major part of this section, and describes not only his own arrest and release, but also that of J. Hartley, another Methodist preacher jailed in Talbot County, Maryland. The period covers February through April, 1780, and represents in candid fashion the pressures and persecutions exerted on the Methodists. The Conference, meeting in Baltimore April 24, 1780, gave affirmation to the question regarding preachers freeing their slaves. Although some statesmen condemned the practice of slaveholding as did religious leaders, the practice was a continuing source of contention for preachers like Garrettson.

SECTION VII.

An Account of my Travels after I was released from Prison.

After preaching in a variety of places in the Jerseys and Pennsylvania, with great freedom; in the fall I returned to the Peninsula, (which was my second visit) and we had a blessed quarterly-meeting at Mr. W's. I travelled largely through this country all the winter; and many were gathered into the fold. I would say something here of the beginning and progress of the work of God in Dorset county—a place where they were generally of the church of England; and universally enemies to the life and power of religion. The work began by the means of a young woman who was niece to, and sometimes lived with judge E. of Dorset: her sister was wife to the honourable Mr. B.[94] I am not certain whether it was on a visit to Queen Ann's or Dover, that she fell in with the Methodists, by whose means she was convinced and converted; and afterwards became a pious follower of the blessed Jesus. When she returned to her uncle's in Dorset, they began to think she was beside herself; however, the Lord blessed her endeavours in favour of her sister Polly, and a few others. Her sister was soon set at liberty in a powerful manner, and had as great a zeal for God as her sister Catharine. Shortly after, their sister B. became as blessed a woman as ever I saw; and I have not a doubt but that she lived and died a bright witness of sanctification. Mr. B. was brought into the faith, with two young lawyers who were studying under him, and several others of the family; who were the fruits of the labours of these pious, I may say, blessed women. To return; some time after Mary's conversion, she went to visit H. A. Esq. who was a relation of hers. As he was a man of fashion, and an entire stranger to inward religion, he was much afraid she would drive his wife out of her senses. He undertook to shew his *visitor* that the Methodists were not in the right way; and for this purpose he chose an old book written by a Puritan divine, an hundred and fifty years ago: but he had not read many minutes before conviction seized him, and the tears flowed from his eyes. He withdrew and read, till he thought he must go among the Methodists with his book, and compare it with theirs. He did so, and found the Methodist publications to agree in substance with that. On this occasion I first met with him at Mr. W's. After he had laboured some time under distress of soul, the Lord gave him rest—he felt the burden of guilt removed—and now expressed an anxious desire that I should come to the county where he resided, being determined to stand-by the cause as long as he lived.

Thursday Feb. 10th, 1780, I arose very early in the morning, and addressed the throne of grace. My dear Master wonderfully refreshed my soul, and I felt a willingness to suffer any thing, whatever the Lord might permit to come upon me, for his work's sake. I opened my mind to Mr. Francis Asbury who was at Mr. W's, and he seemed very desirous I should accept the invitation. He then commended me to the Lord in prayer, and I set out in good spirits with a strong hope that good would be done.[95] The first day I got half way, and had a comfortable night. February 11th was a day of deep exercise. Are others distressed in the way that I have been? I travelled on seemingly with the weight of a millstone. I wept bitterly as I passed along, and several times stopped my horse, intending to turn back, but was still urged on my way. I got to my dear friend Mr. A's,[96] some time before night; and the burden which I felt all the way, left me at his door. The dismission of it was perceptible, for my spirit did rejoice in God my Saviour. I was conducted into a private room, where the Lord let me know that I was in the very place he would have me to be.

In the evening the family were gathered together for prayer: I shall never forget the time: I suppose about twelve white and black were present. The power of the Lord came among us: Mrs. A.[97] was so filled with the new wine of Christ's kingdom, that she sunk to the floor, blessing and praising the Lord. And many of the blacks were much wrought upon. This night was a time of great refreshment to me.

Saturday 12. About thirty of the neighbours were called together; and the word seemed to melt their hearts. I had not the least doubt, but the Lord had called me to this place.

Sunday 13. Near an hundred gathered: the field, though in the winter, seemed ripe for harvest; and my gracious God wrought wonderfully in the hearts of the people; so that some who were enemies before acknowledged it to be the truth.[98]

Monday the 14th, accompanied by my friend, I went to the other part of the county. The field is ripe.[99] One man was deeply affected only by seeing us. I preached at colonel V's, a clever man,[100] who afterwards became a great friend to us and himself too.—The fields are white for harvest—The devil is angry—The wicked rage, and invent lies and mischief. The county court was sitting, and some of the heads of it were determined, by some means or other, to clear the place of such a troublesome fellow.[101] For a cloak they charged me with toryism: and I was informed, gave a very wicked man leave, and promised to bear him out, in taking my life; and for this purpose he was to lay in wait for me the next day. It providentially reached my ears that night before I went to bed, and as the wicked seemed thus inclined. I thought it expedient to withdraw to Mr. A's[102] where I staid two days; but being pressed in spirit, I could stay no longer; I went to another part of the county. Many came out to hear, and the word was still attended with power; for they began to enquire the way to heaven.

I had a most remarkable vision of the night. And in that vision it was revealed to me what I was to suffer; and that the Lord would stand by me, so that my enemies should not injure me. Hundreds flocked out to hear the word, on one side sinners were enquiring, what they should do to be saved; and those on the other side, how they should manage in order to banish me from the place.

Monday 21. I had great satisfaction in reading a piece that treated on the human soul.—I had much freedom in the word in public, and a blessed family-meeting at my good friend A's; but sorely tempted of the devil. Shortly after (shall I speak the truth? I will without the fear of man, though these things may appear strange to some people) I went to bed, the devil made his appearance upon it: first he felt like a cat,[103] he then got hold of my pillow: I now believed it to be the fiend, and was not alarmed; I took hold of the pillow, and both pulled at it; I cried out, get behind me Satan. And immediately he vanished. I went down stairs in the morning intending not to speak of what had past: but brother A. enquired if I had been down in the night; I told him I had not; "why," said he, "shortly after you went up, I came into the hall, and was at prayer, when I heard some one walk down stairs, and seemed to be standing at the door: as I knew there was none above but yourself, I concluded it must be you that wished to go out; I therefore went and opened the door, but saw no body, and certainly it was the devil." This was about the precise time he left my bed. Poor devil, you are afraid of your kingdom. I then mentioned what had past in my chamber. The little daughter was under some concern of soul, and getting up one night, awoke her parents, and told them she was afraid the devil would carry her away.[104] The soul spirit was wonderfully roused, and very bitter against this dear family.

February 24, I had a sweet and powerful time. After I went to rest I was strangely exercised in my sleep: I thought I saw an innocent creature chased almost to death, by a company of dreadful beings; after a while I saw a cloud about the size of my hand rising in the West, which grew blacker and darker, till it appeared to cover the earth: I thought now, most surely the world is to be at an end. I saw after a while those cruel beings turn pale as death. I saw a person come up to the innocent creature, which they were chasing, and receive it. I awoke rejoicing, but knew not how to interpret this dream.

Saturday 25, my spirit was solemn and weighty: expecting something uncommon would turn up. I withdrew to the woods, and spent much time before the Lord. I preached with freedom to a weeping flock, my friend A. accompanying me to the place. In the evening we were repairing to his house, being about to preach there the next day; but a parcel of men embodied themselves and way-laid me, with an intention to take me to gaol. About sun set they surrounded us, and called me their prisoner. They beat my horse, cursed and swore, but did not strike me.[105] Some time after night they took me to a magistrate who was as much my enemy as any of them. When I was judged, and condemned for preaching the gospel, the keeper of the peace, who sat in his great chair, immediately wrote a mittimus and ordered me to gaol. I asked him if he had never heard of an affair in Talbot county. Brother J. H.[106] was committed to gaol for the same crime, that of preaching the gospel: soon after the magistrate was taken sick unto death, and sent for this same preacher out of confinement to pray for him. He then made this confession, "When I sent you to gaol," said he, "I was fighting against God, and now I am about to leave the world, pray for me." His family were called in, and he said to his wife, "This is a servant of God: and when I die, I request he may preach at my funeral. You need not think I have not my senses; this is the true faith." He then gave brother I. H. charge of his family, and desired them to embrace that profession. Now said I, I beseech you to think seriously of what you have done, and prepare to meet God. Be you assured, I am not ashamed of the cross of Christ, for I consider it as an honour to be imprisoned for the gospel of my dear Lord. My horse was brought, and about twelve of the company were to attend me to gaol. They were all around me; and two, one on each side, holding my horse's bridle. The night was very dark; and before we got a mile from the house, on a sudden there was a very uncommon flash of lightning, and in less than a minute all my foes were dispursed: my friend A. was a little before the company. How, or where, I know not, but I was left alone, I was reminded of that place of scripture, where our dear Lord's enemies fell to the ground, and then, this portion of scripture came to me, *Stand still, and see the salvation of God*. It was a very dark cloudy night, and had rained a little. I sat on my horse alone, and though I called several times, there was no answer. I went on, but had not got far before I met my friend Mr. A. returning to look for me. He had accompanied me throughout the whole of this affair. We rode on talking of the goodness of God, till we came to a little cottage by the road side, where we found two of my guards almost scared out of their wits. I told them if I was to go to gaol that night, we ought to be on our way, for it was getting late. "O! no," said one of them, "let us stay until the morning." My friend and I rode on, and it was not long, ere we had a beautiful clear night. We had not rode far, before the company had gathered, from whence I know not. However, they appeared to be amazingly intimidated, and the foreman of the company rode along side of me, and said, "Sir, do you think the affair happened on our account?" I told him that I would have him to judge for himself; reminding him of the awfulness of the day of judgment, and the necessity there was of preparing to meet the judge of the whole earth. One of the company swore an oath, and another immediately reproved him saying, "How can you swear at such a time as this." At length the company stopt, and one said, "We had better give him up for the present;" so they turned their horses and went back. My friend and I pursued our way. True it is, *The wicked are like the troubled sea, whose water casts up mire and dirt*. We had not gone far before they pursued us again, and said, "We cannot give him up." They accompanied us a few minutes, and again left us, and we saw no more of them that night. A little before midnight we got safe to my friend's house. And blessed be God, the dear waiting family were looking out, and received us with joy. And a precious sweet family-meeting we had. I retired to my room as humble as a little child, praising my dear Deliverer.

During the remaining part of the night, though dead in sleep, I was transported with the visions which passed through my mind. And had a confidence in the morning, that my beloved Lord would support me. I saw in the visions of the night, many sharp and terrible weapons formed against me; but none could penetrate, or hurt me; for as soon as they came near me they were turned into feathers, and brushed by me as soft as down.

Sunday 27th, at eleven o'clock many came out to hear the word, and it was expected my enemies would be upon me; and I was informed, not a few brought short clubs under their coats, to defend me in case of an attack, for many had just about religion enough to fight for it. As I was giving out the hymn, standing between the hall and room doors, about twenty of my persecutors came up in a body, (I was amazed to see one of them, who was an old man and his head as white as a sheet) these were under the appellation of gentlemen. The ringleader rushed forward, with a pistol presented, and laid hold of me; putting the pistol to my breast. Blessed be God! my confidence was so strong in him, that this was with me, as well as all their other weapons, like feathers; as was represented to me in the vision of the night. Some of the audience, who stood next to me, gave me a sudden jerk; I was presently in the room, and the door shut. As soon as I could I opened it, and beckoning to my friends, desired that they would not injure my enemies; that I did not want to keep from them, but was willing to go to gaol. If I had not spoke in this manner, I believe much blood would have been shed. I began to exhort, and almost the whole congregation were in tears; and in a particular manner the women were amazingly agitated. I desired my horse to be got, and I was accompanied to Cambridge, where I was kept in a tavern from twelve o'clock till near sun-set, surrounded by the wicked; and it was a great mercy of God that my life was preserved.[107]

A little before night I was thrust into prison, and my enemies took away the key, that none might administer to my necessities.[108] I had a dirty floor for my bed, my saddle-bags for my pillow, and two large windows open with a cold East wind blowing upon me: but I had great consolation in my dear Lord, and could say "Thy will be done." During my confinement here, I was much drawn out in prayer, reading, writing and meditation. I believe I had the prayers of my good friend Mr. F. Asbury: and the book which he sent me, (Mr. Rutherford's letters during his confinement) together with the soul-comforting and strengthening letters which I received from my pious friends, was rendered a great blessing to me. The Lord was remarkably good to me, so that I experienced a prison to be a mere paradise; and I had a heart to pray for, and wish my worst enemies well. My soul was so exceedingly happy, I scarce knew how my days and nights passed away. The bible was never sweeter to me. I never had

*Dorchester County Jail, Cambridge, Maryland,
where Garrettson was imprisoned. (from
"The Heart of Asbury's Journal," by Tipple.)*

99

a greater love to God's dear children. I never saw myself more unworthy I never saw a greater beauty in the cross of my dear Lord; for I thought I could (if required) go cheerfully to the stake in so good a cause. I was not at all surprised with the cheerfulness of the ancient martyrs, who were able in the flames to clap their glad hands. Sweet moments I had with my dear friends who came to the prison window.[109]

> Happy the man who finds the grace,
>   The blessing of God's chosen race,
> The wisdom coming from above,
>   The faith which sweetly works by love.
>
>   —Charles Wesley

Many, both friends and strangers, came to visit me from far and near, and I really believe I never was the means of doing more good for the time: for the county seemed to be much alarmed, and the Methodists among whom I had laboured, were much stirred up to pray: for I had written many epistles to the brethren. I shall never forget the kindness I received from dear brother and sister Avery. They suffered much for the cause of God in Dorset county, for which (if faithful) they will be amply compensated in a better world.[110]

My crime of preaching the gospel was so great, that no common court could try my cause. There appeared to be a probability of my staying in gaol till a general court, which was near twelve months. My good friend Mr. Avery (Airey) went to the governor of Maryland, and he befriended me: had I been his brother, he could not have done more for me.[111] The manner in which he proceeded to relieve me was this. I was an inhabitant of Maryland by birth and property: I could likewise claim a right in the Delaware state, which state was more favourable to such *pestilent fellows*. I was carried before the governor of Delaware. This gentleman, was a friend to our society. He met me at the door, and welcomed me in, assuring me he would do any thing he could to help me. A recommendatory letter was immediately dispatched to the governor of Maryland; and I was entirely at liberty. O! how wonderfully did the people of Dorset rage—but the word of the Lord spread all through that county, and hundreds both white and black have experienced the love of Jesus. Since that time I have preached to more than three thousand in one congregation, not far from the place where I was imprisoned; and many of my worst enemies have bowed to the sceptre of our Sovereign Lord. The labours of C. P. and C. were much blest in this place, in the first reviving and spreading of the work.

After I left my confinement, I was more than ever determined to be for God, and none else.[112] I travelled extensively, and my dear Lord was with me daily; and my spirit did rejoice in God my Saviour. In visiting the young societies, after I left gaol, we had blessed hours: for many came to hear, sinners cried for mercy, and God's dear people rejoiced.

Friday 24, was a solemn fast, being Good-Friday, the day on which my dear Redeemer gave up his precious life. Three days after, being in a blessed family, I had great sweetness both in public and private; and before I laid down to rest, I was very desirous of being lost and swallowed up in the love of my dear Redeemer, and of feeling the witness of perfect love. After I laid down to rest, I was in a kind of visionary way for several hours. About one I awoke very happy, arose from my bed and addressed the throne of grace. I then lighted a candle and spent near two hours in writing the exercises of the night. I saw myself travelling through a dismal place, encompassed with many dangers; I saw the devil, who appeared very furious; he came near to me and declared with bitterness, he would be the death of me; for, said he, you have done my kingdom much harm: thus saying, he began pelting me with stones, and bedaubing me with dirt, till I felt wounded almost to death, and began to fear I should fall by the hand of my enemy. But in the height of my distress, my dear Saviour appeared to me: I thought him the most beautiful person that ever my eyes beheld: "I am your friend," said he, "and will support you in your journey; fear not, for your enemy is chained." I seemed to receive much strength, and the power of my enemy was so broken, that he could not move one foot after me: all he could do was to throw out threats, which he did loudly, till I got out of his hearing. Being safe from these difficulties, I looked forward and saw a very high hill which I was to ascend; and began to fear I never should be able to reach the top: I entered on my journey, and got about half way up, so fatigued that I thought every moment I must sink to the earth; I laid down to rest myself a little, and seemed to fall into a kind of dose; but I had not laid long, before the person who met me in the valley passed by, and smote me on the side saying, "Rise up, and be going, there is no rest for you there." With that I received strength, and got up to the top of the hill. I then looked back and saw my enemy at a great distance: I was greatly surprized when I saw the place through which I had come; for on every hand there appeared to be pits, holes, and quagmires in abundance. I was much wounded, and all bespattered with dirt; but looked around to see if I could find any house: and at a distance I espied a little cottage, and made up to it: when I got near the door, two angels met me and said, "Come in, come in, thou blessed of the Lord, here is entertainment for weary travellers." I thought within appeared to be the most beautiful place I had ever seen. After I went in, I thought it was heaven filled with blessed saints and angels. One and another broke out "Glory, glory," &c. &c. till the place was filled with praises. One spake to me and said, "this is not heaven, as you suppose, neither are we angels, but sanctified Christians; and this is the second rest. And it is your privilege, and the privilege of all the children of God." With that I thought I had faith to believe, and in a moment my spotted garments were gone; and a white robe was given me: I had the language and appearance of one of this blessed society: I then awoke.

Before this, I had an ardent desire truly to know my state, and to sink deep into God. When I awoke I seemed all taken up with divine things; and spent part of the remainder of the night in writing, prayer, and praises: and had a strong witness of union with my dear Lord. My brother Thomas from Baltimore side came to see me, and travelled several weeks with me: and blessed times we had together; for I believe it was on this visit he felt a witness of pardoning love to his soul.

Upon a certain occasion, I was wonderfully led to think of the place called hell, and was severely buffetted by the devil. "Hell, said he, is not as bad a place as you represent it: how can God be a merciful Being, as you set him forth, if he sends people to such a dismal place for a few sins, to be tormented forever?"—I was earnestly desirous to know what kind of place it was. And the Lord condescended to satisfy me in the dead season of the night. After I fell into a deep sleep, I seemed to enter through a narrow gate into eternity; and was met by a person who conducted me to the place called hell; but I had a very imperfect view of it; I requested to be taken where I could see it better, if that could be done: I was then conveyed to a spot where I had a full view of it. It appeared as large as the sea, and I saw myriads of damned souls, in every posture that miserable beings could get into. This sight exceeded any thing of the kind that ever had entered into my mind. But it was not for me to know any of them. Was I to attempt to describe the place as it was represented to me, I could not do it. Had I the pen of a ready writer, and angelic wisdom, I should fall short. I cried out to my guide, it is enough. With that he brought me to the place where he first met me. I then desired a discovery of heaven: my guide said "not now, return; you have seen sufficient for once; and be more faithful in warning sinners, and have no more doubts about the reality of hell." Then I instantly awoke.

SECTION VIII

Among the prominent issues for Methodism in 1780 was the question of administering the ordinances of baptism and especially the Lord's Supper. As early as the Deer Creek Conference May 20, 1777 this question was foremost. The answer was to postpone until the next conference session. The question was repeated at successive Conferences until 1779 when it was decided to permit several of the older preachers to perform the sacraments and the marriage ceremony. The failure or absence of the Church of England clergy, especially in the South, prompted this decision. Garrettson was present at all these Conferences, but together with the Methodist preachers of the North opposed this innovation. Asbury, Watters, and Garrettson carried this concern to the Conference held in May, 1780 at Mannicantown, Virginia.

SECTION VIII.

A short Account of my Labours and Exercises on the Western-Shore, in the year 1780.[113]

The Methodists being only a society, who were mostly united (with respect to communion) to the church of England; and her ministers (especially in Virginia, and Carolina) in the time of the war were dispersed, so that a large body of people, under the name of Methodists, were in a great measure destitute of the ordinances of the Lord's house. In this case what was to be done? Our dear Virginia brethren thought it expedient to form themselves into a church, and have the ordinances among them; which they did in the year 1779. But it was contrary to the minds of the preachers to the North.

In April 1780, we held a conference in Baltimore; at which brother Francis Asbury brother William Watters and myself thought proper to visit our brethren at the South: and after a tedious journey of several hundred miles, we arrived safe in Manekin-Town; where we found the brethren in conference, fully persuaded in their minds that the Lord required us to be a separate church. We for a considerable time confered together, and much of the divine presence was among us. On both sides it was painful to part. This the great governor of the church would not permit; for when the help of man failed, he interposed his omnipotent arm, and convinced our brethren, that they ought at least to accede to a suspension of the ordinances for one year: till the founder of our society, Mr. John Wesley, could be consulted. A circumstantial letter was written to that venerable apostle of the age, which moved his bowels of compassion toward us: and he was fully convinced, some time after, that he was in duty bound, for the prosperity of the connection in America, to do that thing, which he once but little expected—I speak with respect to his sending over a power of ordination, with his approbation of our becoming a separate, though Episcopal-church. Which he did as soon as the way was open: and it has proved the rising glory of the connection.

Thursday May 11, having accomplished our business and obtained our wishes, we set our faces to the North with gladness of heart, praising the Lord for his great goodness.

Thursday 18, I came to Baltimore, where I was appointed to labour.

Friday 19, I set apart as a day of fasting, and felt my soul sweetly united to the Lord Jesus Christ. I visited brother W. L—'s family, and had great fellowship with them. Surely sister L. possesses the perfect love of God.

Saturday 20, I awoke a little after four o'clock, very much taken up with my dear Redeemer. The company and conversation of God's dear children, are blessings for which I shall never be sufficiently thankful. I have had many sweet moments with this dear family. I returned to town, and preached with freedom.

Sunday 21. As the serpent was lifted up in the wilderness, so did I endeavour to hold up the Saviour of the world to a listening multitude at the Point-chapel. I attended the English church, and heard my old parish minister Mr. West and he delivered a good moral sermon. I think it a pity, for people to be entertained from the pulpit, with compositions without any thing (to the purpose) about repentance towards God, and faith towards our Lord Jesus Christ. O God! grant that I may be always faithful in the great work whereunto I am called. In the evening I preached to about five hundred precious souls with freedom. My trials are great, but I am borne above the world and sin.

Monday 20. I was comfortable whilst exhibiting the truth to a loving people; and the day following I attended a funeral, and found great freedom to preach. The remaining part of this week, I was comfortably employed in preaching, visiting our pious friends and meeting classes.[114]

Sunday 27. I held forth in Gunpowder-neck to many hearers. This is almost as old a society as any in Maryland: it is about 12 miles from where I was born. In the evening I preached to a stiff-necked people; but I believe some good was done. This week was chiefly taken up among my relations and old acquaintances, who are mostly laying in the arms of the evil one; nevertheless I found freedom, by day and night, to offer Jesus to them.[115]

Sunday June 3. With delight I viewed the rising morn; the fields are clad with a beautiful green; the creation smiling, and the birds tuning their notes—surely an immortal spirit ought to praise the Creator of the universe. Many attended my ministry in our old Bush-chapel,[116] among whom were many of my relations, and old companions, some of whom came a distance. I found freedom, 1. to point out the beauty, 2. the order, 3. the strength, 4. the privileges of the church; and lastly, gave an affectionate address, particularly to parents, to tell it to the generations following. Psalms xlviii. 12, 13. I had reason to believe the hearts of some were softened, and some of my relations and old acquaintances began to think that I was not beside myself. I cried the same day to many precious souls. *Cut it down, why cumbereth it the ground?* Luke xiii. 6—9. The week following temporal business somewhat interfered with my spiritual concerns; but I trust the one thing needful was not neglected.

Tuesday 5th, eight hours passed sweetly away in closet-exercises. I want to drink deep into the spirit of holiness. In general my sweetest hour in the twenty four, is from four till five in the morning. I can heartily recommend this hour to all who can receive the saying, especially if they want close communion with God.[117]

Sunday 10. At the Fork-chapel I found freedom to hold out the willingness of Christ, to save all who unfeignedly devote themselves to him: and afterwards Mr. Gough's gave a lively exhortation to the Christians to stand fast in the faith: but I fear some who were present, have turned aside. In the afternoon I preached at his house, from, *Fear not little flock, for it is your Father's good pleasure to give you the kingdom,* Luke xii. 32. 1. Who are the flock? 2. Why small? 3. What fears are they troubled with? and then concluded with an affectionate address. I felt a sweetness in my own soul and several thought it good to be there.[118]

Sunday June 17, I preached two sermons: the first in a private house, and the second in the Dutch church at Rister-Town.[119] Part of my retired hours was taken up the week following, in the study of the Revelation. This book is not to be understood but by the same spirit with which it was written. It was not written without tears; with tears we must sit at the feet of Jesus for an understanding of it. I know but little: I must set out afresh, and earnestly seek more grace and knowledge.

Monday, my dear friend C. rode with me to Mr. V's, where the Lord favoured us with a public visit. My dear Lord used me as an instrument to revive his blessed work in this neighbourhood; for many souls were brought to experience his precious love. I still pursue my study of the Revelation, and see a great beauty in it.

Thursday 21, was a very dull day to me, especially the former part of it.

Sunday 24, was a day of gladness, and I preached with freedom. Monday I met brother Watters and brother Tunnel. I preached with freedom, and one soul was set at liberty. Tuesday morning was a refreshing time to me. I am happy in visiting the sick: it is a most comfortable thing to have an interest in heaven on a dying pillow.[120]

Sunday July 2. I have again returned to Baltimore-Town, and have great fellowship with the dear disciples of our Lord in this place; and the word is sweet to many. I have been once round the circuit; and although some of the societies are in a dwindling state, yet considering them collectively, we have reason to praise God for what he hath done, and is doing among them. I found great freedom in my illustrations on, *This man receiveth sinners*, Luke xv. 2. 1. What sort of sinners doth Christ receive?— Broken hearted, penitent ones. 2. On what conditions does he receive them?—Obedience—*Believe in the Lord Jesus Christ, and thou shalt be saved.* 3. What does he do for those whom he receiveth?—He saves them from the guilt, power, love, and practice of sin. I preached a few miles from town, and the Lord displayed his convincing power. The Christians were all alive, and sinners crying aloud for mercy; so that my voice was almost lost. When I departed, I left one youth, who had been very wicked, struggling as for life; and his companions weeping around him. I know not how many were set at liberty: I felt the power of faith, and returned to town, where I preached with freedom to near a thousand people. The next day in the country, whilst I was first describing who we are to understand by the king's daughter: and secondly, in what sense she is all glorious within: one soul was new-born. Tuesday 6, I again visited brother Lynch's family, and found great freedom in pointing out the state of holy souls: and in class I had a comfortable time with the pious members: for there were about twelve professors (and I trust possessors) of sanctification.

I felt myself much refreshed, and strengthened in the faith. I had sweet moments in preaching to and visiting the Deer-Creek friends.[121]

Monday 17, having been sent for, I visited aunt B.[122] my father's sister, a very old woman; and she appeared to be near her end. I know not how many years she had been a communicant in the Episcopal church; but all this will not avail, if we do not become new creatures. My father had eleven brothers and sisters, the most of whom lived to be old. They are all gone to a world of spirits except one, and she is on the borders of the grave. My heart melted within me. After prayer I left her, and she appeared to have a tender heart.

Sunday 23. The worth of precious souls lays with weight upon me. O! for a trumpet voice, on all the world to call! After preaching at the Fork-chapel,[123] we had a comfortable love-feast; and at Mr. Gough's we had a profitable watch-night.

Sunday 30, brother Cromwell[124] and family accompanied me. At seven o'clock we had a love-feast; about two hundred of our brethren were present, and our Saviour was in the midst. Afterwards I preached in the Dutch church. About thirty of our friends accompanied me about eight miles to another Dutch church, where I preached to many with freedom. Many went with me three miles further to Mr. Vaun's, where we had a watch-night. The labours of this day were wearisome to the body; but I was strong in faith, and willing to give my little all to God. The next day a crouded audience assembled at the same place: some time before, and whilst the people were gathering, my mind was uncommonly exercised: but I found great freedom whilst inforcing, *Think it not strange concerning the fiery trial, which is to try you, as though some strange thing happened unto you.* The cloud was dispersed, and I felt myself uncommonly sweet and comfortable. This dear family drink deeply into the blessed Spirit. I went to bed very happy: but my night visions were uncommonly strange: I thought I was taken dangerously ill, and expected shortly to be in eternity. I doubt not, but I felt just as dying persons do. I appeared to be surrounded with thousands of devils, who were all striving to take from me my confidence; and for a time it seemed almost gone. I began an examination from my first awakenings—then my conversion—my call to preach—the motives which induced me to enter this great work—my intention, and life from the beginning. In the time of this examination, every fear was dismissed, and every fiend vanished; and a band of holy angels succeeded with the most melodious music that I ever heard. I then began to ascend, accompanied by this heavenly host; and thought every moment the body would drop off, and my spirit take its flight. After ascending a vast height, I was over-shadowed with a cloud as white as a sheet; and in that cloud I saw a person the most beautiful that my eyes had beheld. I wanted to be dislodged from this tabernacle, and take my everlasting flight. That glorious person, more bright than the sun in its meridian brilliancy, spake to me as follows, "If you continue faithful to the end, this shall be your place; but you cannot come now; return, and be faithful: there is more work for you to do." Immediately I awoke, and my spirit was so elevated with a sense of eternal things, that I thought I should sleep no more that night. Great, and glorious discoveries have been made to me, both sleeping and waking; but all the promises of heaven and eternal glory, have been conditional. In scripture we have a little, but significant word, *if*—If you are faithful until death, you shall have a crown of life. I would advise all the children of God, to be very careful and watchful, and continue. in well-doing until death. Some suppose that we ought not to put any dependance in dreams and visions. We should lay the same stress on them in this our day, as wise and good men have done in all ages. Very great discoveries were made to Peter, Paul, and others in their night visions. But is there not a danger of laying too much stress on them? We are in danger from a variety of quarters: let us therefore bring every thing to, and try it by the standard; taking the Spirit for our guide, and the written word for our rule, we shall without doubt go safe.

Tuesday August 2, I preached with great freedom to a crouded audience, and a minister of the reformed church of Holland gave an exhortation in the German language; as there were several present, who did not understand English.

I paid the town of Baltimore another visit; and was then under a necessity of crossing the Chesapeak-bay agreeably to the desire of Mr. F. Asbury. During my absence brother Daniel Ruff supplied my place. In many places during my travels through the Peninsula, we had great displays of the power of God; for thousands gathered to hear the word. The devil was angry, and he and his agents spread many most scandalous reports; some of which were carried across the bay, and reached the ears of my relations: and some of the carnal ones believed the reports. My manner was, to go straight forward in the line of my duty. When I returned, many gathered, at the Fork-chapel, from all quarters; and among the croud, I espied my old uncle T. who had heard, and believed the reports; and was determined, as I understood, to detect me in the midst of the people. Never shall I forget the day; for the Lord made his arm bare, and we had a precious refreshing shower; and the heart of my dear old uncle was tendered, and tears flowed down his face. After he left the Chapel, he said to some of his acquaintances, "surely my cousin is belied." He came and begged me to go home with him; which I did. The next day he followed me five miles; and the tears flowed plentifully. When we were about to part, he asked me what compensation he should make me, for the benefit which he had received. "Will you," said he, "receive a suit of clothes?" I thanked him kindly, telling him that I had as much clothing as was necessary. He then put his hand in his pocket, and pulled out eighty continental dollars, which at that time were worth about 20 hard dollars; at first I refused; but he would not be denied. So I took them, and some time after gave them to brother S. a man who needed them. When we parted he told me, he expected to see me no more—It was so; for some time after the Lord called him away.

I continued in this circuit till the following spring, and enjoyed precious moments. Many were added to the society, and many brought into gospel-liberty: and some received the second blessing. I trust I grew in grace and knowledge during my stay: and felt myself an unprofitable servant, and very unworthy of the many favours which I received from the precious, loving followers of Christ in this circuit.[125]

SECTION IX

From January 1781 until the next Conference in May Garrettson made his junket into the area around York, Pennsylvania. This work among the Dutch (probably German) and English settlers was unusually successful according to Garrettson's record.

SECTION IX.

An Account of my Travels, Exercises, and Success, in forming what is called Little York Circuit.

For some time it was on my mind to visit Little York, and the country round. The way being open, on Monday the 24th of January 1781. I set out, and travelled till evening: and then put up at a tavern,[126] about twelve miles from the town to which I was bound. I lectured in the family on the seventh of Matthew; and the Lord began his work: that night Mr. Worley a gentleman from the town, lodged at the same tavern; and in time of family-worship, the Lord, in mercy, laid his hand of conviction on him.

Tuesday 25th, I went on to town, and in the afternoon the bell rang, and I preached in the Dutch church; and the gentleman's lady (who was awakened the evening before) got her heart touched. When he came home in the evening, he spoke to this effect, "My dear, I heard such a man last night as I never saw or heard before, and if what he said be true, we are all in the way to hell." "I expect," said she, "he is the same man whom I heard this afternoon in Wagoner's church; and I believe that his doctrine is true, and that we are all in the way to ruin." "Well," said he, "let us set about our salvation." "I am willing," said she.

Wednesday 26th. As I had sent forward an appointment, I went on about twenty miles, and preached with a degree of freedom.

Having an appointment, I preached at Mr. Gering's,[127] the Lutheran minister; and after meeting we had an agreeable conversation. His mother and sister, whose hearts the Lord had touched, accompanied me to Berlin, where I preached to a large congregation with great freedom. I again had an opportunity, in the evening, to hold up a loving Saviour to the listening multitude.

By this time a persecution had arisen among the people in Little York and around: the enemy of souls had taken an advantage of my two friends, who were awakened: being under deep distress, and sorely tempted by the devil, not knowing what to do, at length they prepared water, and washed themselves; and then put on clean clothes, and concluded that it was the new birth. And after they came from their room, they kissed their two children, who were man and women well nigh grown, and told them they were new born. Being in a great measure bereft of their senses, and the enemy ready to take every advantage, "Come," said they, "old things must be done away, and all things must become new." They then began to throw their old clothing and blankets on the fire; and among other things he threw on a large bundle of paper money. "This," said he, "is an old thing, and must be done away." The neighbours being alarmed, ran in and saved many things: but I suppose they did not sustain less than fifteen pounds less. A minister was sent for, and he desired a doctor to be called; for they knew not what was the matter. A Quaker woman came to see them, and she said, "She did not know of any one that could be of service to them, unless it was the man that was the occasion of it." The cry was, such a man ought not to go through the country: and others desired me to be brought and put into gaol. I was about twenty miles off, and as soon as I heard of it, mounted my horse and got to them as quick as possible. When the neighbours saw me, several gathered into the room. When I entered the house, I perceived that the woman looked strange, and the man was in bed under the hands of the doctor, with several blister-plaisters on him. I sat down by his bedside (she sat an the foot of the bed) and asked him what he wanted—"To be new born," said he. Taking out my little bible, I read and lectured on a chapter; and sensibly felt that the Lord was present to heal. It brought to my mind the time when St. Peter visited Cornelius. I believe, in the time of the exhortation and prayer, the Lord not only opened the way of salvation to those two distressed ones, but several others who came in; and we had a precious sweet time. I desired them to take his blister-plaisters off. Glory to God! he restored them, not only to their natural, but spiritual senses. A good and gracious God has his own way of working among the children of men. Though at first it caused a great distress to lay upon my mind; yet in the end it was for good; many were astonished and brought to a serious consideration. Although the church door was shut against me, a large school-room was opened, in which I preached a sermon on the occasion, to about three hundred souls; and the Lord touched the hearts of many: and my two mad people (as they had been called) were able to rejoice in the Lord: and it was not long till I gathered a loving society.

Wednesday 15th, I preached in Mr. Gering's church, to almost as many as it could hold, from, *If the righteous scarcely are saved, &c.* Shewing, 1. Who are the righteous, and how they are scarcely saved. 2. Who are the ungodly and sinners, and 3. their awful doom. Surely if the righteous are scarcely saved, and the nominal professor not saved at all, the open profane will have no chance for heaven, unless he repents. In the evening I preached to many in the minister's own house, and there was an inquiry how to obtain mercy. In the country Satan began to rage as well as in town. The people began to cry out against their minister, because (as they expressed it) I had turned him to be a Methodist.

Wednesday 22. I had a tedious journey to Colchester; but found the parents of one family (who were awakened when I was there before) mourning for Jesus; and I had freedom to preach to the people. In the morning I set out again for Berlin, and missed my way. I am burdened—surely it is a burden which the Lord hath laid upon me, and it is for the best. I called at an house to enquire for the road—I heard a dismal groaning, and lamenting within. I alighted from my horse and went in; and found the woman of the house wringing her hands, and mourning bitterly. Good woman, said I, what is the matter with you? "Sir," said she, "have you never heard what has happened? I have sold my three little children to the devil, and such a day he is to come for them." I can prove to you, said I, that it is out of your power to sell your children to the devil, for they belong to God. I read and explained to her parts of several chapters; but it seemed all in vain. Her husband came in, and I desired him to get a horse and take her to preaching that afternoon. After he had got the horse, I desired her to make ready, and go to preaching with her husband. "O," said she, "I cannot think of leaving my dear little children in the arms of the devil." After some time she was prevailed on to go. Her husband told me, that she had carried a razor in her bosom for three weeks, with an intent, first to take the lives of her children (before the day came, that she thought the devil was to come for them) and then take her own life. I preached a sermon suited to her condition; and it pleased the Lord to visit her soul in mercy, so that after preaching she came to me in a rapture of joy, blessing and praising God that she ever saw my face. She became a blessed pious woman. I then knew the cause of my being lost. O God, thou art good, and I will praise thee! thou art kind, and I will give glory to thy holy name!

Friday February 24, I returned to town, and the persecution was so hot, that I thought it most expedient to preach at Mr. Worley's a mile out of town. Many gathered, and we had a moving time. The next day we had a powerful season; and the hearts of some of my enemies were reached.

Sunday February 26. I never saw so many out in this place before, and even some who had thought it a sin to hear me. And I never saw a more general moving in any place where preaching had been so short a time. In this county there were, I think, sixteen different denominations, and some of all seemed zealous in their way. In the afternoon I again returned and preached at Daniel Worley's, where one woman was struck under conviction, and cried aloud for mercy. There was a shaking through the whole assembly—I felt the power of faith, and was greatly enlightened in the holy scriptures.

Wednesday February 28, I returned to try the town again, and found the people very still; and we had a solemn, useful time. Lodged at Mr. Sidler's, and felt my spirit much refreshed.

Tuesday March 1. Being desired the day before to visit a distressed man, one who was troubled with an evil spirit; between day-break and sunrise, I called his minister out of bed, and desired him to go with me. We went, and I desired all to leave the room, except the distressed man, his wife, the minister and myself. I then desired him to open to me his case. He said that "for a long time the devil had followed him, and that he had frequently seen him with his bodily eyes." The dear man was under conviction, but knew not what was the matter with him. I told him my experience, and gave him as good directions as I was capable of. I prayed for him, and so likewise did his minister in Dutch; and I understood afterward, that he was troubled no more in the same way, and became one of my quiet hearers.[128]

I visited the country, and experienced great displays of the awakening power of God; for many precious souls were enquiring the way to heaven, both Dutch and English. I again returned to town, and preached to about three hundred people by candle-light; but some were offended. I appointed to preach the next evening. In town there were many soldiers billetted, and the officers declared that if I came to attempt to preach again, that they would have me to gaol—So I understood by my friends; who desired me to decline. I was not afraid of their threats, but in the evening attended the appointment. Shortly after I had taken my text—*Quench not the Spirit*, Thessalonians v. 19. Several officers with a company of soldiers came to the place, but the house was so crouded, none could get in but the officers, who fixed themselves by my right-hand; one of whom stood on a bench with his staff in his hand, lifted up several times either to strike, or scare me; but had a bat, or an owl lighted on the wall, I should have been as much afraid. The devil cannot lead his factors further than the length of his chain. After sermon was ended, all withdrew, and no harm was done. I was surprised to see the same officers come to hear the word the next night; and they were peaceable hearers. The next day I had an invitation to preach to the soldiers; but as I was under a necessity of leaving town, I could not.

Saturday 20, I preached at Mr. H. P's, and the Lutheran minister who met me, gave an exhortation after I had done, in Dutch.

Sunday 21, I preached at the same place at eight o'clock to hundreds. I then rode five miles and preached in a large barn at twelve o'clock, but many could not get in. More then a hundred followed me from the morning preaching, and many of them were crying for mercy. One man came to me in a flood of tears—"Sir," said he, "can you tell me what I shall do to be saved, for I am the wickedest man in the whole county." I exhorted him to put his trust and confidence in God. The general cry among the people was, "This is the right religion."—It did appear to me, as if sects, and names, and parties, would fall; and only the name of Christ be all in all. I rode six miles farther followed by many, and preached with freedom at four o'clock. And in the evening I had great freedom to preach in town. It would be too tedious for me to give an account of every particular; yea, I could not do it. During my stay in this part of the Lord's vineyard, which was a little more than two months, I preached in more than twenty different places: and I then thought, that there were more than three hundred people under powerful awakenings; and many had found the pardoning love of God, and were happy; and I joined about a hundred in society the last week of my stay in the parts, and was very sorry that I could not stay a longer time with the people—Though I was succeeded by a faithful preacher, the work afterwards did not prosper in the manner I expected.

Monday 22, I was to preach my farewel sermon in town, at five o'clock. I found great freedom from John xvi. 33, *In me ye shall have peace*, *&c.* A little after six o'clock I started for Baltimore, to attend the conference; and rode twenty five miles, where I preached; and after sermon rode thirty five miles more, and got into town about sun-set, and heard a sermon.[129]

SECTION X

The next Conference assigned Garrettson to Virginia. He arrived on his circuit June 4, 1781. The war and slavery continued to provoke much persecution of the Methodists. The emotions engendered by the war severely distressed the people.

Garrettson's manuscript journals for March and April 1782 as well as those for October, November, and December 1782 were unpublished. The material for much of 1783 is also included and was previously unpublished.

SECTION X.

A short Account of my Travels till the following Conference, 1781.

Our conference was attended with a blessing. All the travelling-preachers were willing to abide by Mr. Wesley's judgment, respecting the ordinances. I was appointed to Sussex circuit in Virginia: but found it to be somewhat difficult to travel; for it was the time when Cornwallis was ransacking the country. In Virginia it was a time of distress indeed, and there was a call for great faith and patience.

June 4th, 1781, I got into the circuit,[130] and had an appointment at Ellis's chapel. When I entered the door I saw a man in the pulpit dressed in black, and he was at prayer. I soon perceived he was a man bereft of his reason. I went into the pulpit and desired him to give over. After he ended, I gave out his text, and began to preach. But I had no other way to stop him, than to desire the people to withdraw. His testimony was, that he was a prophet sent of God to teach the people; and that it was revealed to him, a person was to interrupt him in his discourse. After a few minutes the people returned, and all was still. I then gave out, *Feed my sheep*, John xxi. 17. I had liberty in shewing. 1. The character in the text—sheep, 2. why the followers of our Lord might be called sheep, and 3. how the sheep are to be fed. 1. The shepherd, 2. the food, and 3. the manner of feeding the flock. The prophet returned home, and that night he told his family, at such an hour, he would go into a trance; and that they must not bury him till after such a time, should he not come to. Accordingly, to appearance he was in a trance. The next day I was sent for to visit him. Many were weeping around the bed. He lay like a corpse, for I could not perceive that he breathed. He was once happy in God, and a sensible useful man. About the time of which he spoke, he came to himself. Satan was partly disappointed; for in a measure, he was restored to his reason, and I took him part of the way round the circuit with me. What was the cause of this? Satan prompted him to think more highly of himself than he ought; and to set himself up for some great one; and so he fell into the condemnation of the devil. I had a hope before we parted, his fallen soul was restored; and some time after he began again to preach Christ; and, I trust, was more humble than ever. I continued on this circuit about three months, and had many happy hours, and some distressing ones. Two things caused a great distress on my mind, 1. The spirit of fighting; and 2. that of slavery which ran among the people. I was resolved to be found in my duty, and keep back no part of the counsel of God. Day and night I could hear the roaring of the cannon, for I was not far from York, during the siege, or taking of Cornwallis. Many of our pious friends were absolutely against fighting, and some of them suffered much on that account. Some of them were compelled, or taken by force into the field; though they would sooner lose their own lives, than take the life of any human creature. I saw it my duty to cry down this kind of proceeding, declaring that it was not precedented (to compel persons to fight contrary to their consciences) in the oracles of God. I was, in a particular manner, led to preach against the practice of slave-holding. Several were convinced of the impiety of the practice, and liberated their slaves; and many others, who did not liberate them, were convinced that they ought to use them than they had done. Had it not been for those two evils which laid so heavy on me, I might have been more popular among the people. I preached at a quarterly-meeting at Mabery's chapel, where there were about two thousand present, of all ranks; and being pressed in spirit, I cried, *Do justice, love mercy, and walk humbly with thy God.* There were more than a thousand people who could not get into the chapel: some of those without called out for an officer to take me. After meeting was ended, I walked through the midst of them, but no one laid hands on me. During my stay in this circuit, many backsliders were reclaimed, and though my trials were great, I had many refreshing seasons.[131]

Saturday and Sunday August 12 and 13, I attended a quarterly-meeting in Nancy-Mond circuit; and travelled several times round it, possessing a great love for the people. Mrs. G. (a woman of note) and her niece, came out to hear the word; both were convinced, and became famous for piety.

Friday 25, I preached near a place called the Desert. I am informed that this wilderness is twenty miles broad and fifty long; and in the middle of it is a lake three miles wide and five long; in which is abundance of fish of various kinds. I am also informed, that when the Indians were driven from this part of Carolina, many of them fled to this desert, in which they found a small spot of high land, where they lived mostly on roots and fish, till they were driven out by the wild beasts of the desert. I am farther informed that it is inhabited by panthers, bears, wolves, and wild cats in abundance: and that they are of a very large size.

I am now in my element—forming a new circuit—and I have pleasing prospects. I preached in one place, and there was a great shaking among the people. I preached again the next day, and the power of the Lord in a most wonderful manner came down. I was somewhat surprized—the rich are brought to mourn for Christ. Several fell under the word. A major was so powerfully wrought on, that I suppose he would have fallen from his seat, had not the colonel held him up. A large society was united in this place, mostly of the rich. About this time I received a letter from Mr. F. Asbury in which I was informed that he could not visit the south, and that it was his desire I should see to stationing the preachers.[131]

In November I began my autumn visitation. Saturday and Sunday 3d and 4th, the Brunswick quarterly meeting was held; at which about twelve preachers met, and had their different appointments. We had a blessed time at this meeting. I travelled (by the desire of the brethren) largely through the circuits, and my dear Lord was powerfully present in many places to heal. I met with much trouble from several who were not willing to give up the administration of the ordinances.

Tuesday January 29, (1782) I unexpectedly met Mr. F. Asbury (as he had concluded it was best to come down) who requested me to visit the circuits on the north side of James river; which I promised to do, as soon as I had fulfilled my appointments already made. I did not accomplish this till the month of March, for I had to visit my new circuit, where I had crouds to hear the word; and several of the English churches were open; and many enquiring after eternal life.

March 14. Having finished my rout, I crossed James river, and entered Fluvannah circuit: and felt my heart closely united with the dear children of God, some of whom have emancipated their slaves. I found them in great confusion about the ordinances at the Brokenback church, and favourably hope that my visit was for good, for I was greatly drawn out in preaching the word.

Saturday 23 and Sunday 24th, I attended my brother Richard Garrettson's quarterly meeting; and we both had great freedom to preach the word, and a precious powerful time. This meeting was held at colonel F's, a most precious man; one who speaks boldly for his master, and has liberated many slaves. My brother travelled several days with me, and we had sweet times together.

Saturday 30th of March, I travelled on my way to Hanover circuit, and had some very agreeable conversation with a gentleman on the road, who appeared to be desirous of salvation; though at first very unwilling to let it be known.

Sunday 31, I preached in the Presbyterian meeting-house at Ground-Squirrel; but I do not know of any good done, except prejudice removed. I past round the circuit, preaching day and night with a degree of success, and my spirit was daily refreshed.

Sunday 5, April I preached in the church in King and Queen. We had such a shout in the camp of Israel, that my voice was lost. Saturday we had a powerful meeting at dear brother S's. The good old man told me, it was revealed to him several months before, that I should preach in his house. (I have heard much of you, said he, and have had a longing desire to see you.) I perceived that the Lord had blest my brother Richard's labours in this place. I set several days apart for retirement, and earnestly desired to drink more deeply into the Spirit of God. O, for a closer walk with my heavenly friend! It is not enough for me to preach to others, I need food daily for my own soul. Lord, give me a constant hungering, and thirsting after thee.

Saturday 11, as I was on my way to my appointment, my chaise turned over, and the horse being scared, broke the chaise and harness, so that I was under a necessity of borrowing a horse and saddle. The next day I preached in the church, and my chaise being fitted up, I set out on my way, accompanied by brother D. We rode all day through the rain, and on Wednesday we got to Surry, where conference was to be held. My reward is not with man: if it was, I should be poorly off. We settled our conference concerns as far as we could, and adjourned till the third Tuesday in May: when it was to be concluded in Baltimore. On Sunday I attended the quarterly-meeting in Sussex with Mr. F. Asbury. When I came to Leesburgh I found the small pox very brief; and when I got into Baltimore-Town it was more so; and my scruples being removed, I was inoculated; for which I have had no reason to repent. My labours in Virginia the past year were not altogether in vain. I think my dear Lord made me instrumental in uniting to us many of our brethren, who had disagreed with us about the ordinances, both preachers and people. I can say it was a year of humiliation; and humbly believe I grew in knowledge as well as grace.[132]

SECTION XI

In this brief account of his work before undertaking his mission to Nova Scotia, Garrettson describes his efforts in the Peninsula territory. This material includes the events surrounding the founding of the Methodist Episcopal Church. The manuscript journal offers somewhat more detail of these events than any of his published material, and is included in this section as well as remarks about his departure for Nova Scotia.

SECTION XI.

A short Account of myself till I embarked for Nova-Scotia.[133]

My time was mostly spent in the Peninsula; and glorious displays of the goodness of God we had. I never saw a greater meeting than we had at Barrot's chapel, in the fall. It was the desire of brother F. Asbury that I should go to Redstone,[134] in order to form some circuits there. I was willing to go in the spring, but I felt an unwillingness to expose myself in the dead of winter, in the back settlements, where all were strangers to our doctrine and discipline. I never was able to determine, whether I was right or wrong in refusing to go at that season. However, I suffered much in my mind; wishing many times afterward, that I had taken up the cross.

In August 1784, I received a letter from brother F. Asbury in which I was desired to prepare for a journey to Charleston, as quick as possible. At that time I was travelling in Talbot circuit, and had great freedom among the people. Our dear Lord was laying a foundation for, and carrying on a most glorious work. I have no doubt but hundreds were awakened, that summer, in the circuit. Dear brother M.[135] (who was called the weeping prophet) travelled with me; and the Lord owned his labours. The most of my time, during this station, was spent in Kent, Sussex, and Talbot circuits; where we had glorious gatherings to the society. It was not uncommon to see from one to four thousand people at a quarterly meeting; and I was ready to conclude, that the whole Peninsula would flame with the glory of God. I was resolved, by the blessing of the Lord, to leave the circuit as quick as possible, and set out on my journey to Charleston. Which I did after the Tuckehoe quarterly meeting, at which I preached my farewel sermon to a numerous croud, bathed in tears. I went as far as Dover, and intended to stay at Richard Bassett's Esq. a few days. The evening following a friend came to my room, and informed me that doctor Coke had arrived, and was below. I went down, and received him and brother Whatcoat as welcome messengers; and accompanied them the next day to a quarterly-meeting held at Barrot's chapel. Dear Mr. Wesley had gratified the desires of thousands of his friends in America, in sending a power of ordination, and giving his consent to our becoming a separate church. About fifteen preachers were present; and it was concluded that I should go through the continent, and call a conference at Baltimore immediately. Within six weeks, after travelling upwards of twelve hundred miles, I settled the business, besides preaching almost every day, once, and sometimes twice, and made my return. The preachers being gathered, our conference began on Christmas-day, and we acceded to the method proposed by Mr. Wesley: and men were set apart, and consecrated for the different orders of the church. And instead of Charlestown, I had an appointment to take charge of the work in the East. I was tempted (if it was a temptation) to think that the nomination was partial; however I was resolved, with the blessing of the Lord, to go as long as my strength would admit; and where, and every where, as might be thought best. Under exalted thoughts of the Deity and a sense of my own unworthiness, my will was subject, and my heart revived: and I felt a willingness to be the servant of all. I am convinced, that a small degree of grace will not do for a Methodist preacher.

SECTION XII

Garrettson's appointment to travel in Nova Scotia represented the new church's first venture into mission beyond the new nation. Other than the printed Journal very few of Garrettson's manuscript notes remain, and they are simply repetitive of the account in the printed Journal. Several letters between Garrettson and John Wesley, Thomas Coke, and Francis Asbury help round out the account of the Nova Scotian endeavor.

Garrettson and Cromwell sailed in February 1785 and returned to this country shortly after April 10, 1787. Thomas Coke had requested his return in order to attend the Baltimore Conference.

SECTION XII.[136]

A short Account of my Travels, and Success through the
Province of Halifax

About the middle of February, accompanied by brother C.[137] I embarked for Halifax in Nova-Scotia. The weather for two days after we set out was very pleasant; but the wind shifted, and it became extremely cold; and withall we had a storm for several days, so that we almost despaired of life. A strong impression was on my mind, that we should be spared to do some good in that country: and so it was, for after tossing fourteen days on the ocean, we safely landed in Halifax, and were kindly received by P. M.[138] esquire, and a few others. Brother C. went on to Shelburne, and I continued in the city. My good friend Mr. M. hired a large room, and had it furnished with seats and a pulpit. I preached to as many as attended, almost every night in the week, and three times on the Lord's-day, during my stay; and that with a degree of freedom; and I trust a few were awakened, and some were united in society.

Having repeated invitations, I set out in the latter end of March on a journey through the country. In two weeks I travelled about three hundred miles, and preached twenty sermons (though the snow was deep) to many attentive hearers; and I trust some were brought under a serious concern about their souls; and a few old Methodists, who were emigrants from Europe, rejoiced to hear that glorious sound, which they had been accustomed so often to hear in their native land. When I returned again to Halifax, I found freedom to preach to the people, but laboured under many trials. My few kind friends in Halifax were not willing that I should leave them. The harvest is great, and the labourers are few. I must go where there is a probability of doing the most good. There are thousands of poor souls in the wilderness who are destitute of a spiritual shepherd—yea, I fear in the open field of ruin.[139]

May-June I again left Halifax and rode to Windsor, where I preached on the 20th of May, to many who seemed to pay attention to the word. Saturday I rode twelve miles, and lodged at Dr. M. S. Bourn's: and the day following I preached in the court-house to about an hundred people, from, *I will show thee mine opinion:* the greater part appeared to be well pleased; but none convinced of sin. Several followed to hear the word at the new court-house about four miles, where I preached in the afternoon from, *Is there no balm in Gilead; is there no physician there? why then is not the health of the daughter of my people recovered?* I found freedom in answering the questions proposed by the prophet, especially the last. The way is open for the recovery of man—but man is unwilling to accept of proffered mercy. I rode several miles, and preached in Cornwallis at six o'clock; and there appeared to be a small moving on the minds of individuals. I staid a few days in this town, and preached several sermons; and I doubt not but there were several powerfully awakened; and about twelve, whose hearts seemed to be touched, joined in society.

I travelled through Wilmut, Granvil, Annapolis, and Digby, and had many to hear, but few were willing to give their hearts to God. In Digby they were destitute of a minister of any denomination, and I fear of religion too; and in my opinion they were but a small remove from it, in Annapolis— true they had Mr. B. for their minister; but his discourses were not adapted to the awakening of sleepy sinners. Can these dry bones live?—O! that there may be a shaking, and a little army raised up to praise the Lord! Many took me to be their enemy, and would not come to hear the word. I had many sorrowful hours, and shed many tears on account of the wickedness of the people; but my dear Lord comforted my soul.

Sunday June 5, 1785, I preached to many in Mr. Eaton's barn; at eleven o'clock I administered the sacrament to a few. In the afternoon I preached again. Monday I preached at Horton, on the freedom of the will: and Tuesday met brother Cromwell at Windsor. The day following about twenty of our friends, after sermon, communed with us; and we had a feast of love. Brother C. went on his way to Cumberland, to supply brother B's place; for I had written to him to come to Halifax; and the Lord made him a blessing to the people in that city. After spending a few more weeks in those country-towns, with a degree of liberty and success, I returned to, and spent some time in Halifax: and found that brother B's labours had not been in vain.

Tuesday July 26, I embarked for Liverpool, and landed safe on Friday, and had a time of refreshment whilst preaching in the meeting-house. Captain D. who has since gone to heaven, some time before any of us came to this town, met with a little tract, written by Mr. Wesley, called the character of a Methodist, and having a great desire to hear one of those men, sent to Shelburne, and desired brother I. M. to give them a visit; which he did shortly after: and many of the people were very fond of his doctrine; but he was much opposed by a company of warm professors of religion, who, were the followers of one Mr. A. One Lord's-day he went into the meeting-house to preach, and a party of those zealous disciples were determined if possible to prevent it; and in all probability would, had not the magistrate interfered: Colonel P. as mild a man in nature as any to be found, as well as a wellwisher to all religious persuasions, reasoned very coolly with them, but to little purpose, till another magistrate spoke more roughly, and then they gave over, and left the house. After this they did not attempt an open attack, but strove to prejudice the people against us.

When I came to town, I found that by the preaching of brother M. and brother Cromwell the Lord had begun a work, and they had united twenty in society. In this town there were about one thousand inhabitants, besides little children. I was much pleased with the people, and found great freedom to preach the word. I began to preach at five o'clock in the morning; and the people being mostly raised amongst, and accustomed to the ways of the Presbyterians, rather thought it to be a work of supererogation. I staid in the town about four weeks; during which time I preached three, and sometimes four sermons on the Lord's day; and frequently on other evenings: and visited from house to house. When I departed I left forty in society, several of whom had found pardon, and several were under deep distress; and I can say for my own part, it was a precious season.

In August I embarked for, and arrived safe in Shelburne, where I found sixteen members of society of whites, and some blacks, who were united by brother Cromwell. In this town there are many precious souls, mostly refugees, and prone to evil as the spark is to fly upwards. In this town we had a little preaching-house which was built by Mr. W; and would accommodate about two hundred people. During my stay my manner was as follows, viz: In the morning to preach in Shelburne at nine o'clock: then to walk to Burchtown three miles off, and preach to the black people at twelve o'clock: (there were about five hundred in the town who were able to attend, and they had built themselves a church) then to return and preach in Shelburne at five o'clock, and likewise by candlelight. I had not preached long till our church would not contain the people, so that many went away for want of room. Mr. W. minister of the church of England, gave me an invitation to preach in his church; which I did three Sabbaths at five o'clock: and then there was no more place for me there. So I stood on a large rock in the street, and cried, *On this rock will I build my church, and the gates of hell shall not prevail against it*, Mat. xvi. 18. Our friends soon enlarged our little house, so that it would accommodate three or four hundred; but still it would by no means hold as many as wished to hear. Agreeably to my desire, the blacks of Shelburne built themselves a little house at the North end of the town, and I preached to them separately, in order to have more room for the whites.

Our dear Master began to carry on a blessed work; but the devil and his children were angry. They frequently stoned the house; and one night a company came out, and strove (as it stood by the brow of a hill on pillars) to shove it down.—Whilst I was preaching to near four hundred people by candlelight, they were beating underneath, to get away the pillars— In the midst of my preaching I cried out, *Without are dogs, sorcerers, whore-mongers, idolaters, and whosoever loveth and maketh a lie*. The company ran off with a hideous yelling, and we were left to worship God peaceably.

During my stay in and around Shelburne (which was six weeks) numbers, both white and black, were added to the society; and many tasted the good word of God, and felt the powers of the world to come.

Being under an engagement again to visit the new societies where I had been, I embarked for Liverpool. Shortly after we hoisted sail (a man-of-war lay in the harbour) an officer said to his fellows, "He is going," and they cried amain, "Hail the Methodist parson! hail the Methodist parson!" Our captain paid no attention to them; but they followed us with a bullet from a cannon, though we passed on unhurt. I touched at Liverpool and staid two weeks, and found the work of the Lord prospering under the ministry of brother I. M. From thence I went to Halifax, and found the work prospering under the ministry of brother B. I staid two weeks, and preached with a small degree of freedom. I want to do good! I want to live to the honour of my dear Lord! I want to be all glorious within! When, O when will my warfare with Satan end? Not till my work is done! I resign—Lord, I am willing to wait thine own good time.

My custom was to travel mostly by sea, in the summer; and by land, in the winter: and the Lord was with me.

I spent the most of this winter in the different towns between Halifax and Annapolis; and there was a gathering to the society. My mind was often troubled with people of a disputatious turn of mind; and was grieved at the hardness of their hearts. Whilst in the wilderness, surrounded by the impious, my mind was staid on my dear Lord.

In the spring 1786, I paid Liverpool my third visit; and from thence went to Shelburne, and found that a black man, by the name of M—t, from England, had done much hurt. Surely if lady Huntington had him put into the ministry, (as he gave this account) her ladyship was much deceived in the man; or else he has since become an amazing bad one. I left near two hundred blacks in society, and at my return I did not find half that number. When I went to their town, I called them together, and informed them of his character. Many of them were convinced of their error, and returned to the society; so that in the whole we only lost about twenty persons. I likewise applied to their colonel, who was a black, or rather a yellow man, to have him put out of the town, which he consented to; so there was once more a prospect of prosperity among them.

A town called Barrington lay heavy on my mind, and I had a great desire to visit its inhabitants. This town lies about thirty miles to the South West of Shelburne, having no other than a small foot-path which leads to it; so that I was under the necessity of going by sea, or on foot. I set out with A. E. for a pilot, as he had been there. I preached at Port-Roseway, where we had a small society. From thence we went to Cape Negro, where we were kindly entertained by old Mr. S. who I trust had a love for our Saviour. With freedom I preached to a few families, and the Lord began a good work. From thence I went to Barrington; and after wading good part of the way nearly half-leg deep in mud and water, we got into town about three o'clock on the third day of our journey from Shelburne. I did not know of one person who would receive me, so I sat down on a large stone in the town, not far from the meeting-house. Their former minister who had left them, I was informed, had written a letter in which he said, there was one Garrettson going through the country, who was a dangerous Arminian; and advised them to be careful. I desired Mr. E. my companion and pilot, to notify the inhabitants, that a stranger had come to town, and intended at an hour by sun to preach in the meeting-house. The hour commenced and I had about twenty hearers; and appointed to preach the next day at the same time. The people all withdrew, and there was no one to say, Will you go home with me? I told my friend, he must get a home if he could, and I went to the house of a gentleman who asked me to drink tea, but not to stay all night. I asked him if there was a boarding-house, or tavern in town; he said there was not, and it was not convenient for me to stay with him, or he would make me welcome. However, rather than stay out all night, I went to another house; and gave myself an invitation, and was not denied.

The next day about thirty came out to hear; and I then had an invitation to an house. The day following I appointed to preach morning, afternoon, and evening; but the people were much afraid of being deceived. My mind was greatly distressed; and I was almost ready to leave the place; for the people looked very coldly on me.

About an hundred came to hear; I preached two sermons, and concluded not to preach in the evening, as I had an invitation to go home with Mr. S. a very clever man, who lived on a little island about seven miles off: in this man I found a friend. On this little island I preached several sermons with freedom: and began to think, that the Lord had a work for me to do.

The following Friday I went to another little island, to Mrs. D's, who had a friendship for religious people. Whilst I was on this island, a Mr C. came; whom I invited by a messenger to attend my ministry, and speak after me; but this he refused. In the evening I preached on the mainland, not far from the meeting-house, to a few; but pride and unbelief keeps out the word. Saturday I attended the ministry of Mr. C. To-morrow, said I, (after meeting was out) I have an appointment in the meeting-house; and the days are long enough for us both to preach: this he refused; but appointed to preach in a private house. This kind of conduct in him astonished the spectators; but still the people were afraid of the Arminians.

Sunday. This morning my mind was amazingly distressed. I was afraid the Lord had not called me to this town. I mourned in secret, and intreated the Lord to make it manifest that he had sent me to this place, by a display of his convincing power among the people. The hour came, and I repaired to the meeting-house; none were present but my pilot (and he was greatly shaken, and in doubt which way to go) and two others. My distress of mind was to be sensibly felt. I withdrew to a little wood, a quarter of a mile from the meeting-house, and intreated the Lord, if he required me to preach in the place, to send out the people and bless his word. As I was again ascending the hill, toward the meeting-house, resolving within myself, that if the people did not attend, and if the word was not blest, I would leave the town, and conclude that I was not called thereto. But I saw the people coming from every part of the town, and in a short time we had a large gathering, and immediately the cloud broke from my mind, and with a glad heart I ascended the pulpit stairs; and the word of the

Lord seemed all open to me. I preached, and the flame ran through the assembly: in the afternoon I preached again, with the same freedom. Among two or three hundred people, it appeared as though there were but few present, but in a greater or less degree felt the flame. After meeting was ended, they came around me on every hand in tears; and I suppose I had invitations to more than twenty houses.

Having an appointment at Shelburne, we set out; but after I got there I staid only a few days, and returned to take care of the awakened souls. And in my return, I called at Cape Negro; and the Lord began a blessed work in several families there. When I got to Barrington, I found many hungering after the word. I took the town in rotation, and visited the greater part of the families; and I went to but few houses, at which there had been no awakenings. Mrs. A. and two of 'squire H's sons' wives, had experienced the pardoning love of God; together with several others. Now it was that many were willing to be called *Arminians*, and join society.

I paid Cape Negro a visit, and found Mrs. S. under deep conviction, and several others; I preached with freedom, and returned, accompanied by near a dozen, and among the rest was old Mrs. S. under deep distress of soul, who walked nine miles; and the next day she was baptised; and what was much better, she received remission of sins; and returned home on Monday praising the Lord. Mr. A. who had been at sea, and had never heard a Methodist, came home in the midst of this stir; and the Lord touched his heart, and he wept at his feet. Mrs. D. (wife to the 'squire) and several others were powerfully wrought upon. I visited them; and Mrs. D. said, "I am afraid there is no mercy for me! when I was eleven years old in England, under the preaching of Mr. Wesley and Mr. Whitefield, I was convinced; and Mr. Whitefield received me for a convert, but now I am a gross backslider." A young woman under deep distress, who was at her house, retired, and was resolved not to rest till her soul was blest: and so it was, for about three o'clock the Lord gave her a new heart, and put a joyful song in her mouth. She came where I preached in the afternoon, full of love, and went all round the house among the young people; and talked to them, to the admiration of all present. I preached from, *Our entrance in unto you is not in vain*. I visited Mr. A. who was under deep distress. "O! said he, what an alteration there is in the town—the people do not look like the same."

By this time the Lord had raised up a young preacher, J. M. who came to me, and was helpful in the work. I continued in Shelburne, Barrington, and the adjacent settlements around, till Autumn; and our dear Lord did great things for many. Being under a necessity to visit the East, I left J. M. to take care of the new-born children; and embarked for Liverpool; where there had been a blessed work under brother I. M. I think he informed me, that the Lord made use of the sudden death of our worthy friend captain D. to begin this revival. I find a great alteration in this town. The first time I visited the people here, we only had seven communicants; the second time we had twenty; the third visit we had near forty; and now we have more than sixty. Many in this town were taught to believe, that none ought to commune but such as have the witness of their justification. In my third visit, two women came to me on Saturday evening, and said, "we wish to commune to-morrow if we can get admittance." They said it was pressed on their minds as a duty. I believe they were mourning after a Saviour; and told them, I was willing that they should commemorate the death of that Saviour, whose most precious blood was shed for the remission of their sins; and desired them to expect a blessing at the table. That night my enemies got hold of it, and it ran through the town that I had admitted two unconverted women to the table. The next day we had a precious time at the communion, and the Lord visited the souls of those two women whilst at the table: the change seemed visible to many of the spectators—and our enemies, when they heard of it, were ashamed. I went to Halifax, Windsor, Horton and Cornwallis, where I spent the winter; except a few excursions through a few other adjacent settlements. In Horton, this winter, I favourably hope the Lord did bless my weak endeavours—I preached the word with freedom in different parts of the town; and many were added to the society. There are many in that town that are near to me, and I shall not soon forget the kindness shewed me by Mr. and Mrs. C. Mr. and Mrs. S. and several others. O! that our good and gracious God may look on all those who show kindness to his children; and grant them the sanctifying influence of his holy Spirit. I received a letter from Dr. Coke, in which I was requested to attend the Baltimore conference. It was with reluctance I came to this country; but I now feel a willingness to labour and suffer in the cause of God, among this people. I came to Windsor; where I had great consolation. Mrs. S. was a woman of a most excellent spirit, and her husband was a very kind man. Dear Mrs. S. I understand has since gone to Abraham's bosom—she is amply compensated for all her labours of love—*I was hungry, and ye fed me; naked, and ye clothed me; sick, and in prison, and ye came unto me*— The members of Christ's body—his children—are near to him. I came to Halifax, where I found our good friend Mr. M. busily employed in building us a church. Of all the women which I have met with, I have not found one more kind than Mrs. M. but she is now no more: and my heart was glad, when I heard that her faith was strong in her last moments. I travelled, laboured and suffered, in this country, a little more than two years. My dear Lord was with me by land and sea. After all, I am an unprofitable servant—my greatest wish and desire is, to do something to promote the interest of my dear Lord's kingdom. Monday April 10, 1787, I bid my Halifax friends farewell; and so leaving my dear Nova-Scotians, embarked with captain Wilson for Boston. I think I left behind about six hundred members of society.

SECTION XIII

Garrettson's printed Journal concludes with his account for the period from April 1787 to 1790, his Journal being published in 1791. Garrettson obviously returned expecting to be appointed General Superintendent of the Methodist work in British America, mainly Nova Scotia, and apparently the West Indies as well. The plan was never consummated although initially approved by the Conference. Methodist historians have never really resolved what actually happened.

Failure of this plan to return Garrettson to Nova Scotia prompted a temporary appointment to the Peninsula. Finally, he assumed the major work of his remaining ministry as Apostle to the North and became the founder of Methodism from New York City to the Canadian border.

SECTION XIII.
THE CONCLUSION.

Sunday April 16, I preached in the cabbin with freedom. The wind was high and contrary, so that for the preservation of our lives and vessel we came to anchor between two islands. I had an opportunity of preaching on each island; and gave a few books to the poor, and left many in tears, whose hearts the Lord had touched. On Wednesday 19, I landed in Boston: preached a few sermons with freedom, was kindly entertained by Mr. S. and on Monday 24, took the stage for Providence. Here I staid at Mr. Snow's, who is a godly Presbyterian minister. The bell rang the next day at six o'clock, and I found freedom to preach. The evening following I preached again to many serious hearers, in Mr. S's meeting-house. I had some conversation with a deist, who appeared to be good natured in his way. I sailed to Newport,[140] and had freedom in preaching two sermons there, one in Mr. F's meeting-house, and the other in Mr. T's; and the people behaved very well—A gentleman came to me after sermon, and said, "You have a great gift, but I will hear you no more; for your doctrine I do not like." From Newport I sailed to New-York, where I had an opportunity to preach in the Methodist church on Sunday April 30. After spending a few days agreeably there; I took a saddle-horse, and rode through the Jerseys, and had an agreeable time among my old friends; and so came to Philadelphia on Saturday.

On the Lord's-day I found great freedom in preaching there to a people very near to me; and was rejoiced to find the church in a prosperous way. I then pursued my way to Baltimore: where many of the dear servants of God met in conference. It was the desire of Mr. Wesley and others, that I should be set apart for the superintendency[141] of the work in Nova-Scotia—my mind was divided—man is a fallible creature—In the end I concluded not to leave the states; for thousands in this country are dear to me. On the whole we had a blessed conference, and my appointment was to preside in the Peninsula.

Sunday May 14th,[142] I preached at the college; and after visiting some of my relations, I set out on my way to fulfil my appointment.

Friday 19th, I called on that loving society at Duck creek Cross-roads, and had great freedom to preach the word.

Saturday 20th, I got to Mr. B's, and on Sunday preached with freedom in the Methodist church in Dover. I visited B. and P. and found them still in a backsliding state. This week was spent joyfully among a people whom I had not seen for a long time.

Sunday May 28, 1787. I preached in Tuckehoe church to about a thousand people. Many happy moments I have had in this Neck, in years past, and we have not forgotten old times. A spiritual gale ran through the congregation—my consolation, and the consolation of the people was so great, that I appointed to preach in the same church the next day;

and had near as many hearers as there were the day before. After sermon I rode on my way, and unexpectedly met a congregation of about an hundred, who came out to meet me as I passed; I preached a short sermon to them: and went to colonel H's, where I was rejoiced to meet brother C. and many other of my old friends; and had great freedom in a lecture on the parable of the prodigal son, to a crouded audience who assembled in the evening.

Tuesday 30th. At Talbot court-house I was surprised to see the gathered multitude from all quarters. I suppose there were above five hundred more than our little chapel could hold. Lord keep me humble! I fear many had a greater desire to see the servant, than to partake of the crumbs from the Master's table. Many were disappointed, for I had very little liberty. The people in this part of the country seem as if they would be all Methodists. It is a small thing to be a Methodist in name only; but it is a great thing to love the Lord with all the heart, and our neighbour as ourselves.

Wednesday 31. In the forenoon I preached to that little persecuted flock at brother Rigby's; and in the afternoon, I had a blessed time at the Bayside-chapel. I preached in Miles-river Neck; and the day following about four hundred attended my ministry at Bollingbroke chapel. This society will not hold their fellow-creatures in bondage. A great harmony subsists among those people, and I feel my heart united to them.

Saturday June 3. I crossed the river into Dorset, a place where I desired to be. Sunday 4. At brother McKeels I met so large a congregation, that I was under a necessity of withdrawing to the shade for room. Some time ago there was a great work of the Lord in this Neck; but I am informed the work is now rather at a stand. What is the cause? Those preachers whose labours the Lord particularly blest in this revival, were lively and powerful; and there was much of what some call wild-fire among the people: the cries of the distressed were frequently so great, that the preacher's voice was drowned. I was informed that those people had been visited by some, who had but little friendship for what some call hollowing meetings; and the work began to decline. The danger lays on both hands; and blessed is he who knows how to steer aright. I am never distressed in hearing convinced sinners crying for mercy; though they were to cry so loud as to be heard a mile. And I doubt not, but the children of the Lord are so happy at times, that they are almost carried out of themselves, and constrained to shout forth his praises.

Sunday June 11, I preached in our new chapel on Taylor's island, to abundantly more people than the chapel could contain. Many on this island love God.

Tuesday 13, I preached on Hooper's island, and we had a precious shower. Before our meeting ended five souls were new-born; three of whom were sisters. There were many awakened at this meeting; and great cries were amongst the distressed. There was as little confusion as I have ever seen, where there was so great a power felt.[143]

I continued in the Peninsula till May 1788; during which time I was seldom a day without preaching, and frequently twice, or thrice, in a day; and that with great freedom. I cannot say that there was a universal gathering; but I trust the church was edified and built up in the faith. During this year, I travelled through and preached in every county on the Eastern Shore, which are three of Virginia, three of Delaware, and eight of Maryland.

It was on my mind to go to Boston, and with the approbation of Mr. F. A. I set out on my journey in May 1788. When I got to New-York, I found brother H. at the point of death. The harvest being great and the labourers few, I was prevailed on by brother D. to stay till the York conference, which was to be held in October. During which time I staid mostly in the city; except some excursions through Long-island and New-Rochelle circuits. Before the sitting of conference, I had received invitations from a variety of places; and letters came to conference, in which we were intreated to send help to several places. I was conscious to myself, that it was not expedient for me, at that time, to pursue my way to Boston; though I had an eye to that place.

At the conference I was appointed to take charge of the Northern district; which at that time consisted of New-York, Long-island, and New-Rochelle circuits.[144] After conference ended, I set out to the North with about twelve young preachers to form circuits; and our dear Lord opened our way, in a most surprising manner: although much evil was said of us. Many houses, hands, and hearts were opened; and before the commencement of the winter, we had several large circuits formed; and the most of the preachers were comfortably situated; and sinners in a variety of places began to enquire, what they should do to be saved.

Satan and his children were much alarmed, and began on every hand to throw out threats against us. Some said, "They are good men;" others said, "Nay, they are deceivers of the people." A stranger from the new state, on his way down the country, informed the people that we were spread all through the country through which he came. This sudden and universal spread caused some person to say, "I know not from whence they all come, unless from the clouds." Others said "The king of England hath sent them to disaffect the people; and they did not doubt, but they would bring on another war." Whilst others gave it as their opinion, that we were the false prophets spoken of in scripture; who should come in the last days, and deceive if it were possible the very elect. Among others, the ministers of the different denominations were alarmed, fearing lest we should break up their congregations; and frequently coming to hear, some of them openly opposed, declaring publicly that the doctrine was false. The power of the Lord attended the word, and a great reformation was seen among the people; and many enabled to speak freely and feelingly, of what God had done for their souls. My custom was to go round the district every three months, and then return to New-York; where I commonly staid about two weeks. In going once round I usually travelled about a thousand miles, and preached upwards of an hundred sermons.

Tuesday June 9, 1789. I left New-York accompanied by brother N. to East-Chester; and in the evening had an opportunity of hearing Mr. F. A. and Mr. W. and the word was powerfully felt. The next day I accompanied them to New-Castle; and sat with delight under the word. The morning following we parted; and the remainder of the week I spent mostly in writing.

Sunday 14. I found liberty in preaching to a solemn company in our new church at New-Castle, on Naaman's Cleansing; and in the afternoon I heard brother Lee at Bedford; and closed the meeting with an exhortation. Here we joined a society. The people were brought up in the Calvinian line, but many are convinced that such a system does not reflect glory on the Deity; and they are willing to flee from it, though there are two ministers who use their strength in opposition.

Monday 15th, I found great freedom to preach to a loving society, formed by brothers M. and B. at Mr. H's, and had reason to believe that many of them were engaged for the salvation of their precious souls. Their singing was delightful.

Tuesday 16th. In the morning I found my mind free in preaching the word at Stony-street church; and in the evening the Lord was with us at the English church at Peak's-kiln; and I had a comfortable night at Governor Van Courtland's. This is an affectionate family; and they seem very attentive to the word of the Lord.

Wednesday 17th, I rode ten miles and preached to a people gathered from the mountains; and then went to brother Jackson's, about twenty miles, and had great liberty in the word. There seemed to be a silent struggling among the people, whilst I endeavoured to dwell on the deep things of God. I visited dear brother Cook, and found him near death. But his soul is happy in God his Saviour.

Thursday 18th. Accompanied by a friend twenty-five miles, I met brother F. A. and brother W. at doctor B's, where I heard a good sermon, and an encouraging exhortation; as I also did the day following Saturday we parted, and I had a tedious day.

Sunday 21. The sun this morning arose with his usual lustre, and dispersed light through all the lower creation. Jesus, the much brighter sun, was precious to me. I preached in a barn, in the morning, at Rynebeck; then rode eight miles lower down, and preached in another barn, and had great liberty; and found a few whose hearts the Lord had touched when I was there before. I returned and preached again at six o'clock: but fear the word had no place in the hearts of the hearers—I was much distressed—dear Lord! man is weak. But when thou displayest thy convincing power, the work is done. I rode to and spent the most of this week in the city of Hudson. In this place I have had some sweet moments, and been greatly encouraged; but I now feel the need of patience—have I spent so much labour for nought? Have none been benefited by my ministry in this place? Some have been made angry, but a few also have been benefited—I am clear in the matter, having warned, invited, and handed out the promises with tears. So I let the matter rest with the Lord, who said, *O Jerusalem! how oft would I have gathered you, and ye would not?*

Monday 29. Accompanied by one of the preachers, I rode on to brother B's, and on my way I stopped and preached in a cool summer-house, made of green boughs, to near two hundred precious souls, who seemed to drink in the word. I am fully convinced (and it is an observation which I have made these many years) that poor people in general are more fond of the gospel than the rich. And this is agreeable to the doctrine of our Lord. I had a precious sweet time among those people. More than twelve months ago, I was solicited to preach among them; but never had an opportunity till now.

Tuesday 30. I preached in Mr. V. D's large barn to many serious hearers: and perceived that the Lord was carrying on a work on the patent by the instrumentality of brother C—, a young preacher who had just entered the field.

Wednesday I rode 14 miles to Albany. Some time ago I petitioned the assembly (as they were then sitting) for liberty of the city-hall; access to which I have had ever since; but many in the city seem much set against the Methodists. The hearts of a few were touched, and several joined in a society which, has gradually increased ever since.

Sunday July 5, I preached in Schenectady at 10, and at 3 o'clock in the English church: and in the evening in a spacious hall, and had great hope that good would be done in the town. Prejudice hath taken deep root in the hearts of these people; at present, I fear there is very little vital piety in the place.

Monday July 6. I set out on a journey to the North, and on my way I overtook an old gentleman, who said, "I expect you are a minister. Oh! it is a blessed work, if you are called to it. I am a follower of Christ, and know my peace made with God." How, said I, do you know that? "By the spirit which he has given me." Do you, said I, know that your sins are forgiven? "O Yes." Do you, said I, live in sin? "Yes, we are all sinners." Pray, said I, how can you know your sins forgiven, if you live in sin? "I have the imputed righteousness of Christ, and it is no more I that do it, but sin that dwells in me." Don't you, said I, swear sometimes? "Swear, yes, and have been drunk too, many times since I was made a new creature, but my comfort is, I cannot fall." What, said I, would become of your soul if you were to die drunk? "Die drunk! what, would you think to see the sun fall? was it ever known that a saint died drunk? impossible!" Well, said I, according to your doctrine, if you always keep yourself intoxicated with strong liquor, you will never die. Sin made man mortal; but I cannot find from scripture that drunkenness makes him immortal. "Sir," said he, "I perceive you are a rank Arminian, and I would not go the length of my foot to hear you preach, for you are an accuser of the brethren; and hold out a very uncomfortable doctrine to God's dear children." Pray, said I, what denomination do you profess? "I am an old Englishman, and a convert of Mr. Whitefield's, and a new-light by profession, from the soul of my foot to the crown of my head." After I endeavoured to set his danger before him, I wished him well; and riding thirty miles I found great liberty to preach my dear Lord's gospel, from the language of the gaoler, *What shall I do to be saved;*

I travelled and preached through the country, and many gathered to hear the word; but many were much afraid of being deceived by a false prophet, so termed by some. I preached in Ash-grove, where we have many kind friends who have built us a church. When I first came into this settlement, I found some emigrants from Ireland, who had been acquainted with the Methodists; but there were very few of them, who retained the power of religion; though I soon perceived, that the doctrine was as a slave to a festering wound. Backsliders were healed, and many, who had never been acquainted with those men before, were brought to experience the faith which justifies the ungodly. In several places in this circuit, the Lord made D. D. instrumental in the conversion of souls.

Saturday and Sunday were the days of our quarterly-meeting; and a precious sweet time we had. It was held in brother R's barn, and I think we had an addition of about twenty communicants. I baptised eight adults in the house, and one by immersion; also several children. We had about two hundred present at the love-feast, most of whom were young converts. In the evening I had a conversation with a woman who informed me, that she was brought to experience the love of God not far from Boston; and being surrounded by the Baptists, they strove to persuade her to renounce her infant baptism, and enter more deep into baptismal water. By their continual solicitations and arguments, her mind became confused, so that she was in doubt respecting the matter, and earnestly prayed to the Lord to shew her his will. One night after she had thus prayed, she went to bed, and not long after her eyes were closed in sleep, she thought she saw our dear Lord with his arms extended and an infant presented to baptism. She awoke without a doubt or fear, respecting the validity of infant baptism. Some time after this, in the state of Vermont, she had an opportunity of hearing the Methodists, who, she immediately perceived, preached the same doctrine which the Lord had taught her; and she had never before met with a people with whom she could join.

Monday July 14. After I had ended my visit through Cambridge circuit I came to Albany, where I met the small society; and the next day rode to doctor H's. My horse being very lame, and I not able to get another for a few days, either for love or money, I set out on foot; and after I had walked near twenty miles, I came to Spence town, with my lame horse hopping behind me; and had at captain Salisbury's a precious sweet time among the people. In spite of all the opposition, our gracious God has carried on a blessed work around this place. Tuesday I preached in Sheffield, where I was greatly opposed; but the Lord has plucked a few brands from the burning. The day following I dined at colonel B.s, of Canaan: and in the afternoon held forth in the Presbyterian meeting-house. The people of this town are mild and catholic. Their former minister (Mr. T.) was a catholic man, and did not do as some have done—prejudice, and harden the hearts of the people against other denominations; especially Arminians, as we are called: our dear Lord by the instrumentality of brother W. brother B. and others, has convinced, and converted a number of souls in different parts of this town; so that at present we have several classes.

Saturday 18, our quarterly-meeting began. Souls are flocking to Jesus. The number of disciples increases. Jesus rode in his gospel-chariot, in Mr. C's barn on the Lord's-day, whilst I was declaring, *The ransomed of the Lord shall return, and come to Zion, &c.* Brother B. assisted me in the administration of the supper. In this part of our Lord's vineyard many have been much troubled with Antinomianism: but the dismal gloom is vanishing away. I continued round on my regular plan, till on Thursday July 23, I came to Sharon, where I was met by a number of precious souls; to whom I preached in the afternoon in the open air, for want of room in the house. Surely the Lord has a work to do in this town. Mr. S. says we are leading souls to hell: but, blessed be God, many will not believe it.

Friday 24. This was a sweet morning to my soul—I continued writing successively till two o'clock exclusive of some intervals. The day passed sweetly away. When I looked at my watch, I perceived I had scarce time to get to my appointment; and rose from my seat in haste. The man of the house had gone out, and left the horse tied in the meadow by a long rope, to be handy when I wanted him. I took the bridle and went out, in order to make ready for my journey: and not considering him to be a borrowed horse (mine was too lame to be used) when I took hold of the rope, and began to gather him to me, he was scared, and began to run; and by some means I was entangled in the rope—how it was I cannot tell, but I felt myself in the utmost distress: I lay by the fence bereft of the use of my senses as well as limbs. For a long time I could not tell who, or what, or where I was; till at length I saw in my hat (as I had been striving to get it to lay my head on) the two first letters of my name, and knew who I was; and immediately called on the name of the Lord, who gave me power to rise up, and walk to the house. A physician was immediately sent for; and when he came, he found me much bruised, my right shoulder dislocated, and almost every joint in my hands and arms much strained. After my shoulder was set, and blood let, I was restored perfectly to my senses. Many of the neighbours gathered in: and I think in all my life I never had a greater sense of those words, *Thou shalt love the Lord with all thy heart.* Those around expected me to die. But as I lay on my bed I was constrained to cry out, *Perfect love casteth out fear.* Now, said I, I know there is a reality in the religion which I have been recommending to others, for these many years; as well as a truth in the Methodist doctrine, so called. I had such a love for the doctrine and cause, that it seemed as if I could freely have gone to the stake for it. I did not dare to murmur; but cried out, *Lord, it is good for me to be afflicted.* I was never more reconciled to the dealings of a good, and gracious God. I was constrained, and that in a flood of tears, to exhort all those around to fly to Jesus: for I saw a fulness in him for every creature. But one thing induced me to indulge a desire to stay longer in this world; and that was to be instrumental in doing good in the church.

Saturday 25. I desired a friend to make ready a carriage; for I had a longing desire to attend the Dover quarterly-meeting. That evening I got as far as Oblong, where I lodged at the house of an old doctor, and received much strength, and in the morning I got to Dover church, and was enabled to administer the supper to many of God's dear children: and afterward to preach with great liberty. I was attended by brother L. to my appointments, till I got to North Castle; where I thought it most expedient to decline attending my New England appointments, for I could by no means ride on horse back; and the roads were too rough for a chaise; and withal I could only get in and out with help; and that with a degree of pain. I withdrew to the city of New-York, where I staid about ten days; and then met my appointment on Long-Island; and had a precious sweet season. After I had fulfilled my appointments on the island, on Wednesday August 19, accompanied by a friend, I returned to the city; and had a favourable hope that my affliction was sancitfied for my good; and it also proved a blessing to some in the town where it happened. Surely the Lord is preparing me for some severe trial. The church in this city is gaining ground under the ministry of brother Moriarty and brother Cloud.

Sunday 23. I was resolved, God being my helper, to devote this day without reserve to him: and was very happy both in public and private.

I preached two sermons and several hours past away in solitude.

Friday August 28th. Having finished a piece of writing, I again set out on my journey round the district; and found a gradual gathering to the church in almost every place—the society-members as well as communicants, greatly increased. My mind was much exercised frequently; but I could find my all in the Lord Jesus. In my return I visited several towns in Connecticut, to which I had not been before; and found enlargement of heart to preach among the people.

Thursday November 19th, I returned to New-York, on my way to the council held in Baltimore: which journey was rendered a great blessing to me. When I left Baltimore I was resolved, God being my helper, to be more than ever engaged in the glorious work; and it was my earnest prayer, that, as in the South, the flame might break forth with us. I felt something of it in Philadelphia; and when I came to New-York, I preached with an enlargement which I had never felt in that city before; and had faith to believe that the brethren would have glorious times; and so it was;

for a few days after I left the city, the work, in a most extraordinary manner, broke out: first in a prayer-meeting, and then in the congregation; and I saw and felt something of the same flame, in many places round the district, in my winter visitation.

I had to encounter a variety of difficulties. In common the church-people do not oppose us in doctrine: but in this place, where we had a good society, one of this order of men went and preached, and spread books; and the minds of several were much confused; and they concluded they would not commune with us any more. I preached from these words, *We preach not ourselves, but Christ Jesus the Lord, and ourselves your servants for Jesus's sake.* When our dear Lord sent out his servants, he said, *Lo I am with you to the end of the world.* Who is he with? The pope?—the carnal bishop? By no means. He will be with all his faithful ministers of all denominations, even to the end of the world. Our Lord displayed his power, and there was a shaking among the people; and those wavering ones had their doubts removed, and drew near to the table. "It is a pity," said one, "that you ever separated from the church." It is a greater pity, said I, for the church-people, so called, to live without inward religion: should there be a reformation and turning to God, among your ministers and people, we shall stand a better chance to come together. I was brought up in the church, and have a great affection for it; and it would do me much good to hear of a turning to God among the members.

June 2, 1790[145] I set out on a journey to Boston, and so round the district. And on Tuesday I preached with liberty at New-Rochelle from, *O my dove, who art in the cleft of the rocks,* &c. My greatest freedom in the subject was when I inforced, *let me see they countenance, let me hear thy voice, for sweet is thy voice, and thy countenance is comely.* Crouds attended the word. On Sunday I suppose there were a thousand under the word at Bedford, whilst I inforced, *Friend, how camest thou in hither, not having on a wedding garment?* The day before a multitude gathered in King-street; as soon as I entered the house, I saw a man who was almost dead with the cholic: I desired him to drink a pint of cold water; and when he had taken it, his pain was gone. Monday 7, I cried to a listening multitude, *All scripture is given by inspiration of God,* &c. The next day the house was crouded, and about an hundred without. The people seemed to drink in every word. Wednesday I declared to a solemn company at Singsing, *Now the just shall live by faith,* &c. And in the evening at G. C's I had much freedom to preach the word. Thursday 10. Oakley's church was filled from end to end. I had much satisfaction in explaining the first psalm. In the evening I found great freedom to declare. *He that is born of God doth not commit sin, for his seed remaineth in him, and he cannot sin because he is born of God.* David lost the seed of grace out of his heart, before he committed the act of adultery: no doubt he was an adulterer in his heart before he left the house-top. If we keep ourselves that evil one cannot hurt us. We passed on over the Fishkiln mountains through Oswego, Rynebeck, and Nine-partners; and had an opportunity, every day, to preach the glorious gospel to hundreds of precious souls.

Sunday 20. About a thousand met in Sharon, and I found it to be an high day.

Monday 21. In Cornwall I trust several were awakened; one in particular who did not rest till he found peace to his soul. The next day I unexpectedly met a large congregation in the English church in Litchfield; I found freedom in preaching from, *Enoch walked with God*, Gen. v. 22. I went and preached in the Presbyterian meeting-house about two miles off: and our heavenly Father has raised us up some good friends. The next day I preached in the skirts of the town from, *Whom he did foreknow*, &c. Here I met with trouble from a disputatious Antinomian; however, I went on, and preached at the house of a goodnatured drunkard, and talked to him about his soul. His wife and daughter are lovers of our blessed Lord.

Monday 28. I preached to about five hundred people in Hartford with satisfaction. Thursday July 1. After a tedious journey we came to Boston. I preached several sermons, and had no doubt but the Lord will, sooner or later, give us a people in this place. From Boston I went to Providence, and staid a few days; and preached several sermons with liberty. On Monday morning I preached my farewell sermon a little after sunrise, to more than two hundred people. I have great fellowship with Mr. Snow as a Christian minister, and several of his people, as followers of Christ; for they appeared like Methodists to me. I have some reason to believe that my journey to this town was not in vain, for as I went out, some met me in tears, desiring to know what they should do to be saved.

I again passed through Farmington, Litchfield, Cornwall, and Canaan; and was happy to converse with many new-born souls. A woman in Canaan told me, that about seven years age, a man of a low stature came to her one night when she was asleep, dressed in black, and as she thought surrounded with a light brighter than the sun; he took out a book, and enquired for her name; and she saw him write it down in golden capitals; and told her that if she was faithful in the service of God, she should have a crown of life. In the morning she told her husband the dream, and that she should surely see that man. "I went to hear every strange minister who came into the town," said she, "and saw not the man till you came." And she knew me as well as if she had been acquainted with me seven years; and had no doubt but the doctrine which I preached was the light which she saw around me. And when she went home, she told her husband that she had now seen the man.

I continued my journey through Hudson and Queman's; from whence a distressed man followed me to Albany, and under the word he found peace to his soul. In Albany I have encountered many difficulties, in raising a little church; which is now likely to be finished. I held a quarterly-meeting at Clifton-park; and from thence advanced toward the new state; and found the work increasing in most of the societies. I had one and sometimes two quarterly-meetings to attend every week; and many were encouraged to press on in the narrow way. Having finished my rout, in October I returned again to New-York: where conference was held. At this conference our new Northern district was divided; and I have continued in the Albany district ever since. I have met with trials of a peculiar nature, part of which I once thought I never should have encountered. I wish at all times to be resigned to the will of my heavenly Father—hitherto I have had an heart to bless them that curse me, and pray for those who persecute, and despitefully use me. One thing I have taken notice of, which in some instances has been admirable. More than two thousand have joined the society—more than a thousand have been really born of the Spirit—more than eight thousand have been brought to see in a measure the propriety of our doctrine and discipline, and a reformation in a variety of places has taken place—hundreds, if not thousands, in the back settlements, who were not able to give an hundred a year to a minister, and could seldom hear a sermon, may now hear a sermon at least once in two weeks; and sometimes oftener—withal some of the ministers have lowered their salaries, and are more assiduous in their labours. If you will take pains to enquire among them, at least some can tell you that their congregations are larger: and where they had one, now they have two church members.

Respecting the doctrine taught among the Methodists,[146] I have not doubted of the truth of it, no not for a minute since I first embraced it. Respecting other denominations, I am willing to think, and let think; but this I say, I would not have any one be of this or the other persuasion merely because their parents brought them up in that belief. Touching unconditional election and reprobation, I never did believe it; and I am persuaded I never shall whilst I retain the use of my reason. What! to suppose that the Judge of the whole earth should unconditionally from eternity, destine part of the human race to eternal flames! If any man can persuade me to believe it, then it will not be a hard matter to make me believe, that he has unconditionally set apart a select number, (whom he calls the elect) for eternal felicity: and of course do what they will, it is impossible for them to lose their election, or as some term it, to fall from grace. If this in reality be the plan of the gospel, I acknowledge myself to have lived to the present time a stranger to it. I have not conversed with any man, since I have been acquainted with men and things, that could be consistent in supporting such a doctrine. And thus it is, that they so often contradict themselves. The holy scriptures have a beautiful harmony when rightly understood. God spoke a number of intelligences, called angels, into existence—beings capable of using aright, or abusing their moral agency—many of them did the latter, and were justly punished. God also made a creature, called man; and surely, though he was liable to fall, yet he was capable of standing; the former he chose, and incurred the just displeasure of his Creator. And in justice Jehovah might have punished Adam and Eve with eternal punishment for their own actual rebellion. And as the sin of their posterity was a seminal sin, so their punishment would have been a seminal punishment. Sing, O heavens! and give ear, O earth!—Instead of hell, we hear the voice of the eternal God in the garden to Adam and his whole posterity, *The seed of the woman shall bruise the serpent's head. I saw*, said St. John, *in the right hand of him that sat on the throne a book written within and on the backside, sealed with seven seals.* Though there was not any finite creature either in heaven or earth, able to open the book—to undertake the redemption of man—the Son of God, the second person in the ever adorable Trinity, appeared as a lamb slain from the foundation of the world. This precious Saviour was promised for Adam and Eve, and their whole posterity. As saith the angels to the shepherds, *Behold I bring you glad tidings of great joy, which shall be to all people.*

In the first Adam we lost our will and power to do good. In Christ, the second Adam, we are graciously restored both to a will and power; and with a great degree of propriety, the Lord may say, *choose life, that you may live.* Cain's punishment was just, for sin laid at his own door. Moses made a wise choice. Paul was not disobedient to the heavenly vision. The blind man went to the pool and washed. Bartimeus cast away his garment, rose, and came to Jesus. And we are exhorted by our Lord and his apostles, to *repent and believe the gospel. O Jerusalem! Jerusalem!* saith our Lord, *how oft would I have gathered you* &c. *I have called, but ye have refused,* &c. *Behold, now is the accepted time,* &c. The blessed Spirit, whilst we have a day of grace, is always ready. *I stand at the door and knock,* &c. Sinner, hear the voice of the eternal God, and lay aside your vain excuses. No longer cry out, I can do no-thing. For if you are not careful, you will do enough to damn your precious soul. We offer Christ to all upon earth, who have not sinned away their day of grace. Why, O! why should people be angry with us for preaching deliverance to poor captive souls—souls that are fallen— souls for whom Christ died—souls that must perish everlastingly without a change—Christ has merited every thing we need—Oh! then, dear souls, comply with his conditions—repent, believe, obey, and you shall live. The privilege of a Christian is to be made holy. God hath promised it to his faithful people. I wish to sit at the feet of my Redeemer, and if any one should receive any benefit from what I have published to the world, give God the glory whilst your unworthy servant sits as in the dust, earnestly praying to God that he may ever be humble and faithful.

Amen and Amen   F.G.

PART I
NOTES AND MANUSCRIPT MATERIAL

1. Freeborn Garrettson's Manuscript Journal gives his birthdate as August 15, 1752, but the *St. George's Parish Register* 1681 to 1799, p. 208, located in the Hall of Records, Annapolis, Maryland, gives his birth date as October 17, 1753. Allowing for carelessness of hand copied records, Garrettson's own record should take precedence.

2. *Garrettson Ancestry.*

Skordas, in *The Early Settlers of Maryland* notes the earliest Garrettson was Richard transported from England 1665. Book II, Folio 309. Richard may have been Freeborn Garrettson's great grandfather.

Freeborn's father was John, born February 7, 1706, son of Garrett Garrettson and Elizabeth Freeborn, married December 5, 1702 (See below). Other children of the first marriage on record: George, b. November 26, 1703; Elizabeth, b. April 30, 1704; Sarah, b. December 30, 1708 (?); James, b. October 15, 1709; Sophia, b. November 15, 1711; Freebourne, b. February 15, 1713. *St. George's Parish Register*, p. 18. Obviously they are not all recorded, for Garrettson mentions in his Journal that his father had eleven brothers and sisters.

Freeborn's father married Sarah _____ and had the following children: George, b. March 20, 1743; Sarah, b. December 25, 1747; Elizabeth, b. December 20, 1749; John, b. December 16, 1751; Freeborn, b. October 17, 1753 (August 15, 1752); Richard, b. December 5, 1755; Thomas, b. December 12, 1759.

Freeborn's grandfather, Garrett Garrettson, was remarried March 12, 1760 to Mrs. Susannah Robinson, widow of Capt. Daniel Robinson. Brumbaugh, G.M. *Maryland Records.* Vol. 2.

3. Considerable confusion has existed regarding Garrettson's birthplace. Actually a place not far from Perryman in Harford County, Maryland (at that time a part of Baltimore County), was the site of his birth, a place called Bush River. Much of this area is occupied today by the Aberdeen Proving Grounds. It is a low, flat expanse of land jutting out into the northern end of the Chesapeake Bay.

The St. George's Parish, which Garrettson attended as a youth and his family before him, has remained active since its origin in 1671. The old Spesutia Church of this parish where Garrettson was baptized has been on its present site of Perryman since 1718. The present building, set under huge trees and surrounded by an old burial ground (earliest stone 1790), was erected in 1851. The previous building was begun in 1758 when Garrettson was six years old.

A red brick vestry, built in 1766, stands in the church yard and has gone unrecognized as a landmark in Methodist history. Here Garrettson in 1775 defended his interest in Methodism before the vestrymen and the parish priest, the Rev. William West.

4. *Freeborn Garrettson's Education* was for that day well above average. His education continued with more or less regularity until the age of sixteen with the offer then to complete his study at Newark, Delaware in the Presbyterian Academy. This was one of the few good secondary schools in the Middle colonies and abounded in classical learning and Calvinist theology. He rejected this opportunity and opted for a course in surveying, finally becoming manager of a farm about 10 miles from his father's home.

Regarding Garrettson's early education, the references are not precise, but it is possible that he received some of his training in his own parish school. St. George's parish was the center of education. The vestry house in the church yard was used as the parish school for many years and each rector conducted a school. Church schools flourished at Sion Hill near Havre de Grace, and at Trappe, near Dublin. There were also itinerant teachers who boarded in local homes and held classes.

5. "I went to hear Mr. Strobridge and Mr. Williams." Manuscript Journal.

This is Robert Strawbridge (b. ___ d. 1781) a local Methodist preacher who came to America from Ireland in 1760. He organized the first Methodist Society in Maryland probably during 1763. He had probably been ordained by a German minister and therefore qualified to administer the sacraments.

Robert Williams, a local preacher from England, came to this country in 1769. John Wesley gave him a permit to preach in America under the direction of his missionaries. Williams arrived before Boardman and Pilmoor and preached first in Wesley Chapel, New York City. He died in Virginia September 26, 1775.

Wakeley, J. B.—*Lost Chapters Recovered from the Early History of American Methodism*, New York: Carleton & Porter, 1858.

6. *Russell's Seven Sermons*. Robert Russell, an English Divine, wrote this work which became popular among the Methodists of Wesley's day.

7. Religious reading which added fuel to Garrettson's examination of his thoughts and motives, intensifying his sense of lostness included the work of:

JAMES HERVEY. (1714-1758). Before his Calvinistic convictions, Hervey had been one of John Wesley's companions at Oxford. A pious, spiritually minded individual, his writings emphasize the practical aspects of spiritual religion.

Hervey's Works, Philadelphia, W. W. Woodward, 1810.

JOSEPH ALLEINE was a non-conformist born in 1633. His work, *Alarm to the Unconverted*, was widely used as a manual on practical religion.

BENJAMIN KEACH was a Baptist minister born in England in 1640. The work Garrettson studied, *The Travels of True Godliness and Ungodliness*, is written in dialogue form.

8. FRANCIS ASBURY (1745-1816 had a profound influence on Freeborn Garrettson and was a close co-worker. Asbury reached Philadelphia October 27, 1771 in answer to Wesley's second call for help for America. Asbury soon became the leading force in American Methodism and its first bishop.

9. RICHARD WEBSTER. Webster was among the earliest Methodist local preachers in Harford County, Maryland. Beginning in 1774, he settled near Abingdon, Maryland, and served several circuits for 50 years. Calvary Chapel built in 1821 was one of his efforts.

10. "One night, as I sat by him, he seemed to be deep in thought; I find, said he, that there is something wanting. I think there was a great change in him, before he died, tho he said but little." *Manuscript Journal.*

11. "(Mr. West) who was a very upright man in his outward deportment, and had a great zeal according to his light and knowledge . . . began to think that his doctrine would suit me better than the doctrines held out by the Methodists." *Manuscript Journal.*

12. GEORGE SHADFORD (1739-1816) was "admitted on trial at the British Conference of 1768; admitted to the Traveling Connection in 1769; and in 1772 was persuaded by Capt. Thomas Webb to volunteer for service in America. Unable to renounce his allegiance to Great Britain, he returned to England in March 1778."

Barclay, W. C. *Early American Methodism 1769-1844* Vol. 1, p. 43. The Board of Missions and Church Extension of the Methodist Church: New York, 1749.

"Many are the times that I have sat behind the door of Bush preaching-house in tears, and my poor foundations would tremble; especially under the preaching of Brother Shadford." *Manuscript Journal.*

BUSH PREACHING-HOUSE. "In 1769 the oldest Methodist church in Harford County, Maryland, was constructed in the "Forest" on what is now the road from Stepney to Carsin's Run. It is said to have been the second Methodist Meeting House in America. It was called Bush Chapel, after the town of Bush, which was the county seat of Harford County from 1773-1782." C. Milton Wright. *Our Harford Heritage* 1967.

13. DANIEL RUFF lived near Havre de Grace, Maryland. He was received on trial at the Philadelphia Conference 1774 and ceased traveling in 1781. Asbury counted him one of his most dependable assistants.

Clark, Elmer T. *The Journal and Letters of Francis Asbury*, Vol. I. Nashville: Abingdon Press, 1958, p. 348n.

14. ". . . as I stood with my Psalm book open, just about to begin to sing, it appeared to me, as if some person stood by me, and said, it is not the will of the Lord that

you should keep your fellow creatures in bondage, . . . (I stood amazed) . . . I paused about a minute, afraid to go in worship, for the person appeared to be waiting for an answer." *Manuscript Journal.*

Garrettson, as will be seen in his Journals, remained an opponent of slavery, suffering rebuke and persecution because of his position. One of his publications entitled, Do-Justice is a denunciation of slavery.

For a description of slavery in the time and place where Garrettson worked, see: *Life and Times of Frederick Douglass*, London: Collier-Macmillan Ltd., 1962, pp. 55-56.

15. "In the fore-noon I attended the church (St. George's)—before the service began, the people were gathered in little companyes—the old men talking about the price of grain, their farms and crops, and the younger people about horseracing and the like etc, etc. This is the church in which I was raised, and to which I was begotedly attached; but I was impressed. "There is no spiritual food in this place for your soul" *Manuscript Journal.*

16. "I went about 10 miles . . . to be in class meeting." *Manuscript Journal.*

17. *Deer Creek* is a tributary flowing into the Susquehanna River in northwest Harford County, Maryland. A number of Methodist families resided here not the least of which was Henry Watters, whose home was headquarters for Asbury. p. 50 Clark, E. T. *Journal* . . . Asbury. Vol. I.

The Deer Creek Friends Meeting House, established 1734 was also a site of Methodist visitation . . . *ibid.*

18. "About 12 were gathered, and this was the first time that I attempted to give a publick exhortation." *Manuscript Journal.*

19. "about forty people (mostly Black people) came together . . ." *Manuscript Journal.*

20. "I suppose nearly 20 poor sinners were on the floor crying for mercy." *Manuscript Journal.*

21. "One Lord's Day whilst I was holding a meeting among the poor blacks." *Manuscrpit Journal.*

22. ". . . not that I was an enemy to the country, no . . ." *Manuscript Journal.*

23. "The Colonel desired me to walk with him, he wanted to have some conversation with me. I found him to be a reasonable man, I told him what God had done for me, and he seemed to be satisfied; but there were others who were much more trying than he; but it all worked together for my good. The Colonel had not been long from me, before he returned, and said, he wanted to have some more conversation with me on the subject. I conversed with him, till he seemed almost persuaded to be a christian. I conversed with many of them with tears, and some seemed to be affected, and others mocking, said, he is a fool." *Manuscript Journal.*

24. John Wesley's position regarding the American Revolution set up circumstances which made all American Methodists suspect of loyalist sympathies. This was a primary factor in their abuse and persecution. Wesley, was an outspoken Tory and supporter of the crown. Most of his missionaries in America subscribed to that position also. The burden of abuse fell upon Asbury and the young men of the native itinerant ministry. For a fuller discussion of Wesley and the war see: Simpson, Robert Drew, *Freeborn Garrettson, American Methodist Pioneer* Ph.D. Thesis, Madison, New Jersey, Drew University, 1954, pp. 51-61.

25. MR. WEST (the St. Georges Parish minister).

26. "You have no right," said he, "to break thru my lines. There are many unconverted sinners in your parish said I and I think you ought to be thankful for a helper." . . . "I am sorry," said he, (rising from his seat) "that this gentleman has come to disturb us today." "I can assure you Mr. West this was not my intention; you first introduced the conversation, and I think it my duty to vindicate the precious truth of my Saviour's gospel . . ." *Manuscript Journal.*

27. T. R. (Thomas Rankin) was one of the eight missionaries John Wesley sent to America in response to Capt. Webb's appeal at the Conference of Leeds in 1772. He

was a strong disciplinarian. Coming to America with George Shadford in June, 1773 he returned to England in 1778 in the midst of the American Revolution.

MR. D. (Dallam's). Probably Josias Dallam who lived near Aberdeen, Maryland, on the present site of the Aberdeen Proving Ground. This was a staunch Methodist family whose home was a center for Methodist preachers including Asbury.—*Asbury's Journals*, Vol. I, p. 59.

MR. R—(Martin Rodda) one of Wesley's missionaries who remained less than 3 years in America, and because of pro-British sympathies returned to England shortly after the out-break of the Revolution.

28. "I was not called to marry. When I went downstairs, I met the object in the hall, and told her, that I was convinced that the Lord had a greater work for us to do, and gave up the whole matter." *Manuscript Journal*.

29. In the audience that day was the officer's thirteen year old son, Ezekiel Cooper. Cooper became a prominent Methodist preacher and close friend to Garrettson. In a note quoted by Nathan Bangs in his *Life of the Rev. F. Garrettson* p. 45, further information is revealed which does not appear in his printed Journal nor in available manuscript notes.

"After I left Brother Ruff, I was wandering along in search of an opening for the word, in deep thought and prayer, that my way might be prosperous. I came opposite a gate, the impression was sudden—turn in, this is the place where you are to begin. It was the house of Rev. E. Cooper's mother, and the officer was his stepfather. Ezekiel was about thirteen years of age, and as he has since informed me, he received a divine touch which he never lost, and some years after, he was happily brought out to testify of the forgiving love of Jesus, was called to the work of the ministry, and to eminent usefulness in the church of God. There is great cause of thankfulness for my feeble efforts in this little excursion."

30. D— R— (Daniel Ruff) . . . Cecil County, Maryland.

31. T— R— (Thomas Rankin).

32. "My exercise was so great the next day that after we returned from the preaching house, to Brother Moor's for dinner, I fainted (—yea, it was a kind of swoon—) and sunk to the floor." *Manuscript Journal*.

This occurred at the Baltimore Conference May 21, 1776. The political unrest in Philadelphia necessitated the move to Baltimore.

33. "I joined this blessed connection as a preacher on trial at the May Conference 1776 and forever blessed and praised be the Lord's name for it, and I trust I shall praise him to all eternity." *Manuscript Journal*.

34. MR. MARTIN RODDA.

Frederick Circuit, the birthplace of American Methodism, embraced all that territory north of Baltimore which afterwards comprised Frederick, Montgomery, Carroll, Washington and Allegany counties.

Armstrong, James Edward, *History of the Old Baltimore Conference*, Baltimore: Kings Bros. 1907, p. 25.

35. Thomas Weatherington's — *Manuscript Journal*.

36. Martin Rodda (and continuing references to Mr. R.) *Manuscript Journal*.

37. FAIRFAX CIRCUIT, Maryland was newly established, having been added at the May 21, 1776 Conference in Baltimore. Three preachers were assigned at that time— Watters, McClure, and Fonerdon.

38. "SHEPHERDSTOWN, originally called Mechlenburg, has been called the oldest town in present West Virginia. Named for its founder, Thomas Shepherd, Methodism met strong opposition here in the early period." *Asbury's Journal* Vol. I. p. 430 note.

39. T— R— (Thomas Rankin).

40. "Brother Watters and Brother Tunnel" *Manuscript Journal* (Gatch was also in this group). The Brunswick Circuit was designated at the second conference on May 25, 1774 in Philadelphia. Formerly it had been Petersburg in Virginia.

41. "Miner's in Fairfax." *Manuscript Journal*.

42. *June 5, (1777)*—"called at an inn for some refreshment where I had an opportunity to pray within, and exhort the family and many officers that were present; they begged me to preach in the neighborhood." *Manuscript Journal.*

43. "*Tuesday 10:* I preached at a schoolhouse to a cold dead set of Presbyterians, I hope my Lord reached some of their hearts." *Manuscript Journal.*

44. Col. Taylor's.

45. The Rev. F. Poytress. (Francis Poythress).

46. "The hearts of the people in an uncommon manner, was attached to me; they begged of me to settle among them, offered me money by the handfuls, and a seat of land if I would settle. This portion of God's word came into mind, woe be unto you when all men speak well of you for so they did of the false prophets, these thoughts caused me to mourn in secret. O how powerfully the devil tempted me . . . *Manuscript Journal.*

Sat. 14. I preached to a small _____ with little liberty, I exhorted in the evening. I trust the word was owned and blessed.

Sun. 15. The lord sent his word home with energy to the hearts of the people. I felt my spirit abundantly refreshed . . .

Mon. 16. This day I labored under much hardness of heart. I perceive all prosperity is not the best, I want to be humbled.

Tues. 17. I am under the afflicting hand of providence; not in body but in mind . . .

Wed. 18. I am still wading thru distress of soul, the devil is an unwearyed enemy . . .

Thurs. 19. O Lord I am opprest, undertake for me.

Fri. 20. This morning I am sorely exercised all the way to meeting; I had scarce openned my mouth before the cloud broke . . . the whole house was filled with the power of God; three souls was espoused to Jesus . . .

Sat. 21. The past night, and this morning I had a time of rejoicing." *Manuscript Journal.*

47. MABRY'S CHAPEL in Virginia.

48. "*Sun. 22.* But why will you not take the oath? 1. I never swore an oath in my life, not even before I profest religion, (not that I condemn those who are not conscience bound, with regard to it). 2. The oath appeared to be too severe. 3. I want to have nothing to do with the affair, and lastly I wish to be on the safe side—Our blessed Lord, and his apostle St. James, tells us not to swear at all." *Manuscript Journal.*

49. The circuit in North Carolina was divided at the conference in Leesburg, Virginia in 1778 into three circuits—Roanoke, Tar-River, and New Hope. This circuit together with the one in Virginia were the only new ones reported. Actually for that year a total loss of 873 members and 7 preachers was recorded. This reflects the pressures of war and anti-Methodist sentiment.

Sweet, W. W. *Methodism in American History.* The Methodist Book Concern, New York 1933, p. 92, 93.

50. "Brothers Hartley, Littlejohn, Cooper." *Manuscript Journal.*

JOSEPH HARTLEY, later jailed in Talbot County, Maryland, for preaching.

JOHN LITTLEJOHN and EZEKIEL COOPER.

KENT MEETING HOUSE was the first meeting house built by the Methodists on the Eastern Shore of Maryland in Kent County about nine miles below Chestertown in 1774. Jesse Lee records that neighbors opposed to the Methodists smashed the rafters during the night, but the workmen undaunted completed their work.

Lee, Jesse. *A Short History of Methodists,* Baltimore: Magill and Clime, 1810, p. 50.

51. "In Queen Anne County Joseph Hartley was bonded in amount of $500 not

to preach in the county, and in Talbot County (Maryland) was whipped and committed to prison." Barclay, W. C. *Early American Methodism*, Vol. 1, p. 48.

Hartley, Sussex County, Virginia, was received on trial in 1776. He died in 1785 and was buried near his residence in Miles River Neck, Talbot County, Maryland.

52. The reference is to a Methodist layman, Chauncey Clowe, a resident of the Peninsula, who raised a company of three hundred tories in a plan to march overland to the Chesapeake to join the British fleet anchored in the Bay. Clowe and his company were apprehended and Clowe was hanged, but not before the reputation of the Methodists was worsened by his conduct. It was at this time that the Methodist preacher, Martin Rodda (here referred to as Mr. R.) was discovered distributing the King's Proclamation on his circuit. Before he could be arrested he fled to the British fleet.

53. "In March, 1778 he (Asbury) took refuge in the home of Judge Thomas White, a prominent magistrate and a Methodist. Pursuit followed him even into his place of asylum. Judge White was imprisoned on the sole charge of being a Methodist, and for a time Asbury sought concealment during daylight hours in the depths of a dreary swamp." Barclay. *Early American Methodism*. Vol. I. p. 49.

JUDGE THOMAS WHITE (1730-95), Kent County, Delaware, lived near Whiteleysburg. Asbury was in hiding there from November 9, 1778 to April 20, 1780. The White family were early Methodists and gave it prestige and protection on the Peninsula. Asbury named him among his best friends in America. *Asbury's Journal*, Vol. I., p. 253.

54. "I now began to travel at large through Kent, Cecil, Queene Anne, and Talbot and also in other counties in Maryland and in the Delaware State." *Manuscript Journal*.

55. "John B_____n":—John Brown. *Manuscript Journal*.

56. "I told him that I freely forgave him and begged of him never to persecute the people of God anymore." *Manuscript Journal*.

57. ". . . preached at 11 o'clock at Brother Randal's." *Manuscript Journal*. The Randall mentioned could have been either John or Harry who lived near Worton, Maryland. In John's home Robert Strawbridge is reported to have preached the first Methodist sermon on the eastern shore of Maryland in 1769. *Asbury's Journal*, Vol. I. p. 89.

58. "Preached several sermons at Thomas' and Scotton's." *Manuscript Journal*. Both of these families opened their homes to Methodist preaching. Asbury's Journal records frequent visits to them. The old Forest Chapel meeting house in Delaware became Thomas Chapel in honor of, and tribute to, the contribution of the Thomas family to Methodism in that area. *Asbury's Journal*, Vol. II, pp. 260, 299.

59. "I do believe that some of the first sermons which I preached on the bay side, and in Mil's River Neck, and at other places will never be forgotten." *Manuscript Journal*.

60. "SISTER PARROT AND SISTER (BOROFF?) *Manuscript Journal*.

61. KENT ISLAND, Queen Anne's County, is the largest island in Chesapeake Bay. This appears to be Garrettson's first visit there.

62. "Mush Million, Mother Kill, and several other places around . . . at Brother Williams." *Manuscript Journal*.

63. "Under a large spreading oak." *Manuscript Journal*.

64. "Old Brother Lewis." *Manuscript Journal*.

Barratt's Chapel and Methodism. p. 18, 19 refers to this incident as follows: "In October, 1778, Freeborn Garrettson preached with his usual virility in Murderkill (Motherkill) at the house of David Lewis, and among those converted or awakened to self-consciousness were Philip Barratt, Sheriff of Kent County, and his brother-in-law, Jonathan Sipple, Coroner of Kent, whose house became a preaching place as well as Philip Barratt's. After his death in 1780 his father, Waitman Sipple, Jr., took his place. This often resulted in from two to three hundred people being present, which was more than could be comfortably accommodated, especially on Sundays or during revivals. . . . A regular place of meeting was sadly needed, and it was to supply this want and to have a fixed place of public worship where regular services could be held that determined Philip Barratt to erect this chapel."

65. C. B. "CALEB BOYER." *Manuscript Journal*.

CALEB BOYER, converted by Garrettson on this occasion, was an itinerant from 1780-88, and was an effective leader of the Peninsula Conference. The family home was located near Magnolia, Delaware. *Asbury's Journal*, Vol. I, p. 292.

66. "Many of the people in these parts were Presbyterian; but they were con-vinced that they had the name without the power." *Manuscript Journal.*

67. "I likewise preached near the house of Parson Thorn, who appeared friendly for a time. I lodged several times at his house, but I fear the seed was sowed among thorns." *Manuscript Journal.*

The PARSON THORNE mentioned was apparently Sydenham Thorne, Rector of Mispillion Church which was located some distance to the west of the present Milford, Delaware. Asbury was also a visitor in his parish. *Asbury's Journal*, Vol. I, p. 392.

68. "MR. SHAW's." *Manuscript Journal.*

Probably Richard Shaw whom Asbury mentions as "a striking instance of the power and goodness of God. . ." *Asbury's Journal*, Vol. I, p. 262.

69. "The free school or the academy as it was called." *Manuscript Journal.*

70. "MR. P_____ "Mr. Pryor, a merchant . . . Mr. Lockerman, a very rich man." *Manuscript Journal.*

Possibly Theodore R. Lockerman of Talbot County, Maryland.

71. "MR. SMETHERS." *Manuscript Journal.*

72. DR. MAGAW." *Manuscript Journal.*

DR. SAMUEL MAGAW (1735-1812) became rector of Christ Church, Dover, Delaware in 1767. A friend to the Methodists, he gave them their first frame meeting house in Delaware called originally Forest Chapel. *Asbury's Journal*, Vol. I, p. 299.

73. "My youngest brother, Thomas." *Manuscript Journal.*

74. "I traveled till the setting sun. I was in a vicious part of the world, where they threatened my life. I met with an old Negro man—hired him to conduct me to a poor man's house where I thought I would be safe. I rested very comfortable with the poor man." *Manuscript Journal.*

75. JOHN WHITE—"Joney White." *Manuscript Journal.*

Probably John White, brother of Dr. Edward White and nephew of Judge Thomas White. *Asbury's Journal*, Vol. I, p. 335.

76. MR. NALLUM. *Manuscript Journal.*

77. MR. PARROT's. *Manuscript Journal.*

78. BROTHER PEDICORD—Caleb B. Peddicord was received as a preacher at the Deer Creek Conference May 20, 1777. He was rich in song and eloquence. He died in 1785.

79. BR. HARTLEY. *Manuscript Journal.*

80. DR. WHITE—Dr. Edward White, nephew of Judge Thomas White.

81. MR. NALLUM. *Manuscript Journal.*

82. "SISTER RIDER." *Manuscript Journal.*

83. "Respecting the people in this place, Mr. Garrettson makes the following observations in his notes to this part of his journal, (this material appears to be lost from the Manuscript Journal) that an admirable change soon took place for the better in this region of the country. When he first went among them the people, their land and houses, with but few exceptions, were poor. What was worst of all, they were destitute of even the form of godliness. Many of them preferred fishing and hunting to cultivating the land. After the gospel came among them, religion spread rapidly, and the people became industrious and happy; left off gambling, tilled their land, built houses, and attended to their spiritual interests, so that, says he, "after a few years, in retracing my footsteps in this country, I found that my younger bretheren in the ministry who had succeeded me, had been blessed in their labours, and everything appeared to wear a different aspect. Experience had taught many that there is nothing like the gospel in its purity to meliorate both the temporal and spiritual condition of man; and my prayer is that it may find its way throughout the whole world, to the destruction of idolatry and infidelity."—Bangs, Nathan. *The Life of the Rev. Freeborn Garrettson*, N.Y.: Emory & Waugh 1830, pp. 85, 86.

84. Garrettson made a note about the Quaker principle which was not included in the printed Journal and has been lost from the Manuscript notes. It appears only in Nathan Bang's *Life of Garrettson*, pp. 89, 90 and is included in Appendix I Note 84.

"It is said, in favour of silent meetings, that Job's friends waited in silence seven days, and then they began to speak. Why was this silence? Before Job's affliction he was thought to be a very good man. His friends were in council to make up an opinion respecting his case. It was a received opinion with many in that country and age, that the Almighty would not lay so heavy an affliction upon a good man. From such an opinion, their decision must be, that Job was a bad man, or that his Maker dealt unjustly by him: but the judgment of the counsellors was, that the Almighty was perfect in wisdom and goodness, and that Job was a bad man; and having made up their minds on the occasion, they began to load Job with accusations of base hypocrisy, and to preach to him repentance, or banishment from the presence of God. Had they known how to reconcile those deep afflictions with the mercy and goodness of God, they might have begun their discourse when they first approached Job, and not have accepted a false vision.

"I grant, in several instances, the prophets waited in silence; but who cannot see the difference between foretelling future events, and declaring those sacred truths of the gospel which have been revealed to every regenerated child of God, and especially to his ministers? Before a person professes to be an ambassador of Jesus Christ, he must know that he has a commission from him, and the pious man with the commission, receives a holy unction, and if he is faithful, he will be taught every necessary truth, and certainly he will be taught to be instant in season and out of season. I know that the nearer we live to the fountain head, the more plentifully will the water flow. A Christian minister should always have the holy spark with him, and certainly he should have the faculties of his soul so well regulated, as to know when to speak, and when to be silent. I myself one day heard three men speak, after brooding over it for nearly an hour, and I verily believe I have heard a pious sister in a lovefeast speak more to the purpose in fifteen minutes. What would you think of E. H., who by some is cried up to be a great man, after professing to have waited a considerable time for the Spirit, rising up and declaring that there is no more merit in the blood of Jesus Christ, than in the blood of any common animal, and inveighing against almost all the duties enjoined by the Christian religion? I speak thus, because I think it a pity that any respectable society of professing Christians should be imposed on by such men, and such doctrine. . . ."

85. "Calling me Mr. Preacher in a deriding manner I immediately stopt at his request the flesh being weak and the surprise sudden, I found the flesh wanted to *jump*; but . . . when I reflected I knew I was in the hand of the Lord, and the hairs of my head were numbered. . . . After a moments reflection I was encouraged to look to the Lord for strength. . . . But I was followed, I heard the drum beating some distance behind me, the mob swearing, guns firing one after another. Glory to God . . . he conducted me safely to my appointment." *Manuscript Journal.*

86. "I think I never met with harder trials in all my life than I did this morning. I was much troubled and the night passed with corrupt nature. I was scarcely out of my bed, before I was so tempted I thought I was the impurest creature in the world. I seemed to be miserable, I was tempted that I should sin against God, if I attempted to preach his gospel. I thought I was too unholy. I labored all this morning under hardness of heart. I had but eight miles to ride to preach in a new place. After I got there, I went into a barn and mourned . . . my hard heart, it was a great cross to me to preach. Satan told me that God would never visit me again. A very large congregation came together blest be God he gave me to know that the devil was a liar. I can shout my joys upon the banks of deliverence. If we was not tempted how should we know how to comfort the tempted follower. Lord make me humble, and when I stray from thee in the least, let me hear thy voice, and know that love is near. I returned to Mr. T. and met the society. My soul could praise my God, to see such an alteration in the neighborhood within two months. I examined the society and I had reasonable hope they will retain a sense of the need of a savior. I had six miles to travel two of which I went by water, it was a very tedious journey against wind and tide." *Manuscript Journal.*

87. "I thought I would have given the world if I could have been exempt from preaching (it was such a cross) I thought I was not fit to preach." *Manuscript Journal.*

88. "I had some conversation with an old calvinist (the judge of the court). We disagreed in sentiments. I fear he has no vital religion." *Manuscript Journal.*

89. "Here is a den of thieves and vile persecutors. Several of their rulers came to lay in wait for me, the night before they took Brother Nelmus (Nallum) out of (his) house (the man where I preached) and dragged him through the street, and abused him very much, and intend to duck me in the creek." *Manuscript Journal.*

90. "Immediately after preaching the Mob was racing and marching through the street, but God had, through the sermon, opened the eyes of one of the magistrates, so far, (although before he was a persecutor) that he took my part, and stopt them. Lest they should assault me in the night, I thought it prudent to leave town. Many of the dear persecuted followers of Christ followed me to Brother Bird's, here we had a blessed prayer meeting . . . this night I rested in peace and happiness." *Manuscript Journal.*

91. *The week of June 14, 1779,* is summarized in Freeborn Garrettson's printed Journal as follows: "All this week I spent in preaching and visiting the young societies." Nathan Bangs also omits references to this week's activities.

Monday the 15th (14) (1779)—This morning I was much tempted. I walked about the field and in the woods, and could not enjoy that comfort that I desired. I was much tried with drowseyness. I could scarcely read one chapter without being ready to drop with sleep. I seem to be a cumberer of the ground. I got no comfort at all, 'til I began Meeting. Blest be God the gloom burst and the Lord paid me a sweet visit. Reexamined near 30 very close, endeavored to strip some that was covered with their own righteousness. In the whole we had a blest meeting. Some of the friends tarreyed. We spent some time singing praises of God. I enjoyed some sweet moments, there are two happy souls in this family and others near the Kingdom.

Tuesday the 16th (15)—This morning conversation in publick hindered me in a measure from private retirement. As I was about to leave the friends they wanted some conversation. I rode 12 miles and preached to a crowded audience with uncommon liberty. I think good was done in my Master's name; met the Society with near 15 strangers, rode 6 miles with a stranger in order to preach at his house the next day. This evening I was very dull and heavy.

Wednesday the 17th (16)—I preached to an unexpected congregation. I had much liberty. This is a strange doctrine to the greater part of my hearers. They listened with great attention. I had some conversation after meeting with the woman of the house. She gave me a Christian experience. She also told me many things that seemed strange to me. She said she knew when she was to dye and what death she was to dye. She told me she was to be put to death by false witnesses and that in a short time.

Thursday 18 (17)—This morning I had sweet peace. I conversed with the woman of the house. I think the Lord had done a great thing for her. She told me that he had pardoned her sin and she knew the very time. She also told me that at the same time he made it known to her what death she should dye. She was to be put to death by false witnesses and that in a short time.

I rode 12 miles and preached to a small audience with some liberty. A baptist preacher held forth after I was done. This evening I spent in visiting the sick. I had some satisfaction in talking and praying. This night I was troubled with an impure heart. . . Lord, wash my soul and body in clean water, and make me clean.

Friday—I preached at _____ with little liberty. The baptist preacher held forth, we had a very long meeting. I hope some good was done, as this was a day set apart for fast, blest be God I seem to be humble. I want a deep work of grace carried on in my soul, I'm determined to press after it. I was very happy in family prayer, there seemed to be a great stir in the family. This night I rested in peace.

Saturday 20 (19)—Blest be God, when I awoke I felt the love of Christ in my heart. The baptist continued with me, we both went to the appointed place, we both held forth. I hope good was done in the name of the Blest Jesus. I lectured in the evening with much happiness. Glory be to God I laid down in peace . . .

"I stood on a table in the midst, under the trees. I preached from these words, Solomon made himself a chariot, etc. Song of Songs 3:9,10. . . . In my discourse as I understood two blind guides was to preach at the said place in opposition, I took occasion to point out the character of a true preacher and I warned the people against blind preachers. . . After I had preached the Baptist preacher held forth. I thought much more of his discourse, than I did the day before."—*Manuscript Journal.*

92.   Again both Garrettson and Bangs omit the Journal for the week of June 21, 1779, through July 11 except for occasional notes for the last week. The following is Garrettson's Manuscript Journal for that period. JUNE 21, 1779 THRU JULY 11.

Monday, June 22, (21) 1779—This day I have set apart (as there is great talk about Society Meeting) for meeting Societyes and reading and explaining the rules of society. I suppose several hundred came together.

I read and explained the rules much to the satisfaction of the people. I joined many in Society.

Lord be praised for his goodness. It was blest day to my soul. I lodged with an old baptist. I had great satisfaction, although we differed in regard to externals.

Tuesday 23 (22)—This morning very early, after family prayers I had some conversation about the final perserverance of _____. About two hours by sun I met the Society, was very happy, many of them when we was parting stood around me in tears. I rode 8 miles and preached to a crowded audience. They seemed to be very hard. I rode 4 miles and preached at five o'clock to another crowded audience. I had much liberty, it was a powerful time. I believe sinners was brought to tremble. Others enquired, what shall I do to be saved? My soul was happy in God and my savior. I visited a distressed, afflicted man, his soul unconverted. I was happy in advising and praying with and for him. This night in peace I went to my bed but I was troubled with dreams.

Wednesday 24 (23)—I found my soul very dull and heavy and so I continued all the morning. I preached to a very crowded audience. I preached in the orchard. I was very happy in the latter part of my sermon, many in tears. I rode 12 miles and held forth in evening to a very small audience in a strange place. Many are hard and blind.

Thursday 25 (24)—I rode 12 miles, 6 of which was in company with a blind clergyman. Some weeks ago he was hired to preach at Salisbury against the truth of the gospel. I attacked him about it, he made his excuse by telling me he was wrong informed. I begged him never to assert false reports for the truth. I preached in a strange place and he was in tears. I had a hope good was done.

I had some conversation with a blind old woman, her language was very disagreeable. I rode six miles to _____. I exhorted the Society, my soul was happy. I rested in sweet peace.

Friday 26 (25)—This day I was very dull and heavy until I began to preach. I had a good time.

Saturday 27 (26)—I preached and dined with the Rev. Mr. Thomas _____ Williams and met Society.

Monday 29 (28) (June 1779)—I spent the morning in reading and writing. This evening I had much satisfaction in visiting our friends.

Tuesday (June 29) evening I preached with much freedom; a doctor who came some distance was deeply affected, he and his lady. We had much of the Presence of God in our private meeting.

Wednesday (30)—it being harvest time I had a small audience, mostly females, mostly all humble seekers. We had a very tender meeting. Brother Avery met me at this place. We rode as far as Brother Shaw's, met Brother Asbury; they left me in the morning. I was very happy amongst the dear children of God. This day I preached to near as many as the house would hold. Blest be God, he was with us. I think we had a very solemn class meeting. This evening I paid my dear friends a visit, gave an exhortation, and enjoyed much of the goodness of God.

Friday (July 2, 1779)—I rode 6 miles out of town and preached with much happiness, returned and held forth in town at an hour by sun. If I know my own heart, I enjoy a sense of the love of God.

Saturday—I set this day apart to meet three classes. I did in town with much happiness. After meeting the Societies I preached to them and as many more of the Town that saw proper to attend. My time was so taken up in Publick, that I had very little time for private except morning and evening.

Wednesday 8 (7) (July)—I went to town in order to preach. Mr. Bradley, Esq. had my horse and carriage taken care of as the people were very busy about saving their grain. I had but about 100 hearers, mostly all the great ones in Town, except a few that would not come through prejudice, from hearsay, all that did hear was much taken both rich and poor, though Satan began to rage in a few of the baser sorts. An advertisement was set up at the door a little before I began to preach. Mr. Wilson, a disenting minister (to my sorrow) throwed out some aspersions against me. I dined at Squire Rodney's. (Squire Rodney was probably Thomas Rodney (1744-1811) brother of Gov. Caesar Rodney.)

Friday 10 (9)—This evening I exhorted near 30 of the neighbors that came in, most of them were black.

Saturday 11 (10)—I preached at quarterly conference with much liberty to a crowded audience.

93. The period for September 29, 1779 to February 8, 1780 is summarized in Garrettson's Journal as well as in Bangs. The following represents the significant material Garrettson included in his Manuscript Journal but did not include for printing in the summary for this period. It included his travel beyond New Jersey and Pennsylvania into Delaware and Maryland. The material needs to be interwoven with Sections VI and VII.

"*Sept. 22, 1779*—This morning I left the City of Philadelphia, and set out for the lower Jerseys. I preached by candlelight at Br. Chews with very little happiness. The next day I had a very good time at a School House."

"*Oct. 1*—I preached at a little town with some liberty; in the evening I held forth at Gordens. I had much sweetness. Blessed by God. I spent the evening very comfortably at Capt. Sterlings. Sunday 2 (3), I met with various temptations and trials. I gave a lovefeast in the morning. Glory be to God, it was a blessed time to many precious souls. My soul was refreshed. At 12 Q.C. I preached in the barn from these words: "Behold the Lamb of God that taketh away the sin of the world." It was a very powerful time. In the evening I held forth at Woodstown. It was a blessed time indeed. I lodged at the house of a Moravian. It seemed to be a precious family. I had much comfort.

"*Mon. 3 (4)*—I rode many miles to Mr. Sterlings. In the evening preached with more freedom at Salem in the Court house; the people seemed to be much melted. I lodged with a very kind friend, though his family was very much divided."

"*Oct. 4 (5)*—This morning I left and rode to a few of the neighbors with satisfaction. We rode 6 miles; I preached by candlelight. I was much distressed, but Glory be to God in family prayer the Lord paid us a sweet visit."

"*Wed. 5 (6)*—I returned to Salem and preached to a crowded assembly with much freedom. I praise God for his love. I rode about 6 miles to very kind friends, in this family my spirit was refreshed."

"*Thurs. 6 (7)*—The word was attended with much power morning and evening. Glory be to God, this is a day of love to my soul."

"*Fri. 7 (8)*—This morning I set out for the City."

"*Monday 10 (11)*—I rode 10 or 12 miles to hold a Watch Night. I preached, and heard many of our young exhorters with much satisfaction."

"*Tuesday 11 (12)*—This day I had a tedious journey to the city. I preached by candlelight to a crowded audience."

"*Wednesday*—I rode 12 miles out of the city and preached at _____ Church."

Thursday 13 (14)—Preached at Chapel at twelve o'clock and in the evening by candlelight.

Friday 14 (15)—This day had a tedious journey to Philadelphia.

Sunday 16 (17)—I preached about sunrise, about 9:00 met class at 2 o'clock and preached at 6 o'clock. I still am tried. I fear God has not called me to the City.

(October) Monday 25—I set out to Tren-Town. (Trenton, N. J., heard George Whitefield in November 21, 1739. Capt. Webb preached there in 1776, but it was Joseph Toy from Burlington, N. J. who organized a class in 1771. The first Methodist meeting house in New Jersey was built there on the corner of the present Broad and Academy Streets. Vol. I, Asbury's Journal, pp. 31, 76.) I had a very tedious journey. I was so weary I could not preach.

Tuesday 26—Brother Ruff and I gave a love feast. A blest one it was. In the evening I preached with liberty.

Wednesday—This morning we parted. I rode to Philadelphia and preached.

Thursday 28—I gave a love feast in the City. In the evening I preached my farewell sermon. Blest be God it was a blest time. I never saw so many tears shed in the City in my life.

Friday 29—I set out for Dover (Delaware) lodged at my kind friend Brother Furnace's. (Brother Furnace was Robert Furnace who owned a tavern in New Castle. There Asbury preached his first sermon in the State of Delaware. Vol. I—Asbury's Journal, p. 26.)

The Lord be praised, we had a comfortable time, his family, myself.

Saturday 30—After a tedious journey of between 40 and 50 miles we got to Dover. I preached, we had a blest time.

October Sunday 31—This morning I can praise my God. I preached at sunrise to near the [Dover, Del.] courthouse full, we had a blest morning. I preached at 11 o'clock in the open air, the sun shining on my heart to a crowded audience. At 3 o'clock I preached to near a thousand mostly affected. O for a thousand tongues to sing my dear Redeemer's praise the glories of my God and King the Triumphs of His Grace. This night I rested as if in the arms of my blest Jesus.

Monday 1, 1779—I set out to Brother White's to quarterly meeting. Many of our preachers were present. We had a blest day.

Tuesday, November 2—Near 2000 came; I think this was as great a meeting as ever we had in America.

Wednesday 3—This morning after taking my leave of the brethren I set out for Baltimore, after a tedious journey I reached as far as Kent near the bay. I was very weary.

Thursday 4—After a tedious while I was landed on the other shore. I lodged at a very kind friends.

Friday 5—I went to my brother George's to sorrow I found him a stranger unto the Lord, blest be God he gave me a heart to pray for him. At night I lodged at an old uncles. I found him a stranger to the Lord.

Saturday 6—This morning while I was at prayer in the family we had a melting time, the family was in tears. I went to Mr. Gough's. There I met with many of our preachers.

(Henry Dorsey Gough was from his conversion a close friend to Asbury and numerous Methodist preachers. A man of wealth and position, his estate Parry Hall, about twelve miles northeast of Baltimore on the Bel Air Road, was a center for Methodists. His wife Prudence Ridgely Gough was equally friend and supporter of the Methodist cause.)

Sunday 7—I preached in the Fork. Many of us was happy in the breaking of bread together.

Monday 8—Several of us set off to quarterly meeting at Deer-Creek.

Tuesday 9—I think I heard as deep experience as ever I heard in my life; many testified of a second work. After love feast I preached from these words "Mark the Perfect Man", Psalm 37:37. Glory be to God, His power came down in a wonderful manner. Many souls did praise God. I think I never spent an evening happier in all my life. God's servants did rejoice together.

Wednesday 10—I spent in visiting my relations.

November Thursday 11—I preached at Brother Presbury's (George Prestbury). There I insisted on the freedom of slaves. I perceived some was much tryed.

Friday 12—I crossed the bay with a very pleasant gale. Glory be to God for peace of mind. Though I meet with many trials, my God stands my friend, and I hope I shall ever trust in him.

Saturday 13—I had a very tedious journey. I rode 40 miles to Brother Shaw's. There I met with Brother Asbury. As iron sharpeneth iron, so does the face of a man his friend. Praise be God he refreshed our spirits. Many are the afflictions of the righteous, but out of them all does the Lord deliver us.

Sunday 14—I rose about daybreak and bowed before my God to crave a blessing on the day. About sunrise I set out on my journey. I had 20 miles to ride. I missed my way. About 12 o'clock I got to the place and being very weary, I was too debilitated to preach. Glory be to God He enabled me to preach a short sermon. I rode 5 miles and preached to six or seven hundred. This was a wearisome day.

Monday 15—Glory to God I preached to a blessed and happy people. I felt much of the love of God.

Tuesday 16—I felt a composed mind. I was requested to preach from these words: "One Thing I know whereas I was Blind now I See." I never was happier in my life, many tears were shed. I trust much good was done in the name of Jesus.

Wednesday 17—This morning I visited a very pious family, the woman was groaning for redemption in the blood of Christ. I preached at Brother Shaw's with much happiness. We had a blest Class meeting. This evening I went to Mr. Nagoui's. Spent the evening on religious subjects.

Thursday 18—I preached at Wells with happiness. Met the Class. Turned out three members for selling liquor at a horse race. Lord have mercy on them, cast them not away. I rode to Dover, spent my time very happy in exhorting the Dover friends.

Friday 19—I rode 7 miles, preached from these words, "Thou art weighed in the balance and found wanting." They are a poor but desirous people. I returned to Dover.

Saturday 20—This morning I visited an awakened widow, she formerly was a persecutor but now very comfortable. I had some conversation with a young student, he seems to be under a concern for his soul. After breakfast I went to Mr. Boyer's. I spent the evening in religious conversation by candlelight. I held a Watch Night, Jesus is with us.

Sunday 21—I met the Class in the morning, we had a blessed time. I preached at 11 o'clock and after preaching I gave a love feast to about 200 of the friends. I went to Dover and preached in the evening to a crowded audience with great freedom, all seemed very attentive. By candlelight I lectured at Brother Wile's. We had a blest time. This evening Brother Thomas met me, I was glad to see him.

Monday 22—This day I met with a few struggles with the enemy. I rode several miles and preached at 2 o'clock by candlelight to a poor, but ignorant people. We are all blind and ignorant by nature. Lord open their blind eyes. I met with very hard trials this evening. I was so tempted and tryed, I went to bed without family prayer. After I lay down, conscience lay hold of me. I think I never suffered much more in a small time in my life. I was much disturbed with dreams. In the morning when I arose, I seemed to be miserable, I went away much distressed. I thought I would give anything could I be exempted this day from preaching. O how miserable I felt. Glory be to God whilst I was in my introduction, the Lord visited my soul with His love and blest be His Name, it was a blest time, many hearts were much tendered. In the evening I preached at Brother Alfrey's to about 25 Lukewarm Followers. I met them in Class. (Lewis Alfrey lived in Fieldboro, Newcastle County, Delaware. In 1779 he was one of the four preachers with Asbury on the Delaware Circuit. But his name disappears after that year.) Vol. I—Asbury's Journal, p. 260.

Wednesday 24—Several of us went to Meeting. I preached with more liberty and sweetness. I trust good was done. I lodged at my old friend Weatherby's. The old woman is a precious follower of the meek and lowly Jesus. I had a blest evening.

Thursday 25—I met with a few temptations, after a while they blew over, I held forth at Scotton's with much freedom. We had a blest private meeting.

Friday 26—This is a very wet morning; Brother James _____ with me. We rode 4 miles to the Chapel through the wet, about 20 of the poor followers of Jesus came together. We had a very cold time; we rode 4 miles through the wet to Brother Black's, this evening the Lord refreshed our spirit, I was refreshed to see a good work in the family.

Saturday 27—I went a few miles, preached and returned, and preached in the evening by candlelight. I had a blessed time. There was this night a natural birth in the Family. O that there may be many spiritual ones in the Family and in the neighborhood. Lord grant it.

Sunday 28—This is a very cold day. I rode about 10 miles, preached at 11 o'clock and began immediately a second sermon about 12 o'clock. It was a blessed time. I rode 5 miles to Mr. White's, and preached at 4 o'clock. I had very little happiness. This evening I felt myself _____, and solemn in visiting Billey White. He is dangerously ill. Lord convert his soul. This night I rested in peace.

Monday 29—I preached and gave a Watch Night, it was a good time.

Tuesday 30—I feel my mind much composed. I held forth to a small audience with much freedom. I rode 6 miles, held a Watch Night at Brother White's. I preached with much satisfaction.

Wednesday, December 1, 1779—I met Brother Asbury. We had a comfortable meeting together.

Thursday 2—This is a very rainy day. We tarryed at Brother White's together. I had some agreeable conversation with a young gentleman that was awakened in a very dark part of God's vineyard by reading one of his father's old Books. He came 40 miles and brought his Book. He thought there was not such a Book in the world. He gave me an invitation to his house and neighborhood. I could not give him a direct answer. Lord direct me in this matter.

Friday 3—I was happy at the thought of taking my (circuit). I preached at Brother Law's on the new birth. I hope good was done. I can rejoice in the work in this part of God's vineyard.

Saturday the 4th—I seem this morning to have a comfortable hope I shall have a blessed day. I rode 5 miles and held forth to a crowded audience with great happiness. Glory be to God my soul is very happy. In the evening I was comforted in holding a Watch Night.

Sunday the 5th—I arose some time before day, my heart seemed very hard. The day was dark, cold, and snowy. I rode 6 miles and preached to about 20 people with very little happiness. I rode 5 miles to Mr. _____ and lectured to about 15. I had some degree of comfort. I was refreshed in the Family. I rested in sweet peace.

Monday 6th—I arose in the morning about day. My mind seems dark. I spent some time in reading, prayer, and meditation. I set out cold as it was, preached a funeral and had a very uncomfortable time, the house was filled with smoke. One of our greatest persecutors was tendered. He condescended so far as to go in the Classroom. Lord open his eyes and give him to see his danger.

Tuesday 7—Blest be God this morning. I arose about daybreak, travelled to the preaching place. I preached a funeral over three persons from these words: "The last enemy that shall be destroyed is Death." 1st Corinthians 15: 26,1. I showed when death became an enemy. 2. To whom death became an enemy. 3. How death is to be destroyed. Blest be God I had some sweetness. This is a young people but I trust very serious. I had some comfort in instructing them in secret.

Wednesday 8—This morning I woke at my usual hour, five o'clock, but to my shame, I may say sloth overcame me. Instead of rising, Satan got an advantage and lulled me to sleep. When I awoke, by the crowing of the cock, day was breaking. I spent half an hour in secret, part of which was by my bed and part in an outhouse. After family prayer I visited a kind friend. We rode to Brother Joseph Turpin's. I preached with liberty from those words: "Now the just shall live by faith; but if any man draws back, my soul shall have no plea save in Him." Hebrews 10:20. We had a blest Class Meeting. Its about four months since I preached at this place. There is great altercation for the better. My brother Thomas and I spent several hours in reading the Holy Scriptures with other Books. I went to my bed about 10 o'clock. I prayed to the Lord he might grant me to awake at 5 o'clock. I woke within a few minutes of the time before I felt temptation. I spent about three quarters of an hour in my chamber in prayer and meditation. Glory be to God he has given me to see the need of living nearer to my blessed Master. I have often made covenants with the Lord, and broke them. I am determined with His grace from this moment to give myself wholly up to His service. Lord stand by me I pray thee. Part of this morning was spent in striving to convince a person of

that cruel practice of slave keeping, but almost in vain. I went on my journey, preached with happiness to a small audience. A few days ago the
Lord laid his hand upon the old woman of the house and one of her daughters.
The old woman got _____ crippled out of her chair and the young woman
had her thigh broke by a fall from her horse. Blessed be God I hope they're
both under a good work. I spent some time agreeable with the Family.
Went to my bed at 9 o'clock, rested happy 'til 2 o'clock. I was troubled
with dreams. I arose at 4 o'clock, spent half an hour in prayer in mediatation,
my mind is very wandering, my heart is wicked. O when will the time
be that my soul shall be humbled in the dust. Blest be God, I hope this
family will devote themselves to the Lord. I was very happy in prayer for
them. I rode about 8 miles. Preached to a small audience of poor people
with very little liberty. I met with various kinds of temptations. I went
to a house to visit a poor family. I think I never visited a _____ family
in all my life. The old man was upwards of 70, roped up in his sins, his
son in despair, and had been for many years. I asked him if I should pray
for him. He answered me, I am in a state of reprobation. His wife, I fear,
was in her sins. I was in prayer for them.

At Brother Moore's we fell in conversation about this man. (Joshua
Moore, a leader in the Broad Creek Society.) I was informed that he was a
great reader, and one that seemed to have a light of the Holy Scriptures,
and seemed to be upright in his conduct. I understood, when he was in
the field one day the devil appeared to him in his bodily shape and tempted
him to curse God, and as I understand he denied the Holy Scriptures.
He went home and told his father if he would lend him the bible he would
deny the devil. From that very day he went into despair. He lays, they
tell me, months together without drinking. I think it was rendered a great
blessing to me, my visiting this distressed family. Lord help me to watch
and pray.

Saturday the 11th—I arose a little before day, I had much happiness
in meeting two Classes. It was a time of refreshing. I went home with my
kind friend. I went to bed between 9:00 and 10:00, slept comfortably;
rose between 4:00 and 5:00 very happy. Spent 2 hours in the morning
reading and praying. I enjoyed much happiness 'til breakfast, after I seemed
to be rather dull and heavy. I preached with much liberty. Many in tears,
my soul was much refreshed. After dinner Satan got an advantage. I laid
in the bed, and in a short time fell asleep, and slept half and hour. When
I woke I blushed to think I spent a glorious Sabbath in sloth. I spent some
time conversing with the family. After prayer I retired to my room. I read
3 chapters in the Bible, prayed and went to bed. Blest be God for his fatherly
protection.

Monday 13—I woke about daybreak, spent the morning in conversation,
went 4 miles, preached to a poor but very desirous people. I returned to
Brother Moore's to hold a Watch Night. I preached on the 10 Virgins

with much liberty. Had an opportunity of hearing two young exhorters Brother C. and Brother M. I had much satisfaction and gave them notes. I was by this time very weary.

Tuesday 14—I arose about an hour before day, spent the morning very comfortably. I rode about 5 miles, the wind blew excessive cold, I preached in a cold open room. The people seemed to be excessive cold. I preached a very short sermon with little liberty. After sermon I prayed with an old woman that was bedridden. I met the Class, rode 1 mile to a kind friends, exhorted by candlelight. I was taken very ill with a violent pain in the head.

Wednesday 15—This morning I found myself very poorly, I did not rise 'til after daybreak. I spent the morning very dull and heavy. I seemed to be very loath to undertake my journey. I pled with the Lord, if it was his blessed will to strengthen my body, by giving me health to persue my journey. Rode 5 miles and preached with much freedom from those words "What Is Man?" After preaching I rode 10 miles to Brother Rider's. Several families came together. We had a blessed meeting.

Thursday 16—This morning I overslept my time. I arose a little before sunrise. I felt his love in family prayer. I preached at 1 o'clock with little liberty. I had a degree of happiness in Class. It is 4 months since I was here. Many sinners have been brought to the knowledge of God.

Friday 17—I was lively in prayer. I rode 10 miles and preached. It was excessive cold, my audience small, this is a blind part of the world. Lord open their eyes. I rode all the way back to Mr. Rider's. This was a tedious day.

Saturday 18—The day was excessive cold. About 11 o'clock I set out to Sister Fletcher's. At 1 o'clock I preached with liberty.

Sunday 19—I set out at 10 o'clock to my appointment, the day being very cold. I began to feel we would have a very cold meeting. But it was a blessed time. I went to Mr. Bird's. I found great alteration for the worse. Had very little comfort in the Family. The Baptists had been among them and confused their minds. Many disputes arose about baptism.

Monday, December 20, 1779—This morning my mind seems to be discomposed, I went thru the cold, preached with little liberty, and met the class. To my sorrow I found them much confused, one was for Paul and another for Appolios, (Apollos) and I fear too for Christ. All this confusion was about baptism. I gave a lecture on the head. After I begged of as many that were desirous to continue in Methodist Society to speak. Out of 25 I joined about 17, turned out the old leader, and appointed Brother Flitch. Although Satan desired to sift the class, I hope he will be disappointed. Lord keep these dear souls together. Glory be to God, this is a blessed evening to my soul, the family is very poor but humble. I have much happiness in opening the travail of a soul to a few disconsolate ones. I went to bed with peace of mind. Glory be to God for it.

Tuesday 21—It was sometime this morning before the morning cloud burst, the day was exceeding cold, I travelled eleven or twelve miles, preached with liberty at 1 o'clock _____ the Watch Night by candlelight. The Lord was with me. Glory be to His Name.

Wednesday 22—I set out on a very tedious journey, much ice in the way. Bless Be God, I arrived to the place a little after one, it was a great cross to me to preach, but Glory be to God it proved a great blessing. I met the Society all unconverted, but the woman of the house. I met with great exercise of mind and I went out to prayer, my heart seemed to be hard but blest be God he visited me in the _____.

Thursday 23—This morning I had a tedious journey, much ice to cross, about 1 o'clock I got to the place, I preached with liberty. I insisted upon Christ being Savior of the whole world, when I met in the Society I found there had been much disputing about baptism.

Friday 24—I rode to Brother W's, preached with happiness on the great necessity of perserving on the ways of holiness. I found there was great disputes concerning baptism, a very great rent like to be made in the Society. I spoke largely on this head. Lord do not let Satan sew the seeds of discord among thy people. But keep them humble at thy feet at this hour.

Saturday 25—This morning I preached to a crowded audience at 9 o'clock upon the activity of our Lord. 12 o'clock I preached to a crowded audience a funeral over one of our sisters that went triumphantly in the faith. She was convinced by me telling of a dream in the time of preaching. I rode 4 miles, left the Society by candlelight. We had a refreshing time.

Sunday 26—This morning there seemed to be a cloud over my mind, I begged of the Lord to remove it. I preached at 11 o'clock to a crowded audience, the cloud broke and I received a sweet visit from the Lord. By promise I was to give a love feast after preaching. I begged of the Society to come in as they had never seen the like before. They were in doubt, they began to inquire whether I was scriptural. I saw they had no faith, this text came to my mind, "Whatsoever is not of faith is sin." A lamp came upon my spirits, I endeavored to lift my head to the Lord. The people came in. As it was a new thing I took pains to explain the rise and nature of it. The bread and water went around, I was afraid the Lord was not with us, my soul seemed distressed. I groaned in the Spirit on account of unbelief. Whilst the third person spoke the Lord broke in upon my soul. I was enabled then to praise the Lord. Glory be to God we had a general melting amongst the people. Glory be to God he took away their doubts and fears with regard to this means of grace. I think there was never such a day seen before on the Sound. Believers rejoiced in the love of God, sinners smote on their breasts saying, "God be merciful to me a sinner." My soul doth magnify the Lord. By candlelight I held a Watch Night, the house was much crowded. I had great liberty. Blest be God, this has been a happy day to my soul. I lay down happy in my God and slept very comfortably.

Monday 27—Being weary, I did not rise until after daybreak, I find my mind much composed. I retired in the wood, spent some time in prayer to God to grant a blessing on the day. I was accompanied by many of our friends, when I came to the place I found there was a crowded audience, many could not get in the house. They paid great attention. I hope good was done in the name of the Lord Jesus. I endeavored to meet the Society but could not for the multitude, I told the Society to meet me at Brother Evan's at night. Such a multitude flocked in, I could not meet the Society, I gave an exhortation. Glory be to God I find my soul very happy. I went to my bed very poorly though happy in the Lord.

Tuesday 28—When I awoke it was raining very hard. I was disappointed though I had two places to attend. The first was disappointed. It stopped raining in the evening so that I rode 6 miles. The night was so dark I had but few. I was very happy in conversing with a humble child of God.

Wednesday 29—Being much weary from the past day, I kept my bed 'til sunrise, I find myself very heavy. I rode 10 miles to a place near Blackford, preached to a desirous people with a degree of happiness. I parted with many of my dear friends. I rode 6 miles, met with kind friends, rested in peace.

Thursday 30—Preached Brother Rider's funeral. I had some degree of happiness. Friday I preached with little happiness. Saturday was a day of rest. I am much tempted, Satan wanted to persuade me that it is a man practice to go about preaching the gospel, I proved the devil to be a liar. I was in a furnace all the day, I think it was a day of distress.

Sunday, January 2nd, 1780—I am in a furnace, sometime ago I did not think I should meet with this distress, I seem to be a burden to myself, I was brought to search myself to know the cause, I found I had not been diligent as I ought to have been. I held forth at 12 o'clock to a crowded audience. I was almost blinded with the smoke. I had very little liberty, within a few minutes I held forth again, many was brought to their tears. Glory be to God, this evening he set my soul at liberty to praise Him.

Monday 3—This morning I was out of my bed before day, Blest be God I am in a heart to praise Him. I rode 5 miles through the ice, the wind blew very hard and cold. Very few attended, I preached a funeral from these words, "The Sting of Death is Sin." I had a degree of liberty. Met a young class, I hope there is a good word in many of their minds. I had much love for the people.

Tuesday 4—This is a day set apart for private devotion. I had sweet conversations with the Holy Spirit before the day ———. I was very happy in family prayer. Glory be to God, I see a great beauty in holiness. I think with the help of the Almighty to devote my soul and body a living sacrifice to God from this day. Lord help me to live more to thy glory. I conversed with several persons with satisfaction. Especially the woman of the house. She told a very remarkable thought she dreamt before she heard the gospel. She was like Cornelius, often prayed, but did not know what she wanted, or what to do 'till the Lord sent the gospel by us, and then her dream was interpreted to her, and she received us as joyfully as Cornelius did Peter. Here are 9 children, all very desirous. I went to my bed in the love of God, and all mankind. Glory be to God for his goodness. This is a sweet night to my soul.

Wednesday, January 5, 1780—I awoke this morning about 3 o'clock, arose a quarter after. Blest be God Jesus is with me, I find an heart to pray for God's children. O Lord stand by them and bring them through every trial. I find uncommon freedom in prayer for the unconverted, especially my unconverted relations. Lord open thou their eyes, enlighten their minds. O give them to behold the beauty of a redeemer; let their souls be ravished with His humanliness. Thou art all fair, O! Jesus, though the inpenitent can see no beauty in Thee. I rode to Brother Shys the day being cold and snowy, few came out, the Lord was with us. I preached from these words, "Is there no balm in Gilead, Is there no physician there?" Why then has not the health of the daughter of my people healed. Jeremiah 8: 22. In class meeting we had a blessed time. I rode 9 miles and preached from these words, "I will arise and go to my Father." Luke 15: 18. My soul was happy in God my savior. This night I was happy.

Thursday 6—I feel myself very dull and heavy. I find some comfort in family prayer. I rode 5 miles to Brother Ward's, preached to a small audience with liberty. Rode home with Brother Rogers. I hope there is good work on his mind. I had much happiness in his family.

Friday 7—I feel some sweet rays of the Holy Spirit, preached at Brother Bradly's (this was probably *Gitting Bradley*, a charter member of Moore's Meeting House located between Laurel, Delaware, and Sharptown, Maryland. p. 307 Vol. __ Asbury's Journal) with much happiness. One soul was converted under preaching, and many comforted. We had a glorious class meeting, much love among the people. God is carrying on a blessed work in this part of the vinyard. Glory be to God I was comforted in this family. I want to spent my life on this earth in the service of my blessed Master.

Saturday 8—I met my brother Thomas. I met the class at Brother W. (Ward). We had a blessed time. I preached by candlelight. My blessed Master refreshed my soul.

Sunday 9—I am much tryed. It seems like death to me to preach. O! the cross is heavy, I must take it up. I preached from these words. "Now the Just shall Live by Faith, but if any man draw back, my Soul shall have no pleasure in Him." Glory be to God it was a powerful time to my soul, and I trust the souls of others. In the evening I held forth at Brother B's. I had not free access to the hearts of people. I rested this night in sweet peace.

Monday 11 (January) 1780—I'm sorely tempted of the enemy. I went to the _____. Glory be to God I preached with much liberty. In the evening I visited with Sister Smith, she seemed to be at the very point of death.

She was very happy in the Lord. "Oh! said she," my dear Father, if I was but able to tell you how good God is to my soul, He is love."

I asked her if she was afraid to die, "God is love, I am not afraid to die. Glory be to God He is good to my soul. I am not worthy," said she, "of the least of His favors." She began to tell me how the Lord wrote first upon her mind. It pleased the Lord to cause an earthquake that struck the house. The house trembled, and it was brought to her mind that God could in a moment dash her to pieces, and send her soul to hell, in an instant she was struck with the power of God. She thought she saw the pit of hell ready to swallow her soul. Her sins stared her in the face, Satan told her there was no mercy, she was such a wretch, God would not have mercy on her soul. In this agony she fell at the feet of the Lord and cried for mercy, in this distress she continued for many weeks, not one spiritual guide. The language of her heart was; "I am undone forever." "Oh," said she, "the horror of my soul." One day when she was all alone the Lord appeared to her soul's comfort, that distress was taken away, and peace and joy flowed into her soul. In a short time she heard of the Methodists, she went some distance to hear Brother Asbury. She witnessed his doctrine and returned rejoicing. When I came around she joined into Society. It is but a few months since she received this change. "Oh," she said, "I have had many trials but I hope it will not be long before I am rid of them all." I asked her if she felt sin in her heart. "Oh yes," said she, "I am troubled with the remains of sin." I begged her to look to the Lord and he would cut short his work. I had much freedom to pray for a total deliverance from sin. Glory be to God for his goodness, He paid us a sweet visit. This night I rested in sweet peace.

Tuesday 10—I asked her if she was happy. "Happy? Oh yes," she said, "my soul is happy. I am made a new creature whilst you were at prayer, the Lord cleansed my heart from sin, now I love Him with my whole heart. Oh God how good thou art, thou art love." I left her praising, of the best of friends. I have no doubt that I shall meet her in glory. Lord grant it.

I visited Brother Sipple (William Sipple was the father-in-law of Phillip Barratt (1730-84). Garrettson converted Barratt in 1778. The chapel bears his name). He was very weak in body but very happy in soul. I preached at Brother Purdins with much liberty. Glory be to God here are many mourners. Many joined in Society and I lodged in a blessed family. Glory be to God this is a day of comfort to my soul.

Wednesday 12—The weather being cold and I missed my way, to my grief the people were disappointed. I preached in the evening in Dover with liberty.

Friday 14—I met class in Dover and we had a blessed time. I preached in the evening with little liberty.

Sunday 16—I preached at Brother Boyers with much liberty. Glory be to God I trust he is carrying on a blessed work among the people. In the evening I went to Brother Sipples. He was dying to all appearance. I asked him if he was happy. "Glory be to God" said he, "my soul is very happy." He told me he wanted to hear me pray once more; when I was done he broke out in praises to God.

I think I never had a solomner time since the goodness of God in all my life. I went home with Brother Furby (Caleb). Glory be to God I am happy, and most of the family is.

Monday 17—This morning my soul doth rejoice in God my Savior. I spent this day in visiting the sick. I visited Sister Smith, she is very weak but Glory be to God very happy in His love. Angels are waiting around her bed to take her happy soul away. Oh what a blessed thing it is to live the life of the righteous. I went to Brother Furbys, Glory be to God my soul is happy in God my savior.

Tuesday 18—I went to Brother Williams on my way to the sound. The Lord refreshed my spirit. Glory be to God.

Wednesday 19—I went as far as Shockley's. I heard Brother Cromwell with happiness. (The Cromwell family lived in Green Spring Valley, Baltimore County. Joseph and James, brothers, became preachers. James served with Garrettson in Nova Scotia, and later was a presiding elder in New Jersey, James became ill and located in 1793.) This is an evening of comfort.

Thursday 20—I set out on my journey to the sound, the morning is excessive cold and I rode six miles, I think I never suffered more with cold in all my life. When I went to the fire, I thought I should have fainted, I was so overcome. I was covered up warm in bed. It was 'til late in the night before I got to my journey's end. Blessed be God for christian friends.

Friday 21—I preached at Brother Laws with very little satisfaction.

Saturday 22—I rode eight miles, preached at a new place, it being a new thing I had met very few hearers.

Sunday 23—I held forth at Gray's with much success both morning and evening. I trust there was awakenings. I praise God for his love.

Monday 24—I preached to a crowded audience with much liberty. In the evening by candlelight I preached to a crowded audience. I hope good was done. Glory be to God, my soul is happy.

Tuesday 25—I held forth to a crowded audience with much liberty at Mr. Hills. Spent the evening in prayer and meditation.

Wednesday 26—I delivered two sermons at Brother Evans with much freedom. It was a powerful time . . . I feel sweetness within, very little tempted.

Thursday 27—Glory be to God this is a day of power, there is a shaking amongst the dry bones . . . We had a blessed time in class meeting.

January 1780, Friday 28—I preached in a poor forest to a poor simple people who never heard the gospel in their lives, many in tears. I held a Watch Night about four miles off. Many came from far.

Saturday 29—I met three Classes. In the evening I went home with one that had formerly been an enemy to us. One that set up a meeting in opposition to our Society. He came to me and made this confession that he had been an enemy to God all of his life and begged to join in Society.

Sunday 30—I think we have a glorious day. I never saw such a crowded audience, mostly all in tears, many joined in the Society. Brother Laws and I set out to quarterly meeting, we rode as far as I.G. We spent the evening very happy.

Monday 31—We rose out of bed at 4 o'clock, set out on our journey about seven in the morning, very cold, I had some profitable conversation by the way with an old man. We got to the place about 11 o'clock. Meeting began at one o'clock. Brother Asbury, Brother Cromwell, and myself held forth. We had a blessed time. Glory be to God for His goodness. This evening was spent very happy together. We spent our time talking about the work.

Tuesday, February 1, 1780—Glory be to God is in our love feast. Brother Asbury and myself preached in the evening. I am sensible how God was in the midst of us. It was a blessed day. We spent the evening talking about things of God.

Wednesday 2—I set on my journey to Kent.

Thursday 3—I got as far as Brother White's visiting the sick.

Friday 4—I had an opportunity of hearing Brother Hartley.

Saturday 5—I preached with liberty. Went home with Brother James.

Sunday 6—Held forth to a crowded audience in the evening. Glory be to my God, my soul is very happy.

Monday 7—I preached at Brother Furby's. From these words: "My little children in whom I travel in pain, 'til Christ be formed in you and so forth." Glory be to God one soul was converted, others built up in their most holy faith, no tongue can express the glory I feel.

Tuesday 8—I preached to a crowded audience from these words, "Behold now is the acceptable time. Behold now is the day of salvation." Salvation came to the house. Grace rested upon the people. It was as good a day as ever I saw. Lord make me more holy. In the evening _____ Caleb Boyer and myself held forth at a Watch Night. It was a blessed time to many souls.

Wednesday 9 (February, 1780)—This morning Brother F. and myself set out to Brother Whites. In the evening I attended an exhortation by Brother Asbury, at the putting of Mrs. Elizabeth Peterkin in the ground. It was a solemn evening. God was with us. She died triumphant in the faith. I preached in the evening by candlelight, a solemn awe rested upon the people. The thoughts of going to Dorset caused me to have a gloomy, sorrowful night.

Thursday 10—This morning I arose very early, and went before my God for a blessing on the day.

94. Mr. Bassett—The honorable Mr. Bassett was an eminent lawyer in Delaware. After his conversion he became a member of congress and then appointed a U. S. judge. Finally, Bassett was elected a governor of the State of Delaware.

Bangs, Nathan, *Life of the Rev. Freeborn Garrettson* p. 105.

95. "Brother Asbury with the family joined in prayers for my protection . . . it was pressed upon my mind to travel thru Dorset." *Manuscript Journal.*

96. Mr. Avery—Garrettson consistently spells the name in this fashion in his Manuscript Journal. The name in fact is Thomas Hill Airey and Mrs. Airey.

97. Mrs. Avery.

98. "In the evening by candlelight instructed about 30 black men and women, they were very attentive." *Manuscript Journal.*

99. "Mr. Avery and myself set out to visit Mr. McCrain's congregation." *Manuscript Journal.*

100. "*Tuesday 15*—I preached at Major Vickers to about 30 persons." *Manuscript Journal.*

101. "Satan began to rage, the court ordered me to be taken and brought neck and heels. No man laid hand on me . . . This evening Mr. Avery came from court to meet me: he informed me that the whole court was throwing out their threats . . . Satan has gone almost the length of his chain without hurting one hair of my head." *Manuscript Journal.*

102. "I should have been in gaol before now I suppose if my friend Avery had not been Justice of the Peace." *Manuscript Journal.*

103. "Sometimes I thought it was a cat, at other times I thought it was a great rat. . ." *Manuscript Journal.*

104. "They up and told what had happened to their eldest daughter. A few nights ago, she was afrited. She got up in the night and awoke her parents and told them she saw the devil and that he grinned at her. (the child is about six years old). In the morning she came to her mother and asked her what she must do to be saved, for said she I am so wicked I am afraid the black man will come for me." *Manuscript Journal.*

105. "They shook their fists in my face and their clubs over my head and swore what they would do to me." *Manuscript Journal.*

106. Brother J. Hartley. A Garrettson note about Hartley is as follows: "Brother Hartley, a dear good man, and an excellent preacher, was so pressed in spirit, he could no longer contain, and the rulers laid hands on him, and confined him in Talbot jail: (Easton, Md. from July to October, 1779) but he preached powerfully through the window. The blessed God owned his word, and he was instrumental in raising a large Society. He was confined a long time, till finally they thought he might as well preach without as within jail. Shortly after he was set at liberty, he married a pious young lady, and located. He did not live many years, but while he did live, he was very useful, and adorned his christian and ministerial character. He died in the Lord, and went to glory." *Manuscript Journal.*

107. "I think I never saw anything more like hell in all my life, if the damned had been loose, they could not have been wickider, cursed and swore (altho it was the saboth) . . . I find an heart to pray for my enemies." *Manuscript Journal*

108. "I had one friend or I should have been put in the dungeon." *Manuscript Journal*

Garrettson was placed in the Dorchester County Jail, Cambridge, Maryland, February 27, 1780.

109. "*Tuesday 29*—I was sweetly drawn out in prayer and meditation, most of my time was spent in writing letters to my friends." *Manuscript Journal*

Wednesday, March 1 (1780)—Many came to the window and others out of mock . . .

Thursday 2—It is pressed upon my mind to preach, but the weather being cold, and no notice given I thought I would defer it a little longer, as my friend Avery set off this day to the governor in order that my grievances might be redrest. I thought it expedient to let it alone till his return . . . I commonly breakfast on bread and water mixt with a little syder. I sup on the same . . .

110. *Sunday 5* . . . Many came this day to see me, some from far: the wicked threatened to beat them, would not let them come near the prison window . . .

Monday 6—This day I was visited by my brother Thomas, received a letter from Brother Asbury, it was spirit and life to my soul. He (Thomas) stayed with me two nights; we was very happy . . .

Wednesday 8 . . . This evening I spent in reading the life of Mr. Welsh . . .

Thursday 9 . . . I now perceive a great alteration in the town. They begin to pity me and wish I was gone. Some of my enemy converses with me at the window and begs for the lone of some books. I spent the day in writing to my dear friends.

Sunday 12 . . . this day I had an opportunity of conversing with many of my dear Talbot friends . . . I read a sermon of my own writing, the first that ever I penned.

Monday 13—My friend Avery returned from the govenor and Council. I had much favor shown me. . . . I think this is the 16th day of my confinement, I think I never spent 16 days happier in all my life. I prayed with about 15 of the Town people, took my leave of them and went to my dear friend Avery's." *Manuscript Journal.*

111. The following note appears in Bangs, but not in the printed or *Manuscript Journal.*

"Mr. and Mrs. Avery were remarkably kind, and sent me everything that was necessary. My brother, Thomas, who lived about 100 miles off, heard of my imprisonment, and come to see me, and brought a letter from Judge White to Mr. Harrison, a gentleman of note, who was the greatest enemy I had in town. After reading the letter, he not only invited my brother to put up at his house, but went out and got the prison key, let my brother come in, and next morning he came to the jail and invited him out to breakfast, and told me he would do anything he could for me. Before this he was as bitter as gall. One day when an old Quaker friend came to see me, he came and abused him, and strove to drive him away: the Quaker made him ashamed of his conduct. My enemies sent a spy, who feigned himself a penitent, and as I was coming downstairs to converse with him through the window, it came powerfully to my mind, he is an enemy sent if possible to draw something out of you concerning the war. He cried and said he was a miserable sinner, that he was afraid he would go to hell, and wanted to know what he should do to be saved. I told him to leave off swearing and drunkenness, and return, and I would give him further directions. I afterwards found he was the very character I had supposed." pp. 113, 114 Bangs, Nathan—*Life of the Rev. F. Garrettson.*

Correspondence related to the arrest, imprisonment, and release of Garrettson in 1780 may be found in Appendix I.

112. *Wednesday 15 (March, 1780)*—I set out to Dover, had a tedious journey . . .

Friday 17—I set out from Mr. Tokes? met Brother Asbury. I had an opportunity of preaching at W. Law's.

Monday 20— This morning, my dear friend Avery went with me to the governors as I was let out of jail upon condition that I would appear before _____ Caesar Rodney, the governor of Delaware. We was introduced by the Rev. Mr. Megau (Magaw). He was very kind, I praise God for civil rulers . . .

Tuesday 21—I left Dover in order to go on my way to Lewis-Town. I had an opportunity of hearing Brother Asbury with satisfaction . . .

Wednesday 22—I rode to Brother Shaws, preached with much light of the holy scriptures.

Thursday 23—I rode to Brother Virgins ?, had a disagreeable time in preaching, for the smoke.

Saturday 25—I preached at the Landing with love to the people . . .

Wednesday 29—I rode to Lewis-Town . . . By appointment I was to preach in the court house. Just as I was beginning to preach, a man came to the house (Woolf by name and Woolf by nature) with a bell in his hand, he disturbed the whole house so that I was obliged to give over, and went about a mile out in the country, the people followed me . . .

Thursday 30—Preached at 12 o'clock at S. A. Smiths with much happiness . . . I went home with _____ Whealbank . . .

Friday 31—Rode out as far as Mr. Fishers, without any notice near 50 came together. *Manuscript Journal.*

113. *April 1780*—Sunday the 1st (2)—My soul this morning is "Happy in God my Saviour." I went to the appointment, there was a crowded audience came together, I preached two sermons with much liberty. I trust that some will praise God for the day in glory. One sermon I preached from Ezekiel 18: 27. The second I preached from these words: "Marvel not that I said unto thee, ye must be born again;" many hard hearts were melted; I was much tempted while I was preaching, although my soul was happy; these people in general are very poor, and blind, they have been in times past as sheep without a shepherd. Lord have mercy on them and open their eyes before it is too late.

Monday 2 (3)—This morning I spent in writing till near 11 o'clock, then rode six miles and preached a funeral to a crowded audience. Glory be to my dear savior, I trust much good was done in his name. The people was mostly in tears. I went home with G. Rider, bless be the Lord, this was a night of comfort to my soul, the Lord poured down his spirit in family prayer. This night I went to bed happy in my dear Savior; it appeared my soul was happy all night. I seemed to walk in among the dead in solitary places and through gardens beautifully set out with flowers of all colors, and finest of all sorts. Bless be my dear Jesus, my soul was exceeding happy.

Tuesday 4 (5)—I met with very little exercise this morning. Part of my time was spent in writing. Bless be my Savior, I enjoyed sweet peace, when I rode through the rain to meeting. Preached to about a hundred with much liberty. Many of them never heard before. I praised my Lord for peace and joy in the Holy Ghost. This night I rested as it were in my dear Lord's arms. Oh sweet Jesus, loving Savior thou art all fair.

Wednesday 5 (6)—I rode 15 miles part of the way through the rain, the creeks were exceeding high, my horse and carriage were very near swimming. Glory be to God he in safety brought me safe through every difficulty. I had much liberty in preaching to a small audience from the Word . . . my soul enjoyed sweet communion with my dear Lord Jesus. These are poor but blessed people. Glory be to God for choosing such to be heirs of eternal glory. Glory be to my dear Lord, there is a sweet calm, yet I know my soul hungers after the love of my dear Jesus. I want a greater depth of love.

Thursday 6 (7)—This morning I spent not as profitable as I might, I read very little. My mind was drawn out in service of my God as I went to meeting. I had a sweet time in meditation. A little before I preached I felt the power of temptation—the world seemed rather dark, but glory be to God, before I began I had much light on the holy scriptures and much love to the people, I hope good was done. I went to Brother L. Glory be to God I had a blessed evening. God dwells in this family. This evening I went to bed very happy in my Lord; but the enemy tried me after I went to bed, but in vain; my dear Lord is my friend; and I can truly say it is my meat and drink to do his blessed will.

Friday 7 (8)—Glory be to my dear Lord I met with my friend Asbury, we spent some time very agreeable together. I preached with much love to the people. I hope the Lord is carrying on a blessed work among the people in these parts.

Saturday 8 (9)—This morning I am sorely tempted of the devil. I preached at 11 o'clock with much freedom to a poor but humble people. In the evening I had an opportunity of hearing Brother Asbury. The evening was very wet.

Sunday our meeting began, we had a blessed time. They came from every quarter.

Monday 10 (11)—I think we had as agreeable a love feast at 8 o'clock as ever was set. Glory be to God his power came down amongst us and many praised the dear Lord. I think at our Watch evening, I never felt more of the power of God in all my life. Sinners trembled, mourners were comforted, and God's dear children was built up in their holy faith.

After meeting I set out on my journey to the Conference which is to be held in Baltimore town, several of us rode several miles in company. Many tears was shed among my dear friends in our parting.

Tuesday 11 (12)—I rode 20 miles and preached at 12 o'clock. My dear Lord was with me, I rode eight miles and preached by candlelight. I think good was done in my dear master's name.

Wednesday 12 (11)—Glory be to God for his goodness. My soul is happy in God my Savior. This day by appointment I am to give a farewell sermon to my dear Broad-Creek friends. I had in the morning a lively expectation of having a blessed meeting. But I feared the people looked too much at the preacher. Many flocked together from various quarters, I preached and gave a love feast; in the whole I trust it was a time of profit. In all I was sorely tempted of the devil, and my fear gave way to him in temptations which gave me to doubt of the work of santification, I was brought to write in secret for a considerable time, but blessed be my dear Lord Jesus it was not long before he visited me with his love.

Thursday 13 (14)—This morning I am under the power of temptation, I went to Sister Turpin's ?, preached with much liberty, Glory be to my dear Lord Jesus, he is a God of love; in the evening I went to Brother Brown's and met a Class, Glory to God my soul was exceeding happy in my dear Lord Jesus, I rested this night as in the arms of my dear Jesus.

Friday 14 (15)—My whole heart seems to be given up to the Lord. Oh what a blessed thing it is to love Jesus. After discharging my duty in the family I set out to Mr. Laws. I preached with much happiness, many in tears. After preaching I rode nearly 17 miles to Brother White's, preached by candlelight. I hope good was done.

Saturday 15 (16)—My mind this morning is much harried, but blest be God my soul hangs on my Jesus. I rode 20 miles, preached at Brother W's., oh we had a sweet time, Lord be praised. In the evening I rode five miles and held forth at Brother L's, glory be to God for his sweet presence. Oh Lord, I praise thy dear name that I love.

Sunday 16 (17)—My soul is still happy in the Lord. Praise the Lord oh my soul, let all that is within me praise his holy name. A crowded audience came together at 11 o'clock. I preached a farewell sermon, I took my text out of Paul's second Epistle to the Corinthians, the latter part of the last chapter. Glory be to God my soul is exceeding happy. Many tears were shed at that parting. Lord grant that I may meet my dear children in heaven. I rode six miles and preached in the evening to a hundred or more than was ever seen before at this place. Glory be to my dear Jesus for his goodness, there were many wet eyes. After preaching I went to my dear friends. I spent the night exceeding happy, Glory be to God.

Monday 17 (18)—I set out this morning very early with my dear friends to quarterly meeting. Blest be God it appeared as if the whole country came together. Our meeting held about three hours. I was much pleased, I think good was done in my Master's name.

Tuesday 18 (19)—Our love feast began about eight o'clock, it was a love feast to many precious souls. Public meeting began at 12 o'clock. The Rev. Mr. Megan (Magaw) read prayers and the Rev. Mr. Neal (This is the Rev. Hugh Neill, a former rector at Dover but in charge of St. Paul's Church, Queen Annes County, 1767-82. The participation of Magaw and Hugh Neill in this service at Thomas Chapel helped reduce tension and prejudice against Methodists for they were clergy in the Established Church.) [p. 307, 345, Vol. 1, Asbury's Journal] . . . delivered a very warm discourse. I held forth after him and Brother Asbury concluded the meeting. Glory be to the Lord, I think I never saw a more powerful time in my lifef blest be my God many seemed to be groaning for redemption in the blood of a crucified Jesus. Oh my soul is in raptures, I want words to utter the praises of my dear Lord, and Savior Jesus Christ.

Wednesday 19 (20)—I conversed this morning with several under great distress of soul, oh what a love I seem to have this morning for souls. I rode many miles to Brother Shaw's, I met Brother Asbury, Brother Peddicord, Brother Cromwell. I preached with much sweetness from these words, "And ye now therefore have sorrow, but I will see you again, and your heart shall rejoice, and I will give you a joy that no man taketh from you. John 16:22." My soul was drawn out in sweet communion with my dear master, tears of joy flowed from my eyes; oh what a melting time, when parting with my dear, humble friends. Oh I hope to meet them in a better world, where we shall never part. About sunset I rode about four miles to visit a family that desired my company. I had some sweetness, but I met with my trials.

Thursday 20 (21)—Very early this morning I returned to Brother Shaw's. At eight o'clock we parted. Brother Asbury and Brother Cromwell went round today, and Brother Peddicord and I myself set out to go across; we went as far as Brother Sadler's. I preached with much love to the people. Oh that I could praise my God for his goodness, his love and power was felt. I met my dear friend A. (probably Airey and wife) and two of my brother laborers; we rejoiced together and I spoke of the goodness of God—we rode after dinner about eight miles, I praised my God for the journey. We had been in the house but a few moments before the neighbors flocked together in being in Queen Anne County. The devil's people are much enraged against me. As soon as they came in I began to exhort, the love of God flowed into my soul. I exhorted a considerable time and went to prayer, Glory be to God on High. I had not been praying many minutes before the power of God in a wonderful manner came down upon the people. Oh my Lord keep me from boasting, keep me humble in the dust, about 30 black and white came together and I think near 20 of them was pricked in their hearts, and cried out, "What shall I do;" one found the love of God, oh what a night of happiness to my soul and the souls of my dear laborers that was with me. We all continued in prayer till near 10 o'clock.

Friday 21 (22)—This morning they came together again and joined in class. We rode to New-Town. I had an opportunity of attending the worship of God in church, after divine service was over I preached to a crowded audience. Glory be to God for his goodness to my soul, I expect there will be glorious work in this town. Lord grant it. In the evening we held a Watch Night at Kent Preaching House. I seemed to be much wearied. Saturday we all crossed the bay on the way to Conference, this evening I met my dear Asbury at Mr. Gough's.

Sunday 23 (24)—I preached a funeral about four miles off. Mr. Gough held forth after I ended. I think there were 500, they stood out in the hot sun, they behaved exceeding well, an east wind blew and the sun shone exceeding hot in my face, which caused it to be very disagreeable; but glory be to my Jesus I was able to cry aloud and to lift up my voice as a trumpet. I heard Brother Gough's exhortation with satisfaction. I rode home with him and preached with liberty at his own house. At four o'clock about a dozen of my brother laborers was present. We spent the night exceeding agreeable.

Monday 24 (25)—We all set out to Baltimore to Conference.

(The Conference of 1780 met at the new Lovely Lane Chapel in Baltimore. It was a particularly difficult time for the Methodist Societies. The northern preachers were in favor of administering the sacraments. The northern preachers as a rule maintained the attitude established by John Wesley that Methodism was but a society within the church of England, and as such the preachers were not permitted to administer the sacrament.

The southern preachers were opposed to this limitation for at least two reasons: (1) It was especially difficult to utilize the services of the established church since many of their clergy were either absent or held in low regard. (2) In the south, there was in most places no settled ministry of any denomination. The southerners, therefore, undertook to administer the sacrament in their own right.

This question was first raised at the Deer Creek Conference May 20, 1777. The next year the Conference deferred action still another year. War conditions in 1779 prevented northern delegates from attendance. The southern group decided for administration of the ordinances. Several of the older men were appointed to this task.

Their next Conference was scheduled for May, 1780. The preachers north of Virginia were gathering in Baltimore in April, 1780. All the elements of schism were present. The northern group were firm in their position that they could not continue in fellowship with the southerners unless they agreed to suspend all their sacramental administrations for one year. All would meet after that period of time to reach a final decision. F. Asbury, William Watters, and Freeborn Garrettson were appointed to relay this action to the southern conference to be held the next month in Mankintown, Virginia. Asbury wrote in his Journal (p. 347, Vol. 1) "Myself and brother Garrettson are going to the Virginia Conference, to bring about peace and union.")

Tuesday 25 (26)—A 6 o'clock conference began. The preachers seemed much united in love. Two of our Virginia brethern was present, who had taken on themselves to baptize and administer the sacrament.

Wednesday 26 (27)—We set at six o'clock, what brotherly love was among us, ourselves was exceeding happy. In the evening we was to consult what was best to be done with our dissenting brothers in Virginia. We made it a matter of solemn prayer and fasting. When we came together much of the power of God was among us; we all with one (mind) concluded it was best to disown them if they would not return. Oh! it was a cutting thought; to think of losing so many of our dear brother laborers, there was many sorrowful hearts, many sympathetic tears was shed. Lord Jesus unite us together seemed to be the language of each heart.

Thursday 27 (28)—We all met early in the morning, we spent many hours together, the conference consented that Brother Asbury, Brother Watters and myself should attend their conference in Virginia. This was a heavy sorrowful day to me; but Glory be to God we joined in prayer together and it seemed as if the power of God in a wonderful manner came down. Oh, the goodness of God after prayer with one consent we all agreed to have a union conference next spring in Virginia. Oh what union of spirit was among us. We had the love feast at 12 o'clock, it was a love feast indeed to our souls, preachers and people prayed and wept like little children. Oh Lord we will praise thee for they goodness, Oh Lord we lift up our hearts to thee. We had a blessed watch night together and so parted praising and blessing God. Oh Lord go with my dear brothers.

Friday 28 (29)—I continued in town. I had some degree of sorrow when I parted with my dear brothers Richard, and Thomas, as I hope the Lord will bless them. In the evening I went to Brother Moore's. Oh it was a blessed evening, we took sweet council together. This night I went to bed with my heart filled with the love of God.

Saturday 29 (30)—This day I sat out apart for prayer and writing and meditating. I can say this moment, that if every hair on my head were tongues I could not sufficiently praise my dear Lord Jesus; I do not feel sin in my heart. Yet I am sensible my shortcomings are exceeding many and that it is my privilege to go on from one degree of grace to another. I preached by candlelight at the Point with some degree of light.

Sunday 30 (31)—I feel my mind in some measure refreshed. I heard preaching at six and nine o'clock at twelve I attended church. At three o'clock and seven I held forth. I praised my dear Lord Jesus for the comforts of his holy spirit. I hope this has been a day of comfort to my soul. I rested this night as in the arms of my dear Jesus.

Monday, May 1st, (1780)—I praised my God for his sensitive goodness, after breakfast I set out on my journey to Virginia. Lord give us a blessed journey. I preached two sermons this day as I journeyed. Blest be the Lord, though it was a day of trouble, yet it was a day of love to my soul, I spent the evening with three of my brother laborers.

Tuesday 2—I waited at Brother W's for my friend Asbury. We set out, had a tedious journey to Brother Adams, blest be God for refreshing both soul and body.

Thursday 4—We stayed and rested. Brother Asbury and I held forth to about a hundred that came together, we had the company of the Rev. Mr. Griffith.

Friday 5—Brother Asbury and W. Watters set out with me this morning; we had an exceeding tedious journey. About sunset we took up our quarters at a tavern. I had some conversation with a Calvinist, after we joined in prayer Glory be to God we spent the night very comfortably.

Saturday 6—Being much refreshed we set out on our journey, after traveling nearly 30 miles we came to a kind friend, a congregation came together, I hope good was done.

Sunday 7—I prayed God for health and peace, I preached with a degree of happiness. I trust good was done, many was in tears, I conversed with several in tears after preaching. I traveled 20 miles, met my brother travelers and I praised God for some degree of comfort.

Monday 8—We sat out on our journey, after a tedious worrisome travel we met our brethren.

Tuesday 9—Conference began, there seemed to be nothing but love; at first I thought there would be union, in the evening they seemed almost to demand further ordinances. We was about to part. Oh what distress I felt. I thought I should not sleep one wink. (The Conference of southern preachers heard them out. Asbury in his Journal [pp 349, 500, Vol. 1] describes the process and events. No conclusion was reached. The committee withdrew and one hour later, the Conference rejected their conditions. The next day the Conference reconvened. As Asbury, Garrettson and Watters met in prayer, the Conference reconsidered and accepted the plan to suspend administration of the ordinances.)

Wednesday 10—We all met, and Glory be to God to the comfort of all the brethern we came upon a union, had a blessed love feast and parted praising God.

Thursday 11—I set out on my journey to Baltimore, had three tedious days journey.

Saturday 13—Got as far as Brother Moore's.

Sunday 14—I preached with happiness.

Monday 15—I preached at _____ I feel my soul happy in my God.

Tuesday 16—I spent this day in retirement. I enjoyed sweetness.

Wednesday 17—Brother Rowe set out with me this morning for Baltimore, after a tedious journey we got as far as Brother W's.

Thursday 18—With no small comfort we got in town, I hope the blessed Jesus_____.

114.   "I rode to Mr. Gouges (Goughs) . . . in the evening I met Brother Dudley at Col. H_____. *Manuscript Journal.*

115.   *Tuesday 29*—I preached in the Neck where I was brought up, I had little happiness.

Wednesday 30—I continued among my old neighbors. I am much distressed. A prophet is not without honour save in his own country and among his own kin.

Thursday 31—. . . I rode to Brother John's . . . I had some conversation with . . . a christian hearted Quaker, my soul this evening is drawn out in prayer. *Manuscript Journal.*

116.   BUSH CHAPEL was erected in Bush Forest and was the second house of worship (Methodist) in Maryland. It was located in Baltimore, later Harford, County, in 1769 or 1770 about six miles from Aberdeen. Armstrong, G. E. *History of the Old Baltimore Conference*, King Bros. Printers, Baltimore 1907 p. 9.

117.   *Friday 8 (9) June*—. . . I lodged this evening with my brother George . . .

Saturday 9 (10) June—I preached at a strange place to a people that was destitute of the power of religion; they behaved exceeding well, a few tears was shed . . . *Manuscript Journal.*

118.   *Tuesday 12 (13) June 1780*—I rode 10 miles to Brother Weatherinton's, dined, and rode six miles and preached to a well affected audience . . . *Manuscript Journal.*

Thursday 14 (15)—I preached to about 40 cold hearted professors.

Saturday 16 (17)—. . . In the evening I rode 5 miles and preached to more than got in the house . . . I joined 10 in class. I hope they will do well; I rode seven miles to Brother Cromwell's. *Manuscript Journal.*

119.   "RYSTAR-TOWN" (Reisterstown, Maryland)
This town is 18 miles from Baltimore, Maryland. It was settled by Germans. Asbury's Journals, Vol. 1. p. 190.

120.   Cromwell rode with me about eight miles to Squire Vauns . . . (Vaughn's).

Wednesday 20 (21) June—I rode near ten miles to Brother Polston's in Frederick County, preached to a crowded audience . . . from the 12th chapter of Matthew, verse 35. I think it is near four years since I preached at this place . . . there is a great alteration for the better. There are 20 in the class . . .

Tuesday 27 (28) June 1780—I rose at my usual 4 o'clock, spent some time in private . . .

Friday 30—. . . I held forth at Brother Evan's with freedom, good was done . . . *Manuscript Journal.*

121. I preached at Mr. Gough's, met Brother Dudley in the evening.

Sunday 9 (July)—I preached a funeral over one of our departed friends . . . in the evening I preached with little happiness at New-Town by candlelight. I exhorted the Black people. Being harvest time, my congregations on Monday, Tuesday and Wednesday were small . . .

Sunday 16—. . . at 2 o'clock I preached and gave a love feast at a Deer-Creek preaching house . . . *Manuscript Journal.*

122. "Aunt Brown . . . I rode seven miles to Brother Dallam on my way." *Manuscript Journal.*

123. FORK-CHAPEL or Meeting House was located near the forks of Gunpowder Falls near Fallston, Harford County, Maryland. Robert Strawbridge organized a Society here, and the chapel was built in 1773. p. 189, Vol. 1 Asbury Journal.

124. . . . I preached to about 400 people with much liberty . . . M. Goughs.

Monday 24 (July)—I rode to a Mr. Randal's, dined, and went to preaching . . .

Friday 28—I visited a kind friend, rode to Fisher's preaching house.

Saturday 29—Brother Wetherinton rode with me to preaching . . . I stayed this night at my good friend M. Cromwells. *Manuscript Journal.*

125. This material appears in summary in the printed Journal. The following is the Manuscript copy for the period.

Friday—August 4, 1780—I rode 14 miles this morning, met Brother Watters. I preached with liberty and gave another love feast.

Saturday 5—This day God's word was spirit and life to the people.

Sunday 6—This morning the task lays heavy upon me. I have to ride 25 miles and preach three sermons. With much love I held forth at two o'clock to a crowded audience. Many tears were shed. Now I set out to Baltimore Town, got in town about sunset, the day being exceeding warm, I was very weary, but blest be God he enabled me to preach by candlelight with much sweetness. If any good is done God shall have the glory.

Monday 7—I set out to Gunpowder. Quarterly Meeting began at three o'clock.

Tuesday 8—At 10 o'clock we had a comfortable love feast; we had a powerful watch evening. I trust many went home rejoicing in God.

Wednesday 9—I rode 16 miles in visiting my friends and relations.

Thursday 10—I set out this morning for Kent; I traveled 25 miles by land and seven by water to New Town. Glory be to God for a kind friend. I praise God for a night of comfort.

Friday 11—I left town about eight o'clock, rode 10 miles and preached to 200 people with much freedom, many in tears. I rode 15 miles to Squire White's.

Saturday 12—About sunrise we set out to Quarterly Meeting. Several of us held forth to about 1000 people. It was a blessed day.

Sunday 13—We had our love feast at eight o'clock. There was at least 1000 present. A joyful time it was. I think there was near 2000 that attended 11 o'clock to public preaching. We had three sermons and one exhortation.

Monday 14—I rode as far as Squire White's, visited the sick. Glory be to God for humbling me under a sense of my unworthiness.

Tuesday 15—My trials are very great. I preached to near 400 all very solemn.

Wednesday 16—I preached near the drawbridge among my old friends to a crowded audience, on the necessity of purity. Glory be to God his power was felt, many seemed to be in search for holiness. It is four months since I was among my dear Mother-kill friends. They hung around me like children their mother. I had a blessed time this evening in Class.

Thursday 17—I visited a humble family and my way of preaching held forth with liberty to a crowded congregation. I have no doubt that great good was done in my Master's name. I rode near 20 miles and preached at Squire White's, what a blessed time we had.

Friday 18—Two of my dear friends set out to Bolingbroke Quarterly Meeting. In my way I had an opportunity of hearing part of a sermon with very little satisfaction. We had a tedious journey to Brother Dennies.

Saturday 19—Early this morning we set out on our journey. We got to the place about 10 o'clock. The meeting began about 12 o'clock, there was about 1500. I preached with freedom and heard several of my brethren with much comfort.

Sunday 20—Our love feast began at nine o'clock. There was a powerful time. It appeared as if the whole country came together at 11 o'clock. I think at least there was between two and three thousand. Four of us preached and one exhorted. Glory be to God, Bolingbroke never saw such a day before. I think the devil's kingdom was well shaken. When I left Baltimore County it was with an intent to visit all the circuits between the two bays. Oh Lord thou knowest my weakness. The undertaking is exceeding great, be thou my strength and wisdom. I am first to visit the upper circuit.

Monday and Tuesday—I continued in Bolingbroke preaching to two crowded congregations with much success.

Wednesday 23—On my way I preached at _____ Miles River on the necessity of being blessed cleansed from all sin. I am now with my kind friend Mr. Barrot.

Thursday 24—I held forth near Talbot Court House with liberty to a crowded audience. In the evening I rode _____ miles and preached with freedom at Mrs. Askin's to a crowded company.

Friday 25—I preached in the midst of the confusion in vindication of infant baptism. After preaching I desired our friend to retire to a private room. I dropped many hints to one of their preachers present, he opened not his mouth, but a private member did. I excluded five from society that had been dipped. I hope some of them are christians but very troublesome ones. Lord have mercy upon us all. This day when I began to preach I was almost disheartened with a toothache, but blest be God as soon as I got warmly engaged my pain was eased and my soul happy.

Saturday 26—I spent part of this day in writing. In the evening I preached to about a hundred with much freedom of mind. The Baptists has caused great confusion in this class. I had a blessed time this evening with Mrs. Askin's. I met my friend Avery. (Airey).

Sunday 27—I preached two sermons to near 500 people. I left many in tears.

Monday 28—Glory be to God this morning I parted with brother Avery (Airey) and many others of my dear friends rejoicing in the Lord.

I rode 12 miles and preached with liberty to about 100. The next day I rode 25 miles preached a funeral over one of our friends that died, I trust happy in the Lord.

Wednesday 30, 1780—This morning I am much troubled with a toothache; I preached in the Fork with very little satisfaction on account of the rack of pain of body. This evening by candlelight I was to preach but could not. I think I never suffered so much pain in my life for the time. It came to my mind how much the damned must suffer in hell. Glory be to God about midnight I got a little ease so that I fell into a sweet sleep.

Thursday 31—Glory be to God I woke with ease and peace of mind. I travelled 15 miles to Broad Creek and preached with much liberty to my dear friends from these words "Feed My Sheep"—John 21:17. Many of my Quantico friends came to see me, many tears of joy was shed.

This evening I had much sweetness in visiting and praying with the sick. Oh Lord let not the smiles of the world lift me up with pride with the language of my heart. My dear friends hung about me like children their mother, the Lord keep me in the dust _____ I rested this night at Brother Moore's as in the arms of Jesus.

Friday, September 1 (1780)—Many of my friends accompanied me 10 miles. I preached near Salisbury, where I had been much persecuted, to a crowded audience. Many came from far. Mr. Car I understood had been preaching against the doctrines of perfection. I preached from the 5th chapter of Matthew and the vindication of it I believe to the satisfaction of all present. Glory be to God it was a time of love. We had a sweet time in class and we rode 10 miles to preach with much liberty, it being late many returned home. This evening I had the company of Brother Wyet.

Saturday, September 2—I cheerfully set out on my journey, rode 22 miles and preached to near a hundred more that could fit into the house. I think it was a time of refreshing from the presence of the Lord. This evening I feel myself very weak in body yet I have peace of mind.

Sunday 3—I preached at 11 o'clock to about 500 with a degree of happiness. In the evening at four o'clock I held forth to near 300. It was an evening of power.

Monday 4—I preached under the trees where I preached yesterday morning to almost as many as I had on the sabbath. Brother James Cromwell and I held a Watch Night at A.M.

Tuesday 5—Arose this morning about daybreak in order to set out on my journey. About sunrise Brother Cromwell and I set out on our journey. I rode 22 miles and held forth to about 100 people. At 11 o'clock I rode afterward seven miles and preached at Tamor's at three o'clock with great liberty. I have often experienced that the more I do for my Master and the nearer I live to His glory, the more the devil buffets me. Oh Lord give me strength.

Wednesday 6—I rode about 10 miles to preach amongst my old friends. Near 400 came out to hear me. I preached two sermons with great liberty. In the evening I went to my dear friend Furbys. Oh! it was a night of comfort to my soul.

Thursday 7—I preached to about 300 near the drawbridge. God's dear children rejoiced much to see me. Lord Jesus keep me humble. I have a reason to hope I grow in grace.

Friday 8—I held forth at Brother Andrew Purden's with much freedom from Matthew 5:48. Lord establish me in the doctrine of perfection.

Saturday 9—I preached at my friend Shaw's to near a 100 or more than got in the house. In the evening by candlelight to more than the court house could hold, and the house was so crowded the Governor stood all the time. Glory be to God his power came down and many tears both for joy and sorrow were shed. This is the first sermon I have preached to my Dover friends for many months. My soul was happy in God, my Savior.

Sunday 10—I exhorted to about 20 of my friends a little after sunrise before I left town. I rode 10 miles to the chapel, preached two sermons, one after the other to I think upwards of 1000 people. The first sermon I had not much freedom: but Glory be to God the second my soul was filled with love. "He shall save his people from their sins" was the text. God's power came down in as wonderfull a manner as I ever saw it. I think almost the whole congregation was in tears; I have no doubt but great good was done. This evening I lodged at Squire Lockwood's. They all seemed to be enquiring the way to heaven, I trust with their faces Zionwards.

September 1780—On the 11th I rode 20 miles and preached to more people than could get in a large house in the midst of my opposers; all was still and composed, in general they consented to the truth. Oh what a glorious work God is carrying on in this county.

Tuesday, 12—I preached to a crowded audience of rich and poor, learned and unlearned, in New Town, from 1st Samuel 2:30. Whilst I was treating of the day of judgment, the dear Lord preached by lifting his voice in thunder, a dismal cloud came up; the house seemed to be filled with lightening. Oh what a day it was. Lord be praised the house was filled with the glory of God; rich and poor cried for mercy, God's dear children rejoiced in his love.

Wednesday, 13—I went through the midst of my persecutors, preached and met class with much liberty. I had some pious conversation with two pious young women. I have no doubt they enjoyed a state of sanctification. I have met with little persecution since I came over. Lord I praise thee for thy goodness.

Thursday 14—I rode near 30 miles without any refreshment, my horse was exceeding weary, the carriage being heavy in order to preach near Tuckehoe. Just as my horse was taken and I got into my room the constable came with a warrant to take me before the general court. Glory be to God providence ordered itself, that I preached my sermon, went away unmolested. There were two or three hundred, they were almost to a man on my side. I think it was a time of refreshing for the presence of God.

Friday 15—My companion Brother Kent is exceeding poorly, we travelled to the next preaching, many more came together than the house could hold. I preached with little liberty. After preaching I exhorted with great freedom. In the evening by candlelight Brother White assisted me in holding a watch night. It was a time of power.

Saturday I crossed the river and preached to a small audience with freedom. In the evening we had a blest time at Sister Askinses. God is carrying on a blessed work in this place.

Sunday 17—I travelled eight miles by land and one by water in canoe and preached to about 500 people. Glory be to God for the light of his blessed word. I rode 12 miles and preached in the evening to at least a thousand people. Oh what a solemn time there was, and all paid due attention, many both rich and poor in a flood of tears. Immediately after preaching a friend informed me the constable was laying wait to take me to jail. I rode about ten miles after preaching, out of the county; Glory be to God for this day. I rested this night as in the Lord's arms.

Monday the 18th—I spent partly in reading the Holy Bible.

Tuesday 19—Brother Kent set out with me on my journey to New Town, rode about 20 miles to Mr. White's. I had much happiness in conversing and praying with Mrs. White who was exceeding weak today but strong in spirit.

Wednesday 20—We rode 15 miles to New Town, stayed at a kind widows. Blest be God for a time of refreshing!

Thursday 21—I rode to New Town and preached to about 200 with great sweetness.

Saturday 23—I crossed the bay, got as far as my brother George's. Oh what a change since I left him. His soul is happy in the Lord. Blest be God for giving all my brothers to taste his goodness.

Sunday 24—I rode 15 miles to Bush Preaching House. With much liberty I preached on holiness. Preached at Deer Creek out of the 12th chapter of Revelations. I praised God for the light of his holy word. This evening I was very happy at Brother Bull's.

Monday—

Tuesday 26—I was exceeding happy in visiting the sick and the distressed.

Wednesday 27—I spent in company with an old Presbyterian 'till 12 o'clock. Rode 10 miles to my brother George's and exhorted to a few.

Thursday 28—

Friday 29—Met Brother Ruff and Brother Gough. Preached with Freedom.

Saturday 30—I was happy in preaching a funeral over one of our pious friends. It was a time of love.

Sunday, October 1, 1780—With much happiness I held forth to a company of Christians showing the necessity of being cleansed from all filthiness of flesh and spirit. In the evening I held forth to about 400 mostly hardened sinners.

Monday, 2—My soul was happy showing complete salvation wrought for poor sinners.

Tuesday 3—Blest be God for giving me to feel the power of faith in time of preaching. I hope good was done. We had a comfortable time in class.

Wednesday 4—I visited from house to house and met with some comfort.

Thursday 5—I feel humble and happy this morning. I preached to about 50 poor but very desirous people. My ideas was very clear, my soul happy and it was a melting time among the people. I exhorted in the evening with great freedom.

Friday 6—I preached at Rock Run to an attentive audience with love, light, and freedom; joined 10 in society. I rode to Brother John's, whilst I was in my room, he came to me and said one of the wickedest women in the neighborhood had come out to hear and if you can be a means of converting her you may—. I replied, "God's power is sufficient." A crowded audience came, I preached from these words "Watch therefore"—Matt. 25:13. God laid his hand in love upon the woman, so that she slept very little that night. "Oh," said she, "I am in hell and am afraid that there is no mercy for me." I think God began a work in her that night that shall in glory end.

Saturday 7—I exhorted about 20 at Brother W's.

Sunday 8—I have a lively sense of the favor of God. I held forth to as many as could crowd in the preaching house. Many of my relations and old companions, and others came from far. I blessed God for a great light in preaching on the great salvation; being my farewell sermon many tears was shed. In the evening I preached to a company of solemn christians, I prayed God for peace and solemnity in the congregation.

Monday 9—I spent in visiting from house to house. I trust not in vain. In the evening I held a watch night. It was a night of power.

(Notes from 10th of October through Friday the 22nd are crossed out yet in part are legible. There are references to places for preaching and visitation, for instance, he visited his brother George. He makes reference also to a visit to New Town and preaching there to 400 people. On the 16th there is a reference to a visit he made to his sister and preached there to a small company. The manuscript journal begins again with his edited notes for Wednesday the 10th continuing:)

I had a tedious ride to Carsons, I did not find the friends as I could wish.

Thursday, 11—We returned to Deer-Creek. I blessed God for a sweet meeting both in public and private.

Friday 12—My spirit is sorrowful and in the evening I met Brother Roe. We had a comfortable watchnight. My spirit is refreshed.

Saturday 13—We went in company. I held forth at 12 o'clock, in the evening we held a comfortable watchnight.

Sunday 14—Many came from various quarters, we had a blessed time. I preached on Solomon's chariot. I read two disorderly persons out of Society. In the evening I preached at Mr. Gough's with freedom to about 100 black and about 20 white people.

Monday 15—I paid my Uncle Tolley a visit. I parted with him in tears; in the evening with little freedom I preached to 30 people. I feel myself uncommonly tempted of the devil.

Tuesday 16—I am much exercised this morning. I preached to a crowded audience. About 40 of us had much sweetness in the breaking of bread together in token of our love.

Wednesday 17—My trials are exceeding great yet I bless God for a humbling sense of his goodness. The hearts of the people are exceeding hard. This is a night of exercise, though under the cross I find comfort.

Thursday 18—I preached three sermons with little success I fear. I am still sorely tempted of Satan. Lord in thine own time deliver me, I feel myself resisting to his will.

Friday 19—I am still under exercise. I preached at 12 o'clock on Satan's limitation; in the evening Brother Owings assisted me in holding a watch evening, it was a time of profit.

Saturday 20—I did not spend as much of this morning on my knees as I ought. I preached with little light in the word, rode to Brother Cromwell's, I blest God for sweet peace.

Sunday 21—I went and preached at Ristertown, in the Dutch Church, I had much light and liberty. I think sinners trembled, God's people was happy. Here are many living witnesses for Jesus.

Monday 22—I preached with great success, joined eight in class.

Tuesday 23—I preached to a poor, but desirous people. I had great light in the holy scriptures.

Wednesday 24—I held forth on Pipe-Creek with great liberty. We was much comforted while breaking bread one with another.

Friday 26—I have joined near 20 in class who I trust are much engaged.

Monday 29—I met Brother Foster. After I had done preaching and the people gone, the woman of the house said her house never was before in so glorious a manner perfumed with the glory of God. I think I never in all my life saw so solemn a class meeting. Glory be to God for giving the mistress of this family to love Him with all her heart and the master to groan for full redemption in his blood.

Wednesday 31—This day was set apart to break bread together at Mrs. Randon's. Glory be to God it was a precious time. In the evening we had a very comfortable Watch Service at Captain Stone's.

Thursday, November 1 (2), 1780—My mind is refreshed with the love of God. I had a sweet time in preaching Matthew 13:33 in the evening on the same words in Baltimore Town.

Friday 2 (3)—We broke bread together at Brother Lynch's, I trust the little flock was fed with the bread of life. Many in this neighborhood professed the second blessing.

Saturday 3 (4)—I rode 20 miles, preached and broke bread with about 40 of my friends: rode about seven miles and preached to about 100 of the black people, joined 12 in class; Glory be to God we joined together in hope of meeting one day in heaven.

Sunday 4 (5)—I preached a funeral over one of our friends in Gunpowder, who died in the faith; in the evening at New-Town. I feel a little good was done: by candlelight we spent two hours watching and praying.

Monday 5 (6)—This morning my mind is much troubled, occasioned by my horse straying from me: as quarterly meeting begins this morning, I borrowed a horse and set out, we had I trust a comfortable meeting.

Wednesday 7 (8)—Brother Roe set out with me to the eastern shore: we crossed the bay between 12 and 3 o'clock with a pleasant gale: we had an exceeding powerful time by candle with near 300 who seemed to be very much engaged. I have no doubt but much good was done.

Thursday 8 (9)—With much satisfaction I hear Brother Roe hold forth in New-Town: in the evening I exhorted to 200 on Lazarus and the Rich Man.

Friday 9 (10)—This day I spent in visiting the sick with much satisfaction. One lay under the afflicting hand of providence was wrought upon in a very powerful manner; she was not only wrought to receive the love of God, but her bodily disorder was suddenly removed; in a short time after the first visit I visited her again. She cried out, "I blest God at ever I saw your face: in a short time after you went from the house, that burden under which I labored was taken away, and peace and joy flowed into my soul: the pain of body is removed and I have ever since been as composed as a little infant." Glory be to God my soul cannot help praising his holy name: I preached with very little satisfaction, the preaching house being very open and cold

Saturday 10 (11)—I rode 30 miles to Quarterly Meeting, held forth to about 1500.

Sunday 11 (12)—I think we had the greatest meeting that ever I saw. While breaking bread together I saw the power of God in a wonderful manner came. I think at 12 o'clock near 4000 people came together, I preached with little satisfaction to myself, but heard my brother with satisfaction.

Monday 12 (13)—Some of us had a conference at Mr. White's. It was a time of distress.

Tuesday 13 (14)—This evening I preached at I. W. We had a glorious time.

Wednesday 14 (15)—I set out on my way to Baltimore, preached at Brother Sadler's. We had a time of refreshing.

Saturday 17 (18)—I held forth at New Town.

Sunday 18 (19)—I preached to a crowded audience in New-Town, in the evening a funeral in Kent Preaching House.

Tuesday I crossed the bay with a ———— gale. The rest of the week I visited the friends and read my bible. I was much exercised the whole week.

Sunday 20 (26)—I preached in Gunpowder Preaching House in New-Town with a degree of happiness. I spent all this week in preaching and meeting classes.

Sunday 30 (uncertain date)—Being a very rainy day I had small congregations in both morning and evening.

Monday, December 4 (1780)—I had a sweet time at Deer Creek.

Tuesday 5—I preached with liberty at a new place. The remaining part of the week I had small congregations, the people not knowing I was coming around.

Sunday 10—Today I had a tedious journey. The Lord repaid me for my trouble in giving me a sweet time in preaching on charity

Wednesday 13—We had a solemn season. The remainder of this week I travelled to preach with liberty through the Barrons.

Sunday 17—I blest God for a happy time in preaching in a Lutheran Church.

Monday 18—I preached to about 150 many of which was happy in God. Tuesday I preached to the same audience. Glory be to God for peace of mind.

Monday, December 25—being the day on which my dear Jesus came into the world I preached to a crowded audience with freedom. Glory be to God, I spent the Christmas in the service of my dear master. In general I had many to hear, my soul is happy, but many are the trials I meet with.

Sunday 31—I blest God for a trembling sense of His goodness to my soul. I preached in the morning at the Point to a genteel audience. In the evening by candlelight I held forth in Town, I think there was at least a thousand, the house was so crowded the floor broke down; I think I never saw a prospect of more good being done in Town.

Monday, January 1, 1781—I held forth at Brother Fergo's in the morning. Returned to Town and held forth to another crowded audience. The people paid due attention. I had sweet communion this evening with my dear friend Brother More. We took sweet council together.

Tuesday 2—I held forth at Brother Lynches.

Tuesday 17—I preached in a cold house, a cold day and to a cold people.

Monday 23—I had a sweet time in exhorting and praying with a quaker family.

126. "This morning I set out to Pennsylvania in order, if the Lord opened the way to form a new circuit. I lodged at a dutch tavern, I was of very little service to them, not understanding the dutch language." *Manuscript Journal.*

LITTLE YORK CIRCUIT: Daniel Worley was present in the tavern when Garrettson led in family worship. He was awakened, and the next day his wife was also awakened. Out of these contacts and those in the Lutheran Church the next day came the beginnings of the Little York circuit. "The first society was organized at the house of Daniel Worley, in York. Soon about 100 souls were added to the church; and, at the ensuing Conference, Little York became the second circuit in Pennsylvania." pp. 50, 51 Armstrong, J. E. *History of the Old Baltimore Conference . . .* King Bros., Baltimore 1907.

127. His mother and sister rode with me five miles to Beer-lene (Berlin) . . . I preached at Beer-lene to a crowded audience. In the evening I held forth by candlelight to almost as many.

Friday 27 (26)—I rode several miles and preached to a crowded audience at an old Quaker house: many of the Quakers flocked out, many tears was shed; the people began to inquire into our rules; after being somewhat acquainted with them, several begged to join; I told them to take—time to count the cost—In the evening I rode many miles and preached at an old dunkard's. I met with two that I hoped were christian. *Manuscript Journal.*

Tuesday 31 (30) (January) 1781 . . . I rode back to my friend's, Brackins . . . I rode and preached at one William Thomson, a profane man, I bid his house farewell 'till he gets a better heart . . .

"The uproar in the county by this time was very great, one cryed out one thing, and another an other thing, some who before confessed great friendship for me, shut their doors, and cryed out against me, calling devil and false prophet but glory be to my dear Lord who stands by his cause, where one door was shut ten was opened . . . I began (to) see the wisdom of God in permitting it to happen." *Manuscript Journal.*

Saturday 25 (24) February 1781—I preached five miles out of town. Some of my greatest persecutors was from Town; They appeared after the sermon very friendly; in the evening by candle-light, I had at least 200 hearers and we had a remarkable melting time.

Sunday 26 (25)—I preached to the largest audience that I ever did in this part. Some came out, who before thought it was a sin to hear me preach, the general cry was, I never heard the like before. In the evening preached at S.W. where I had preached the last evening to as many as could crowd in three large rooms; Monday I returned and preached at my friend J.W. in sight of York, at night I had a meeting at D.W.'s (Daniel Worley's). I trust many will forever praise God for this day and evening. A woman was struck with a trembling, she cried out, unless we repent we are all lost. After the meeting I went to her and asked her if she thought Christ was willing to save her, she said she saw a fellowship in him and was determined to lay at his feet.

27th (26)—I preached to a curious audience at a new place, with much freedom. In the evening I had a crowded audience. *Manuscript Journal.*

Wednesday 28 (27) Tues.—I rode about 40 miles to York and preached with much freedom to a crowded audience by candlelight.

Friday 30 (Wed. 28th Feb.?)—I met my dear friend Ebert—spent a few hours together.

128. *Sunday 4 (March 1781)*—Many of various denominations flocked to hear the word, and with great attention morning and evening.

Monday 5—I rode to McCollisters Town, I was received as an Angel . . . much refreshed in reading several letters my dear Baltimore friend, I rode many miles to Abits-Town, where were many scoffers of religion, in proportion I think this place is as wicked almost as Sodom.

Sunday 11—I rode 12 miles and preached with great freedom to my York friends. I have been about four weeks in these parts, and . . .

Monday 12—I rode 32 miles to Brother Vaughan's and preached to about 300. *Manuscript Journal.*

Wednesday, March 15, (14) 1781—I preached in Brother Geering's church to a crowded audience with great freedom. In the evening I preached in his own house to more than it could contain; Glory be to God for his goodness in sending down his power upon the people, so that almost the whole congregation both Dutch and English was brought to cry for mercy. By this time his parishioners began to cry out against this, some said he was turned Methodist.

Thursday 16 (15)—I preached in Berlin Town to a crowded audience. I am informed there is a great altercation in this place since I preached here. I hope many are under conviction.

Friday 17 (16)—I preached, many of my hearers were Quakers. I hope the dear Lord is carrying on a glorious work in the neighborhood.

Saturday I preached at an old German's, I think many here are inquiring the way to Zion. Many were open opposers of the truth. My dear master was so present and precious that their mouths were stopped. The cry was among others who would not come out to hear, "He is driving people mad;" Glory be to God the more the devil raged the larger was my congregation; Blest be God many were all around crying. The man where I lodged who was a sensible Englishman, he told me in the morning he was so distressed that he did not get one wink of sleep and desired all night to awake me to pray for him. He was afraid the devil was coming to carry him away. His wife in the same condition.

Monday 20 (19)—This morning when I got out of bed and came out I saw my dear distressed friend. My soul did magnify the Lord. I prayed with and commended them to the Lord. I preached with much freedom at 12 o'clock and in the evening we had much of the divine presence. Sinners trembled before God's word. I preached to a company of Lutherans and Presbyterians. There was a shaking among the dry bones. Some who were persecutors cried out at the truth and I will not befriend any longer to fighting against God's word.

Wednesday 22 (21)—I had a tedious ride to McCollister's town. I did not begrudge my journey for I found one gracious family who were convinced of sin when I was there before. Their souls are mourning for Jesus. I spent the night 'til two o'clock in writing letters to Baltimore Circuit.

Thursday 23 (22)—Early in the morning I set out to Berlin Town, I lost my way.

March 1781—Work around York, Pennsylvania. There was I diverted but to a poor distressed family; the woman of the house had got under distress of soul for sin, and the grand adversary had persuaded her that the day of grace had passed and that such a day the devil would come for her and her three dear little children. When I came in the house I found her wringing her hands and crying, "Oh my dear children what a pity it is that the devil should have them, she did not seem to be as much concerned for herself as for her children. I now blest and praised God for turning me out of the ride (?). I opened my bible and began to open God's holy word, tears running down her cheeks. Good woman said I, the devil shall not have you nor your dear children for I will pray for you and God has promised to hear his people's prayers; Oh, said she, who knows but he will: We went to prayer, after which I begged of her to go with me to preaching, which she and her husband readily did. I took my text in Luke the 12th chapter, 32nd verse, and endeavored to adapt the subject to her condition; I did not speak to her after the meeting but was told she went away praising God. After I rode as far as York, the persecution was so high that I was not permitted to preach.

Friday 24 (23)—I preached at my friend Worley's. I had many from Town to hear. Almost all the people was in tears, prejudice was in a wonderful manner removed.

129. *Sunday April 1, 1781*—This was a day of labor; hearts as hard as flints. I preached in the evening, we had a melting time.

Monday 2—I preached and joined the Class. My spirit was refreshed among them.

Tuesday 3—I rode and preached in McCal-Town morning and evening, joined the Class—Lord let thy word spread. On my way to York I called in and preached at Berlin with much freedom, joined the class. Glory be to God we had a time in York to be remembered. I feel my mind sweetly drawn out in a service of my God.

Thursday 5—I preached at Brother Worley's and joined a prosperous Society. In the evening I preached in Town. Next day in Dover at 12 o'clock and 3 o'clock in Buttstown and by candlelight in York, this was a precious day to my soul, that he sent me into these parts, hundreds are seeking Jesus.

Saturday 7—was a day of power both morning and evening. In the evening I joined a very large class. In this neighborhood the Dutch and the English are alarmed.

Sunday 8—I was happy in visiting my good old friend; at 11 o'clock I preached to some hundreds, God's love came down. How powerfully present Jesus was in the many joined in Society. This night my soul is happy.

Monday 9—My dear Lord has permitted the enemy to buffet me. Lord give me presence.

Tuesday 10—I had a tedious journey over to Cumberland, my Lord _____ me for my trouble.

Wednesday 11—I think this is the greatest day of trial that ever I met with in these parts, the Lord Jesus stand by me. It is hard labor to preach to these people. Lord have mercy on them and open their eyes. This evening I lodged at a Dunkers. He and his wife and children appeared to be lovers of Jesus.

Thursday 12—At 11 o'clock I preached at an old Quaker's, at 5 o'clock at a Lutheran's, and by candlelight at a churchman's. I hope I did not labor in vain.

Friday 13—With great freedom I held forth at Squire Smith's, and in the evening at Mr. Pettit's, both before and after preaching; I was exceedingly tormented with a toothache which caused me to have it drawn.

Saturday 14—A Dutch minister met me at Mr. Hollerpeters (?). After preaching to several hundred he gave an exhortation in German.

Sunday 15—I find my mind calm and serene. I preached to some hundreds at 12 o'clock. By candlelight I preached in York to a crowded audience. I think I never saw but one such day in my life and the people flocked from one place to the other in great droves on horseback and on foot.

Monday 17—Two of my friends set out with me from York to Quarterly Meeting. We rode 45 miles to attend a sermon at 3 o'clock.

Tuesday our love feast began.

Wednesday 18—My dear friends set out with me to York. We had a tedious but happy journey. I met with some opposition on the way from the town's squire.

Thursday evening I held forth to my York friends with great freedom.

Saturday 20—Morning and evening I preached to a crowded audience of poor sinners crying for mercy. Saturday was a blest blessing to the souls of hundreds. I have preached but a few sermons in this neighborhood and I trust sinners are crying for mercy.

Sunday 21—I have to ride 12 miles and preach a sermon this day at 8 o'clock, 12 o'clock, 3 o'clock and 7 o'clock. Glory be to God I shall never forget this day, and I think hundreds will remember it in eternity. I plan to begin my fairwell sermon next morning at 5 o'clock. Monday—Day was *broke* when I got out of bed; I begin to preach about 8 o'clock. We had a glorious meeting. I preached and _____ York circuit. I parted with my dear friends. A little after 6 o'clock I rode 25 miles to preach to a small audience. After preaching I rode 35 miles to Conference. This was the greatest day that ever I went through where I met with many of my brethren.

130. *Tuesday, April 23 (24)*—Conference began a precious day we had, not one _____ thing among us.

Wednesday 24 (25)—the same.

Thursday—likewise.

Glory be to God all are sweetly united, except one preacher, who intends to administer the ordinances. My lot is cast in Virginia, where I expect to meet with troublesome times. Lord stand by me.

Friday I spent in Town.

Saturday visiting my relations.

Sunday in hearing preaching.

Monday my brother Richard set out with me on our journey. Got as far as Baltimore.

Tuesday—parted both having different appointments to supply, I am much exercised.

Wednesday—I an comfortable at a kind friend's. I intend to stay several days 'til my brother comes up with me.

Sunday, May 5, (6) 1781—I preached on my way.

Monday 6 (7)—I crossed the Potomac, lodged at Brother Adam's.

Tuesday 7 (8)—I set out on my journey, I lost myself. Oh the distress I expected to have had to lodge in the woods.

Wednesday 9 (10)—Got to a kind friends. My mind was refreshed.

Thursday 10 (11)—I got to a Baptist's who used me exceeding kind.

Friday 12 (11)—I reached to my Brother Richard's circuit.

Saturday 13 (12)—I thought to have got to Amela but could not _____. Stayed at a kind friends. Attended church, preached with liberty, returned and preached at a friends where I lodged the other night.

Monday 15 (14)—I set out on my journey, got as far as Brother Gatch's.

Tuesday 16 (17)—I got with great difficulty as far as Brother Tinney. I stayed 'til the Lord's Day, met Brother Dudley, preached several sermons with great freedom. Saturday evening Brother R. and a few other friends had a private watchnight. I wrote a long letter to Brother G. I hope he will have the desire to fret.

Monday 22 (21)—I set out for Sussex the times were so exceeding distressing. I could not get along on my journey, stayed at a friend's.

Tuesday I set out, rode about 10 miles, I found there was danger on every hand, people on every side moving, I did not know what course to take, to get clear. I rode near 20 miles out of the way to get out of the noise of war and other distresses. Got to a kind friends where I stayed 'til Thursday.

In the morning my kind friend set out with me 15 miles on my way, where after much trouble, having a creek to swim, I got to my dear old friend Gilbens. Glory be to God for bringing me back to this pious family. I think it is about three years since I left them. I rejoice to see all their faces Zionwards. I stayed in the family several days, preached two sermons with a degree of freedom.

Sunday 20 (appears to be out of sequence)—I preached with much freedom at the preaching house. Rode to Brother Jones, preached in the evening. I think I was never in a more distressing place, my horse was in danger of being taken. This week I spent in setting the circuit in order.

Saturday (June 16, 1781?)—My helper met me and rode several days in company; preached several sermons for me, the preachers being much scattered and many circuits without preachers, I thought it expedient to send Brother Parks in the lower circuit and to endeavor to supply this circuit myself.

Sunday, June 17—we had a solemn feast of love. At 11 o'clock I had the largest meeting than I have seen since I came to Virginia and I believe was the most good done. In the evening I had a crowded audience, the power of God was among us.

Tuesday 19—I was much distressed and as I was on my way to my appointment it was a great cross for me to preach, my soul was warmly drawn out with exhorting and praying with about 20 negroes.

Thursday 21—I preached to a company of backsliders. In the evening I had freedom in preaching a funeral over a child, part of my subject was to prove the justification. I praised God for comforting my soul.

Friday—The next day I rode eight miles to the Bushel's Chapel. I had liberty in stressing the necessity of keeping experience void of offense for God and man. I returned to my friends after meeting and settling some matters on three classes. This evening I am troubled with a drowsy spirit.

131. *Thursday, June 28, 1781*—If I know myself it is my soul's desire to do God's blessed will. I find a degree of liberty in preaching to a small audience at 11 o'clock. Rode six miles and preached to a lively happy people at 4 o'clock. We had a profitable meeting.

Friday 29—I set this day apart for fasting and prayer, I never was more powerfully tempted in my life, I was in great measure robbed of my comfort, I mourned all day over a hard heart, I fear I grieved the good spirit.

Saturday 30—I preached a sermon with great freedom.

July 1st (1781)—I rode 10 miles and met about 30 in Society, at 9 o'clock. Preached at 11 o'clock. After preaching I met 20 in class, rode six miles and preached at 4 o'clock. After preaching I rode four miles home with Brother Howard. I bless and praise my God for a precious day, my soul this day is drawn out in love.

Monday, July 2—This morning I am under a degree of exercise, I preached to a very lively people, insisting on a deeper work of grace, I examined about 12 penitent, my soul is so much refreshed in public exercise, but returned to my friends much dejected; my spirit at dinner was lighter than it ought to have been, and my conversation not so well seasoned as was required, which caused me to moan in sorrow. Lord have mercy upon me and make me more solemn. My God joined his love into my soul while exhorting, and praying with and for the family.

Tuesday 3—I find a backwardness to duty this morning but my dear Jesus gave me a gracious visit. I rode about eight miles and preached to a small audience. I began to preach from these words, "Blessed are the meek for theirs is the kingdom," I had not been preaching five minutes before a part of the people was nodding. The day was very warm. I was much tempted, I began to exhort them to lift up their hearts to God, stressing the devices of Satan: all I could do I could not keep their eyes open, 'til I came to the application; forever blest be God in the close of the sermon. The Lord broke in upon the people, all seemed to be in a flood of tears. I had much satisfaction in instructing about 90 serious persons. This evening I exhorted about 50 negroes, I fear Satan got an advantage of one; she fell down, thumped her breast and puked all over the floor. I gave over exhorting, and went to prayer; after prayer I endeavored on the ___ ___ to lay down the Plan of Salvation, showed them that they may be converted without falling down, or hollouring. I believe some of them was weak enough to think they could not be converted unless they fall. My dear Lord and Master was powerfully present, I think there will be a glorious work among the poor negroes.

Tuesday, (Wednesday) 4—My spirit was very heavy this morning. I set this day apart as a day of abstinence. O Lord let it be a day of humility. I have a stubborn heart to conquer. I fear I have not that nearness to my God, that I enjoyed in months and years that are past. Lord keep me from sliding back. I am more than ever convinced, that the kingdom is taken by violence.

Wednesday, (Thursday) July 5—Brother _____ attended me to the appointed place. Found very great backwardness to speak for my master, but whilst holding forth the Lord stood in the midst, and while I was insisting on a pleasant salvation, the Savior paid us a sweet visit. I fear satan got the advantage of two women, they cried out, so that I was obliged to stop and speak to them. By candlelight, I heard Brother Nils with satisfaction. This evening I was taken very poorly; in the morning I had very little expectation of preaching. I set out to my appointment, and what with the head, and toothache, I was in much misery. It pleased the Almighty to remove the pain, so that I had a comfortable time. I rode several miles, and preached a second sermon with great satisfaction, the holy word was opened, and my soul much refreshed. This evening I visited Sister Nule who was in a very declining way. I hope as the body decays, the inward man is strengthened day by day.

Friday, July 7, (6) 1781—I was accompanied to Lains, F.H. by Brother Howard, blest be God for restoring him to soundness of mind. O how precious God was to my soul, and the souls of the people whilst I was preaching from these words to about a hundred. "Many see the afflictions of the righteous; but out of them all the word shall deliver Him." Psalm. After preaching many of our dear friends spoke boldly in love feast. It was a feast of love to many souls. There are many in this neighborhood under the afflicting hand of kind providence. After meeting I rode about 12 miles, met with many _____.

Saturday 8 (7)—I praise God for giving me sweet peace, whilst preaching two sermons.

Sunday 9 (8)—At 9 o'clock I held a love feast, at 11:00 preached with light, rode seven miles and preached with freedom, showing the devices of the devil. I hope my dear master gives me a growth in grace.

Monday 10 (9)—My soul is sweetly drawn out in the nearness of my God, I preached to a crowded audience with a tender heart, I hope good was done. I had a precious, sweet time, whilst preaching to about 15 christians on the wisdom of God in delivering his children. I think I can say I never was more moved with pity, than visiting the negroes in their quarters, they were laying on the floors without a spirit, and I fear their souls dead. My heart was filled with love and sorrow, whilst conversing with their master and mistress insisting on better usage, or give up their religion, for without doing so we would be done by where there is no real religion.

Tuesday 11 (10)—I had an opportunity for hearing a good sermon delivered by a servant of God, except one part however did not appear to be orthodox. He rather in the former part of the discourse went on a quaker theme. Preached justification to be a gradual work. At 4 o'clock I preached with great freedom of soul to about 25 mostly solemn deep Christians showing the devices of satan, and the _____ of Christian living in love, and the danger of not speaking with note of encouragement to press on in the narrow way. I have a hope they have advanced in the divine life since I was here this day a fortnight. This evening I enjoyed peace of soul.

Wednesday 12 (11)—By appointment I was to preach at Bushel's Chapel* but the alarms are so great that the people was afraid to come, five of us got together, we had a very comfortable meeting—I went to Brother (Potten's)?

BUSHEL'S CHAPEL—According to Jesse Lee this was Boisseau's about 12 miles from Petersburg, Va. in Dinwiddie County. Asbury made frequent visits there. Mr. Boisseau built this chapel commonly called Bushill's. It was the third Methodist chapel built in Virginia. p. 56 Lee, Jesse, Short History of the Methodists.

Thursday 13 (12)—I had an opportunity of hearing a sermon with a degree of satisfaction; in the evening I had an opportunity of preaching to a loving people with freedom. This evening I have a deep sense of the goodness of God.

Friday 14 (13)—We set out very early this morning, I was somewhat exercised, my head seemed somewhat numbed by reason of pain. I preached with a degree of liberty, about four loving souls broke bread in token of our love. This is a Christian hearted family.

Saturday 15th (14) of July—I find sweet and calm; I had the happiness of preaching to a tender hearted audience. Brother A. (Asbury) gave an exhortation. After meeting rode about four miles to Brother B. E. If I know my own heart, it is the desire of my soul to do the Lord's will.

Sunday 16 (15)—I was much comforted whilst instructing about four black ones, my soul's desire is their salvation. At 11 o'clock I was drawn out in the spirit of preaching to about three hundred. In the evening whilst preaching to about one hundred, the power of God came down; He laid his hand upon several; one in particular: She was standing with her child in her arms, when she was struck. She fell to the earth and her child under her; at first she loudly cried out for mercy, but shortly laid quiet; with a half an hour after I ended my sermon when going away I heard her praising God. I praise and bless my dear God for his goodness: when first I came into this circuit very few seemed willing to suffer for Jesus, Blest be my God, of late some has, and others willing to suffer if called there unto. I hope my dear master is reviving his glorious work. O God pull down the devil's kingdom.

Monday 17 (16)—This day God opened the holy scriptures unto me, I had freedom to preach to about 150. About 100 of us spent about an hour in speaking of the goodness after breaking bread in token of our love and the people was humble, but we need a greater degree of grace.

July 18 (17)—I know what it is to be assaulted by the grand enemy the devil. For several days I have been much tried with a drowsey spirit: O that this flesh was conquered. Lord help me to live a self-denying life. This day was spent partly in visiting friends. I have reason to complain of my shortcoming.

Wednesday 19 (18)—This morning my mind is sweetly drawn out in the service of my master. Part of this day was spent in reading, writing, prayer and self-examination, part was spent in endeavoring to convince two of our friends of that iniquitous practice of slave keeping. Glory be to God, not in vain, one of them had about 20 and the other 12. One promised their freedom, and asked to settle them on land, and the other promised their freedom some years ago. He sold one, he promised if he could not free him. His intent was to give him the money that he sold him for. O God, open the heart of thousands to let the oppressed go free. Lord enlarge my heart faithfully to discharge my duty with regard to this particular as well as the salvation of souls—at 4 o'clock I had an opportunity of hearing one of my brethren preach, my mind seems stayed on God my Savior.

Thursday 20 (19)—This morning the disagreeable news of two of our horses being taken came to our ears. Lord grant me patience. One of my brethren helped me this evening in holding a watch night, it was I hope a profitable time. My mind is calm.

Friday, July 21, (20) 1781—By appointment I am to preach a funeral over one of my pious friends. I preached from these words "Behold, the Perfect Man." It was a precious time. I think proper to speak a few words with regard to his life and death. His parents had 15 children grown to the years of men and women; he was the 14th child. I expect in his youthful days he lived as other young men. About seven years ago it pleased Almighty God of his great goodness to send his glorious gospel into this part of the world by despised people called Methodists; he heard the joyful sound with gladness, and was brought to experience redemption in the blood of Jesus: after a few years he was convinced of the need of holiness: he was brought to experience the second blessing, I believe his brethren did not doubt his experience, for he was a man of great piety, admired by all his brothers. This _____ despised by the impious class of mankind. His walk was as becomes the gospel. I believe neither by what I understood, friends nor foes could lay anything to his charge. Last May this dear saint was called to suffer for his master: he was altogether adverse to shedding blood. He was forced out into the field as a soldier, torn away from his dear wife and children. They used every means they could to make him take a gun; they threatened him bitterly, after this they marched him two days without giving anything to eat or to drink, when he could get an opportunity he would kneel down in the crowd and pray for his enemies. They threatened to beat him, all in vain. After this a day was set apart for him to be shot if he did not submit: he was brought forth, if I mistake not, blindfolded, and the men chosen, their pieces (guns) charged, and had not power to shoot. They gave him a few more days to consider, all this while kept in confinement; but when he was brought forth again, they had not power to shoot him. They kept him in punishment for several weeks, but all in vain. All this while the Lord kept him in his arms. His company was (_____) Jesus with Daniel in the lions den. After they saw they could do nothing with him they let him go: he returned home to his family praising the God of Shadrack and Abednigo. In a short time after his return I came into the parts but he was laid under a severe spell of sickness, supposed to be occasioned by the hard usage he met with, his soul was happy in God his Savior. Sometime in his sickness he was lightheaded, but his whole talk was about Jesus. I visited him a few days before his departure, death was strongly working upon him; I asked him if he was happy, he said "yes." His face seemed to shine like the face of an angel. He longed to be disolved and be with Christ. I believe in a rapture of love he left all his dear friends behind. He has gone to the arms of Jesus. O that we brought _____ _____ follow the good examples of our dear brother Hargrove.

Saturday 22 (21)—I preached his wife sister's funeral. She died happy. Her last words while she was in her senses was "I have fought the good fight" etc. I think I never had greater freedom to preach since I came to visit. I hope good was done in the name of Jesus.

Sunday 23 (22)—I find much freedom in my mind this morning. I preached at Lain's house at 11 o'clock with great freedom. I rode eight miles and preached at E. P. house showing the dreadful consequences of being excummunicated, several troubled ones was present, thought I had boldly excluded from Society and others who had been disorderly. This evening I find my mind much exercised.

Monday 24 (23)—I spent in retirement I hope with profit.

Tuesday 25 (24)—I had great freedom whilst explaining the travels of the children of Israel to about a hundred black and white. I went home with old Mr. Ivey. I was about an hour by _____ assaulted violently by the devil. I was nearly scarcely able to read half a page before I was ready to nod over the book: I walked about, went to prayer—still powerfully assaulted until family prayer and Blest be God the cloud broke, and we had a sweet time.

Wednesday 26 (25)—This morning I was severely assaulted by the devil. I fear I did not bear up under my trials as I ought, I went mourning for hours but Glory be to God whilst I was laying down the narrowness of the way to heaven, and in encouraging the friend to hold faith, my dear Lord gave me a sweet sense of his love. This evening I can truly say I was laid in the dust, the language of my heart, O that I could love God more. My Lord knows I am not worthy of this good bed. In the morning I set out accompanied by several of our friends to the other preaching house; I had not been long there before my brother Richard Garrettson and Brother Joshua Dudley came to meet with Brother Allin: my heart in a moment was filled with rejoicing. I heard Brother Richard with satisfaction preach from these words "Enoch walked with God" and he undertook to show what is implied in walking with God and how a walk with God may be maintained and three motives to induce us to walk with God.

Friday 28 (27)—We rode to Brother Tuckers. I was much shut up in preaching. We had a comfortable time while breaking bread together.

Saturday 29 (28)—Our Quarterly Meeting began by Brother R (Richard) preached. We had a good meeting.

Sunday was a glorious day to many souls.

Monday—I set out on my way to Sussex Quarterly Meeting. I had an opportunity of hearing my brother Richard preach.

Tuesday, (July 31) August 1—I preached with freedom, we rode about five miles and held a watch night. I had an appointment and an opportunity of hearing Brother Dudley and Brother Richard both preach after which I spoke freely by way of exhortation.

Wednesday, August 2 (1) (1781)—I had great freedom after preaching.

Friday 4 (3)—With satisfaction I heard my brother Richard, after preaching we rode to Brother E.'s.

Saturday 5 (4)—Meeting began: we had a crowded audience. Our meeting was comfortable. I had happiness whilst examining and giving license to the local preachers and exhorters.

Sunday 6 (5)—At 9 o'clock we had a comfortable feast of love. Many happy souls feasted with us: from 12 o'clock till 4 o'clock. The evening was spent in preaching and exhorting. The word had due worth on the minds of the people. I can truly say a day of refreshment to my soul.

Monday was a day of rest; about 8 o'clock I departed with Brother Dudley and Brother Richard.

Tuesday—this is a day of sorrow: I sensibly feel the corruption of my heart, if ever they were taken away, I fear they had returned. I preached to about a hundred serious Christians.

Wednesday 9 (8)—I feel distressed in mind on account of my many shortcomings. I am sorely buffeted by the devil much troubled in private prayer with wanderings. I rode to my appointment and Blest be God he gave me access to the hearts of the people. I think it was a time of profit. I fear the family has very little religion. O blest be God in a small degree my mind is refreshed in private.

Thursday 10 (9)—Brother Norris set out with me to Quarterly Meeting. We had to go through the camp where several of our friends were under guard for not bearing arms. I believe our master's kingdom is a peace and joy in the holy ghost (Romans 14:17). He has chose his children out of the world. If his kingdom was of this world then would his servants fight. I believe he will stand by all those who keep their trust in Him. We got belated and called in a house where we was miserable; though our bodies was kindly entertained. The woman of the house had under _____.

Friday 11 (10)—I was blest with an opportunity of preaching to a crowded audience with freedom. After meeting, my very heart was pained to see no more religion in the family. I was accompanied by several of my friends to Brother W. in Carolina. My mind still pained to see no more religion.

Saturday 12 (11)—Our quarterly meeting began, I had freedom to preach and satisfaction in hearing an exhortation.

Sunday 13 (12)—The Lord very much favored us. I had great satisfaction in speaking on the _____ victory. It was in general a time to be remembered. My mind this evening seems calm and serene.

Monday 14 (13)—God being my helper I intend to travel a few months in these parts. I set out to my appointment. I had a tedious journey and many was the trials I met with on my way.

Wednesday 16 (15)—I got to the first place. I appeared to have no door opened. The people here has just religion enough to make them miserable.

Thursday 17 (16)—I went to the next place distressed and came away the same. This evening I was comfortable in a good man's house. Next day I preached to a loving people but under a degree of dejection. This evening I was too miserable with the toothache until near midnight. My dear master removed it—I think it worked together for my good. I was reminded of hell. If we cannot bear pain in a small member how shall we endure soul and body to burn in hell. O God make these people humble and holy.

Saturday 19 (18)—I praise God for a comfortable time.

Sunday 20 (19)—I preached at Nansemond, Va to a crowded audience. My dear master stood by me, I think satan was angry. In the evening I preached in a private house and I am well assured the power of God was amongst the people. My soul rejoices in God my Savior. There are some good people in these parts. My mind is sweetly drawn out to love God. I see beauty in following Christ.

Monday 21 (20)—By appointment I am to preach a funeral. About 10 o'clock I was taken with a violent fit of toothache except I think I never was a wrack of misery. I had almost laid aside all hopes of attending the funeral. I thought I would trust in the Lord. I rode to the place in much pain. A crowded audience of both white and black came together. Soon after I took my text the pain left me and a glorious time we had. The greater part of the congregation was _____. In the evening I held forth to a small audience about six miles off, there seems to be a searching among the hearts of believers. This was a sweet night to rest.

Tuesday 22 (21)—This morning the family under great exercise. Satan wants my confidence. Lord help me to hold fast the shield of faith. I had some sweet rays while preaching on the leavening of the whole lump. This evening I have covenanted with my Lord to live more in heaven.

On the 23rd (22)—I rode 15 miles and preached in a new place to more than the house could contain. I think good will was done here.

On this Thursday 24 (23)—I preached to _____ audience. Several, know God, others _____. I preached to a crowded audience, mostly strangers to Jesus. The woman of the house was in a despairing condition. I could not persuade her but her day of grace was past.

Friday 25 (24)—I preached on the edge of a place called the desert.

Saturday 26 (25)—I had a tedious drive to the other parts of the circuit where I had a more sensible audience to preach to, and gave private advice after preaching to about twelve who had been lately awakened and brought to know Christ and others who were seeking salvation.

Sunday 27 (26)—I preached in the courthouse to about 300 blacks and whites. I had great freedom in opening up and illustrating on the fallen and on the talents. (Matt. 25:15). In every particular manner, the poor _____ were affected. Some of the rulers were out, there being a very sudden death in the neighborhood, and a soldier who was taken and died in a few minutes, who seemed to be somewhat concerned. In the evening I had great freedom in lecturing on the parable of the Prodigal Son. We had a very moving time. I can truly say I had a deep sense of the goodness of God as I have had since I left Baltimore. I went to bed happy in my God: but truly I was buffeted by the devil, and in my sleep I awoke distressed. O when shall I be so happy, and so holy, as never in the least degree to feel sin. Lord if it be my privilege never to feel the desires of the flesh give me no rest until I obtain the blessing. I want to be pure. This morning I have set a resolution to fast and pray. O God, wash my body in pure _____ and from all my idols do thou cleanse me. O that my garments more and more may be _____ in the flesh.

Monday, August 28 (27) 1781—This morning I spent in retirement, I had freedom in the evening to preach to a small audience. Very little true religion here.

Tuesday 29 (28)—I am this morning exceeding tormented with a pain in the tooth. My mind is very much discomposed. I rode eight miles farther in Carolina and held forth to about a hundred souls, the greater part of which were very ignorant of the plan of salvation. There are about 12 in the class, all but two strangers to the pardoning love of God. I exhorted them to seek Christ. I had a conversation with a _____ Antinomian, I hope in some degree God clutched at his heart—without any invitation, about 30 came where I lodged. I had great freedom, showing them the way to heaven: many in tears—I had my hand this evening on an old book, for which I have a reason to believe God; with happiness I read in it till about 11 o'clock. I never received more light in God's word for this length of time: my dear Master gave me refreshing sleep.

Wednesday 30 (29)—With the assistance of God I am determined to be more faithful than ever: I am with grace of God, this night set out on a journey over Chowan River: I am _____ into a new place, where I have an invitation. Lord give me good speed— I rode eight miles, and came to a small creek, where I had to go near two miles upon a—ridge through a dismal swamp: after crossing the ferry I shortly got to my appointment where a crowded audience came together, I preached with great freedom; the

Colonel of the county said he would pray join these people, for he never heard the doctrine, it was what he was always aiming at but didn't know how to come at it: there was a general meeting among the people—I gave out to lecture by candlelight, I expect the best part of a hundred came together, the Lord wonderfully broke in upon the people. Several poor sinners cried out for mercy, there was not many dry eyes in the house. I went to bed happy in my Lord; but Satan tempted me in the morning, so that I am very much distressed: he wanted me to cast away my confidence. I prayed in sweet frequency, all dull and heavy. I rode nine miles to Winton, N.C. courthouse where I had a comfortable opportunity of preaching to about 70 souls: I think I have not preached to so _____ people since I left Baltimore: they behaved exceeding well and I have a reason to hope the words sunk deep in the hearts of people: I had several kind invitations to dine: after dinner I set out on my journey: my _____ Brother Arnol took me to a kind widow's house: I was much refreshed while conversing with her son-in-law who was the son of a doctor. Nature improved will go a great way: Lord show thy frame of love.

September 1, 1781—I praise God for the pleasantest and _____ sleep that I nave met with in a long time. I was preaching the whole night in my sleep, seemingly very happy—I rode about 15 miles to _____ Gregory's where I had a kind invitation, I have a prospect of good here. The woman of the house, Mrs. Gregory, professes faith.

Sunday 2—There is a great burden upon my mind. I went to the place of preaching much tempted, but glory be to God in a short time after I began to preach the cloud burst, and a glorious time I had when the people first came together. They appeared as if they came to see a tragedy. Shortly after I began that lightness seemed to be removed and the whole congregation seemed to be as solemn as death, and mostly in tears, I was sensible of how the power of God was among the people. I gave an evening lecture at Mr. Gregory's; it was a time of solemnity. I had great freedom in describing the new birth. My soul is comforted under a hope that good will be done in the name of Jesus.

Monday, September 3 (1781)—My mind is very comfortable. I rode three miles and preached with freedom, but not attended with that divine energy.

Tuesday, September 4—This morning I find a degree of comfort: by appointment I am to preach in the church. About 130 came and I had much freedom to preach from these words, "Simon, Son of Jonah, lovest thou me"—John 21:17. I did not hear of one of the whole congregation but what thought well of the doctrine. A man and his wife, who was formerly the clerk of the church and great persecutors, was convinced last Sunday: gave me an invitation home with them where I was very kindly used:

Wednesday 5—They both attended me eight miles preaching, where they seemed much convinced especially in class meeting, we had a previous meeting I trust _____ went home with sorrowful hearts. I think my resolution is still strong to double my diligence, this evening I find my soul much refreshed. I'm much troubled with a wandering mind. I feel I do not love God as I should.

Thursday 6—This morning I seem heavy and dull, private prayer rather seems a cross to me: I desire to have a greater delight in retirement. When shall I be dead to this world. I rode 12 miles and preached to a small company of penitents: O Lord comfort _____. Before I went to bed my mind was refreshed but was a great part of the night troubled with worldly dreams.

Friday 7—I preached to a company of poor but I trust pious souls. I hope it was good for the people that they came together.

Saturday 8—I'm much distressed; this morning there is some wanting.

Sunday 9—My mind seems much clouded, I had a company of hard hearts to preach to, in the evening I preached, had very little comfort; the hearts and minds of the people seemed to be filled with time so that there is but little room for the gospel.

Monday 10—I find my mind much distressed, I have a spirit of sympathy for our dear friends, who for conscience sake cannot join in the war—several they have beat, I fear they have caused some to blaspheme—Glory be to God others stand fast, and are determined to go to the stake if called there onto. They have the promise of God, I will not leave you, etc. I had an opportunity of preaching a funeral sermon over one of our friends, who I trust died in the faith. I visited one of the friends who was very poorly, just came from the camps of the ungodly, from under guard. He seems to be much given ———.

Tuesday 11—I'm discouraged on account of the blindness of the people.

Wednesday 12—I think this is a day of great profit to my soul.

Thursday 13—Glory unto God I'm much comforted under the expectation of living nearer to God.

Friday 14—Lord be praised, for a precious day to my own, and get the souls of others we had a very happy time whilst breaking bread in token of love.

Saturday 13—I was refreshed whilst, answering a letter to a brother in distress.

Sunday 14—I was much dejected this morning and for several moments after I began to preach, but Glory to God the cloud broke and we had a precious time, my soul feels humble this evening, and I find freedom to reprove sin.

Monday 15—I'm sweetly drawn out in prayer and waking I had a very comfortable time in preaching to a small audience. I was enabled to lay down the narrowness of the way—I now have a comfortable hope I advanced in the divine life.

Tuesday 12—I am to preach at a new place. My audience was made up of officers and their wives. I think there was good impressions made upon their minds; I had an invitation to preach in the church.

Wednesday 19—I preached to a crowded audience. I hope great good will be done in this neighborhood.

Thursday 20—With great freedom I preached and gave a love feast, and a precious meeting we had, I went home with old Mrs. Gibson who has been lately awakened, a very sensible old lady.

Friday 21—I preached at a new place, with a degree of sweetness and the ——— to the old lady's.

Saturday 22—Whilst I was preaching the power of God was amongst the people. This is a night of affliction, my soul has ———.

Sunday 23—I had an opportunity of preaching in the Courthouse with great freedom ——— the Colonel of the Countys heart to so much tendered, he gave me a loving invitation.

Monday 24—I preached in a church near the Colonels to about 150. Many tears was shed. I dined at Major Baker's and lodged at the Colonel's.

Tuesday 25—I set out in my journey over Chowan River, (N.C.) and had an opportunity of hearing Brother King.

Wednesday, September 26, (25) 1781—I spent in retirement, I praise God for sweetness of mind.

Thursday 27 (26)—I preached to a well behaved audience in the Courthouse, great attention was paid to the word—the next day I held forth at Mr. Hill's. I bless and praise God for his goodness, I trust several are brought to cry for mercy, I have a hope the gospel will spread through these parts.

Sunday 30 (29)—I preached two sermons in Buckhorn Church and one in a private house with great freedom. The people are in some measure awakened in this ——— my mind is slowly sweetly drawn out to love God.

Monday 31 (October 1, 1781)—I had great freedom in preaching two sermons.

Tuesday, October 1, (2) 1781—This is a precious time to my soul, I preached to about 100, about 20 of which were Christians, and I hope prayerfully going in the ways of God.

Wednesday 3 (4)—I preached in a penitent family with much freedom.

Thursday 4 (3)—It was the same.

Friday 5 (4)—I preached and held a love feast; it was a time of comfort.

Saturday 6 (5)—was a day of distress.

Sunday 7 (8)—I had much sweetness in the morning, and in the evening I had a very grand audience who gave good attention. This night in sleep I was wonderfully tryed.

Monday 8 (7)—I preached among my old friends, where I had a very large audience.

Tuesday 9 (8)—I preached a sermon for Brother Bonham. I had a time of refreshment, it is two or three months since I saw these people before, I rejoice to see them going on in the way.

Wednesday 10 (9)—The unexpected news of the death of Brother Barker came to my ears: about two months ago I gave him a lecture to make trial of his gifts. Shortly after this he was taken as a six month soldier, and was carried away, the cross was too great for his grace and higher demand in his place and came back, and was taken sick immediately and died. This portion of scripture came into my mind, "He that seeks to save his life shall lose it:" He was visited by the friends and I understood was in distress, but some day before he died the Lord gave him a sense of power, and he sent for Brother _____ to rejoice with him: and he had a hope God received his soul—I preached his funeral to a crowded audience from the 25th chapter of Matthew, verses 14 and 15. I bless God for much freedom. At the grave we had a precious time _____.

Thursday 10 (11)—I set out on my way to Nancy Munn, (Nansemond, Va.). I travelled till near sunset. I saw it was out of my power to go to the place I intended, I _____ to seek some place to lodge, I came to a widow's house, she was not willing to entertain a stranger. I went a little farther, and called in at an old man's house, he told me he would entertain me if he had not made so short a crop of corn. I went several miles farther, the man told me he had but just lodging for his family: by this time with some difficulty, I got to the house, they were afraid to entertain a stranger, though they told me where they thought I could get lodging—I perceived everyone was freer with his neighbor's house than his own—however I went, and was kindly entertained, and had a reason to hope the woman loved and feared God.

Friday 11 (12) —I got to preaching in due time, and had a precious meeting.

Saturday the 12th (13)—I had a good time.

Sunday 13 (14)—I held forth near two homes with a great happiness—met the class and appointed to keep next day as a fast.

Monday 14 (15)—I felt myself humble this morning.

Tuesday 15 (16)—I travelled several miles, and preached in Cypress Church (Nansemond Co., Va.) with great freedom.

Wednesday 16 (17)—I preached a funeral to a crowded audience. I believe my dear Master was among people. I held forth by candlelight with great freedom.

Thursday 17 (18)—Blest be God for a glorious time in the preaching and meeting Class—in the evening I went home with an old gentlewoman who is under deep distress.

Friday 18 (19)—My dear Master was with me. In the evening I held forth in the old widow's. The black people are much engaged.

Saturday 19 (20)—This is a day of power.

Sunday morning and evening I preached my farewell sermon, I had two large congregations with rich and poor.

Monday 21 (22)—was a glorious day.

Tuesday 22 (23)—I preached to _____ congregation—lively happy souls.

Wednesday 23 (24)—I preached through Winton County and preached two sermons in the courthouse with great freedom. Next day I travelled, I crossed Hill Ferry and after preaching to a small audience in the church I went to my good friend Gregory's, who was greatly effected, I prayed with them and crossed the ferry to be nearer Nancemond where I had to attend a Quarterly Meeting Friday the 25th (26). I rode about 40 miles to a funeral over an open grave, rode four miles and held a night watch. I am very weary, Quarterly Meeting began next day. Glory be to God we had much of his power—I have been in this part about two months, I bless God, I have not labored in vain. About ten good houses has been opened for preaching, and I trust many hearts have received Jesus both rich and poor. I am humbled in the dust before God, I am poor be thou my riches—I am ignorant. I want a thankful heart, Amen, Lord Jesus bless me.

Monday, October 24, (29) 1781—After Quarterly Meeting I sat out on my journey to Sussex, I preached after riding near 30 miles to a small but pious congregation with great liberty.

Tuesday 29 (30)—I attended Quarterly Meeting in Sussex. We had a sermon and two exhorters. I had great satisfaction in our meeting of private business. Especially whilst examining into the conduct of local preachers, and exhorters is when I found them all unspotted from the world.

Wednesday 30 (31)—I trust I feel as _____ sense of the goodness of God; our love feast began at 9 o clock, Blest be God, of a truth it was a feast of love. Many pounds was collected for the support of one who was a widow in need, they that give to the poor lend to the Lord. After the love feast I preached with great freedom, after two of my brethren spoke, we broke up praising God.

Thursday, November 1 (October 31) (1781)—I set out on my journey to Brunswick. Several, both preachers and people went with me. On my way after riding about 20 miles I preached to about 100 souls at Squire Jone's.

From _____ went forth to _____. I had much freedom in pointing out the sewer, the seed and the ground. After dinner had two of my brethren accompany me to Colonel Gibbin's, where are many precious souls.

Friday 2 (1) (1781)—I preached in Mr. Malry's Chapel. It being a rainy morning my congregation was small. I rode to a kind old friends where we was kindly entertained. I was very weary, but my Lord refreshed my soul. I am now about 10 miles to Brunswick Quarterly Meeting.

Saturday 3 (2)—Four of us set out to meeting by appointment. The preachers are to meet here to change, after I got to the chapel I received a letter from my old friend Brother Asbury, wherein he informed me that he could not come down this winter, and desired me to stand in his place. My own charge was very great—Lord give me grace and wisdom for so great a task—several of my brethren spoke, about ten of us went to a kind friends where we stationed the preachers, Blest be God, we laid at each others feet and at the feet of Jesus, all contented with his station. I am to go through five or six of the circuits, Lord keep me at thy feet.

Sunday 4 (3)—Blest be God at 9 o'clock we had a glorious feast of love—at 12 o'clock our public meeting began. I had as much freedom to preach as ever in my life. Psalm 40:12, 13 walk about Zion and so forth. Our Master was at the head, I think in general we had as good a meeting as ever I saw in Virginia.

Monday 5 (4)—I set out to go through Amela (or Amelia). In my way I preached at S. Y. Chapel, among my old friends. It is as near four years since I preached to these people. Some have turned aside: Blest be God for keeping their faces heavenward. My soul rejoices to see their faces.

Tuesday 6 (5)—I visited my dear old friend O. M. I trust the old people are going on in their journey. I hear with sorrow one of my old friends has turned aside.

Wednesday 7 (6)—I preached with freedom at W's Chapel. God enable me to preach very close, here is a good people; but I fear many others are on the sand. I visited my dear friend, and brother _____ Drumgoole who has been at the very point of death who is now recovering.

Thursday 8 (7)—I held forth with freedom to a crowded audience. I hope my dear Lord and Master was in the midst.

Friday 9 (8)—We rode near 20 miles, the day being cold. We had but about 60 hearers at W. O. Chapel. Here are Christians deep in experience.

Saturday—Amelia, Va. Quarterly Meeting began, here I had my hands full. Several of the local preachers had been breaking the rules—I mean administering the ordinances. I took them aside and told them plainly if they would not come under discipline they could not be of us. My greatest trial was from I. J. a traveling preacher who had gone out of the line of the gospel. His accusers was brought face to face; I did not know whether to send him to a circuit or not, he acknowledged his fault, we thought he might be dropped another quarter.

Sunday, November 11 (*10*)—This being a wet day few came out, we omitted the love feast, I preached to about a hundred with great liberty, then there was great rejoicing.

Monday 12 (*11*) *and Tuesday 13* (*12*)—I set apart for retirement. I commonly meet with the greatest trials at such times but blest be God he is with me.

Wednesday 14 (*13*)—I continued in retirement.

Thursday 15 (*14*)—I preached to a very pious audience. These people have been joined together five years and come as I understand there has not been one _____ so as to hinder their union.

Friday 16 (*17*)—This day I felt a great unwillingness to preach, but blest be God, my soul was refreshed.

Saturday 17 (*16*)—This is a day set apart for private, for retirement; I find myself much troubled with drowsiness and dryness in my private devotion. This evening I was much refreshed whilst conversing with a pious young woman who was liberated, as she was coming from school, when very young, and brought to Carolina and sold, who of late has fell in with people called Methodists. This brought to my mind that part of God's word where Joseph was sold, as God provided his friend, so he has this young woman's. I have often covenanted with my God, but O, my short comings; they are so many, I am ashamed before my God to think how little way I have got in my journey. O! that I have grace to spend the third part of my time in sweet reading, writing, praying, and meditating. Then I should have nine hours for publick, and seven for my bed. O God, enable me to be more given up to this. There has, in months that pass, a practice stole upon me—(the use of tobacco). I find it to be a burden to my mind. With the grace of God from this time I am determined to make an oblation of it. I bless and praise God for giving me mind drawn out in love to him, and all mankind. This evening as yet I find my soul prospering before God.

Sunday 18 (*17*)—This morning I feel a tender heart. I preached to a crowded audience with liberty. I was exceeding exercised before and after preaching—we had a comfortable time whilst breaking bread together. The wicked are prejudiced against the gospel.

Monday 19 (*18*)—I had a tedious journey, but few to preach to, we had a comfortable time.

Tuesday 20 (*19*)—I rode many miles, at a cold home to preach in, cold hearts to preach to and my own soul distressed, on account of the unhappy ones among them. I preached my first and I fear my last sermon to them: mostly being inclinable to a disunison from Methodism. In the last of my sermon I had freedom in showing the devices of the devil, and also the danger, and consequence of backsliding from the ways of God.

Wednesday 21 (*20*)—I rode to Brother Finney's—had a degree of freedom in opening, and explaining some parts of the Revelation. We had much comfort in conversation this evening. I trust the family will remember this night.

Thursday 22 (*21*)—The past night I was drawn out in contemplating on the sacred word, till near midnight after I went to bed, so that I overslept myself this morning—being somewhat elated, and losing myself, I was much distressed—though Glory be to God, he paid me for my trouble. With liberty I preached morning and evening. I feel we had a greater designation of the word of God. This evening I got to the house of a dear friend and _____ had a sweet time.

Saturday 24 (*23*)—I am sensible of my shortcomings. Lord give me engagedness in thy ways.

Sunday 25 (*24*)—Being a very wet day, there was but about 100 attended preaching. The power of God was amonst the people.

Monday, November 26 (*25*)—I travelled through Brunswick circuit (Va.). On my way I preached to a small audience out of the Rev. 15:2. I saw as it were a sea of glass mingled with fire, etc. God's word for many reasons may be compared to a sea of glass, is mixed with love and terror. I had freedom in the family whilst speaking of the impropriety of slavery, and was well pleased to hear a young gentleman, strenously insist on the injustice of it.

Tuesday 27, (*26*) *November 1781*—I had great freedom to preach from "Feed My Sheep"—John 21:17. There is some confusion in the class, occasioned by the Baptists.

Wednesday 28 (27)—I had a tedious ride through cold rain and had but four hearers besides the family.

Thursday, November 29 (28)—I rode through Mecklenburg, Va. circuit and I preached at Quarterly Conference. It is about four years since I was in these parts, it grieves me to hear of many who run wild, that have turned into open sin. Lord Jesus reclaim poor backsliders.

Friday 30 (29)—My soul is rejoiced to see the faces of my dear friends (who meet at B. B.)

Saturday, December 1, (November 30) 1781—This is the day set apart as a day of fasting. Blest be God for humbling my soul before him.

Sunday 2 (1) (December 1781)—I bless God for sweetness in my soul. I rode to Preaching, many came out to hear, I was much comforted, whilst reading the morning service (the people mostly were of the church) prejudice was much taken away, so that they heard with great attention (in this parish the minister has deserted, and turned to the Presbyterians). There is much disputing about religion, and a very little of it in reality in the parish. Glory to God I think this day his word was attended with power, few dry eyes were left. This evening was spent greatly to my satisfaction in a family against slave keeping. Parents and children going hand in hand to do their Savior's will. O what a precious thing is this. Lord raise up thousands such families as this.

Monday, December 3 (2), 1781—My soul is as much distressed as the weather is very cold and in a house where they keep a parcel of naked slaves.

Tuesday 4 (3)—I am still distressed being confined to the said family by reason of snowy weather. A few neighbors came together, and I was set at liberty to speak freely of the cruel usage of slaves.

Wednesday 5 (4)—I rode many miles, they not having knowledge of my coming. I gave an exhortation on the _____ of holiness.

Thursday 6 (5)—I spent the day retired.

Friday 7 (6) —I preached on charity and the end of the law, to a company of holy, happy souls. I think it was good for me to be among this people, especially with the man of the house, being a man of great faith, love and zeal.

Saturday 8 (7)—I had the company of Edward Wood, a young gentleman (who was a captain lately brought to know God, whom I expect will be a bright light—a few things relating to his experiences as follows viz: About eight years ago he was brought under conviction, had some tender feelings, and received the Lord's Supper at the hands of Reverend Mr. McRoberts—about six years ago he went as an officer in the army. About six months ago he returned. The Lord laid to his convincing power; the devil persuaded him his day of peace was past, so that he was driven out of his head under despair. Several of our preachers, and private friends visited him from time to time (after several weeks)—one night about midnight, there was a great struggle in his soul to God for mercy: He heard as it were the words, "Come unto me all ye that labor etc." with several other portions of scripture, one after the other imparting the same, in an instant he was restored; his _____ dropped off, and peace and joy flowed into his soul. After this "The Saints Rest" was brought into his hand, he was much comforted in reading it; shortly after this he got again under doubts and fears. One evening as he was contemplating in the field, with great distress, this portion of God's word came to him when our Lord spoke to unbelieving Thomas. In an instant he saw the love of God as it were, great streams poured into his soul, so that his doubts and fears in a moment vanished, and said he, "I have been happy in God ever since." Sometimes it appears as if I am all spirit; I cannot doubt—shortly after he joined in Society—I think he is a happy, saint-like young man—the reason of my giving these few lines is because I think the Lord intended him for a light in his church. "O," said he, "I often feel the blood of Jesus as great drops washing my soul." My spirit was refreshed with him.

Sunday, December 9, (8) 1781—It being a very wet day I kept my room all day, and I hope it was a day of profit to my soul.

Monday was a day of trouble.

Tuesday 11 (10)—Was a day of distress, few came out, the people are most prejudiced on account of the disorderly walk of S. B. a young exhorter.

Wednesday 12 (11)—The clouds broke, I have not had a greater time since I left Sussex, Va.—in this family my mind was much refreshed.

Thursday 13 (12)—was a sweet day to my soul, I preached with great freedom, next day was spent in refreshment like the evening, then I had a great light and liberty in preaching a watch night sermon.

Saturday 15 (14)—I rode to Colonel Bedford's (Charlotte Co., Va.) where I had great liberty in opening up and illustrating on the talents—I am not sensible, I live beneath my privilege—O God wash my soul and made me holy.

Sunday 16 (15)—Glory be to God, my soul is refreshed, I rode to meeting—this neighborhood seems to be full of Antinomian and Calvinist—. Shortly after I came into the room, a friend came to me and told me that he thought people in the neighborhood thought Mr. Wesley and his preachers built altogether upon works: begged of me to preach on the subject. Immediately a portion of God's word was handed to me which was: "But wilt thou know, o vain man, that faith is dead without works." James 2:20. I showed a true gospel faith with the necessity of its being productive of God; I endeavored to vindicate for justification. (1) Infant—(2) By family—(3) By works before the world—(4) By works at the day of judgment—Glory be to God, it was a day of power. Christ encourages! (they) hung down their heads, confounded. God's work seemed to be all laid open to me, I can truly say the spirit of God was upon me.

December 1781, Monday 17 (16)—I had a tedious ride near 20 miles, but blest be God he gave my soul his holy spirit, and in refreshing the people. I have got among my old friends, but many have turned aside since I was in these parts which is about four years and three months: but blest be God for a few who are faithful.

Tuesday 18 (17)—Part of this day I spent in writing a good man's will, as he was going a distance from home, when I came to a division among the negroes, at first I thought I could not pen it: I used my influence in showing him the injustice of slave keeping, he went aside to consult his wife and continued near an hour, I was exceeding happy whilst praying to the Lord to open his eyes to strip him of self: he returned (self was too strong) and told me he did not see it his duty. Oh when shall we be entirely clear of this man, self, that sticks so close to us, Lord give us the perfect knowledge of our own hearts.

Wednesday 19 (18)—After receiving some refreshment both for soul and body I set out a journey of about 300 miles to visit the Societies in Pittsylvania. My dear old friend accompanied me to the river, I crossed it in safety and in due time I got to Parishes Circuit my first appointment, where was the chapel near full of poor though I trust honest hearted souls. I had much freedom in opening and illustrating on talents (Matt. 25:14, 15). My spirit was refreshed yet sorrowful, whilst conversing with one whom I was acquainted with four or five years ago, who was then a very pious soul but as of late with Peter, denied his Lord. She went away weeping, Lord reclaim backsliders—I was rejoiced to meet my good friend Brother White.

Thursday 20 (19)—Brother White intends to travel with me 'til Quarterly Meeting. We set out about sunrise, rode 20 miles and arrived to Brother Baker's where the people was visiting. I had great freedom in preaching on charity and the end of the law. (Timothy 1:5).

Friday 21 (20)—was a day of exercise, I find blest be to God it is good for me.

Saturday 22 (21)—We set out on our journey in the rain, we got as far as an old Baptist preacher, Mr. Harris, he loves God. Oh what a precious thing it is to feel the love of Jesus.

Sunday 23 (22)—Had an opportunity of preaching to many of the old friends that moved from the north.

Monday 24 (23)—I set out on my journey.

Tuesday 25 (?)—I missed my way, and was disappointed in preaching my Christmas sermon. My mind was much exercised.

Wednesday 26 (?)—I rode 30 or 40 miles. I never was in such a place before. The people in general live poor and I fear lazy.

Thursday 27 (26)—I preached to a crowded audience with much freedom. My dear master sent home his word with freedom.

Friday 28 (27)—My soul is refreshed, I rode to Meeting, and blest be God we had a sweet time, these are a poor but loving people. My soul was much refreshed in the family.

Saturday 29—I have been exceedingly exercised about returning back, but I think the further I go the more I am encouraged. I preached this day to a crowded audience. I believe many will remember it through all eternity. Glory be to God, I felt the power of our Father.

Sunday 30—I preached in Gilford Circuit, Va. Some of the professors of religion in these parts know very little of the substance, and as little _____, I showed them various ways in which we may grieve the good spirit and the consequence.

Monday 31—I had much freedom and exhorting about 30 souls—as I lost my Bible my mind was much disturbed.

Tuesday, January 1, 1782—I had freedom in preaching my first sermon in the New Year; this day I have covenanted with God to live nearer to him than ever. Lord carry on this work in my soul.

Wednesday 2—I preached to a crowded audience with great freedom.

Friday 4—I was refreshed in preaching to my old friends who moved from the north. Blest be God I hope their faces are Zionward.

Saturday our Quarterly Meeting began. I had freedom in preaching.

Sunday 6—The divine presence was with us in our love feast. I preached the first sermon, the power of God's sweetened word—I took my leave of preachers and people, and was accompanied 20 miles on my way by Brother Sutton, one of my old Maryland friends. Next day I was to preach his departed companion's funeral. I lodged this night in an old Antinomian's, by opinion, I know not what he was in practice. His conversation much disturbed my mind being so repugnant to the word of God.

Monday 7—We rode near 30 miles. Blest be God we had a glorious time. Two Baptist ministers was present. I was accompanied after preaching by several friends to Mr. Harris's, a Baptist minister, it was 8 o'clock when I got there. Near 40 souls expecting me was waiting to hear the word and a blessed time we had.

Tuesday 8—My soul is much refreshed and the conversation I had with the old gentleman is very agreeable. He is not in the general spirit of his persuasion. I rode 20 miles to Burches Creek Church, where I had a large audience. _____ I had much freedom, people behaved very well, the word had weight upon their minds. This evening I lodged at a lawyer's. He seemed very desirous, his wife is a precious woman and his sister, and her sister's little daughter, who is about 10 years of age. _____ seems to be very happy in the Lord. I had liberty in lecturing to about 20 this evening. I blest God for refreshing my soul in this family.

Wednesday 9—The lawyer accompanied me to Boyd's Church, (Halifax Co., Va.) on Dan-River. Mr. Thomas was one of my hearers. There was more people than I expected. I hope good will be done in these parts. I rode 10 miles to preach by candlelight. O how I was distressed what with the fatigue of body and Satan's temptation but Glory be to God I had not been speaking long before the cloud broke, and I was wonderfully strengthened in body and soul, Glory be to God I did not spend this day for naught. O God give me fortitude.

Thursday, January 10, 1782—I rode seven miles and preached with great freedom. After preaching I rode near 20 miles, and preached. I think I was never much more outdone, what with the fatigue, and Satan's powerful temptations.

Friday 11—My mind is refreshed in this loving family, I was accompanied by the friends to Quarterly Meeting. I rode 15 miles and preached, after sermon we rode 15 more, it was dark when we got to our journey's end. Glory be to God he bears me up under my trials, I care not what I suffer so I can win souls and get safe to heaven; after riding 150 miles and preaching 8 or 10 sermons in five days, I find myself weary. Lord strengthen me.

Saturday 12—Our Quarterly Meeting began, I preached with light but little sweetness.

Sunday 13—Our love feast began at 10 o'clock, continued two hours and a powerful time was had. I began to preach at 12 o'clock, Glory be to God his power was displayed, I think if ever I felt the power of God whilst speaking with satisfaction. I heard two exhortations. I trust we parted triumphing in the faith.

Monday 14—I preached a funeral on my way to Roan-oak (Roanoke, Va.) Quarterly Meeting. I had great sweetness. At night I preached with much freedom upon growing in grace; these are poor but happy souls.

Tuesday 15—This is an exceeding cold day. A cold house and a cold class.

Wednesday 16—I labored almost in _____, I had sweet communion with this family.

Thursday 17—I had freedom to exhort about 20. I rode about 10 miles and preached by candlelight—it is about four years since I left this part of the circuit. I find religion very drooping. My old friends being glad to see me and blest be God for a few names.

Friday 18—By appointment I am to preach at Eslings Quarterly Meeting where I was formally threatened to be put in jail, the rage of Satan is not yet over; a few days ago one of his children set out for the house so I was obliged to preach in a private house and a blest meeting was had. I had been travelling and preaching day and night for a considerable time: having had but little time for reading, and very seldom a private _____: Blest be God this night my room is sweet to me and Glory be to God in the name of my dear Master I think he is precious to my soul.

Saturday 19—This morning I find my mind refreshed, at 9 o'clock I set out to Quarterly Meeting. I preached at the tabernacle with great freedom to my old friends.

Sunday 20—We had a comfortable love feast and at 10 o'clock I preached with freedom. At 1 o'clock I heard a sermon and an exhortation with satisfaction. We had a crowded audience and I hope good was done, I lodged at my old friend Colonel Taylor's, and rejoiced to find him and family in the _____ to have _____.

Monday 21—I preached about 15 miles off, I was so drawn out, I did not know when to leave off. Many hearts too was softened, I rode three miles and preached to a small audience with freedom.

Tuesday, January 22, 1782—O my God what will become of many of our friends. Some of them seem to be in a fighting and slave keeping spirit. This day I preached to a crowded audience with happiness in my soul and hope good was done.

Wednesday, January 23, 1782—I preached out of the _____ with great freedom.

Thursday 24—My soul is much drawn out in preaching to my old Carolina friends, after preaching we rode 10 miles and had a comfortable Watch Night.

Saturday Quarterly Meeting began at Roan-Oak (Roanoke, Va.) Chapel. I showed the majesty of living a holy life inwardly and outwardly.

Sunday 26 (27)—I characterized the righteous and the wicked and discoursed between them. Malachi 3:18.

Monday and Tuesday being troubled with a toothache I had it drawn. I unexpectedly met my old friend Brother Asbury, (Brother A.) who requested me to travel through the Circuits over the James River as there is like to be great division among the brethren. I promised so to do after supplying a few _____ appointments.

Wednesday 30—I set out to Sussex.

Thursday 31—With great freedom I preached a funeral showing the majesty of being in readiness for the solemn hour of death.

Saturday and Sunday (February 2, 3, 1782)—I attended Quarterly Meeting, it being wet weather we had but few hearers, but Glory be to God he was with us.

Monday I set out to _____ Circuit, rode 20 miles and preached to a solemn and deep people with great freedom of soul; God of a truth is among this people. The next day I rode 20 miles and described the faith and the affliction of God's people and Moses' wise choice (Hebrews 11:24, 25). I rode five miles and preached by candlelight to a crowded audience. Glory be to God it was a time of solemnity. Many will remember it.

Wednesday, February 6, 1782—I described what we understand by the works of the devil to the extent of Christ being manifested (2nd John 3-8). The meeting was made up of what is called the better sort. Glory be to God I hope he has not sent me a warfare at my own charge—the next day I travelled through and preached in Winton where I met with a degree of interruption by a Bland, I may say, a wolf in sheep's clothing. Blest be God he comforts my soul by making fresh discoveries of his infinite goodness to me.

Friday 8—I travelled through Gates County.

Saturday 9—I preached with great freedom at Mrs. Gibson's to a crowded audience. We had a comfortable time.

Sunday 10—I find my mind much staid on my dear Lord, I preached to as many as could crowd in Cyprus Church, the people generally behaved very well and gave great attention.

Monday 11—I travelled through Nansey Mun (Nansemond, Va.) and countries with great freedom preached two sermons.

Tuesday 12—I travelled 35 miles and held a Watch Night. Next day I preached with freedom at Ellis' Chapel (Sussex Co., Va.).

Thursday 14—With great freedom I opened the Nature of Justification by Faith to a Christless audience. I blest God I think I did not labor in vain. I find myself very weary. A friend was kind enough to lend me his carriage.

Friday 15—I set out through Sussex Circuit, preached on my way at Brother P's. He rode with me _____, where we spent two or three hours with many of our friends watching and praying. Glory be to God this has been a precious day to my soul.

Saturday—Jesus is sweet to my soul. I preached at my old friend Smith's with great freedom.

Sunday 17—In the morning I preached at B. Chapel and in the evening at P. Burg— Glory to God for humbling me under a sense of his goodness and my unworthiness. I tarried the next day and preached in the evening. We had a powerful time—the next day I rode 10 miles and preached on evil speaking with the consequence after I met the Class I moved to praise God for his goodness. Sometime before there had been a great disputing in the Class. I hope my Lord united their hearts together.

Wednesday 20—I preached and examined about 25, I hope humble souls, and rejoiced to hear of others. Rode six miles and preached a Watch Night sermon.

Thursday 21—This morning I spent in reading a piece in vindication of infant baptism—rode 12 miles, preached with great sweetness—rode six miles and held forth at night to a crowded audience. Glory to God he gave me a weeping spirit, I have no doubt that good was done.

Friday 22—Rode two miles and explained (to about 100 souls) the Apostle's Doctrine, etc.—Acts 2:42. After breaking bread with about 40 and rejoiced together in the hope of eating bread in heaven I went on my journey rejoicing.

Sunday 24—I rode to Ellis' Chapel Preaching House and held forth with freedom. I bless God for a sense of his goodness.

Monday 25—I had a tedious day.

Thursday 28—I bless God for a sweet time—all the week was spent very comfortable.

Sunday, March 3 (1782)—I had great freedom in preaching and think we had a powerful love feast.

Monday I went on my way and preached to a gospel hardened set.

Tuesday 5—I was greatly exercised though my mind was much clouded, but blest be God the cloud broke and he gave me great freedom to preach.

Wednesday 6—Was a sweet time to every soul present that knew God.

Thursday was a time of power. I'm sensible God was with us.

Friday 8—I hope the hearts of Christians was searched.

Saturday 9—I had a large audience and hardened sinners trembled.

Sunday 10—I showed the analogy between the awakened and unwakened sinners and the necessity of their being convinced and brought to Jesus. In the evening I showed the necessity of walking with God. I am now on my way over the James River to visit Hanover and Fluvana Circuits (Va.).

Monday 11—I got as far as Mr. Garrats.

Tuesday to White Oak.

Wednesday 13—to Brother Finney's.

Thursday 14—to Grangers.

Friday 15—I crossed the James River.

Saturday 16—Preached at B. E. Church. Here is much confusion.

Sunday 17—I preached at Forks Church to several hundred I think with much liberty, as ever I did in my life. I do not remember I saw a smile on one countenance.

Monday 18—I had very poor encouragement.

Tuesday 19—I met with good people at Dr. Hopkins.

Wednesday 20—Travelled all day.

Thursday 21—Preached and gave a love feast to a well behaved people.

Friday 22—Glory be to God my soul was refreshed.

Saturday 23—My Lord was with me and blest people. I blest God there was not so much confusion as I expected, this evening I met my brother Richard Garrettson.

(Asbury gave Richard Garrettson a license to preach on April 14, 1779. Richard continued until retirement from the traveling ministry in 1783.)

132.   *Sunday, March 24, 1782*—Quarterly meeting began. Glory be to God I have not saw many such two days since I came to Virginia.

Tuesday 26—I had great freedom in preaching to an audience of what is called the better sort.

Wednesday evening by candlelight I held forth to a crowded audience.

Thursday 28—I had a day of rest and preached in the evening by candlelight. We had a time of power. I had a very tedious journey to Hanover.

Sunday 31 (March)—In the morning I preached in the Presbyterian Church and had a Watch Night Service in the evening at Brother Grangers. I know of no other good being done and prejudice removed from the minds of the people in general.

Monday, April 1, 1782—I rode near 40 miles and preached with a degree of freedom.

Tuesday 2—We had a blessed time, I did not know when to give over. I expect I preached three hours and left the people in tears hungering after more.

Wednesday 3—I rode eight miles and preached at 12 o'clock and in the evening in the same room to more than double the number. I blest God for this day. His power was greatly displayed. Several sinners were concerned and God _____.

Thursday 4—I was sent for by one that was brought under distress the day before. She had a company collected by 8 o'clock. I held forth to them and rode 30 miles and preached at 5 o'clock. Glory to God for his goodness I have not felt so much of the divine presence for many months. I fear in these parts the annababtists are enemies to our great Master's cause: A house built with deceit cannot stand.

Friday 5—When I first set out from Ground Squirrel I had a sensible manifestation of the love of God and witness, my journey was of the almighty. This day my dearest Lord displayed his almighty power, I was in a _____ to cry aloud. I think we had a glorious Class Meeting. Brother Devrieler met me as if to continue with me for several days. Our spirits are refreshed together—in this class they have lost their leader who is one of the General Stewards: the baptists has poisoned his mind with their doctrine, and into the water he has gone and out of Society we have turned him. I fear this sect has lost the power of religion and is after a party, this their persecuting spirit demonstrates. I mean those of them in this part of the country.

Saturday 6—I find my mind wandering and am under grevious temptations, I rode to my appointment, a serious audience came together, I now speak in the presence of the great Jehovah. I have not seen or felt so powerful a solemn occasion for many months. I can truly say it appears as if the house were filled with the glory of God. Great freedom I had and preached on the necessity of holiness.

Sunday, April 5, 1782—I preached in the Old Church—there was such a crying that I was once obliged to stop preaching; I expect several hundred was melted into tenderness, yea, saint and sinner wept much. In the evening about 100 attended church. The power of God came down as to exceed as possible Saturday's meeting at the same good old man's house, Brother Stedman. As he told me he prophecied of my coming into this county, long before I came; I blest and praised God that ever I set foot in this King and Queen's County, I cannot leave the people yet, but have consented to stay among the people all this week.

Monday 6—I had freedom (1) in describing the law (2) in showing how we may use it unlawfully (3) the use of it. I praised God for light and liberty, 2nd Timothy. I find my mind sweetly drawn out in the service of God with as great desire to do my Master's will as ever.

Tuesday 9—I preached not far from York-River to a crowded audience. When first they came together they seemed very careless, but Glory to God, I had not been preaching long before his power came down among the people. The congregation was mostly made up of poor unawakened sinners: my Lord made bare his almighty arm. There was very few dry eyes left. The general cry was I never heard the gospel in this manner before. I left them and went to Mr. Garrett's and preached a Watch Night sermon. A solemn awe rest upon the people. This day two women walked 20 miles after the gospel.

Wednesday 10—With great freedom I preached a sermon on charity. About 40 of us broke bread together in token of his love and charity, not without a hope of breaking bread in heaven.

Thursday 11—Friday 12—I have set apart as days of retirement. I'm sensible I do not enjoy that close walk with God is what I desire, I want always to feel myself all holy.

Saturday 13—I have an invitation to preach a poor man a sermon who has been bedridden for a long time. On my way my carriage turned over, my horse got much scared, run away and broke the gear so that I was not able to ride any further. I borrowed a horse and saddle, rode to the place and blest be God we had a very comfortable time.

Sunday 14—This day although the baptists had their two meetings on each side, and as many people as the church would hold, and Glory be to God we had a solemn session. Poor sinners in tears—this evening we went as far on our journey as _____ where our horses left us.

Monday 15—About 3 o'clock we got our horses and set out on our journey, it rained very hard, we called in at several places but could not get lodging, at last we called at a home of a doctor where we were kindly treated.

Tuesday 16—In the evening we got down to James River, the wind exceeding high and the river near three miles wide and the boat very bad. Glory be to God he brought us safe over just as the sun was setting. We rode seven miles to a kind friend.

Wednesday 17—We got to Sussex where Conference was held—the badness of the weather prevented the preachers from coming as soon as they ought.

Thursday 18—The preachers was stationed.

Friday 19—The Reverend D. Jarrett preached and administered the sacrament and a blest time it was to many precious souls. Glory be to God for his ordinances. After we had a comfortable love feast with our business being done, we adjourned 'til 3 o'clock 'til the third Tuesday in May in Baltimore Town—some of the preachers went on their circuits and others to attend Baltimore Conference. I went 30 miles on my way.

Sunday 21—Sussex Quarterly Meeting began.

Monday 22—I rode as far as M. Town.

Tuesday I went to Ground Squirrel.

Wednesday 24—I preached with freedom. Rode 15 miles when our horses got away.

Thursday 25—I rode as far as Mr. Walters.

Friday 26—We rode between 30 and 40 miles where we was kindly entertained, next day we got as far as Brother Fornardens.

Sunday 28—I preached. I hope good was done.

Monday 29—I got into Leesburg where the smallpox was very bad. In times past I have been _____ against innoculation; in some measure my doubts are removed.

Tuesday 30—We rode 15 miles. I had great freedom in showing a few pious souls the necessity of growth in grace. Blest be God for his loving kindness in giving me a deep sense of his goodness and my own unworthiness. I rode eight miles to a kind friends, the next day I went to _____ as a favor to Brother Howard. Next day I got into Baltimore Town. The smallpox being very bad I was _____ to go under the doctor's hands and receive it. After some time I consented.

Friday May 3 (1782)—I was innoculated.

Saturday 4—I seem _____.

Sunday 5—I was enabled to preach morning and evening. Glory be to God for _____.

Monday 6—I seemed _____.

Wednesday 8—I was much cast down.

Thursday 9—The physick goes very hard with me.

Friday 10—I'm hardly strong enough to pray in the family.

Friday 17—I think I never endured more in my life, in one week, distress of body and mind. Lord give me grace.

Saturday 18—Brother Asbury and several others of the preachers came to town. I praised God for allowing me to hear a good sermon.

Sunday I praised God (pocks is just out) for giving me strength both morning and evening to attend preaching. I praise and blest God for his goodness this week; my mind is more sweet.

Sunday 26—I was able to appear in publick, I glorify God for it.

Monday 27—I visited my friends.

Tuesday 28—I left town and rode as far as my brother G's. where I stayed 'til Friday the 31st. A little after sunrise I set out and rode about 45 miles to York where I was joyfully received amongst my York friends.

Saturday, June 1 (1782)—I preached with a degree of freedom.

Sunday I held forth at 8 o'clock and 12 o'clock and 4 o'clock with great freedom.

Monday 3—Blest be God we had a very powerful time by candlelight.

Tuesday 4—I rode 45 miles and preached at Kells at seven in the evening.

Wednesday I set out on my journey.

Thursday 6—I spent in taking some bonds.

Friday 7—I got down to the ferry about 4 o'clock. We crossed in about an hour.

Saturday 8—I rode to New-Town.

Sunday 9—I had great freedom in preaching at 10 o'clock and at four I preached at Kent Chapel, a funeral over a daughter of the Rev. Mr. Harris. I blest God for freedom.

OCTOBER 1782

Friday, October 18. I am now about to take my leave of my dear kind A. M. friends. Just as I began to preach in P(otato) Neck, the enemy of souls sent a man to disturb the meeting. He was disappointed. Some lovers of truth bore him off by force. We had a comfortable time.

In the evening we spent some hours in watching for the coming of Christ. I trust He came into many hearts.

Saturday 19. This is a solemn season. I preached a funeral over one who had been a great rake; his pious brother thought he died a pentient. Rich and poor were melted in a flood of tears. After preaching I was powerfully tempted by the enemy. This evening we lodged at Doc(ter) Robertsons, who seem to be very penitent.

Sunday 20. Our horses got away which caused great exercise. However, we got to the chapel by 10 o'clock where we had a cold Love Feast. Blessed be God. In time of preaching he gave us good measure. Here I took my leave of the p(reachers).

Monday 21. Many of our friends set out to Quarterly meeting near the line of Virginia. After riding we got to Squire Downings, a dear child of God. *Tuesday 22.* Next day our meeting began and a powerful time we had.

Wednesday 23. The day following meeting ended. I can truly say to my great satisfaction I have seldom seen such a powerful time from the beginning to the ending. When I first came into these parts, about 8 weeks ago, we had but about 8 in society and the neighbors much prejudiced. Glory be to God. Prejudice is wonderfully rolled away and there are several prosperous classes. O! that the gospel may prosper.

Thursday 24. My brother laborers set out with me to the Sound—rode 40 miles and held a Watchnight.

Saturday 26 and Sunday 27. Our Quarterly Meeting was for Sussex. There was a large concourse of people. Glory be to God for His divine presence. Here I took my leave of my sea-side friends. Many tears were shed. I was reminded of Paul's parting.

I now speak in the fear of God. I have been in these parts about 5 months. When first I came there was only a six weeks circuit. Now blessed be God. There are two comfortable four weeks circuits. With all there has been added about 200 to the number. Who shall have the glory? Lord, grant that the crown may be put on the head of the dear Redeemer. So shall worms of earth lay in the dust.

Monday 28. I set out to Delaware Quarterly meeting. Preached at Blackford.

Tuesday 29. Glory be to God. I have communion with my Saviour, Preached and broke bread together; better bread was broken to our souls.

Wednesday 30. Rode near Salisbury, preached and broke bread, bid my friends farwell and so rode 12 miles and preached a Watchnight sermon.

Thursday 31. The day was very wet. About 200 of my B(road)—Creek friends met me. I spent two or three hours with them, took my leave, and rode 12 miles through the rain and had a comfortable watchnight.

NOVEMBER 1782

Friday, November 1. I was accompanied by about a dozen friends; rode 20 miles and preached near Johnstown to a crowded audience. Blessed be God for an ingathering of souls here. Rode 12 miles where I got a com-

fortable night's refreshment. Glory be to God, for supporting both man
and beast. I am as clear of pain or tir(edness) as if I had been sitting in
a warm room.

Saturday 2. About 20 preachers met. Our meeting ended Sunday evening.
I expect there were not less than a thousand of the friends out to Love
Feast by sun rise. I think I never saw more of the power of God.

Monday 4. I began the circuit. My mind is much exercised. Lord, teach
me Thy will. I think I never preached a sermon with more sweetness in
my life. I have never heard of one jar in this class of about 60 members.
They have been joined about 3 years. O! what a sweet thing it is to love
Jesus.

Sunday 10. I preached in Dover at 9 o'clock from is all well. I think
many were convinced all was not well. Among the rest a lady who thought
but little of this way was struck, who shortly pulled off her fine headdress.
Can now walk miles through the mud rather than miss hearing a sermon.
In the evening at 3 o c I preached to a crowded audience in the Court
House. This evening I indeavoured to examine myself. I fear I did not
warn souls so faithfully as I might. If ever I am spared to see another Sabbath, I'm determined to be more faithful.

Monday 11. The people could hardly crowd in the house. I gave notice
to preach at night 2 miles off. The house was well stowed and I was informed there were not less than 30 out, cold as it was. Jesus paid us a powerful visit. My voice was almost lost with the cries of the people. In this place
it is a new thing.

Tuesday 12. I rode about 10 miles and preached with great freedom.
It is about four years since I was among these people. They have increased
from about 40 to 60, many of them are renewed in love. I want more faith.
O! that I was more dead to the world.

Wednesday 13. I rode down in the neck and preached near Delaware
Bay. 4 years ago I preached in this house, when the whole neck appeared
to be in Egyptian darkness; I never visited them till now. Though I labored
as I thought to little purpose (now there are more than 2 scores professing
to know Jesus) many dating their conviction from that day, which encourages me to draw the bow at a venture and leave the event to the Lord.

Thursday 14. I rode 12 miles and preached from Rev. 15:2. There are
about 100 members belonging to this Preaching House. I fear if they do
not get more religion it will go bad with them.

Friday 15. I preached not far from Dividing Creek—this friend keeps
slaves. However, it did not hinder a blessing from the congregation. One
boyish young man in scarlet was cut to the heart and cried for mercy and
begged to join with God's children.

Saturday 16. At 12 o'clock a crowded audience attended at the Crossroads, all much taken.

Sunday 17. Though the morning was very wet I attended and preached
at Blackiston Chapel. In the morning I was in low spirits, but glory to

God. He paid my soul a powerful visit. There was a great shaking among
the people. I was the first that preached the gospel in this place to about
50 souls. The day will be remembered through eternity. Now many are
inquiring the way to heaven; they have gotten a stately house of worship
near finished.

Monday 18. I preached in the neighborhood of Chaney Clow. I preached
here about 7 years ago and there seemed to be a prosperous work (Clow
being leader) but the enemy got an advantage. Clow comenced (being a)
captain and drew off a Tory company which broke up the class and preaching was taken from them. Of late we have brought it back and I expect
there are more than a score souls in Christ. I warned them against all
unlawful riots. *Tuesday 19.* The next day with great freedom I preached
a funeral in the forest over an infant. I find my mind sweetly drawn out.

Wednesday 20. I preached and rode to Dover. Glory to God. I hope
all goes on well here and the next day I set apart to visit from house to
house and blessed be God, I trust not in vain.

Friday 22. I rode 12 miles in the country and preached at the house of
a zealous Baptist and returned to town where I met Br. Gill. My mind is
refreshed.

Sunday 24. I preached at the Forest Chapel with great freedom, visited
one of the sick friends. This visit was sanctified.

Monday 25. I met Br. Cole; preached morning and evening.

Tuesday 26. Visited some of my old friends. I think next day preached
with as much freedom as ever I had in my life. Blessed be God. I met with
crowded audiences.

DECEMBER 1782

Sunday, December 1. I preached at the Buck Chapel in the morning
and a funeral in the evening. It was a day to be remembered.

Monday 2. I had as many as could hear. The house being well filled.
I preached every day this week except Thursday.

Sunday 8. I preached morning and evening in Dover. I expect with
more success than I have for many years. I must confess I have not had
so much freedom in my own soul for some weeks.

Monday 9. Br. Jones set out with me to the Neck where I preached
with great freedom and in the evening by candlelight, I preached to as
many as could crowd in the house. Next day was as solemn a time as I
have commonly met with. I find a loving spirit among the classes and hope
the work is deepening, as well as spreading.

Saturday 14. Being earnestly solicited by Mr. Bassett, the lawyer and
others, I set out to Cecil County with a desire to form a new circuit.

Sunday 15. I preached at Mr. Tomsons with a lively hope of answering
my expectations.

Monday 16. Being a very cold snowy day, I kept my room.

Wednesday 18. I preached with satisfaction at the Lawer's sisters and dined at Squire Lawsons. Having an invitation in Turkey Point Neck, set out on Wed.; held forth at the Head of Elk. The people appeared to believe what I said by their behaviour. *Thursday 19.* Next morning I received a very kind letter from the minister of their town (being present at the evening sermon) to preach at his stated preaching place. *Friday 20.* Next day I got down in the Neck and preached at Colonel Helands, to about 30 of the grandees. This day I labored under a disadvantage. Hard by on either side there was either a grandee, baal or burning. Those who came out seemed very attentive and gave their assent to the truths that were delivered. It is very amazing while we set at dinner, I asked an old lady how she liked that new doctrine. She answered as well as the rest, very well. But when I began to make an inquiry how matters stood between God and their souls, they could not bear it. I returned eighteen or twenty miles to Mr. Tomsons. I am much distressed for the people in this county. Being conscious they are in the broad way. O Lord, sent thine enlightening illuminating spirit among the people.

Sunday 22. I preached in the morning not far from Bohemia Ferry. Glory to God, not in vain. My dear Master found a way to their hearts. At 3 o'clock I preached to a crowded audience with great freedom. I had invitations from some of the great ones. Having but a short time to stay in the circuit, I want to do all the good I can.

Monday 23. I set out to Dover, preached on my way and found my spirit refreshed. I got into Dover and held a Watchnight to as many as could crowd in the court house. *Wednesday 25.* Christmas day in the Brick Chapel, I had freedom to cry to a multitude of souls "His name shall be called wonderful counciller." This way I desire to live and dye declaring the council of God to the children of men.

Thursday 26. I rode five miles through a steady rain and with great sweetness I cried to a few hungry souls." Little children, let no man deceive you, he that doeth righteousness is righteous even as he is righteous." I John 3:7.

Friday 27. I met G____ N____. We had a good time. It is a matter of rejoicing to think what God has done for hundreds of precious souls in this part of the vineyard.

Saturday 28. I preached a funeral over our dear departed Br. Smith, who lived for years a life of piety, was a man of great affliction, bore it with Christian fortitude, though he measurably lost his speech for many months before his death. I visited him several times in his sickness, and though he could not speak so that I could understand him, my soul was refreshed and by the signs he made, and the tears that so plentifully flowed from his eyes, I had not a doubt or fear but his soul was transported with joy. Happy he lived; happy he died, leaving a family happy in God, and glory to God; I have not the least shadow of doubt but his soul is happy at God's right hand. O! that all my dear friends and children may make so happy an end. I rode to Br. Barratts and spent two or three hours watching for the coming of Christ and blessed be God; we found Him in our hearts.

Sunday 29. I held forth again in the B(rick) C(hapel). this week I spent in preaching and visiting the friends. My soul is sweetly drawn out to serve God and if I had a thousand tongues I would employ them all in praising my dear Master.

JANUARY 1783

Sunday, January 5, 1783. I have once more come round to my Dover friends. Surely God is among these people—the last Sabbath I preached here before; God in mercy laid His hand upon one of the greatest persecutors in the town, finding no rest day nor night; he cried mightily to God (both he and wife were convinced and brother's wife) who are now going hand and hand with the brethren happy in God, and he is resolutely bent upon building a brick chapel. Shall we not give the glory to God who can change the hearts of lion like men and women in so short a time. Have great freedom both in preaching, exhorting, praying and visiting the friends. God has and is doing great things for the people in this town.

I visited Sister Bassett who has been a long time under the afflicting hand of divine providence. I think she is one of the happiest women I have met with. I believe her to be a living witness of sanctification. Her soul seems to be continually wrapped up in a flame of divine love. Seven of this family are happy in the love of God, four of which enjoy that degree that have cast out fear. Surely God has a church in this house.

Monday 6. I set out to visit the societies through Kent and Newcastle. I generally preach once and twice every day, besides meeting the classes and bless God for the sweet consolation. Many are happily going on to perfection. Something very strange happened one evening while I was praying in a good man's house. When I rose up from prayer part of the skirt of my coat was gone. What did it I cannot tell; no one was near me, but a little dog—if he gnawed it, he swallowed it. Nothing of it was to be seen. I had great freedom to preach several funerals this week over a person who had from time to time been convinced by our preaching and had grieved the Holy Spirit, consenting and assenting to the truth. They lived; how they died, God knoweth.

Wednesday 8. And also as I returned from New Castle, I preached at Duck-Creek Crossroads with great freedom and hope good will be done. There is a small, but lively class of white and black. I think if I know myself, I have set out in the new year to live a life of devotion to God.

Sunday 12. I bless God for a deep lasting sense of His love to my soul while preaching at Blackstone's Chapel.

Monday 13. I set out on my journey but the weather being so frosty and slippery I had hard work to get along. The flesh cried, "ease, why will thou destroy thyself." Blessed be God. He inabled me to ride and preach every day, though few came out. Blessed be God; His promise was verified.

Sunday 19. I spoke with freedom to several hundreds. "All are yours and ye are Christ's and Christ is God's." I think a particular door was opened. A great discovery was made to me of the beauty of Holiness. The Christians, black and white, seemed to be going on joyfully to do the will of God.

Monday 20. Brother Cole met me. I heard him with a degree of satisfaction. In the evening we met and watched for the coming of Christ a few hours—I preached with liberty. We had much of the divine presence.

Tuesday 21. I rode to and preached at White's Chapel. My mind seemed at first to be much clouded, but the cloud in a short time broke and we had a melting time. This reminded me of the Quaker who says we are not to open our mouths but when we have a particular moving of the Spirit. Respecting this, my own experience teaches me to the contrary. When I have felt the most freedom of mind, to open my mouth, I have not been so favored as when the cross has been great. Yea, at times, when it has appeared like death to open my mouth, I have boldly resisted the foul spirit and God has in a wonderful manner poured out His Spirit upon the people. "Be instant in season and out of season."

Wednesday 22. The enemy of souls this day sent a drunken man to disturb our meeting. Shortly after I began, he spoke. I was determined the devil should be disappointed had him put out, and the door shut. After the meeting ended, he came to me, broke out in tears and said he was a poor miserable Sinner and desired me to pray for him. He was afraid of going to hell. I understood afterwards that in times past he was under conviction and the devil had harried him into drunkenness.

O! what a pity it is for men to make brutes of themselves. God gave me a heart to pity and pray for him. The day following I had great sweetness in preaching at 11 o'clock and also to a crowded audience at night. I was powerfully tempted by the enemy about sunset. News came that a woman on her way to meeting fell down and broke her arm. "Ah! said the enemy, you and your night meeting is the cause of this." I felt a degree of distress, but the cloud broke and I preached with great freedom.

Friday 24. I preached at Greens Chapel, met class and rode to Dover and preached with great freedom. Next day rode 11 miles and met about 80 of the society. Returned and held a Watchnight at Brother Boyers. And a blessed time it was.

Sunday 26. I preached to about 600 souls from Acts 2:42. "As they," etc. About 300 of the brethren spent two hours with me, breaking bread in token of love and speaking of the goodness of God. I do not think I have been so out done for many months.

Monday 27. I set out to visit my Somerset friends, rode to Johnstown; next day got to my first appointment and preached with great freedom.

Wednesday 29. Quarterly meeting began at Moores Chapel.

Thursday 30. I preached our dear old friend I(saac) Moore's funeral.

Friday 31. I returned to Johnstown.

FEBRUARY 1783

Saturday, February 1. Sussex Quarterly meeting I opened up and illustrated on the talents. Having an appointment at the Brick Chapel, I set out on my journey.

Sunday, February 2. This day exceeds for cold any we have had this winter. I rode 30 miles and preached two sermons. In Dover I had great liberty.

Monday 3. At Boyers and at night in a new place.

Tuesday 4. Our own Quarterly Meeting began at the Forest Chapel. Though it was a very wet day, abundance came out. I preached with great freedom.

Wednesday 5. We had a powerful time. Many in Love-Feast spoke boldly of the goodness of God. This evening I find my mind much distressed. Not knowing which course to take to be the most useful, my mind let me in some degree to travel out to the back parts; it being the desire of the conference. However, my mind not being altogether free, I spent much time in prayer. About 9 o'clock the cloud broke and it seemed as if I had the most freedom to pray and pay my Sussex friends a visit.

Saturday 8. I set out on my journey.

Sunday 9. Preached at Whites Chapel.

Monday 10. Preached a funeral in the neighborhood. In the evening Brother Prior met me to accompany me round the circuit (who is under exercise about the ministry).

Tuesday 11 and Wednesday 12. We had a tedious journey.

Thursday 13. With great freedom I preached a funeral to a crowded audience. Hard hearts were much melted, from these words: "Then shall the dust" etc. Ecles 12:7.

Friday 14. I preached to a loving class, though the neighborhood is much troubled with the Nicolliton doctrine, from these words: "Little children, let no man deceive you." 1 John 3:7. Glory to God. My soul was much drawn out; I have no doubt but good was done. One joined society.

Saturday 15. I preached in a neighborhood much confused by the Anabaptists. God's power was felt, His word sunk deep in the hearts of the people. I hope some were convinced of the poisonous nature of the Calvinist doctrine. Three joined the little flock. We rode as far as Mr. Haskins. I am as ever determined to do and suffer the will of my dear Master.

Sunday 16. My mind this morning is sweetly drawn out to do my Master's will. This day I preached to not much short of a thousand souls. God's power was displayed in a wonderful manner. Few dry eyes were left. At three I preached a funeral about a mile off, nearly the whole congregation followed me, where I had great liberty in showing what is implied in being prepared for death and the blessings consequent. Glory be to my dear Master for this day. I think many souls will date their conviction from this day. It is better than two years since I preached in Caroline before. There was as well as now a prospect of great good, but the Anabaptists keep the people halting between two opinions. O! that our great Master would lay too His almighty arm and shake the devil's kingdom. They have drawn off several of the class.

Monday 17. I find my mind this morning sweetly drawn out; rode six miles. Preached with freedom. Here is a young but happy class. I laid my head this night upon my pillow in great fear. Great discoveries were made to me in my sleep. God gave me (I think) a token of His spreading His glorious gospel in New England. How short I cannot tell—it seemed as if I tasted some of the sweets.

Tuesday 18. This morning I had some consolation, in private devotion. I rode 12 miles. Brother Pryor exhorted first. There came in two stout, able men whom I took to be the men that came out about three years ago when I preached in Dorset not far from this place, in order to take me to jail. Satan was telling me the whole time till I came to the application I was to be taken to jail that day. I proved him to be a liar. I had but little freedom to preach and less in class meeting. I fear these souls are not engaged. We dined and set out on our journey, lest the fresh should be so high we could not cross in the morning. The road was exceedingly miry being accompanied with several friends, we got to Mr. Adam's about sunset, where our spirits were refreshed. It is a matter of thankfulness that we have a private room this evening.

Wednesday 19. Being a wet day but few came out. I had freedom to preach from "Purge out the old Leven," etc. 1 Cor. 5:7. I think I never was in a much deader class meeting. I fear some of these have lost their first love.

Thursday 20. I am under deep exercise this morning. I rode to Mr. Wheatley's without eating anything. I had light and liberty to speak but not sweetness. O that my dear Lord may break in upon the people. My soul this evening is humble and hope to be more given up.

Friday 21. I set out this morning under a divine sense of my obligation to God for past and present favors. Preached at Mr. Cannons. We were favored with much of the divine Presence in our meeting. The man of this house some months ago was a violent persecutor. The lion is turned into a lamb. I think we are getting ground very fast of the devil. This evening we went to Brother Browns.

Saturday 22. This being a very wet day I kept my room, spent the greater part of the day in writing letters to my Christian friends.

Sunday 23. I feel a great degree of dullness. Many are the difficulties we have to grapple with in this wilderness. The congregation came together about 400 in which number I expect there were about 100 in society, whose souls were hungering after God. I believe saint and sinner were divinely touched. Glory to God. My heart earnest pants for a greater nearness to my Lord.

Monday 24. How shall I give an account for this day. Reading seemed a burden and also prayer.

Tuesday 25. I preached to a loving lively class with great freedom. My heart was very tender, both in preaching and meeting class. Lord, stir me up to run the Christian race. The man of this house seems to be greatly distressed for holiness and wants instruction. Lord, give me wisdom.

Wednesday 26. I visited a cripple. They heard of my coming and I expect there were victuals enough prepared for 20 or 30 hearty men. O that they have made that preparation to have entertained Jesus. I fear all are strangers to his redeeming love. I preached at 12 o'clock to a little gospel hardened company.

Thursday 27. I spent several hours this morning on my knees, reading, praying and meditating. I think I enjoy a solemn sense of God's love to my soul. At 12 o'clock I preach at Widow Jumps; my soul was distressed. I fear these people pray very little. O God lay too thy hand; and rouse poor sleepy sinners and lukewarm Christians. I was much comforted in the 5 o'clock hour of retirement. I was severely tempted about midnight.

Friday 28. I bless God for peace of mind. I preached a funeral to a crowded audience over an old woman that died suddenly not far from Marshy Hope bridge.

In the evening I preached a Watch night sermon with a degree of freedom. Brother Prior continues with me and I have no doubt but God has set him apart for Himself. He increases fast in gifts.

MARCH 1783

Saturday, March 1. I rode 12 miles and preached to about a hundred souls, many of which are hungering after Christ. Many can say it was good to be here.

Sunday 2. Glory to God. I feel my self drawn out in sweet composure of mind. Preached at Johnstown to a crowded audience. I felt the power of faith. Met a loving class and joined four in society. My mind for some time has been calm and undisturbed. I now have a lively hope I grow in grace.

Monday 3. Brother Prior receiving lines from his father (being unwell) I consented for him to go home a few days. I went to my preaching place. The day being very cold and snowy I had but a small audience, but I had great freedom. And the divine Presence was sensibly felt. This evening I feel myself very comfortable in this friend's house.

Tuesday 4. I preached in the forest to as many as could crowd in the house. Many were admitted into the room to see our class meeting. My heart pitied them. When I examined into their hope I asked one if he thought he had communion with God. He answered, "yes." I asked if he was converted. I found him as great a stranger to God as if he had never heard the gospel. I asked an old white headed man what he thought of the matter. "Sir," said he, "what position is the soul in the body?" "This question is not the point in hand." "Does Christ dwell in your soul?" "O how it pities me to see as old a man as you so great a stranger to Christ."

I asked another, how the state of his soul was (who was a Presbyterian). "Cannot," said he, "a man be a Christian and know nothing of it?" O God have mercy on poor blind souls.

In the evening I preached with great freedom, mostly all in tears. My heart is tender and my eyes full of tears, while dispensing the glorious gospel of my dear Master.

Wednesday 5. I preached at Mr. Harris' to a crowded audience. I have not preached here this two years before. I fear the people think more of me than my dear Master. O! what a pity, so kind a people should live in sin and go to hell. Few comparatively have a sound experience. I hope the Word was attended with power.

Thursday 6. I began this morning to read Nicodemus on "the fear of man." I had not read long before I was so overpowered with sleep I did not know what course to take. I rode to the preaching place where was a crowded audience. Many more that could get into the house. While I was preaching, I thought surely these people must all be convinced. The house seemed to be in a flood of tears. How is it, I fear, they weep, sin and repent. When I was in this neighborhood three years ago, they were in the same condition. Near 30 in society and not more than 2 believers. O God, thou must do the work—lay too the hand to Thy power. What is to be done? My soul is distressed for the people. Many, I fear, who live in sin appeared to be as glad to see me as if I had been their father. I always endeavour to preach as plain home truths as I possibly can. This has been a day of temptation. Satan wanted to persuade me my life was a life of misery, but glory to God. I am sure one soul is of more value than 10,000 worlds. Lord, give a more earnest hungering after all the mind that was in Jesus. I have been troubled with a drowsy spirit. O! that I may be able to give an account before my Master of the improvement of this comfortable room. God gives me great favor in the sight of the people, though an unworthy unprofitable servant.

Friday 7. I preached in the Neck a little below Lewis-town. I was surprised to see the multitude that came together of all ranks, as they had not seen me for some years. They came out with great expectation, thinking to hear something more than common. Whether the work was real or superficial, I cannot say; we had a melting time. In the evening I went home with a kind friend, who lived about 10 miles off. He took pains to send for the neighbors; about 30 came together and a precious time we had.

Saturday 8. Although it rained without the least intermission the house was nearly filled with people and a most glorious time we had. I think the woman of this house has as great a depth of piety as most I have conversed with. The last time I conversed with these people was shortly after I came

out of jail. Which was the greatest night that ever I met with since I received justifying faith. I had no doubt but at that time God in great mercy
deepened His work. However, my evidence respecting holiness at times
has been clouded ever since. It is a great thing to love God with all the
heart.

Sunday 9. The wind blew very high so that after I went to the preaching-
house, I could not preach in the house. I expect there were three or four
hundred that could not get in; many of which could not hear my voice
so as to understand; the wind was so high. Great attention was paid. In
the evening I went to the suburbs of Lewistown. Here I was obliged to
preach in the house. Few more than the women got in. I think I have
seldom seen a more grand audience in Philadelphia. They were serious
and some deeply affected. Without any invitation or notice of meeting,
many followed me to Squire Wheelbanks where I lodged—among the
rest, a young woman under deep distress desired some conversation I
found her almost ready to dispair. With great freedom I preached to as
many as were present, both black and white. Glory to God. We had a
great time. After meeting the young woman told me God had comforted
her soul. In this place they have had little of our preaching since I left
them about three years ago. I have occasion to hope, as I had then, God
in mercy will raise up a people here.

Monday 10. I rode 10 miles into another Neck above town, where they
have stood it out a long time, without inviting the gospel. God in mercy
has opened one house; His word went home like a two edged sword. Speedily,
I hope (to) many hearts and houses. I expect one who had been the most
profane in the neck with tears begged to join in this way; said he believed
(though he was ashamed he had been so great a persecutor) them to be the
people of God and the right way to serve Him. With that several others
broke out and made a humble confession with that I read the rules and
joined a class. Others said they were convinced it was right, but would
wait some longer and count the cost.

Tuesday 11. Glory to God. I preached with great freedom, where Brother
Pryor met me. One of my old disciples came to me who had turned Calvinist in my absence. If this was all it would not be so bad, but I fear he had
turned from God.

Wednesday 12. I rode to my appointment. The people wanted me to
preach out of doors. The wind being so high and the day cold I got as many
women to go in the house as it would, the men stood out and I stood at the
door and preached with no great deal of comfort. I fear the people looked
more at me than Him that sent me.

Thursday 13. A very wet day. I rode six miles, got dripping wet. I do
not repent my trouble. The room wanted but little of being full. I joined
a class and rode to Brother Braidey's.

Friday 14. The enemy of souls is striving to break into this class. I preached with freedom. Some misunderstandings were rectified and the friends parted in great union.

Saturday 15. I preached to a mixed multitude.

Sunday 16. I find my mind sweetly drawn out. In the morning I preached a funeral over three open graves. I expect there was not much short of 600 souls and in the evening seven miles off to near as many. I think this has been as high a day as I have met with for a long time. I am informed many were deeply affected who never heard us before. I returned to my old friend, Mr. W_____s.

Monday 17. Crossed the creek and preached to many souls, mostly strangers to our doctrine. All seemed to pay solemn attention. In the evening Brother Pryor assisted me in holding a Watchnight. Glory to God. We had a time of great power.

Tuesday 18. I had a tedious ride, but the Lord paid me well for it. I had great freedom in opening up the deep things of God. 1 Peter 5:10. "The God of all grace Make you perfect, establish, strengthen, settle you." I think I never saw greater beauty in a text in my life. I want the three last things. To be established, strengthened and settled (as a house on a rock) in the doctrine and experience of sanctification.

Thursday 20. With great freedom I preached a funeral over one of our friends, who for many years has maintained the gospel in his house. Surely she is now reaping her harvest. Those that give a cup of water are not to lose their reward.

Sunday 23. I find my mind drawn out. With great freedom at W_____ Chapel I showed the necessity and benefit of Christians uniting together in society to receive the word of exhortation and w(eep) over each other.

Tuesday 25. To a small audience I reminded them of the glorious work God has carried on in the earth and that He ought to have the glory. Psalms 115:1. "Not unto us," etc.

Wednesday 26. I preached a funeral over one of our pious friends who has for many years adorned the gospel. Yes, there are two open graves, one a youth. I expect there were more than a hundred souls that could not get in the house.

Thursday 27. At 10 o'clock I preached a funeral a few miles off and at one, began to preach after riding six miles. This is a day of great comfort to my soul.

Friday 28. Preached and had a comfortable Love-Feast.

Saturday 29. My soul is drawn out in prayer. A crowded audience came together. I have not had more sweetness in preaching I know not when. I have not the smallest doubt but God applied His word.

Sunday 30. I preached a funeral at the old burying ground at 9 o'clock. Over an old woman who formerly was a Nicollite preacher. A spirit of weeping ran through the congregation.

At 12 o'clock I began to preach at Mrs. H_____'s. I am sure I never preached to so large a congregation in this place. I do not believe there was one less than a thousand souls; some came not less than 20 or 25 miles. I am surprised the people seem so very fond of preaching and yet there are very few in society. Although Monday was a wet day the house was crowded. What with riding through the rain and preaching long, my throat next morning was very sore.

APRIL 1783

Tuesday, April 1. At 11 o'clock I was obliged to preach in the open air a funeral; one woman sunk to the ground under conviction. God left a witness for Himself on most of their hearts of the truth of what I said. In the evening I preached to as careless a people as ever I did in my life. Next day I heard a young preacher on trial and was much pleased; in the evening, I preached a funeral with satisfaction.

Thursday 3. Many came out. I fear these people do not love God as they once did.

Friday 4. I had great satisfaction, particularly after preaching while examining the class. There are some members here who hold slaves. O what a pity, God's people should be so blind. I fear if they do not give them up, they will be forsaken.

Saturday 5. I preached Mrs. Handay's funeral who died triumphing in the faith. In the morning after she was laid out, there came a dove into the house, lit upon and fluttered over her a considerable time, and returned. Was not this an olive leaf of peace. Glory to God. We had a solemn, sweet time.

Sunday 6. As many came together as could well crowd into the Fork Chapel. Our love was confirmed together by breaking bread. We did not part without feeling the power. I set out at 3 o'clock, rode 14 miles to I_____ T_____ and preached to a crowded audience before dark. I leave two young friends in my place.

Monday 7. I set out to Lewis Town, held forth to a loving people, after riding 15 miles. At 4 o'clock I preached not far from town to a neighborhood of well behaved people on a good conscience. Rode to Squire W_____ B_____.

Tuesday 8. I had great freedom to preach at Mr. Shanklands. Some of our greatest opposers were present who behaved very well. By candlelight I preached again with great freedom. I have no doubt but the fruit of this day will be seen in eternity.

Wednesday 9. I rode 6 miles out of town, preached, and returned, and preached to as many as could crowd in a large hall. I believe there were but five of the society present. Before I was done preaching it appeared as if they were half of the society. Several cried out. After preaching, I inquired who they were. I was informed they were some of the first rate in town. This has been a glorious day to me. I bless God that He put it into my heart to take this trip.

Thursday 10. I set out in my return to I_____ T_____. Being informed some persons who were awakened last night desired some conversation with me, I called at Mr. W_____ B_____ where they came. One was the great lawyer's niece, who appeared to be in deep distress of soul. I asked her if she saw herself a sinner. She broke out into a flood of tears. "O yes," said she, "a great sinner." I exhorted and prayed with much freedom, hoping her captivated soul would be set at liberty. Set out and got as far as Wm. S_____ y_____.

Friday 11. Was a day of exercise; got as far as St. John's Town.

Saturday 12. I preached on backsliding and at night spent about 2 hours with about 200 souls watching. It was a time of great power.

Sunday 13. I preached to a crowded audience. The Christians were happy. I think we had as comfortable a Love-Feast as I have commonly seen. A great day of consolation to my soul.

Monday 14. This morning my heart was drawn out in prayer. I rode four miles and (preached) with great freedom (on) "This is the love of God that we keep His commandments" 1 John 5:3. These people are much engaged.

Tuesday 15. I rode to my appointment and held forth with a degree of freedom from Mat. 7:1. "Judge not that ye be not judged." I have a reason to hope that the society is more engaged than they were the last time I was here before.

Wednesday 16. I preached to a crowded audience with great freedom. Surely the time will come when these people will turn to God. This night the enemy of my soul assaulted me. For a few minutes I sensibly felt the power of darkness. I rose out of my bed, wrapped myself in my great coat and slept on the floor. This body must be kept under. I rather suffer anything than feel the motions of sin. I am determined to mortify the deeds of the body.

Thursday 17. I had great freedom to preach in the forest to a crowded audience. Our dear Master came among us in great power. Glory to God. The time is coming to favor these people. I rode near 15 miles to (Lewis) town; was to preach at Squire W_____ B_____, but the night before his daughter ran off to be married which caused great confusion. Blessed Be God. The people came together and I had a sweet time.

Friday 18. I rode a distance and preached a funeral; rode back to town and with great freedom, preached to a crowded audience.

Saturday 14. I preached again to the same audience.

Sunday 20. Held forth to the same people at 9 o'clock; rode out in the country and preached at 10 o'clock; returned back and preached at 5 o'clock. I adore and praise God for this day and hope many souls will praise Him through eternity for it. By this time the people of the world in a flouting manner begin to cry out, wool will be very cheap this year. Why? Because the young women are burning their head dresses. I hope the foundation is laid for a glorious work of the Lord in Lewistown and round about.

Monday 21. I rode 20 miles and preached to many with great freedom. Several who had been under great doubts and fears were enabled to praise God from a sense of His pardoning love to their souls. In the evening I went to Mr. T_____, but had so little satisfaction. Set out on my journey.

Tuesday 22. Glory to God. We had a high day. I parted with many of my dear old friends not knowing whether I should ever see them again. Rode near 20 miles to Mr. Whites.

Wednesday 23. I set out for Kent Island, preached a funeral on my way to a good people.

Friday 25. I preached in Tuckahoe Neck where I almost first began the ministry. A wonderful change since then. God, give me great freedom.

Saturday 26. Next day not far from the Island. After preaching I crossed the ferry and was very kindly received at old Mr. Richardsons where Quarterly Meeting began next. I held forth both days and can truly say they were days of great power. In the evening (I got a friend to ride my horse round) I went on board the boat (Others were about three score friends on board); we sailed in about three hours 20 miles with a sweet gale. Glory be to God. My soul doth magnify his dear name. Was received with open arms among my dear Talbot friends.

Monday 28. (As it has been some time since I was in this place before) the people came out from every quarter and glory to God, a great time it was. Immediately after preaching, about 50 of us went on board the boat again, crossed a wide river, where I preached to almost double as many as could crowd in the room. I had great freedom in pointing out a Christian's walk. I was wonderfully glad to see the good old woman, Mrs. Parrot, well and steadily going on towards heaven.

Tuesday 29. Morning. I set out, accompanied by several of the friends to Dorchester. Preaching was to begin at 12 o'clock. Having 20 miles to ride, exclusive of a ferry two miles and the boat the other side and with all a contrary wind, we were too late for preaching.

Wednesday 30. Next day I preached not far from where I was imprisoned to near 500 souls. There is a glorious change since I was here before.

MAY 1783

Thursday, May 1. I crossed over to Bolingbrook, where I preached to about 400 souls, with great freedom. God has a precious people here. Having such a love for the people, I gave out to preach in my return next week. Blessed be God. This evening I rode as far as my old friend's Mr. Airey, where I met Brother Roe and Brother Metcalf.

Friday 2. and Saturday 3. I preached in the circuit with great freedom.

Sunday 4. I preached at Mr. Airey's to between 1,000 and 1,500 souls, although the morning was somewhat wet. O! God keep my soul in the depth of humility.

Monday 5. With great freedom I preached a funeral in the neighborhood.

Tuesday 6. I returned over to Bolingbrook, and preached to almost as many as a chapel (30 by 40 ft.) could hold. My soul was much refreshed.

Wednesday 7. In my way to Kent, I preached at Talbot Courthouse to about 300, although it rained without intermission. Mostly hardened sinners, few but what seemed to be in tears. Some of which were at Balliard's before night. So powerful does the enemy of souls strive to pick up the good seed. In the evening I held forth at Brother Hartley's. In my return I preached next day again at the courthouse with not so much freedom as yesterday.

Friday 9. I preached at Collins and returned to Mrs. Haskins where I held forth on Sun. to a crowded audience. I do not remember that ever I preached a sermon in this place but I had a hope of great good. This day we had a powerful sense of the divine presence. The whole congregation was as affected as is common to see a company of Christians. Several poor sinners came to me to know what they should do to be saved.

Monday 12. I returned to Mr. Whites and *Tuesday 13.* to Dover, where I sat with pleasure under the sound of the gospel.

Wednesday 14 and Thursday 15. I preached in Dover.

Friday 16. Morning I took my leave of my dear Dover friends who are dear to me and in my way, preached with great delight in Greens Chapel.

Saturday 17. Quarterly Meeting began at (Thomas) W(hite's).

Sunday 18. Was a very high day to many souls. I do not think there were less than two thousand souls. After the house was filled, three of the preachers took the remainder of the people in the woods. Two of my brethren spoke in the house before me. Just as I began, they were dismissed in the woods, so that I had the whole congregation. I was obliged to speak so loud in order for all to hear, I got somewhat hoarse, but glory to God; it was a sweet time to me and many others.

> "The opposers admire
> The hammer and fire
> which all things over come
> the hard rocks for to break
> and the mountains consume"

Monday 19. I set out on my way to Baltimore Conference. I had 8 days before me. I preached in the Forest Chapel to about 300 souls from "Finally, brother, farewell," etc. 2 Corinthians.

A little before I began a woman was taken very ill, was carried out into a little house. After preaching I went to see her, commended her to God in prayer, came away not expecting she would live five minutes. This portion of Scripture came to my mind: "Watch, therefore, for you know neither the day nor the hour wherein the son of man cometh." Mat. 25:13. One great comfort was she had adorned a state of sanctification for many years. We rode into Queen Anne's Circuit, and I preached by candlelight to a crowded audience, both white and black. Here I met with S. Dudley from the Virginia Conference who informed me of the marriage of my brother Richard Garrettson. For a few moments my soul seemed to be overwhelmed with sorrow, but that portion of scripture came to me concerning David's grief for his child. Immediately the cloud broke and my soul was inflamed with a divine sense of God's love. In my meditations, I inquired of my Master, what improvement I was to make of this unexpected scene. The resolution in the name of my dear Master was to be more faithful. (As I expect His usefullness in a measure will be buried) in his work. Lord, give me grace and strength to supply his lack of service. Glory be to God. I am more determined to live a life of celibacy and spend and be spent in the cause of so good a God.

Tuesday 20. I preached in a barn to a crowded audience near Mr. Sudlers in Queen-Annes Circuit. O! how precious was Jesus to my soul. In the evening I preached in Newton and in the morning I set out to a Quarterly Meeting in Still Pond. I held forth with freedom both days. I fear some offense was given in time of Love Feast.

Thursday 25. I returned back to Newton and preached at 6 o'clock.

Friday 23. Morning I returned to Mr. Sudler's where I spent Saturday in retirement, preparing for Conference.

Sunday 25. I preached at 8 o'clock in Coupages Barn in Queen Anns County to a crowded audience with great freedom. Rode 12 miles and preached in a large chapel to as many as could well crowd in. Glory to God. I am sensible I felt the power of faith. Rode 15 miles and preached in a private house at the Head of Chester to an unawakened, but well behaved audience. Rode 4 miles to a friend's house, visited the sick, and rode 1 miles, where I had a comfortable night's repose. I bless and adore my God for this day. O! that the crown may be put on the Redeemer's head and that I may lay in the dust at His feet.

Monday 26. My friend set out with me after a tedious journey, I got around to Newtown in Harford County.

Tuesday 27. We got to (Baltimore) Town. *Wednesday 28.* Next day Conference began. About 60 of the preachers met. I hope in the spirit of the gospel. This evening Brother Watters preached a good sermon. Next morning I preached with little freedom. In the evening Brother Asbury preached a good sermon. Many attended the word. We had much good preaching and praying.

Thursday 29. I was much pleased with a sermon preached this evening by Brother G(lendenning). Brother A(sbury) preached a sermon in the morning—a few exceptional things. This day we closed our business, had a Love Feast. I preached a sermon and the most of the preachers dispersed.

Saturday 31. I being weary, thought it expedient to tarry a few days in town.

JUNE 1783

Sunday, June 1. With great freedom I preached to the people at the Point.

Wednesday 4. My lot being cast in Talbot Circuit, I set out on my journey, was taken exceedingly ill on my way, but through the amazing mercy of God, He brought me to Kent Island.

Saturday 7. Evening. Where I preached next day two sermons with great freedom.

Monday 9. I feel a degree of comfort though grieviously tempted by the enemy. When I stood before the people, it felt like death to preach, from a sense of my unworthiness. But glory to God, He made His arm bear and a melting time we had. On my way to Tuckahoe, this evening, I met with one who had been a Calvinist preacher in Ireland. If I mistake not (one) who had made shipwreck of faith and put out of the ministry. Still strong in the Calvinist doctrine; once in grace always. After a long conversation he seemed something humbled and desired me to preach in the neighborhood.

Tuesday 10. I find myself hardly able to sit up. When the people came, was enabled to preach with great freedom. Glory to God. Here are an honest hearted people.

Wednesday 11. I bless my Lord. He has removed my complaint which was a pain in the head, attended with fevers. I rode a piece in Caroline and preached to a poor, but religious people. I meet with conflicts, but thanks be to God, for grace to withstand the enemy of souls. This evening my good friend Magers came to me, with was not a little comforted together.

Thursday 12. I rode and preached in Talbot not far from the courthouse. These are a poor but good people, the enemy of souls is striving to take an advantage. Jealousies seem to be the side through which he is indeavouring to break. I had the parties face to face and found it to be only suspicion and hope the snare of the devil was broken. This evening I rode to Mr. Parrots, where I preached next day with sweetness. And the day following I had to myself to visit the friends, but was not as diligent as I ought. Drowsiness stole upon me. Lord, forgive me many ommisions.

Sunday 15. I preached at 9 o'clock. When first I began it seemed to be hard work (being somewhat tried with the friend for not providing something to stand on) but in the application, the cloud broke and we had a great time. Having to cross a river two miles wide and no other vessel but a small canoe, we trusted the Lord, set out at 10 o'clock, attended church and sacrament. Mr. Gordon gave an excellent sermon and after church I preached with great freedom. Mr. Rain met me. We had some agreeable conversation.

Monday 16. This morning, feel myself very heavy. I rode and preached on the Bayside to a loving people, though I fear religion is not much deeper than it was 3 or 4 years ago when I was among them. They were mostly young people and a spirit of marrying got among them and those who married out of the Lord turned out but poorly. I was sorry for one young woman, who was pious, who married an unbeliever, has entirely forsaken the way and means and is in the fashions of the world.

Tuesday 17. This morning I am assaulted by the enemy but blessed be Jesus. He is my rock. I preached in the Neck to a crowded audience and blessed be God. We had a time of refreshing from His presence. I find cause to exclude one member. By her the gospel has suffered and yet she would confess her fault and seemed penitent. She is one that says, I go, sir, and went not.

Wednesday 18. Next day, I preached to a hardened set. Blessed by God. I hope some of their hearts were tendered; there are a few humble faithful souls in society, much persecuted and dispersed. It did me good to see how faithfully they stood by each other. The man of the house is as blind as a stone respecting his bodily eyes, but glory to God. I believe he views the Redeemer by faith. I was very much surprised the next day as he rode with me to preaching. The boy (who was his pilot) went to sleep and his horse took a wrong road. He presently discovered it and whenever he came against a wheat or corn field, he would say this is either good or bad corn, or wheat; when he would come against a house, he would say such a man lives here; when the boy was near a road to turn out, he would say, "Take that left or right hand path." When he got near the gate, he would say, "Boy, open that gate." He can go about his own plantation or to which room of his house he pleases or desk, or chest. He told me he could count money, by the feeling. He is of a blind family; the blindness commonly came on them about 20, or 22. I think he is a precious happy soul. He praises and blesses God for spiritual eye sight. His wife has her bodily ages but her spiritual eyes are out. She is as blind spiritually as he is literally.

Thursday 19. I preached in Hopkins Neck to many precious souls. I was much quickened among them. After preaching I visited a beautiful damsal, about the age of 14. The only child of her tender father who appeared to be under a deep decay and a little expectation of her staying in this world much longer. (Her mother a few months ago went out of the world triumphing in the faith and by all accounts is now in Abraham's bosom praising God). God refreshed my soul abundantly while praying for this damsel. After prayer I asked her if she saw her way clear into the other world. "Bless be God," said she, "I do." I asked her if she were willing to die. "I do not," said she, "want to stay here any longer." I asked her if she thought she was prepared to die. She replied, "God loves me and I love him." "I know," said she, "he loves me." I said, "do you know your sins forgiven." "I have not," said she, "the witness, but I believe I shall, before God takes me." Said I, "are you willing to die when you were first taken." She replied, "no." I asked her, "Why?" "Because," said she, "I was a sinner." "I knew God was angry with me." "I was under distress of soul, but the Lord has turned His anger away." "How did you feel," said I, "in time of prayer." "My soul," said she, "was happy." (I had the witness she was a favorite of heaven) "Child," said I, "I believe God loves you; look to him now for a witness." "I am looking," said she, "for a bright witness." "I believe God will give it to me."

I left her, my heart was full of love, hoping one day to meet her in glory.

Her father accompanied me near a mile. I asked him if she had been under serious impressions any time before she was taken sick. He said, "from the first of the preaching coming into the neighborhood, she had a great love for the way and wanted to join society, but the preachers thought she was rather young." "But," said he, "since her sickness, she has gone through deep distress." This night my soul was transported with joy when meeting the black class, a company of humble, happy souls.

Friday 20. I called in (on my way) at old Squire Lucoms (a rich old man) whose heart, I fear, is on the world. He was once in society, but turned out. I am much surprised to see some carnal men so fond of the gospel. Surely this man wants to go to heaven, but in his own way. I rode 15 miles to Bolingbroke and met the class.

Saturday 21. Met a very happy class. I heard of my good old friend Brother Cole, being dangerously ill with the small pox. I set out to visit him, but the river was so rough and like to be more so I turned back.

Sunday 22. I preached in Bolingbroke Chapel at 9 o'clock and 12 o'clock with great freedom. All behaved very well, but one of the great ones who went away and mocked (as I understood). I think it was a time of great power. I know I have not had so much freedom to speak for a long time.

Monday 22. I rode 12 miles when first I began to preach, I was very much tempted and labored, for a considerable time, without feeling any powerful operation of the Holy Spirit, but glory to God, in the winding up, I was sweetly drawn out and I hope good was done. Many hard hearts were tendered and brought to weep bitterly. One Calvinist was much offended at the first prayer, because I prayed for all. We are commanded to pray for our enemies.

Tuesday 24. I had great freedom to preach. I went with a doctor who ran well in the (way) for a time, but has turned to the wallowing in the mire.

Being harvest time I had but few to preach to this week.

Sunday 29. In the morning I preached in the Orchard to many precious souls. And in the evening I preached a funeral. We had a great power of God. In Tuckahoe the people seem very friendly both rich and poor.

Monday 30. I am rejoiced to converse (of one) who was a few weeks ago a great enemy to religion. Now has a broken heart.

JULY 1783

Tuesday, July 1. After preaching two colonels came into my room who appeared to be under distress of soul, who desired next day to come into class.

Thursday 3. I went on the Island.

Friday 4. I preached with freedom.

Saturday 5. Was a day of great comfort.

Sunday 6. A little after sunrise, I met a large black class, but little genuine piety. At 10 o'clock I preached with great freedom and also at 4 o'clock in the evening.

Monday 7. I preached not far from Q(ueen)town. Prejudice in these parts seems to fall very fast. The neighborhood increases.

Tuesday 8. I preached not far from the Bridge with great freedom, here the work spreads wider and deeper. Here are some pious souls.

Wednesday 9. I preached in Talbot Circuit a funeral over the doctor's wife's sister. There was abundance, both rich and poor. We had much of the divine Presence—hard-hearted sinners trembled. At 4 o'clock I preached to a multitude in the Orchard, about five miles (distance). When I first began, I had but little freedom, but in the winding up, there came a great power of God among the people. Few hearts but what were sensibly touched. After preaching we had as powerful a Love Feast as I have seen for many months. This has been a great day for consolation to my soul.

Thursday 10. I visited and preached to a society down the county, where I found confusion, the damning sin of jealousy. A bad woman crept into this society, whom the devil has made an instrument of doing much hurt. I turned her out with two others. They are a poor, but well meaning people in this class.

Friday 11. I rode to Miles River.

Saturday 12. Met class.

Sunday 13. Preached at Brother Hartleys with great freedom. Crossed the river and preached with as much freedom as ever I did in my life. (At the new building). The house was 30 by 45. Many who could not get in to hear went away. It grieved me much to see this house lay without windows, doors, floor, seats or any such thing. I purposed to make a collection when I came round for the finishing the house.

Monday 14. I visited the people on the Bay-side. I fear these people are not as much engaged as they ought to be, but perhaps more than they have in time past.

Tuesday 15. I preached on "Come, for all things are now ready," to a crowded audience.

We broke bread together—in the evening I had a meeting among the trustees of the house to know what was to be done. I appointed a new manager.

Wednesday 16. I met with a small company at the blind man's. Blessed be God. I can speak in great comfort of a little humble, persecuted company united in this Neck.

Thursday 17. I preached a funeral (over a young damsel of about 15 years old) to a large audience. I have no doubt but she is gone to glory. The squire of this (Hopkins) Neck invited me home with him. I hope he wants to be saved.

Friday 18. Being a rest day, I thought I would give it in part to the preaching house. I crossed Miles River a little after sunrise and called a meeting and made a collection of three thousand foot of plank and sent it over to the house with a letter desiring them to get it in order for preaching against (the time when) I came round. In the evening I rode to B(olin) b(roke) and met a class.

Saturday 19. I was somewhat distressed when I heard of a lie the devil had passed about on a dear good man. It is as follows. As he was travelling the road, he met with a strange woman (as they both were going one way and to one place). He asked her if she was willing to have some conversation; from thence he asked her if her soul was converted (the woman and her husband professed Quakerism). She was much displeased. When she went home, she told her husband she met a Methodist Preacher who she was afraid would behave rudely. He being an enemy to the people called Methodists and being a little warm in liquor ran where there was a small gathering of the devil's children and told that a Methodist Preacher had attempted to ravish his wife on the road and that there was proof of it. One of the company leaped up and cracked his feet together and cried out, "Hurrah! for the Methodist preachers." It shortly spread through the neighborhood. I spoke in public and told them I believed it to be a lie. However, the good friend called a . . . .
. . . .
. . . .
. . . . a Saviour's merits, for a time almost ready to dispair of mercy. At last it pleased God of His great mercy and goodness to set her soul at liberty. She received a clear witness of His pardoning love. Sometime after this, she was powerfully convinced of the necessity of sancification and earnestly sought it by day and night, till it was pleased (to) God of His great mercy to speak the second time, "Be clean." She appears now to be established. She is a slave, who hires her time of her master. She is very industrious, pays her hire, and keeps herself well clothed. I have frequently seen her at five sermons running. It is uncommon to see her many minutes together idle. She commonly carried her work with her. She hires a room and boards herself and lives alone. She rises several times in the night to pray and particularly at 4 o'clock in the morning. In short this is her experience; my trials are many, but every moment I'm happy in God, having an abiding witness.

At 10 o'clock I preached. Crossed the river 1 o'clock and began to preach in the new chapel at 2 o'clock.

AUGUST 1783

Monday, August 11. I set out for Quarterly Meeting; on my way I preached several sermons and visited the classes; found them standing fast in the Lord.

Thursday 14. Quarterly Meeting began at B(oling)b(roke) Chapel. I expect there was not less than a thousand souls. I preached both days with great freedom. The last day we made a collection of near 20 pounds for the preachinghouse.

Saturday 16. Brother Major set out with me to Delaware Quarterly Meeting. On my way I preached at 10 o'clock, at 2 and at 7 o'clock. This was a precious day to my soul.

Sunday 17. I preached at 11 o'clock with great freedom in T(ucka)h(oe) Neck. Rode near 20 miles.

Monday 18. I got in time for the feast. I concluded the meeting with a sermon on sanctification. I believe the devil was present. Just as I began a horse broke loose (I was preaching under the trees), which for a time caused a great disturbance, but the devil was disappointed.

Tuesday 19. I set out to a Quarterly Meeting, held in Queen-Anne.

Wednesday 20. It began.

Thursday 21. It ended. The first day I spoke with freedom; the next day my soul was much comforted in preaching from these words: "As the apple tree among the trees in the wood, so is my beloved among the sons. I sat down under his shadow with great delight and his fruit was sweet to my taste." Song of Solomon 2:3.

As there seemed to be a necessity, I was entreated to attend Sussex Quarterly Meeting.

Friday 22. I set out, rode 30 miles.

Saturday 23. Meeting began. The weather being exceedingly warm and the congregation large and but little air came to me, I was scarcely ever more out done in preaching a sermon (as I had an appointment the next day near 20 miles off) I settled my business and that evening rode 15 miles.

Sunday 24. I preached with great freedom in (Tuckahoe) Neck to a large neighborhood of souls.

Monday 25. I feel myself exceedingly poor, but blessed be God for a humbling sense of His great goodness to my soul. I find a willingness to spend and be spent in His good cause. This morning I set out on my way to Kent Island. preached every day with great freedom. It does my heart good to hear of poor sinners crying out for mercy.

Sunday 31. I preached morning and evening on the island. I feel a very great nearness to these souls, and yet think the time is coming greatly to favor them.

SEPTEMBER 1783

Monday, September 1. I preached at the ferry and rode to Brother Youels— his wife was (to appearance) near eternity. Her soul was in a rapture of love. "O!" said she, "Brother Garrettson, I know God has sanctified my soul and I long to be dissolved and be with Christ." I had (after a while) faith to believe she would recover and shine longer in the church.

Tuesday 2. I again set out to visit the society through Talbot, I find comfort when ever I call upon God. I have been drawn out in adoration, while contemplating on the goodness. There are well on to a thousand members in this circuit and blessed be God. There are but few jaring strings among them. Shall we not adore God for this. O! Jesus continue their hearts knit together.

Friday 5. I think this evening we had a great time. O! how precious Jesus was to the Christians.

Saturday 6. Was spent partly visiting the sick.

Sunday 7. This morning I was sweetly drawn out. The eighth hour was spent in meeting a black class. The 10th in preaching. Two hours in travelling. The first and part of the second hour in the evening in preaching, the third and fourth in conversation and the fifth in private prayer. I laid my head this evening on my pillow, blessing and adoring God, for this day.

Tuesday 9. God showed a miracle. I came to my appointment, much afflicted with a pain in my tooth and head. I thought I would endeavour to pray with the people. I did so—and desired them to lift their hearts to heaven for me and if God enabled me I would speak a few words (to the company of faithful). In a few minutes I was as perfectly delivered from pain as ever I was in my life, and I never had greater strength and power in my life. Was this chance or the answer of prayer?

This evening to meet the class in the town, but so many strangers came out, I omitted meeting class and preached with a great plainness on evil speaking.

Thursday 11. I bless God for a good degree of health. A few days ago Squire Bannings' daughter was taken ill and snatched off suddenly. His desire was that I should preach her funeral. A large number of souls came from all quarters, both rich and poor. I preached with great freedom. I believe great good was done in removing prejudice.

Friday 12. Rode to Bolingbroke.

Saturday 13. Preached with freedom.

Sunday 14. My soul is refreshed among these people.

Monday 15. I set out on my journey round to T(ucka)hoe) Neck and found great freedom. All this week in preaching every day and meeting the classes.

Sunday 21. My heart was sweetly drawn out in preaching to a large number, many of whom were penitent mourners. This week my congregations were not so large on account of great afflictions among the people. I was exceedingly poor and expected every day to lay by, but thanks be to God, He stood by me till I got to the island. There I rested a few days and took physic.

Sunday 28. Though weak in body, I was inabled to preach 2 sermons with great freedom. The devil's kingdom on this island has been shaken this summer.

Monday 29. I preached with freedom to a new class and had an opportunity of sending a letter to my Brother Richard in Virginia.

Tuesday 30. The congregation was small, but very happy. This evening Brother Major met me. His piety is rendered a blessing to me.

OCTOBER 1783

Wednesday, October 1. I preached at the Widow Lowders on the gospel mystery. The remainding part of the week was spent in visiting and preachint to the societies in Talbot.

Sunday 5. In the morning at 9 o'clock I preached at Brother Hartleys and in the evening at the Brick Chapel on backsliding. This evening I retired in order for self examination.

Monday 6. I preached at Brother Lamdens.

Tuesday 7. I preached at Brother Dennys in the morning and a funeral in the evening. While I was preaching the funeral, a man (who was not much acquainted with the doctrine) said, "You preach all to me." After a while he got up. "I go" and he, "before you quite condemn me." We had a solemn season.

Friday 10. I met Brother Asbury.

Saturday 11. Heard him preach.

Sunday 12. We parted, he to the Bayside Chapel and I, to B(oling) b(roke) Chapel. In the evening we met again, had a comfortable time. In the morning we parted. He set out for Dorset and I for Queen Anne.

Monday 13 and Tuesday 14. I preached with much freedom. Glory be to God for the prospect I see in this part of God's vineyard.

Sunday 19. My appointment I was to preach and hold a Love Feast in the Neck. (I was astonished to hear that Mr. Hughes, an Anna-baptist minister, had made an appointment close by). The day being very wet, I omitted having the Love Feast. However, there were as many out as the barn could well hold.

Monday 20. I have but one time more to go round the Circuit before I leave the parts for a season. This day I preached in the Widow Wooters barn, to near as many as it would hold.

Tuesday 21. The people came to friend Grifins from every quarter, many tears were shed. My heart was much drawn out.

Wednesday 22. I preached my farewell sermon at Tizzars. There were near 200 horses and carriages besides near as many on foot. The Word sank deep; in short, there seems to be a universal stir in the neighborhood all round, among both rich and poor.

Thursday 23. I rode to the Island.

Friday 24. Preached with but little liberty at Crab-alley.

Saturday 25. I rode down the Island, preached with great freedom, broke bread together; had a great time of power.

Sunday 26. Was my farewell on the Island. I attended, the people attempted to get in the house, but I suppose not more than one-fourth part could. "Finally brethren farewell" etc. 2 Corinthians, last chapter. We had a blessed day indeed, parted in hope of meeting in glory.

Tuesday 28. I preached at Brother Sweets with great freedom to as many as the house could hold. Rode 4 miles. Preached with freedom.

Wednesday 29. Brother Major met me at Widow Lowders. O how good God was to the souls of the people. I think I never preached with greater freedom in all my life. We broke bread together and parted.

Thursday 30. Preached at Widow Lowders and

Friday 31. At Brother Hartleys and . . . .

NOVEMBER 1783

Saturday, November 1. I rode to Bolingbroke in order to meet all the classes. A sweet time it was. I was under a necessity of excluding one member, for tale bearing.

Sunday 2. At 9 o'clock we broke bread in token of love. At 12, preached to a solemn audience and in the evening by candlelight had a Watchnight I expect there were not much short of 300 souls.

Monday 3. I conversed with two African slaves. One was the daughter of a king. In short her attire when she came in showed it, for her ears, nose and hands were loaded with gold. I asked her if she expected to go to her own country. She said "No, not till she died." She proferred her gold to one who would bury her decently when she died. Several friends set out with me to Quarterly Meeting.

Tuesday 4. It began. Brother Cole preached.

Wednesday 5. I believe this was a good day to many souls. The Brick Chapel would not contain the people. Meeting ended and we parted.

Thursday 6. I tarried behind to preach the funeral of a dear old saint. (I. Danny) And blessed be God, it was a day of comfort to my soul. I preached from these words, "I have fought the good fight, etc." Paul to Timothy. After service was over, I crossed the river, walked two miles, then rode 20 and preached by candlelight.

Friday 7. I preached in T(ucka)h(oe) Neck to about 300 souls. Many crying out for mercy. I rode 8 miles and preached by candlelight to as many as could well get in a large house. I have been travelling in this circuit about 6 months and have abundant reason to praise and bless God for what he has done for and by me. I put the crown on the Redeemr's head and desire to lay humble in the dust. Prejudice has universally fell, many souls have been convinced, and many brought savingly home to Jesus. There has been an addition (in the space of time in the circuit) of 200 souls, besides, I expect the circuit is, at least, 300 better in preached houses. Shall we not praise God for this. My lot is now cast in Queen Anns, Kent, and Cecil for three months.

Saturday 8. I set out for Kent, got as far as Newton.

Sunday 9. I preached in the lower preachinghouse. The house is much shattered, yet I fear not as much as the classes. O what a flourishing prospect here was about eight years ago when first I began my ministry among them. Yea about six years ago I preached 20 or 30 sermons with great freedom and I may say there was a universal revival. They were seeking the mind that was in Jesus. But where are they now? Some gone back to Egypt, others degenerated into a state of formality. I believe if God has sent me among these people, He will bless my labors.

Monday 10. I rode 15 miles and preached to about a hundred souls with great freedom. Half the number professed the love of God. By candlelight I met a company of blacks. I think in this place there are about 65 black people in society, 31 of which are free. I hope I never shall be reconciled to slavery.

Tuesday 11. I preached near the Head of Chester to a few barren ones. I gave out to preach at night. I praise God for it, for I had double the number and thanks be to His name, He was with me of a truth.

Wednesday 12. I preached in Frederick town to a few good souls. I visited an old church woman (as she called herself). When I asked her if she had made her peace with God, she replied she had always endeavoured and the other day, the minister came and gave her the sacrament and she hoped all was well. An utter stranger to the new birth. We prayed and I left her. O what a pity men and women should content themselves without the power of religion.

I think I met as sensible a black class as ever I did in my life. My soul was much comforted.

Friday 14. I preached with very little freedom to about 20 souls and rode 15 miles to I. Sudlers and was much comforted in meeting a happy black class.

Saturday 15. I set apart for private exercise, but was much interrupted by the enemy of souls. I find my mind variously exercised.

Sunday 16. If I know my own heart, I'm engaged for heaven. I did not preach with that sweetness I could wish, but desire to be thankful. I rode this evening as far as Squire Logwoods on my way to Delaware Quarterly Meeting held in the Brick Chapel. The first day I preached with a degree of freedom. The second day Brother Asbury preached a good sermon. In the whole it was a good time. I find my mind somewhat distressed. I accompanied Brother Asbury as far as Dover. We both held forth at Lawyer Bassets.

Monday 17. Next day I accompanied him as far as the Crossroads where was likely to be a degree of persecution, but was prevented. In the evening I returned back to the lawyer's and preached with freedom.

Thursday 20. I preached a funeral in town over a young woman, who

I fear lived without God. I know not how she died. This evening Mr. Basset's family accompanied me to visit a pious saint, near the point of death, who the devil buffetted in the time of her affliction. He wanted to rob her of her confidence. At other times he persuaded her that God would cast her off because she had not a witness that was sanctified. I believe the visit was rendered a blessing. Glory to God, I find my spiritual strength renewed.

Friday 21. I set out to Queen Anne's.

Saturday 22. Preached with freedom.

Sunday 23. I had a cold day; a cold barn to preach in, cold hearers and found myself cold.

Monday 24. I kept my room the most of the day. I did walk about half a mile and preached about half an hour to about 2 souls from "He that's born of God doth not commit sin."

Tuesday 25. I rode about six miles and found a loving people to preach to—mostly seekers.

Wednesday 26. This morning was partly spent in writing to two of the assemblymen in Annapolis, who were then setting. They wanted me to cross over and give them a few sermons. I wish it was in my power. I rode 8 miles down into a Neck where I preached with much freedom. There are but few sheep in this place. Yet they want feeding. On my way to Newtown, I met an old gentleman (I could not have thought there was so blind a man in this county) "Well sir," said I, "what think you of this late new stir in religion" (he was a churchman). "O!" said he, "it's hypocracy." "Why, they judge people." "How do you know my heart?" "Why," said I, "the tree is known by the fruit." "Suppose," said I, "you saw a man drunk, what would you think of?" "Why," said he, " 'tis wrong, but his heart may be good." I told him he must be born again or he would never see God in glory and so parted.

Thursday 27. I preached to a few pious souls.

Friday 28. I was sorrowful. I long to live nearer God.

Saturday 29. I met class in Newtown.

Sunday 30. In the morning I visited the sick. At 11 o'clock I preached to the house full with freedom. Rode 8 miles and preach at 3 o'clock. My soul is sweetly drawn out. This is a sweet night of rest.

Monday 31. I met a small class and rode to Eastern Neck Island.

DECEMBER 1783

Tuesday, December 1. Preached with some freedom.

Wednesday 2. Rode to the island and met two classes.

Thursday 3. Met 2 classes.

Friday 4. Preached with freedom.

Saturday 5. I visited poor John Beck. Five years ago I thought he was called to preach (I believe he was) I sent him on the circuit. The enemy took an advantage, got him in a notion that he would shortly die with a pain in his loins. He got him from one extreme to another, till I think he is an object as much to be pitied as ever I saw. Once he was a young man of great piety, now, I fear, he has not one spark. He continually lays on his bed with victuals by him. He has eaten till he is the fattest being I ever saw and still consents if he was to walk, he should shortly die with his old complaint. I fear he gives way to various passions. When I advised him for his good, he laughed, and said, "You think so." "Ah," said he, "you are one of Job's comforters." I prayed with and left him with grief. O my God, ever keep me from the snares of the wicked one. Glory to God. This day I preached with great comfort and rode six miles.

Sunday 6. I find my mind variously exercised. I want a greater depth in religion. I see a field I never travelled through. "I drink and yet am ever dry." O for a greater deadness to this world. I am sure if ever I get to heaven it will be through much tribulation. Some may think the preachers are in no danger. They are spectecles for men and angels and butts against which the devil casts his firy darts. Sometimes I'm almost ready to cry out, "Why me? Why me? Lord."

In this neighborhood (Still Pond) there has been several deaths within a few days. One very sudden. I did not expect many hearers today as there are several funerals in the neighborhood; but we had a houseful and a blessed time we had. There are well on to a hundred in this society, most of which professes to know God.

Monday 7. I went to my appointment, which was to preach a funeral. The cross seems very heavy. I took it up, preached from these words, "They that were ready went on with him to the marriage and the door was shut." Mat. 25:10. My dear Master stood by me. Poor sinners trembled and the few disciples rejoiced. When I went to the grave, I found freedom to show an ancient custom among the heathens in burying their dead (as the man buried was a great drunkard) who had judges, if the person to be buried had lived an immoral life, his body was either burnt or given to the beasts. This was looked upon as a disgrace and was a terror to the survivors. How is that holy institution abused? What can I say of the person decease? You know his life! Several persons came out this evening to family prayer, whose hearts were touched.

Why should I distrust a good God? I want to live and die at the foot-steps of the blessed Jesus. O what a bright grace is humility. I want more of it. I'm not saved from ignorance nor short comings, neither from mistakes and infirmaties of various kinds. Yet I believe it to be a Christian's privil-edge to love God with an undivided heart and his neighbor as himself. Not while he willfully or willingly keeps slaves in bondage. Why? Because the Lord has said, this is the fast that He requireth, "To love the bands of wickedness to let the oppressed go free," etc. Isaiah 58:6. O that my head was water and mine eye a fountain of tears, that I might weep over those souls who are in love with oppression.

Tuesday 8. I preached morning and evening with freedom.

Wednesday 9. I preached in Fredrick Town. Some of the people looked angry. I was much comforted.

Thursday 10. I rode 12 miles to Brother Tomsons and preached with freedom to a crowded audience. I rode the same distance back to Hynsons.

Friday 11. I preached to a few souls and rode to Sadlers where I met my brother Thomas. My soul is much comforted.

Saturday 12. My mind is sweetly drawn out. I rode 3 miles and preached with great freedom on the 5 chapter and 1 verse of Revelation. "I saw in the right hand of him that sat on the throne, a book written within, and on the backside, sealed with seven seals." I took this text with trembling.

Sunday 13. The day was very cold so that I could not preach out. The house did not contain near all the people. My soul was drawn out in great love.

A Journal of the Life of F. Garrettson from Jan. 1, 1784.

Thursday 1—My mind is much distressed, the weather was very cold, the people did not come out to preaching.

Friday 2—I rode to J. Randals, I had been there but a few minutes before word came that old Mrs. Gooding was dead, and was requested to preach her funeral, I preached a short sermon and went immediately; the people was waiting—I had much freedom. A few weeks ago the daughter departed, both happy in the Lord.

Saturday 3—I met the Class of Angus—at night I preached with great freedom to about 200 souls, some of which _____.

Sunday 4—My Lord was with me, in particular whilst we was breaking bread in token of love, the power of God came amongst us. O! what sweet time we had. I received a letter of the death of our worthy friend, Mrs. Bolton, in New-Town, and was requested to preach her funeral.

Monday 5—Accordingly I attended, when a number of precious souls assembled, both rich and poor. I had great freedom, good attention was given to the word and I believe impressions made on many hearts. Perhaps it would not be improper to speak a few words of her life and death. In her natural state, she was much beloved by the poor, for her acts of charity, and benevolence. A good man came to me a few minutes before I began to preach: if you (said he) want to speak anything of her character, you may be assured she _____ the best of any woman in the town. About four years ago, the people called Methodists began to preach in the town; she was convinced that her morality would not save her and after a time joined in Society, and continued a steady member, but had no witness of sins forgiven. She had a long lingering spell—at first she was not willing to die (I visited her several times) but blest be God, when he in mercy visited her soul with a sense of sins forgiven—she seemed perfectly resigned to leave a tender companion and six or seven children behind to go to Jesus. A few words in the close of a letter: Mrs. Bolton departed this life last evening. As long as she had her senses, (which was almost to the last) she met death with an undaunted courage and I believe she is now with Christ in glory. O! who would not bear the cross of a few years for a crown—cold as the weather was, I travelled through Sussex County—visited the Societies and witnessed to Queen Anne County much—and preached.

Sunday 11—Preached Sunday the 11th at Sudlers with sweetness. I visited the Classes and found them going on steadily. I feel the want of more faith.

Sunday 18—Though the day was exceeding cold, the barn was crowded at Gannons, and I had great freedom. We had a comfortable love feast.

Monday, but few came together.

Tuesday 20—Mr. Downs came to the preaching place with me. The weather being extremely cold and the roads so covered with ice, some places were bare and some were not. I thought it impracticable to go any further on horseback; left my horse and took it afoot, we had several miles to go, the snow being very deep, and very little track, made the journey very tiresome, Glory to God he paid us for our trouble, more people came than I expected.

Wednesday 21—We set out again, travelled on horseback part of the way; the ice filling the road to such a degree we was obliged again to take it afoot. Many precious souls came to hear the word. There seems to be a great stir on the minds of rich and poor. I was surprised to see one of the governor's council there, who walked at least five miles, and attended again that night two miles off where I had well on to 200 hearers by candlelight and blest to God a powerful time we had. The rich was generally out. I have not the least doubt but God is carrying on a great work here.

Thursday 22—I preached a funeral, was poorly and did not attend my evening appointment, but sent a young man to supply for me.

Friday 23—I almost despaired getting along for the ice either on foot or on horseback, however a way was opened—I got as far as New Town Ferry where I was stopped, as far as I could see—I thought the _____ I would go over on the ice, before I got far from the shore, I saw it would be tended with danger, and returned, and rested contented that night. In the morning I mustered together the ferry—before 9 o'clock in the evening got over, by breaking the ice. I rode 12 miles and had a comfortable Watch Night.

Sunday 25—Cold as it was, we had a blessed love feast at 10 o'clock. Preached a funeral at 12 o'clock. Rode eight miles and preached in New Town at 3 o'clock, crossed the ferry and rode to Brother Gold's where I was happy and thankful—.

Monday 26—I rode to Brother Coupages where Quarterly Meeting began. Brother Moir (?) preached a joyful sermon. In the evening it began to snow, and blow and continued 'til the next day and evening. I was surprised to see so many out—we had a comfortable time in love feast, and Glory to God I was comforted in preaching to a company who I believe was hungering after Jesus. In all the days I ever saw, I think I never saw one to exceed this for snow and cold—after meeting my friend M. S. set out with me, I wanted to make on my way to my appointment which was 15 miles off. By the time we had travelled a half mile was tired, and glad to take lodging with our kind friend Brother Elliott.

Wednesday morning (January 28)—I thought I would make the other push—we mounted our horses a little after sunrise—after riding about a mile (the snow being so excessive deep, and no track) I thought it impractical to make any farther push to get to my appointment, and so made the best way we could to a friend's house.

We came at last down to a creek, where we seemed to be at a loss what to do, not knowing whether the ice would bear. I thought I would trust God. I made a push and got safe over, my dear good friend and companion (who was almost ready to faint with the cold) followed: we had not travelled more than two miles when we came to a house almost spent. Who would take all this pains that really believed in the doctrine of unconditional election, and reprobation.

Thursday, Jan. 29, 1784—I set out for Dorchester County. I travelled almost all day, and got but about 10 miles. The roads was so wonderfully filled with snow. My friend (Colonel Kent) could scarce find the way.

Friday 30—I had hard work to get to an appointment—not being able to reach Bolling-Brook, the ferry being shut: I returned and _____.

Sunday, February 1 (1784)—Preached in T. H. Neck. There being a considerable thaw.

Monday I preached with great freedom in the Neck.

Tuesday I crossed the ferry.

Wednesday as the rain fell in great abundance and froze hard, I almost dispaired getting on my journey. However after getting my horse rough-shod, about sunset we set out and rode about 15 miles.

Thursday reached Colonel V. where Quarterly Meeting was held, I had but little freedom to preach being much fatigued.

Friday (February 6)—I had a sweet time whilst preaching to a crowded audience of rich and poor.

Saturday 6 (7)—I spent retired at my old friend Mr. A.

Sunday 8—I had great freedom in declaring, O! Earth, Earth, Earth, Hear the Word of the Lord.

Monday 9—Many came out and my soul was much refreshed. I do not find as deep a work among the members as I could wish.

Sunday 15 (February)—I have no doubt that some hearts was touched. One came out at night for advice who seemed to have as much as he could _____. Comfort in Jesus was what he wanted.

Tuesday 17—Yesterday the Neck got so alarmed that I had most of its inhabitants today and a blessed time we had. I continued preaching by day and night this week with great comfort.

Sunday February 22—I preached a sacramental sermon to our friends at 9 o'clock—and then attended church where the blessed sacrament was decently and reverently administered. The evening I had freedom to preach.

Monday 23—I preached off the island in the Narrows, to a well behaved audience, several sinners were convinced and a backslider reclaimed.

Tuesday 24—I preached on another island to a people ignorant, but willing to be taught. Returned and preached to about 60 souls by candlelight, one of the church vestrymen who was convinced yesterday, and got the word so fastened to his mind, when he got about half mile from the house, his burden was so heavy, he fell and cried for mercy, so that the neighbors was alarmed—the family where I was, heard him, and thought it was a canoe turned over, and so forth. However he came out the next morning to inquire of me what he should do to be saved—joined Class. I prayed for him and believe he went home happy in the Lord.

Monday morning he was an enemy, now in Christ. O! what can God do when he lays to his hand.

Wednesday 25—I called on Captain Cane. He is a strict Church-man, and I hope desirous to be a Christian—but must be convinced first. It snowed very hard. Many considering came out to preaching.

Thursday 26—I preached to a poor but desirous people.

Friday 27—I had freedom to show the necessity of building on the Rock.

Saturday 28—In the morning I met the Class of young women. They have got a mother in Israel to be their leader. In the evening I met the Married Women. In this neighborhood there are many precious souls going on joyfully to do the will of their Father.

Sunday 29—Many came out, though it was excessive cold, one poor hardened sinner was brought to cry for mercy.

Monday, March 1 (1784)—I preached at night with great freedom.

Tuesday 2—A crowded audience came together. I had freedom in showing the different kinds of ground in which was sowed. I rode near 20 miles and preached with freedom by candlelight.

Wednesday 3—I was greatly comforted in preaching and speaking to a company of precious loving souls. The remainder part of the week was spent at Mr. Avery's in retirement.

Sunday (7)—Harry (Black Harry Hosier) met me, and preached after I ended.

Monday 8—As there was a degree of persecution against Harry I thought it expedient to leave him behind. A large congregation came together—Blest be God the word was attended with power. At night I preached to near a hundred black people—many good souls _____.

Tuesday 9—Though the day was wet and cold many came together. Blest be God I believe the word sunk into the hearts of many.

Wednesday 10—I had as tedious a ride through the mud as ever I had in my life. I preached morning and evening with freedom.

Thursday 11—I went to Mr. Ward's and held forth with freedom to a well behaved congregation. We had a very sweet time. My mind was much refreshed in retirement.

Friday 12—A crowded audience came together. Blest be God for a sweet time. After preaching two came to me upstairs under deep distress. One said, "Sir do you not know me?"—I said "No." "Why" said he, "I thought you did. You looked at me all the time of your preaching, and I thought you was speaking to me." This was the first time of his hearing the word by the Methodists. (He had been a Persecutor). "I think" said he, "what I have heard of these people are lyes, I'm now determined, to let my neighbors say what they will, I'll seek the salvation of my soul." Said the other, "a few nights ago I thought I saw one of my deceased neighbors come to me and called me by my name and to me he was in hell and said 'you will die in a few weeks and go there to. He fell on his knees and cried out for mercy." Blest be God he can work with or without means.

Saturday 13—I rode as far as Cambridge, Md.

Sunday 14—Though the weather was cold we had as many as could crowd into a large house, and a solemn time it was. I adore and praise God, though the weather was exceeding cold, I travelled and preached every day with great freedom, on Friday there was near 300 souls, deep impressions was made on the minds of many.

Sunday 21—I preached on Taylors Isle. I could not have thought so many souls could have got together as the ice would not properly bear. I have not seen so powerful a time since I came to the County. Surely God has a great work to do here.

Monday 22—I preached at Mr. Traver's who was brought through a sound conversion a few weeks ago. Harry preached after me. There are many souls brought to cry to God for mercy. Blest be God it is now a spring season with the Islanders. O that Jehovah may carry on his glorious work.

Tuesday, March 23, 1784—I preached on another Island not far off. Harry was to preach after me, but there was such a crying to God for mercy, I thought it was best to have a private meeting and give instructions to as many as desired. Glory to God it did my heart good to see what a change was brought about with a space of four weeks. One turbulent tempered, is converted, who has the appearance of an angel: when I was here four weeks ago she wore a head dress, now in tears she goes on her knees to tell her experience.

Wednesday 24—The audience was small, nevertheless I hope good was done.

Thursday 25—We had a sweet time, I endeavored to point out the way, and the narrowness of the way to heaven.

Friday 26—I fear that most of the people in this Neck are fast asleep.

Saturday 27—My soul enjoys great consolation. At night I preached to several hundred—"Behold he comes with clouds." Rev. 1:7. My tongue is not able to express what a sweetness my soul enjoyed whilst preaching. The people were so exceeding filled with the new wine, they were constrained to break out in praises to God. One sunk down under the divine power, so that she was carried into another room. My soul, don't delay Christ's calls, rise and follow thy Savior and bless the glad day.

Sunday 28—Harry and I both preached (for want of room) in the open air. One persecutor was out to the heart, many in floods of tears.

  O! to grace, how great a debtor
  Daily I am constrained to be
  Let that grace now like a fetter
  Bind my wandering soul to thee.

Monday 29—We both preached in a hardened Neck but good I hope was done.

Tuesday 30—Harry preached a good sermon after me, from the Barren Tree.

Wednesday 31—I had great freedom in preaching a funeral. At night I returned and preached at the widow Wheatley's, O! what a time, my soul was ravished with a divine sense of God. The word was in the midst.

Thursday, April 1, 1784—Blest be Jesus, he is precious to my soul. I was able to speak freely on the _____ of the children of Israel.

Friday 2—To a large audience I preached a funeral, many hardened sinners was out, and appeared very solemn. The Class here much resembles the primitive christians.

Saturday I met the Class at Mr. Avery's.

Sunday 4—Preached with great freedom. Rode for 12 miles and preached at 4 o'clock in a small village to a stiff-necked people. I fear they are too proud for the meek and lowly Jesus.

Monday 5—My mind is much drawn out.

Tuesday 6—I had a comfortable time whilst hearing Mr. Finley preach Mr. _____ funeral. Truth is sweet to me.

Wednesday night I held a Watch Night, a very comfortable time.

Thursday 8—Preached to a poor but loving people.

Friday 9—I have an appointment at Col. Richardson's as I understood from his consent. When I went I found the doors all locked up, and he and his wife fled. Several hundreds came out. The wind was too high to preach out, went to a neighbor's house and I had a comfortable meeting, Will he not lay uneasy on his bed!

Saturday 10—A sweet time I had in preaching—in the evening I went to Cambridge, and on Sunday preached in the air for want of room in a large house, the wind was so high it was very disagreeable. At 4 o'clock I preached with great freedom in the _____ Neck, surely God is about to cultivate it.

Monday, Tuesday and Wednesday, was spent in the other Neck with great satisfaction—they are a young but growing people.

Thursday I had a sweet time whilst preaching at Colonel Viccaro's, I was somewhat grieved to hear of a misunderstanding between two of the Society.

Friday—My soul is comfortable.

Saturday 17—Blest be God he enabled me to preach on the narrowness of the way Christians are travelling.

Sunday 18—I preached on the Island of Taylors and in the evening at Benjamin (Kene's)? In the morning I think I never preached a sermon to my comfort. Glory to God the congregation was mostly bathed in tears. In the evening I found much barrenness.

Monday 19—I went to St. James Island but was disappointed, for I did not begin to preach till near an hour after the appointment and the people kept dropping in until I was almost done. My spirit was grieved within me.

Tuesday 20—I returned to the other Island and preached my farewell sermon. And a glorious time we had. I praise and adore Jehovah's name for his great goodness in sending me to this County again.

Wednesday April 21—I went on my way, preached and had a love feast at Mr. Kenes, I had a sweet time.

Thursday and Friday I spent in preaching and meeting Classes.

Saturday 24—My time was taken up partly in Meeting and conversing with friends.

Sunday 25—I preached my farewell sermon at Brother Todd's. After breaking bread with two or three hundred of the brethren, we parted.

Monday 26—I set out on my journey to Somer-set to visit my friends and to attend Quarterly Meeting. I preached several sermons on my way to Cambridge where many attended and at B. I'm sorry to hear some of my friends walking disorderly, however I had great freedom to preach.

Tuesday 4th of May (1784)—Meeting began and a precious sweet time we had. Blest be God I trust his children are pressing on in the narrow path. The first day I had great freedom to preach from these words, "Many are called but few are chosen," Matthew. The second day from, "Feed my sheep," John 21:17. There was a divine flame in the assembly.

Thursday 6—I set out on my return to Dorchester, preached at the Fork Chapel with great freedom.

Friday 7—I preached at 11 o'clock and again at 3 o'clock. Rode to Mr. _____ Avery's.

Saturday 8—Quarterly Meeting began. There was about 500 souls. I had but a dull time in preaching. But in the whole we had a very good time.

Sunday, May 1784—We had our love feast at 9 o'clock and a sweet time it was. I expect in publick preaching there was not less than 4,000 souls.

Monday 10—I set out to conference (I have about 20 sermons to preach on my way). I had a sweet time at the Bolling Brook. I was accompanied by Brother Major who exhorted every day after me. I feel a divine sense of God upon my heart.

Tuesday 11—I held forth morning and evening. The friends about the side are much stirred up.

Wednesday 12—I preached in the morning at Widow Lowder's, and in the evening at John _____. The largeness of each congregation forced me to preach in the air.

Thursday 13—In the morning I preached to several hundred at Col. Harpers, (?) and in the evening at Mr. Griffin's and lodged at Squire Down's.

Friday 14—I preached at 11 o'clock to about 250 souls and in the evening I preached at Captain Cooper's funeral. I never saw a much better day than this—if I know my own heart there is a hungering and thirsting of my soul after God. This Neck at present seems very hungry for the word.

Saturday 15—I met with several of the preachers on their way to Conference. I preached with great freedom at Mr. White's house. After dinner several of us set out for Dover (Delaware).

Saturday & Sunday (May 15, 16)—were the days of _____ Quarterly Meeting. There was a great gathering. The new Preaching House was open. Surely God will reward his children for building so noble a house for his worship. I expect it will not hold (when the gallerys are done) much less than 2000 souls. I found great freedom to preach the second day. The friends here are ripening fast with glory.

Monday 18 (17)—I preached at the Barrett's Chapel. (Barrett's Chapel in Kent Co., Del., was a frequent preaching point, but was especially noted in Methodist history as the place where Asbury met Thomas Coke, Sunday, Nov. 14, 1784. At that meeting Coke presented John Wesley's plan for forming the Methodist Episcopal Church.) O what a sweet day it was. The friends was very comfortable.

Tuesday 19 (18)—I preached with great freedom at the Forest Chapel. Many flocked out to hear.

Wednesday (19)—I preached in Queen Annes at the Brick Chapel to a crowded audience. I was applied to preach the funeral of Squire Benton's wife. (the man who once joined Mr. Brown) to get me to jail. Who would have thought this man would have had his wife buried by a Methodist. O! the goodness of God, he can and does change the lion into a lamb. O Jesus go on in this glorious work-a vast number of souls attended both rich and poor. We had a sweet powerful time. After preaching I rode 20 odd miles into Circuit and the next day crossed Bohemia, Elk and Susque-hannah ferries into Hartford County where I tarried at Mr. Dillam's, where I preached next day. Many of my old school mates, relations and old neighbors were out. In the evening I held forth in a new brick chapel in the country village near where I lived. I once thought I never would feel the cross in this manner again. An abundance of my relations and acquaintances both rich and poor came out to hear the word. I can truly say this had been a day of _____ to my soul. This night I lodged at my eldest brother's and in the morning I set out to Baltimore-Town about an hour by sun.

Tuesday, May 26 (25) 1784—Conference began. We sat together several days without a jarring _____. O what can God do for men. We had a sweet meeting

Saturday I set out to the Circuit as my lot was again cast in Talbot Circuit.

Sunday I preached at Fork Preaching House and in the evening at Captain (Well's?).

Monday I was taken up in writing bonds and deeds, settling temporal matters at my brother's.

Tuesday, June 1 (1784)—I was accompanied around the bay by some friends and the first night we lodged at R. Tomsons. Being somewhat fatigued I tarried in Queen Annes a few days.

Sunday morning and evening I preached. I was lamenting to myself lest I had done no good, but to my great comfort a few days after I received a letter part of which is as follows, viz "Blest be God I believe great good was done when you was with us. Several was convinced and nine has since you left us found peace with God. I acknowledge it was great comfort to hear of the work going on amongst the rich as well as the poor."

Monday 7—With great freedom I preached on Election to some Calvinists—Matt. 22:14—"Many are called but few chosen."

Tuesday 8—I entered the Circuit where I had great freedom, and in the evening I preached Quarterly Meeting to as many as could get into a 30 ft. barn. The first time I went around the Circuit I had great freedom.

Wednesday 9—I preached at the Widow Lowdens and Thursday the 10th.

Sunday 13—At the Bayside Chapel the friends seemed to be going on a much as formerly. The week was spent in preaching and meeting the Classes.

Sunday 20—I had a sweet time morning and evening. This week was spent as usual— the houses in general are full in the week—I find myself drawn out sweetly. God seems to be carrying on a work.

Sunday 27—I preached in Tuckahoe, I expect there was not much short of a thousand hearers, rode and preached in the evening at Queen Anne County. I preached several sermons here amongst our young friends.

Sunday July 4 (1784)—I preached on the Island with great freedom, several sermons. I perceived some of our friends was falling into a spirit of dressing. I took occasion to enforce Mr. Wesley's rules or rather advice respecting dress. When I came again to the Island I was surprised to see the alteration. Some who was very gay I found setting in the congregation as plain as I could wish. I found the friends this week happy. I find many trials.

Sunday 11—I had great freedom morning and evening. The people flocked out this week from every Quarter.

Sunday 18—I preached at the B. Chapel at 8 o'clock to about 400 souls. At 10'clock I preached with great freedom at the Hole in the Wall to about 600 souls and at 4 o'clock at Talbot Court House to not less than a thousand. I may say this was a day of exercise and a day of comfort since I did not labor in vain. There seemed to be such a great work of God, I thought I would come a week before my regular converse. My soul is happy and I'm well persuaded many are beginning to enquire of the way to heaven. After spending the week very happy in preaching and meeting Class.

Sunday 25—I had a precious season in the Neck. Love feast 9 o'clock, preached to a Class of _____ number of souls. At 11 o'clock, again in the evening I spent a few days very happy at Queen Annes and so went on my way to Kent Isle. Seemed as if the whole Island came together and a sweet time I had at every meeting. I think the Lord will do something for this people. This week I had a sweet time as I came around in preaching and holding love feasts.

Sunday, August 1 (1784)—11 o'clock I preached at B. D. Chapel—a precious time and at the Court House 1 o'clock. I was surprised to see as many souls of all sects and rank. Many Quakers attended, I've not seen so powerful a time this summer. In times past this has been a hardened place but glory to God, hundreds I think have had their eyes open this summer.

Monday 9—I preached at the Bayside Chapel. O my God what a sweet time I had.

Tuesday 10—Several hundred came out. I publickly insisted on the freedom of slaves. A powerful time we had. One good old man came to me and desired me to write him a manumission, he saw it was wrong to keep slaves, and he was willing to save his soul. O! that Christians was convinced of this odious practice.

Wednesday 11—I held forth at 12 o'clock at _____ and in the evening at a wicked village called Oxford, perhaps one of the most abandoned places in the county. Many came out and paid good attention, some tears stole from their eyes.

Thursday 12—I had a sweet time.

Friday I set out to Dorset Quarterly Meeting.

Saturday 14—Began about 8 o'clock. Hundreds of people came together. We had a good meeting, I think I had as much freedom to preach as I have had in a great while.

Sunday 15—May be called a great day. I cannot tell how many thousands of souls were present. My soul was much drawn out in preaching to them.

Tuesday 17—Our Quarterly Meeting began at B. Brook. Many of our judicious friends can say they never saw the like in this part of the world before. I can say it was a good meeting to me. I think I never had more freedom to preach in my life. Tuesday evening at the meeting at Brother Mores and I set out to Carline Quarterly Meeting held at Jons-TN (Johnstowne). We rode four miles and next day reached the place. Meeting began. We had a good sermon the first day and an exhortation, a shower came up which prevented me from preaching. The next day we had a good love feast—I had great freedom to preach, two exhortations were given, and we parted. I was very glad to see many of my old friends, especially to see them happily going on in the ways of God. I rode about 15 miles to my good old friend, Mr. White's.

Saturday I rode to Mr. Sharp's.

Sunday 22—I preached in the Neck, the wind was very high, and I was very poorly. I had not as sweet a time as I could have wished. I have a hoarseness occasioned by preaching so much in the open air. I rode eight miles and preached with freedom at Chop Tank with a degree of freedom. I am at present very unwell, but blest be God I am resigned to my master's will.

Monday 23—With a degree of freedom I preached at Keets in the town to about a hundred souls. Here is a sweet loving Class.

Tuesday 24—Blest be God for a sweet time this morning in my own soul. Preached at Mr. Griffins in the Queen Anne Court House, the day being sweet but few attended. I had the freedom to preach the word.

Wednesday 25 August—This morning I found freedom to speak freely to Mr. Griffin about his slaves and was glad to find him very teachable, and readily consented for me to write him a manumission determined to give them their freedom. I rode to and preached with freedom in _____ Bard to about 120 souls. These are poor but a loving Class already going on to perfection.

Thursday, August 26, 1784—I preached a funeral at the Church, many attended and I had liberty to try to set their house in order for many shall die and not live. I hope this day will be remembered in eternity. This evening I visited a small but blest Class in the Neck, here I began to put a plan through the Classes for the raising of funds in the Circuit to encourage the building and finishing. I believe many will praise God for this institution through eternity. I wonder why I never fell on this plan before.

Friday 27—I preached on the island Saturday evening and Sunday morning. I preached on the lower end of the island with great freedom.

Sunday evening I preached on the Island to the largest audience perhaps I ever saw in private preaching on the Island. The whole Island was together, rich and poor, I do not remember I saw a smile on but one face. O! what does God intend to do here?

Monday 30—I rode about 18 miles and preached the funeral of Mr. Kent who once did not care for Divine things. Last summer he came to hear me preach a funeral. God laid his powerful hand and opened his eyes (he was a man of note) and gave him to see the necessity of religion, when he went among his old companions (not to partake with them) but to "sin it down" said he. This is such a day—"from this day" said he, "I am determined _____."

Tuesday 31—I had great freedom to preach at I. Keet's, the widow of poor Mr. Kent attended meeting under great distress—she cried out to God for mercy, joined Society and I hope will soon be happy in God.

Wednesday, September 1 (1784)—Preached with freedom at Widow Lowder's.

Thursday 2—I had a sweet time in preaching from "Wash and be Cleansed."

Friday 3—I preached in the forest to a very wild set of beings and went home with a man of note who some weeks ago was an enemy to the people called Methodists and is now under deep distress of soul.

Saturday, September 4, 1784—I met Class at I. Hartley's, here are some good people.

Sunday 5—I had great freedom to declare the counsel of God at 10 o'clock from

David's last advice to Solomon. Crossed the river and preached at 3 o'clock with freedom in the Bayside Chapel, blest be God for this night's refreshment.

Monday 6—I preached at Brother Lamdens, with a sense of God in my heart. I believe it was profitable to the people.

Tuesday 7 (September)—Glory to God we had a sweet time. I had freedom to preach. I now began to prepare for a journey to Charles Town, S. C. Went around the circuit and commended my dear friends to the Lord and precious times we had together. I held the Quarterly Meeting at Tuckey-Hoe new chapel. A blest powerful time we had. I took my leave of the people and rode as far as Mr. White's, where I had an opportunity of preaching with great freedom. The next day I went as far as Dover to Richard Bassett's where I intended to tarry a few days to gather my books, and prepare for my journey. In the evening news came to my room that Dr. Coke was come. I found a spirit of rejoicing when I went downstairs, I was somewhat surprised when I heard Mr. Wesley's new plan opened (respecting ordination). I thought I would sit in silence. I thought it expedient to return with him to a Quarterly Meeting held in Kent County, where I expected to meet Mr. Asbury, and a number of the preachers. About fifteen met.

We sat in Conference. It was thought expedient to call a General Conference to Baltimore, and that I should decline my journey to Charles Town. I was appointed to go and call the Conference. I set out to Virginia and Carolina—a tedious journey I had. My dear master enabled me to ride near 1,000 miles in about five weeks and preached going, and returning, constantly. The Conference began on Christmas day. We with one consent fell in with Mr. Wesley's plan. Sixteen were ordained, and I was appointed for the spreading of the gospel in Nova Scotia, instead of going to the south, which was a considerable cross. Nevertheless I was willing to take it up, in conformity to the voice of Conference.

134. The Redstone country is west of the Allegheny mountains. First settled by Marylanders, Richard Owings went out in the fall of 1783. Asbury assigned John Cooper and Samuel Breeze in the spring of 1784 and two months later Asbury himself made the journey. *Asbury's Journals*, Vol. I. p. 462.

135. Brother M. was John Major who died in 1788. He was from Virginia and was one of the first missionaries sent to Georgia. Major was an unusual character. As Jesse Lee said: ". . . what he lacked in words, he generally made up in tears. Sometimes he wept from the beginning to the end of his discourse." Lee, Jesse—*A Short History of the Methodists*, Magill and Clime, Baltimore 1810, p. 137.

136.
The weather being extremely cold I was near three weeks before I got to New York. About the middle of February Brother Cromwell embarked with me for Halifax, a dismal storm we had—the vessel small and deep loaded, we was well nie under water for hours during the storm. Cold as it was, we was ten days without fire to do us any good—I never saw such a dismal time before. I had the amazing goodness of God; he brought us safe to Halifax. We were greeted in kindness by Mr. Marchington, a true friend of the gospel. A few received us with kindness. I had a convenient place set apart for preaching. I hope the Lord gave me a few souls. I joined a Class—I tarried in the City four weeks, preached commonly six times in the week. Having an invitation I went to Windsor where I met with friends, joined about 15 in Society. Though the snow was deep I got as far as Granvil, Annapolis and Digby.

"*Dear Brother*
"God in his wisdom has altered my station from the south to the north, and I am now on my way as far as Mount Holly (N.J.). There seems to be a loud call for the gospel in Halifax, Shelburn, and many other places in Nova Scotia. I am willing, and want to go in the power of the blessed Spirit. I hope I shall have an interest in the prayers of all my dear friends. I shall never forget you for the acts of kindness you have showed. Lord grant you may ever continue an humble, zealous follower of the Lamb, that I may one day meet you in glory everlasting.

"Blessed be God, my mind is sweetly drawn out in the work of the ministry, and I hope I shall ever be little and mean in my own eyes, and that I may ever be rising higher and higher in the divine image. Brother Kent informs me that the work seems still to prosper, which rejoices my heart. O that Jesus may still go on in the power of his Spirit. Give my kind love to sister Hopper, and to all inquiring friends. I hope you will write to me often: direct to Halifax. I am more and more convinced that our new plan is of God. I hope and trust the Lord is about to raise up a glorious church.

"I commend you to Jesus, trusting you will be faithful unto death. In great love believe me.

"Your friend,

"F. GARRETTSON."

I

Dr. Coke: —

"*Halifax*, 1785.

"*Rev. and dear sir*,—After a stormy and dangerous passage of thirteen days, we arrived safely, at Halifax, where we met with a kind reception from Mr. Marchington, and a few other poor sheep in the wilderness. As yet I do not know as much of the country, or the state of affairs, as I shortly shall, God being my helper.

"A few days ago brother Cromwell set sail for Shelburn. Brother Marchington has hired a house at ten dollars a month, that will contain about three hundred souls. I have preached five sermons. The number has increased so that we now have our little apartment filled. I cannot speak of any visible good, more than that they seem to hear with attention and solemnity, and I have joined a society of seven or eight members. Shortly after I came to town, I waited on the old rector. 'Sir,' said he, 'you are on a blessed errand; I will do what I can in assisting you. I desire to see the gospel spread.'

"The next day I waited on his excellency, the governor, accompanied by Mr. Marchington. I found him very accessible. After telling him my business, from whence I was, and by whom I was sent: 'Mr. Wesley,' said he, 'is a good man—a very good man. How long do you purpose to stay?, I told him twelve months, or two years. 'I am glad you called upon me: you have my approbation, and whenever you call for my assistance, if I can help you I will.' I could but humbly thank him.

"God willing, on Monday next I purpose to take a tour through the country, to collect, if possible, the sheep so widely scattered. I believe there are many precious souls who desire to hear us. I am well assured we shall have hard work this year; but who would not labour, and suffer in so good a cause. I bless God for health, and as great a desire as ever to do his blessed will, and spend and be spent in the best of causes. We shall, as the people are poor, do little in the sale of books. Indeed I expect we shall be under a necessity of giving some of the small tracts away. The travelling here is extremely expensive. The packet has no less than four or five dollars for carrying a person from Halifax to Shelburn, and as much to Annapolis or St. John's Town: besides long journeys by land to the different towns and settlements. I am fully persuaded that our voyage to this part of the world is of God; the very time when preachers of our order ought have came. But if possible we must be assisted, for our preachers are left without horses, and but four pounds a piece. Next year I trust the people will be able to support the gospel. When I am more acquainted with the country, I shall send on another letter to conference. By the grace of God I shall do all that lies in my power to promote the Redeemer's kingdom.

"Dear sir, I remain your affectionate friend and brother,

"F. GARRETTSON.

II

"To the Rev. Dr. Coke."

In another letter he says, "The secretary sent for me, to know whether it would not be expedient for me to take the oath of allegiance to his majesty; but on my objecting to it, and stating my reasons for so doing, he told me there was not the least necessity: he also told me if there should happen any disorders in our meeting, to apply to a magistrate, and I should find favour. So far is well, is it not? My congregation has been increasing ever since I came; so that on the sabbath evenings many return home for want of room in the house. The last week night I preached, the house was nearly full. For two nights we had a little disturbance. On one night the stones flew, and one stone of nearly a pound weight was levelled at me, but missed its aim, and struck out two panes of glass near my head. This is but trifling, if I can win souls to Jesus."

III
AN UNFINISHED LETTER TO MR. WESLEY.

Halifax, April 20th, 1785.

"*Rev. and dear Sir,*—Known to me, yet unknown, I have many things to write, but am afraid of burdening you, or of taking up your precious time, which I believe you are redeeming moment by moment. I bless God that I ever heard of your name, or read your numerous works. Close doctrine and discipline I dearly love. This spring is fourteen years since I was powerfully convinced without the use of human means. The doctrine of the first Methodist preacher I ever heard was as precious ointment to my poor wounded soul. I was sure he was a servant of the living God. I have been travelling in your connexion nine years, during which time (I desire to write it with humility) God has granted me health, so that I have seldom missed preaching the whole of that time. My lot has mostly been cast in new places, to form circuits, which much exposed me to persecution. Once I was imprisoned; twice beaten; left on the high way speechless and senseless; (I must have gone into a world of spirits, had not God in mercy sent a good Samaritan that bled, and took me to a friend's house:) once shot at; guns and pistols presented at my breast; once delivered from an armed mob, in the dead time of night, on the high way, by a surprising flash of lightning; surrounded frequently by mobs; stoned frequently I have had to escape for my life at dead time of night. O! shall I ever forget the Divine hand which has supported me. O that I could love my God more, and serve him with a more perfect heart. It was three years from my conviction, before I was brought through the pangs of the new birth. Eight months elapsed after I was called to preach, before I was willing to leave my all and go out. I wanted to live in retirement, and had almost got my own consent to sell what I had in the world, and retire to a cell. God withdrew himself from me. I was very near desperation, for I was travelling, as it were, alone. I betook myself to my room, except when I was wandering through the woods and fields, ill I was worn away to a skeleton; and all this time I was kept from unbosoming myself to the lovers of Jesus. Strong impressions I had to go forth in Jehovah's name to preach the gospel. When I thought of it, I was pained to the very heart: it seemed like death, so great was the sense I had of my weakness and ignorance. By day I was drawn out in the study of the Holy Scriptures, and in the night season, when fast asleep, preaching aloud, till I have been as wet with sweat, as if dipped in a river. O! what a precious time I had when I gave up my own, to the will of God. I saw there was no other way for me to be saved. I was determined, if required, to go to the ends of the earth; yea, I promised the Lord if he would stand by me, and required it, I would go to the very mouth of hell. Blessed be God, he has been very kind and good to me ever since.

"The second year I travelled, I was powerfully convinced of the necessity of holiness. For a considerable time I waded through deep, but sweet distress. I had a discovery of the purity of the law, and the impurity of my own heart: being conscious it was my privilege to become pure in heart, I determined not to stop short of it. Sensible I was it came by faith. I was under deep exercises to preach no more, till I received that blessing. There was a time when I had a greater nearness to God, but I did not receive the witness till a twelve-month afterwards.

"F. Garrettson."

IV

"*Dublin, June*, 26, 1785.

"*My dear brother,*—Dr. Coke gives some account of you in his journal, so that although I have not seen you, I am not a stranger to your character. By all means send me, when you have opportunity, a more particular account of your experience and travels. It is in no way improbable that God may find out a way for you to visit England, and it may be the means of your receiving more strength, as well as more light. It is a very desirable thing that the children of God should communicate their experience to each other; and it is generally most profitable when they can do it face to face. Till Providence opens a way for you to see Europe, do all you can for a good Master in America.

"I am glad brother Cromwell and you have undertaken that labour of love, the visiting Nova Scotia, and doubt not but you act in full concert with the little handful who were almost alone till you came. It will be the wisest way to make all those who desire to join together, thoroughly acquainted with the whole Methodist plan, and to accustom them, from the very beginning, to the accurate observance of all our rules. Let none of them rest in being half Christians. Whatever they do, let them do it with their might, and it will be well, as soon as any of them find peace with God, to exhort them to go on to perfection. The more explicitly and strongly you press all believers to aspire after full sanctification as attainable now by simple faith, the more the whole work of God will prosper.

"I do not expect any great matters from the bishop. I doubt his eye is not single, and if it be not, he will do little good to you, or any one else. It may be a comfort to you that you have no need of him: you want nothing which he can give.

"It is a noble proposal of brother Marchington; but I doubt it will not take place. You do not know the state of the English Methodists. They do not roll in money like many of the American Methodists. It is with the utmost difficulty that we can raise five or six hundred pounds a year to supply our contingent expenses, so that it is entirely impracticable to raise five hundred pounds among them to build houses in America. It is true they might do much; but it is a sad observation, they that have most money have usually least grace. The peace of God be with all your spirits.

"I am your affectionate friend and brother,

"J. WESLEY."

V

"*Shelburn, April* 25, 1786.

"*Rev. and dear Sir,*—Some weeks ago I left Halifax, and went to Liverpool, where the Lord is carrying on a blessed work: many precious souls of late have been set at liberty to praise a sin-pardoning God. There is a lively society. Allen's small party oppose us warmly. The greater part of the town attend our ministry, and the first people have joined our society.

"A few days ago I came to this town, where I met dear afflicted brother Cromwell, and was glad to find him able to set out for Liverpool and Halifax. A negro man by the name of Morant, lately from England, who says he was sent by lady Huntingdon, has done much hurt in society among the blacks at Burch town. I believe that Satan sent him. Before he came there was a glorious work going on among these poor creatures, now (brother Cromwell not being able to attend) there is much confusion. The devil's darts are sometimes turned upon his own miserable head.

"Our chapel in Shelburn is not able to contain the congregation, and at present our friends are not able to build a larger. If I thought it right, I could wish, yea, beg for fifty or sixty pounds from England to promote the building one. Blessed be God, there are some precious souls here; but I expect many will be obliged to move to other places for want of business. The people in Halifax have had very little preaching of late, at which they are much tried. It is impossible for us to supply half the places where they want us. I have written to Mr. Asbury for help, but with no certainty of obtaining it, as the work seems to be spreading among them.

"I am an unprofitable servant, but blessed be God, the desire of my soul is to be instrumental in spreading the glorious gospel. I find a willingness to spend my all for God. I meet with many difficulties, but a moment's contemplation of the eternal world weighs down all. A man who labours for God in this country, needs a greater degree of grace, fortitude, and wisdom, than I possess. Dear sir, if you are disposed to send books to be given to the poor, or for sale, the sooner the better: let me know the conditions, and I will do the best in my power. The Saint's Rest and hymn books are wanted; the small select hymn book would sell; some pieces displaying the nature, manner, and doctrine of the Methodists; your journals and sermons; Mr. Walsh's Life; dear Mr. Fletcher's works have been a blessing in Cornwallis and Horton. I would to God they could be spread all through the country. I wrote in a former letter for some of the new prayer books adapted to the kingdom.

"We have bought two horses, which will do for the present. In some places the people will be able to support the gospel. In general they are poor; but in my opinion this country wants nothing but pure religion and industry to make it desirable. I have seldom seen a better spring in Pennsylvania or Maryland. The winter has been very moderate, except a few weeks. Much of the land is very good, and I am informed they get from twenty to forty bushels of grain from an acre; and hay and vegetables in great abundance.

"I want to die to the world, and live wholly to God. This is the constant prayer and desire of your unworthy servant.

"F. Garrettson."

VI

TO THE REV. FREEBORN GARRETTSON.

"*London, Sept.* 30, 1786.

"*My dear brother,*—I trust before this comes to hand, you and Dr. Coke will have met and refreshed each other's bowels in the Lord. I can exceedingly ill spare him from England, as I have no clergyman capable of supplying his lack of service; but I was convinced he was more wanted in America than in Europe. For it is impossible but offences will come, and of yourselves will men arise speaking perverse things, and striving to draw away disciples after them. It is a wonderful blessing they are restrained so long, till the poor people are a little grounded in the faith. You have need to watch over them with your might. Let those that have set their hands to the plough, continually pray to the Lord of the harvest that he would send forth more labourers into his harvest.

"It is far better to send your journals as they are, than not to send them at all. I am afraid it is too late in the season to send books this year, but I hope Dr. Coke has brought some with him to serve you for the present. I was far off from London when he set sail. Most of those in England who have riches love money, even the Methodists, at least those who are called so. The poor are the Christians. I am quite out of conceit with almost all those who have this world's goods. Let us take care to lay up our treasure in heaven. Peace be with your spirit.

"I am your affectionate friend and brother,

"J. Wesley."

VII

"TO THE REV. FREEBORN GARRETTSON.

"— — *Nov.* 30, 1786.

"*My dear brother,*—You have great reason to be thankful to God, that he lets you see the fruit of your labours. Whenever any are awakened, you do well to join them together immediately. But I do not advise you to go on too fast. It is not expedient to break up more ground than you can keep; to preach at any more places than you or your brethren can constantly attend. To preach once in a place, and no more, very seldom does any good; it only alarms the devil and his children, and makes them more upon their guard against a first assault.

"Wherever there is any church service, I do not approve of any appointment the same hour; because I love the Church of England, and would assist, not oppose it, all I can. How do the inhabitants of Shelburn, Halifax, and other parts of the province, go on as to temporal things? Have they trade? Have they sufficiency of food, and the other necessaries of life? And do they increase or decrease in numbers? It seems there is a scarcity of some things, of good ink, for yours is so pale that many of your words are not legible.

"As I take it for granted you have had several conversations with Dr. Coke, I doubt

25

not you proposed all your difficulties to him, and received full satisfaction concerning them. Commending you to him, who is able to guide and strengthen you in all things, "I am your affectionate friend and brother,

"J. WESLEY."

"P.S. Probably we shall send a little help for your building, if we live till conference. Observe the rules for building laid down in the minutes.

"I see nothing of your journal yet. I am afraid of another American revolution. I know not how to get the enclosed safe to Dr. Coke, probably you know: on second thoughts I think it best not to write to him at present."

VIII

"A LETTER FROM MR. GARRETTSON TO MR. WESLEY.

"Halifax, March 10, 1787.

"Rev. and dear Sir,—I received your dated London, September 30th. As I have not had an opportunity of writing for a long time, I shall be the more particular in this. By a storm Dr. Coke was driven to Antigua, and it is not certain when he will be here. We are much disappointed, but hope it will all work together for good.

"My time this winter has been spent mostly in Horton, Windsor, and Cornwallis. In the former there has been a divine display; many convinced and converted to God. A few months ago the place was famous for the works of the devil—now for singing, praying, and hearing the word. If the work continue much longer as it has done, the greater part of the people will be brought in. I have had a blessed winter among them. The work greatly revives to the west. James Mann (a young man God has lately given us, whose praise is in the churches) writes, 'God is carrying on his work in a glorious manner in Barrington; the people flock from every quarter to hear the word: many have been convinced, and about fourteen have been set at liberty, some of whom were famous for all manner of wickedness. The fields here seem white for harvest.'

"Brother Cromwell has had his station in Shelburn, but is very poorly: he writes, 'There seem to be very dull times in this town: hundreds have the small pox, &c. The Lord enabled me to go on as far as Cape Negro. I could only stay to preach a few sermons, &c. It would do you good to see the dear people, some rejoicing, and others mourning. In this way they continued good part of the night: depend upon it there is a blessed revival here. I returned to Shelburn very poorly, and expect, if God spares my life, to go home early in the spring.

"Brother John Mann at Liverpool writes, 'I am greatly comforted under an expectation of an ingathering here: the society is very lively; several added, and several lately converted,' &c. Dear sir, it would cause your heart to rejoice to know what a deadly wound Antinomianism has received in the town of Horton. My dear Master has given me one of the first lawyers in Cornwallis, and his lady.

"Brother Black is very steady and zealous in our cause, and has gone for a few weeks to the country. I can say this for Halifax, they are very kind in supporting brother Black's family: I think they give a guinea a week, and they have got a famous chapel nearly ready to preach in; it will contain a thousand people. Religion, I fear, is not very deep as yet.

"William Grandine, a young preacher, whom I mentioned in a former letter, has returned to his friends. I am under a necessity of going to the west to relieve brother Cromwell. I know not what will become of the young work in Horton: God can raise up or send us a preacher. Poor Cumberland is still mourning for want of one.

"I have received no books since I came to the province. We thought it expedient to have about fifty pounds' worth printed, as the printer was at leisure this winter. He printed several tracts very reasonably. Shall I ever see your face? Lord grant that I may be found worthy to meet you in heaven. So far I have been kept by the power of the Spirit, and I hope I shall never bring a reproach on the good cause. I want to be more given up to the work, with a greater nearness to God.

"I remain, as ever, your affectionate son,

"F. GARRETTSON."

"P. S. Since I wrote this letter I received one from brother Mann at Liverpool, saying, 'The Lord has broken in, in a wonderful manner, among the people, especially among the young. Within a few days twenty have been set at liberty: nine were converted one night.' Surely the Lord will do great things for us.

IX

"A LETTER FROM MR. GARRETTSON TO MR. WESLEY.

"*Shelburn, Sept.* 25, 1786.

"*Rev. and dear Sir,*—Lest my other letter did not reach your hand I send this, My time this summer has been spent principally between this and Barrington, which has occasioned me many fatiguing journeys through the woods, many times half leg deep in mud and water. Blessed be God, he has supported me under all my difficulties.

"When I first made my entrance among the people at Barrington, Satan strove in every possible way to hinder. 1. The people were dissenters almost to a man. 2. There was a party of those they call New Lights, who stood in opposition, and a preacher of that denomination warned the people against me, telling them I was legal and destitute of faith. 3. A letter was sent by a Calvinist preacher who had ministered among them, warning them against an American. For a few days I was under great exercise about leaving the town, despairing of ever being the means of planting the gospel under these and other disadvantages.

"The second sabbath I preached among them many came out to hear, and a recommendatory letter was written on many hearts. Before, I had scarcely a place to lay my head; since, I have not wanted friends. I visited a small harbour a few miles off, where there were about ten families. We had a divine display of the goodness of God: very few were left behind. Of these families I have joined sixteen in society, ten of whom know the pardoning love of God to their souls. About thirty young and old have been baptized. One man cried out bitterly against his wife; went out to hear; was cut to the heart, and now both are rejoicing in the Lord. At the head of the harbour we had a gracious display; very few families escaped conviction more or less. I visited almost every family, as also on the two islands, and most of them were willing to submit to our American plan, as it is called. At the head the meeting house stands where I have joined a prosperous society, as also at another harbour. Blessed be God, there have been many as clear and as powerful conversions in this township, as I have seen in any part of the States. At different times this summer I have spent about eight weeks in the township, and have formed a small circuit, able, and willing, to support a preacher. There are about fifty members, twenty of whom I favourably hope have experienced the love of God, and many who are not in society are earnestly seeking. I appointed four leaders and two stewards. I am so far on my journey to Liverpool, and I expect to meet the Doctor in Halifax, in which place we are to hold a conference the middle of next month.

"My hope revives for Shelburn; there has been an addition, and the society has become more lively. I have given them my consent to take one hundred pounds on interest toward building a church. Most of the coloured people whom Morant drew off have returned. I shall not be satisfied till we get a preaching house in this place. I must beg some from Europe and some from the States.

"Some months ago I received a letter from Mr. Asbury, in which he intimated the desire they had of my being ordained to superintend the work in the north. I answered the letter. A few days ago I received one from *the Doctor* on the same subject. Three considerations caused doubts to arise in my mind in relation to this important question. 1. The great desire I have of seeing England sooner or later. 2. My unfitness for so great a work. 3. There are many in your connexion so much more fit for the place. I love the connexion, and want to do every thing in my power to promote it. Perhaps when I shall receive a letter from you, and meet with the Doctor, more light will be cast on the subject. Don't think hard of my not sending my journal.

"I have not heard from brother Cromwell for some time. Brother Black informs there is a moving in Halifax. I desire your prayers and counsel. God is love, and I wish to be more humble.

"I still remain your affectionate, though unworthy son,

"F. GARRETTSON."

"FROM MR. WESLEY TO MR. GARRETTSON.

"*Macclesfield, July* 16, 1787.

"*My dear brother,*—I have your letter of March 15, and that of May 20. In the former you give me a pleasing account of the work of God in Halifax and other towns in Nova Scotia; and indeed every where except poor Shelburn, from which I had an excellent account a few years ago. Shall the first be last? What could have occasioned the decrease of the work there? St. Paul's advice is certainly good for all Methodist preachers—that it is good for a man not to touch a woman; and 'if thou mayst be free, use it rather:' and yet I dare not exclude those who marry out of our connexion, or forbid to marry; but happy are those who having no necessity laid upon them, stand fast in the glorious liberty. I commend you for laying as little burden upon the poor people as possible.

"Before I had printing presses of my own I used to pay two and thirty shillings for printing two and twenty pages duodecimo. The paper was from twelve to sixteen shillings a ream. I do not blame you for printing those tracts.

"But you do not send me your journal yet: surely you have had time enough to write it over. Dr. Coke seems to think you are irresolute, yet not willing to take advice. I hope better things of you, and your heart says to God and man, what I know not, teach thou me.

"I am your affectionate friend and brother,

"J. WESLEY."

XI

"A LETTER FROM MR. GARRETTSON TO MR. ASBURY.

"—— —— 1786.

"*My very dear brother,*—I had the pleasure of receiving yours dated Charlestown, January 15, 1786, and considered the contents. I had strange feelings on reading the account of poor G——g, but was happy to hear of my dear old friend, brother Cole. I fear there is a wide door open for the last b——p to do us much hurt. O that our dear Lord and Master may lay to his hand, and let the blind world know that there is a God in Israel.

"I have seen neither brother Cromwell, Black, or Mann, since last fall, though I have frequently conversed with them by letter. My time this winter has been in Halifax, and in the different towns between that and Annapolis. In Cornwallis the last time I was there I put a chapel on foot; there were nearly five hundred dollars subscribed: how they will manage I know not. On my return I put one on foot in Windsor. In this town God has given us a loving society. A few friends are willing to build one at Annapolis, though they have had very little preaching for six months. This day they began to draw stone for building a church in this town also. It is to be the same size of that of Mr. White, except a pitch higher. I have preached several sermons in Dartmouth, a new town, six miles from this. They seem very desirous, and made an offer of erecting a small house of worship, if we would pay attention to them.

"God willing, what time I have to stay in this town I expect to spend as follows, viz. Sunday eight o'clock preach in our little chapel, which will hold about four hundred persons; ten o'clock preach in the poor house, where there are about a hundred people;—I gave them books which attached them to me; I hope great good will be done among them;—at twelve o'clock in the preaching house; four o'clock in a private house by the dock yard; and by candle light in the chapel. I preach every night in the week: Friday visit the prisoners. After all I feel myself a poor needy creature. You desired me to send our minutes. I wanted to have a little conference in this place the first of April, and to have sent a full account to your conference: but this cannot be, and as I know brother Cromwell's mind, I shall give you as full an account as I can. Halifax, where there are forty members, will employ one preacher; Horton circuit will employ another, where I left sixty members; Annapolis circuit will employ another, where I left nearly one hundred members last fall; but how they are now I know not. In these three districts I expect brother Cromwell, brother Black, and brother Grandine, will be stationed. This brother Grandine is a young man we have taken on trial: I think he will be a preacher Brother Mann must take his station at Liverpool, where there are about forty members.

"There is Cumberland, where there is nothing but sin and the devil to hinder our gospel. This place would employ two preachers: however, one at present would do. There are about fifty members. In and around Shelburn there are between two and three hundred members, white and black. Much hurt has been done by a black man sent by lady Huntingdon, as brother Cromwell was not able to attend them constantly. Then there is the city of St. John's, and the country all around: I suppose there are twenty thousand souls. A few of our friends are scattered in that part; but in all that space there is only one clergyman, an old church parson. I was informed by a respectable man from the east, that there are hundreds of souls entirely destitute of the gospel. I have heard very little from Newfoundland: Mr. Wesley has sent brother Megary there, as I am informed by Dr. Coke. So you may see we are in want of three preachers. I made bold to open matters to Mr. Wesley, and begged of him to send one preacher from England, as a number of people would prefer an Englishman to an American. Many have refused hearing me on this account. However, this prejudice would soon wear away. The Lord knows I am willing to do every thing in my power for the furtherance of the gospel: but as to confining myself to Nova Scotia, or any part of the world, I could not; a good God does not require it of me.

"There are several thousand coloured people in this province, and the greater part of them are willing to be instructed. What do you think of sending Harry here this spring? I think he would be very useful. I have no doubt but the people will support their preachers in this country. It would be very well if the preachers who come would bring money to pay their passage; for we have but little money in hand, having been under the necessity of buying two horses.

"Next week I purpose to go to Shelburn, where I expect to meet brother Cromwell: if we think it expedient, and have an opportunity, one of us will attend conference, where we can state matters fairly. I send this letter lest I should have no other opportunity. A preacher will not do here unless he is able to take a circuit. Let him be in orders.

"Yours in love,

"F. GARRETTSON.

"P. S. In Horton the Lord has given us a kind friend, though not converted, Mr. Crane. He and his brother-in-law have offered two hundred dollars toward building a church in that town. There are many places I should be glad to visit, if there were preachers to supply the places already mentioned. Dr. Coke wrote to me to visit Newfoundland last fall, but it was not practicable."

The following anecdotes and reflections are from the pen of Garrettson's daughter, Mary.

"Thus has my dear and honoured father ended his notes to his printed journal. When they were commenced and when ended I cannot precisely say, but I think it is one of the last testimonies which he has left, probably written very near the close of his devoted life. His memory was stored with a rich fund of anecdote, and I regret exceedingly that of many passages of his life he has left no record. His journals while in Nova Scotia, except those in print, are I believe lost. I have been able to find only short notices of his labours while there, and among my earliest and most pleasant recollections are the details which my dear father used to give me of his residence in that region of frost and snow. I well remember the delight with which I used to climb his knee, and the importunity with which I used to beg for a story, about *Nova Scotia;*—and in riper years—but those halcyon days are for ever flown: tears will not recall them. At one time in order to attend his appointment, he rode through an unfrequented country, the hail driving in his face until nearly benumbed, he was obliged to lay the reins on the neck of his horse, and leave the animal by his own instinct to keep the road. There was no visible track, and turning out of the road in that country exposed the traveller to the greatest fatigue, as his horse sunk in the mass of unbeaten snow. At length he arrived at the only house he had seen; his horse stopped at the door, and he had only life enough left to walk in and throw himself on the bed. None but children were within, who covered him with plenty of bed clothes, while he lay almost insensible for nine hours, and had nearly forfeited his valuable life by too great eagerness in his Master's cause.

"He had often to cross the St. John's whose tide recedes, leaving its bed nearly empty, and again comes roaring up with great velocity and force, sweeping every thing before it, and elevating on its waves the vessels and ships which it had left dry. During its recession its bed is fordable; but in winter the crossing is dangerous on account of the large masses of ice it leaves behind. On one occasion his guide, instead of leading him up the river, went down, and they were not apprized of their danger until they saw the tide fast roaring toward them. The guide shrieked out, 'Put spurs to your horse and make for the nearest land!' He did so, although uncertain whether it would be accessible when attained, for the shores thereabout were very bold and rugged. His horse was fleet; the shore was accessible; he outrode the wave, which swept over the back of his horse just as he had set foot upon the land. I have often heard my father say that if he had only been half the length of his horse's body behind, he should have been swept off like a feather on the tide."

It appears that Mr. Garrettson continued to travel and preach in this province until April 10, 1787, when he embarked for Boston, Mass., leaving as a testimony of his fidelity and success in his Lord's vineyard, about six hundred members in society. After a perilous passage of three days he arrived in Boston, where he was kindly received by a few pious friends.

137. C. or CROMWELL (further references to C. or Bro. C. are to James O. Cromwell.)

Nova Scotia. Methodism was not new to Nova Scotia. The story of Methodist work there really begins in 1772 with the influx of English settlers from Yorkshire. Many others followed in the next two years. A number of them were Methodists. Numerous Loyalists, fleeing the American Revolution, swelled their number. Most of the work for the Methodists fell upon the shoulders of William Black, a new convert. By 1781 Black was traveling widely through Nova Scotia and New Brunswick organizing classes, love feasts, and preaching services. Within this year he appealed to the Conference in England for help. Wesley had no one to send, but Thomas Coke promised help from both England and America. Black came himself to the Christmas Conference and renewed his plea. The new Methodist Episcopal church answered in the persons of James O. Cromwell and Freeborn Garrettson. Smith, T. Watson—*History of the Methodist Church in Eastern British America*, Halifax, N. S. Methodist Book Concern, Vol. I, 1877, p. 153.

138. P. MARCHINGTON. This may be Philip Marchington of Pennsylvania who is mentioned by Lorenzo Sabine. Marchington was a Loyalist who spent part of the war in New York. There is record of a Mr. Marchington involved there with the Methodists in 1783. He settled in Nova Scotia and died in Halifax in 1808. He was a merchant. Sabine, L. *The American Loyalists*, Boston, Chas. Little & James Brown, 1847, p. 442.

139. *Friday, May 20, 1785*—I preached in Windsor to a crowded audience with great freedom.

Saturday 21—I rode 12 miles to Norton, sleighed all night with Dr. Booling—whom I found to be a religous, sensible man.

Sunday 22—at 9 o'clock I preached in the Court House to about 100 souls—I will join _____ curiosity brought these people out to hear—the general cry was "after preaching" "if this was Methodist doctrine it is agreeable to truth." Many of them followed me to the Baptist meeting house where I preached at 1 o'clock. When I came in the old gentleman was holding forth. My Lord gave me freedom to show that there is balm in Gilead, and that there was a physician there, and also I showed why the daughter of the people was not received or revered (Jeremiah 8:22) Many tears was shed.

Monday 23—I preached at Mr. Eatons. A sweet time I had, the cry was "if this is Methodist's doctrine I will be Methodist."

Tuesday 24—In the evening I preached at old Mr. Woodworth's, who was awakened by Mr. Whitfield 40 years ago—the dear old man is convinced of the possibility of falling from grace. O what a powerful time we had. About 12 souls was brought to cry for mercy. After meeting they continued some time hanging around each other inquiring what they should do to be saved.

Wednesday 25—I preached a few—of showing the necessity of Society meetings. Twelve joined and a precious time we had. Blest be God I hope the Calvinism and Antinomianism will get a wonderful stab.

Friday 27—I set on my journey to Annapolis. Preached at Captain Vowins in the evening.

Saturday 28—I rode 15 miles and preached at a house on the road with a degree of freedom and rode to Mr. De St. Croix's to a small audience and in the evening preached at Mr. Bath's. We had a divine presence.

Sunday 29—I preached with freedom at Granville Chapel at 11 o'clock and at 2 o'clock rode 12 miles and held forth at Annapolis Court House.

Monday 30—I held forth about five miles out in the country with freedom—I had some conversation with the Rev. B. I have never conversed with man farther from the truth than he.

Tuesday (May 31)—I held forth in the Court House. People in this place seem to be strangers to the life and power of religion.

Wednesday (June 1, 1785)—I preached in Digby about 20 miles from Annapolis and Thursday returned and held forth in the Court-House again.

Friday I preached and went on my way.

Saturday I rode 20 miles and preached at Mr. Bowins and rode 25 miles and held a Watch Night at old Mr. Eatons.

Sunday (June 5, 1785)—I preached in his barn to a crowded audience and at 11 o'clock administered the sacrament again at 3 o'clock.

Monday 6—I preached at Norden with freedom on the freedom of the will some approved, and others did not. In the evening I met Brother Cromwell at Windsor and Tuesday and Wednesday we had a Quarterly Meeting at Mr. Tomson's and a precious sweet time we had in time of sacrament and love feast, there are some souls in this place growing in religion.

Thursday 9—I preached with freedom at New-Port.

Friday 10—Falmouth and Saturday at Major Crains.

Sunday 12—At 9 o'clock I preached to a crowded audience in the Court House in Norton—rode five miles and preached at the Baptist meeting house with freedom and rode seven miles and preached at the Presbyterian meeting house at 5 o'clock. It was a precious day.

Monday (13)—I rode to the end of the town and preached with freedom. The people are all talk there but it is all chaff to me.

Tuesday (14)—I held forth in the heart of the town to a well behaved audience at Mr. Fox's, this N.N. wants to go to heaven without the cross of Jesus.

Wednesday (15)—I held forth to a gentile audience, some lovers of Jesus. I had great freedom. An antinomian said after preaching, "I understand you deny ritual sin, and say that a saint can fall away." I asked him if he was the saint or knew he was in grace—I do not know what I am. Then said I, "you cannot fall—if you will seek till you get grace, I will talk to you on the subject, for you can't fall"—what said he to you blackard—I can blackard as well as you, and so went away, as naaman.

Thursday (16)—I preached at Mr. Woodworths to a crowded audience. A little before preaching there came two old Calvinists in my room. Said one of them, "I came before preaching to have some conversation with you, for I understand you hold with falling from grace, I heard it and did not know how to believe it. I should be glad to know whether to deny perserverence of the saint—I answered, "I do not, my desire is that they should persevere. I do not hold with man's prospering in wickedness"—neither do I believe that a man can have grace while he lives in sin." Let's take the bible and see what it said there. I read part of the 15th of John and part of several chapters in Hebrews, part 1 in Peter, and where Paul was afraid of being cast away. Now said

I this is the condition that the other _____ we have not a promise for any but such who persevered in the end, and we have had many unhappy instances of men running well for a time and then turning back—read the 10th chapter of Ezekiel. Now what harm can there be in enforcing our Lord's, the Prophet's, and Apostle's Exhortation— very good said he—What should we do it for, if there is no danger—what harm can there be in the doctrine—Suppose you are a Christian and suppose your neighbor is one also—you believe in the unconditional perseverance—your neighbor believes in the conditional perseverance—whose sin? is the safest—if you are right, surely he cannot fall. I never said he saw so much before he said. They stayed to hear the sermon after- wards, said he, I never heard these men before—but they are better than I thought.

Friday (17)—morning I set out to Granville. I had not gone far before a man came running out. Said he, "I like part of your doctrine well but part I do not." What part don't you like—"you say sir a saint may fall. Will you answer me one question, said I—do you know that you was ever converted. I do, said he, Pray tell me how matters are at the present between God and your soul. Why, he said, it is a winter state. But, said I, are you now not living in open sin against God? He paused awhile. I asked "in the fear of God and desired an answer in truth. Yes, said he, I am living in sin and yet you say you cannot fall. I believe that because you have fell. If this is what you call a winter state, I call it living in the arms of the wicked one. You may talk if you will about your past experience, but I would not give one stone for your chance of heaven. Dying in the state you are reconciling Christ and Bilial together—O! said he I shall be raised up at last. You will, said I, but it will be to be cast in the lake if you do not repent—he seemed much affected, and went away.

Saturday (18)—evening I expounded the 7th Chapter of Romans to a few Antinomians.

Sunday 19—I preached in the Presbytery Meeting House the opposite side of the river from Granville to a number of precious hearers. I was invited to the home of an old gentleman to dine who makes a high profession of religion. Whilst we was talking at the table there was about a dozen present. I understand, said he, you preach per- fection. I answered, I do, and have for a number of years and shall continue unless I get a new bible. Why sir, said he, Paul was not perfect—he complains of a thorn in his side—the heart is the place for sin, said I—not the side. But see, said he, in the 7th chapter of Romans I am carnal, and that sin dwells in me, etc. I endeavored to open the matter. Well, said he, if we say we have no sin, etc. I endeavor to open it also—pray said I, let us come to the point at once. Do you believe that an unholy creature can enter into heaven—no—pray where is sin to be destroyed, at death—you must hold death as part of the savior or with a purgatory after death or come to perfection this side of the grave. He sat amazed and seemed to give up. We rose from the table. I went to prayer and went on my journey and preached at 6 o'clock in the court house. When I left the old man's house he desired me to make his house my home. I left Fletchers—shortly after I received a few lines from him to this effect: I believe you to be a servant of God, I hope the Lord will bless you and those that sent you here, I wish to see you at my house at every opportunity. I thank you for the book.

Monday (20)—I preached again.

Tuesday (21)—I went to Digby where I was greatly encouraged. Believe good work to be done, I joined a Society.

140. NEWPORT, RHODE ISLAND.

"In the morning I set sail, and the evening I came to New-port and preached in the Meeting House to several hundreds, with freedom. The next evening I had an in- vitation and preached to many more people than we had the night before. Surely there are some Christians in this town. In the morning the wind was fair, so that we sailed for York (New York), and arrived within 48 hours, where I had opportunity of preaching in the Methodist Church on the Lord's Day with a degree of freedom. *Manuscript Journal.*

141. The reading from the *Manuscript Journal* is particularly interesting.—"I was elected to be set apart as Bishop (this word crossed out and written over it the word 'Superintendent') over the work (in the) West Indies. My mind was under very deep

exercise, and I was not willing to take that office—1. I was not acquainted with all the preachers especially those who were lately from England. 2. A qualification. 3. I was not clear that I had a call wholly to leave the states. The Methodists in every part of the world are one. I am not ashamed to own Mr. Wesley under God, as the head and founder of the Methodist Church. I want to do all the good I can. I resign. My mind is easy. Oh God, stand by thy people. I am persuaded in my mind that if we are faithful, everything will be made plain. I preached several sermons in Baltimore with great freedom and blessed be my good and gracious God for the love which I feel for him and I am determined through his grace to devote my whole time and talents in his service." *Manuscript Journal.*

142. *Sunday 14 May (13)*—I preached at Abington Church with a degree of freedom, blest be God for carrying on work in this place.

Wednesday 17 (16)—I set out on my way to the peninsula. My Conference appointment was to preside over the work in that quarter. I rode about 20 miles, and had an opportunity of preaching at the head of Elk with freedom. Our good work never took deep root in this place.

Thursday 18 (17)—I rode to Dr. Boshels and called a few Presbyterians together, and I preached to them with some happiness. I found the old doctor to be a sensible man with a head full of religion and very fond of talking about it; but it was not in my power to convince him that he was not a Christian. Our gracious God has brought his son to know Jesus.

Friday 19 (18)—I came to Duck Creek Crossroads and preached several sermons to these dear loving people, and the words seemed to sink deep into their hearts. They have just laid the foundation of a new church, and they somewhat resemble the builders of the Temple at Jerusalem.

Sunday 21 (20)—I visited and preached to my old Dover friends. They do not prosper as well as I could wish, but I bless God that some of them are zealous in our dear master's cause. O! what will become _____ they once seemed to run well but where are they now.

June 1, 1787 (May 30, 1787)—I preached in Miles River Neck. This is a place where I have enjoyed many precious hours; but some of those who were very dear to me have gone into a world of spirits. Sister Parrot, her sister-Nancy and Sister Bruff are in Abraham's bosom. There are a few faithful souls left but individuals I fear have lost their first love.

Friday June 2 (1)—I visited and preached to about 400 of my Bolling Brook friends. We had a sweet time. For several things, this church exceeds many that I am acquainted with. 1. They are a very plain, solemn people. 2. There is a great degree of harmony among them. 3. They seem to care for each other. 4. Slavery is almost banished from among them, and 5. They love to hear the word.

Monday, June 5 (4)—I had a comfortable meeting at the bottom of the Neck, found that there had been a revival.

Tuesday, 6 (5)—I preached to a solemn company in Col. Vicker's. These people set out for heaven in a moderate way, and they seem to continue. The Colonel's was the second house in the county at which I preached at my first spreading of Methodism here, and he has continued a faithful friend. I spent the remainder of this week in visiting among my old friends, and preaching every day with much satisfaction. When I first made my entrance among these people, they knew not their right hand from their left, but now they are for the religion of Jesus. After I ended the sermon (this is in reference to Tuesday the 13th (12th) and the visitation to Hooper's Island) I desired the Society to go into the other room in order that we might have a Class Meeting. When they withdrew, I found that those who made a noise were strangers, some of whom had seldom heard the preaching. I desired the leader to meet the Class whilst I held the meeting with those who were not in Society, and a wonderful time we had. Several on the floor struggling for mercy, and before the meeting broke up several were powerfully set at liberty. There were four sisters who had been prejudiced against the Methodist, three came out to hear, and one would not come. The three who came out were convinced, and converted before they left the house. Their souls made happy they went home to tell their prejudiced sister what great things the Lord had done for them; but behold that same power which found them out in the church ran a mile and found her walking through the fields (it was about the same time) she was struck, and groaned for redemption so when they went home to tell her about what God had done for them she was able to give the same account of herself; so that four sisters were converted that day. Glory to God the Island is all alive. Glory to God his praise rings through this county. Who would not praise the Lord.

Sunday 18 (17)—I preached at Dodds Church. We had a solemn time. After I went around the Dorset preaching day and night to multitudes, both white and black; I set out from my good old friend T. Avery's. I preached and crossed over at Vianer? and on Wednesday visited and preached among my dear children in Quantico, and the next day had a blessed time with the Church on Broad Creek, and a blessed time I had. Glory to God my soul is happy and I am determined to devote in our dear master's service.

143. Journal for the 10th of July, 1787.

I set out to visit Worcester, rode about 35 miles and preached in the Line Church. As soon as ever I opened my mouth to sing I sensible felt the powerful presence of the Lord. The people seemed to be all in a holy flame. These are poor, but blest people.

Tuesday (July 10, 1787)—I rode 20 miles and preached in the Sound Church. These people are not in the state they were a few years ago—the Society is much richer, and have less religion. I found freedom to declare unto them my mind, with respect to their lukewarm state, and I trust there were some _____ meltings amongst them.

Wednesday, July 12 (11)—I rode 20 miles and preached at Brother Conaways. This is a young growing Society. There was a shaking amongst the people and the Lord began a great revival. Brother Conaway has become a zealous, faithful preacher, and the Lord owns his word. I passed through Somerset and found great freedom to preach the word.

Saturday 15 (14) and Sunday 16 (15)—We held our Quarterly Meeting for Somerset Circuit at Quantico Church. Multitudes flocked, both rich and poor. White and I being prest in spirit cried aloud. The word was too hard for some of the rich. A few weeks ago, when I preached at this place the wife of a rich man was powerfully convinced but they would not let her rest 'til she shook off her conviction, and then she could sit pretty secure at the communion of the Presbyterians.

Monday 17 (16)—My good and gracious God enabled me to preach at Vinson's near Salisbury to a few precious sheep, who are, and have been much harassed by the Annabaptists, and though they turned several aside, yet those that remain stand fast, and the little company begins to increase. When I first preached in this town, there was a blest gathering for good; a large Society seemed to be going on joyfully until the Baptists came and set them against each other, and sometime after this it pleased the Lord to remove Brother Hitch to a blessed eternity who was the leader, and a pillar in the Society, so that I was afraid that it would have been torn to pieces but blest be God, there are more than 20 who seem to be established in the truth.

Tuesday 18 (17)—I preached at a new place, with a degree of freedom. The place seemed awful because of the presence of the Lord, and in the evening I rode a considerable distance and preached. The people in this part of Worcester are not friendly to our pure religion.

Wednesday 19 (18)—I entered Snow Hill, a place where they were going (some years ago) to beat me for visiting a prisoner under sentence of death. After this they received the word in the Court House, and then turned it out, so that I preached with freedom to about a hundred under the trees. This town is made up of church people, and Presbyterians. We have Societies all around the town but not one member within. In the evening I went to good Sister Manemore's where I was comfortable in body and mind.

Thursday July 20 (19)—I preached at Brother Pernal's where I had as many hearers as the house could accommodate, and a sweet time we had. These are a loving, religious people.

Friday, July 21 (20), 1787—I had a comfortable time at Brother Mashel's. There are some lovers of our dear Savior in this Society.

Saturday 22 (21) and Sunday 23 (22)—We held our Quarterly Meeting at W.D-GS and I think this meeting will not soon be forgotten. Brother Downing is one that endeavors to do as he would be done by, and has set the example to the Virginians of the Manumission of Slaves. We had sweet preaching, a sweet love feast, and sweet communion with our blest friends. In this neighborhood there is a large prosperous Society. The slaves that Brother Downing set free seemed to be honest and industrious.

Monday 24 (23)—I preached near the Ferry at Brother Melvin's. I set out the next morning preaching every day in my way to Dorset Quarterly Meeting and Saturday and Sunday we held our Quarterly Meeting.

144. This is the Journal entitled "My First Journey through New York State after the Conference May 26th, 1789—January 20, 1790."

I preached several sermons in the City (New York), and had much consolation among the children of God, and as I was appointed to preach in the State of New York I left the City, rode to West Chester accompanied by my good friend, Brother Wigton, and in the evening had joyful opportunity of hearing a sermon from Brother Asbury. I think we had much of the divine presence. I accompanied him and Brother Whatcoat where I had another opportunity to hear the word. The remainder of the week was spent at Brother Lyon's in writing.

Sunday, June 14 (1789)—I had a sweet time in preaching to the North Castle Church from Naaman's Cleansing. I felt much of the divine presence, and in the evening I heard Brother Lee, and it appears that they are for the time considerably advanced. I was much taken with the kind family, and likewise with the Society in general. They have made an amazing progress in learning our Tunes.

Tuesday 16—I rode about 12 miles, and preached in Oakley's Church at Stony Street. I did not find my mind enlarged when I first began but in the latter part of the sermon the cloud was taken away and the Word seemed to reach the heart of the people. In the evening I preached at the Old English Church at Peakskill, and lodged at Governor Cortland's. I think the old lady is a follower of our blessed Savior, he is very kind, and one of their daughters professes faith. I felt my mind sweet, and my resolution firm. I rode 10 miles and preached at 11 o'clock, then rode to Brother Jackson's about 20 miles and preached with great freedom. There seemed to be a silent struggling among the people whilst I dwelt on the Lord knows how to deliver the godly of their _____. I received dear Brother Cook, as one of the dead, for I never expected to see him again this side of eternity. Dear man, he is very poorly, though I trust his soul is happy.

Thursday 18—Accompanied by a friend about 25 miles, I met Brother Asbury and Brother Whatcoat and had the pleasure of hearing another sermon and an exhortation at Dr. Bartlet's, and the next day we all rode to Rhinebeck together where I had another opportunity of hearing a sermon and exhortation. I fear we shall never do anything with these people. They are mostly Dutch, and I fear that they are fast asleep in carnal security. In the morning we parted, and I spent the day in Dr. Tillotston's.

Sunday 21—I can lift up my head this morning and praise the Lord. I preached in Rhinebeck in a barn at 11 o'clock, I rode eight miles and preached in another barn. We had a melting moving time. There I found a few souls who were convinced when I preached here last fall; I left word for the assistant preacher to take this place into the circuit. I returned to Rhinebeck and preached at an hour by sun. But the hearts of the people seemed as hard as flint.

Monday, June 22—I lodged at Mr. Livingston's, and Tuesday I rode to Hudson where I stayed all the week and spent my time mostly in writing.

Sunday 28—I preached in this _____ little city. I do not know what to think of these people. I think they are in a very poor way. In the evening I crossed the river and preached with freedom in the house of a kind Dutchman. I have an expectation.

Monday 29—Accompanied by a friend I rode to Queman's (Coeyman's) Patent, and preached among the mountains in a kind of house made with green bushes—it was very pleasant, and many attended, and a sweet time we had. This is a new place,

I was sent for more than 50 miles to preach in this place sometime ago, and never had an opportunity of attending them before. I blest God for a refreshing time among these poor people. The disputatious Annabaptists strive to hinder in this place but think there are some seeking souls. I had freedom in baptising a family of church people.

Tuesday 30—I rode about eight miles to another part of the Patent and preached in a large barn to about 200 hearers. Mr. Van Dyke the one in whose house I preached seemed very kind. I had great freedom to preach and I had no doubt but that good was done. The people seemed to be attentive. After I had ended the sermon an old Annabaptist got up, I suppose to witness to the truth according to their custom, but I desired him to sit down, that I did not approve of such irregularities in our churches. I had some conversation with him after the Word and found him to be a very forward man. This has been a _____ day to me. I lodged at Mr. Blaisded's who is part owner of the Patent. The family are very desirous of being Christians.

July 1 (1789)—I rode 14 miles to Albany where I had an opportunity to preach in the City Hall. This seems as yet to be a poor place for Methodism.

Thursday, July 2—At an hour by sun I called a few of my friends to endeavor to set up a Society, and had a ray of comfort among them and by candlelight preached in the City Hall again. The next evening Brother Bloodgood preached in a private house to about 200 within and without.

Saturday I rode to Schenectady and lodged with John Gorie? who formerly was a Local Preacher in Ireland. He still retains love for the people.

Sunday, July 5—I preached in the English Church morning to a family and in a private room at 7 o'clock. There are about 300 families in this town, and they have a Dutch and Presbyterian minister but very little religion. They have no Episcopal and the congregation has almost dwindled away. I found freedom to preach and found several who appeared very kind.

Monday, July 6—I rode about 30 miles to Brother Rowlands, Esq. near Tomhannock. In my way I met an old man. In the evening I got to my kind friend, Brother Rowlands, Esq.

Tuesday 7—I preached in the barn to about 50 with a degree of freedom from the language of the jailor "What shall I do to be saved?" People seemed to be somewhat affected. Our gracious God hath brought several souls to know him in this neighborhood. I am much pleased with Brother Rowland and family.

Wednesday, July 8, 1789—I preached at Hoosick? In this place the people are mostly Dutch so that I had but a few hearers. I had freedom and baptized one adult and three children. I think the time is coming to favor these people. My mind is sweet and comfortable.

Thursday, July 9—I preached in Ashgrove New Church and I think we had divine breathings after the Lord. The poor Society, consisting of about 50 members, have since last winter built the most elegant church according to the size of it that I know in the connection. They are very little in debt. They all set about it as if they were building for their own family, and they were greatly assisted.

Friday, July 10—I was exceeding poorly so that at 10 o'clock I could scarcely stand to preach, and in the evening likewise. Saturday I preached at 11 o'clock not far from Chase's Bridge with much freedom, and at 4 o'clock our Quarterly Meeting began in Tomhannock and Brother Rowland's. We had a very sweet time and about 20 new communicants were added. We had about 200 present at the love feast and I baptized eight adults and one by immersion and several children.

Sunday 12—On Sunday evening after meeting broke up I had a conversation with a woman: she told me that she was brought up to be Presbyterian, being dedicated to God in her infancy in baptism, she was strictly brought up and she thought within herself that she had been baptized, that she ought to be a Christian and lived a moral life until she was 14 years of age, about which time it pleased the Lord without the instrumentality of anyone to shine into her heart and her insight and give her a sight of herself and reveal Christ to her pardoning of love. She was led on as it were alone, only surrounded with the Annabaptists who strove to persuade her to renounce her baptism and go into the water. They told her that the Presbyterians were entirely wrong and that she could not be saved after all unless she entered deeper into baptismal water, which was very inconsistent for they beheld me a Christian and their principles led quite the reverse. They teased her continually till her mind was much bewildered, and she was almost ready to renounce her infant baptism. She thought she would inquire of the Lord and to let her know by some sign what was His will, and one night after prayer she went to bed and her eyes were closed; she saw Christ with his arms extended and an infant presented to baptism and immediately after she saw a beautiful branch of a blue color in each hand. He gave her one of them and immediately after she saw herself on her knees and the devil appeared in a very frightful form; he appeared to be in the shape of a lion and had a face like a horse. She could not tell what was this signification of two branches or the devil, but every doubt was removed respecting infant baptism. Sometime after this she went near 100 miles to Granvel in the state of Vermont to see two of her sisters, who had moved there. In this town I met with her and the very first Methodist sermon which she heard, she was convinced that it was the true doctrine and that the Methodists were the right people and would not leave the house until she had joined the people and brought out her sister, a stiff Calvinist, who was likewise, and joined the Society, likewise the third sister, so that in a very short time they were as much established in Methodism as if they had been acquainted with it for years. The town of Granvel is overwrought with Antinomianism, and I met with much opposition, as well as my brethren; but Glory to God in the midst of Antinomian preachers, and people, and persecution, the Lord in the short time raised up a Society of near 30 members, and I expect the _____ the whole lump.

Monday July 13—I rode 20 miles to Albany and had a meeting among the few of my friends in the City.

Tuesday 14—I rode to Dr. Hamilton's who believes as we do touching the principles of religion, and his wife professes to have had an experience.

Wednesday 15—My horse being very lame, I knew not what to do, for I could neither hire, buy or borrow a horse; so I set out on foot, travelled almost 20 miles with my poor horse hopping after me and got to my appointment, which was at Captain Salsburyes in Spencer-Town, and a very sweet time I had, surely I did not think much of the fatigue.

Thursday 16—My horse was a little better, so that I rode him a good part of the way— as I had many miles to go, and the road bad and I missed my way. Part of the people were gone when I got there, which was great trouble to my mind, for a large number had come out. Sheffield is a bigoted place and with a _____ wicked.

Friday 17—I rode about 12 miles to Colonel Burrel's and dined, and at 2 o'clock preached at Canaan Meeting House to a well behaved congregation. There is great difference between this and the Town of Sheffield. In this town the people in general do not seem to be prejudiced, and we have had some awakenings by our own instrumentality. After preaching I rode six miles and preached in Salisbury a little before sunset to a crowded audience.

Saturday, July 18—Our Quarterly Meeting began at J. Conklin's. We had a very dull time. There are great awakenings in this neighborhood, and we have formed a Society which will grow and prosper.

Sunday 19—I began to preach at 10 o'clock to about 300 people from "The Ransoms of the Lord shall return and come to Zion" etc. We had much of the divine presence. Brother Bloodgood assisted in the administration of the sacrament and I believe the Lord was with us. The minds of this people in this place have been much confused with Antinomanism, but I trust the gloom is blowing over. Many seemed to stand ready, both here and in Salisbury, to join the Society but they are fearful. I had some agreeable conversation with some serious friends in the evening.

Monday 20—I rode to the Pine Plains. On my way I called at Squire T's—had a long conversation with his wife, and other old predestinarians, and found them very strenuous for the unconditional desires and warm for sin. The squire is almost persuaded to believe as we do. In the evening I preached from "I saw the Dead, Small and Great, stand before God," etc. (Rev. 20:12) Great attention was paid to the Word, and there's great alteration in the place. In the midst of errors, we have planted a Society and it grows. Seven have been converted.

Tuesday 21—I spent in visiting several families with a degree of freedom. The next day I preached morning and evening and baptized two adults with freedom. In the morning a member of the Presbyterian Church made much confusion in the congregation. I was informed that he was set on by his minister. It is thought by well meaning people that he is afraid of losing his salary.

Thursday 23—After spending several hours in meeting I rode to Sharon (Connecticut) and for want of room in the house I preached in the open air, and a divine time we had. The Presbyterian minister of this town is a streneous opposer of our doctrine in the way of worship.

Friday 24—I was sweetly drawn out in writing to about 2 o'clock in the evening. As the man of the house went out early in the morning, I went out in the meadow to catch my horse. He was tied with a long rope to feed in the edge of the meadow; as I had hold of the rope gathering him to me, he gave a sudden jerk; by some means the rope got around my arms and body so that in less of half a minute I was entirely bereft of my senses; how long I laid in this situation I know not, for no person was near me. I knew not who I was or where I was, after laying in almost as much pain as I had been racked on a wheel for a considerable time I suppose rolling from side to side I made an attempt to lay my head on my hat for a pillow and saw the two first letters of my name in my hat—immediately I knew myself, and cried out, "Is this poor Garrettson—where is he and what is the matter?" I received a small degree of knowledge and rose from the earth and walked in the house and was laid down on the bed. Providentially a skillful surgeon was at hand, who came to me, and found my right shoulder dislocated. My left wrist, thumb, arm, shoulder, and several fingers much strained, my body much emaciated and many contusions on my head several _____ and my shoulder was put in place, blood was bled, and my other wounds were bound up. Immediately after I was bled, I recovered my senses perfectly as ever, and was able to look up by faith to my dear Savior and received a strong confidence in Him. Many of the inhabitants of the town came to see me, and my soul was so happy that I was constrained to exhort all who came near me with tears. I think I never had so strong a witness of perfect love. I was enabled to bless God for the affliction and would not have had it otherwise. I do believe it was rendered a blessing to the town.

Saturday 25—I _____ a person to borrow a carriage; he did carry me as far as the Oblong and the next day to Dover where I received strength to preach to a large congregation in the church and administered the sacraments to about 20, and it was a powerful time. The two following days I rode about 40 miles across the mountains, almost impossible for a carriage, and I suffered much pain but my mind was sweet and calm.

Wednesday 29—I rode to Mr. Braidays still accompanied by my good friend and brother, A. Lyon, who took tender care of me for I was not able to comb my own head, or put on or off my clothes, or even get in or out of the carriage, without much pain yet I was able to preach with much strength and freedom.

Saturday and Sunday the 2nd of August (1789)—was the days of our Quarterly Meeting at North Castle Church and we had a great meeting, perhaps the greatest that we have ever known in this side of the North River.

Monday the 3rd of August—I seemed to grow worst, and thought it expedient to take a passage and go by water to New York, and on Tuesday I safe arrived and stayed a day during which time I only preached two sermons.

Tuesday 11—Being a little better in my appointments coming on Long Island I rode 10 miles accompanied by a friend and preached in New Town by candlelight with much freedom.

Wednesday 12—I rode to the Court House in Hampton Plains and preached to about 60 or 70 people. The people seemed careless at first being a new place but before I was done, seemed much more attentive, except one man who left us.

Thursday 13—Rode to Hempstead Harbor, begun to preach about 3 o'clock in a paper mill to a considerably large congregation on, "If any man think himself something, when he is nothing, he deceiveth himself, but let a man prove himself," etc. Rode about 3 miles and began preaching at candlelight to where we had more than the house could hold and a very solemn time while I spoke from Rev. 1:7.

Friday 14—Rode to Oyster Bay, a little village inhabited by New Lights and Anti-baptists; began preaching at Colwell's in the evening but my hearers being mostly Calvinists they could not stand my doctrine very well. It seemed to make them _____.

Saturday, August 15, 1789—The members, and those that were permitted, gathered about 8 o'clock. We had the supper of the Lord, about 70 communed—to their soul's comfort I trust. After this Love Feast began, and several spoke feelingly, we had a calm melting time. Began public preaching to a large congregation at 11 o'clock. They appeared attentive while I discussed the perfect man from Psalm 37:37. We closed public exercise a little before 3 o'clock. O may a lasting _____ be made in the minds of these people so that the fruit may be seen many days hence. Amen.

Sunday 16—Set out about 4 o'clock and rode 17 miles accompanied by several friends to Brother Combs where I met with a loving family.

Monday 17 August 1789—This morning I felt my mind but full. The people gathered at three and I found freedom to preach and I trust we had a useful time. Religion on this island (Long Island) is not in as prosperous state as I could wish. There are many who care not for any of these things.

Tuesday 18—I preached by the edge of the plains at a good old brother's to a well behaved audience, and there seemed to be some divine breathings among the people. I was assisted in dispensing the Word. O when shall I see the life and power of religion among these cold hearted professors. I feel I am distressed. O for an outpouring of the blessed spirit.

Wednesday 19 August—I rose early this morning and addressed the throne of grace, and felt a sweetness of spirit, and after commending the kind family to the Lord, accompanied by a friend I rode near 30 miles and got safe to New York about 1 o'clock. In this journey there through the island I met with many trials and bodily afflictions. The sea air, however, I thought was of service to me. This was a day of much comfort to my soul. In the evening I found great freedom to preach to a solemn company. I think the church is gaining ground. I have about 10 days to stay in the city and much to do.

Thursday 20—I spent about five hours in writing. Part in reading, a short part in solemn prayer. And in the morning met the Bands. But before the meeting was concluded I so sensibly felt my weakness I was scarcely able to support myself and thought I should have fainted and fallen to the floor, but my blessed Lord was good to my soul.

Friday 21—I preached in the church on the temptations of the devil, and the goodness and wisdom of God in delivering his people. I retired to rest with a calm mind.

I have reason to bless God for this day. Dear Brother Cook has gone to Abraham's bosom. He was a dear good man. Some of the last words I heard him utter when he appeared nigh unto death was "I feel myself an unprofitable servant; but I was in precious _____ but to my soul. I am now reminded of what I have often told the people in my preaching of the happiness of dying saints. I now see angels around my bed waiting to convey my happy soul to heaven." He was able to commend all around a lovely savior. He had a tedious illness but blest be the Lord his happy spirit is now with Jesus.

Monday, September 7, 1789—I rode 25 miles to Brother Bartlets. Where I spent a comfortable night though not without inward trials. The enemy of souls goes about like a roaring lion seeking whom he may devour but blest be God Jesus is my friend, and I am borne up under my peculiar situation and am more happy in station than a king upon his throne.

Tuesday, September 8—I fell in with Brother B. _____ D., and A. _____ T. _____. I found a considerable degree of freedom in preaching not far from the Cold Springs and each of my brethren gave an exhortation. Brother A _____ T _____ is a rough plain preacher and the Lord owned his word in Brother Rowe's barn to many hearers and Brother A _____ gave an alarming exhortation and blest be the Lord. We had a shaking time and a precious class meeting. This is just beginning here. Sinners tremble, and a few are converted.

Wednesday 9—I preached with satisfaction in Rhinebeck but it was a day of trial as well as the two following. There was a cause. Lord give me wisdom. Lord grant me to do in all things the perfect will. I trust my eye is single. O that my body may ever be full of light, and that the cause of God may lay so near my heart that I may never take a single step to hurt my usefulness in the church of God.

Friday 11—My mind continues under deep exercise. I rode to and preached at Doctor B _____ T's with freedom. Our gracious God has given us many good friends in this neighborhood.

Saturday 12—I preached at Pine Plains to as many as could crowd into the house. The people were much affected—there was weeping and moaning through the whole assembly. In the close of the sermon I requested all who were determined for the kingdom of heaven to arise as a witness of their intention. I believe there was not more than a dozen of the whole congregation but what rose in tears, and those who kept their seat seemed deeply ashamed. I was obliged to hasten away as I had to preach that night at Mr. Smith's and we had a very solemn time. Their minister had left them and the flock was scattered, only the pious women remained and they gladly joined our Society.

Sunday September 13—I preached at Salisbury and baptized three daughters of Mr. Eldridge. There seems to be a considerable excitement in this town. Many of the women have joined us; but the men though very kind, stand at a distance. There is a sense— when their hearts are truly broken up, they will gladly come forward. In the evening I met Brother T. and preached to his congregation, and gave out to preach at the same place the next day. Many came together. And while preaching to them many shed tears. I desired as many as wished to see our Doctrine spread to withdraw, and would explain to them the nature of our Society. About 40 separated, some of whom I admitted. An old Calvinist asked me to preach a sermon on "He that is born of God doth not commit sin, for his seed remaineth in him and he cannot sin because he is born to God." A large house was immediately offered, and I gave out that I would attend the following Wednesday. After preaching a sermon in the skirts of the town on Wednesday 16th, agreeable to my promise I attended a large congregation. I have seldom had more light and freedom in the holy scriptures. After the meeting was closed, the general cry was, "If this is not the meaning of the text it has no meaning at all." Sometime before a certain minister had spoken from the same text but told his hearers that the unpardonable sin was spoken of there, and likewise that sin was not imputed to the elect. There was a pure seed within them and though the flesh sinned with David, Lot, etc. yet by Christ's imputed righteousness the Lord, the soul, was pure.

Thursday 17—I preached again in Salisbury from: "Unto me all ye that are weary and heavy laden, give you rest." Many seemed to be earnestly engaged, the weak faith of some was strengthened.

Friday 18—I preached in church at Canaan and at night among the mountains to abundantly more than could crowd into the room. Here is a young growing Society. I had some conversation with Mrs. Rothburn who told me that she saw me in a dream seven years ago. "I dreamed," said she, "I saw a person coming toward me who was surrounded by a very bright light. He came to me with a Book in his hand and asked my name and wrote it in his Book of golden letters. Told me I must presevere if I hold out to the end I should receive a crown of life." He then swiftly departed from me with the same light shining all around him. I told the dream to my husband and every strange preacher who came to the town I hoped would be the person; for I expected sooner or later to see him. When you first came to preach last summer in Canaan Meeting House I met you at the door, I know you to be the very person, your deep look and countenance were as familiar as if I had been acquainted with you for many years. When I went home I told my husband that I had seen the person and that the pure doctrine which he brought was the light which I saw shining around him." She appeared to be an earnest inquirer after the narrow way. O 'tis a blessing that this doctrine ever shone in this town.

Saturday 19 September—I rode accompanied by a young preacher to Salisbury, preached in the schoolhouse and lodged with a kind friend.

Sunday 20—A good part of the town came together. I expected to have the sacramental sabbath but there was a neglect of preparation. I preached two sermons. Many people thought we should never be able to spread our doctrine in New England but blest be God his power is sufficient to break the hardest rock and to subvert errors and this he is doing in a wonderful manner. This was a very barren wilderness. Now many can praise the Lord.

Sunday, October 3 (4), 1789—I preached to a very large congregation in Oswago. I was powerfully drawn out. There appeared to be general shaking among the people. This solitary place begins to bloom as the rose. Brother Jackson and his family all appear much engaged. In the evening I preached not far from Poughkeepsie. The people thronged together to that degree that it was too crowded. This circuit has been formed about twelve months and now we have about 300 members and many of them happy in God.

Monday 4 (5)—Went to the next appointment, a new place where we have no Society, and myself scarce able to speak on account of a severe cold. But any way our blessed Lord reached the hearts of some and I could say it was good for me to be here. A few days before, a minister came into this neighborhood to preach and after he had taken his text informed the congregation that God required of a man that which he could in no means do. Many of the eastern states have fallen in with what they call 'new divinity' and I think it is new. Man can neither repent, pray, believe or have a good desire before regeneration. Some asked me what use preaching was in this case.

Tuesday 5 (6)—I found great freedom to preach in the Nine Partners to a good Society, mostly taken from the _____ community. I found my mind comfortable at Brother Lyon's, an honest hearted kind man. All the family appeared desirous to enter into life; several have found peace with God.

Wednesday 6 (7)—I preached from: "The axe is laid at the root of a tree." The people here are mostly German and although their Pastor is unfriendly to us yet some have been brought to know the Lord. At night I preached at Dr. Bartlett's—a sensible loving man who has lately embraced religion and is appointed one of the general stewards of this circuit. Surely the Lord has in a short time done great things for the people to this place though we are surrounded with opposition. Our gracious Lord owned his blessed word and many now rejoice in his love.

Thursday 7 (8)—I preached at Squire Lewis's and at night at Pine Plains. Jesus rides prosperously through this land, shows his saving power in plucking sinners from the burning. Though the two following days my trials were great I trust I was useful in dispensing my master's gospel among the mountains.

Sunday 10 (11) October 1789—My appointment this day was in the city of Hudson in a house our friends had appropiated to our use; but an old church minister came in and wished to know if we would give it up to him for half a day. As he was an old man I consented and heard him read over his notes. I think though on the subject of repentance I do not recollect hearing the name of Jesus once mentioned. In the afternoon and in the evening I found it pleasant to open the way of salvation by Jesus Christ and I think the Lord was with us. When I was here before I invited 18 into Society and now they are doubled. Some of the members are very desirous of building a church but I thought it best to put it off a little longer.

Monday 11 (12)—My appointment lay on the west side of the North River; the preacher on the other side was waiting to go with me but the river was so choked with ice that I could not cross, and so rode around by Albany and didn't fall in with my regular appointment 'til Thursday noon at an old English Methodist's where I had a sweet opportunity to hold up Christ crucified to many and this evening preached in Albany. We have lately formed this circuit and many are inquiring the way to heaven.

The following Saturday and Sunday we held a Quarterly Meeting over the Mohawk

River, and we had as many people as we could find room for and we had refreshment from the presence of the Lord. We have lately joined more than a hundred in this new circuit, and many found peace to their souls. Brother Dunham is a bold useful preacher.

Monday 18 (19)—I set out to visit Cambridge circuit in Vermont and preached in the morning at Newton, and with difficulty and danger crossed the Hudson on the ice; I preached to a crowded company in the evening. In this neighborhood our dear Lord has brought many to him and many are seeking to know what they should do to be saved.

Tuesday 19 (20)—We had a precious sacramental occasion at Brother Knowlands. This good old gentleman has followed Jesus many years but never could meet with people to his mind 'til he found the Methodist and now he is established and can rejoice the day long and a good part of his neighbors have embraced the faith.

Wednesday 20 (21)—I rode 20 miles and preached with freedom and communed with about 50. People in this town have lately built us a church. I think they began and nearly finished it in a little better than a month and I thought they a little resembled the builders of Solomon's Temple. Accompanied by preachers and friends I rode about 20 miles to Greenfield, where we had a joyful time together.

Sunday, October 24 (25)—I preached with great freedom, administered the Lord's Supper, baptized about a dozen young converts. I then returned 20 miles back to Granvel, preached and had a love feast with my young converts, and desired any who had anything on their mind respecting our ordination to meet me in the enjoining room to speak their minds freely. Dr. Hatch and others did and told me that they were perfectly satisfied.

Monday 25 (26)—I rode 30 miles and preached at Ashgrove at night and had a love feast. I rode 30 miles and preached at New City. The young man they hired for their minister is a great enemy to this way. His influence is not extensive. We have no society in this place.

Wednesday 27 (28)—I lost myself in the woods and was belated. I suppose that I rode 30 miles instead of 20. However the people waited and we had a most precious time.

Thursday 28 (29)—Accompanied by Brother Wigton and another friend who came 20 miles to meet me, I rode 20 miles and preached at Wilmington New Church and I trust the Lord was with us.

Saturday, November 21, 1789--I got safe to Philadelphia and was gladly received by my friends, Mr. and Mrs. Baker.

Sunday 22—With a freedom of spirit I inculcated the truth to many precious souls. I feel much united to the pious in this City.

Monday 23--Rode on to Chester where I was kindly entertained by Mr. W. (Whiting?) an old disciple of our Lord; and then rode to Wilmington where I had a sweet opportunity to force the apostle's words "but grow in grace;" the children of the kingdom informed me they had not had so sweet a time for months. It was good for me to be here. My poor heart felt much of the love of Jesus.

Tuesday 24—I rode 40 miles, and had another precious opportunity to preach at night to the brethren in Duck Creek. I lodged at my old friend McClain's and had sweet consolation.

Wednesday 25—I rode to Dover and had great happiness in preaching. O my soul, what days of felicity dost thou enjoy.

Thursday 26—I rode 20 miles to Quarterly Meeting held at Choptank in their New Church. When I went in Brother Everett was preaching. After I preached and we were favored with much of the power of God. In the time of love feast I sat down in the pulpit, looking up, praying to God if there was any extraordinary power among these people, I might partake of it. They had been speaking but a few minutes; before the power came down in a very remarkable manner, and glory to God I enjoyed it to the comfort of my soul, and was satisfied it was of God. Great part of the saints brought out in loud ecstacies so that the whole house rang, and then they continued until time for public meeting. Brother Asbury gave us a precious sermon and ordained six pious men to deacons orders.

Afterwards I found great freedom to preach. I accompanied Mr. Asbury to Mr. White's glad once more to see good sister White. I heard I should never see her again in this world.

Saturday, November 28, 1789—I rode to Queen Annes and stayed at Brother Bradley's and Sunday's Quarterly Meeting for that circuit began. I rejoiced to see many of my old friends and had a great freedom to declare, "leaving the principles of the doctrine of Christ." Heb. 6:1. Several exhortations followed. The next day the house was crowded so that we were under the necessity of omitting the blessed sacrament. We had a charming love feast, and I found much freedom to preach and also to hear. On the whole we had a great meeting. The next day I thought it best to take a water passage to Baltimore, and after waiting all day I parted with my sulky, and Wednesday and Thursday rode on horseback around the bay about 90 miles, and got to Town at sunset.

Friday, December 4th 1789—We met in council. I was happy to see many of my old fellow laborers from all parts of this extensive continent. We had many prayers, and a sweet conference.

Saturday 5—Sweet prayers, and sweet union with Jesus. Preached at night with liberty tho under the cross.

Sunday 6—I sat with pleasure under the Lord, had a joyful time at the Lord's table.

Monday 7—Our council continued—not on discordant—

Tuesday 8—We continued all in harmony.

Wednesday 9—Sweet conversation—every night we had a sermon and several exhortations. Among the rest, I found freedom to speak. O how wonderful the power of God came down—I suppose there were more than a thousand people present, and the whole congregation agitated, the voice of singing, praying, exhorting and crying for mercy and singing the praises of God, and most exultant strains were heard in every part of the church. This continued 'til three in the morning. I know not how many were converted, or how many sanctified.

Thursday, December 10, 1789—This was to be the concluding day of our council. Part of it was spent in telling our experiences and giving _____ of the work of God in our Districts. At night we had another blessed meeting which continued until after midnight.

Friday 11—Most of our brethren left town. At night I preached with much comfort.

Saturday—I took my leave of the brethren, and rode as far as Cokesbury and preached at night.

Sunday 13—My soul is happy. I preached in the College Chapel a little after sunrise and 10. At 3 o'clock rode seven miles and preached to a crowded audience at my brothers. Here I met Brother Ruff who gave a warm exhortation. I rejoiced to see my brother face Zionwards, and several of his family, lately brought into the faith. I spent four days visiting, and preaching among my relations, and had more satisfaction with them than I ever had before. Surely the Lord has heard my prayers for them; for flame has broke out among them which has run like a flame in dry stubble. Many of them have felt power and are humbling witnesses for Jesus. O who would distrust so good a God.

Thursday 17—I again took my leave of my native land, and set myself to the north. Determined God being my helper to be more than ever engaged in his glorious cause beseeching him to grant a blessed _____ might be kindled in that cold clime. In any way I had a sweet time, glad once more to be at Wilmington New Church, and I trust the Lord was with us.

Sunday 20—This day I was much drawn out in prayer. I preached two sermons in Philadelphia and the Lord attended with his power in the evening so that the cries of the people made the place ring 'til 10 o'clock. The next morning I found myself unwilling to leave the City but appointments were such that I must away. After a journey of 100 miles on Christmas Eve I arrived in New York. During my stay I preached two or three times every day and I think I never spent a better Christmas in my life for the Lord was powerfully present with the people. When I spoke of the great revival of the work in the south many of the friends seemed in full expectation of it and so it was; for

I left the City but a few days before for the word broke out in a great powerful manner in a prayer meeting and after that in the church.

Thursday, December 29, 1789—I left the City and rode 'til late in the night, and the next day I preached at North Castle. As the weather was cold we had not as many as would fill the lower part of the church. At night we had a watch night at Mr. Gown's, when I had the opportunity of hearing several of our young exhorters. In this circuit the members have increased to near a thousand. Glory be to God, many of them are happy in his love. I preached to many not far from Bedford. This is a growing and going Society. The minister in Bedford is much opposed to us. I rode through the rain six miles accompanied by several friends. We had to cross a rapid river, one friend and myself got safely over, the others returned being too timid to cross. I preached to a few. We had a precious season.

January 9, 1790—I rode about 30 miles through a very mountainous country, and preached to a prosperous Society the next day.

145. Garrettson set off on a tour through some parts of Connecticut and Massachusetts on his way to Boston. The following extracts from his journal are given:—

"Having stayed a few days in the city, on Wednesday, June the 2d, (1790) accompanied by Harry who is to travel with me this summer, I rode as far as Miles's Square, and preached to more people than could get into the house. In the evening I rode to brother M.'s, at East Chester, and felt myself not so much drawn out as I could have wished.

"*Thursday 3d,*—the appointment was in New Rochelle church, where I preached from, 'O my dove which art in the clefts of the rock, &c. I had a degree of freedom while comparing the Church to a dove; but more while speaking of the rock and the secret places of the stars; and when I came to speak on the latter part of the text, 'Let me see thy countenance, let me hear thy voice; for sweet is thy voice and thy countenance is comely,' I was much drawn out, and a small moving ran through the people. In the evening I retired to brother S.'s and was very comfortable in a kind family, and blessed be God I felt my soul somewhat refreshed.

"*Friday 4th,*—we had a solemn meeting at the Plains. Though it was a wet day many came to hear the word; and gave great attention. My mind is sweetly drawn to love the ways of the Lord. I found great freedom to describe the pure in heart.

"*Saturday 5th,*—we met in King-street: more people gathered than the house could contain, and I found great enlargement in speaking. Harry exhorted after me to the admiration of the people. When I came into the house I found a man extremely ill with the colic. I ordered him to drink a pint of cold water, and he was relieved in less than three minutes. I returned to Brother C.'s and was very comfortable.

"On the Lord's day we met in North Castle church, where I was surrounded by a listening multitude while I explained, 'A King shall reign in righteousness,' &c. I found great freedom to speak the word, and we had much of the divine presence. Again in the afternoon I was enabled to expatiate on Matt. xxii, 12, 'Friend, how camest thou hither not having on a wedding garment?' I think there were more people than I had ever seen together in this place. I suppose Bedford court house would not have contained half the people, so that I was obliged to stand under the trees: many of the rougher kind of people attended, some of whom did not behave very orderly. It is not common to be threatened with stoning in this country; the children of the devil would threaten a long time before they would venture on such a work, for the laws are very strict and the greater part of the people favour religion. In the evening I retired to brother L.'s, and I trust enjoyed the company of my blessed Master.

"*Monday 7th,*—preached at brother B.'s in the manor to a crowded audience from, 'All Scripture is given by inspiration of God,' &c. I had great liberty to point out the benefit of our glorious dispensation. Our dear Lord owned his blessed word, and my spirit did rejoice in God my Saviour.

"*Thursday 8th,*—many more came together at brother H.'s than could crowd into the house: we had a joyful season; my own spirit is filled with sweetness. The people of this circuit are amazingly fond of hearing Harry.

"*Wednesday 9th*,—I rode to Sing Sing and had an attentive audience while I enforced, 'Now the just shall live by faith,' &c. I have not preached a sermon with more sweetness since I left New-York. In the afternoon, at General Van Courtland's, near Croton river, I had great comfort while declaring, 'It is God that justifieth, who is he that condemneth?'

"*Thursday 10th*,—though a wet day, the church at _____ was well filled and I had much pleasure in describing the walk and prosperity of the blessed man, Psalm i, 1, 2, 3, and in the afternoon the old English church was nearly filled. I showed that, 'He that is born of God doth not commit sin,' &c. Harry, though it was a heavy cross, exhorted afterwards. I lodged at the old governor's, where I was comfortable with a kind family. The governor was gone far to the west to make a treaty with the Indians.

"I highly approve of the conduct of our statesmen respecting the poor Indians. On the frontiers of other states they encroach on the Indians' property; here they have made a large purchase from them, and it is a rare thing to hear of an Indian's killing a white person.

"*Friday 11th*,—I rode over the highlands and at three o'clock preached to a large congregation among the mountains: in this place our gracious Lord has raised many from the dead. I felt my heart much alive among the people while I explained St. John's advice to and account of the church of Philadelphia.

"*Sunday 13th*,—our horses gave us the slip, so that we had to send five miles after them, and just as I was determining to set out on foot the man brought them to the door. We got to the place in good time; but the day was very wet and the house so very leaky that we had a disagreeable time at Fishkill. In this place the Lord hath given us a few good souls, and I trust that we shall have a precious gathering.

"Monday, early in the morning we set out and called on the son of the widow at whose house preaching was the day before: he was in deep distress of soul, and I trust it will not be long before he shall be set at liberty. In the afternoon I preached to a crowd of people from Ezekiel's vision of the dry bones, and I trust there was a shaking among the people who came from almost all parts of Oswago, some perhaps from curiosity to hear Harry.

"*Tuesday 15th*,—I had but a small congregation assembled in a barn at a new place among the Presbyterians: the next day I preached at (Rhinebeck,) and spent the day following comfortably with my old friend, R. Sands, Esq.

"*Friday 18th*,—I advanced toward the Cold spring, and preached at my good friend Rowe's from, 'Loose him and let him go.' Spent an hour with Dr. Bartlett and had a comfortable meeting at Mr. Lewis's. Jesus is precious to me; his ways are delightful.

"*Saturday 19th*,—I rode to Mr. Herrick's, where I preached in the afternoon. I had great freedom to preach from 'In hell he lifted up his eyes,' &c. Harry exhorted after me with much freedom.

"*June 20th*.—This day I was met by a Churchman who desired me to come and pray with his family: I did so with freedom; then rode on to Sharon, where I preached to about one thousand people under the trees from, 'O my dove, thou art in the clefts of the rock,' &c. I was much drawn out and great attention was paid to the word. The devil strives very hard to hinder the spreading of the gospel in this town: but blessed be God, many are under awakenings and I think the kingdom of Satan will be greatly shaken.

"*Monday 21st*.—This was a day of great trial to me arising from a very plausible story told of one who I believe was entirely innocent of the charge. My heart was pained within me, but I could not convince those who were the accusers of his innocence. In the afternoon I was obliged to preach in the open air again for want of room in the house.

"*22d*.—This morning I called a few together and examined into that strange affair, and am convinced of the innocence of the accused. I rode about fifteen miles and preached in the Presbyterian meeting house to some hundreds from, 'If the righteous scarcely be saved, where shall the ungodly and sinner appear.' It is encouraging to see such hearers affected under the word. I am informed that when I preached in this meeting house last spring Mr. G., who was one of my hearers, was very much touched, and a few weeks ago died a penitent. I have great hope for the people of this town. I had a comfortable time at R _____, Esq., who has a friendship for us.

"*Wednesday 23d,*—I rode about twelve miles to Litchfield, and was surprised to find the doors of the Episcopal church open and a large congregation waiting for me. I preached from, 'Enoch walked with God,' and I believe good was done. I left Harry to preach another sermon and went on to the centre of the town; the bell rang and I preached to a few in the Presbyterian meeting house, and lodged with a kind Churchman.

"I preached in the skirts of the town where I was opposed by _____ who made a great disturbance. I told him the enemy had sent him to pick up the good seed, turned my back on him, and went on my way accompanied by brother W. and H. where I found another waiting company, in another part of the town, to whom I declared, 'Except ye repent ye shall all likewise perish.' In this town we have given the devil and the wicked much trouble; we have a few good friends.

"*Friday 25th,*—we rode fourteen miles through the rain, many people gathered, and I found freedom to declare, 'If we say that we have no sin we deceive ourselves:' several were in tears, and there was a shaking among the people. The squire and several other Calvinists came out to converse on the disputed points of unconditional election and reprobation, the freedom of the will, and the perseverance of the saints. I had to discourse with them until nearly midnight, and I believe some of them were much shaken. We have hard work to plant what they call Arminianism in this county: we stand in need of the wisdom of the serpent and the harmlessness of the dove.

"*Saturday 26th,*—I rode a few miles and preached to a company of people assembled in a barn; my text was, 'But deliver us from evil.' I had a considerable degree of freedom in enforcing the necessity of being delivered from all sin; some believed it and some did not; among the rest one good old man who came a considerable distance on foot, said the Lord is with us and I am satisfied. A few weeks ago he was a warm pleader for the unconditional decrees; but now he sees differently.

"*Sunday 27th,*—I preached in Farmington to about three hundred people, and had great freedom in showing that Christ tasted death for every man, and that as the way was open, if they did not repent they would justly be damned. There are a few precious souls here who cleave to our doctrine and have united to our society.

"*28th,*—we set out for Boston, rode fifteen miles, stopped at Hartford, and preached in the court house to five or six hundred people, who seemed to give great heed to the words which were spoken: while Harry gave an exhortation some rude people behaved very uncivilly. The two following days we travelled and arrived at Worcester about four o'clock, where I was kindly entertained by Mr. Chanler, but the people appeared to have a small share of religion: I went from one end of the town to the other and could get no one to open the court house and gather the people. I went to the house of the Rev. Mr. B_____. I was asked to take tea. I drew near, and inquired if it was not customary to ask a blessing? No, said he, not over tea: I then drew back from the table: his countenance changed, and he said in a very short manner, 'You may ask a blessing over your dish.' Pinching want might drive me to eat and drink in such a case. I had an hour's conversation with him. It is lamentable for masters in Israel to deny the power of religion.

"*Tuesday, July 1st, (1790)*—we rode through a very pleasant country; I never saw more elegant buildings in a country place than those that surround Cambridge, and the college has an imposing appearance. I got into Boston, about seven o'clock, after riding forty-eight miles. I boarded Harry at the master Mason for the Africans, and I took my own lodgings with a private gentleman, who had been a Methodist in England, but has, I fear, fallen from the spirit of Methodism.

"*Sunday 4th,*—I attended church in the morning, and gave great uneasiness to the people with whom I lodged on account of my not communing. I never in my life saw such a set of communicants, dressed in the height of the mode, and with all the frippery of fashion—so much of the world in their manners and appearance that my mind was not easy to look on. In the afternoon I preached in a meeting house which had formerly belonged to Dr. Mather. Monday evening likewise in the same place. Tuesday I went from end to end of the town and visited several who were friendly, a few of whom were formerly Methodists, but I fear they are not such in practice. I engaged the use of the meeting house, and a place for a preacher to board, and on Wednesday set out for Providence. I had rode but about thirty miles when I met brother Lee, and while we were sitting on our horses talking, an old gentleman rode up and asked us to go to his house and preach that night: we went and had a comfortable meeting, and I also preached the next morning: after dinner we parted; brother Lee consented to go to Boston and make a trial there until I could send another preacher. I reached Providence about five o'clock; the bell rang, and I had an opportunity of preaching in good old Mr. Snow's meeting house.

"*Friday 9th*,—I had a sweet time in retirement, and in the evening addressed a larger congregation than I had the night before.

"*Sunday 11th*,—with freedom I preached in the morning at six o'clock. I officiated all day for good Mr. Snow, and at six Harry preached in the meeting house to more than one thousand people. I appointed to preach the next morning at five o'clock, and I suppose three hundred people attended to hear my last sermon. I had a sweet time in Providence. I have no doubt but the Lord begun a good work in many hearts. I left many in tears. I left town about nine o'clock, rode about thirty-five miles, and lodged at Colonel P——'s, whom I found to be a very kind man, and I trust the family were stirred up: the daughter seemed to be much affected.

"*Tuesday 13th*,—I rode forty-five miles to Hartford, and preached the next evening to as ill behaved an audience as I have ever seen in New-England. The people of this place, with a few exceptions, seem to be fast asleep in the arms of the wicked one. The following night I preached again, and some of what are called the gentry behaved so ill that I was under the necessity of breaking up the meeting and declining to preach by candle light.

"*Sunday 18th*,—I preached again in the state house, to a few who gave attention. I rode to Weathersfield and preached at eleven o'clock, and likewise at two o'clock, and then returned and preached at Hartford at five o'clock to about two hundred people. I am apprehensive from the state of religion in this place that the ministers do not enjoy the life and power of religion; they seem to be so smoothed over that they cannot with any degree of patience bear to hear of the carnal mind, or any mention of hell.

"Thursday, I preached with freedom at Farmington, and on Tuesday morning I gave an exhortation on the subject of baptism, and baptized fourteen adults and children, and we had a sweet time, and then rode to Litchfield and preached to a serious company. I have no doubt that the Lord has begun a good work in this town. Brother W—— is a very acceptable preacher in this new circuit, and the Lord owns his labours.

"I lodged at Mr. O——'s, and had a long conversation with him and his brother, who related a very singular circumstance, which was as follows:—The brother (as they both informed me) was intended for a Presbyterian minister; he had gone through his course of study, and as a probationer he had begun to preach, and I doubt not from what he informed me but that he was acquainted with inward religion. He fancied that if he was called to preach the Lord would endue him with a gift of miracles, and he concluded that he would preach no more until he obtained that gift. He began to fast, and after he had fasted eight or nine days, ministers, people, and physicians came around him, telling him that he would shortly be a dead man unless he took some nourishment—at another time they endeavoured to force him to eat, but to no purpose. He told me that he did not eat a mouthful of victuals during forty days, and only drank water and a few times a little small beer. He likewise told me that nothing went through his body for forty days. His brother, who I trust is a man who fears the Lord, professed to be an eye witness of the truth of this statement; he was with him most of the time, and said that during the forty days he did as much work as he himself was able to do, who eat four or five times a day. When we would come in from work, said he, he would take nothing but a little water or a little small beer, and then go to work again. From the tenth to the nineteenth day of his fast, he seemed somewhat feeble, but after that he grew strong and looked nearly as fresh and well as he ever did, and continued to labour hard during that time: after the forty days were ended, he eat as hearty as usual, and found no injury from it, though the physicians warned him that in so doing he risked his life. Before this he was much exercised about the doctrines peculiar to Calvinism, and had renounced them. When I saw him I found him a believer in the same system of free salvation which the Methodists hold out, and he has begun boldly to preach again.

"Saturday I rode as far as Cornwall, and preached at Squire Rogers's. I found that the Lord had begun a blessed work in this town when I preached here before, so I rode to Canaan, where I was comfortable.

"*Sunday 25th*,—I preached in Canaan to about five hundred people, from Matt. xxv, 14, 15, the parable of the talents. The Lord was with us: the work in this place is moving on. I have circulated a subscription for the building of a church here. Brother Bloodgood was with me; as it was too warm in the house I preached in the open air. Harry preached after me with much applause. I rode in the afternoon and preached in Salisbury, in a part of the town in which I had never before preached, and I think I have never seen so tender a meeting in this town before, for a general weeping ran through the assembly, especially while Harry gave an exhortation. The Lord is carrying on a blessed work in this town.

"*Monday, July 26th*,—I preached on the whole armour of God, with freedom, and in the afternoon at brother Haywood's from, 'If our gospel be hid it is hid to them that are lost.' One careless woman was brought under concern, so that shortly after she went home she returned and opened to me the state of her mind, and appeared to be in great distress indeed.

"*Tuesday, July 27th*,—between two huge mountains the morning appeared very beautiful, and I was very much delighted with the prospect when the natural sun had arisen and illuminated the earth with his bright beams, but one much brighter Sun doth arise to cheer the mind, even the Sun of righteousness. At four o'clock I preached on another beautiful mountain, in a Presbyterian meeting house, to about three hundred people who gave heed to the things spoken. The people on this mountain are so far convinced that they appear to receive the gospel. When we first came to this mountain the people were much prejudiced, but are now more reconciled, and there is a prospect of a society.

"*Wednesday, July 28th*,—I had a sweet time at the furnace, and sent on Harry to supply my afternoon's appointment. I rode twelve miles with two disciples, and had an opportunity to see a distressed woman, Mrs. L——n, who has almost lost her reason. I endeavoured to converse with her, but I was too late. They are very much engaged to give her medical aid, but a revelation of the love and favour of God alone can relieve her.

"*July 29th*,—I rode to Hudson, where I found the people very curious to hear Harry. I therefore declined preaching that their curiosity might be satisfied. The different denominations heard him with much admiration, and the Quakers thought that as he was unlearned he must preach by immediate inspiration.

"*Friday 30th*,—I spent part of the day in planning a new church in this city, and in the evening preached to several hundred people with considerable freedom from, 'Him that honoureth me I will honour,' &c., and I think I never witnessed a more solemn time in this place. The people of this city drive away their convictions by the love of the world. I have frequently seen fine prospects here which were soon gone.

"*Saturday 31st*,—crossed the North river, rode twelve miles, and preached among the mountains. The Lord is deepening his work among these poor people. The society is young, but growing."

(The Manuscript Journal for June 2nd, 1790 through July 31 is reprinted verbatim in Bangs, pages 208-219). Garrettson's *Manuscript Journal* continues in its *day by day* record as follows:

Sunday, August 1, 1790—Accompanied by a friend I rode 8 miles and preached on a high mountain to about 500 people, who gave very good attention and I trust good was done. I rode 8 miles further, and preached in a large barn (in pencil there is written in, Van Dyns. Previously where he is preaching on a high mountain the name Brother Coeymans is written in pencil), to about 600 people and the Lord was with me. The young Society seems very prosperous in this place, and our kind friend Brother Blasdill is appointed a leader. Sister Blasdill is a mother to the preacher.

Monday the 2nd of August—I rode a few miles to the west of Albany among the Dutch and had but few hearers for their Domeny had been crying down the Methodists at a surprising rate, informing the people that we were deceivers and robbers. Blest be God many know that we have instrumentally undeceived many, and robbed the devil of many of his subjects, and his ministers of much of their worldly honor, and convinced many that they are after the flesh.

Tuesday, August 3, 1790—I preached with considerable freedom to a small congregation of Dutch and English. In this neighborhood the people seem as hard as rocks.

Wednesday 4—I preached at Aswell's, and rode into Albany and preached with freedom to as many as could crowd into the house, and the next day I spent in visiting our few friends, and preached again at night with freedom.

Friday 6—I preached in a barn 10 miles west to the city to many, some of whom came a distance to hear the Word.

Saturday 7—Our Quarterly Meeting began and we had the presence of our dear Master. This week I spent in visiting the Cambridge Circuit, and on Saturday and Sunday our Quarterly Meeting.

146. These concluding pages of the printed journal are not found in any presently available Manuscript and obviously represent F. G's personal reflections especially concerning unconditional election. This is not surprising for it was one of the major battlegrounds in his ministry. His final words are an appeal to all so minded to receive Christ.

PART TWO

THE GARRETTSON JOURNALS
1791-93, 1805, 1807, 1809,
1817-21, 1824-26.

NOTES

Thursday, March, 3 1791—After enjoying a happy season in New York I set out about 10 o'clock, rode about 40 miles and preached with freedom to about a hundred people at General Courtlands.[147] My mind this day without deep exercises. My dear Lord did comfort me.

Friday 4—A good part of the day I spent in writing. In the afternoon rode to Gov. Courtland's, whom I found very kind, and the old lady the same solemn godly woman whom I left here once before.[148]

Saturday 5—This morning my mind was calm and sweet. I rode to Oswago where I met with trials. I resolved to do my duty, and stand fast in the liberty of the gospel.

Sunday 6—I preached two sermons with freedom.

A JOURNAL FROM THE CONFERENCE IN NEW YORK, MAY 17, 1791

"We had a convocation consisting of about 30 ministers and preachers and it was a time of union and consolation."[149]

Tuesday, June 7—I left New York, and had an opportunity to exhibit truth every day during my journey to Albany.[150]

Saturday 11—I got into Albany and found that Brother Wigton had been useful in an enlargment of the congregation, and _____ in taking over our new building. I've had much trouble in getting our poor little society in the city a convenient place erected for their worship; but I hope to accomplish it.

Sunday, June 12—I opened our New Church, which was not quite covered in, and only a loose floor laid, from these words: "On this rock will I build my church, and the gates of hell shall not prevail against it." *Matthew*. The following week was spent in the City, partly preparing my Journal and partly in collecting money, for and in looking after the building. Brother W. and I went through all the streets in the City, and did not collect 40 pounds from strangers in the whole. I hope the time is coming to favor this place.

Wednesday 22—I left the city accompanied by my friend Mr. Crosfield from New York in order to visit the Societies in the western settlement.

Friday 24—We got to Johnstown, New York where I found freedom to preach in the evening.

Sunday, June 26—I preached two sermons with freedom, and rode 10 miles through a heavy rain to Mayfield, and preached to a very desirous company, In this new settlement I stayed several days and found great freedom among the poor people. Blest be God, the poor have the gospel preached to them.

Saturday, July 2, 1791—Mr. C. met me, and the next day we had our Quarterly Meeting at Johnstown, and a sweet time it was—we had about 30 communicants most of whom are young converts. A week ago I drew a draft for a church in this town and our willing friends have nearly got out the timber already.

Monday 4—I agreed with a gentleman for a lot to set the house on, in a beautiful part of the Town, and paid part of the money down before several of the Society, in confirmation of the bargain, and set out again for Albany, accompanied by Brother N. and my old friend C.

Tuesday 5—We arrived and found the workman busily employed on the church. I have a great desire that the gospel should take _____ in this City, but find little freedom.

Sunday 10—I preached three sermons to the people in the New Church which is completely covered in, and the floor laid.

Monday 11—I left the City, and preached at Coeyman's with a considerable degree of freedom on: "Grow in Grace." I do not feel as happy and solemn as I wish.

Tuesday 12—I rode to Hudson, and found freedom to inculcate truth in the Court House. I was resolved to get rid of the incumbrances on our hands respecting our building—called the male members of the Society and we concluding we had better exchange our lot and frame for Mr. Jenkin's lot and house already built 40 feet × 24 completely finished— he supposed himself to have favored us with about 50 pounds. I felt myself well satisfied, for I am sensible the Society was not able to finish our own house.

Wednesday, July 13—I rode to Mr. Latham's and preached to a few, and the next day I had a considerable degree of sweetness in preaching to a serious company at the Pine Plains.

Friday 15—I preached at Mr. Eldridge's in Salsbury. I felt a degree of liberty.

Sunday 17—In Canaan[151] I found a degree of liberty in opening our New Church from: "On this rock will I build my Church,"—the building is beautifully situated on a large flat rock by the side of the road. In this part of the town, we have a Society of some who are lovers of our Lord. In the afternoon I rode to, and preached in Cornwall at Roger's Esq. and felt my mind drawn out in the Word.

Thursday 21—Our Quarterly Meeting began at Farmington, Conn. where Brother Asbury met me and delivered a lively discourse and I found much liberty of speech, and we had a comfortable time both in time of communion, and love feast. My mind is calm, and I have great sweetness in prayer.

Friday 22—We rode to Litchfield, and preached Christ to a serious congregation in the English Church, and lodged at the house of Mr. Osborn who is a friendly Presbyterian. Our dear Lord is with us.

Saturday 23—We rode to Cornwall and dined with Mr. Rogers, and in the afternoon had freedom to exhibit truth to many precious souls in the Presbyterian Meeting house and lodged at Mr. Wadsworth's.

Sunday 24—In the morning I staid behind, and in the house of Mr. R. declared with freedom "compel them to come in that my house may be filled," we had a moving time. I rode to Canaan and in our New Church, to many precious souls, opened on the first Psalm and went on and met Brother A, and Brother D. at Colonel Burrell's, where we were comfortable together.

Monday 25—Mr. A.[152] preached to a cold hearted people in Barring in the afternoon and I preached in the evening. The next day we had a sweet time at Weagen's, and the day following our Quarterly Meeting began at New-Britain.

Thursday, July 28, 1791—Many serious people met us at Bethlehem and the day following went into Albany and continued until Monday morning. Brother Asbury preached five sermons with freedom. Many of our country friends met us; we had a little Conference, and one of our Brethren was set apart for the Office of Deacon. We travelled through Coeymans, Hudson, Rhinebeck, Nine Partners, with a degree of freedom and on Saturday our Quarterly Meeting began on a huge mountain not far from the Oblong where a vast crowd assembled. The Meeting House though large would not have contained a third of the people, so that we withdrew to the woods, and though many were disorderly, many drank in the Word. I found it to be impractical to attend to our love feast. We travelled through Salsbury, Sharon, Oblong and Dover, and on Saturday, August 7 and 8 we came to Oswago where we had but a dull Quarterly Meeting. At our love feast, and likewise at our Lord's Table several seemed sweetly drawn out in love to our dear Lord.

Wednesday 9—We set out and travelled through Fish-kill and crossed the mountains (many attended the Word) and on Wednesday came to Peekskill and lodged at Governor Courtland's. In the morning I was under the necessity of parting with the Bishop.

We had a comfortable time together. I felt almost a continual calm in my soul, and it was with a degree of reluctance I left him. I find in him the qualifications of a primitive Bishop.

Thursday 10—I set out for New York, where I staid one week and had liberty to preach the Word, and had sweet communion with my dear New York friends Brother Whatcoat and Brother Morrell who are precious to me.[153] I feel myself drawn out in the cause of my dear Lord; but have many things to trouble my mind. I am sometimes ready to wish for a more retired life; but feel the willingness to bear the burden which our dear Lord Jesus came to lay on me.

Wednesday 16—I left the City, and travelled 40 miles and preached in the evening at General Courtland's. I had a degree of freedom. Sister V. V. is a living follower of our dear Lord.

Thursday 17—I rode 10 miles and breakfasted at the Governor's, rode 20 farther and preached in Oswago. My dear Lord so wonderfully supports me that I seldom feel weary.

Friday 18—I rode 20 miles accompanied part of the way by Brother Everard to Dover where I met Brother Moriarty and we had a sweet time. The day following we rode to Sharon, and I found I had much freedom to preach to those loving people.

Sunday 20—Sunday morning at 10 o'clock I met the people at Canaan. I know not what to think of the people in this Town. They are civil—but the slackness of their attendance, discovers a dislike either to me or my doctrine, or manner of delivery. God has not sent me to smooth people over with untempered mortar. I fear many of those people want to go to heaven without the cross, which cannot be. In the afternoon I preached with freedom at Cornwall, the hands of some of our friends are hanging down on account of the circuits being free. This I could not help—the preacher who was appointed to it did not come, which was a trial and grief to my mind; but I have sent a young man who I trust will be a blessing to the people. Their _____ taken exeeding poorly, but travelled around the Litchfield Circuit and supplied or fulfilled my appointment and returned the Sabbath following and held a Quarterly Meeting in Cornwall, when our friends were greatly encouraged and strengthened and I trust the two young men, Brother Swain and Brother C. will be rendered a blessing to the people.

Monday 29—I went through the lower, and upper part of Canaan. I preached a sermon for dear sister _____ who was just beginning to recover from a severe spell of sickness from "many are the afflictions of the righteous." She is a true penitent, but does not know her sins forgiven. I had much freedom.

Monday I had to settle a troublesome affair between two of our friends, so passed on to Barrington where they think it a great favor to hear us. I understood that many in the main street had laid themselves under an obligation that the first who went to hear the Methodist had to pay a bottle of Rum. Brother Dillon, a preacher of Stockbridge Circuit met me there.[154]

Thursday we went to Stockbridge, and preached to a stiff-necked people, the day following I preached in another part of the town in a house where I found the family no credit to the gospel, the congregation in general counted themselves unworthy of eternal life from those words "we did not do many works then because of unbelief," and so took leave of the family and we moved the preaching to Mr. Barn's a little to the west where I preached in the evening from "the wicked watched the righteous and seeketh to slay him" with great freedom. There I felt myself at home.

Saturday, September 3, 1791—I entered the State of Massachusetts and met Brother Green and we had a powerful orderly meeting. The work in this Circuit is just beginning. Brother Green accompanied me several days, and I visited several of the towns, and found a beginning work, which I hope will grow and prosper. Surely the Lord will bless the labors of Mr. Green for he is a precious humble soul. I met a sensible man and he was a Shaker, but had left them, and had joined us. Of this man I received a most full, satisfactory account of those people called Shaking-Quakers than I had ever done before. I had been at a great loss to know how, or from what they sprang. This man convinced me they were the relics of one Mr. Bell in England who was formerly a Methodist preacher, who fell into enthusiastical notions, and was by Mr. Wesley excommunicated. He held, though we might be as perfect as angels, or Adam in paradise, he carried matters so far, that he professed that on such a day, such a part of London would be sunk which mightily alarmed hundreds, if not thousands in the City. Once he was a man of great faith, but where is poor deluded Bell now? His followers were dispersed and after a time a few of them came over and settled in Niscauna, and were preaching for a time, until the Mother (as she was called) professed to have _____, and a few entered on their new work which consisted mostly in dancing, shaking, turning around and (as they said talking in unknown tongues) together with the cohabitation as husbands and wives. This new scheme with great rapidity for a time was carried on, so that people of note were taken in among them, and among the rest several ministers. As they professed to be in the same state of purity, which Adam and Eve were in, whilst in state of innocency professed not the least degree of shame whilst both sexes were dancing together (what they call working out their salvation) as naked as they were born. I have conversed with several judicious men who have left them, who have informed me that whilst among them they hated everything which they thought to be sinful and—thought they were doing right.

Wednesday, September 14, 1791—I preached with a considerable degree of freedom on the subject of election: "Many are called, but few are chosen." The greater part of the congregation were well satisfied, but a few were not. In the afternoon two students in divinity, came out for a dispute. One of whom asked me if it was agreeable to me to be asked a few questions. "I want to know the difference between foreknowledge, and an unconditional decree. If God foreknows the salvation or damnation of every individual, this knowledge is definite and cannot be altered." Inspired writers spoke to _____ creatures, though of an infinite Being, and as they spoke to _____ creatures their expressions were adapted to their weaknesses; were we to speak to and of the Supreme Being we should say that there is neither fore, or after; but from and to eternity a present now. When the Deity revealed to the prophets, some hundreds of years before it came to pass a matter of the crucifixion of his dear son, and the person who betrayed Him, it was actually before him that he saw the determination of the will of the betrayer, and murderers, and according to the determination of their wills, it was revealed to the prophets, and surely of their wills if their wills had not determined in his crucifixion it could neither have been seen, or foretold, and although (speaking after the manner of the Holy Scriptures) God foreknows all things, yet he does not unconditionally decree anything, leaves his rational creatures to act freely. "I want to have some conversation about the will before we enter that subject, we ought to know what the will is. I wish you would tell me." "The will is a passing of the soul." It hath for once missed the mark. You might as well have said the eye was the ear. It is the dictate of the soul. You must follow your studies long before you will be capable of a dispute on polemical divinity." "Pray sir, what do you say the will is?" I think the power of the soul to choose good or evil. When God placed Adam in paradise, and gave him the power of choice. After he chose the evil and fell that our choice was forfeited. He promised the Messiah man—Adam, and his whole posterity was again graciously restored to a free choice, and now good and evil is set before him. This is not unnatural, but preaches freedom of will—a freedom purchased by Jesus Christ. By this time more than forty of the inhabitants of the town had gathered, and even listening, "I wish you would tell me how the soul is brought to Christ." It is now time to begin public meeting, where I shall open that matter to the congregation. I withdrew to the room where the seats were prepared and I gave out "one thing I know whereas I was blind, now I can see." I had great freedom and hope good was done.

Thursday 15—I preached near Lebanan Pool,[155] and the next day went into Albany, and preached in our New Church to a few with a degree of freedom. I continued in the City 'til the Saturday week. On the Lord's Day I preached to many serious hearers, morning, afternoon and night; when will the people of Albany turn to God.

Saturday 24, 1791—I left Albany and attended a Quarterly Meeting at Captain Groosbeck about 20 miles to the north of the City. I felt a great freedom to speak.[156]

Monday 19—Accompanied by Brother Green, I rode to Dr. _____ who is converted to the faith, and in the evening I preached in a large schoolhouse to as many well behaved people as could crowd in, and I found great freedom together with a hope my labors were not in vain. We lodged at B's Esq. who I found to be a sensible man, but held some strange sentiments. He believes that the body was fallen, but not the soul—for it was pure from the hand of God. One, was this true, the soul not in _____ need a Savior so that those who die in infancy by no means _____ redeeming. Two, the creation was not finished in six days. Three, the Almighty would be under necessity of creating pure begotten bodies or they would be mere animals. "How then does the soul _____?" Every species both of human and animal creatures have a power of beginning beings after their own kind. I cannot conceive that infants partake of Adam's sin, neither do I suppose that it would be just in God to punish them for it. John says, "Behold the Lamb of God who taketh away the sins of the world." John 1: 29. The sin of the world, in the singular—original sin—knew a child in the first Adam and you view it a child of wrath; but you would in second Adam [as] Jesus Christ, you view it angelically holy, "what would have become of Adam's race had not a Savior been provided." The sin of his _____ posterity was _____ seminal—in the seed and their punishment would have been equivalent to the crime. It would not be more than nonexistence, since the crime was not actual, or sensibly felt _____ with the punishment. Adam _____ _____ _____ inevitable ruin, and not justly for his own actual but first he opened a way for him, and his unborn posterity—the Savior was provided. Man in Christ is graciously restored, to a free choice, _____ _____ _____ for their own actual deservings. "I never heard anyone reason this on the subject before. I cannot _____ give up my opinion 'til after a more mature consideration."

Tuesday 20—We rode in the sleigh with our friendly doctor (and his two young men rode on horses) to the next town which lay ten miles to the east, and I preached to many serious hearers. Our dear Lord has awakened several, we have a blessed prospect. The people at whose house we staid were very friendly, and one daughter who was under religious concern was so taken with Quarterly Meeting that she was pressed in spirit and wrote beautifully in verse the state of her mind, and the son's wife who was driven almost into black despair by the Calvinist system has through the instrumentality of Brother Green and brought to experience the love of God. This said the old lady was the same work that was laid out four years ago by New Lights, and my minister and others just despise you, I will give you the right hand of fellowship.

Wednesday 21—We're still accompanied by the doctor and the young men to Pownel in the State of Vermont where I preached to many serious hearers, and as I found the Lord had begun a good work, I appointed to meet the distressed or such as desired it, and in the evening set up a Society. I did, and about 12 gave in their names. Mr. Angel, the gentleman in whose house I preached, presented a petition to me signed by about 80 of the principle persons in town to let us know it was their wish and desire to let the Methodists continue to preach in the town.

Thursday 22—Finding it impractible to attend my appointment through as a severe storm. We staid at Mr. Angel's and the next evening felt freedom to offer Christ to as many as could crowd into the room.

Saturday 24—My new, though kind, friend Mr. A. thought best for my horse to stay at his house, and for him to convey me for several days in the sleigh. There I departed with dear Brother Green, and we rode 40 miles and got into Albany before sunset.

Sunday 25—What with the swiftness of my passage not being much accustomed to that way of conveyance, and the severity of the weather, I found myself unable to preach more than one sermon. Brother B. stood in my place and preached the other two.

Monday 26—We went to Nescaunia, and I found great freedom among a loving people. Sister Fradenborn and family are still on their way to heaven.

Tuesday 27—We returned in the morning to Albany, and dined and set out for Tomhanock, and the next day my friend A. left me, and I preached at Mr. Grosbeck's from, "By faith Abel offered to God a more excellent sacrifice than Cain, etc." Heb. 11: 4. I spoke of Abel's offering and where he excelled that of Cain's. The effects of it ———— take witness that he was righteous and God accepted his gift.

Thursday 29—I preached at Brother Milks, Esq. who by faith Noah being warned of God moved with fear, prepared an ark for saving his house. Heb. 11: 7, etc. I hope that good was done.

JOURNAL FOR 1792- '93

Saturday, December 15—I left Philadelphia, and rode to Burlington (N.J.), and lodged with our worthy friend Mr. S————g, and on the Lord's Day found freedom to preach two sermons in our new church. In time of the intermission, I felt very heavy, and sorely tempted by the evil one, and found it somewhat difficult to keep my mind fixed on the right object.

Monday 17—I rode about 30 miles, and stayed with a kind friend, on the day following reached Elizabethtown, (N.J.) and had some agreeable conversation with Mr. and Mrs. M————c. Though he is not a Methodist, I think him a sincere follower of our Lord, and a kind friend to the Methodists, though his sentiments do not exactly tally with theirs, yet we are nearer to his mind than any other people.

Thursday 20—We sailed from ———— at eleven and reached New York by one, and the following evening I preached in the old church with a small degree of freedom on perfection. The conversation which I had this day with Mrs. L. Livingston was very agreeable. The Lord sometimes works by means, and in ways, which are strange to man, in bringing about his purposes. I am entirely willing for the Lord to do with me what seemeth Him good; but wish to increase in submission to his good pleasure. My mind is now fixed on that matter, and think the sooner it takes place the better.[157]

Saturday 22—I had a conversation with Brother Tillotson and know not what effect it had or may hereafter have with him or others.

Lord's Day 23—This morning was not an easy matter for me to fix on a subject, my mind was not fully determined till after I ascended the pulpit. I had but little freedom. In the afternoon the Lord was with me in the New Church whilst preaching from Revelation 3: 12. I drank tea at Mr. S's in the evening, and felt myself poorly. Part of the evening was spent in conversation with my good friend ————. We can fix on nothing certain, respecting time or places. The Lord does all things well and we shall yet see his stately footsteps in the whirlwind, as well as in the earthquakes, a small voice. I have often said, "Let patience have her perfect work and so forth."

Monday 24—I left the City and rode through the rain to Sing Sing, N. Y.[158] and declared to a small company in the evening. It is appointed, "Once to die, and after death the judgment." There was no visible moving among the people.

Christmas Day, Tuesday 25—As the roads were very slippery occasioned by the rain, and frost, I was ———— of having my horses shoes roughed, which brought me too late to Oswago (N. Y.) for my appointment. This day my mind was drawn out in deep thought. Jesus is the fairest among ten thousand.

Wednesday 26—I preached from, "Except ye be converted, and become as little children and so forth"—Matthew 18, after which I rode to Dover, and preached in the evening with freedom. A drunkard disturbed the congregation till he was put away. I fear this Society is not lively. Some souls felt the power and I had freedom to press the necessity of a close walk with God.

Thursday 27—After an agreeable time with Brother and Sister M_____y the young preacher rode with me to Sharon (Conn.) where I preached to a crowded audience from, "The kingdom of heaven is like treasure hid in a field, and so forth"—Matthew 13. This Society is united to each other, and I trust are in a prosperous way. The Lord was with us. I was sweetly drawn out this evening in writing letters whilst all are still, and hushed to sleep in their different apartments. A deep sense of God rested on my mind, and an awful eternity was before me. Solitude is a fine exercise with me whilst Jesus is my chief joy.

Saturday 28 and Sunday 29—was our Quarterly Meeting in Pittsfield (Mass.)[159] I preached the first day on Isaiah 16: 16, "Behold I lay in Zion for a foundation and so forth." It is about 15 years since I preached on this and it seemed sweet to me, and we had a solemn time. We had several lively exhortations. I spent about three hours in the evening with the publick members of the circuit in conference, and it was a useful time. There have been an addition of upwards of a hundred members the past quarter in the circuit. The following day a large meeting house was well filled and I had freedom to preach on "By whom shall Jacob arise, for he is small,"— Amos. We had about 150 communicants, and the best of all was the Master of the feast was with us. In the evening for my encouragement a good old gentleman said I had greatly improved in preaching since I was there last, and that he thought me a very glowing man; but this was no proof to me: I wanted greater evidence of it than man can give.

Monday, December 31—was a remarkably stormy day. I rode in a sleigh accompanied by three preachers and others, to Lanes-Borough, and agreeable to a vote of the congregation at meeting previous to this, I preached in the old Episcopal church to a large assembly considering the inclemency of the weather. The doctrine of the gospel was very clearly opened to me, and several parts appeared to be tendered. The Presbyterian minister who was present gave me an invitation to lodge with him, but I was previously engaged. In this town we have no Society, but several seem to be under considerable awakening, and are greatly encouraged, for some have _____ the _____ plan, but the church people are great advocates for the line of succession.

Tuesday evening, January 1, 1793.—We rode to Adams, (Mass.). This year was begun by me with seven conflicts from satan. I could scarce read a paragraph without being in a kind of sleep, and the senses so numbed I could scarce understand what I read. Before my appointment came on, I was ready to conclude I should not be able to stand to speak to the people. Many came to hear, and I was happy, and enabled to speak with freedom. In this town we have a small Society in which there are some lovers of God.

Wednesday 2—In Williamstown (Mass.)[160] the room was crowded. I preached to a persecuted Society from, "Yea and all they that will live godly in Christ Jesus shall suffer persecution," Timothy 3: 12. 1. What is it to be in Christ? 2. What to live godly? 3. What is meant by persecution? I have no reason to doubt but good was done. The time has come to favor this town, and several do bless God for those blessed opportunities.

Thursday 3—Brother (D. or B.) and I continued together. I rode in the sleigh with _____ to Pownel (Vt.), and preached to many. The work in this town continues to prosper; but I was much grieved on account of the complaint lodged against one who ought to have been a pillar in the church. Our gracious God knows the hearts of all.

Friday 4—We went on to Ashgrove (N. Y.).[161] I blessed God for arrival in this circuit; upwards of an hundred have been added in the past quarter.

Saturday 5—Quarterly meeting began. Five preachers were present, to whom I wholly gave up the public meeting, and the Lord was in the midst. I had a long and comfortable conference with the preachers and other public friends. Till now the preachers did not in the general get half their quarterage; but at this meeting they got their full pay, and there were six, or seven pounds to spare for the contingencies. The leaders and preachers seem all alive.

Sunday 6—Our love feast began a little after sunrise; but the strangers pressed forward to that degree, that we could not refuse them entrance: the dead could not bury the dead, and the burdens fell on the living, which greatly retarded the sweet consolation which otherways been experienced. I preached for the second time on, "By whom shall Jacob arise for he is so small." The power of God, as in ancient times, ran through the crowded assembly. Many declared they had never seen, or felt so powerful a time. The work of the Lord does, and will prosper _____ I feel a revival of it in my own heart.

Monday 7—We rode 15 miles and there were four preachers with me. I gave up the evening meeting to three of them, and I took Brother S_____m with me to Brother M's, Esq. where I had a comfortable night's repose. Dear man, he is much _____ and disappointed in two disobedient children. Children owe much to their parents and ought by all means to obey them in everything lawful. The following day we had a solemn sacramental occasion at B_____d's, Esq. As the preachers continued with me, I again gave up the evening meeting to them. I suppose 200 were present, we had two sermons, and an exhortation. We are now near Pittstown at which place the Lord is carrying on glorious work. O Jesus ride on properously in thy gospel chariot.

Wednesday 9—This morning I parted with three of the brethren, and Brother Dillon and I set out for Albany, to whom I gave up my evening appointment.

Thursday 10—This evening I preached to a clever congregation, and find an alteration in the place for the better. The work has been gradually increasing ever since conferences. The society is alive. The congregation is enlarged, and the society about doubled since my last visitation. I am greatly encouraged, and have no doubt but the building of this house was of God. Our God can work, and none can hinder. O who is like the God of Jacob. Thou are good O God and I will praise thee. O God thou art merciful, give glory to thy name.

Friday 11—I left the city and attended my appointment not far from Mesiannia. This Society stands in the liberty of the gospel, and the past quarter there has been a considerable revival, and several members added. Mrs. D_____n is alive to God, and proves a blessing in her family, and the Society. One of her sons is brought into the faith, and seems zealous for his master, though a wild youth a few months ago. Our God can break the most obstinate heart.

Saturday 12—From Schenectady I took the sleigh and rode about 20 miles to Brother Snow's, where we held the Quarterly Meeting for Saratoga circuit.[162] I was greatly comforted with the public members of the circuit in conference and the meeting continued till late, so that I could not lay down till after midnight; but the time was not tedious, God is calling and sending forth several to speak in his name, the examination of whom took up much time. I have no doubt, but their way is of the Lord.

Sunday 13—_____ more than the house (which was not small) could hold gathered a little after 9 o'clock to whom I declared, "Set thee up way _____ marks" 1. In the first place showed who these way marks are. 2. we are to know them. 3. their use, and lastly the application. In the first of the meeting we were greatly troubled with _____; so that I was under a necessity of giving over for a small season; shortly after which it subsided, and the melting power of God came down, and we had a memorable season. After which the communicants withdrew into one room, and whilst I was administering to them, the preachers were employed in exhortation, so that all could hear, and we had a little heaven on the earth. It would do the heart of the Christian good to see the glorious work the Lord is carrying on through this country by the instrumentality of those despised intinerants. I have stationed a lovely young preacher in this circuit for the ensuing quarter, and I look out for a great gathering of the church.

Monday 14—Two of the preachers left me, and I rested at Mr. Brown's and found a kind affectionate family.

Tuesday 15—We rode to Johnstown and I preached in the evening from Matthew 13: 41 but had not much freedom—the work of the Lord is by no means in a flowering state in this place. In general the wives of our brethren are in opposition to religion by which means several I fear have been turned out of the way; but a few faithful souls remain.

Wednesday 16—I was accompanied in a sleigh by two preachers, and one young convert 30 miles to Springfield, In this town the work of the Lord has lately broke out. 25 have joined the Society, and several have found the Lord. The work did not seem to be attended with power; but I had liberty, and comfort in my own soul. The words of my choice was, "Now we know that God heareth not sinners; but if any man be worshipper of God, and doeth His will, him he heareth," John 9: 31. I feel for the preachers in these back settlements, for although the people are kind, yet they often have hard fare, and seldom a private room; but it is a most growing country.

Thursday 17—We are now five in number, four in the sleigh and one on horseback. We traveled through a severe snow storm about 11 miles, and met a kind family, the snow being deep, and the storm severe, who attended our evening meeting. The subject matter of my sermon was, "He that is dead is freed from sin," Romans 6: 6, 7. Here we have a comfortable room to ourselves. I am disappointed in paying the Indians a visit _____ my time will not admit of it. I pray for a greater degree of patience under suffering. If I cannot fare roughly for a few days how must the poor people endure it continually. At every place they endeavor to make me as comfortable as possible, and express a thankfulness for my visit.

Friday 18—We still pursue our journey to the west, and find tedious travelling. About 12 o'clock we called at a cottage when the woman helped us to stable, water, cups and milk and we dined on a dish of good green tea, and cake of our own, and after prayer we found ourselves greatly refreshed, and the poor woman seemed well pleased with a few small pieces of silver together with a word of advice. She seemed willing to receive instruction. We got to the intended place, and I preached to about a hundred souls from "Buy the truth and sell it not." Proverbs 23: 23. First, what is truth. Secondly how to be bought, and thirdly, enforce the exhortation by the truth and sell it not. There are some hungry souls in this place. I lodged in the house of a kind friend, with whom I was formerly acquainted. There we were troubled with a few disputatious Baptists. Am I willing to suffer in the cause of Christ? Were I not I should be a most ungrateful creature.

Saturday 19—We still pursue our journey to the west, our number has increased to seven. We dined with a brother who moved from Albany. As soon as the neighbors had knowledge of us, the little house was filled, and several were in tears. We rode three miles farther to the appointment, about an hundred gathered, and several with whom I had been acquainted in New England who seemed as much rejoiced to see me, as if they had been my children, came from far. Our God will work, and who can hinder. I preached from, "The spirit of the Lord is upon me." Luke 4: 18. This appointment is in Whitestown where the Presbyterians have built a most elegant meeting house, the construction of which I am informed cost seven hundred pounds. A _____ came for the first time to hear, and gave me a kind invitation to his house. As I was other ways engaged, he staid several hours and we had an agreeable interview and though we could not agree in the disputable points, yet we agreed to disagree. As yet we have no Society in this town, but several are under awakenings.

Sunday 20—I have no place to retire except the woods, and the snow is rather deep. This morning as many people as could crowded into the house, although there were two other meetings in the town. I preached from "From my maker is thine husband." Isaiah 54: 5. 1. I showed what must pass between Christ and the soul before we can say our maker is our husband; 2. being thus espoused to Christ by the living faith, what is our duty to him, 3. point out the objections generally made to this match. The dreadful consequences of the denial, together with the general invitation to come to Christ. I accept the overtures of mercy. I was afterward informed that such _____ was never before known in Whitestown. The flame ran from heart to heart. About 20 of our scattered flock, some of whom came 20 or 30 miles, drew near to the table after which we had another sermon, and exhortation. A stranger came to me and said "I never heard a Methodist preach till yesterday; I came 20 miles to seek food for my soul, and I had heard much of the Methodists, and read their books, and blessed be God, he blessed me with a ministry of sins forgiven. God is with you, and I intend to offer myself as a member of your church. I now see the goodness of God, in scattering the Methodists through this new country." Some of them have stood as way marks, and by their books, prayers, and admonitions, in a variety of places, a people are prepared for our entrance among them. Though they have but small houses they receive us with tears of joy and thankfulness, and show a willingness to communicate with the last morsel of bread. I do not suppose I should have been happier in a popular part of the world around. A part of the world crowded by thousands. O that our God may raise up, and send more shepherds among these people, after his own heart; for the cry of many is, "come over and help us," and that with power evident enough to move the heart of a rock. After dinner we rode three miles to the south part of the town, and found as many waiting as could crowd into two large rooms, to whom I cried, "Who hath believed our report?" Isaiah 53: 2. I found great liberty but the people in this part of the town are hard, yet it was thought the hearts of several were moved.

Monday 21—I am now at Esquire _____. We have a large house, and a full table—I am distressed—does Israel's God dwell here? I found freedom to pray—O this strictness, what call is there for so much ado about religion?

Can we not go to heaven in our father's religion: The cry is we cannot fall from grace: How strange! What to see people kneeling, weeping, and agonizing in prayers before the Lord—the old people are very kind; but I am distressed. We rode six miles northward in the same town, and saw some of the fruits of our yesterday's labors. As many as could crowd into a large room met us, many of whom were under deep distress. I gave out "Blessed are they that mourn: For they shall be comforted." One, I illustrated the Christian character—Two, the exercise of gracious souls— the various causes of sorrow—Three, offer the promise _____. We rode a mile where it was for us to dine, but we had but little time for dinner; for the house was soon filled, and several were crying for mercy. I examined and admitted about a dozen in the Society for the first that ever joined the Methodists in this town. We rode six miles farther, and in the evening I gave out to a stubborn people, "Almost thou persuadest me to be a Christian." Had I been endeavoring to split rocks with a pick axe for an hour and a half my labor would have been as easy; but not as useful, for I was met in the morning by one whose heart was broken, and he wept bitterly and declared that God had given him to feel his fallen condition, and I am informed the hearts of several others were touched.

Tuesday 22—We now leave our kind friend, and set our faces toward Albany. At present we are only four in company, for we left one preacher to nurse the children. After riding 30 miles we came to Springfield, I am tempted of the devil—Lord give me continually to watch and pray. I am now blessed with a private room, and the people are kind. These western territorities populate very fast, and the land is very level, clear of stones, and fertile, and the price of the land is daily on the rise.

Wednesday 23—I visited a friend this morning who has lately emerged from the kingdom of darkness with no small degree due to his wife who was brought up a Lutheran; but now happy in God. I was interrogated by two Baptists: Why should professors of religion plead so strenuously for sin? I am resolved to cry it down both by precept, and example. At 2 o'clock I began to preach to about an hundred, had a time of liberty, and sweetness, and one of my antagonists seemed humbled, and broken in heart. About 20 communed. I am satisfied with respect to the reality of the little works being of God. Several souls are hungering after righteousness, and some are comfortable in the love of God; but there is a degree of persecution.

Thursday 24—I have only one preacher with me, and we turned our faces toward the Delaware, and after we passed the Cherry Valley other preachers met us. I shall not soon forget kind friends, at whose houses we dined, for parents, and children, have been lately brought into gospel liberty. Between 3 and 4 o'clock I began to preach at the house of an old gentleman who was formerly Quaker but now the whole family are Methodists, and several of them have been baptized. I gave out for my text, "And yet I show unto you a more excellent way." Corinthians 12: 31. I am well pleased with this family and the Society. God has done great things for many of the people in this neighborhood. Now I have a private room, and prayer is sweet, especially for a particular friend with whom I hope to enjoy many sweet moments in the company of.

Friday 25—Nine of us set out for Quarterly Meeting. This is a morning of deep distress, and humiliation to my soul. O God keep my soul from sin. We travelled near 30 miles through a very new and mountainous country; at about 6 o'clock we came to the desired town, and one preacher accompanied me to Whitmore's, Esq. This morning from 4 till 5 o'clock I was mostly drawn out in meditation on humility, and it was a profitable season. Part of my time from 5 till 6 I was sweetly drawn out in private prayer, but before 1 o'clock I was most severely attacked by the enemy of my soul. This evening I see great beauty in the perfect, meritorious righteous[ness] of Jesus Christ; He is just such a savior as I want, and I am able through his grace to cast my whole soul upon him, for in him there is plentious redemption. O for that purifying stream to flow continually to my heart.

FREEBORN GARRETTSON'S JOURNAL FOR FEB. 1793-MAY, 1793

Wednesday, Feb. 6, 1793—I travelled to and spent the evening in Hudson[163] at Brother Wighton's, and had access to the throne of grace, found the Society much as formerly. I fear the people in this place are fast asleep in carnal security, but I bless God for a few names in the Book of Life, who I trust will ever walk worthy of their Christian calling, and at last enter the celestial court.

Thursday 7—I have a measure of the divine presence this morning. Met Brother W. and preached at N.C. The little company seemed very impatient. I had very little freedom, and felt a hard spirit towards a prayerless people, whom I fear (a few excepted) are on the brink of ruin, and feel not their danger; for if they did they would flee for refuge to Jesus Christ.

Friday 8—I rode to Canaan. I am exceeding poorly with a sick headack. Since I was last at this house, I find Brother C. has made choice of a frank companion, and I trust they will walk hand in hand to spiritual Canaan's peaceful shore, to bask in the beams of redeeming love forever.

Saturday 9—I continue so poorly. I do not think it expedient to attend church, and indeed there was no immediate call, for several preachers were present. This day passed away all alone in affliction, and solitude. In the evening the travelling and local preachers, together with the stewards, leaders and exhorters met me, and I was enabled to hold a comfortable conference with them, and found freedom in opening few of our regulations at the General Conference. We had the presence, and the power of God among us. I fear the work in several parts of this circuit is on decline. Though blessed by God, there are some little movings in some places.

Sunday 10—Want of sleighing caused our congregation to be much smaller than otherwise it would have been. I am much better today, and feel very happy, and I never had so much freedom, and power of speech in Canaan. Our dear Lord was with us at His table. For the first time our good old friend Col. B. L. communed. Our old antagonist William V. Y. was quite calm, but I fear the poison of asps is yet under his tongue, and his mouth full of bitterness; but he is afraid of the love of man. When we consider ourselves surrounded with beasts, as ferocious as those at Epheseus, we may bless God for civil rulers, and wholesome laws. This unhappy man disturbed the whole meeting, at our last Quarterly Meeting in this place. Our dear friends parted in great peace. I rode to the north end of town and preached to many solemn hearers in the evening, and several of our preachers followed the discourse with affecting exhortations. This little Society is closely united, and I have great hope of a revival.

Monday 11—I called on Brother C. and rode to Sharon, and preached on the witness of the spirit with freedom. I do not see that fruit, which my heart panteth after. Here I seem to be shut in by a severe storm. I now go but slowly on, for the snow is very deep—some places to my horse's side. On my way to Rhinebeck[164] I visited several friends, and go under some severe trials, I did not lose sight of the horse. We have great need of patience, and perseverance, that after we have done the will of God, we may receive the crown.

Friday 15—I am disappointed: my good friends did not return as expected. Dined at William S——, returned in the sleigh. How do I stand it? Is my eye single? Do I love God supremely? In many aspects I am imperfect; but blessed be God, according to my small degree of knowledge I can answer in the affirmative, and glory to his dear name, I had rather suffer the loss of all things, than dishonor God, or ruin my own soul. The world is as a mere bubble on the water.

Saturday 16—Hugh M—— began at Row's Church.[165] We have very disagreeable weather, but we had many friends whose hearts were fired with love. I had a deep sense of God's love whilst preaching the word from Matthew 5: 4. O Lord how is it that thou art so kind to so unfaithful a preacher. The duty I owe the church is not all: I must stand before the eternal judge. I labor in the vineyard of my dear Lord; but I have a soul to save or lose. This night the house of our good friend rings with the praises of God, and I have sweet fellowship with the pious company. My soul thou waterest from on high; but make it all a pool, string ____ ____ in the ____ well I ever cry spring up within my soul.

Lord's Day 17—The rain was excessive from morning till night, but it did not hinder the attendance of many, but we had a cold, disagreeable time, respecting the outer man; but God was in his word, and at his table. I was comfortable whilst in ——, Matthew 5: 4—"blessed are they that mourn." The meeting is broken up and the people gone; I am in retirement. The lovely Savior is precious to me, and I have access to the throne of grace.

Monday 18—Took the sleigh and went to Brother S_____ where I staid two days. Mrs. S_____ is unwell, and Mr. S_____ is from home. I have a lively hope Mrs. S_____ will yet be brought into gospel liberty: but O how hardly shall they that have _____ entered into the Kingdom of Heaven. I trust William S_____ is a travelling Christian.

Wednesday 20—I now set out for New York and at 11 o'clock preached to many serious hearers at Lyons in the evening at Conklin's Esq. Showed that "he that is dead is free from sin." Romans 6: 1. Some of the Presbyterians thought I preached a Presbyterian sermon, and were well pleased. I showed as plainly as I could what was implied in being dead, and freed from sin, and on what conditions we are brought to such an experience. "Not by works of righteousness which we have done; but by his mercy, he saveth us," and that "by the washings of regenerations, and renewings of the Holy Ghost." The rivers are exceeding high occasioned by the rain and thaw, and very dangerous. Brother M_____y was to have met me, but was prevented by the flood. On Thursday I received a letter from New York favored by Mrs. B. which was refreshing. This evening we had a precious family meeting at Governer C. We were all happy and Sister V. V. offered a feeling prayer to the Lord. In piety, she emulates her mama, whom I think a mother in Israel.

Friday 22—I reached Sing Sing and preached in the evening to a small audience with very little liberty. The next day we had a storm; it is impracticable to reach the city this week. I put up with a blessed family not far from King's Ridge,[166] and on the Lord's day I was happy in private, whilst dispensing truth to a small, serious audience.

Monday 25—I reached the city, and took a room with Brother Blecker. I am willing to rest all my conscience with the Lord. A thick gloom hangs over us. I would not turn a straw to please myself, if I conceived it would counteract the will of God; for I believe he does all things well. Matters must come to a crisis. My mind is troubled. I am retired. I read, write, pray, and meditate and in the like exercises have passed several days. I received a letter from my dear friend, and we had several interviews, and we feel clearly convinced, that God has united us, and duty calls us to go forward.

Friday, March 1, 1793—I preached in the old church, it was favored beyond my expectations. The cloud is dispersed from my mind, and the sun of righteousness shines on my soul. Lord keep me from a murmuring spirit.

Sunday 3—This morning I am tempted of Satan. I preached in the old church from "behold I stand at the door and knock," Revelation 3: 20. I was greatly assisted, and the sweet flame ran through the church. One soul was awakened, and the following evening (as Brother V. informed me) at a prayer meeting was set at liberty. Brother Green[167] assisted me in the administration of the communion. In the afternoon I was comfortable whilst preaching in the new church. I heard Brother G. preach a useful sermon in the evening from, "the Lord God is a sun, and a shield." I had a sweet night's rest.

Monday 4—I do business and write letters.

Tuesday 5—Evening I preached with not much freedom on a new subject, "but the wisdom which is from above is first pure, then peaceable, gentle and easy to be entreated, full of mercy, and good fruits without partiality, and without hypocrisy." James 3: 17. My dear friend's mind is perfectly satisfied, and I trust the matter will be settled in June.[168] I hope we will be amply compensated for all the severe conflicts we have had on the occasion. I still write letters, and do business, for I must soon leave the city. I have sweet fellowship with this kind family, they do everything in their power to make me happy and Captain Canowell who lives in this house could not be more kind were I his only son. O Lord reward thy people for their kindness to thy poor creature. I must depart, and leave my dear friend behind, to meet no more till May. O Lord preserve and keep our minds in perfect peace.

Thursday 7—Accompanied by Brother V. in the chaise chair we rode as far as King's Ridge, and I preached in the afternoon, and he in the evening. I am happy in doing what I believe to be my duty. I trust the bread cast on the water will be gathered not many days hence.

Friday 8—I reached White Plains and preached on Revelation 3: 18, "I counseled thee to buy of me gold, etc." I feel fear lest after preaching to others I should become a castaway, might stimulate me to watch, and use self denial and much prayer. There was very little moving on the water. God is faithful to his promises, and if I endure hardships as a good soldier until death, there will be a crown of life for me.

Saturday 9—I reached Croton,[169] and found Sister Van Wike on wings for an eternal crown. At this place Brother Everard met me. I often feel in fear—I do not speak of those which are slavish. The effects of the fall we shall feel whilst we dwell in an house of clay. Happy we, who bear the cross faithfully. The devil is the Christian's enemy, and an unwearied one he is.

Sunday 10—I preached in the new church to a few and rode to Stony Street. I am under heaviness through manifold temptations. I sometimes feel weary but not of the glorious cause in which I hope ever to be engaged.

Monday 11—The riding is exceeding bad; I set out this morning for Oswago. About sunset I got within about five miles of my destined place for the day; but behold the flood had swept away the bridge. I was informed the river was at least 14 feet deep, and there were two long logs laid lengthwise for foot people. A negro man told me he thought he could lead my horse over on those logs. The horse walked over as careful as a human being would, with two feet on each log. I gladly gave the stranger a piece of silver, and went on my way with a glad heart, and got to Brother G's a little after sundown, and was happy with his kind family. It is by faith the Christian feels him that is invisible, and cheerfully bears the cross for a crown. Indeed the Christian's compensation is great, even in this world.

Tuesday 12—I visited the family of Conklin, Esq. And in the evening preached with freedom in the Nine Partners. I repaired to the house of a kind friend. I have two days for retirement. My mind is much deranged. I am all alone. The family remarkably kind. I want no temporal blessing. A neatly furnished room. The door is shut. I bow before my God. A drowsiness seizes me as I read; but my understanding seems numbed. The clouds break, the shadows flee away, and the scriptures appear beautiful.

Thursday 14—Brother M_____y came to me. I preached on, "So then they which be of faith are blessed with faithful Abraham." Galatians 3: 9. I now retire again. My enemy is not dead. I am willing to fight. When our captain goes before, and fights our battle, all goes well. He gives us power to exercise the Christian armor, and in his name we can put to flight the armies of the aliens. I have another whole day to live retired, and drink of the still waters. I expect one day to be rid of this cumberous clay. I am willing to carry it as long as my dear master has work for me.

I preached again with freedom and lodged at Doctor Bartlets. We had a sweet family meeting. I was greatly drawn out in prayer, and the Lord manifest himself to Sister Bartlet, insomuch that she was constrained to praise him. My text the next day at B's _____ V. _____ new church was, "there remaineth therefore a rest to the people of God." This rest remaineth, and that for but one sort of people. The seventh day is a day of rest. The year of jubilee was a year of rest. The millennium will be a time of rest; but the rest alluded to particularly in our text, supercedes all other days, or times of rest and it remaineth; for whom the people of God not nominal, but real Christians of all denominations. We (the people of God) rest from the guilt, power, love, and dominion of sin; but still this rest remaineth, and what is sweeter than rest to a weary soul. In heaven there cannot be the smallest trace of sorrow or uneasiness. O, "angel minds are lost to ponder dying love's mysterious cause." We should think it a great thing to view the whole of this small system at the same time; but how much greater to view meriads of systems, many of which, very far superior to this. But a privilege much greater still to gaze in uncreated light, where bright seraphims cover their faces with their wings, whilst prostrate, crying, "holy, holy, holy, and so forth." In the afternoon I preached at Rhinebeck on, "he that goeth forth and reapeth sowing precious seed, shall come again rejoicing bringing his sheaves with him." Were our _____ _____ most lucrative, we should be all men the most miserable. As ministers, and as Christians, we go forth bearing the precious gospel seed and under various inflictions and persecutions. Glory to God the time is at hand, when all tears of sorrow will be wiped away. It will be a memorable time when all the dear children of God are gathered home to their father's house, where parting will be no more forever. I am happy with this kind family. Many blessed men I am acquainted with; but to say I have met one in every respect equal to Mr. Sands with regard to benevolence, I cannot with certainty. Sister R. is a person of a most forceful mind—Lord grant that she may always be kept in the spirit, and simplicity of the gospel.

Monday 18—I preached in Hudson. I fear this circuit meets with many disappointments.

Tuesday 19—I got as far as Coeyman,[170] and the next day reached Albany. An alteration for the better is evident in several families, and several young people since my last visit have been brought to God. The prejudices of some have reasonably fallen, and a congregation is larger.

Sunday 24—I preached three sermons with freedom. I am informed Brother C. is dangerously ill. I am at a loss to know where to get a preacher to fill his place. I am under anxiety of mind respecting an house. Several persons are much engaged in this matter, very anxious to have me accommodated.

Wednesday 27—Several had never heard the Methodists, they paid great attention in the church whilst I declared from Acts 13: 38, "Be it known unto you, men and brethren, that through this man is preached unto you the forgiveness of sins, and so forth." One person was sure I pointed the sermon at her in particular. I am so taken up I can read but little. A person in this city promises to have a suitable house in order for me by the middle of July, but I hope he will not disappoint me. I hope should the Lord cast the lot of my dear friend and me in this city we shall be rendered a blessing to its inhabitants. I have weighed matters as judiciously as I was able, and I think in the whole, I know of no place more suitable, at least in this district. Lord grant that in every station of life which I may be in my eye may be single, and my whole body full of light.

Good Friday—I attended appointments to Coeyman's and endeavored to deliver a discourse suitable to the day from, "My soul is exceeding sorrowful, even unto death." We had a solemn session. I withdrew to Brother Waldrums. I have just finished reading the French ———, and was happily entertained. These parents, and daughter are lovers of the Lord Jesus Christ. This little room reminds me of that built on the wall for the prophets. Prayer is sweet. I have time to write. All is still and quiet, there being no children to disturb. I have finished (?) (?) (?) account of himself. We did not understand the nature of the unpardonable sin, and I am not confident he is as clear in a Christian experience. I have travelled by land and sea more than one hundred thousand English miles and have been acquainted with a variety of persons, and characters; but dare not say I ever met with one, whom I had reason to believe had committed the unpardonable sin, or sin of blasphemy against the Holy Ghost. I have read (?) sermon on the subject, and am clearly convinced he knew very little of the matter: he goes round it, and round it again, and entirely misses the mark. The author of the epistle of the Hebrews describes it in few words. It is a sinning wittingly, willingly, knowingly, and maliciously against the Holy Ghost. Many feeble minds have been immeasureably perplexed on this subject, when they had no more business with it, than with an attempt to create a new world.

Sunday, 31—Brother Green left me to officiate at Albany. Brother V. is so far on the recovery as to have met me yesterday, but is unable to preach. I preached in the Coeyman Church to many solemn Christians, and we had a love feast. In my way down last winter, I preached in this church, and thought we had a barren time, but now I am informed that several were awakened, who are now happy in God, and indeed there has been since that time a universal revival in the Society, and the flame has spread amongst the adjacent Societies. I feel little willing to labor for, and in the cause of God, and I am happy.

Monday, April 1—Brother Green again returned to me. We held an election agreeable to law for the trustees of the church. How shall we get this church finished. A subscription paper was handed round, and within five minutes those who were present subscribed nearly the required sum for the purpose. In the afternoon I went into Albany, and was favored with great variety of letters from various parts, and amongst the accounts, one from my dear friend. Surely the Lord has done great things for her since we parted.

Wednesday the 3rd—We had a solemn meeting in the church, and the next day left the city. Private prayer is sweet _____. Brother G. is with me, and we are on our way to Tyringham Quarterly Meeting. We met several of the brethren who brought glad tidings of the new circuit. I preached both days with freedom. God is love, and they that dwell in love, dwell in God; for God is love. I have some pleasing accounts from the Boston district. Go on dear Lord, and spread thy kingdom to the ends of the earth.

Monday 8—A large congregation met me in Lenix, to whom I declared, "they have healed the hurt of the daughter of my people slightly, crying peace, peace when there is no peace." Jeremiah 6: 14. The people of this town I am informed have lately given their minister 70 pounds lawful to preach no more to them, and now they have opened the door for us in the heart of the town. An unconverted, lucrative ministry is a curse to the people over whom they are settled, and supposing they were to serve them as Samson did the foxes or stop their mouths, and suffer them to divine for hire no longer, it would be a blessing to thousands. I have great hope for this people. I now retire to Mr. Collin's and leave two of the preachers to speak to the people in the evening. I am unwell. "Lord help me to watch and pray, and on thy strength rely, assured if I my trust betray, I shall forever die."

Tuesday 9—Many came to the meeting house in Pittsfield to hear the word. The subject of my sermon was, "Stand ye in the way and see, ask for the old paths, where is the good way, and walk therein. And ye shall find rest for your souls." 1. The propriety of this exhortation. God never commanded his creatures to do what was impossible. When God commands, he gives power to obey. 2. The duty enjoined. I stand in the way and ask for the old paths—the good old way. I walk in them. 3. The blessings promised—you shall find rest for your souls. Rest from the guilt, power, and love of sin. Rest from the fear of death, and all inbred sin, and finally from all the miseries threatened the impertinent sinner. Rest in the full enjoyment of God in heaven through all eternity.

We had a precious time of communion at the table of the Lord. I am poorly in body, but happy in God. Our friends are about either to build us a house for worship, or purchase the separate meeting house. I advised them to the former; for it will take as much to finish the old, as to build the new one large enough for our society. It has appeared to me, that New England will yet be most famous for religion. The people will hear the word and some get awakened.

Wednesday 10—When I was last in this town, the Episcopal Church was open; but now the door is shut. I insisted too strenuously on justification by faith, without the works of the law; but Presbyterians think we are entirely in the wrong in denying the unconditional decrees, however, their meeting house was open, and many gathered in, and I found freedom to preach, but several were dissatisfied, and demanded a debate on the points disputable between us. I had rather live in peace. William C_____, the minister proposed some questions. I answered as well as I was able. I suppose after disputing near an hour before the whole congregation, I was as near convincing him, as he was me. The grand point is, to distinguish between foreknowledge and an absolute decree. His text was Acts 2: 23: "him being delivered by the determinant council and foreknowledge of God, ye have taken in by wicked hands have crucified and slain." In God's determinant council, he forcefully gave his dear son to die for the sins of the world. Certainly God knew this, for nothing new turns up with him. God forcefully gave him, and you freely, and wickedly slain him. The evasion. Now could it been other ways, when it was revealed, and foretold that Judas was the very man. When God revealed it, in his view Judas was receiving the money, betraying Christ with a kiss, and hanging himself, so that it was neither revealed, or foretold till it came to pass in God's word and he knew that Judas acted freely, and that it was in his power to have done other ways, and then it neither would have been known, revealed, or foretold. Is it not more scriptural, and rational to argue thus, than to confound the divine arrtibutes? If God has unconditionally consigned myriads and myriads of the unborn race over to eternal flames, without any chance, what shall we do with his holiness, wisdom and mercy? The original and actual sins of the human race, which lay on the Son of God, was a load intolerable. See him agonizing in the garden before Judas or his wicked company laid hands on him, till his precious blood and sweat came out in great drops falling to the ground. Did not the angel of the covenant come to his assistance? Had God withdrawn would not the intolerable load have crushed, or crucified the Savior; but the crowd must glut their utmost rage. O how they clamor for his blood. On the cross he cried it is finished—my God, my God, why hast thou forsaken me—the divine nature withdraws, and he expires on the cross.

O the goodness of God to the children of men, experience teaches us, that thus are pious Calvinists as well as Arminians, so called. I rode five miles, and spent much time in self-examination. I am not convinced I gave way to any wrong temper, or strove merely for the mastery, for if I know myself, I want truth to stand and error to fall.

Thursday 11—This is a day set apart by the state of Massachusetts for fasting. Many came to hear the word. We have preached in this town nearly three years, and have formed no Society. They have no settled minister, neither do they want one of the standing order, for they prefer our doctrine, and preaching, and are liberal, but unwilling to bear the cross. I was led to speak hard things, and even to threaten a removal of the preaching from the town. What has God called us to this town for? Not to gather money. Not to gain honor; but to be instrumental in bringing souls to Jesus. I am not certain that this has been done by our instrumentality, after the labor of several years. We can exercise no church discipline in the town. True you are ready to throw in your might to support the preachers once a quarter—this does not satisfy us, we want to see souls coming home to Jesus. Some wept, and after meeting begged to have the preaching continued—this town is adjacent to Williamstown. Pownel. I spent three days in this town. Preached several sermons and administered the communion. For the first time in this circuit, the preachers got their full quarterage. Mr. A. I fear is declining, and will not long be one of us, unless a change for the better should take place. Man may deceive man, but God cannot be deceived. The government of Christ's church rests on his own shoulders, and not on man. When one friend fails, another is raised up to take his place. One may say, what can you do without me. God is dependent on no man. Were the way to heaven passable in silver slippers, we should have many travellers. Some seem to run well for a season, and then sink again into the practice of their old besetments. Comparatively, it is a small thing to live within the outward rules of the church; but God searcheth the heart and it is a great thing to have a pure intention, and to move internally as God would have us. If individuals have turned aside, living, and loving witnesses still remain, who I trust will continue pillars in the temple to go on more out forever.

Monday 15—I am called into Albany. The workmen are busily employed in finishing the church. The person still promises to have my house in order by the middle of July. He appears like a religious Presbyterian. I do not suppose he has the least intention to deceive me. I have received a sweet letter from my dear friend. I could wish myself better prepared in temporals, for such an agreeable Society. I leave the city. Many met me at Cookesborough, to whom I declared from the words of David: "Come unto all ye that fear the Lord, and I will tell you what he has done for my soul." 1. I described a work of grace on a human soul, together with the evidences. 2. Assigned some reasons why a Christian need not be ashamed of such an experience, and 3. concluded with a few inferences drawn from the subject.

The power and presence of God caused tenderness of heart, and weeping to run through a crowded assembly.

I now ride to Cambridge.[171] Our little church rings with the praises of God, and we have a sweet communion. Peace, and harmony runs through this loving Society. The day following I was called on to attend the funeral of a little child at the same place, and as part of the relatives are Presbyterians, we had many to hear who are strangers to the Methodists. A principal part of my subject was to show the nature of infant justification. Those Calvinists who suppose we on any degree deny the total deprivation of man, or exalt fallen nature, are entirely ignorant of our system. One of the fathers of our church judiciously observes, "view an infant in the first Adam, and you behold a child of wrath; but view it in Christ, the second Adam, and you view it as angelicly holy." He is the propitiation for our sins and not for ours only but for the sins of the whole world. Christ himself saith: "suffer them to come to me for such is the kingdom of heaven."

Saturday 20—I am now accompanied by many pious Christians to Arlington, where we purpose to hold our q.m. The English church is open for us, where we have a sweet providential powerful season. Is the devil willing to let our meeting end in peace? No. He assembles individuals of his forceful fellows, with the young priest at the head, whose determination is, no Methodist meeting to be in our church tomorrow. This news did not reach the ears of our people till in the night.

Sunday 21—What have you to do this morning, but first to seek a large barn, for no private house will contain the congregation. "The wrath of man shall praise thee." God frequently brings good out of evil. About 10 o'clock I stood forth and declared the counsel of God from his own words by the prophet Samuel. "Him that honoreth me, I will honor and them that despise me shall be lightly esteemed." I Samuel 2: 30. This old barn is awful, for God is with us. We know it is not the elegance of the place, gives a sanction to our meeting; but the power, presence, and approbation of Jehovah. And our fellowship below in Jesus be so sweet, what nights of rapture shall we know when round his throne we meet.

I now return to Cambridge. Preachers have been sweetly engaged the past quarter, and God has owned them. The temporalizers of this circuit within six months are more then doubled. Glory to God his work prospers.

Monday 22—I am now on my way to Albany. Preached with freedom tonight. I have but one preacher with me. God's dear suffering servant never appeared more near to me.

Tuesday 23—This is the time of our Cookesbush Quarterly Meeting. *Wednesday 24*—I had an opportunity of hearing Brother Wooley preach. He is a lovely young man, and God is with him. Should he continue faithful he will become more acquainted with men and things, and be better qualified to divide the word. I had great freedom in discoursing on Ezekiel's vision—

    I. The state represented by the dry bones. _____
        1. The Jewish Church
        2. All mankind and their fallen condition
   II. God's method in raising those dry bones.
        1. He laid the _____
        2. He brought up flesh
        3. Covered them with skin

In all this we are taught what God has done in redeeming man by his dear son. By nature man has no strength, or activity in a spiritual sense: but in _____ are the strength, and activity of the body. So is Christ to the fallen, helpless soul. As there is not the least probability of life without flesh, so without Christ man has no more hope than the devil. As there is no beauty or comliness without skin, so no performance whatever can be acceptable without the meritorious righteousness of Christ. This may remind us of the fallen churches, or formal preachers who have every ingredient to constitute them happy, yet after all their outward skin, and destitute of the power of religion. God commands us the prophets to prophesy to those dead, lifeless mortals. The way in, and through Jesus Christ is open for the resurrection. As he prophesied there was a noise. Mark you will not hear such a noise as this under the preaching of unconverted ministers; but God attends the words spoken by his servants with power. What kind of noise think you was this? Prophet tells us there was not only a noise; but a shaking—sinners trembling, and crying for mercy. This is not enthusiasm, or madness. Furthermore the prophet informs, as he prophesied, the bones came together, bone to its bone. Till now the bones were scattered through the open valley (which may represent destruction) but now every bone is coming to its proper place, and the bones, sinews, flesh, and skin are knitting together. One poor sinner is called from the tavern, another from the card table, and a third from the honors of the world, and the fourth from their own deceivings: some from one fallen church, and some from another, and no wonder blind guides are exasperated, with those renegade enthusiasts. Now those awakened souls are inquiring what they should do to be saved, and I would not have them take some twinges of conscience, or considerable degrees of penitential sorrow, good desires are doctrinal knowledge for the new birth, as many do: for God says there is no life in them—that is, they are not yet created anew in Christ Jesus, and commands the prophet again to prophesy to the wind_____ spiritual life, and he did, and an army was raised, and stood on their feet, and so a new creation is brought forth, the soul will stand upright.

III. I endeavored to describe privileges of this blessed army. The great power of the Lord was displayed in the midst of a large assembly. In the close of the Love Feast I was happy in informing our friends, that liberality from the societies of the circuit was such that we were under no necessity of making any collection at this meeting. After the meeting Brother C_____d and I rode to Mr. M's within two miles of Albany.

Friday 26—Having spent some time in the city disagreeably, I set out for Saratoga, and on Saturday began a q.m. at the foot of the lake. We had a comfortable time.

Our next q m began the first day of May in Duainsbush. Since my last visit, there has been a falling away in the Society, though I trust the greater part stands fast I was greatly pressed and enabled to cry aloud. We can get very little food for our horses.

I return again to Albany. I have had a full investigation of that strange affair which turned up some time ago in Cambridge. Mrs. W. in the State of Vermont (who professed a deep work of grace, whilst her six children were under innoculation for the smallpox, thought the Lord revealed it to her, that all her children would die unless she threw herself six times in the river, which she attempted in the night, after rising from her bed and going to the river she arose. Five times she repeated the operation, cold as it was, being in the winter season; but was unable to immerse herself a sixth time. She withdrew to the house certain one of her children would die; in this she was mistaken. Her enthusiasm carried her still farther— she came down to her sister D's, in Cambridge, and infused strange notions into her head, and two other members of the Society. The height of it, one who had been a Shaker came to see them, and said they acted precisely like them, or was activated by the same spirit. They went into the water and sat chin deep till they received (as they said) a sign from the Lord that they were as pure as the angels in heaven. Now they concluded that the place was full of witches, and wizards, they were in the cats, dogs, and every part of the house, and then the little child was tormented with pins, and needles by them. They killed all the dogs, cats they could lay hands on, threw them in the fire, and likewise burned all the pins, and needles, and to make it complete _____ they kindled a fire in the yard, in order to burn all the beds, and bedding, and to clean the house thoroughly; then the neighbors gathered and prevented it. The young man, and the young woman were drawn off by them, were quickly restored to their reason, and the two sisters have been measureably restored. Mrs. D. is still of the opinion that the child was troubled with witches.

Friday, May 3—I left the city, rode 20 miles and preached with very little freedom. Mrs. Blodget (Coeyman's Hollow) has been nigh to death, but the Lord has raised her up. She is a witness for Christ, and when all hope of recovery was gone she was enabled gloriously to triumph over death and we have had a precious gathering at this place the past quarter.

Catherine Livingston Garrettson
1752-1849

Mrs. Garrettson was the daughter of Judge Robert R. Livingston and Margaret Beekman.

Wildercliffe, Rhinebeck, New York

Built in 1799 by the Garrettsons, it remained the family home until the death of their daughter, Mary, in 1877. The original house was the rectangular structure. The wings and porch were added later.

"Our house being nearly finished, in October, 1799, we moved into it, and the first night in family prayer, while my blessed husband was dedicating it to the Lord, the place was filled with his presence, who in days of old filled the temple with his glory. Every heart rejoiced, and felt that God was with us of a truth. Such was our introduction into our new habitation;—and had we not reason to say with Joshua, *As for me and my house, we will serve the Lord.*" p. 237, Bangs, N., Life of the Rev. Freeborn Garrettson.

Saturday 4—We set out to q m. On our way we called on a friend.The parents have nine children. Seven of whom know God as a sin pardoning God, the parents are happy. The happy mother told me she thought her seven children were clearly brought out, and the youngest of them is about nine years old. All this family know God, except the two youngest, who fear the Lord is with them. We went on to Brother S (or L) _____y, and I began to preach at 2 o'clock whilst we held our conference in the house. Brother Jacobs preached in the barn.

Sunday 5—We had our love feast, and communion at 8 o'clock. About 20 of our friends spoke, and I must say, I never heard people in general speak so well, for the Lord with them. They were greatly at liberty to tell what God had done for them. I then preached. Brother G. gave an exhortation, and we concluded our meeting. This wilderness begins to blossom as a rose, and the solitary places are glad, for in the wilderness where dragons lay, springs the water a breaking out, and streams in the desert. We now withdraw to Brother Shaw's—the husband, wife profess perfect love. They are humble lovers of Jesus, willing to divide the last morsel, with the servants of God.

Monday 6—I preached in Hudson, and the next day went on to Rhinebeck, N.Y. I am once more happy in company with my dear friend, and find the two families as kind as ever. I hope ever to live as God would have me, both in time and through eternity. I am happy, but I expect to be more happy than I have been for four years past. God's dealings with the children of men sometimes appear strange, and his providences adverse; but I will praise him whilst "All things work together for good to them that love him." No doubt God has seen it best to chastise. No chastisement is joyous for the present, but I hope this will produce the peaceable fruits of the spirit. Lord we are thine, thou hast united us. Do with us what seems the good, only let us be holy for thee, and to live to thy glory. O God give us patience, and hearts to pray for those who lightly esteem and oppose us, and grant that our union may be for the furtherance of each other in the way of the kingdom—married the thirtieth of June, 1793. "Dear love: Do what you please with these lines for they were hastily drawn up on poor paper." F.G.

A JOURNEY TO THE SOUTH 1805

Friday, March 21, 1805—Left home about 3 o'clock; to the sloop, and set sail about sunset, but few passengers, we had a very agreeable time.

Saturday 22—Landed in New York about 8 o'clock and was very poorly with a cold and a sick headache.

Sunday 23—I continued much indisposed and unable to preach though I heard a good sermon in the morning, and another in the afternoon. This week I spent in visiting friends, retirement, collecting some articles to send home, and preached at the North River Church, and likewise in the Bowery Church with freedom.

Sunday 30—In the morning I preached in John Street. In the afternoon to a large congregation in the Bowery, and in the evening I preached again in the John Street Church. In the whole this was a good day. When I left home, my mind was not fully made up in favor of the tour to the south but having written home, I received the approbation of my good partner, and Wednesday was the day fixed on by Mr. Cooper and myself as he had agreed to go with me. We had a very agreeable time, as there was but one in the stage besides ourselves, except once in awhile a few way passengers.

Thursday, April 3, 1805—We dined at Philadelphia.

Friday 4—In the evening I preached in the Academy Church with a degree of freedom.

Saturday 5—Was a day of retirement except a visit to the station's minister, and a few minutes spent with William Green.

Sunday 6—Preached, and administered sacrament in the Academy Church. In the afternoon preached in St. George's Church, and surely the power of God was among the people. I found freedom in opening on Isaiah's fourth sermon, Isaiah 6th chapter. Having received a note from the Africans I preached in the evening. Without a doubt, but that the power of God was among them. This night I rested in peace, and was very happy. Though there has been a very devisive _____ among the Methodists in this city, yet through mercy the work goes on; there are large additions to the community, and many engaged, and happy souls both white and black.

Monday 7—We reached Wilmington to dine, and in the evening I preached from, "Pray without ceasing," and Brother Cooper gave a useful exhortation and in the whole we had an agreeable time. We were courteously entertained at Mr. McClain's.

Tuesday 8—We reached the head of Elk, where I preached in the court-house from Acts 3: 19: "Repent therefore and be converted, and so forth." I have light and liberty and my friend Cooper made the application. From what I can gather, the people were well pleased, but I fear the heart is not given to God. They were kind to me here. We were kindly received, and entertained by my niece and her husband, Mr. Taylor. She seems to be a well disposed woman, and at times has serious exercises of mind. She is certainly a very affectionate, kind woman and I hope will be brought to experience the power of religion.

Wednesday 9—In the afternoon we took the stage, crossed Susquehanna and rode as far as Poplarville. Left the stage, walked a mile with our baggage to Mr. G Dallam's [?] at about 11 o'clock. After disturbing part of the family, and getting a little supper, we withdrew to rest in peace.

Thursday 10—We visited my niece, and her husband took us in a chair to Abington where I preached with freedom in the evening, and Brother Cooper applied the discourse—We had a very good time. Here we lodged with Mr. Osborn, who married my cousin Betsey Garrettson. They were both extremely kind.

Monday, July 1, 1805—Yesterday with freedom and power, thanks be unto God for his kindness. My love to God increases. I feel more strongly attached to the work than ever. There is a strange thing happening here. A man bereft of his reason says he has been remarkably visited and continues so yet, and yet never _____. He takes up the cause of religion boldly, by bearing testimony to the faith in our public assemblies where he is most regular. The most unhappy consideration is he makes himself _____.

Thursday 4—Monday afternoon I was taken ill with an ague and with a fever which still continues. It has weakened my body so that I am not able to attend to my appointments. O that this occasion of confinement may be sanctified to me. May it be a time of recollection and self examination, self abasement. I feel the Lord near to support me in my vicious trials. Thanks be unto his holy name forever. Friends are exceeding kind to me. O what condescension, may God reward them a hundred fold in this world and in the world to come. I am often astounded at the kindness of my friends to so unworthy a creature as I am. I find though I want of much grace to bear up under such heavy burdens. Adversity brings its own antidote. _____ _____ _____ _____ needs a skillful hand to prove it. O Lord do thou help me for Christ's sake.

Monday 15—My ague having left me I preached twice yesterday with freedom and power. Some parts were liberated. Thanks be unto God. I feel to devote my little all to God through grace, but I find frequently power basements, which make me stagger almost, but I hear a voice saying, "All things shall work for good to them that love God," and I know that I love him. His service is delightsome to my soul and I find that I increase in stability.

Wednesday 17—I am yet striving to move in the circle of duty and the Lord meets me at every turn. The blessing of the Lord it maketh rich _____ no sorrow with it. For the pure—love of God reigns in the soul we have perfect enjoyment. But I fear continues my wine mixed with water _____ some earthly good shares in my affliction. Death seems often a great terror to me, which makes me fear that all is not as it should be. My only refuge in this respect is to fix my faith in this manner—I believe that now I have peace with God through Jesus Christ, and I am endeavoring to be conformable to the image of God both inwardly and outwardly, and in this I find peace and joy.

I believe if I am faithful in improving my talent God will perfect the work in my soul and when I am right God will cut me down and give me grace to stand the shock. That he now supplies my wants he will also supply them in the hour of death. This is the antidote which I use to ease the pains of death, and then by grace I am striving to die daily and am praying that as my outward man decays, the inward man may be renewed day by day. If I miss my mark I am gone forever, but I cannot doubt upon those principles for I have God's word, that he will give grace and glory and no good thing will be withheld from those that walk uprightly even as an eagle stirreth up her nest _____ _____ fluttereth over her young and spreadeth abroad her wings, taketh them and keepeth them, so doth the Lord shelter those that trust in him. O my soul trust thou in the Lord for he is thy shield and thy exceeding great reward. God give me to see some little fruit in my labors which were more than compensated for all my toil. I esteem it though greatest of all blessings to be instrumental in saving souls from death, but if after I have preached to a man I myself should become a castaway, how intolerable my misery? How deep my hell? How endless my torment great God be merciful unto me a sinner. Let my own soul be fed with those truths which I have ministered to others through Jesus Christ.

Monday 20—I arrived at the Bay of Quintic [?] from the Niagra circuit and felt my spirit much refreshed at meeting with my brothers in this place. I scarce ever met with so joyful a meeting. They truly seemed as if they loved me in the bonds of the gospel. May God remember them for good and spread his spirit over them by night and by day. I wish to devote my all to God and his church. May the Lord keep me from dishonoring his cause for Christ's sake.

Thursday, August 9, 1805—Last Saturday I came to this circuit. This time the Quarterly meeting began. One woman after meeting who attended meeting was suddenly taken into eternity. On Monday I preached her funeral and it was a very moving time: Bless be God. O that we may be prepared for this summons. This day I preached with liberty to a small company. I find my mind insensibly drawn at times from God, but it gives me pain. O Lord do thou help me to keep an even balance in my mind, that I may always do those things that are well pleasing in thy sight. I do not feel such a sweet heavenly frame as I would wish, or as I have felt at some times though I am often enabled to rejoice in God my savior. I think the reason must be that my mind is too much attached to the world. Lord do thou fill my heart and my soul for Christ's sake.

Friday 15—Praise be to God, I am still permitted to pray in faith and find faith to live in the Son of God. God gave me a happy season yesterday in preaching. Salvation through faith in the Son of God is the theme which I delight to dwell upon; a truth which my soul feeds and lives upon. Well might the apostle say that he counted all things but lost for the excellency of Christ. I wish every man in his senses will follow his steps herein and by so doing will feel his soul sweetly attracted to the view of the heavenly mansions. There are many things which afford some degree of delight, but nothing short of Christ can satisfy an immortal spirit. In surveying the creation of God we are much pleased with its variety, order and harmony, but even this in time becomes insipid, considered, an abstract from God we can find no object worthy of adoration, but if the judgment brings previously informed _____ God, and if the heart has become touched with a feeling sense of _____ love, we may derive both influence and comfort from everything we see. Now when we consider that all this is only as the commitance of the redemption of Christ are only the fruits of his resurrection we must surely allow that everything that may be called excellent is in him. It is very certain that nature itself is not sufficient to bear up and sustain with a manly and becoming fortitude the occasions and works which adversity brings upon us. Only _____ is the mind.

Tuesday 20—I kneeled down before God and earnestly pled with God for my witness of his love to be bright. I was asked: do you believe that I am able to do this? I said, yea Lord, thou hast all power but I would not believe for a _____ I was wanting in the venture of faith at that instant but I believe God would accomplish his work, but it seemed it must not be then, but God saith now is the time. What was lacking then was in me. I believe that God is willing to save me now but the thing to believe he does save me now. This is the direct act of faith which brings an immediate answer to prayer. I have frequently found myself wanting in this venture of faith, yet this I believe to be the faith of the gospel nevertheless I believe that prayer of the faithful is always answered.

I asked the Lord for a blessing. Now perhaps what I call a blessing at this time the Lord does not. Therefore it gives me one in disguise. I am cut to the heart by the powerful application of some truth _____. I am humbled under a deep sense of my own unworthiness. This makes me loathe myself and long for a still deeper self abasement. Whatever God sees needful he shines upon my soul. I am comforted above measure with a sense of his goodness. I feel at the same time, wholly of grace which makes me thankful to God for his unspeakable gift. Now my heart is wholly given up to God and I have that measure of faith which brings peace to my soul. and that peace is heightened from a sense of sanctifying love. Let me ask what I will, it shall be granted because I am agreeable to the will of God. I ask resignedly and in faith. This then is the model of my prayer: "Lord, if my heart desires anything that in thy wisdom, would be hurtful to me, that with-hold; if thou seeth anything which I need, and am insensible of it myself, that give, and thus may I always be supplied from thee who art the fountain of wisdom and goodness." Thus then is my faith; I believe it will always be answered for the sake of Jesus Christ. Praise be God that he has taught me the mystery of faith in the Son of God. This is the life of my soul. The joy of my heart. Thank God I feel my prayers answered. It is answered _____. Jesus has come into my room—I have been waiting. His love disperses the gloom and makes all within me rejoice. Yesterday I was riding along the road, such a sense of the majesty of God resting upon my mind that I felt all that solemn awe that dares not move in all that silent heaven of love. Early it may be said that he is glorious and holiness—it is good to be absent from the body and be prepared with the Lord. For a while last evening the scene seemed changed, a kind of inward shrinking seized upon me, a fear that the Lord was angry with me. I now feel, thank God, that he is love to my soul. O that I may be saved from the great transgressions. In the evening I have just been preaching. Such a time of rejoicing I have not had for a long time. Before I began I wrestled with the Lord in secret all my might for his _____ and it came like a flood upon my own soul and the souls of his people. Glory and honor be unto God forever for his unspeakable mercy and loving kindness. My text was Psalm 16: 11. I felt such a spirit of prayer last evening as I have not felt for some time. Such arguments were handed to me that could not but believe the Lord would answer my requests and according to my faith it was done unto me.

Monday, September 6, 1805—I never labored under greater embarrassments of mind than yesterday. At both appointments it seemed blessed the beloved of heaven was impenetrable but in the evening the clouds dispersed. God showed that he would answer prayer but it was in a still small voice, but though small, it was sweet and welcome. Blessed be God my soul feels devoted to God at present and I find powerful besetments at times, but God deals with me as a tender father with his son. When I want encouraging he does it by some means, and when I want humbling he brings it to pass; and I find I cannot praise him as perfectly as I would, yet I do as I can. O my Father do thou take me into a sacred nearness to thyself that I may be kept pure from the great transgressions. I cannot but observe that in resolutely resisting the first notion of a temptation which often troubled me I received power against it and it hath not troubled me since. O that I might always observe this _____.

Saturday—My soul has been much blessed of the Lord of late. I have been endeavoring to water those souls of the _____. I am certain that my soul increases in spiritual might and I have but one choice, and that is to render all my words and actions to the advancement of the work of religion. This I know is the will of God towards me in striving to do this my _____ blow swiftly away. Time seems to be on the wing. Once time seemed to run so slow.

Some remarks by way of journalizing from my leaving my station in New York in April, 1807.

Thursday, April 23—We set sail in Captain Shultzes' sloop, and landed after nineteen hours sailing with our family, accompanied by Brother Ezekiel Cooper after a long absence from our country residence. We spent the time happy in reading, prayer, and social converse.

Sunday, April 26—Brother Cooper gave a sermon in the church. Our social amusements continued till Thursday morning, when Brother Cooper sat out with me to Conference. Got as far as Hudson and had a religious meeting in the Presbyterian Church in the evening, and the next day through the deep mud we got to Coeyman, where the ministry sat in Conference.

Sunday May 3—In the morning the General Superintendent preached a funeral sermon in memory of our respected friend and father Richard Whatcoat.[172] In the afternoon I tried to preach on, "Is the Lord with us or not?" Conference ended.

Saturday, May 9—During its continuance we had very rainy weather; however we settled our concerns, and several of us spent the Sabbath in Albany. Mr. Phobus (Thevos)? who was stationed here, has been a means of raising this country to a greater degree of respectibility than formerly. Yet I fear it is not entirely free of tatlers.

Monday, May 11—Ezekiel Cooper and I set out on our return; lodged at Hudson, and Tuesday dined at my house.

Thursday—we went on to Newburg. I started a few days behind with my family. The people at this place are as careless as ever. I sometimes have a little freedom to preach. I was favored with a passage of about 15 hours down to New York. In the city I spent some time agreeably in Brooklyn, at both which places I preached with freedom, and returned by water again to Rhinebeck. This is my third trip this spring and I think in all of them together I was only 45 hours on the water.

Sunday, May 31—I preached in the Rhinebeck church with a degree of freedom. I fear I do very little good, yet duty calls to be striving.

Tuesday, June 2—My dear wife and I set out in an open chair to the Sharon camp meeting, and left our daughter at home to keep house. We arrived on the spot a little before sunset. Many of the children of the evil one have gathered with the pious.

Wednesday 3—I pointed out the construction of the Gospel Church, her doctrines and usages (Acts 2: 46). The impious threatened to decamp Israel.

Thursday 4—This morning I preached from I Corinthians 1: 22. Perhaps I have not been more let out in preaching for 20 years. Our brethren seemed to get into the spirit of the work—darkness gave way and victory from this morning was obtained by the followers of Jesus. Glory to God, we had a display of justifying, and sanctifying grace, and it seemed as if the devil and his followers crept behind the bushes. The work continued gloriously all day and night, and next morning we parted. How many were justified or sanctified is not for me to say. My wife and I arrived safe at home in the evening.

Sunday 7—Preached at Rhinebeck and administered the sacrament. We had a comfortable time. I enjoyed the society of my family at home till Friday morning, when I set out on a northerly tour. Preached with freedom at Hudson and rode to Albany.

Sunday 14—Preached three sermons with a degree of freedom. Monday rode to Pittsfield, where we had a formidable camp-meeting. Two of the preachers and several others became as dead men before the Lord. I had freedom to preach the word. Brother Dillon told me he had received a gift from the Lord to labor day and night with very little food or sleep without wearysomeness. I believed it, for although he was laboring almost continually day and night through the meeting, when we concluded on Friday morning he seemed as fresh as at the beginning and I thought more so. I rejoice to say that I doubt not but many were both justified and sanctified at this meeting.

Sunday 21—I preached and spent the week about home and although I am blessed with an amiable wife and daughter and servants religious, and attentive, and every terrestrial good necessary for life and godliness, together with the beauties of creation, and a delightful season of the year, beautifully situated on the banks of the Hudson, I was anxious to be going in that glorious work, in which I have sweetly labored for more than thirty years. I find that no terrestrial thing can satisfy an immortal mind, a mind soaring to heavenly things, and a thirst for the salvation of sinners.

Sunday, June 28—I set out early for Pokeepsie, and preached with freedom morning and evening. Monday rode to Croton. Tuesday evening preached in Tarrytown. Wednesday rode to New York; visited and on Thursday evening preached with freedom, and we had a time of refreshing. Friday rode to New Rochelle.

Saturday 4 and Sunday, July 5—Attended Quarterly Meeting at White Plains. I had freedom, and power in the word both days. Sometimes young men will esteem their fathers. All do except Novices. I lodged at the house of Brother Fisher and Brother Hibbard's.[173]

Monday, July 6—Brother Mathias accompanied me to Rye and we stayed with good old Brother and Sister Holstead, who was a christian in the Presbyterian Church; but as he thought, for purer doctrines, and greater privileges came over to the Methodists. The parents and children sweetly unite in the good work. *Tuesday* about 20 of us crossed the sound to Long Island camp-meeting. We had a large gathering from New York; but not as large from the country, being a busy season of harvest. Thursday in particular was a great time, and I think the evening exceeded anything I have seen, except one evening at Rhinebeck last fall. Whilst preaching on the subject of holiness, a woman under a sense of the holiness and perfection of deity sunk down helpless as a corpse and lay so for about 24 hours and came too with all the signs of solemnity, and deep communion with God, though her power of speech had not returned, and did not till about eight hours after, when she came to me solemn as death, and praised God for the use of her speech. Tongue cannot utter, said she, what I felt, and some things I am forbid to mention. Several others lay speechless, and helpless. I sat by them for the opportunity of conversing with idle spectators, who passed to and from through the camp. "Tell me sir, said one gentleman, was you ever in that way?" "Now you constrain me to speak of myself" said I. You must bear with me whilst I give _____. It was two, three, or thirty years ago, having struggled under a call to the ministry in an itinerating way for about ten months; I attended the Methodist conference, and was presented for examination, and received a license from Mr. Rankin, the superintendent in behalf of the Little Conference. When we adjourned I had but just entered the parlor of Mr. William More, at who's house several of us lodged, then under a sense of the greatness of the work I had just engaged in, together with the purity and brilliancy of deity, and my own weakness, impurity, and ignorance, I sunk as helpless as a corpse to the floor, and was taken up by several of the preachers, and carried upstairs and laid on a bed, and one of the brethren prayed. I had my senses, but lost as it were in vision. When my strength and speech returned, I said surely I have been in heaven, and was sorry to return. I was never able fully to describe the fullness of the joy and happiness I than felt. We read that Daniel and the apostle John became as dead men before the *Lord*.

A little before midnight I formed a new ring, and shortly after I saw an elderly man without the ring who had fallen, and lay prostrate, and almost as cold, and helpless as a dead body. I inquired, and found he had not been long in the camp, a mere spectator. I had him taken up, and carried to a tent. Some hours after I called to see him, and found him in the same situation. I was told before morning he arose happy in *God*. We have glorious seasons indeed.

Friday, July 10—The meeting broke up about 11 A.M. and about twelve we went on board, and sailed about 15 miles in crossing the sound to Rye. As the wind was against us part of the way. I next set my face towards Fishkill Hook to attend a Quarterly Meeting. Left Rye about half after three. I rode about 25 miles to Croton, and on Saturday got to the Hook.

Sunday 12—We had a precious love-feast. I preached a sermon from, "And they went forth and preached everywhere, the Lord working with them, and confirming the word with signs following amen." Mark 16: 20. The power of the Lord was so wonderful, a circle was formed without. I concluded my work was done for that time, and left the work with the brethren.

[Freeborn Garrettson's Journals from 1809 through June 1817 are lost. The only record is to be found in Nathan Bangs, *Life of the Rev. F. Garrettson.* Both that record and Bangs remembrance of events are inserted at this point.

In the year 1809 Garrettson made a visit to his friends on the eastern shore of Maryland. The record begins with June 12, 1809.]

"Last Saturday about two o'clock, I went to the ferry to cross at Powles Hook, and drove near where the boat lay; a crowd of people being around. The horse began to back; and convinced I could not recover him, I leaped immediately out of the chair, and within the twentieth part of a minute after, horse, chair, and baggage, were all in the water. The horse was active, and swam with the carriage for life. Many people were engaged with boats, and got off the harness with only cutting the girt; so that the harness was not injured; the horse was extricated unhurt, and shortly after the chair was taken up, and every individual thing, without the smallest damage, except getting wet, and the small end of the shaft broken. I crossed on to Newark, and got there by the middle of the afternoon, and found none of my baggage seriously injured, excepting my precious little Bible. It was a heavy jar jumping out of the chair, but I am nearly as well as ever. The affair was most remarkable; first—one hour before it happened I said to a friend, I will put this pocket book into my packet, lest something should happen, in which were notes and valuable papers. Second—my escaping the tenth or twentieth part of a minute before the chair and horse went over. Third—the horse, chair, baggage, and harness unhurt, except the shaft. Fourth—my mind was kept as calm and collected as at this moment. All these things considered, we may see the superintending hand of God, and be led to adore his holy name. No doubt it was permitted for good, and I believe, I shall profit by it."

From thence Mr. Garrettson passed on to Bellville, from that to Newark and Trenton, in which places he preached, and thence to Philadelphia. Here he preached with much liberty and satisfaction, and was greatly refreshed in the society of his old friends. After spending some time in this place, preaching and visiting, he passed on to Wilmington and to Elkton, where he had the happiness to find his niece, Mrs. Taylor, in the fear and love of God. Under date of June 22, he makes the following reflections:—

"In the afternoon I met a large society, after which I inquired if any were members thirty years ago, when I rode that circuit. They told me not one. 'O! my friends,' said I, 'probably all of you will be in eternity before the end of thirty years more. You see the necessity of training up your children for the church, in order to keep a succession of faithful members, as our children and children's children must perpetuate the memory of Christ on earth; and so from generation to generation be transplanted from the militant to the church triumphant, that the upper region may be peopled with blessed millions to adore the Saviour eternally.' "

The following account of this tour was communicated to Mrs. Garrettson in a series of letters which he wrote during his absence. It will doubtless be read with interest by those especially of his surviving friends in that part of the country, as well as by all others who delight in seeing "the good hand of God" on his servants.

"Friday 23. I leave my horse to rest, and Mr. Presbury accompanies me to Baltimore. My sister Elizabeth died about thirty years ago, and left an only child. I saw her about a twelvemonth ago, but she is now gone.

"Saturday I spent mostly in retirement, except to visit some friends.

"Sunday, 25. This morning I preached at Old Town, in the afternoon at Light-street, and in the evening was to be at the Point; but as the weather was so excessively warm, I thought I could not go in justice to myself. The congregations here do not increase much: indeed they are rather smaller. The extravagance of some of our people has had a greater tendency to fill other churches than their own. Mr. D_____d's congregation they say increases very much; it seems a half way house. I am willing God should work when, where, and by whom he pleases. I have met brother Jesse, and he sent on my appointments to Washington and Georgetown.

"Monday 26. I took the stage, and in the evening arrived at Georgetown; had a large congregation. Our friends are much engaged. Brother Roszel is the stationed minister. The weather remains very warm. 'Tis well I got a loose thin garment before I left New-York. I lodge at Mr. Elison's, a very worthy family. Here I have a large cool room. They are some of my old Eastern Shore friends.

"Tuesday 27. To-day Mrs. Foxal sent her carriage for me, and kindly gave me the use of it while I stay. In the afternoon I went to town, and stopped at Captain Lewis's, where I found Jesse Lee, the chaplain, nursing his leg. On his way from Baltimore the day before, his horse fell, broke the shaft of his gig, threw him out, and one of the screws bruised and cut his leg very much. I am fearful it will go hard with him if the hot weather continues. I preached in the evening to many people with a degree of freedom.

"Wednesday 28. This morning brother Smith, the city preacher, went with me to the navy yard, and I thought well of the improvements. Dined at Captain Lewis's. He is not a member of society, but his daughters are. I was well pleased with the family. In the afternoon brother Elison came for me; I intended to go and hear the debates in congress, but they had adjourned for dinner sooner than usual. This evening I preached in Georgetown again; here we have a respectable society; and had I been an apostle they could not have treated me much better.

"Thursday 29. I went to breakfast with an old Eastern Shore friend, brother Gruntree. He is an old Methodist preacher. Here brother Parrot and his lady, my earliest friends, came to see me, and took me to Mrs. Foxal's.

"Friday 30. I left my hospitable friends, and came on in the stage, laden with members of congress and others, to Baltimore.

"Saturday 31. Mr. Hollingsworth gave me a kind invitation to stay with him; so that I am now most comfortably retired in a large airy room. This afternoon I had an interview with Richard Garrettson, my nephew. He gave me a particular account of his father's landed estate, which has been for years involved in law. Their title was thought by the first lawyers to be good, and there was no probability of their losing the suit. He tells me the first person that entered a claim died very suddenly before the trial came on, and likewise the second; and lately a third person renewed the suit, and died suddenly, and left his pretended right to no one. The suit is fallen.

"July 2. My to-day's appointment was announced last week in the public paper. I had much freedom to preach in the new church this morning.

Mr. Colvil, with his five motherless children in deep mourning, came around me in tears; it was an affecting sight. In the afternoon I preached in good old Mr. Otterbine's church. I am not in Rhinebeck now, but where thousands think it a privilege to hear an old Methodist preacher. Mrs. Gough drank tea with us at Mr. Hollingsworth's, and talks of taking me to my appointment at Mr. Presbury's where I left my horse. It was published in all the churches to-day for my last sermon in the new chapel. On Tuesday evening I heard brother Shin preach. He is a good preacher, and is stationed here, and appears deeply devoted to God.

"July 4. This is the day of great parade in the city. Some of the Methodists were warmly engaged in it. From what I understand it was conducted with as much decency as the nature of the thing would admit. The language of my heart was, Turn away thine eyes from beholding vanity. In the evening I preached in the new church to a large congregation, and we had a time of power. I have known the society here in a more flourishing state. I fear politics has done hurt to the cause of religion.

"Wednesday 5. This morning I left my kind friends accompanied by brother Hagerty, in his gig, to Presbury's church, where I left my horse, and had an agreeable time and freedom to preach. This is a blessed family; his mother was my father's niece, and I knew her thirty years ago deep in piety; but she has long since gone to glory. Her son is now treading in her steps.

"Thursday 6. Accompanied by my cousin Presbury and other relatives, we repaired to what is called the Camp Meeting Chapel. It is beautifully situated in a forest, at a distance from any house. As I rode up, my mind was solemnly impressed when I saw such a number of horses and carriages fastened to the trees, and the people waiting to hear the word. I had a sweet time in speaking from 1 Cor. vii, 21. While the gracious Lord was visiting the people with his heavenly grace, we had a little shower to refresh the vegetable creation. It seems this chapel is one of Mr. Gough's last acts of kindness to the poor. I went home with Mrs. Gough. There are some handsome improvements about this venerable mansion, and the garden excels any thing I have seen. At present the parlour family is very large, there being much company. While they enjoyed themselves in the hall, Mrs. Gough and myself sat in the parlour, talking over old times. At nine o'clock the bell rung, and about fifty of the family assembled for prayer in the chapel. All the gentlemen and ladies were present morning and evening. The riches of the world are good, if made a good use of. Who can tell how these pretty things will be employed a few years hence?" (Mrs. Carrol and her mother were both out of health; and since both are dead.)

"Friday 7. My appointment to-day is in Harford, at Belle Air court house. I came to the place a little after 3 o'clock, and found there had been a misunderstanding. A large gathering had been there at 11, and were gone. We went to Mrs. Montgomery's, and had a little gathering at five.

[Dined to-day at my eldest brother's widow's] Brother Galespy, the circuit preacher, met me there, and he and my nephew came with me to my niece Mrs. Norris's, and spent the night. She and her daughters are very friendly and desire to enjoy religion.

"Saturday 8. This day the preacher and my nephew, F. Garrettson, left me. [Here I have one sister living; she is old, and her memory is so totally gone, that she does not know her own children; but gives no trouble whatever; and sits and knits without speaking a word, unless spoken to. A few nights ago she called her daughter, and told her she should die soon, and requested her to bury her by her dear husband. I think I never saw a greater picture of innocence. This afternoon I go to Abington.]

"Sunday 9. This morning a very large congregation assembled from almost all quarters. My mind was sweetly drawn out. The church was much crowded, and many of my relatives were present. Preached from Psalm xlviii, 12, 13. I told them I had come several hundred miles to invite them to come to Jesus, and to inform them that after following the Lord between thirty and forty years, I found religion better and better. I preached about an hour and a half, and scarcely knew when to give over. There was no loud noise, but the whole assembly were melted into tenderness, while I entreated them to meet me in heaven, for thither I was bound. In the afternoon I rode seven miles, to what is called Bush chapel; but it would not contain the people; so I preached in a grove with freedom. Glory to God, I have lived to convince friends and foes that I am sincere at least.

"Many descendants of my ancestors were present. Some of you have wondered where I have been, and what I have been about. Excuse me if I make a small digression to inform you. When the sermon was ended, many gave the hand; among the rest was good old brother Watters, 80 years of age, and brother Herbert, 90, who had made an effort to come out. Indeed they looked like ripe shocks, fit to be gathered home. Mr. Allen, minister of Spesutia church, who was a hearer, said he wanted some conversation. I requested him to fall in with me at some other place, where we could have more time together. He said he would. I went home with my cousin R. Garrettson, and found my mind sweetly composed after the labours of the day. There are very few families in this country, at least in the interior part of it, to whom I might not have access. Indeed if I were an angel I could not be treated with a greater degree of kindness. I rejoice to find Dr. Hall, who is stationed in this circuit, very much followed. It is in his power to do much good through the blessing of God.

"Monday 10. I preached in a church in Bush River Neck, near the Chesapeake Bay, and not a mile from the place in which I was born, and within half a mile of where I believe the first church in Maryland was built. From what I can learn, it was built by an ancestor of mine more than two hundred years ago. It was the height of harvest, or there would have been more hearers than the church could contain; however, it was pretty well filled. I had some freedom to preach from James i, 24. A Colonel Mathews was present, whom I have not seen since we were boys. I requested him to go with me to Mr. Chancy's, where I was to lodge. I wanted to talk with him about new things and old; he gave me his company some hours. He is not acquainted with Jesus, but seems to have a respect for religion.

"Tuesday 11. This day I spent in visiting my relations in the Neck. None of them oppose religion, and they generally think well of Methodism. They are, I believe, moral and industrious, and have a fulness of this world's moral and industrious, and have a fulness of this world's goods. I told them freely my errand among them, and that they wanted but one thing to make them a happy people.

"I appointed to preach at Miss Griffiths. One of the young ladies went to give an invitation to our relatives there; they said they should be glad to see me, but they had not time to attend the meeting. I sent a message to them, begging if they would not meet me on earth, they would strive to meet me in heaven. In this place I had but a small congregation. Here parson Allen met me again, and stayed all night. When alone, I inquired with regard to his knowledge of divine things experimentally, and the manner of his preaching. I told him he was appointed to serve a people who were near to me by natural ties, as the greater part of his congregation were my family connexions. I begged of him to declare the counsel of God faithfully, to attend to regular church discipline, to visit from house to house, to have meetings in different parts of the congregation, and to exercise extemporaneously, both in prayer and exhortation, and show the people that there is something wanting besides profession and morality. He said he would do the best he could, that he wished my time was not so short, and would be glad I would stay some days at his house.

"Thursday 13. This morning I parted with Mr. Allen, and yesterday I parted with brother Galespy, (who had faithfully attended me to every place,) and my affectionate Harford friends, and was accompanied by some relatives to the ferry. I crossed, and went on to the head of North-East *********. I have just received a letter from brother Cooper; he says he must leave the Peninsula soon, and I must by all means come on and help him. I shall, God willing, be at Smyrna, Del., the 27th of this month.

"July 14. This morning I left North East, came to Elkton, and preached at five o'clock to a small congregation. My niece and her husband were very kind to me, and my mind was easy and free. I am not of that service to people as I wish to be. *This* always was, and I fear always will be, a poor place for religion.

"Saturday, 15. I rode to Mr. Canaan's, where I found several of my old friends and acquaintances still in the profession, and I trust happy in the enjoyment, of religion. We had a comfortable time together; the conversation turned mostly on the subject of falling, jumping, shouting, and clapping. I made free to speak my sentiments. Mr. Canaan was with me; but Mrs. Canaan had her fears, and asked if I had ever been at a camp meeting.

"Sunday 16. A large congregation assembled in Bethel chapel. While we were singing the first hymn, a woman shouted and jumped amazingly. Before I gave out my text to prepare the assembly for an attentive hearing, I told them I had come a great way to communicate gospel truths to them, and I requested a patient hearing. I was led to give a display of the wisdom and goodness of God, and to open to view our duty in resigning up our all to him, to the evidencing the power of religion experimentally, and likewise to display the external marks of inward religion. I told them a ministry of this kind was necessary to keep up a pure flame; without it they could not expect to prosper, and that there would be an evaporation that would leave them a mere sound, without the vital flame. The congregation was still and attentive till I ended the sermon, and then one jumped and shouted. I thought it a great favour that there was stillness and attention till I ended my sermon. Mr. Basset dined with us, and in the afternoon I rode home with him, and spent an agreeable evening; but I find my friends are growing old like myself. Mrs. B. is a pious woman, and he is full of zeal and love. He would have gone with me, but his many concerns prevented. He told me that wherever his influence extended he did not suffer a drop of distilled liquor to be used. His house and table are very plain; and he says he feels it to be his duty to do every thing in his power for the cause of God.

"Tuesday 18. I rode after dinner 22 miles to Smyrna, preached with freedom, and lodged at Dr. Ridgeley's. His wife was daughter to parson Harris, and was among some of my first spiritual children about Chestertown, thirty years ago. Here I met an old friend, one of Judge White's daughters, who has stood fast in the Lord more than thirty years. In the vicinity they are making great preparation for a camp meeting, to begin next week. I went to the spot, where I suppose fifty men were employed in seating the ground. They thought it would take fifteen thousand feet of plank, and there seemed to be great anticipations of glorious times.

"Wednesday 19. I rode to Queen Ann's. When I rode up to my old friend's, brother Segar's, I told him to take a full view of me, and try to recognise some features; but he could not. I made myself known, and we had a season of much happiness.

"Thursday 20. This dear friend intends travelling with me till I return from Smyrna. We went on, and dined at Thomas Wright's, and after dinner lodged at Mr. Fediman's. He did know me, and that was all, for he had to consider a long time. Several friends came over this afternoon, and we had some religious conversation, and some politics. Upon the whole it was an agreeable time. Brother Segar is a pillar in the temple.

"Friday 21. We came to Centreville, and in the evening the church was nearly filled. I preached, and then went on to Mr. Kanard's to lodge. This is a respectable and kind family.

"Saturday 22. I spent the day retired, and had an opportunity to read and write.

"Sunday 23. I had hearers from five to twenty miles, and should have had a great congregation had there been general notice. However, the church was filled morning and afternoon. There is a large, respectable congregation in and about this place. I can say, glory to God, this was a high day. I had the privilege to see many of my old friends and their children. Some of the blacks were in raptures. My intention was to go down the Peninsula, for about three or four weeks, on the Chesapeake side, and up on the other side, and I had my appointments about fifteen or twenty miles apart, by which means I might have an opportunity of speaking to thousands and tens of thousands, perhaps for the last time, and seeing many of my old friends; but I found the country filled with notices for camp meetings. I was pressed by Mr. Basset and others by all means to attend them. I am now going on my way to Smyrna, where the first begins.

"Monday 24. I leave my kind Centreville friends, and am to preach in the English church, which is almost an unheard of favour in this country; but it was the desire of the vestry. In this neighbourhood I was beaten by Mr. Brown years ago, and now a near relation of his is the principal vestryman. My appointment was at four o'clock, and though a wet afternoon, the church was crowded above and below with Methodist and church folks, white and black, and we had a moving time. This meeting was at Church Hill. I do indeed love the Lord Jesus.

"Tuesday 25. At four o'clock, in the Methodist church near Saddler's cross roads, I had uncommon freedom to preach. A large church was filled above and below. Indeed it looked a little like quarterly meeting. I preached on Peter's denying Christ. We had a very powerful time; but the enemy took advantage of a weak minded black man in the front gallery, who cried aloud, stripped, and struck his fists together, and declared he would not see his blessed Master treated in that sort;—that he would fight for him till he died on the spot. I desired them to take him out, and not let him return till the meeting closed; which they did in less than two minutes. My soul is happy; Lord, keep me humble. The children and grandchildren of old friends show me the same respect that their parents would if alive.

"Wednesday 26. I had great freedom to preach to-day. I left you at Smyrna; I again resume my detail:—There were about thirty preachers present, local and travelling, and seats provided for about three thousand. There were two hundred and sixty tents. I lodged every night on the ground, in Dr. Ridgeley's tent. We had fourteen sermons in the course of the meeting, and very powerful speaking. I preached with great freedom on Friday, from Isaiah's vision, vi, 8; and on Sunday, from 'I am not ashamed of the gospel,' &c, Rom. i, 16. M'Claskey, Chalmers, and M'Combs, delivered some able discourses. The meeting increased every day till Sunday, when there were about five thousand people. I did not see one disorderly person on the ground from first to last; scarcely a single thing to drink except water, and sometimes a little milk with it, or molasses and vinegar. They had tables, beds, curtains, carpets, and provisions, and servants, in great order. We had a solemn, profitable season, but no particular outpouring of the Spirit, and very few converted, awakened, or sancitfied. The people in this country must be either Methodists or nothing, for there is scarcely a minister of any other name. At this meeting I saw a great many of my old friends with pleasure, and I trust with profit. Good Mr. Basset seems taken up with divine things. At parting they had a manoeuvre, which some of us old men did not feel free to join in, marching round the camp, blowing five or six trumpets, and singing by turns.

"Tuesday, Aug. 2. At eight o'clock the meeting closed. O! what a blessed day it will be when friends meet to part no more for ever! Brother Chalmers, a respectable old preacher from Baltimore, travels with me. My appointment at night was in Dover church, and it was well filled. My text was, 'Grow in grace.' Brother Chalmers exhorted, and we had a good time. Lodged at Mr. Basset's.

"Wednesday 3. My appointment was at Barret's chapel, at three o'clock. About three hundred people were assembled, many more than I expected, as they had but short notice. I spoke from, 'But one thing is needful.' Brother Chalmers exhorted, and the Lord was with us. I am still among my children and old friends. A woman belonging to the community of Quakers was present in a state of depression; whom her friends sent in hope of relief. I conversed and prayed with her, but left her in the same state, despairing of the mercy of God. Here I met with many kind friends I had not seen for four or five and twenty years. Many of my old associates are gone to glory, but their children and grandchildren have taken their seats in the church. We stayed at Judge Barret's. His brother was a dear friend of mine, and a spiritual child, but long since gone to rest. I hope the children will tread in the steps of their pious parents.

"Thursday 4. We went on to Milford, and got on the camp ground by ten o'clock. Seats were prepared for about two thousand. Meeting opened at three—a small congregation, and a small sermon. Friday the congregation increased. I preached from Peter's denial of Christ. Saturday the congregation increased. Brother Chalmers preached a good sermon:— not a great many, and mostly young. Sunday about three thousand. I preached from 'Walk about Zion,' &c, Psalm xlviii, 12, 13. Had much freedom;—about one hundred and fifty tents. Here I met many dear old friends from fifty and sixty miles round, and we were happy together. We had three sermons each day, but I cannot say we had any extraordinary work either in conviction or conversion. Those who do not profess religion behaved well. No intoxicated person, nor even the smell of liquor, on the ground. A few noisy, jumping, dancing Methodists, did, I fear, more hurt than good. An empty sound is very disagreeable to me; a shout, when the power of God is in it, is sweet to me. I have never been at a meeting where there were more fruitless human exertions, though I did what I could to prevent them. I begged them to wait for the Master, and let him take the lead. Extravagance was carried to the greatest height among the blacks, for many of them continued it for hours together. Such things, when the power of God is not in the camp, tend to dissipate the mind. The most I can say of this meeting is, there was great attention paid to the word preached. During my stay I got accommodations at my friend Shockley's—a rich friend, who was within call of the camp ground, where my friend Chalmers and I retired for lodging. It is a blessing to have able, wise, and prudent rulers in the church; but to my grief, I say we have some whose zeal and imprudence go far beyond their knowledge; but, thanks be to God, there are men of piety and knowledge to check their precipitancy, or we might soon bid farewell to good old Methodism. Glory to God, I think it will stand, though encumbered with many disagreeables. There are thousands in this country deeply pious. The Methodists have the whole business to themselves in this country. There is scarcely a minister of any other denomination.

"Monday 7. I had an appointment at Dover to-day at three o'clock. We started early this morning, rode twenty-two miles, and got in by twelve o'clock. I feel a little weary. The church was nearly filled. I discussed two heads of doctrine—the lowest and the highest degree of Christian experience. Brother Chalmers made the application, and we had a precious season. This town looks old:—in fact, there are very small improvements made in any part of this country, except in matters of religion. We stayed at Mr. White's, brother to Dr. White, an old friend. We had a number of my good friends to tea.

"Tuesday 8. To-day I preached at Blackstone's chapel. Dined at Ringold's. At three we had a large congregation. After speaking more than an hour on the various parts of prayer with great freedom, while the power of God was graciously displayed, and I was much spent, I asked brother Chalmers to speak on the duty and benefit of prayer, which I had promised to do if strength permitted. He did so in a very pertinent manner, for he is an excellent preacher. He began travelling when he was sixteen, about twenty years ago, but has been located several years. Brother Whitby, a worthy man, where we now lodge, (who was once a travelling, but is now a local preacher,) said, For your encouragement I can tell you that under the sermon you preached in our chapel, as you went down, a poor sinner was awakened, who has since found pardon, and is now happy in God.

"Wednesday 9. My appointment is at Chestertown in the evening. My good friend Chalmers leaves me this morning. As Basset's camp meeting begins to-day, and he expects to meet his wife from Baltimore, I have no other chance to see my old friend, Dr. Anderson, who is very ill from a fall from his carriage. I think it a small thing to go twenty-five miles out of my way to see so worthy a member of the church, and the fruit of my poor little labours more than thirty years ago. I rode twenty-five miles, and dined at Chestertown, at brother Harris's. In the evening I had the church full of serious hearers, and to my agreeable surprise the Doctor was among my audience. I had a most sweet season among my friends. My sermon was from Psalm xlviii, 12, 13. 1, I spoke of the church ministry, beauty, and order; 2, her strength and fortitude; 3, her privileges; 4, her testimony.

"Thursday 10. Our worthy brother Burniston accompanied me to the camp ground.

"Friday 11. A very rainy day. I preached in a large tent, on the necessity of holiness. Mr. Harris fell under the word, cried for mercy, and found peace. He is not a member of our church. Brother Chalmers got under such a deep travail of soul for holiness, that he fell under the power of God, and lay for hours; and when he came to, rejoiced in the perfect love of God. I was requested by some of my old friends to call this meeting; among others was Mrs. Bruff and her sister Ward. These holy women are full of the perfect love of God. This meeting held several hours. I likewise called a meeting in the preachers' tent at the same time;—the tents rung with the praises of God. The poor blacks seemed almost ready to fly. There is, nevertheless, a probability we shall have a great meeting. Many of our good friends have come from Baltimore. I must leave you. This minute I have been conversing with Mrs. Bruff;—she tells me, at the above-mentioned meeting three besides Mr. Chalmers were brought out, and several led to feel the necessity of holiness. My dear love, there is a struggle in the camp I will tell you more when we meet. God bless you and yours. I am in the cause of God; nothing else would reconcile me to so long an absence from you. I remember you at the throne of grace;—there also remember me;—I can only stand by grace. While I am writing, prayer, praise, and shouting are all around me."

Some account of my travels and labors from the Middlebury Annual Conference in 1817 till the ensuing Conference in New York.

I wrote, as it was not convenient at the time for me to attend Conference, informing the superintendents if they thought best, I was willing to be continued on the minutes as I was last year—to minister as my health and strength would admit without any particular charge. Perhaps this is the most useful relation in my advanced time of life, I can bear to the _____ though I was resigned if it was thought best to take a regular station. The preachers treat me as a Father, and seem like I should favor myself a little after a long servitude _____ this side of the grave—the crown is before and I begin ever to stretch for it—souls are of infinite _____ and are hurrying into an awful eternity.

Sunday 16—The brethren having returned from Conference we had two sermons, and sacrament in Rhinebeck but being a very rainy day, we had but a small _____, I was pleased in hearing they had an agreeable time at the Conference, and that general satisfaction was given in the appointments to the different stations the world may stand astonished, whilst viewing this wonderful machinery, spread over the widely extended continent, in harmony, walking by the same rule and minding the same things. The following week I spent mostly at home. Precious time passes swiftly away. I have an agreeable family and everything the world can give to make domestic, social, or retired life agreeable; but I am burdened and wish so to be, unless when I _____ hit on the Lord, who bore all for me, and has sustained me many years. I retire _____and meditate—my mind is after precious souls. O that my own Vineyard were better cultivated! I see the mark, and am reaching forward. I am assured, the completion of the promises are attainable. I am contemplating ministerial tours southward.

June 23, 1817—I preached with freedom in the Rhinebeck church. I feel as if the Society is on the rise. It would do the hearts of some pious ones about this place good, could they see the wilderness and solitary places bud and blossom as the rose. Sunday schools, if carried on in a proper manner, will be a blessing to the world. In order thereto pious teachers must be employed, and the lambs of the flock must be taught the fear, and service of God, and brought to his house, and taught to keep his holy day.

Monday 24—My good friend wanted to visit Mrs. Van Ness at Kinderhook, and my daughter was anxious to visit Dr. Nott's family,[174] and I had a hope of doing some little good in _____ the churches. In the evening we got as far as General Armstrong's. Baptized his little grand-son, and the next day we arrived safe to Kinder-hook, and the following day my daughter accompanied me to Union College, where we were kindly received. This institution is blessed with a worthy president and professors, and I would hope the institution will be a blessing to society, and give pleasure to its patrons.

Thursday 25—In the evening I preached with freedom at the Methodist Church, and likewise the following evening heard the word. Ministers of the different denominations in Schenectady, seemed friendly to each other but I feel religion is not in a flourishing state. The Methodists are so few in number, and not very rich, have by considerable exertion built a church, and continue to support a minister, for which they deserve great credit. Other denominations have been friendly in assisting about their house. After staying and preaching a few sermons in this place we went to Troy,[175] and was kindly entertained at Mr. George Tibbett's.

Sunday 28—With freedom I preached in the Methodist Church morning, afternoon, and evening, and can truly say it was a good day. About 30 years ago when first I visited this country, there was very few houses in this place, and now it is a flourishing little city with four churches, and good congregations. The Methodists have a good house, and about 300 church members. Brother Spuer was rendered a blessing to the people the two past years, and as Brother Lucky is stationed among them, I hope in future he will be rendered a blessing to them. I was happy to find the different denominations friendly to each other. Indeed I trust party spirit will die away.

June 29, 1817—We returned to Judge Van Ness' in Kinder-hook, and the day following got safe home. Retirement is sweet; I love my family and find the cross more heavy than ever to leave them. The great ones have set themselves violently against the blessed work of reformation. I have labored to do them good, but all my efforts seem to be as water spilt on the ground. That cannot be gathered. They do not openly persecute, and perhaps I might have more hope of them if they did. They would bear with me if I would let them alone; but how can I, as a messenger of God let them sleep over hell, and not strive to awake them from their slumber. Several weeks, or may I say months of the warm season were spent about home, and I only preached twice a week in the church on the Lord's Day, except one tour through part of Connecticut, where I had precious sessions by day and night and several visits to New York, Pough-keepsie, and a few other places in the state. I have had sweet seasons in reading, writing, and family devotions, as well as in public. Although I have not kept a daily, or even weekly journal, I trust my time is not run to waste. I feel daily that God is good, and I will praise him. From the 20th of June till the 9th of December, 1817, I travelled about 1,000 miles, and preached when, and where I found an opening, beside officiating regularly in the Rhinebeck church on Lord's days when home.

Thursday, December 9, 1817—Being pressed in spirit, though under a great cross in leaving a precious wife and daughter, I set out on a tour to the south. I passed through a critical examination previous, to know my motives, and whether it was my duty at my 66th year and consequent infirmities, to leave a quiet, plentiful habitation and a most agreeable family, to encounter the storms of the winter, and to bear my own expenses. A little before sunset I bid adieu to my friends, family, and habitation and went on board the steam, and by sunrise in the morning found myself in New York, 100 miles on my way.

Wednesday 10—I lodged at Brother Hall's in the city.

Thursday 11—Accompanied by Brother Rut_____ at 8 o'clock we took the Elizabeth steamboat, and a line of stages and slept at my old friend, Brother Robinson's Being persuaded I heard Dr. Dun_____ farewell sermon as a physician, and as a minister he was beloved by the people, and indeed I was sorry he thought it his duty to remove to Phil-adelphia. For four years past his labors had been a blessing to the church in Trenton. Saturday I spent in retirement, and blessed be God in my mind sweetly drawn out in his cause, and hope to live and die a witness for his name, and in his cause.

Lord's Day 14—At 11 o'clock the church was nearly filled. I preached from, "Blessed are the pure in heart, for they shall see God."—Matthew 5: 8. We had a precious, solemn season. My own soul was refreshed and I felt as if good was done. In the evening from Genesis 22: 14, Abraham offering up Isaac. Suppose we view Isaac hand and foot on the altar, and his father with his hand lifted up ready to give the fatal blow. Is this not an awful representation of the fallen, guilty state of man and the knife the justice of God leveled against the fallen sinner. Hear the voice of God to Abraham (similar to Adam after his fall)—Abraham spare thy son, I have found a sacrifice—vengeance shall fall on my own son, to rescue the culprit—he looked round and saw the lamb caught in the thicket; with joy he unloosed his son, and brought forth the typical victim, shed his blood, and actually offered him up. David beautifully said, "Mercy and truth have met together, righteousness and peace hath kissed each other." The offering up of Isaac represents the need of a savior, and the lamb the atonement he made for sin. I never had a better day in the city.

Monday 15—My appointment was sent on two days previous to Burlington I preached in the evening. The church was crowded above, and below—indeed the people stood I think at the door, and in the aisles that a person might have almost walked on their shoulders, and we had a solemn season. I stayed at our old friend, Mr. Sterling's. He is a very old man, and confined to his bed, and perhaps will never leave his room till carried out. He appears to be innocent, and happy. He has been a great support to Methodism in this city. It is a good thing to be on the Lord's side.

Tuesday 16—I took the steamboat, and went into Philadelphia and put up at Brother Green's. A kind hospitable friend, and an old minister of Jesus Christ. He traveled and labored till he was worn down, and then married and located, and has since been greatly prospered in the world.

Thursday 18—Preached in St. George's Church. Had not a very good time, but considerable attention was given to the word.

Friday 19—Preached in the Academy Church, from "Search me O God and know my heart, try me and know my thoughts, and see if there be any wicked way in me, and lead me into the way everlasting."—Psalm 139: 23, 24. I had freedom in the word, first to show that a state of sinning is incompatible with the state of salvation; second, the doubt expressed in the text; third, the best method to solve that doubt. The next day I spent in retirement, contemplating the infinite perfections of deity, and praying for a blessing on his blessed word.

Sunday 21—I preached again in St. George's Church and in the afternoon in the Academy—we had a good day. Monday—visited friends.

Tuesday 23—In the evening preached with freedom in St. John's to a large congregation with much freedom from, "We preach Christ crucified and so forth." Brother Cooper stayed with me at Mrs. Bassett's—she is the same pious heavenly minded christian she was many years ago.

Wednesday 24—Being Christmas Eve we had a Watch Night in St.

John's Church. I preached with freedom on the occasion, and several of the station's preachers continued in singing, praying and exhortation till midnight, and we had a great time of refreshing. This church was only built last summer and now we have a large congregation, and many souls converted in this part of the city. I again lodged at Mrs. Bassett's.

Thursday 25—We see another Christmas Day. I preached in the morning at Ebenezer Church from, "Unto us a child is born and so forth"—Isaiah 9: 6. The government of the son of God and his divine, and human nature, and his ability to sustain that character. An able counselor as well as a wonderful counselor—for he is the mighty God, the everlasting Father, the Prince of Peace. Equal with the Father, being from eternity. In redemption, salvation and government He is the Father of His Church. In the afternoon I preached in the Asbury Church from, "I bring you glad tidings and so forth." I can truly say it was a good day in Wilmington so in this place Brother Sharply both itinerant ministers.(?) It seems they both in part, support their families on their private purse. Their wives are pious, and resigned to the dispensations of providence, in calling their husbands to go into the vineyard to call sinners to repentance. Our people are too slack, in making provision for their ministers, and indeed in part it is our own fault—we have made the ministry of the word too cheap. "The mouth of the ox that treadeth out the corn should not be muzzled, and they who preach the gospel, should live of the gospel." This evening I was in doubt whether it was my duty to ride in the dark 30 miles to Abingdon, and whilst I was thinking of it, two stages arrived, and one of them concluded to tarry till morning, which I considered good providence in my favor, and paid for a _____ seat to start in the morning at daybreak.

Saturday, January *10,* 1818—I had a pleasant ride to Abingdon—only one with me in the stage. My friends are very kind.

Lord's Day 11—I preached morning, afternoon, and evening, in the church not with that freedom I could wish. I fear the kingdom of Jesus does not prosper in this place. Some of the old people drop off and the young people seem either too gay, busy, or idle to submit to the cross. What can be done? Our plan seems incomplete. Circuit preaching only comes round once in two weeks, in which case there can be but a small part of ministerial duties performed, especially as it respects the youth, and rising generation. We baptise the infants, and I fear too little care is taken of them afterwards. It is right to take the lambs into the fold, but they should be taught the rules, and regulations of the family, and to become actually interested in the promised inheritance. There are two parts in baptism; the first is the outward form, or sign; the second is the thing signified, grace in the covenant; but in persons who come to the age of discretion, there must be repentance, and faith in Christ, or a death unto sin, and a new birth into righteousness, and a coming forward, and actually and personally uniting in all the _____ of the church. The head of the church is of long forebearance, and so should his ministers be; but he may, and in justice will disinherit them, and cast them out forever, if they repent not, and why should the rising generation slight offered mercy and trample under foot covenant blessings? *God* for Christ's sake is willing to save, the covenant stands open from year to year, and a merciful *God* is unwilling to cast off forever.

Monday 12—I stayed at Mr. Hollis's, and wrote. I had the pleasure of receiving a letter from home, and hearing of the welfare of my family.

Tuesday 13—In the evening I preached at Mr. Mather's and was well pleased with the family. God's people have sweet union with Jesus, and each other.

Wednesday 14—I rode to Mr. R. Garrettson's, and met with several of my relatives. I find it a greater cross to speak plain to my relations, than to strangers. I came on an errand of love, but O how far I come short. Lord Jesus stand by thy feeble dust, and give him some seals to his feeble ministry.

Thursday 15—At 12 o'clock I preached within a mile of the spot where I was born—mostly young people, and distant relations. It seems to be almost an entire new set of people, and indeed there were very few in the congregation I had any knowledge of. My native country scarce makes any improvement, indeed in some instances there is a declinnation— generally the houses are very poor, and the land's wearing out, and the inhabitants appear to be not as prosperous as they were 40 or 50 years ago. I fear there is a great degree of indolence, and dissipation among the youth, especially the young men. I am sorry to say, education is amazingly neglected.

Friday 16—I rode to Boosby Hill, and preached in a school house. The Society here is not as large as it was 45 years ago. I was comforted under an impression that it had been a nursery in which many trees of righteousness had been raised many of whom had been transplanted in heaven, whilst others had removed to different parts of the back settlements where they have invited the gospel, and have been a means of establishing other nurseries larger than this—for this was among the first Methodist Societies on the continent. I stayed with my old friend, J. Dallam, who has stood as a good friend in this society for many years, without being a member— though the first and second Mrs. Dallam were precious members.

Saturday 17—This morning I returned with my niece, an old friend came in to see me, who said his father William Herbert, was yet living and in his 104th year, and that his mother a short time ago went home happy in her 97th year. This family was among the first Methodists in the state.

Lord's Day 18—I preached in what is called Bush Church. This house was built of hewn logs, and has been standing almost 50 years. The church in John Street, New York, was the first ever built on the continent for the Methodists, and I believe this was the second—it seems to be sinking into

ruin. I was enabled to cry aloud, "Who will rise up, and rebuild the temple?"
—the old people have dropped off, and are dropping off, and I fear the
rising generation will not be zealous for *God*. Should they neglect the courts
of the Lord's House—he may be justly displeased, and cast them off. I
administered the sacrament assisted by Mr. Toy to about 60, and we had
a solemn season. I rode to and preached in the Abington Church in the
evening with freedom. I bless the giver of all good for health, and freedom
to work in his vineyard. I lodged at Mr. Billingsley's. Mrs. B. is a mother
in Israel, and he is a worthy brother. O when will there be a shaking among
the young people.

Monday 19—I rested at Mr. Hollis', and he took me to Bellair, and
Tuesday I preached in the court house to many and in the evening at
Mrs. Norris'. I find it a cross to speak plain to my relatives. They are very
kind, but I fear they want the one thing needful.

Thursday 23—I preached at Mr. Richardson's in the evening. Every
part of the house seemed to be filled, and the next day I rode to Baltimore
and put up at my old friend Smith's in Gay Street. O for a spirit of prayer.
I find a glorious work going on in this city.

Sunday 25—In the morning I preached in the Light Street Church
to a crowded congregation, and I had a precious time, the people were
very solemn and melted into tenderness. After preaching 17 came forward,
and joined Society. In the afternoon I had a crowded assembly at Eutaw
Church and a great time. I was sweetly let into the gospel. In the evening
I heard Dr. Jennings—he is much followed—prayer meeting continued
till late in the night—in the morning I inquired from all the churches,
and found that 230 had joined Society, and many were hopefully set at
liberty.

Tuesday 27—I preached at Eutaw again on Wednesday at the Point
Thursday Light Street—Friday Old Town—churches crowded, many
converted. This was a blessed week's labor to me; I never had more liberty
to preach. My time was fully taken up preaching, in visiting my friends,
who were very attentive. I have mostly lodged among my family connections except at Mr. Smith's and Mrs. Gough's.

Sunday, February 1—I preached a sacramental sermon after which between 50 and 60 advanced to the altar to give in their names to join Society
—we administered the sacrament to about 400, and a sweet time we had.
In the evening I preached at Old Town perhaps 1,500 or 2,000 present.
Brother Rossel thought it the most powerful time he had known. I left
the church about 9 o'clock and it appeared in every direction that prayer,
praise, singing, mourning and shouting were at the same time going on.
This day in all the churches, 130 joined Society. The word is sweet, and
it is easy to preach. The churches will not contain all who wish to hear.
I am happy to find that the preachers, and people are heartedly engaged
in the blessed work. I hope it will continue rapidly to spread till the earth
is filled with the glory of *God*. I have seldom seen a work so _____ with

so little persecution, or ill natured expression. The congregation seems awed into silence. This evening I stay at my cousin Morehead's. This week I spent mostly in retirement, except to pay some visits and to preach Wednesday night at the Point, and Friday night at Old Town. Great attention was given to the word.

Lord's Day 8—I feel myself to be very unworthy. In the morning I preached in Light Street to a crowded congregation from "Charity never faileth." In the afternoon to nearly 1,000 Africans—many stood at the doors, and windows, as their church would not contain them all, from "Where unto you have attained, walk by the same rule, and mind the same things."—Phil. 3: 16. In the evening at Eutaw—the church was very much crowded; several were brought into liberty. This to me and others was a good day. This morning one of the stationed ministers preached a sermon in Eutaw Church which was much talked of. The heads of which I received from a preacher who heard the sermon, as follows: "And they ran violently down a steep place and were choked in the sea." 1. When the devil cannot do a greater evil, he does a less—when he could not take the life of Job, he laid as heavy affliction on him as he was permitted. So when he could stay no longer in the possessed he requested permission to go into the swine and so forth. 2. Those whom the devil drives he drives rapidly. a. the swine represents the wicked. b. the devil employs drovers. c. who he employs. d. the devil, and his drovers drive the swine rapidly down a steep place. He showed who are the devil's drovers—such as dancing masters, heads of theaters, ring-leaders in card playing, horse racing, unconverted ministers, wicked rulers of every description, such as Congressmen, governors, assemblymen, magistrates, and so forth, and so forth, and so forth. 3. The market to which the devil drives his wretched herd—into the sea, or lake—a. to hell. b. the dreadful market.

Monday 9—Was the day appointed for me to leave the city; but the weather being extremely cold, I was persuaded to stay two days longer. I did, and Wednesday evening had a blessed time in preaching in Eutaw Church on the experience of holiness.

Wednesday 11—I rode with Mrs. Gough to Perry Hall, and had an agreeable time in the evening in preaching a short sermon to her servants on, "Stand fast in the Lord." Philippians 4: 1 I stayed in Baltimore a little more than two weeks and preached 14 sermons to crowded congregations, and I am an unprofitable servant. I long for a greater nearness to the blessed savior, and to be more useful. My good friends think more highly of me, and treat me with a greater degree of attention than I am worthy of. O for a closer walk with *God*. I hope I can commit my family to the protection of a kind Father—the cross of leaving them so long is sensibly felt. Nothing but a sense of duty would induce me to do it. Surely it is not for ease, riches, or honor. I wish to please *God* in the execution of my duty—I desire above all things to spend my few remaining days, striving to serve the interest of the church.

There are many in Baltimore imminently pious, but as it is the case everywhere, too many are too superficial. I pray that the blessed God will give grace, and wisdom to the official members of this church.

Thursday 12—I travelled through the forest, and preached and came on Saturday to Abingdon.

Sunday 15—Preached three sermons at Abingdon with less freedom than I have had since I left home. The weather was very cold. Monday and Tuesday I rode through the forest, and visited friends and Wednesday the 18th Mr. Hollis took me to Susquehanna where I took the stage, and came on Thursday to Philadelphia. I stay at Mr. Manley's, and am very hospitably received.

Sunday 22—Preached two sermons—morning in the Academy Church, and in the evening at St. George's. Many came to the altar to be prayed for. Thank God, he is carrying on His blessed work in this city. I never feel better than when I am employed in my master's vineyard.

Monday 23—I took the stagecoach and came to Trenton, and preached in the evening with great freedom to many hearers. Could these people be properly attended to, I have no doubt but a blessed work would break out—but the circuit preachers can only attend in the regular course of their circuit—I advise them to apply to conference for a stationed minister. Tuesday evening I preached again. I have no doubt but many hearts were touched, and I had strong solicitations to stay longer. My heart is enlarged, and I had strong drawings to stay a few days longer, but my passage was bespoke to depart in the morning.

Wednesday 25—This morning I took the stages, rode 50 miles, and preached in the evening at Elizabethtown with freedom.

Thursday 26—Thursday morning came into New York, where I continued near four weeks, and had much liberty in communicating the sacred truths of the gospel alternately in the church, and in the latter part of March, returned to Rhinebeck after an absence of about four months, through the mercy and goodness of God, had a happy meeting with my family.

SOME ACCOUNT OF MY LABORS FROM THE CONFERENCE HELD IN TROY (N.Y.), JUNE 6, 1819

In the conference, several things very disagreeable turned up. I fear occasioned by a few aspiring men. In times past our conference has been famous for peace and harmony, but I fear seeds of discord are sown. We sensibly felt the need of the wise, decisive hand of an Asbury, in the exercise of our episcopacy. In an individual or two there seemed to be a disposition to crush their betters to the _____ and establishing themselves, and in a measure our young bishop tamely submitted to it.

I returned from conference, and staid a few weeks at home, and only preached two sermons a week and on the Lord's Day in our Rhinebeck Church, with a degree of freedom, but I fear with but a small degree of good—duty urges to stand on the walls of Zion and give warning. I set out on a contemplated tour to the south about 200 miles. Visited Kinderhook, attended a camp meeting at Nescaannia, a Quarterly Meeting at Troy, visited Pittstown, Lansingburg, Schenectady, and attended a Quarterly Meeting on the borders of Spencertown, and so again returned home during this tour of about two weeks. I had great sweetness in the preaching of the Word, preaching one or more sermons at every place generally to full congregations. I am now officiating in my little Rhinebeck congregation. I contemplate a tour through the New England states; but the vehicle preparing for the journey is not quite ready. I attended a Quarterly Meeting in Amenia, we had a good time. I returned home. I found several of our friends on a visit from New York and several from Maryland. I was happy to see them. I am pleasantly situated in life, a family very agreeable and every essential to make life desirable, and I find the more I stay at home the greater is the cross to go. I tended a Quarterly Meeting at _____ Church.

August 18, 1819—All things being in readiness for my eastern tour, having engaged John Lucky, a young man who professes to be under impressions to preach, to travel with me, about 9 o'clock I bid my family and visitors farewell, called at a friend's house and dined. They are anxious to have preaching here. I told them if possible I would send on the preachers. In the evening I preached with freedom in Poughkeepsie.

Thursday 19—The weather is extremely warm. We set out in the morning, and after riding a mountainous road for upwards of 30 miles, we came to Peakskill[176] as the stars appeared; having no previous appointment, a few friends ran to and fro, and called nearly the lower part of the church full before 8 o'clock. In this place we have a revival of religion. I preached with freedom, and likewise in the morning at five to a goodly number. To strive to do good is my element, and I bless God, the word, and duty are sweet.

Friday 20—I rode to, and in the evening met a congregation at Tarrytown. Some of our principle friends left this place, and the few left are feeble. O Jesus, support thy cause—lift up the hands that hang down and strengthen the feeble knees.

Saturday 21—It was my intention to run into the city today and spend the Lord's Day there, but a fear that I should unfit myself for the service of the church as well as injure my horse, I turned aside and lodged at Brother Millar's, who has lost his good mother. She died I think in her 92nd year. Her house, I believe, was my first home in this county.

Lord's Day 22—In the morning I found freedom to declare the council of God at the White Plains and in the afternoon at New Rochelle. I am sure in part of Mr. Beecher's moral wilderness; however, we think the gospel had a glorious spread in this county, and within a distance of eight miles of the place where I now stand we can count six or seven respectable Methodist churches, and congregations, and many men and women of undoubted piety. O that our fellow creatures would lay aside their bigotry, and superstition and cleave to righteousness and true holiness.

Monday 23—I rode into New York, and put up at Mr. Suckley's.[177] The parents are in Rhinebeck, but some of the dear children were at home and the housekeeper all of whom were very attentive. I have allotted four days to stay in the city. My mind was impressed with this text, Joel 3: 13, "put ye in the sickle, for the harvest is ripe." I delivered a sermon on these at three of the churches on the same text, and I hope they were attended with a blessing. I could have shed tears over the Society. I have never known them in so trying a situation; I fear owing to a want either of wisdom or piety in those who have had the rule over them two years past had there been a suitable change last conference, the breach might have been made up. I am clear—I gave my mind decisively. My advice was followed only in part. When men become self-important it is time to take them down. My prayer is that all things may be overruled for good.

Saturday 28—I left the city and rode to New Rochelle Sunday, preached in the new church in the morning and in the church at Rye afternoon. Lodged at Mr. Holsteads. Here I met many of my old friends. I have not been in this place before, for several years. It has been a good day.

Monday 30—I rode to Stamford accompanied by Brother Day and Brother P. Smith, and had freedom on the love of God. We all lodged at Brother Seleik's—a kind hospitable family. I find that my horse is rather light for the carriage, and should be willing to have chains for when heavier. The people suffer much with the drought. Very little green herbage for the cattle. The spring is very low and a scarcity of water and I fear many are low in religion.

Tuesday 31—We went on to Brother Day's in Norwalk,[178] and in the evening preached in the new church with a degree of liberty to many hearers. I am certain, those who do not soften under the word will grow more hard.

Wednesday, September 1—Rode about 20 miles to Stratford here the appointment did not reach the place till I came, but some were diligent in spreading it, so that I had a good congregation by candlelight, and had a good time.

Thursday 2—I preached in New Haven to nearly a church full of people, and stayed at Brother Hibbert's. I have an anxiety for the Methodists have a better church, but the Society is small and poor, and I have hard work to support their stationed preacher.

September 3—I rode 22 miles, and preached in a school to a small congregation in Durham. Brother Ames and Brother Harris are stationed on this circuit. I fear they have dull times. I stayed at Brother Swathel's. He is one of the general stewards of the circuit, and a very kind friend. Mrs. Swathel is, I hope, pious but greatly afflicted in body and mind, and has been for many years.

Saturday 4—I rode to Middletown, and put up at Brother Jewet's, the stationed preacher.

Sunday 5—I preached morning, afternoon and evening to full congregations. I was requested to preach in the evening on the resurrection. The youthful part of this congregation appear to be full of levity and I fear have very little religion. The Society have built a good church, and I doubt not but there are some pious people. In this city there are five respectable congregations. Presbyterian Church, Baptists, Independents, and Methodists. There seems to be no special revival of religion. The different sects seem to be at peace with each other, and peculiarity of their opinions seem to lay dormant.

Monday 6—I crossed the Connecticut River, and entered the bounds of the New England conference and after riding between 20 and 30 miles on tiresome mountainous roads. I preached with great liberty in the Methodist Church in the town of Hebron. In this town there is a good revival. Souls coming to Jesus. I stayed with Brother Burris, a pious wealthy respectable local minister. I feel myself much united with this pious family. They are largely in the way of manufacturing cotton, and one of his sons carried on the carriage making business there I got some necessary repairs to my carriage.

Tuesday 7—We set out for New London, and dined at Brother Whitelsey's, a pious local preacher he has built a decent little church near his house. Whilst dinner was making ready. He and myself repaired to the church for prayer and had a refreshing time together. I am much attached to the simplicity and piety of this family. I feel as if surrounded with heavenly light. The work of the Lord is going on in this neighborhood. They have lately had a camp meeting, which has been greatly blessed. We got into New London about 5 o'clock after riding between 20 and 30 miles. I fear my congregation will be disappointed—till now I have never visited this city—the people are in great expectation. What can a poor _____. God can work, and what he does, is well done. In the evening we had a full congregation, and I found liberty to speak. There are about 250 members in our church in this place, mostly poor and with hard struggling they have built and completely finished a handsome church, that will seat about 1,000 people.

Wednesday 8—I spent partly in writing and visiting friends and dined with an old disciple, and preached again in the evening to a large congregation, where I informed the congregation that I would leave the city next day and appointed to preach in the morning at sun-rise on the doctrine of christian perfection.

Thursday 9—I rose this morning a little after 4 o'clock and after spending more than an hour in retirement I repaired to the church about sunrise, and had a solemn sweet season in disseminating some truths to about 200 attentive hearers. I was kindly entertained at Brother Kent's, the stationed minister. He is a worthy, dispassionate man and beloved by the Society.

About 10 A.M. Brother and Sister Kent accompanied me about four miles to Mr. Millar's, a gentleman aged 78, and appears to be friendly to religion, though he belongs to no church. Several of his daughters, and I believe, one son are young converts brought in during the late revival in New London, and are very happy in their first love. I had much conversation with the old gentleman. He said he was happy in the change which had taken place in his children. I exhorted him to seek God in good earnest till he experienced the same change in his own soul—he seemed to have the old New England tune. I told him people were under a great mistake— although Christ has _____ everything to make us happy, yet many things through the grace of God were enjoined on us to do, we cannot expect salvation unless we with faithfulness do our part. Here I found an excellent garden, and a great variety of good fruit. I spent about three hours very agreeably at this place.

After spending some time in prayer, we bid a kind family farewell, and rode 10 miles to Norwich and preached to many who came to hear— the church was nearly filled. I lodged at the house of a respectable local preacher who had done a large part toward building the church. This edifice is erected on the bed of the river surrounded by water except a piece of made ground for an entrance. After church a pious woman asked me if anyone had requested me to preach on the Lord's Prayer. I answered her in the negative. She told me that she had prayed to God that I might explain that blessed prayer. I told her when I went into the pulpit and before it lay with such weight on my mind that I did not dare refuse a discussion of the subject. She believed it was of God in answer to prayer. She was particularly exercised on that petition "Thy will be done on earth as it is done in heaven." It seemed her husband was under exercises about going out as a traveling minister and her mind was under deep exercise about his going into the work. This is a large town built at the head of a navigable river with four churches belonging to the four leading denominations of New England: Congregational Church, Presbyterian, Baptist, and Methodist. There Brother Hide, the ruling minister of the circuit, met me and gave some pleasing accounts of the work of God on his circuit. Two camp meetings have been rendered and a blessing to many. The following towns he mentioned as having been visited; Glastonbury, Conn. on the Connecticut River, Middle Haddam Parish, East Hamton, East Haddam, Colechester, Eastbury, Marleborough, Hebron, Norwich, Landing and several other places. Several _____ have been the subjects of convicting and regenerating grace, and many stirred up to seek sanctification. I have no doubt but that the blessed God is carrying on his work in this New London district.

Friday 10—We traveled near 30 miles, the road rough and hilly, crossed over the line into Rhode Island state and preached in a free meeting house to a small congregation, and they appeared to be as hard as sticks. Here a lower class of Socinians have spread their poisonous doctrine. Almost every part of the town I conversed with some of them, but found them ignorant and positive. The woman of the house where I lodged, was one of that association. She thought it cruel, when I told her there was no salvation in the Socinian plan.

Saturday 11—We rode about 22 miles to Providence. We passed a Baptist meeting, what they call a religious association. It looked more like a fair than anything else. It was supposed that on that ensuing Lord's Day, more than 5,000 people would assemble, and that buying and selling, and different kinds of diversion would be carried on.

Sunday I preached morning and afternoon in the new Methodist church and administered the sacrament. Mr. Wilson, the Presbyterian minister, requested me to preach in his new meeting house—which I did to a large congregation in the evening. This meeting house is larger than our John Street Church in New York. Mr. Wilson was once a traveling Methodist preacher. He retains his old methodistical principles, and I trust piety and usefulness too. There are about 150 members in connection with us, and though in general they are poor, nevertheless, they have built a decent house that will seat about a thousand people. They are a happy growing society, and I was happy among them. Their stationed preacher appears to be a worthy young man, and well received. The Baptist congregation have come out, minister and people, for Socinianism in this place. Except Mr. Wilson and the Methodist congregation I view religion in an awful state. O blessed God support thy tottering cause.

Monday 13—I rode 15 miles to Bristol, and in the evening a large church was nearly filled, though they had but a few hours notice of my coming. As a letter was not received till a little before my arrival. We have a large pious society in this place. I preached on christian perfection with uncommon freedom, and we had a powerful time. They sing sweetly in this congregation. Unpleasing to tell, the only Baptist minister in the town has lately come out pointedly in favor of Socinian principles, and there is a wonderful commotion in a large congregation, and I believe the largest meeting house in the place. The majority decided in favor of their heretical minister and they keep the meeting house afloat and distressed. They say the Episcopal bishop is pious, and makes a worthy stand against the heresies of the times. I bless God the Methodists stand as firm as a rock in the old Apostolical and Wesleyan doctrines. Perhaps the time is coming when they will be the principle pillars to withstand the spreading contagion. It appears that many are convinced of the impropriety of Calvin's _____ decrees, and not knowing where to fix the line of demarcation, have run wild into universalism or something worse. The deists are rather ashamed of open infidelity and are smothing it down to unitarianism.

Tuesday 14—I bid my kind Bristol friends farewell. I stayed at Brother Wardel's. They are both kind and engaged in the work, and rode to Warren. Here our people have a handsome church handsomely painted and neatly finished. The Society is small, and the hire of the pews will hardly support a minister. The unitarian Baptist minister was present. I preached from Hebrews 10: 38, "Now the just shall live by faith, but if any man draw back my soul shall have no pleasure in him." We had a sweet time. I feel for this loving Society. Their stationed preacher is far gone in the consumption, and can preach but little. I rode to Somerset. In the afternoon preached in another handsomely finished Methodist church to a good congregation from, "We preach Christ crucified and so forth." I stayed at Brother Bredins. This is a pious gentle family in which I felt myself at home.

Wednesday 15—We started about seven and traveled through many towns, roads rough, and the land generally poor, about 30 miles to Easton, and put up at Tinkham's—a respectable located minister of our Order. Here I met Brother and Sister Hedding come on a visit from Lynn. I was very glad to see them. I expect their company several days. The people ran together from all parts in the evening, and filled the church, and among them was the settled Presbyterian minister. He came over to see us before meeting, and gave me a kind invitation to his house. They say he is fully in the Hopkinsian plan, but a clever respectable young man. I had a good time, and I hope good was done. I see it to be my duty to hold forth an Almighty Savior and give his character as fully as I am able according to the scriptures perfect God, and perfect man.

Thursday 16—We rode 14 miles to Dorchester, and put up at Brother Otheman's, a pious wealthy French gentleman, who a few years ago moved from Boston to this town. He embraced Methodism some years before he left Boston. When he moved to this place he opened his house for preaching. At first very few came out to hear, and it seems the wicked were so angry with his introducing Methodism in the place that they frequently stoned the house in time of preaching; however the blessed Lord began his work, and a good society was formed. After his house was not large enough to contain the congregation, he built a handsome church at his own expense. His son some years ago was called to the ministry among us, and is this year stationed in this congregation. He appears to be a promising young man. Notice of my coming was spread abroad, and in the evening I preached to the church nearly filled and we had a sweet time. This is a loving society. The Presbyterian minister in this town has turned Socinian. I exhorted our young brother to stand fast in the Lord, and visit and preach from house to house. I exhorted the old French gentleman, his father, to stand fast in the Lord, and that if he and his son were instrumental in spreading the pure evangelical doctrines of the gospel through that populous town, they would meet their reward in heaven. The old gentleman seemed almost happy enough to fly away. I was very much pleased with this family. O how wonderful that our blessed God should send a person from France to America to be regenerated and be a means of raising such a society in the midst of the heresies of the times, and stands as a shining light in the midst of such a town as Dorchester. Mrs. Otheman is cordially going with her husband.

⸗ *Friday 17*—Accompanied by Brother and Sister Hedding, we left this kind family, and started for Lynn, passed through Boston, and about twelve after riding 16 miles on a good road, we came there. They had not heard of my coming; but messages were dispatched around the town to give information.

In the evening at the ringing of the church bell a good congregation came together. I preached from Joel 3: 13, "Put ye in the sickle, for the harvest is ripe." I had great freedom of speech. 1. What it is for the great harvest to be ripe. Some marks of the ripe or ripening state of the great harvest. II. What is to be done when the great harvest is ripe. A very great change has taken place in this town since I preached here about 11 years ago. Then the Methodists had but one small church. Now they have two. The one I preached in was very large—about seventy by eighty feet neatly finished with square pews, an elegant steeple and bell which is the only one in town. I took occasion to tell the congregation they had swerved from the plain simplicity of primitive Methodism. Some of the pious brethren next morning acknowledged the justness of my remarks, and assured me that that part of the congregation which were not members of the church would hear it so, or they would not contribute. Brother Hedding and Brother Mudge are stationed here; and they are worthy ministers, and the congregations are happily united under them. In this town old Calvinism is buried, and I hear of no appearance of Unitarianism. I have reason to believe the society is in a prosperous condition. They have paid for their elegant church and had a surplus of money to put on interest to assist in supporting their ministers. The blessed God is doing great things by the Methodists in the eastern states. They and the Episcopalians will be I think the main pillars to rebut false doctrines. O that our blessed Lord may keep them pure in life and doctrine. I thank God for this tour among these good people.

Saturday I rode to Cambridge, three miles from Boston I put up at my old worthy friend, Brother Black. This is a pious, worthy family with whom I feel myself at home. They are at the elegant country seat where they spend their summers. In a particular manner, the Lord has blessed the family since they embraced Methodism, and bless God that ever they received it. They have five daughters and three sons. The young people sung sweetly this evening.

Sunday 19—I preached three sermons in Boston to large congregations with freedom. The following week travelled upwards of a hundred miles, and preached in the different towns, and had great liberty, especially in Old Hartford, These people, I hope, will submit to the gospel.

Sunday 26—I preached in Goshen, and Cornwall, and on Monday and Tuesday rode home, and through mercy found my family in health.

In this tour I was out six weeks, travelled eight hundred miles and preached about 60 sermons. I thank God for his sweet company, and presence every day. I do not want to be employed in a better work.

THE JOURNAL BEGINNING DECEMBER 1820—

I left my home the latter part of December 1820 and came to New York, and labored with freedom in the church during my stay.

Saturday 29—I took the post chaise and rode between 60 and 70 miles to Trenton.

Sunday 30—I preached and heard two sermons and had a strong hope of good words.

Monday, January 1, 1821—

In the morning I found my leg a little swollen, and had fears that it would _____. I rode an easy carriage to Philadelphia and put up with Mr. Pounders, where Brother Cooper lodges. I saw it necessary to be under the direction of a physician, for I found my leg much swollen, and enflamed. Dr. Sergeant[179] visited me and ordered a poltice, for a _____ was inevitable. The family were very attentive, and did everything in their power to make me easy, and comfortable.

Sunday, January 7, 1821—The week was spent very much in solitude, without leaving my chamber, and frequently under very severe exercise of mind, but in the whole I found Jesus precious.

Sunday 14—I am still confined to my chamber, and my leg worse. I am deprived of the privilege of attending church, or leaving the room. However I had the privilege of the company of my kind friends, who more or less visited me daily, and my attentive doctor visited me once and twice a day, whose company, and conversation was very agreeable and edifying. I had a solitary week, and some severe buffeting of the enemy, and was frequently very low spirited, and perhaps at times something a little bordering on what is called hypochondria. However in the whole, I derived benefit in the sanctification of my affliction; for I had a fine time for reflection and self-examination.

Sunday 21—The bruise by the use of the milk and bread poultice is removed and the ulcer now appears about as large as a dollar. I was in hopes I should be able today to attend church and preach, but close confinement is still my lot. All is right in the order of God—he knows what is the best for his creatures. Three sabbaths forever gone, whilst I have been resting in silent solitude, contemplating the wonders of redeeming love, and the mysterious beauties of the various parts of the sacred scriptures. O redemption how deep, how mysterious. Deity O how unsearchable! Three hypostaces or distinct subsistencies in one glorious incomprehensible divinity, co-equal, co-substantial, and co-eternal. I have had the week past, a great travail of soul. My exercises were various, but the most weighty part particularly concerned myself—I saw infinite perfection in God, His law and works, and I saw myself as a mere fallen, imperfect speck in creation. I inquired, what motive led you at this period of life, and at this season to leave your home? Was it for money? No. Was it for ease or honor? No. Was it because you thought yourself a great preacher? No. I was called of God 46 years ago to be a minister and the blessed God has told me frequently, that he called me for life, or as long as I was able to work in the vineyard. I did some years ago tell the Lord I was growing old, and infirm, and begged him to let me rest in peace, with some little occasional labors about home. The blessed God restored me to my hearing almost as perfect as ever, strengthened my intellect, and renewed me in soul and body and told me I must go. Be sure it is a great cross to leave one of the most agreeable families in the state, and easy circumstances —I can stagger under it for Christ's sake in casting in a mite toward promoting the interest of His kingdom.

Sunday 28—Another Lord's Day has come, my good doctor gave me liberty to appear in church. I did so, and stood on one leg, and preached in St. George's to a large congregation with liberty from, "Put ye in the sickle for the harvest is ripe." Joel 3: 13. 1. What is implied in the harvest is ripe? 2. Some marks of a ripening state for harvest. 3. The injunction in the text put ye in the sickle, and so forth. I stood about an hour in the sermon on one leg, and I know the God of the harvest was with me, and I have some reason to believe we had a profitable refreshing time.

Thursday, February 1—Having an appointment previously published, the church this evening was nearly filled, and I had liberty from these words, "Christ hath once suffered for sin, the just for the unjust, that he might bring us to God." I Peter 3.

Friday, February 2, 1821—I left Mr. Pounder's kind family and went to Dr. Chandler's. Here I am blessed in a kind, attentive family and every necessary accommodation.

Sunday 4—This morning I preached in Ebenezer Church, to a crowded congregation, and administered the sacrament assisted by Dr. Chandler, and it was a precious time. In the evening I had a good time preached in the Academy Church from Hebrews 6: 4, 5 and 6. My leg is recovering fast. I spent the week mostly retired, and nursed my leg, wrote letters, and read the sacred scriptures and history at intervals and received several letters from home. It gives me great pleasure to hear that my family are in health and happy. I have already stayed longer in Philadelphia than I intended and had serious thoughts of returning homeward. I feel anxious. O to know and to do the will of God. At an official meeting of the ministers, preachers, stewards and leaders, a committee was appointed to wait on me, and request my longer stay in the city, which I received as a call in Providence which I could not reject, and thanked them and agreed to stay two sabbaths more. God is good and I will praise Him.

Sunday 11—I preached in Ebenezer Church in the morning and St. George's in the evening. Crowded churches. I love God, His cause and people.

Sunday 18—Morning at the Academy I preached on the "Fruits of the spirit," and in the afternoon at St. John's on "Charity never faileth."

Monday 19—At Salem Church, from "But one thing needful," and we were very much crowded at night.

Tuesday 20—Preached at Nazareth Church from wisdom, righteousness, sanctification and redemption—house full.

Wednesday 21—At Ebenezer, house full—I suppose between twelve and fifteen hundred people.

Thursday 22—At St. George's more people than last night.

Friday 23—At the Academy lower part of the house nearly full.

Sunday 25—Morning, Ebenezer—aisles and every place full. In the afternoon in the Methodist African Church—many went away for want of room, and some stood without—and in the evening I preached my last sermon in St. George's. It was thought by some that nearly 3,000 people crowded into the house—every place above and below was filled. I have been remarkably favored the past week. I preached eight sermons, and the blessed God was with me. Why have I been so honored with crowds of people to hear a poor, old bruised reed in Philadelphia? Not because he is a great preacher—either for antiquity's sake or because they tasted the good word of life, must have been the cause. O that I may sit at the feet of Jesus and wonder and adore the riches of grace. I frequently groan for full salvation. I wrote home and consulted my good wife about going farther to the south, and received for answer she would not prevent my doing the will of God, and I made up my mind to go on. Brother and Sister Chandler were very attentive to me, and I shall not soon forget them; he was kind enough to attend me with his carriage to almost all my appointments by day and night.

Thursday 28—I bid farewell to the city. Dr. Chandler accompanied me to the steamboat, and about twelve we started and before daybreak we were in Baltimore. I was received very kindly by my old friends, Mr. and Mrs. Job Smith in Gay Street.

Sunday, March 4—I preached in the morning at Eutaw Church with freedom, and administered the sacrament to about 300 assisted by Brother Haggerty and Brother Birch. In the evening I preached in Light Street Church to a very crowded congregation. I had great freedom, and the people were very attentive and apparently much blessed.

Monday 5—I visited Mrs. Gough, and she wished me to take up my abode under her roof whilst I stayed in the town, which I agreed to do. Brother Shin has his abode here. He has in time past been greatly afflicted in mind even to derangement: but at present seems perfectly restored to the rise of his mental faculties, and health of body. He was a man of very strong reasoning powers, and it is supposed that his immeasurable exercise of those powers on abstruse subjects was the cause of his derangement, particularly in laboring to reconcile the infinite mercy, and goodness of God with the eternal torments of the damned. I resign all to God, in full confidence that he will do perfectly right: which not in time will be fully and clearly developed in eternity and even those in misery will acknowledge his justice. I told him I was once immeasurably pushed on the same subject, and how I obtained a deliverance. He seemed determined to lay aside all abstruce reasonings. He has a fine mind and an excellent preacher. Mrs. Gough is a pious old lady, and as diffusive in her charities as a large income will admit of.

Tuesday 6—I preached at Eutaw Church with much _____ and it appeared to be rendered a blessing to a large congregation, and I lodged at Judge Dorsey's.

Wednesday 7—I spent the first part of the day in visiting some friends on my way to my lodging. Dined with company and in the whole it was a pleasant and profitable day; but to be absent for so long from my family is a cross to be felt. I leave them with a good God.

Thursday 8—This morning I was retired and under some disagreeable exercises of mind. In the afternoon I rode to the Point and visited my nephew, Richard Garrettson. They are in good health but have not yet become members of the church. In the evening I preached with freedom to a good congregation.

Friday 9—I returned and dined at Mrs. Gough's with her son-in-law, Mr. Carrol, and her grandchildren and great grandchildren. I was well acquainted with her mother, and now I see the fifth generation. In the evening I preached in Old Town. It was Brother Shin's appointment, and I told the people it was rather a cross to me to stand in the place of another. However, we had a good time, and it appeared that the congregation was not dissatisfied.

Saturday 10—I am looking out for a letter from home, and am rather disappointed. I am now in retirement and never had a greater desire to be swallowed up in the will of God. I am a great debtor to grace. My dependence is only in the merit of Christ, I have no hope or help but there. I am to get a family dinner today with Mr. Brice, President of the bank. O God help me to be watchful and useful.

Sunday 11—This morning I feel comfortable in my mind. Rode to the Point and preached with freedom and returned to Mrs. Gough's to dinner, and in the evening preached in Old-Town with much freedom from, "Mark the perfect man, and so forth." Psalm 37: 37. The church was unusually crowded. We had a blessed time whilst I was opening the way to perfect holiness in the work of entire sanctification. God visited the people and gave us a sweet refreshing season. I speak as if every sermon was my last.

Monday 12—I sent a messenger to bespeak a seat in a public carriage to Harford, As Conference time was coming on all seemed engaged or I might have had a friend to have accompany me on my country tour.

Tuesday 13—I rode to Abington and lodged at Mr. Hollis' and found my niece much afflicted with ague and fever. I trust she is a precious child of God.

Wednesday 14—We rode to Mrs. Norris' and found the family in health and more engaged for salvation and more like Methodists than when I visited them. I am humbled among my friends and relatives for they treat me more like an angel than a week mortal man—God grant them blessings in this world and in the world to come eternal life.

Thursday 15—Mr. Wiley rode with me to Brother Richardson's; we dined and had a social meeting with friends and returned to Mrs. Norris'.

Friday 16—I preached in the evening and on Saturday Mr. Wiley accompanied me to Abingdon where I preached two sermons on the Lord's Day with freedom. Religion is not very prosperous in this place; there seems to be obstacles in the way. O Lord remove them, and shine forth gloriously. At this place my good friends, Mr. and Mrs. R. Garrettson met me, and I was glad to see them. I feel as though I had not followed cunningly devised fables.

Monday 19—Mr. Hollis accompanied me into Baltimore. The Conference is now in session. Several days I spent either in retirement visiting my friends or in the Conference. About 80 of the itinerating ministers were there and had an opportunity of hearing several sermons and among others I heard one by our good old friend Valentine Cook who was educated in Cokesbury College, delivered with the power and simplicity of the gospel. A holy man of a most excellent spirit, and very much beloved, he nearly wore himself out in the travelling connection, located and opened an academy in Kentucky but takes occasional excursions. The preachers in general seemed to profess the spirit of the gospel and began and ended their Conference in peace. I had great fellowship with all with whom I conversed. I was solicited to preach one more sermon before I left town, and it would have been my mind so to do, but as G. R. had the management of appointments in part he seemed not so disposed—he is said to be arbitrary and not well acquainted with the rights of man, and with all I was in opposition to some of his sentiments at General Conference last spring. O for the feelings of that pure man of God, Mr. Fletcher, when he said, "Make me little and unknown, loved and prized by God alone." What a great, great thing it is to set out right in the Christian ministry, and still greater to persevere to the end with a single eye to the glory of God, and to sit humble at the foot of the cross.

Saturday 24—I took the steamboat touched at Annapolis and spent a few minutes at Brother Emery's, then went on to Easton, and arrived a little after sunset. I had much conversation with the captain, he is a very respectable man, and I was much pleased with some of his sentiments. He said he was principled against keeping slaves or even hiring them, at first he refused receiving the fare of the boat, but I insisted on his taking it, and would not be refused. What a pity such men should miss heaven!

Sunday 25—I preached at Easton morning and evening to the church full, with freedom. God is good and I will praise him. The weather is very cold and changeable, the land in the country appears to me to be wearing out fast.

Monday 26—My good Brother Jenkins accompanied me to Cambridge and Dorset; we had to cross Choptank, a wide dangerous ferry, but after travelling 16 miles we came to my old tried friend, Dr. White, about one. The people had no knowledge of my coming, but the news soon spread and in the evening the church nearly filled, and we had a good time. 40 odd years ago I was cast in prison in this town for preaching the gospel, and 16 sweet days I had and perhaps did more good than I should have done had I been out.

Tuesday 27—This morning Brother White offered his services to accompany me to Somerset. We dined at Vienna and got to Quantico before night after riding 30 miles. We rode in a light covered wagon, or dearburn, as they call them in this country.

Wednesday 28—I visited my brother's homestead which has lately been sold—a large valuable farm and grand buildings. My brother left a handsome estate but it seems the executors failed and his widow and children lost more than half of the estate, however they may yet be comfortable, if they take good care of what is left. This morning Brother White preached at Brother Ryder's to a house full of people. Brother White is a good man and a good preacher.

Thursday 29—I preached at the church to a good congregation with liberty. I stayed at Mr. Evans—I had a pleasant time with my sister and children, and thanks be to God they all seem bound for glory. Thomas, the youngest son, has just married and they seem to be well suited to each other. They have both joined the church, bought a farm and just began housekeeping. John, the eldest son, who has been unfortunate in the world seems happy in religion, and it is supposed he is under a call to preach. The pious mother has been under deep affliction, but seems borne up by the grace of God. It is about 42 years since I first preached in this neighborhood, and joined a large society, and bless be God I met with some of my spiritual children; the many others are I hope gone to glory while the aged are bending like the ripe corn for the sickle.

Friday 30—This morning I left my youngest brother's widow, and children, and we had a melting time. We rode 12 miles to Vienna, when I came to the church I was surprised to see the crowds of people for it seemed as if the people were gathered from far and near, so that I suppose one-third of the people stood without for want of room in the church. My subject was prayer and we had a moving time. My country appointments were 11:00 in every place, I was very glad my good Brother White was with me to press home the sermon at every place. O my blessed savior I am in my element though a feeble creature.

Saturday 31—We rode on six miles to Salem where the congregation was much larger than yesterday—it appeared like a Quarterly Meeting.

I was enabled to preach freely from: "Till I die I will not remove mine integrity from me." Many tears were shed. I feel little. I was the first that planted Methodism in these parts, and although but few of my hearers have ever seen my face before, from what their grandparents and parents had told them, they seemed to be acquainted with me. We rode to good old Sister Ward's and dined, then went into Cambridge, and lodged at Dr. White's. The weather is cold and chilling. I do not think I could stand this climate. I feel poorly but the blessed God is with me.

Sunday, April 1, 1821—We had a great gathering of people. I held forth with freedom from _____. Brother White (preached) in the afternoon. I was not able to go out though—I wanted to hear him but I thought it would be too much for me, as I had to preach in the evening which I did on: "Grow in grace, and so forth." It was a rainy night, and yet a large church was nearly filled. My good friend Mrs. White stayed all night.

Monday 2—I feel weak and faint. I parted with my good Cambridge friends. Brother White would not cross the river but went round, and Brother Jenkin was to meet me with a carriage the other side the river and accompany me on. Several friends went down to the boat with me, the wind was very high and squally. The owner of the boat said it would not do to cross and so said the friends which came down with me. It was supposed that there would not be much less than a thousand people waiting at Bolling Broke Chapel at eleven—the ferryman of another boat proffered to carry me over if I would venture, and a stranger who was present said perhaps I shall never see you again; I will accompany you over. I told the ferryman to neat the foresail, and have up but one, and start immediately for the winds seemed to be rising. We had wind and sea abundantly. I got somewhat wet and my baggage—it was a trying time, for it was very cold, but thank God I got safe over and after riding six miles to the chapel found the congregation as numerous as was expected, and we had a sweet season. Here they have lately built a large new brick chapel with galleries—every place was crowded. After dinner we rode to Easton: Brother Scull a worthy minister is poorly.

Tuesday 3—People again at eleven in Easton crowded together and filled the church and I was able to stand more than an hour in my sermon. God was with us, though the weather was cold. The tables of the people are weighed down with rich food, but what is it all to me—one simple dish is sufficient for me. A great many people die young in this country. Though a few live to be very old. I stayed at Mr. Locherman's this evening, my old friend—a tender affectionate family.

Wednesday 4—Today my appointment is at St. Michael's 12 miles distant. Mr. Locherman sent me in his coach. I was accompanied by several friends. I preached from Psalm 48, verses 12 and 13. 1. The order and beauty of the church. 2. The strength of the church. 3. The privileges of the church and, 4. The testimonials of the church. The congregation was attentive and solemn and much affected. Here I met some of my old friends, but a new generation have come on the stage. We rode to Mr. Banning's whose father was an old intimate friend of mine—a very affectionate family. Here they have oysters in abundance within a few hundred yards of the door, or to be brought to the house for 12½c a bushel. After dinner we returned to Easton, and I am now at Mr. Locherman's and about to go to rest in peace, though somewhat weary. O God help me to praise thee for thy tender mercies.

Thursday 5—I preached at the chapel to more people than could get in, with freedom and lodged at Brother Holt's.

Friday 6—Preached at Wye Church—many hearers—many tears and great solemnity. Here my good friend Jenkins left me, and several preachers accompanied me to Brother Bordley's—a local preacher. The land in this country is much worn out with raising Indian corn, wheat, and tobacco. Brother Bordley informed me that he has found a large bed of marl and has taken upward of thirty thousand load of it on his land. It doubles his crops of corn and it is his purpose to cover five or six hundred acres. He informs me that various kinds of shells, bones and petrified fish are found twenty feet which is as deep as they have dug below the surface. There is a probability that marl will be found in various parts of this peninsula. How admirable is the providence of God! I have no doubt but this country was made at, or during the time of the flood, and probably there is a sufficiency of manure in the bowels of the earth to restore her surface to its former fatness and fertility.

Saturday 7—I am very unwell and have been for several days. Thankful for a day to rest at the house of a very kind friend.

Sunday 8—We rode to Centreville. It is a rainy day. I am very poorly with a heavy cold. I feel small and very weak—several travelling and local ministers and preachers at a large country church crowded above and below—I had not the free opening I could have wished, but all appeared still solemn and much tendered. In the evening I had more freedom, and I think more good was done.

Monday 9—I rode to Church Hill. They have lately built us a new handsome church, and it was filled above and below with very attentive hearers. I had great liberty and a very melting time. This afternoon I walked out and viewed the old Church of England built under the reign of the king. I felt sorry to see it deserted and melting away. The door was open and it was a habitation for sheep, hogs, cattle, bats and owls. The field is given to the Methodists, and I hope they will take due care to cultivate it. If not, the Lord may justly cast them off, and raise up another people.

Tuesday 10—I rode seven miles into a place that was called Parson Cane's Parish. The old church is deserted and melting away, but the Methodists have a good brick church and many adherents. The church was nearly filled with attentive hearers, and I seldom see such a sweet season or so much liberty in the word. This is the neighborhood where I was about

42 years ago beaten by John Brown, Esq. almost to death for no other crime than preaching the gospel. I stayed all night at Mr. Elliott's, a wealthy, worthy friend, who has about 2,000 acres of good land under his own inspection and cultivation, and the best of it is he mostly carries it on by hiring for he seems principled against keeping slaves. Mrs. Elliott is a daughter of my old friend Mr. Segar. A new generation has risen up in this place. When I came out of the church I looked around in vain to see the faces of my old friends. Where are they gone into eternity, but thank God many of their children and grandchildren have taken their seats in the church and appear placid and friendly. We stayed at Brother Elliott's who married the daughter of my old friend Segar, who has long since gone into a world of spirits—Brother Elliott is among the richest men in the county, and I felt myself at home in a kind attentive family. W. Allin, the young preacher who travels with me, generally gives an exhortation after I preach. I am well pleased with his deportment, and I doubt not if he is faithful—he will do good in the church.

Wednesday 11—We rode 16 miles to Greensbury formerly Chop-Tank Bridge. The people gathered as if to a Quarterly Meeting and soon filled the church to overflowing. I had freedom to preach; the blessed God knows to what effect, however solemnity to rest on every mind. It is well nigh 40 years since I was at this place, since which time a handsome village risen up and almost a new generation. I tarried at Brother Godwin's whose wife was daughter to my old friend Harrington. This is a kind affectionate family, and had I been an angel they could not have showed a great degree of kindness. About 45 years ago I preached not far from this place and have had many joyful seasons through various parts of this country since my first setting out in the ministry. O what glorious seasons I have had. I can look back with pleasure. Brother Allin preached in the evening.

Thursday 12—Accompanied by several friends we rode to Denton, a county town which has risen since I was here before. "Blessed are the pure in heart for they shall see God," was my text—a crowded audience and solemn as the grave. O how shall I sufficiently praise a good God. I feel my weakness. I am in the midst of kind friends. I stayed with the sheriff of the county. I meet with no people more kind than Marylanders. This day Conference begins at Milford. I have several appointments before I reach the place, and I am anxious to get there in hopes of a letter from home. I have not heard from my family since I left Baltimore. I have precious seasons, though under a heavy cross. The blessed God bears me up. I am reaching forward for something I have not yet attained to. The law is a transcript of divine purity—I want to be all glorious within.

Friday 13—I rode eight miles to Concord—church crowded—all strange faces, except a few of my aged friends. I preached from I Corinthians 1, verse 21, "After that, in the wisdom of God, the world by wisdom knew not God, it pleased God by the foolishness of preaching to save them that believe." The wisdom of God is vast, and knows no bounds, a deep where all our thoughts are drowned.

I. God's wisdom is infinite in creation and redemption.

II. It pleased God in his wisdom after the fall, that man by wisdom should not know God. We cannot read the will of God concerning us in any part of his vast creation.

III. By the foolishness of preaching God saves those that believe. Through the second person and the glorious divinity, God reveals himself to man, by the preaching of the gospel. In him is salvation from all sin, to the humble penitent believer.

This was a good season. I bless God whilst bordering on 69, I have voice and intellect to preach the blessed gospel. I had a sweet night's repose at Brother Houston's and I feel joyful in God.

Saturday 14—We rode to Marshey Hope Bridge Church. I preached to a full congregation with ease and pleasure. It is upwards of 40 years since I preached in this neighborhood before, all strange faces except a few of my old friends. In my younger days I had a precious season in those parts, and the fathers and grandfathers and mothers have told it to the generations following. We rode three miles to the house of Brother Richards, a kind friend, where we were hospitably entertained.

Sunday 15—We rode three miles to Bridgeville and put up at Dr. Caries. I preached morning and evening. The blessed Lord was with me—indeed we had a powerful time especially in the evening. I am sorry to find our people so very remiss in keeping their churches in order—very few of them are finished, and in the construction of them, there is very little uniformity, generally the pulpits are too high, and too small and often a large vacant place is left in the middle of the house.

Monday 16—We rode about 16 miles to Milford where the Conference is sitting. I put up at Dr. _____. We rode through a very poor country, the lands are nearly worn out. I am certain that if the people do not adopt some other mode of husbandry, they may desert their farms, for they will not be able to raise their bread.

Tuesday 17—I preached in the evening with freedom.

Wednesday 18—I attended Conference and found the brethren in harmony, and at three I preached on Christian perfection, and the words seemed to have a salutary effect on the minds of many. It is a sweet doctrine to me. O for more of the perfect love! In the evening I heard Brother Groober preach. He is certainly a very zealous man and loud amens rang through the assembly. I am sure he has uncommon lungs or he would have been in eternity before now. God is good and as we sometimes say, can fit the back for the burden.

Thursday 19—Conference ended this morning and after dinner I. W. Bondly was kind enough to offer to accompany me as far as Smyrna in his gig, and as we passed Fredricka the people insisted on my staying all night and preaching in the evening. I could not refuse, and I had a full congregation and a blessed time.

Friday 20—A note came this morning requesting me to attend Judge Barrett's funeral. As I have an appointment at Dover this evening, I thought the labor would be too much for me, and I got Brother Ryder to attend the funeral. We went on to Dr. Cooper's and met his uncle Ezekiel E. Cooper—and several other preachers where we dined. In the afternoon we went into Dover and got tea at Mr. Comegers who is cashier of the bank. In the evening I preached to a full congregation in a large church. This town has scarcely improved at all for 40 years past. About 42 years ago I preached in this place and joined the first Methodist Society; O what hath God wrought since that time.

Saturday 21—My good friend, Wesley Bordley, continues with me. We rode to Smyrna and put up at Judge Davis'—a kind Christian friend and a pillar in the church of Christ. About 45 years ago I travelled through these parts to preach the gospel and the people were universally in the gall of bitterness and posing the downward road to hell. Indeed it was almost dangerous for a Methodist preacher to pass through this village. But an almost universal change has taken place from the highest to the lowest. O bless the Lord, O my soul, and all that is within me, bless and praise his holy name!

Sunday 22—I preached morning and evening in the church, and Brother Bordley's in the afternoon. We had a blessed day. Several of the preachers were present on their way from Conference. Here I met with Miss Ann White, an old maiden lady, whom I had not seen for near 40 years. She was among our first converts in the Delaware state when she was a young lady. She was the daughter of Judge White, and her brother Samuel was a member of Congress. Thank God she is yet among the followers of Jesus, and I hope will get safe to heaven.

Monday 23—The carriage was provided to take me to Wilmington, 34 miles, for my good friend Bordley returned home. We had a pleasant journey and I put up at Mr. Worrel's, president of the bank. I had no regular appointment, and as I was weary I wanted to hide myself and rest, but they found me out and begged me to preach. Notice was spread and in the evening the church was nearly filled below and above, and I had a sweet time from these words, "Walk about Zion, go around about her, tell the towers thereof mark ye well her bulwark, and consider her palaces that she may tell it to the generations following." Psalm 48, vs. 12 and 13.

Tuesday 24—A young friend and myself hired a gig and we rode into Philadelphia, and I am now with my good friend, Dr. Chandler. Thank God I have peace and consolation. My face is now toward Rhinebeck. I have lately received a letter from my daughter and another from her mother, informing me of a blessed revival of religion in Rhinebeck which is an additional stimulus to urge me homeward.

Wednesday 25—I stayed in the city and visited several friends and read and wrote.

Thursday 26—I started in the steamboat for New York at six in the morning and came by way of Amboy and arrived safe in New York about sunset very weary for we had had a very hard land carriage from Bordentown to Amboy—I never travelled this route before and I hardly shall do it again in preference.

Friday 27—By appointment I am to preach in John Street Church in the evening but hearing that the famed Mr. Moffit (or Maffit) was in town, I sent for him to drink tea with me in the afternoon. As I had a great desire to hear him I requested him to take my appointment which he did. What shall we say for taste, or how shall we account for popular opinion. He has a mild friendly address but is somewhat theatrical in his movements, and as a preacher he can hardly be placed on the scale of mediocrity, however, he has drawn many to hear him and they say he has done good. I lodged at Colonel Few's. Here I met my dear daughter who came down to accompany me home and is very poorly.

Saturday 28—My mind is stayed on God, and I have an unshaken confidence in him. About five we took the steamboat for Rhinebeck.

Sunday 29—This morning we landed about daybreak after an absence of more than four months; I embraced my family, all of us in good health. O Lord how shall I praise thee for thy loving kindness to me, thy poor unworthy servant. We repaired to the church, where I preached morning and evening, and Brother Hunt in the afternoon. Thank God a great change has taken place within five or six weeks—about 50 have joined Society and the greater part of them profess experimental religion, most of whom are young people. The little church is crowded, and if the work continues we shall have to enlarge it. The blessed God began and carried on this work in his own way, and Brother Hunt the stationed minister.

JOURNAL FROM MARCH, 1824 . . .

With the first running of the steamboats, my wife, and daughter accompanied me to New York where I stayed about three weeks, laboring in the city, and at Brooklyn according to my usual way, with much freedom, and I trust not without some success; although there does not seem to be any special work going on.

Thursday, April 1—In company with Brothers Reece, Lindsey, and others, I took the steamboat and about 10 o'clock P.M. we came to Trenton, and next morning arrived in Philadelphia. My good friend, and brother Dr. Sargent having previously given me an invitation to put up with him.

Lord's Day, April 4—Good Brother Reece (a delegate from the British Conference) and myself preached alternately in Ebenezer and Union Churches, morning and evening, and had crowds of attentive hearers. I bless God for this day.

Monday 5—Brothers Reece and Lindsey went on to attend the Baltimore Conference, accompanied by W. Smith.

Tuesday 6—This is a sweet day under the roof of my hospitable friends,

Brother and Sister S. In the evening I preached at St. John's Church, and we had a tender melting season. It gives great pleasure to associate with a pious intelligent society. My good friends where I stay, have a lovely charge—nine sons and daughters, trained in the fear of God, and Thomas, the eldest son, bids fare to be a light in the church. I visited three of my old friends and disciples—Brothers Wood and Wilmore, and Sister Manley, all standing like ripe shocks, bending for the grave. I am happy; but my family are 200 miles distant; but glory to God, I can hear once a week that they are doing well. This cross for Christ's sake I must bear.

Saturday 10—Brother Hannah and Martindale have just arrived from New York.

Lord's Day 11—My appointments for today are at the following churches: Morning—Union, Afternoon—St. John's, Evening—St. George's. Though it was a wet day churches filled. Brother Hannah preached two sermons, and was spoken highly of. I can say it was a good day to me, and though I preached three sermons to large congregations, I was scarcely at all weary when I ended. I think it a singular mercy from a good God.

Monday 12—I left my dear doctor and family for Wilmington. Brother H. was to accompany me; but he came to the boat two minutes too late, and followed the next morning. I arrived safe, and put up at Brother Wood's, a good old Local preacher.

Tuesday 13—I preached in the Wilmington church to a full house, blessed God was with us of a truth. Brother Potts is the stationed minister here, and has been a blessing to the people.

Wednesday 14—I had a very bad carriage to Elkton, and with _____ all a fat young country man, and his wife took the hinder seat and neither age nor anything else would induce them to relinguish their pretended claim, so I had to ride backward, and it so overcame me, that I had to stay a day at Elkton to rest, which gave me the opportunity of having an interview with William Drake, an aged, intelligent minister, one with whom I was acquainted nearly 50 years ago.

Thursday 15—I took the steamboat at eight in the evening and was in Baltimore before daybreak. I put up with my good friend Dr. Baker, who married Mrs. Dicken's daughter, an old friend, with whom I was formerly well acquainted, and who sat under my ministry 47 years ago—she was Miss Yancy. I was happy to see her and to see her so pleasantly situated. Dr. Baker is a pious, valuable Christian. Here I met Brother Reece, and Brother Lindsey again. I am now pleasantly retired.

Lord's Day 18—I am very unwell. I consent only to preach one sermon. I did in the evening with great freedom in Light Street. House full—a very solemn season.

Monday 19—Old friends are near, and dear to me, and blessed be my good savior. I am happy in his love. Whilst I was sitting at tea in the afternoon at Mr. Moreheads, Mr. L. Norris—one of my great nephews came in and said he had come to town with his carriage to take me to the country.

I was glad, for I wanted a tour through Harford. I had a melancholy account from a steamboat which last night burst her boiler and several were killed on the spot, and many others desperately scalded. Be ye also ready. I wish owners of boats would take warning, and not suffer them to run on the Lord's Day.

Tuesday 20—This morning my nephew called for me. We rode about 20 miles to his sister's, near Bell Air. I see a vacancy in this house. When I was here a few years ago, the mother, and her daughter Clarissa, two lovely females received me with smiles; but where are they now—first the sister, and then the mother took their flight to glory, and left four brothers, and three sisters, to mourn their loss. Mrs. Norris, and her daughter Clarissa, were blessed women, and I doubt not but they have gone safe home.

Wednesday 21—I visited, and retired, and it was a good day.

Thursday 22—I preached at Union Chapel, and dined at Mr. Richardson's, and in the afternoon returned to the old mansion. Sophia Norris, the eldest daughter, takes good care of the family.

Friday 23—My nephew Captain Norris offers his service to carry me wherever I wish to go. We started to traverse Bush River Neck, my native place, and I saw many of my haunts when I was a boy, the old Spesutia Church, where I received Christian baptism. Many occurences were brought fresh to my recollection, which transpired more than 60 years ago. I was glad to find that the people had fully repaired the old Church and Vestry house, and that a good fence was kept up around the graves of our ancestors. However, they have no settled minister in what they call the old Parish, neither do they want one, for the Methodists have places of worship and societies in every direction. We lodged at Mr. Ruthen Garrettson's. He has the richest farm I have seen in the Neck. His mother was my mother's sister and my father was his father's brother; he married my eldest sister's daughter—they both have a respect for religion, and I hope will get safe to heaven.

Saturday, April 24—We rode to Abingdon and stayed at F. Hollis's. He married my niece. She professes to be happy in God, and he has a respect for religion; but I fear the world has too great a share of his heart, as I have often told him. He has the good things of this world in abundance. The river half surrounds his large valuable farm, on which is an excellent fishery.

Lord's Day 25—In the morning I preached in the Abingdon Church, and had a sweet solemn time I rode six miles, and preached in a large, handsome church lately built in the forest, under the patronage of old Mr. Webster who was laying very ill about a mile off. I was sent for to visit him, and I found him nigh unto death, joyfully waiting for the last messenger. He was among the first to embrace religion when the Methodists made their first entrance into the place about 56 years ago. He is now about 85 years of age and has been a preacher more than 50 years;

he has a large family of children and grandchildren settled around him, while he like a ripe shock of corn, is waiting for his dissolution. A few days after I left him he took his departure. I had sweet fellowship with him, and bless God for the opportunity.

Monday 26—I spent in visiting my friends in Abingdon. A few came together to the baptism of little Edwin Garrettson, my brother's grandchild. The mother is a young widow, and very handsome, and probably will not be a widow long. Sometime ago, her husband went on a voyage to Havanna, was taken with the yellow fever, called off suddenly, and left a widow, with four beautiful children, and a brother, brothers and sisters, and many other near relatives to mourn their loss.

Tuesday 27—Captain Norris accompanied me to Baltimore, where I found the preachers gathering for General Conference. I lodged at Mr. Morehead's, and met an old relative about my own age—several of her children have experienced religion, but I fear she has not found that blessed change, though she has a respect for good people, and has a desire to be religious. Her youngest son has been a great trial to her. His portion of the estate was $100,000, and in four years, after he came of age, he had run through about $80,000 of it; but it seems of late there is an alteration in his conduct for the better. I sent for him to come and see me, but he sent me word that he was not prepared for such an interview.

I repaired to Mr. Rennel's, the place appointed for me to board during the sitting of Conference, and I am much pleased with the family. (I left home in March 1824 and spent about three weeks in New York and Brooklyn, and went on to Baltimore, visiting Philadelphia, Wilmington, and some other places, and got to Baltimore about the middle of April, and after spending one sabbath, I went on tour through Harford, and visited and preached to many of my relatives, and others, and returned to Baltimore.)

May 1, 1824—General Conference opened at eight. We were four days fixing rules by which session was to be governed. I am, and hope always shall be an old fashioned Methodist. When the apostles, Elders, and Brethren met in their grand Council in Jerusalem, we do not read of their spending three minutes in forming rules to govern their proceedings. They were full of faith, and the Holy Ghost, and their blessed master was with them. Formerly we could do the same without a set of congressional rules, which only had a tendency to perplex, and retard the business of the meeting. We had delegates from every part of the union—north, south, east, and west, from England, and Canada. We have the largest Conference we ever had. As it respects the doctrines of the gospel, we all harmonized; but touching lesser matters, there were various opinions. In the Southern States, slavery is prevalent amongst the Methodists, as well as amongst other Churches, and indeed the laws are against their Emancipation. I tremble for those states. The southern brethren seem to be as much opposed to Pewed Churches in New England, as the Eastern brethren are against slavery; we can prove the former to be a moral evil, which is more than they can do respecting the latter.

Many petitions came in from our people, praying for a lay delegation, and likewise from the Local Ministry, and several were sent in on the opposite side. There seems to be two powerful objections raised to our present plan. 1. The general superintendent's power to station ministers, when, and where they please. 2. The power with which the General Conference is invested, to make laws to govern the whole body, without a fair representation.

How is it possible for 1200 itinerating ministers to give satisfaction to 6,000 of the Local Ministers, and preachers, and well on to half million of the membership, and more than a million of quiet hearers beside, who sit under our ministry. It has been suggested that a plan might be devised to give general satisfaction.

I will transcribe the reflections of an enlightened, candid mind, for more than 40 years. 1. The whole connection in America shall be divided into Annual Conferences, and there shall be one Superintendent in each Annual Conference, and but one, and he shall be invested with every power necessary to carry on the work in his own district, in changing, suspending, and so forth—but he shall be amenable for his conduct at his own Conference. 2. Each district shall be sufficiently small to enable the Superintendent to go once or twice around every year; and if there would be two or more places calling for his attention at the same time, he shall take the liberty to send a Timothy or a Titus to set that matter in order, and then return to his own work. 3. Every Elder, if worthy, shall be a member of the Conference, and shall take part in the government of the Church, but if he is a local brother, and does not give himself up wholly to the work, but follows Secular business, shall not be entitled to the funds of the church, and the Conference must judge of the business he must, or shall follow. 4. The Superintendent shall have the right to call any Elder or any other person from time to time into his counsel, in making of the stations of the brethren, which plan when finished shall be brought into the Conference two days before rises, before the Eldership alone, and the Superintendent shall rest the plan, and every Elder shall be considered as a representative of the congregation he served the last year, and under the weight of the body the stations shall be confirmed, but if it should be necessary to put anything to vote, it shall be done without debate. 5. Every Annual Conference shall be held at the same time— say the 15th of August—and the minutes of Conferences sent immediately by post to the book agents for compilation. 6. Every Quarterly Meeting through the whole Connection shall be held within one or two weeks of each other, say, 1st by May, 2nd by August, 3rd by November, 4th by February. 7. Through the whole Connection two stations or circuits shall be linked together, and the Minister in Charge shall be the presiding Elder, but of the Circuits linked together the Superintending Elders shall hear appeals for each other, unless the General Superintendent is present, in which case the business of the Quarterly Meeting devolves on him as president, or any person who may come with his immediate authority to stand in his place, and the Quarterly Meeting Conference shall Supercede the necessity of a local conference.

II. of the General Conference. 1. All the General Superintendents, if they are all disposed to attend, shall have a seat in the General Conference; but the superannuated, or supernumerary Bishops shall be eligible if elected with the other members. 2. The first thing to be attended to when General Conference assembles shall be to elect a chairman from among the Superintendents, and, the whole body composes the Grand College of Presbiters, with a Cyprian elevated at the head. 3. As our plan is itinerant, and we suppose it would not be expedient to have a lay delegation, we do not think we are authorized to enact any law that touches the terms of communion, or the property of our people, to be binding till it first goes round and obtains a majority of all the members of the Conferences, and the membership. 4. There shall be a power in the General Conference to Station Superintendents, and so forth.

We sat in General Conference four weeks, and one day, and did but little, and indeed there were such a diversity of sentiments touching this government of the Church that I was ready sometimes almost to conclude that we had better amicably divide the work from the Atlantick by Washington, leaving the Genesee (?) and the Canadas in the northern session. In the midst of all the disputations about smaller matters, there was much love, and moderation. I felt myself very much attached to our worthy English brethren, Reverend Reece and Hanna.

June 1, 1824—Our New York Conference began, and after setting about eight days in great peace and harmony, I have reached my family, after an absence of about three months, and blessed be the Lord, I found them in health. After staying about home a few weeks my wife and daughter accompanied me to Albany and from thence to Schenectady.

Sunday, July 4, 1824—I preached two sermons, morning and evening, in the M. Church with freedom, especially in the evening. We are very kindly received and hospitably entertained at President Notts. I feel to be in the way of duty. We contemplate a tour up the Canal to Utica.

Monday, July 5—About sunset we started in one of the Packet boats. We travelled about four miles an hour, drawn by three horses, changing every nine or ten miles.

Tuesday, July 6—About 9 o'clock in the evening we got safe to Utica and put up with Mr. Lynch.

Wednesday, July 7—A good congregation assembled in the evening and I preached with freedom from the words of our Lord to Martha—"But one thing is needful." Bishops George and Hedding came into the church before my sermon ended. We had a good time.

Thursday evening, July 8—Bishop Hedding[180] preached in the evening;

the people were attentive and we were edified. I spent the remainder of the week in Utica but I fear religion does not prosper in the town.

Lord's Day 11—Brother George preached an excellent sermon in the morning, and I preached in the afternoon—the house was full morning and afternoon, and having an invitation, I preached in the Presbyterian Meeting-house in the evening but not with much liberty. There is an astonishing alteration in this country. More than 30 years ago, when I was traversing, and forming circuits through this country, I could only find here, and there a log hut, to screen me from the winter blasts; but now it is a thick settled, and well cultivated country, with many handsome towns, villages and churches, rising up in every direction and coaches rolling, as you would see them in old settled places. I fear the people think more of the world than they do of their souls. I awfully fear for the inhabitants of this fertile country.

Monday, July 12, 1824—This morning we intended leaving Utica, but our daughter on Saturday night took cold which was succeeded by a burning fever, which did not abate until this morning, and it left her too weak for the journey. We found Mr. and Mrs. Lynch very kind, and attentive to us—it will be a blessing if we all get safe to heaven.

Tuesday 13—We leave Utica. I have borne my testimony against the prevailing sins of the place, and feel as if I had done my duty. Brother Peck—a good man—has been stationed in the place two years past— and his friends seem to wish him to stay longer. The Society is small, and in general poor, but not very able to support a minister, and with all, they built their church in an out of the way place. In the town there are five churches, and perhaps not fewer than 6,000 inhabitants and the Methodists have the smallest house and congregation. What is the cause? O God heal our backslidings, and grant that we may be brought back to our former standing. Some men learn to preach, and make a mere profession of it, and get a scant support by it; but I fear they have but few, if any souls for their time. The old gospel plan, was to be thrust out, with a woe unto me if I preach not the gospel. In such there is an ardent thirsting for holiness, and the recovery of perishing sinners, and the blessed God doth own, and bless His word, and precious souls are gathered into the fold.

Wednesday 14—About 9 o'clock we landed safe in Schenectady. Our good friends at the College are very attentive and do everything to make us comfortable.

Thursday 15—I spent a good part of this day in reading Jones' Church History. He certainly views what I call the Novatian schism (about the middle of the third century) in a more point of light than I can. After the death of a Bishop, or the superintending Elder of the church in Rome when the people were about to elect their presiding minister, Novatian wished to have that high station in the church; but when he found he was not elected, he drew off with his party; and they elected and set him apart as Bishop of Rome. If this is not a schism, I am at a loss to know what is a schism.

The church at that time was under the persecutions of heathen Rome, and Jesus Christ certainly had at that period a living body in Rome. I think pride, or something no better must have stimulated Novatian, and his party, to mangle a living body, in rending away its members, and sowing the seeds of discord: the fruits of which was discovered in their union with a heresy, so much complained of by Cyprian, Bishop of Carthage. I dare not date the origin of the Church, which came down to us through the wilderness in succession, pure from the Apostles, from the schismatics, or heretics of Novatian's time. Look through the 4th and 5th centuries, and see the ruling body of the professors of the Christian religion on the left, falling in love with the world, and taking to themselves their own superstitions, and bereft of the spirit of holiness. Look to the right, and see an innocent creature crawling from the old shell, under heavy persecution. The pure Church never united with the whole of Babylon. It is true, whenever there was a reformation, and a coming off from the woman with the golden cup in her hand, the church in the wilderness gave the right hand of fellowship as far as they embraced truth. The Moravians spoke well of the reformation under Luther and others, but did not unite with them, for in that case the more numerous should have come to the life. When Mr. Wesley was first enlightened he was directed to Hurn-Hut, from whence he brought the holy fire, and apostolic succession to England, and had the church in general received this apostle of God, the pure doctrine of justification by faith and sanctification before now, would have prevailed universally.

Friday 16 July 1824—We came to Albany, and Saturday we reached Rhinebeck, and thanks be to God, we found our family in health. A description has been given of the great Western Canal better than I can give with regard to the prosecution of so great a work in so short a time with so little expense, has very far exercised my most sanguine expectations. Indeed it may be placed among the wonders of the world, and yet I have my fears, lest it should not in the whole fully answer the sanguine expectations of the projectors of it, or the citizens at large—for should it stand and bear its own weight that itself will be a greater phenomenon than its first erection. How wonderful to see a vessel of fifty tons burden passing over a bridge, or rising or falling at the _____ between one, and two hundred feet. I enjoyed the pleasure of a comfortable home a few days, and on *Thursday the 22nd* I started in the steamboat for New York. I had a very disagreeable time. I fear we may write on the North-river steamboats—Echabod, the glory is departed. The opposition boat was bad enough to start on the Lord's Day, and the old lines were determined to let them know, that in point of immorality they could cope with them. I fear our sins will bring down the judgements of God on our guilty land.

Sunday 25—I preached and had a precious sacramental occasion in the Allen Street Church; and again in the evening the word was sweet in Greenwich Church. I have had rumatick [rheumatic] pains in my back, and hips. My blessed Lord has been good to me for many years, and I will praise him. I am bending over eternity, and must soon go the way of all flesh. I stay at Mr. Suckley's and am able to go about little, except in a Carriage. I am retired, and have a fine time for Meditation, self-examination, and prayer. I am under many obligations to my heavenly father, and fully sensible that I have nothing in, or of myself to recommend to his favor—Mercy through the merit of Jesus Christ is my plea. The aged as well as the young may say, "Every moment Lord we need the merit of thy death." We may lay up treasures in heaven; but to secure it, we must have supporting grace, not only daily but every moment. Our passions may not be as strong as they were in youthful vigor, yet the assaults are nearly the same, and were it not for the tender compassions of a good God we would not stand. O how infinite is his Wisdom and goodness, and his ways are past finding out.

Thursday 29—I gave a short discourse in Greenwich Church in the evening. After family prayer I spent some time in perusing a small periodical work, called the Teliscope—some things appear calculated to do good, but I fear in a covered way, there is in some particular exceptions, a tincture of that banefull doctrine, called Unitarianism. If so, its deformed head will sooner or later be uncovered. I closed my eyes in sleep a little before twelve. My dreams were not unpleasant, but rather singular for one of my time of life. O God keep me by the power of grace, whether sleeping or waking.

Friday 20—Was a day of solitude, and serious reflection. I am bound for heaven.

Saturday 31—I made visits, and was detained several hours longer than I expected—part of the day was lost, and I was grieved.

Lord's Day, August 1, 1824—My morning appointment was in John Street Church. Light shone on my mind, and I had a sweet time in the Word, and many came to the Lord's Table. Many who came to the Lord's Table, and especially young persons. I had a sweet evidence that Jesus was at his table, and many could say, it was good to be in the church and at the table of the Lord. I am very much afflicted with the rheumatism in my back, and hips. With some difficulty I got a carriage to take me to morning Church, but none offered for the evening, and I had to walk half a mile to preach in Duane Street Church. I was enabled to perform the walk, and had a precious sweet season; stayed all night at Brother Brown's, one of the stationed preachers, and had a sweet night's repose. Brother Brown is a young man of an improving mind, and an acceptable preacher, and I hope he will stand fast in the faith, live long, and do much good.

Tuesday 3—I preached again at Duane Street Church with much liberty, and stayed again with Brother Brown.

Wednesday 4—This morning Brother Clark came with his carriage for me and took me to Greenwich to Brother Rise's, where we held a consultation about my going to Camp-meeting. Poorly as I am, they advised me to make a effort, and go, which I agreed to do, if I got no worse. I stayed a good part of my time at my old friends Mr. and Mrs. Suckley's, where I may be as happy as the prophet was, with his little chamber, stool, table and so forth. Every sermon I preach, I endeavor to deliver, as if it was my last. I often think of my dear old friend, and colleague—Mr. Asbury who spent, I may say the last shred of his life in the service of his great master. I want to do good, I want to be greatly taken up in my blessed master's work, and that my last days should be my best. O wash me Lord and make me perfectly clean. I have had a degree of pleasure in pursuing the history of Eusebious. We may discover a great degree of simplicity in the writings of the old Fathers of the Church. If in our day, we were as much better than the primitive Christians, as we are wiser, we should indeed be like a City set on a hill; but we are very deficient. Many of those were persecuted even unto death, and too, joyfully the spoiling of their goods, but we know nothing of all this—we live under Christian rulers, and have institutions of a homogeneous nature, all sitting under our own vine, and fig tree, none making us afraid, and indeed under such easy circumstances, it is a singular mercy we have any religion beyond a form. Possibly the time is not far distant, till the holy [unholy] alliance will make the protestants tremble, and fly to the wilderness, or mountains for shelter, for the Woman, who some little time ago, sat naked in the street, is clothed and is gathering strength very fast. The Infallible head of the papistical Church, is looking over the world with a sharp eye, and if he can get the bloody inquisition set up generally, he will yet make the Nations tremble, especially if he can get the unholy alliance on his side. Glory to God, he reigneth, and if the infidelity, and backslidings of his people do not call down his displeasure, he will continue to be as a wall of fire around about our heavenly Jerusalem. O that ministers may stand firm in their high calling, and faithfully preach a living gospel with great success, then shall the nations be turned to righteousness.

Thursday 5—I am in retirement. God is good—I greatly admire his perfections. I feel as nothing in his sight. I am full of infirmities, and imperfections. I can only stand by faith in the Lord Jesus Christ. I have heard of laying up a stock of grace for old age; but I am sensible we must gather every day, or suffer loss. We may lay up treasure in heaven, but we must have daily supplies, or suffer loss in our own souls.

Friday 6—My worthy friend, L. Clark, took me to Brooklyn, where I was hospitably entertained with my worthy friends, Mr. and Mrs. Ross. I continue afflicted with pains. It does me good to see how comfortably. our ministers are provided for, and how they are increasing their stock of books and knowledge. It is the prerogative of the blessed God, to send by whom he will send, and we will know that he is not confined to Colleges, or Seminaries, neither are the most shining characters always sent out from thence; nevertheless I am of the opinion that the ministry is among the learned professions, and whenever a young man receives a call from God to the work of the ministry, he should as far as in him lies, lay aside the study of the world, and wholly bend his mind to the study of the holy scriptures, and every other science particularly attached to that great work, and to labor in a particular manner, to enter into the life of faith and God, and to have an acquaintance with ourselves, and the people to whom we preach. This is the way to grow up into the ministry, shining brighter, and brighter, to the perfect day.

Saturday 7—I was profitably employed in reading the history of Eusebious.

Sunday 8—The blessed God is with me this morning. It is a sweet thing to have the holy scriptures opened to one's mind. In the old Brooklyn church in the morning I preached with great sweetness in my own soul, from Hebrews 6: 4 and 5 in the New Church, near the Navy Yard. Revelation 3: 14-20. I had much light and freedom. This evening I rest in God, and feel humble, thankful.

Monday 9—I passed over the river into the city, and spent part of the day in the book-room and dined, and lodged at good old Brother G. Smith's.

Tuesday 10—Rose early and started in the steamboat for Camp Meeting on Long Island. I heard a sermon at two, and another in the evening. Great solemnity rests on the people.

Wednesday 11—10 o'clock about 6,000 present. I never had more freedom to preach. All attention. The power of God was sensibly felt. 2 o'clock Brother Ross preached well—the people were very attentive. In the evening Brother Mason delivered a warm discourse.

Thursday 12—Morning, afternoon and evening we had preaching, and exhortations from the stand.

Friday morning 8 o'clock—We are about to part. The trumpet was blown, and the people gathered around the stand. Mr. Thatcher and myself gave the parting addresses, after which, liberty was given, and several arose and spoke sweetly of the great things the Lord had done for them, and we had a time to be remembered through eternity. A few remarks may be seasonable.

1. Laban Clark was president of the Meeting, and gave his whole time to it, day and night, with a suitable committee, and a Squire who kept order.

2. The preachers were universally in the spirit of the work—preaching, praying, and exhortation, and united as a band of brothers.

3. A solemn awe rested on the Christians in general—many, very many excellent prayers went up to heaven, from the tents, and circles, without unseemly gesticulations, or bold expressions before the infinite holy God.

4. I frequently passed through the Camp, and felt sweetly drawn out, and much pleased with the many pious, and humble addresses at a throne

of grace, and modest exhortations delivered under the influence of the Holy Spirit.

5. I have good reason for belief, that good was done at this meeting. Sinners were awakened, and souls were regenerated, and judgement seemed to sit on the face of the congregation at large.

Saturday 14—I am now in New York, at Brother Stratton's under the operation of medicine.

Sunday 15—I only accepted one appointment. In the morning I heard a useful sermon in John Street—"Live in peace with all men." In the evening I had much liberty to preach in the same church. Our Brother Bushnell has been in a low state of health, and has preached very little since Conference, and at present his recovery is very doubtful. I visited him, and found him very low spirited, and did not desire to say anything to anyone.

Monday 16—I entered the boat at five and was with my family to breakfast next morning, and found them in health. This week I spent with my family, and was frequently under deep exercise of mind. I am never fully satisfied, unless employed in the work of the blessed God.

Sunday, August 22—I preached morning, afternoon, and evening in Mission Chapel, with liberty. O that the blessed work might prosper in Rhinebeck.

Tuesday 24—Brother Coles accompanied me to the Newburg Camp-Meeting.

Wednesday 25—We have peace, and order, and good preaching.

Thursday 26—This morning I preached to more than 5,000 people with great liberty, and I never saw a more attentive congregation. Brother Coles gave a good exhortation after me, and in the afternoon we took the steamboat and came to Rhinebeck. I did not approve of all the regulations at this meeting. Young, inexperienced lads were appointed to keep order, and frequently they were the occasion of disorder. There should be as little parade as possible. Coercion, frequently hardens, when love would soften.

Sunday 29—I preached morning, and evening, in Kingston. Our people have built a very handsome church in this place; but the society is small and the congregation not large; but a few make considerable exertions to support preaching. My intention was to have gone two tours—but was hindered, and I can truly say my mind has not been as fully at rest as I could have wished. O my blessed God, thou knowest the spirit is willing, but this old tottering house.

[NOTE: the following passage has been crossed out in the journal but is quite legible and of interest.]

(I visited Kingston, and preached two sermons with freedom. In and about this place a few zealous friends have built us a handsome Chapel, and finished it completely, and furnished it with lamps, but the Society and congregation are small. Old prejudices, deeper rooted in the heart, are not easily rooted out. The inhabitants are mostly descendants from immigrants from Holland, when the place was first settled. O blessed Lord when will the time come when there will be shaking among the dry bones in this place? Unbelief must give way to the sacred truths of the gospel. In Rhinebeck Brother Coles is stationed, and his labors are very acceptable, and I hope a great blessing will be the result of his ministerial exertions. One sabbath is gone, in silence with me, but thanks be to God, attended his house, and heard two sermons with pleasure.)

I have been several weeks about home, and sometimes preached two or three times on the Lord's Day with freedom. I am sensible to be happy we must be rationally employed, and we must not take anxious thought for the morrow, as saith our blessed Lord. I have time for reflection, meditation, and self-examination, and though, blessed be God, I have not designedly erred, yet in many things I discover imperfections. I have been dejected and felt something like a hypochondriac, when I ought to have rejoiced and given glory to God, for surely I am surrounded with his mercies. Jesus is my friend, and I will praise him. My dear Catherine, always ready to give a word in season, when a melancholy gloom over-spreads my mind, and the smiles and cheerful conversations with my lovely daughter, would awaken sensibility in the mind of a hermit. "Why art thou cast down O my soul, and so forth?" Near half a century ago, I was happy in the perfect love of God, and my labors were abundant in this cause. The blessed Lord has blessed me with many days, and a good constitution, but I fear I have come short of doing as much in his cause as I might have done. I have a glorious advocate, or I must sink. Glory to his name, I will praise him, and yet strive to do something to promote his cause. Unworthy as I feel myself to be. I would not part with my hope of glory for a million worlds.

September 21, 1824—I set out with my wife and daughter, on a tour to visit some aged friends in Westchester County. We stayed two nights at Fishkill, with our kind friends, Mr. and Mrs. Crystie, where we met Mrs. Suckley. My mind is free, and I am happy in God.

Thursday 23—We passed over the mountains, dined at Mr. Hibberts, in Peekskill, and went on to Colonel Few's, where we were met with open arms.

Friday 24—I left my wife and daughter, with an expectation they would meet me the Tuesday following at Governor Jay's. I rode on to the White Plains, and put up at my good old friend A. Miller's.

Saturday 25—I visited old friends and returned.

Sunday 26—I preached to an attentive congregation with much sweetness, and lodged at Brother Barker's. Mr. and Mrs. Barker I trust stand firm in the faith. The Methodists for many years have had the field very much to themselves, but at present the Presbyterians, and what they call Church people, are building each of them a church, near our chapel. A young man from our Society has lately been ordained by the old side Episcopalians, whom they have called to their new church, and he seems to command considerable attention. The Methodists have a blessed Society in this place, and they are numerous throughout this county.

Monday 27—I spent this day, accompanied by Brother Barker, in visiting the afflicted. Dear old Brother Dunewen, is deeply afflicted: his wife has been partially deranged for many years, and lately one of his daughters has gone into the state of derangement, even to madness, and is now in the hospital. He is a pious, and as patient as Job. I passed the evening at Brother Martindales, and felt as if at home.

Tuesday 28—I set out to meet my family. Rode 20 miles, and got to the Governor's just in time for dinner, but my wife and daughter did not arrive till near sunset. Mr. Jay[181] lives like a dignified statesman, and patriarch (as he is) with his children, and grandchildren about him. As it happens to be a time of visitation, there are about 20 to sit at table, and the best of all, is, they fear God, and are engaged in trying to do good. He is about 80 years old, and very feeble. After filling the first offices in the union, in an advanced time of life, they have advanced him to the presidency of the National Bible Society in the place of Mr. Boudinot. He has family prayer attended to regularly morning and evening.

Thursday 30—After a very pleasant visit, we turned our faces toward home, lodged at Brother Mathias'. We were handsomely entertained. I preached in the evening in the Chapel nearly filled with serious, attentive hearers, and I felt an holy flame of love, and believed the word was felt.

Friday, October 1—We recrossed the mountains, and came again to Fishkill to the house of our friend. It is a handsome place, overlooking Newburg and many hills and dales, and fruitful fields. The Methodists have lately built a respectable church in this vicinity. I feel comfortable in my mind, and an ardent desire for the prosperity of the gospel. *Saturday* we reached home, and found the family in health. "Peace be within thy walls O inhabitants of Zion." God has been gracious to my family, many years, and prayer and praise, I trust ascend daily to heaven.

Sunday 3—We repaired to church, and Bishop George delivered an excellent sermon. He accompanied us home. I tried to persuade him to preach in the evening; he thought himself too unwell, so the lot fell on me, and I had a good time. I have been late—touring among these people more than 30 years, and blessed be God I hope not altogether in vain.

This week was spent in a round of duty much as usual when at home.

Sunday 10—I have no particular appointment today, but I heard two good sermons.

Thursday 14—I go to New York. Our dear old friend Mrs. Carpenter is gone, and has left her husband, and family to mourn their loss. However their loss is her eternal gain. She was born in the same month and year that I was. She has gone a little while before me, and I must soon follow. O God prepare me for this solemn event.

Sunday 17—I know the blessed God was with me, and with the congregation, whilst setting forth: "Who is she that looketh forth as the morning, fair as the moon, clear as the sun and terrible as an army with banners." In the evening I preached with liberty in John Street Church from Romans 5: 1, 2.

Monday 18—I took my departure for home and found my family in health. This was a week of deep exercise. Who can correctly philosophize on the cause, and effects of hypocondria. The mind is sensibly affected, as if the imaginary cause was real. A dismal gloom hangs over the mind, and the sensations are painful. It vanishes as a shadow, and leaves the mind solemn, tranquil and serene. We form resolutions to guard against another attack; but unawares the enemy approaches from another quarter, or the same in another form. O Father we need thy help every moment.

Lord's Day, October 24—I rode to Poughkeepsie and preached with much freedom. The blessed God was in the little assembly. I never had a greater desire for the prosperity of Zion.

Monday 25—I am now in retirement. My mind is tranquil and Jesus is precious.

Thursday 28—I go again to New York (from the particular request of the afflicted family) to preach the funeral sermon of Mrs. Carpenter.

Friday and Saturday in sweet retirement.

Sunday 31—In John Street Church we had a crowded assembly of all description of people, especially of the aged and pious. Upon this solemn occasion I gave out "Blessed are the dead which die in the Lord from henceforth, yea saith the spirit for they rest from their labors and their works do follow them." Rev. 13: 14. I considered that part of the text, "In the Lord" to be very euychatic—to be in the Lord, as the branch is in the Vine. Jesus Christ is the Vine, and our departed, aged friend was emminently in the vine. She had a clear evidence of justification by faith, and in an emminent degree experienced the sanctifying influences of the Holy Spirit, and received spiritual nourishment from the true vine, for more than fifty years. I found freedom in setting forth the impressive declaration of the Holy Spirit. "Blessed are the dead, and so forth." This blessed Christian, after a long and useful life, left the world in full assurance of a better state of existence, the 73rd year of her age, lamented by all who knew her. The church, and her family have lost a valuable friend; but their loss is her eternal gain.

November 4, 1824—I left the city and returned home. My nephew[182] has gone on a journey to the south, and I have to attend to many things of a temporal nature, which is not very congenial with my inclination. He has married a wife, and will have to take care of his own family. I hope the blessed Lord will direct me to some suitable person to take charge of our temporal concerns. I gave up the world about 50 years ago, and have been employed about the holy Altar, and I desire so to be as long as I live. For nearly two weeks I have been busily employed about home, and read, and wrote but little; but blessed be God, I have had access at a throne of grace, found liberty to preach on the Lord's Day.

Saturday, November 20—I set out on a tour to the east, and had some precious seasons on the Lord's Day. In some places the Socinians have disturbed the minds of a few, and proselyted, some who I fear had braved it out against the truth, too long. It is an awful thing to trifle with sacred things. I returned home, and found my people busily employed in gathering in and storing away the fruits of the earth. There is abundantly more pleasure in giving than in receiving. We are stewards, and will soon be called to give an account of our stewardship. Lord Jesus be with us in old age, preserve our memory, and keep our souls in perfect peace. O for a useful happy life. O to love God with every power of the soul.

Saturday, November 27—Crossed the North River, and lodged in Esopus.

Lord's Day 28—This morning I am looking to Jesus. Very few are apprised of my coming. Indeed we must with patience bear this neglect also, and one apology to be made is, my letter did not get over till late in the week, and secondly, two of the leading members were absent on business. I repaired to the church at eleven and preached to between 50 and 100, and gave out for the evening, and had a good congregation. This is a poor soil for Methodism. This is an ancient village, and first formed by immigrants from Holland, and their descendants through a succession of ages, seem to retain the profession of their forefathers, and almost think it is a crime bordering on the unpardonable sin to turn from it. There is but little to be accomplished without perseverance. The time may come when many hearts even in this place may be touched, and many souls be truly converted to God, and the kingdom of Christ greatly prosper. The following sabbath I spent in Rhinebeck.

Thursday 9, 1824—I go to New York. Though I have some temporal concerns, yet glory to God, my main end is the service of the church. I inquired after Bishop George. He has just left the city for the south.

Friday 10—I visited several families and walked out to Greenwich Village. I stayed at Mr. Suckley's.

Saturday 11—I returned to town, and retired to Brother Stratten's, after meeting with the preachers in the morning.

Lord's day 12—I had a good time in John Street Church whilst preaching on, "Who is she that looketh forth as the morning, fair as the moon, clear as the sun, (and terrible) as an army with banners" Song of Solomon 6: 10. In the evening in Duane Street Church, we had a blessed shower, and I am informed that some were awakened, and others brought into liberty. I bless God for this visitation.

Thursday 14—I was assured by I.L. if I would go over to Brooklyn, I would have a large congregation. This was on Saturday last, and he would take no denial—I told him if it must be so, appoint for Tuesday evening, and I found even as he said, we had a blessed time. I visited Brother

Ross, and found him in a very debilitated state. His lungs are inflamed, and he has a fever, and I fear consequences. He is valuable but if the blessed God calls him away, he can put another in his place; for he is perfectly independent of his creatures, and knows what is the best for them. This evening I had a perfect retreat at Brother I. Lyon's where they were very kind, and I had a sweet time with my blessed Lord.

Wednesday 15—I recrossed the East River, and walked out to Greenwich, and had the pleasure of visiting several families on the way. I spent this evening with Brothers Rice and Clark, and lodged with the former. Sister Rice is an excellent woman, and has several fine healthy sons, and he is a Boenargis, and I hope will live to do much good. A poor man told me his wife was in a despairing way, and she had a particular desire I should visit her. I did so and found her case pitiable. I asked her what she wanted. She said she was once happy in the perfect love of God, and used to have blessed times in Ireland before she came to this country, and belonged to a band class, and that she had been very happy in this country; could praise God day and night, but said God has forsaken me, and I am a reprobate—there is no mercy for me. I asked her what was the cause of the Lord's forsaking her. She could not tell. I said have you committed any known sin? She said no; but I have not one spark of grace. Said I, do you love good people? O yes, said she, and I would give this world to feel as I once did, but mercy for me is clean gone, and I have thought I had better put myself out of the world, and know the worst, I labored to show how heinous such a crime would be. I endeavored to surround her with a rich cluster of promises, but she put them from her. I prayed with her, and was humble at the feet of Jesus, and felt greatly. I left her apparently as I found her. I thought her a child of God, under the powerful temptations of the evil one. I requested her husband not to leave her alone, and I spoke to several of the ministers and Christian people to pay particular attention to her.

Thursday 16—Brother Rice accompanied me to Town. I visited several families, and at five entered the steamboat, and landed at Rhinebeck a little after daybreak, and again embraced my family. I made but a short stay in the city, but it was a profitable time to me, and I trust to some others. I am received as a father, and they know how to bear with my many infirmities.

Friday 17—I am now in my warm room, surrounded by my attentive family. My dear Catherine was born the same year that I was, and she is only about three months younger than me, but much more active. I bless God for such a friend, always ready to help, strengthen, and console, and the blessed God has blessed us in an amiable daughter, and our domestics, live in harmony and strive to please. "O to grace how great a debtor Daily I'm constrained to be and let that grace now like a fetter bind my happy soul to thee."[183]

Saturday 18—I set out on a little tour accompanied by the principal of our little Academy. Dined with my old friend, Mr. Sands, who was among the first that espoused the cause of Methodism in this vicinity, and was a leader for many years, but has been for some time much afflicted and scarcely able to leave his own door. He has an attentive friend in his eldest daughter, who lives with him, or rather he lives with her, for she has the entire management. In the evening I preached in the house of Brother _____ but few assembled. The old people are pious, but neither their children or neighbors seem to be under gospel discipline. That poisonous Socinian doctrine has crept into a few families and invariably a train of evil follows the propagation of it. Every good person should lift up a standard against it.

Lord's Day 19—I had a good time at Boro Church. The congregation was small, but attentive and tendered. In this place there has been a falling off. A few weak men have been striving to sow the seed of heretical principles. I met the class and some hearts seemed to feel quickening influences. The love of the world is a besetting sin among the farmers. When the hand is shut against liberality, the heart is not open to receive the graces of the Holy Spirit. I preached at the Plains in the afternoon, and also in the evening with freedom. I slept but little, and was very unwell.

Monday 20—I feel a little rested and refreshed this morning. The roads are very bad but having only 20 miles to travel, I reached home to dinner. I now have four days for rest and retirement. O that I may drink deep into the spirit of wisdom and holiness. I read and labored to understand the first chapter of Ezekiel. Was the prophet's vision confined to what was to take place touching the captivity of his brethren, the Jews. He might have glanced at that event; but the spirit carried him far beyond the political polity of the Jewish nation. We may form a chain to suit, as we may suppose, the economy of the Christian church, and that chain may appear beautiful but since the most knowing of commentators, have not the same views, can we assure ourselves, that our chain is constructed agreeably to the design of the Holy Spirit. In a prophetic flight, the prophet's mind was carried from the Babylonian captivity, through a succession of ages, even to the great judgment day, and no doubt he saw in the different ages of the church Christians, under Jesus the Captain of their salvation, worshipping in a glorious manner, ministers and people harmonizing in the order of God as described in the vision.

December 25, 1824—Christmas Day—We must avail ourselves of this festival. More people assembled in our Chapel on the occasion than expected, as some who have been brought up in the Presbyterian way, rather think it leaning to popery. I gave out for my text Isaiah 11: 10. "And in that day there shall be a root of Jesse, which shall stand for an ensign of the people; to it shall the gentiles seek: and his rest shall be glorious. 1. The character of the person. As was predicted he came through the loins of Abraham, Jesse, David. His character is beautifully described—Isaiah

9: 6. 2. His kingdom—he is the ensign—standard—the rallying point—the great conflux to this kingdom. 3. His rest, or reign shall be glorious. I have seldom seen a greater degree of solemnity on the occasion.

Lord's Day 26—This morning we had a good congregation. I had freedom in applying St. Paul's discourse to the Bishops, or Elders in the Church of Ephesus, who assembled at his request. He preached repentance toward God, and faith in our Lord Jesus Christ, and he did not shun to declare the whole council of God. In the evening I opened on that beautiful parable, Matthew 13, verses 47, 48. 1. The gospel is compared to a net. 2. It was cast into the sea. 3. Abundance of fish of every kind was enclosed. 4. It was drawn to the shore. 5. The good were gathered into vessels; the bad were cast away. Amongst the Jews, according to their law, there was a sure criterion. All that had not fins and scales were accounted unclean, and unfit for use, and were to be cast out. At certain periods it is honorable to bear the name of Christ. The mustard seed produced a tree, with large spreading branches, to which the birds of the air of different descriptions resorted for shelter. We live in an age, when it is honorable to take the Christian name, but the time is coming, when men's souls will be tried, and there will be a just discrimination, by an infallible judge, between the clean and the unclean. None will be received to heaven but such as have love to God, and faith in Christ.

Sunday, January 2, 1825—I only preached one sermon last week—at our Watch-Night New Year's eve, and a glorious time it was. Brother Coles followed with a useful discourse. This day I am under deep exercise of mind. The snow storm was such that I did not attend church; I spent the sabbath in silence and solitude.

Monday, January 3—I am cheered and refreshed. Prayer is sweet, and I find it good to be in my study alone. God is love.

Lord's Day, January 9, 1825—I preached a sacramental sermon this morning, and had a blessed season, and the blessed Jesus was at his table, and the hearts of his people were glad.

Monday 10—The world, O to keep the world completely under foot—it requires great care, prayer, and watching. "Be careful for nothing; but in everything give thanks." "We brought nothing into this world, we can carry nothing out." O for a holy walk with *God*.

Friday 14—I am severely buffeted by the enemy and a gloomy melancholy hangs over me, which is not easy to shake off, and it has been so with me at times for several days. The news came to me that our old gardener was nigh unto death. I rode over yesterday to see him, and found him very ill. He is a German and a moral old man, but knows nothing of the plan of salvation, by faith, through the merits of Jesus Christ. He has been in our service many years, and I have often strove to enlighten him, and he always told me he was as good as he knew how to be. I now put the question to him, and read, and explained the first part of the third chapter of John, touching the new birth. He was perfectly in his senses, and looked very pleasant, and said he expected to die last night, and he was not afraid but quite willing to go. I prayed with him, and left in the hand of God. As is customary with our people to come in, for a New Year's present, he came, and I gave him a shirt, and observed, that perhaps he would be buried in it. I felt much and prayed much for him. What are we to think in such a case?

Sunday 16—This is a stormy day, and inexpedient to attend church. Spent the day in family devotion and retirement, and found some consolation in looking at Jesus.

Tuesday 18—This morning I set out on a journey to Beekman Town accompanied by my nephew to settle some worldly concerns, travelled 15 miles, dined at Poughkeepsie, and travelled 16 miles to Mr. Snitekers, and the roads being very muddy and the travelling very heavy, we did not reach his house till sometime in the night; it was very dark, and the way rather dangerous; but through the protecting care of our heavenly Father, we arrived safe, and I had a comfortable night's rest. I spent two days in visiting our tenants, and was agreeably entertained. My nephew took care of the temporal concerns and endeavored to drop a word for Jesus. In this neighborhood, the Methodists, of late, have been much blessed in raising a good Society and the blessed work seems to be spreading. A few years ago, when I was here, darkness seemed to cover the hearts of a worldly minded people, but now, thanks be to God, light is breaking forth, and some are coming into gospel liberty.

Thursday 20—We returned to Poughkeepsie, and in the evening I preached to many with a degree of freedom.

Friday 21—This morning Brother Youngs accompanied me, and we went in search of a suitable place to erect a new church. Our church is too small, and with all it stands too much out of the way. I have been for several years urging this matter, and now the Society seems to be willing to prosecute our wishes. A good part of all our earthly blessings, should be returned to our heavenly Father. We are his stewards, and sooner or later we shall be called to give an account of our stewardship. We returned home, and found the family in health, thanks be to God.

Saturday 22—Rest, and retirement is sweet. In reading Mr. Moore's late life of Mr. Wesley, I was much pleased: It is well written and the doctrine of justification by faith, and a direct witness of the spirit as it dropped from the lips and pen of Mr. Wesley, is beautifully transmitted to posterity. It would be well for our ministers, and preachers to study that subject deeply, and universally, and preach it pointedly and constantly. Justification is by faith, in, and by the infinite merit of Jesus Christ, and so also is sanctification. The blessed God can do a great work in a moment.

Sunday 23—I am under deep exercises of mind: I am called to examine my state. I have no hope, but in Jesus. In his fullness, by faith I rest my all. On this Rock I feel comfort, and safety. In the Rhinebeck Chapel,

I preached morning and evening with pleasure, though no visible appearance of spiritual good.

Sunday 30—Another week is gone—I fear I have done very little good. We have peace in our family, and prayer ascends to heaven, and we are comforted. I again preached morning and evening in Mission Chapel and had freedom in the Word.

Sunday, February 6, 1825—This morning I had a sweet time whilst preaching, and administering the blessed sacrament. The Christians seemed joyful in the Lord. My text was, "He shall feed his flock like a shepherd; he shall gather the lambs with his arm, and carry them in his bosom, and shall gently lead those that are with young." Isaiah 40, verse 11. We may say in great truth that Isaiah was a gospel minister and spoke beautifully of Gospel times. See verse 2, "Speak ye comfortably to Jerusalem (the church) and cry unto her, that her warfare be accomplished, and so forth." This Evangelical Prophet by the spirit of inspiration, saw the blessed Jesus, through his under shepherds feeding the flock with spiritual food, and gathering his lambs to the Church, and gently leading weak, and disconsolate ones to the fold. My heart was enlarged, and mine eyes filled with tears. O that I may always sit at the feet of Jesus.

Monday 7—This day we have given our nephew a settlement, and he is to continue in our country, and have the management of our temporal concerns, which is a great relief to my mind.

Tuesday 8—I am in retirement, and thanks be to God I feel prospects of future usefulness. I want to drink deep into the spirit of holy living for, and in the cause of the blessed God. Many are afflicted in our town. The weather is such as to confine me very much about home; but thanks be to God, I am able to visit the sick, and preach in our Chapel on the Lord's Day two, and sometimes three sermons, and reading and prayer is sweet. I try by faith to look into heaven, and bring death near. I visited my good old friend Mr. Sands. He has been greatly afflicted for many years and cannot stay with us much longer.

March 9, 1825—A messenger brought us word—Mr. Robert Sands took his departure from this world of sorrow about 3 o'clock this morning.

Thursday 10—We attended his funeral. Many assembled on the occasion at his dwelling house, and I had freedom to speak, and we had a solemn time. He was interred in the family burying grounds.

Sunday 13—I preached the funeral sermon to a large congregation from "Many are the afflictions of the righteous but out of them all the Lord delivereth him." Psalms. Mr. Sands was amongst the first to join the Methodist society in Rhinebeck. He was the second person who invited me to his house in this place. I found him a kind, benevolent friend, and it was not long after I came to the place, before he was brought into Gospel liberty, and was appointed leader of the Society in which office he continued as long as he was able to attend. Many of our preachers will long remember his bountiful hand. He was a man of universal benevolence, and uprightness. Let one specimen at present suffice. At the period when Mr. Jay was Governor of this state, between Federalist, and Republicans, so called, politics ran high, and each party seemed disposed to expose the flaws in the character of those who were proposed for office. Mr. Sands was nominated for Senator. I looked over the paper to see what might be said against him and read a very short paragraph which appeared the substance of which is, "A surprise to see good old Mr. Sands forward at the head of his party, and suggested that they thought it would be better for him to stay at home, and take care of his class." He lived a useful member of the Methodist Church about 35 years, and in the 82nd year of his natural life, took his departure to glory.

Sunday 20—I attended the funeral of Mr. C. S. after our morning services in the church. He was a merchant very highly respected as a useful citizen. I have frequently endeavored to inculate the nature and necessity of our holy religion, but O the world. The blessed God will do right. I felt much for him, and I was very glad to hear that there was some alteration in his mind for the better.

Monday 21—We leave Rhinebeck for New York, and in 10 hours we are by the dock. Our old friends are dropping—Brother Hick,[184] and Brother A. have gone home and Brother Carpenter[185]—I fear will not stay long behind. O Lord, sanctify me wholly, and I pray God, my soul, body, and spirit may be preserved blameless to the coming of our Lord Jesus Christ. Amen.

Sunday 27—I preach in Duane Street Church in the morning with freedom. In the afternoon I heard a good sermon in John Street, delivered by Brother B. on the death of old Brother A. In the evening it was my desire to awaken the attention of the people met in John Street on the old Methodistical doctrine from these words: "Behold now is the day of salvation," the two parts of our subject are: 1. A full, and 2. A present Salvation. When in midst the discourse, there was a cry of fire which disturbed the congregation for a time. I had not those free openings, which I expected.

Monday 28—I suppose in the course of the day I walked more than three miles. It is good to go to the house of mourning. I am weary, but joyful in God.

Tuesday 29—A messenger was sent, requesting me to visit the sick. I repaired to the place, the mother and daughter confined to their beds in one room. The old lady told me she had been a cripple eight years, and confined to her bed three years; but blessed be God she said I am happy in his love, and resigned to his holy will, and supported under various and deep afflictions. The daughter was not so strong in faith, yet Jesus at times was precious to her soul. I had a sweet time in prayer, and conversation with them. I dined at Dr. Hibbard's where I met with his father, Billy Hibbard, Sr. He has published a small tract on the Trinity lately, and I am sorry to find he has fallen into that new doctrine lately broached by Dr. C. touching the sonship of Christ, and some other peculiarities from Kid, and others. I know a time when the Methodists were all of one soul, and of one sentiment. If we leave our first principles, I know not whither we shall go. I think it a dangerous thing to attempt to be wiser than what is handed to us in the good book.

Good Friday, April 1, 1825—I preached with much freedom in the Bowery Church. Many hearers, and we had a moving time. I felt much of the power of the Gospel and shed many tears.

Sunday 3—A very cold stormy day. I preached morning and evening on the resurrection of our blessed Lord. John 20, verse 17.

Tuesday 5—Sat to a portrait painter,[186] and preached in the evening on growing in grace. I begin to feel as if I want to leave the city. Our young friend Brown is about leaving the traveling ministry, and going to measuring Calico. Did the blessed God call him to be a minister? How has he disposed of the call? It is a very serious thing to trifle with the work of such magnitude. Did he run without being sent? Or has he fallen from God? I awfully fear. A call to the ministry is for life. I go to Rhinebeck. O blessed God go with us wherever we go. I have omitted keeping a daily or weekly journal for considerable time. I have not been unemployed. I have spent about half my time visiting churches, and the other part has been spent at home, and about Rhinebeck. I bless God for health, and for light and freedom in His word. I measureably see infinite perfections in the adorable Jesus, and I ardently desire to be his humble follower.

Sunday, November 27, 1825—I preached in Mission Chapel with a degree of liberty from Isaiah 41, verse 15. The congregation was attentive. I have been for a considerable time waiting, and praying for a revival of religion in this place.

Monday 28—My intention was to pay New York my fifth visit for the season; but news was brought of the death of our valuable friend, Mrs. Suckley, and that it was her wish to be buried at Rhinebeck, which prevented my departure for the city.

Tuesday 29—This is a day of solemnity—we are waiting to receive the remains of our deceased friend and the mourning family. About 10 o'clock at night they arrived, accompanied by Brothers Stead, Youngs, Roy, and several other friends. Our habitation is honored.

Wednesday 30—After the usual solemnities the funeral procession moved for the Methodist Church, and the place of interment about one. My nephew (F.G.) planned and directed the business and we had great order, and decorum. I shall touch a few particulars in this place. Mrs. Suckley, an old acquaintance, and relative of ours, was awakened and brought into Gospel liberty when in the bloom of youth, after the introduction of Methodism in Rhinebeck. She was sweetly drawn by the cords of love, and this was the prevailing passion of her heart. She was one of those, who in the Apostles sense of the word, thinketh no evil. Her soul was formed in the tenderest mold. She was a woman of prayer and *God* was in all her thoughts. Her communion with Jesus, was intimate, sweet, and constant. She respected the poor, and in her they have lost a friend. Her acts of charity were done in the most private manner, which might have led some to think she was not liberal. She was modest, humble, and unassuming. She was an affectionate wife, and a tender mother. Many prayers have gone up for her children. In her last sickness she said, "God has not shown me His will, whether life or death; but in his good time I shall know: I have much to live for; (here she had a reference to her children) but I cannot form one petition for life. I know it will be best for me to go." Her sufferings were great, but she said her peace flowed like a river. She has gone to rest.

Thursday, December 1, 1825—A little after sunset I stepped into the steamboat, and was in New York about daybreak.

Sunday 4—Having repaired to Brooklyn yesterday I had a good time this morning in the old church to a good congregation on Revelation 20, verses 11 and 12. I am now in retirement at Mr. Suckley's.

Tuesday evening preached at Duane Street Church—but few out—not much liberty; spent the night at Brother Chase's. I retired to my room and studies at Greenwich.

Friday—I have an appointment this evening in the Mission House—full congregation—we had an impressive time. I go into my room—I read, write, and pray. The dear children have lost a tender mother.

Sunday 11—By particular request, I am to preach Mrs. Suckley's funeral sermon. We had a large solemn assembly. Numbers 23: 10, "Let me die the death of the righteous, and let my last end be like his." The blessed God can accomplish his purposes: it appears that Balaam led contrary to his own inclination, by the good spirit to prophesy sweetly of the prosperity of the Israelites, and the coming of the Messiah. I applied the subject to the occasion: 1. In speaking of the experience. 2. The life, and 3. Of the death, and last end of the righteous. The soul of Mrs. Suckley was formed in a tender mold, and she was deep in piety, and she was a woman of prayer. Her charities were done in the most private and unexceptional manner. She was converted to God in early life, and became a member of the Methodist Church and continued a worthy member till she joined the Church Triumphant. She has left a husband, two sons, and three daughters to mourn their loss. O that they may obtain, and retain the life of love and be happy enough hereafter to meet her in glory.

Monday 12—I took my departure, and on Tuesday morning arrived at home[187] to join my family in the praises of the blessed God. The winter I spent in and about Rhinebeck except two short tours. The more I labor in the good cause the better I feel both in mind and body. Part of the winter I was afflicted with my old complaint, which was removed by the use of the Congress spring water. This water has a very salutary influence over my system. About eight years ago, I was restored from a very low debilitated estate, by a free use of it.

Tuesday, March 14, 1826—Accompanied by my wife, daughter,[188] and one servant, we took our departure for New York. We arrived safe, and I had great freedom in preaching the word. I am happy to find the Society in a prosperous state. I have seldom had better, or more free openings, both in preaching and visiting, in the city. We stayed mostly with our kind friends, the Suckleys and Few's. "O to grace how great a debtor. Daily I am constrained to be." One night I had a sweet heavenly vision and seemed to be taught some pure lessons, and I awoke from my reverie very happy in God. The Blessed Lord can teach his people by day or night by his word or spirit or by an intelligent messenger. The word is our rule, by which we must try every impression, or apparition, and the pure impress coincides with the written testimony. Many spirits have gone out into the world, and we are exhorted to try the spirits, whether they are of *God*. His written word is an infallible rule. O that the word of life may be the man of our Council.

After spending about three weeks in the city, I trust employed in doing good, and getting good. On Tuesday, April 4, we returned home and found our family in health.

Sunday 9—Preached in Rhinebeck Church morning, and afternoon with freedom.

Wednesday 12—I stepped into the steamboat a little before sunset, was in New York a little before six in the morning, and immediately stepped into the Jersey boat, and was in Philadelphia a little after sunset. 200 miles in 25 hours is expeditious traveling. We had about 25 miles land carriage, from Washington in Jersey to Bordentown where we took the boat again. The road was extremely rough, and the carriage very hard. We passed the seat of Joseph once appointed King of Spain by Napoleon his brother. He has a large pile of buildings, and a large deer park, his observatory, built something in the form of a steeple stands by the margin of the river. Naturally the land is poor. It will all do, if he can but get safe to heaven.

Brother and Sister Pease gave me a kind reception, and I am well suited to be with them.

Friday 14—This morning Conference opened. I am in retirement, and feel more comfortable in body, then I expected after such a journey. The blessed *God* is good to me, and I will praise him, and strive to live for valuable purposes. In the evening I heard one of the young brethren preach in the Academy Church from Hebrews 6, verses 17-19. I doubt not, but that if he is faithful to his call, he will make a useful man in the church of *God*. It would be well for public speakers to end their sentences in a tone of voice to be heard by the congregation, and also it is very desirable for the congregation to be able to hear the text, and the hymn, or Psalm. After the sermon we had a warm exhortation and prayer. I laid down, and slept in peace till I was awakened by the cry of fire; the light was such that I could almost see to read in my room. We are subject to afflications, and privations in this unstable world, where there is neither sickness or pain, and the gulf that waits the final apostate. I have just received a messenger, inviting me to take a seat in Conference. I have just sent a letter for my family to the post office.

Saturday 15—I spent the day mostly in retirement. I wrote to my good wife and daughter which I expect they will receive in three days.

Sunday 16—I see another blessed Sabbath. I heard a good discourse delivered by Bishop Soule[189] on II Corinthians 1, verse 20. For all the promises of God in him are yea and in him amen under the glory of God by us. His illustrations were: first, the promises, under particulars: 1. In Christ Jesus. 2. Universal. 3. Immutable. Second, to the glory of *God*. In regeneration, sactification, and final glory. Third, By us—the importance of the ministry. After which a number of good looking young men were set apart for the office of Deacons. In the evening the church was crowded. The blessed *God* was with me, whilst on the subject of Ezekiel's holy waters. Ezekiel 47, verses 1-6. I rest in peace.

Monday 17—I was requested to open Conference, after which about five hours were taken up in the trial of a young preacher, in consequence of a breach of promise of marriage, as represented by the young lady. It is a cruel thing for a person, especially a Methodist preacher, after gaining the affections of a female, to desert her, and especially to place his affections on another. "What is man?" Let our young men take warning from this circumstance. A Methodist preacher should never by look, word, or behavior attempt to gain the love of a lady unless he proposes to make her his wife—to do otherwise would be mean, and unmanly. This evening I attended the Missionary Meeting. We had five addresses which were very much to the purpose. I was both pleased and profited and I expect a very handsome sum was raised.

Tuesday 18—This day I spent partly in retirement and partly in visiting old friends and dined at Brother Cooks with several of the old preachers and several of the superintendents, and had a long conversation with Brother Soule concerning the Western Indians. He seems confirmed that they are descendants of the twelve tribes of Israel.

Wednesday 19—I set this day about five hours in Conference, and in the evening heard Brother W. deliver a warm, profitable sermon. I had a sweet night's repose.

Thursday 20—The Conference opened at 8 o'clock—we sat till 1 o'clock. I was really edified. We dined at Brother Commerges, and had a social time. In the evening I heard Brother Merwin[190] preach an excellent sermon from John 12, verse 46, "I am come a light into the world, etc." I can rest my head on my pillow in peace and can say good is the will of my holy Lord. I have not heard from my family since I left home.

Friday 21—Conference opened, and a very distressing case was brought forward; an old Elder was accused of transgression, and suspended from all official services till the ensuing Conference, which will give him a chance to try to clear himself. We dined today at Colonel North's. We had a loving social time, and I believe the blessed God is with (us).

Saturday 22—The Conference sat this morning and finished their session, and then it was to your tents O Israel. I was very much pleased with the good sense, and dispassion with which the business was conducted. The Brethren seemed to be in the spirit of the Gospel, and I hope the ensuing will be a successful year.

Lord's Day, April 23—I heard two good sermons in Union Church, and in the evening I preached with liberty in St. George's. I can say that during my stay in Philadelphia, my mind was calm and stayed on God.

Monday 24—I travelled by land, and water, to New York, and the next day I returned to my family and found them all in health. I want to have very little to do with the world. I never feel so well as when employed in the work of God in his vineyard.

Monday, May 8, 1826—I passed down the river to New York.

Wednesday the 10th—Conference opened and in a good measure we had an agreeable time—however there were some unpleasant things; but this I hope will be over-ruled for good. The preachers received their stations without a murmur at the close of the Conference. I was requested to preach my half Centennial sermon by a vote of the Conference; after which, I was requested by another vote to present a copy for publication.

Lord's Day, May 14—I preached in the morning in Second Street Church.

Friday 19—Conference rose. Our dear brethren seem much engaged in the work, and I can say that I have sweet fellowship with them, and they treat me as a father.

Lord's Day 21—Particular request from the people about the New Church came to me to preach for them in the morning, which I did with great freedom. This is a large handsome house lately finished in the east part of the city. God is working, and I hope he will work till the earth is filled with righteousness.

Monday 22—Bishop McKendree, and Bishop Hedding accompanied me to Rhinebeck, and after having several pleasant days together, they took their departure to go on their way to the Genesee Conference.

Sunday 28—I heard two sermons delivered by Brother B., our new preacher. Lord own his labors and his station, and let there be ingathering to the fold.

Sunday, June 5—I preached at Rhinebeck in Mission Chapel with some little freedom. We have some good members; but we want the holy oil.

Monday 6—As I was appointed by Conference on a committee to try the case of our unfortunate Brother E.S., and as my daughter wished to visit to Union College, we prepared for the excursion, and went on board the Richmond on Tuesday morning, and came to Dr. Notts in the evening where we were kindly received, after a tedious day.

Wednesday 8—I am presently situated, and feel a pleasure in retirement. God is good to me.

[Nathan Bang's *Life of the Rev. F. Garrettson* is the only extant source for the concluding year of Garrettson's life. It is included (p. 313-322) to complete the Garrettson story.]

At the conference of 1826 Mr. Garrettson was continued a conference missionary, and he employed his time in his usual way, making occasional excursions to New-York and some other places, preaching as often as his strength would permit him. Wherever he came he was hailed as a messenger of peace, and as a father in the gospel, both by the preachers and people.

It was in the beginning of the winter of this year that I accompanied him to the city of Hudson, on an invitation from the brethren in that place, for the purpose of opening a new church. Having attended at Poughkeepsie for the purpose of dedicating a church recently built in that place, I went on board the steam boat which came along about 12 o'clock at night. I shall never forget the tender and affectionate manner in which he received me. He was in his birth, but hearing my voice, he addressed me by name, raised himself in his birth, affectionately squeezed my hand, expressing his gladness to see me. Indeed he always seemed revived whenever he came in company with his brethren in the ministry, whom he loved, I believe, "with a pure heart fervently." I have mentioned this circumstance merely to show how sincerely he loved his friends, as well as the readiness with which he obeyed the calls of his brethren to aid them in their work.

It was during one of his visits to the city of New-York, this year, that he sent the letter to Mrs. Garrettson, the last she ever received from him, of which the following is an extract:—

"Yesterday I spent mostly in prayer and conversation; to-day in reading and this evening in writing. To-morrow I expect to be in the book room with the committee.

"I groan for perfect freedom. I have heard people talk of laying up a stock of grace; but, blessed and happy is that person who has a sufficiency from moment to moment, to keep him humble, innocent, and pure. We are every moment dependent upon God. I have no doubt but that retrospection on a long life spent in the service of God, with a continuance in piety, must be very consoling; but I know there is as great a necessity for watchfulness and perseverance as ever. The holy, blessed God knows our various weaknesses, and will in old age put beneath us his everlasting arms. O! to come near to the throne of grace, and touch the hem of his garment by faith, and have every stain washed away. O! to love God supremely."

In 1827 our conference convened at the city of Troy. He attended its sessions with his usual diligence, and among other things supported a resolution, that there should be preaching at five o'clock in the morning, and cheerfully filled the first appointment himself. At this conference he was elected again as a delegate to the ensuing general conference, which was to be held in Pittsburgh, Pa., May 1, 1828. He did not, however, live to see the conference.

Notwithstanding his age, I believe none acquainted with him, who observed his healthful appearance and activity, thought him so near his end. After the close of the conference he persevered with his accustomed zeal and diligence in the discharge of his various duties, visiting his old friends, and preaching once or twice every sabbath. But though his family and friends flattered themselves that he might yet be spared some years to the church, it appears that he had a presentiment that his departure was at hand, and would often speak of it. Whether this arose from any direct impression upon his mind, or from feeling the natural decays of age, or from an impression which he received some years since, I cannot tell. I, however, often heard him observe,—I think he made the remark to me for the first time in the year 1813,—that being unwell a short time previously, he was calling on God, if it might be his will, to prolong his days; when he received for answer, that *fifteen years should be added to his life;* but he observed, at the same time, that he could not satisfy himself whether it meant fifteen years from that time, or so many years beyond the usual term of human life, "threescore years and ten." From whatever cause the impression proceeded, the sequel proves that his presentiment at this time was correct.

On the 17th of August, 1827, after dining with his family with great cheerfulness, and commending them to God in prayer, Mr. Garrettson left home for the city of New-York. On his arrival in the city he preached his last sermon in the Duane-street church, on the words of St. Peter, "But grow in grace," and then administered the sacrament of the Lord's supper to a large number of communicants. It was remarked by some who were present on that occasion, that Mr. Garrettson preached with unusual warmth and energy, a Divine unction attending the word. Thus this venerable servant of God closed his public labours in pressing upon his brethren the necessity of going forward in the "work of faith and labour of love," and in participating with them in "drinking of the fruit of the vine," in anticipation of drinking it anew with them in the kingdom of God.

Soon after he was violently seized with a disease called the *strangury.* Dr. Mott, a surgeon of established reputation in the city of New-York, was immediately called; but though his applications afforded a temporary relief, the disease was so obstinately fixed as to resist the power of all attempts to arrest its progress. To Mrs. Garrettson and his daughter the mournful tidings of his illness were speedily conveyed, and they hastened to the city to comfort him, and if possible to administer relief. But the hand of death had arrested him. I was absent from the city at the time he was taken ill. On my return, hearing of his illness and the nature of his disorder, it immediately came to my mind that "this sickness was unto death." As soon as convenient I repaired to the chamber where he was confined, and had a long conversation with him. He seemed to entertain but slender hopes of recovery, and observed, that should the disease be so far removed as to permit him to live a little longer, he should be a prisoner all his days. Though on the first approach of the disease which was of a most painful character, he manifested some little restlessness, as if nature struggled involuntarily to free itself from suffering, he soon bowed in humble submission to the Divine will, and evinced an unshaken confidence in the mercy of God through our Lord Jesus Christ.

In the conversation to which I have alluded, he unbosomed himself with great freedom, rehearsed the goodness of God, which had been so abundantly manifested to him through every period of his life; at the same time, as was usual with him, expressed himself in terms of the deepest self abasement. At one time he would express his admiration of the perfections of God, as manifested in creation, and more especially in the grand system of redemption, and then cry out with holy rapture, "I am filled with the perfect love of God." With much feeling and emphasis he said, "My hope is all founded in the infinite merits of the Lord Jesus; in this hope I enjoy unspeakable consolation." In this way he lingered, sometimes suffering exquisitely, for about five weeks. He did, indeed, pass through the furnace, but he came forth not only unhurt, but abundantly refined; and he died as he had lived, a witness of *perfect love*. Redemption was the theme of his contemplation through his sickness. Toward the last he became eager to depart—to *go home*.

The following account of some of the last days of Mr. Garrettson is from the pen of Miss Mary R. Garrettson, in a letter to the Rev. Richard Reece of England:—

DEAR AND REV. SIR,—Another memento of your kindness most forcibly reminds us of our obligations, and of the duty of giving you the interesting particulars of my blessed father's last illness and death; a duty which has been long delayed, for as often as it impressed itself on my mind, a sense of my inadequacy to the subject, and the pressure of my heavy bereavement, has most forcibly withheld me from the attempt.

"For several months before his death, my dear father seemed to feel, in an unusual manner, the uncertainty of his own existence; and an impression of the shortness of his stay, made him rather reluctantly consent to an election for delegate to the general conference. Our presiding elder, Mr. Scofield, has since informed us, that during his last visit *here*, papa took him to a little retreat in the garden, where he spent many of his hours in devotion, and after conversing on the affairs of the church, (which ever lay near his heart,) with the spirit of one ready to depart and be with Christ, he said he should not probably live to see the next conference. They then kneeled down and prayed together, when the power and presence of God were felt, said Mr. Scofield, in a manner never to be forgotten by me.

"On Friday, the 17th of August, my dear father left us in usual health, expecting to spend the sabbath in New-York, and to return the ensuing

Monday or Tuesday. I can never forget the last day he spent at home:—a serenity and happiness marked his manner, and the purest love was reflected in all his actions. Our table was surrounded by friends. Some had recently arrived, and others were about to depart. A mingled sensation of pleasure at the coming, and regret at the parting guests, pervaded our minds;—but pleasure was predominant, for fancy painted futurity with the pencil of hope, and the regret we felt was just sufficient to soften her vivid colouring. But my dear father;—the heavenly expression of his countenance during that social meal I can never forget; and I find a mournful pleasure in recalling again and again the events of that last day of family enjoyment. After dinner we kneeled down, and he prayed with us in a manner unusually solemn, tender, and affecting. Almost every eye was suffused in tears:—we parted. The next sabbath was spent by him in the services of the sanctuary, in preaching and administering the sacrament. On Monday he underwent considerable fatigue, but spent the evening at Mr. Suckley's. He appeared to the family to be in unusual health and spirits, sat up beyond his customary hour, although it was his intention to take the six o'clock boat, and dine with us on the morrow. That night, however, he was seized with his last agonizing disorder, and after spending several days of intense pain and extreme danger, he consented to abandon the thought of returning home, and to send for mamma and me.

"On our arrival we were told that the crisis of his disorder had been favourably passed, and that, though lingering, there was every prospect of his ultimate recovery. But though we suffered our judgment to be led captive by our wishes even to the last, no hopes of that kind were implanted in his mind. I believe he knew and felt that his time of departure was at hand. His sufferings at times were unutterable; but through them all were manifested a resignation and fortitude which no agony could destroy. 'I shall be purified as by fire; I shall be made perfect through sufferings:—it is all right, all right; not a pain too much,' he would often say. Daily, and almost hourly, he was visited by some one or other of his brethren, who added much to his consolation during those seasons when the heart and the flesh fail, but when the religion of Christ is indescribably precious; (the recollection of their kind attentions will never pass from my mind;) and as he descended into the dark valley, his views of the grandeur and efficacy of the atonement became more and more enlarged. His disorder inclined him latterly to slumber, and he was often delirious; but even then the same subject was the theme of his discourse. Toward the last his strength was so much exhausted, that articulation became a painful effort; but he would often, in a languid feeble voice, say, 'I want to go home; I want to be with Jesus, I want to be with Jesus.' To a friend he said, a short time before his death, 'I feel the perfect love of God in my soul.' A day or two before his departure I heard him say, 'And I shall see Mr. Wesley too.' It appeared as if he was ruminating on the enjoyment of that world, upon the verge of which he then was:—enjoyments which he said a Christian could well understand, as they began in his heart before he was disembodied. His mind seemed employed with subjects for the sweetest feelings of love and adoration. When asked how he did, he would answer, 'I feel love and good will to all mankind,'—or, 'I see a beauty in all the works of God,'—forgetting that the infirmities of his body were the subject of the inquiry. He had resigned his wife and daughter into the hand of God, and so great was his desire to be with Christ, that parting with us was disarmed of its bitterness. His last sentence spoken, even in death was, 'Holy, holy, holy, Lord God Almighty! Hallelujah! Hallelujah!' After that, though he lingered many hours, he could not speak articulately. Once only, clasping his hands, and raising his eyes to heaven, he uttered, 'Glory! glory!' Many petitions were offered around his dying bed, that he might be permitted to give his last testimony, but they were not granted. For myself, I felt it was not necessary. A holy and laborious life of more than fifty-two years bore ample testimony to the triumph of his soul over its last enemy.

"Never can I hope to give you more than a faint idea of the solemn yet glorious hour when the spirit achieved *that* last victory, and was ushered into the joy of the Lord. Encircled by his kind and affectionate friends, by his brethren and his sons in the gospel, my venerable father lay apparently unconscious of every thing that surrounded him. We *felt truly* that he was only leaving the church militant to join the church trimuphant. Just as the period of his departure approached, one of the preachers broke forth into prayer;—prayer so elevated, so holy, that it seemed to wrap the hearers above all sublunary consideration, and as he commended the dying saint into the hands of God, he prayed that the mantle of the departing patriarch might rest on his surviving brethren. His prayer seemed answered;—a Divine influence pervaded the apartment;—two of the preachers almost sunk to the floor, under a glorious sense of His presence who filleth immensity. My dear mother, with clasped hands and streaming eyes, exclaimed, 'Yes, Lord! we give him up freely,—*freely* give him up to thee!'

"The spirit departed, leaving the body impressed with the sweetest expression of peace and tranquillity; an expression which it retained until the moment when it was shrowded from human observation. We could stand beside those dear remains, and imagine that their appearance of renewed youth and happiness was a pledge of that glorious resurrection, when death shall be swallowed up in victory, and the mortal put on immortality; and we could look on the grave as a sure and certain deposit, until that day when it shall give back its precious seed rejoicing."

Thus as a ripe shock of corn was he gathered into the garner of his God, in the 76th year of his age, and the 52d of his itinerant ministry. He ended his useful life and painful suffering at the house of his long tried friend, George Suckley, Esq., in the city of New-York, about 2 o'clock in the morning of the 26th of September 1827.

His remains were taken to Rhinebeck, his late residence, accompanied by his bereaved widow and daughter, the writer, and several of the preachers on the New-York station, Mr. Suckley, and other friends. These had the mournful pleasure of following the lifeless body into that friendly enclosure, which had so often been enlivened by his presence while living, and while entertaining his friends with gospel simplicity and hospitality, and placed in that mansion which had been dedicated to God, and where He had so frequently honoured his servant with his peaceful presence.

On Friday, the 28th, a numerous circle of family connexions, friends, and neighbours, who seemed deeply affected with their loss, were addressed at the house of the deceased by the Rev. Thomas Burch. Afterwards the procession, which was long and solemn, slowly moved to the burying ground at Rhinebeck Flats, a distance of about two miles, where the funeral service was performed by the writer, and the corpse was deposited in the earth, to sleep till "the resurrection of the just and unjust." A discourse was immediately delivered to a deeply affected audience, who evinced by their conduct their respect for departed worth.

The next sabbath his funeral sermon was preached on these words: "Mark the perfect man, and behold the upright, for the end of that man is peace."

The following inscription is on his tombstone:—

Sacred
to
the memory of the
Rev. Freeborn Garrettson,
an itinerant minister of the
Methodist Episcopal Church.
He commenced his itinerant ministry
in the year 1775.
In this work he continued until his death,
labouring with great diligence and success
in various parts of the
United States
and of
Nova Scotia
He died in peace in the city of
New-York
September 26, 1827,
in the 76th year of his age,
and 52d of his ministry.
"Mark the perfect man, and behold the upright, for the end
of that man is peace," Psalm xxxvi, 37.

PART II

NOTES

147. (Probably Philip Van Courtlandt, elder son of the Governor. Philip had served with distinction in the Revolution, and was a general in the state militia. Asbury's Journals, Vol. II, p. 62n.) My mind this day without deep exercises. My dear Lord did comfort me.

148. Pierre Van Courtlandt '1720-1814', frequently referred to as" Governor," was lieutanent governor of New York from 1777-1795. A member of a rich and prominent family, he lived at the Manor House near Croton, where he entertained Washington and his generals. Whitefield had preached at the Manor House. The house was open to the Methodist preachers and Van Courtlandt gave the land for the first meeting house at Croton and provided a tract for a camp meeting. He and his wife were active in the society but were not members . . ." Asbury's Journals, Vol. 1, p. 727n. Mrs. Garrettson's family, the Livingstons, were closely associated with the Van Courtlandts.)

149. This material is summarized in Bangs, "At this conference of 1791, the district over which Mr. Garrettson had presided with so much honour to himself and usefulness to others, was divided into two: the southern part, including Newburg, Wyoming, New York, New Rochelle and the Long Island circuits, was placed under the over-sight of the Rev. Robert Cloud; Dutchess, Columbia, New Britain, Cambridge, Albany, Saratoga, and Otsego, formed the district of Mr. Garrettson." Bangs, Nathan. The Life of Garrettson. p. 220.

150. ALBANY, N. Y.—Garrettson found a society flourishing here in 1789. He appointed James Campbell to serve there in 1790, and in 1791 Garrettson dedicated the First Methodist Church there on the corner of Pearl and Orange Streets. Albany became a separate station.

151. CANAAN AND CORNWALL, CONN.—These towns are located in western Connecticut near the New York State border. Asbury tells of visiting them in Garrettson's company on August 4, 1800. Asbury's Journal, Vol. II, p. 243.

152. This would indicate that the previous references to Brother A. are to Bishop Asbury.

153. THOMAS MORRELL was a prominent New York and New Jersey Methodist preacher. He was a frequent travelling companion to Bishop Asbury. He served as a line officer in the American Revolutionary army and was seriously wounded in the Battle of Long Island. It was his friendship with Washington which paved the way for an early meeting with the President to bring Methodist congratulations upon the founding of our nation. Morrell's labors took him up and down the eastern coast from New York-New Jersey to Charleston, S.C. He is reputed to have been the first Methodist preacher to have preached in Chatham, N.J.

154. ROBERT DILLON was under appointment as a missionary within the bounds of the New York Conference.

155. Apparently Lebanon Springs about eight miles west of Albany.

156. Continuing the material for the Journal under this day, that is, from Saturday September 24 through Sunday, November 1st is printed in Bangs, pages 224 through 226. There is a continuing fragment of this Journal but there seems to be no way to identify its month or year, however since it seems to be with the Journals for 1791 it is recorded there.

157. This appears to be a reference to his plans for marrying Catherine Livingston.

158. SING SING—Now the name given to a penitentiary at Ossining, New York, on the Hudson River; this was the area of an early settlement. From 1831 it enjoyed some fame as a camp meeting ground.

159. PITTSFIELD, MASS. Asbury described this place in 1792 as ". . . a pleasant plain, extending from mountain to mountain; the population may consist of two thousand

souls. There is a grand meeting house and steeple, both as white and glistening as Solomon's Temple . . ." *The Journal of Francis Asbury.*, Vol. I, p. 725.

Methodism was introduced in Pittsfield during 1790 by Samuel Smith and Thomas Everard.

160. WILLIAMSTOWN—This is the seat of Williams College. Asbury visiting there in 1805 described the place: "we came through Pownall in Vermont, to Williamstown, the seat of the college—containing two houses, one, probably sixty by forty feet; the other, one hundred by fifty feet, four stories, of brick . . . We came away to Lanesborough and onto Pittsfield." *Asbury's Journal*, Vol. II, p. 472.

161. Ash GROVE, NEW YORK—Phillip Embury left New York in 1770 and settled on a farm at Salem, Albany County, New York. He was buried at Ash Grove, later reinterred in Cambridge, N.Y.

162. SARATOGA CIRCUIT (N.Y.) was organized in 1791 with David Kendall as preacher. It was not until some years later that it became a station.

163. HUDSON, NEW YORK is located on the east bank of the Hudson River, about 15 miles below Coeyman's Patent. This town was a focal point of Garrettson's route up the Hudson Valley. Early services were held in a building on Cherry Lane, but a church was built in 1790 at North Third and Diamond Streets. *Records of The First Methodist Church, Hudson.*

164. *Rhinebeck, New York*—Garrettson first preached here in 1788 and was entertained by Mr. Tillotson. His wife was a Livingston and a sister to Mrs. Garrettson. The present Rhinebeck Methodist Church yard is the site of the Garrettson burials.

165. ROWES CHAPEL. This site was located about 12 miles from Garrettson's home in Rhinecliff. It was also known as Rose Chapel. It was erected by John Rowe at Milan, southeast of Hudson.

166. KINGSBRIDGE, NEW YORK, is the probable reference. It is located midway between New Rochelle and New York.

167. LEMUEL GREEN was born near Baltimore, Md. in 1751. He began preaching at age 30 and was admitted to the traveling connection with Jesse Lee and William Phoebus in 1783. He died in 1851. He was a member of Asbury's original council and served among other circuits as a presiding elder in Pennsylvania.

168. Another reference to his impending marriage. There was much opposition to this union on the part of the Livingston family.

169. CROTON, NEW YORK is located on the Hudson north of Tarrytown. The Van Courtlandt's estate is there and they were early benefactors to the Methodists.

170. COEYMAN'S PATENT was a small farming community about 12 miles south of Albany. Garrettson sent John Crawford there in 1789 to begin his work.

171. Cambridge, New York, was an early site of Methodist preaching with Lemuel Smith being assigned to the circuit in 1788.

172. *Bishop Richard Whatcoat* was born in England 1736, and was in class meeting with Asbury in their native land. He came to America with Thomas Coke in 1784 and was elected a bishop in 1800. He died on July 5, 1806 at Gov. Basset's home in Dover, Delaware.

173. *Billy Hibbard* (1771-1844) was born in Norwich, Connecticut, but raised at Hinsdale, Massachusetts. He was received on trial in 1798 and spent most of his ministry in upper New York State and in New England. He was rather eccentric, and was especially useful in difficult situations. He died at Canaan, New York. (Asbury's Journal II p. 353)

174. ELIPHALET NOTT (1773-1866)
President of Union College, Schenectady, New York, and long time friend of the Garrettson family.

175. *Troy, New York*. As early as 1793 there were a number of Methodists in Troy, and in 1795 it was made a part of the Cambridge, N. Y. circuit.

176. PEEKSKILL, N. Y. was named for an early Dutch explorer, Jans Peeke. Whitefield preached there in July, 1770. Garrettson formed a class in the home of Jonathan Ferris in 1788.

177. GEORGE SUCKLEY came to America with Thomas Coke and became one of the most prominent and wealthy citizens of New York City. He became an intimate friend of Freeborn Garrettson. He was a Vice President of the American Bible Society and a leading Methodist. Suckley's mansion in Rhinecliff, N. Y. is next to the Garrettson home. I visited his descendants there in the 1950's and toured the home. It was at the Suckley home in New York City that Garrettson died. Suckley died in New York City June 17, 1846. His wife, Catherine Rusten, of Rhinebeck was also an ardent Methodist. She was an intimate friend of Mrs. Garrettson. She died in 1826. Asbury was also a close friend to the Suckleys. He gave the portrait of his mother to them, and I discovered it in Rhinecliff. The portrait is now in the possession of Drew University.

178. *Norwalk, Conn.* heard its first Methodist sermon in 1787 by Cornelius Cook. For several years the society worshipped in a red school house near the crockery store of Nash Brothers on Main Street, corner of West. (Asbury's Journal 2—p. 344)

179. *Dr. Thomas Sargent* born in Frederick County, Md. in 1776. In 1795 he entered the traveling ministry, and died in Cincinnati in 1883. His appointments included New York, Boston, Philadelphia, and Baltimore. (Wakefield, p. 508)

180. BISHOP ELIJAH HEDDING was born near Pine Plains, New York; became a member of the New York Conference in 1801 and was elected Bishop in 1824. He was born in 1780 and died in 1852.

181. Mr. Jay—John Jay (1745-1829). Statesman and first Chief Justice of the U.S. Supreme Court. He was especially in his later years deeply concerned with religion. Garrettson and his family were frequent visitors in his home.

182. FREEBORN GARRETTSON, JR. has often been mistaken for Freeborn Garrettson's son. He was his nephew. As manager of his uncle's estate, he became closely identified with the Garrettson household and Rhinebeck. Freeborn, Jr. married Elizabeth H. Waters of Somerset County, Maryland, October 8, 1823. He together with his sons, Rusten, Richard G., Robert L., and Lytleton established themselves as a prominent family in Dutchess County, New York. He and his son Richard were members of the New York Assembly. The family home was for many years located at Clifton Point near Rhinebeck. Freeborn, Jr. died at Rhinebeck, November, 1866 at the age of 74. Another Freeborn, Jr., was a probationary Methodist preacher in 1794.

183. These lines are part of the third verse of Robert Robinson's hynm "Come, Thou Fount of Every Blessing." (No. 93 in the 1964 Methodist Hymnal). It was in the hymnal first introduced in 1820 for use by American Methodists. Garrettson quotes these lines three times in his Journal, the first time in 1779.

184. BROTHER HICKS (Paul) was a distinguished member of the Methodists in New York City from the beginning. He came from Ireland and was one of the original New York subscribers. In 1774 he married Hannah Dean. He worked closely with many of the clergy. He died on March 16, 1825. (*Wakefield* p. 542)

185. BROTHER CARPENTER (Thomas), another prominent New York layman, was born in Long Island in 1757 and became a Methodist at age 25. He served in the New York State Legislature, and was one of the first managers of the American Bible Society. He died in April, 1825. (*Wakefield* p. 547)

186. Probable reference to the portrait of Garrettson done by Paradise. A reproduction of this portrait appears as a frontpiece in this book.

187. THE GARRETTSON PROPERTY, Wildercliffe, was a part of the George Suckley estate. The Suckley property adjoining the Garrettson home was known as Wilderstein.

188. MARY RUTHERFORD GARRETTSON was born in 1794, the only child of Freeborn and Catherine Livingston Garrettson. She was handicapped from birth being dwarfed in stature. Mary was a close companion to her father and through her letters and published works we have some personal notes about his life. She was a generous benefactor to the Methodist Church. Personal research in Rhinebeck revealed stories about her which have lived on. One story tells of her practice of holding a fan in front of her face during the sermon. She cut holes in the fan in order to see the minister as

he preached, but she could not be seen. Before her death in 1879 she became blind, but she remained a person of culture and unusual benevolence.

189. BISHOP JOSHUA SOULE (1781-1867) Soule was born in Maine and joined the New England Conference in 1799. After serving in New York City and acting as Book Agent and Treasurer of the Board of Foreign Missions, he was elected Bishop in 1824. He served in the south and became an advocate of southern Methodism.

190. BROTHER MERWIN. This was Samuel Merwin whom Asbury praises for effective preaching in New Haven, Connecticut amongst students of Yale College. (*Asbury's Journal* Vol. II, p. 344).

APPENDICES

BIBLIOGRAPHY

INDEX

APPENDIX ONE

"Substance of the Semi-Centennial Sermon . . ." by Rev. Freeborn Garrettson, New York, *Bangs and Emory,* 1827, p. 8-39.

In prosecuting the intended discourse, I shall,

I. Give a sketch of the rise and progress of Methodism in the world; for we have gone forth weeping, sowing the precious seeds of gospel truth; and,

II. The consoling promise, "We shall come again with rejoicing, bringing our sheaves with us."

I. I am to give you a sketch of the rise and progress of Methodism in the world. I said a sketch; for a subject which has filled volumes, when confined to the narrow bounds of a sermon, can only be called a sketch.

I must begin with that burning and shining light, John Wesley, under God, the father and founder of that section of the Christian church to which we belong. He was born June 17, 1703, O. S.; received a liberal education, was ordained by Bishop Potter, September 19, 1725, and elected Fellow of Lincoln College, Oxford, March 17, 1726. The first years of his life were passed under the tuition of one of the best of mothers, who was, under God, capable of laying the foundation of his future usefulness. The venerable John Wesley was possessed of a sound judgment, great integrity, strong reasoning powers, refined morals, and fine taste. To the man of principle, he united the accomplished gentleman, and I am of opinion, that there was no other person in the world so well qualified in every respect for the great work he was called to accomplish.

Though Mr. Wesley was very useful at Oxford, his ardent desire to be more extensively employed in the promotion of religion, led him in early life to embark for America, to convert the Indians; although he tells us, that at that time he himself was unacquainted with justifying faith. During this voyage he became acquainted with some pious Moravian brethren, and he was convinced that they possessed consolations in religion, to which he was a stranger. His mind was uneasy, for he felt that he wanted something to make him happy.

After his return to England he visited Germany, and spent some time with the Moravian brethren at Hernhuth, where he was much pleased and blessed; and he brought with him to England some of their excellent rules.

The Moravians descended from the primitive apostolical church, and were never contaminated by the superstitions of the church of Rome, and if there is any regular succession from the apostles, I believe that the Moravians have it. I think I understand the meaning of our Lord when he breathed on his disciples, and said, "Receive ye the Holy Ghost; lo, I am with you always, even unto the end of the world." This is the gospel succession, and I have no doubt but that Mr. Wesley received that baptism of the Holy Spirit, for the work of the ministry, and began to preach salvation by faith, through the infinite merit of Jesus Christ. This succession was transmitted from our Lord through the apostles, and a line of faithful messengers sent of God, and reached him who was designed to be the apostle of the Methodists, and I trust there will be a series of pious, faithful ministers till the end of time.

This man of God, filled with the Holy Spirit, began to preach as he had never done before, and the blessed God poured out his Spirit on those who heard the word. Sinners were awakened and converted. The alarm was given, and persecution began. That sweet poet in Israel, Charles Wesley, caught the holy fire, joined heartily in the work, and was rendered a blessing to many.

At this time our apostle seemed to have no concerted plan; but awaited the openings of Providence. Many in London, who were awakened, and those who had received pardon, crowded round this man of God for instruction; he appointed to meet them of evenings, but he soon found that they multiplied so fast, that he could not fully accomplish his purpose alone; and here he was led to take down their names, divide them into classes according to their places of abode, and appoint to each class an experienced person, who was enjoined to meet them weekly, to inquire how they prospered, and to report the cases of the sick or the distressed to him: through the leaders he thus learned that state of the society. Such was the origin of class meetings, which have been kept up, and wonderfully prospered ever since.

It was not long before some of the brethren, like Eldad and Medad, began to prophesy in the camp; and indeed Thomas Maxfield was so filled with the Holy Spirit, and so divinely impressed, that he preached boldly in the name of the Lord, and God owned and blessed his labours in awakening and converting the souls of many. Mr. Charles Wesley being young in faith, accustomed to old established prejudices, and not fully baptized into the apostolic succession, was opposed to lay preaching; his brother John was at first doubtful, and thought to silence Maxfield; but meeting his mother, whose opinion he always reverenced, that blessed woman, the ornament of her sex, and the friend of lay preachers, said, "John, do you intend to stop Thomas Maxfield? I have heard him preach, and I as much believe he is called of God to preach as that you are." Mr. Wesley heard Maxfield preach, acquiesced in the order of God, took him by the hand, gave him license, and sent him on a circuit. This is the origin of lay preaching among the Methodists, and thus the Lord led his servant step by step, until the whole plan was completed. England, Ireland, Wales, and Scotland, lay very near the hearts of the two brothers, and indeed we may say the inhabitants of the United kingdoms were, as it regarded religion, in a very dead and careless state, and needed something out of the ordinary way to arouse them. The harvest was great, and the labourers comparatively few; but the Lord knew what was wanting, and how, and by whom, it was to be done, and he made bare his omnipotent arm, and called, and sent out many faithful heralds of the cross: circuits were formed, chapels were built in every direction, and sinners flocked to the gospel banner. Satan was disturbed, the wicked raged, and persecution was in some places violent: but thank God, in the midst of this raging of the devil, *He* stood by his children, and though they went forth mingling their tears with the sacred truths of the gospel, they were borne up by His mighty power, and frequently had soul-ravishing glimpses of glory, which encouraged them to go on in the blessed work.

In the midst of opposition, Wesley stood firm as a rock. Whitefield, who was his spiritual son, embraced the Calvinian doctrines, and in union with Lady Huntingdon, formed a connection distinct from the Wesleyan Methodist. Her Ladyship (I suppose under a sense of duty) issued a circular letter requesting all who were in her employ, to renounce such and such of Mr. Wesley's doctrines, or to leave it. That burning and shining light, John Fletcher, who was president of her college, wrote to her ladyship, that he had obeyed her order, to leave her house. All this the blessed God overruled for good; as it was the occasion of Mr. Fletcher's most invaluable writings. The Calvinian struggle arose to such a height against what they called Arminianism, that many of their clergy threatened to come in a body to the Methodist conference, and to insist on a recantation of some parts of the general minutes—but they forbore; nevertheless they spared no pains in sending forth their books and pamphlets in every direction.

Mr. Wesley and his faithful sons, like the flying angel spoken of in the Revelation, were going through the kingdom, with a loud voice, crying, Wo, wo, wo, to the sinful inhabitants of the earth.

Mr. Wesley was blessed with the gift of self government, and could comprehend and communicate much, either from the press or pulpit, in a short time, and withal he had that venerable man John Fletcher at his right hand, whose labours never can be too highly appreciated, and I firmly believe, that the scriptural arguments adduced by him and by others against the Calvinian system of infallible unconditional salvation, never have, and never will be refuted, and we bless God for such powerful supporters of the sacred truths of the gospel.

We have gone *forth*, and we have gone forth *weeping*, sowing precious seed. Should it be asked what kind of seed did Mr. Wesley and his preachers sow? I would refer you to his sermons, his Commentary on the Old and New Testaments, his work on Original Sin, and his Appeals to men of reason and religion. His opposers thought he laid too much stress on the faithfulness of man; but fidelity is good, and will expose no one to destruction, and no one ever preached salvation by faith through the infinite merit of Christ more clearly than he did: but if he, with all his piety and wisdom, could not reconcile the doctrines of unconditional decrees and infallible or unconditional perseverance, with the attributes of God and the freedom of a moral agent, is he to be blamed for rejecting them? He believed that Christ, agreeably to Scripture, tasted death for every man, and if any are lost, it will not be because there was no provision made for them, but because of their unfaithfulness. Saint Paul himself was not more clear on the essential doctrines of the gospel—the fall of man, salvation by faith, the trinity, the resurrection, and the general judgment. Why then was he so persecuted, and so shamefully abused, and that by many (I blush to say it) of the clergy? I can account for it only in one way—"the carnal mind is enmity to God." It is true, he believed in Christian perfection;—but it was not perfection in a higher degree than was inculcated by our blessed Lord in his own prayer, and in other parts of His word.

It seems that the design of the Almighty, in raising up that holy man, was, to reform fallen churches and wicked nations, and to spread scriptural holiness throughout the world. Great good has been done, but I trust it is only as a drop to the bucket when compared to what the rising generations will see. Asia and Africa, as well as Europe, will again be visited; thanks be to God, there are some beginnings already: but I must return to America, my native country.

Did Mr. Wesley's labours, direct or indirect, have any influence in America? In answering this question, permit me to take a survey of our toils, our sufferings, and our success.

At an early period Philip Embury, a local preacher from Ireland, came to this country, settled in New-York, began to preach, and formed a society in the year 1766. After awhile the society built a stone chapel in John-street, and wrote to Mr. Wesley for preachers. At this time captain Webb, a British officer, who had a military station in the city of Albany, visited New-York and several other places, and the people wondered much to see the pulpit occupied by a man in uniform. Sometime after this Mr. Strawbridge, a local preacher from Ireland, settled at a place called Pipe Creek, in Maryland, where he began to preach, formed a society, and built a log chapel: he afterwards travelled and preached considerably, and a holy unction followed the word.—When he came into my neighbourhood, I had one evening an interview with him, and after sitting and hearing his anecdotes and family discourse, I left the house with this sentiment—"I place this among the most agreeable evenings of my life." It was the first interview I ever had with a Methodist preacher—I was then seventeen years old. Mr. Williams also, another local preacher, came over, travelled largely, and spread many of Mr. Wesley's books, and a young man by the name of John King, an Englishman, began to preach, and the work of the Lord went on powerfully. Sinners fell under the word, and cried for mercy, while others shouted the praises of God. I began to think that this was carrying matters too far: however societies were formed, souls were converted, and some of the young converts began to speak in public;—Satan was enraged, and persecution commenced.

In the year 1769 Mr. Wesley granted the prayer of the society in New-York, and sent Messrs Boardman and Pilmore, who were the first regular preachers sent by Mr. Wesley to this country. Mr. Pilmore came to Maryland; I heard him, and was pleased, for I thought he was checking what I called enthusiasm. In the year 1771 Francis Asbury and Richard Wright arrived: I heard the former shortly after he came, and thought he told me all that was in my heart, and pointed me to Christ;—for it had pleased the Lord to awaken me about three months before, by means of a fall from a horse. They now began to spread themselves considerably. Boardman paid Boston a visit for a few months, and Pilmore went far to the south, and during the year spent some time in Norfolk, Virginia. Asbury also was busily employed. Messrs. Boardman and Pilmore were called home. But Messrs. Rankin and Shadford came to our help. A divine unction followed Mr. Shadford wherever he went, and he was the means of doing much good.

This year the first American conference was held, and Mr. Rankin, according to Mr. Wesley's appointment, was president. The first American preachers who went out to travel were Messrs. Watters, Drumgole, Ruff, Gatch, Duke, &c.

In the year 1775, Messrs. Dempster and Rodda were sent; but, dear men, they were not very successful. In this year a conference was held in Philadelphia. Daniel Ruff came from the conference to the vicinity in which I lived;—he found me in deep distress, for I was stripped of my own righteousness, and groaning for an interest in the blood of Christ; and it was not long before I received an evidence of my acceptance with the blessed God. I had been seeking religion for more than four years; but the greater part of that time I was resting in a sort of hope, unaccompanied by the evidence of justification, under the tuition of the parish episcopal minister, and very much inclined to the ministry in that church. I was moral, had a respect for religion, and frequently felt the drawings of the good Spirit; but I was a stranger to justifying faith.

It was some time in June 1775, about ten o'clock at night, when all alone, under deep distress of soul, I was enabled to take hold of the promises, and to centre my hope in Christ. The next morning, while alone in the field, praying and meditating, I had a sweet manifestation from God, attended with an impression to disseminate to all around the sacred word of God. I saw clearly that it is past the art of man to make a minister of Christ, and that at least two things are requisite; first a holy union with God; and, secondly, a ministerial baptism from Jesus Christ; and then we may receive his word, "Lo, I am with you," &c.

I began immediately to visit from house to house, and with many tears I testified of the goodness of God; appointed evening meetings in my own, and in other private houses. Under my first public discourse several were awakened, and the second time I opened my mouth to speak at one of my evening meetings, about twenty poor sinners were cut to the heart, and some fell to the floor, and cried for mercy. The power of the Lord was manifested, and he soon gave me a happy society in that place.

Persecution began;—I was beaten by an officer (my own cousin) the next morning, for spoiling his slaves, as he expressed himself; but the fact was, that they began to pray and sing hymns, and it was a terror to him. The Lord was with me, and he gave me a heart to pray for, and to shed many tears over him.

My old instructer, the minister of the parish, was very uneasy on my account; for he thought that I was in an extreme. I lived near the church; and one day, when the vestry and other officers met on church business, I chanced to be among them. After many interrogations from the minister, he said, Who authorized you to preach? and assured me that he would not allow it in his parish, unless I first went home (meaning to England) and took the gown. After a long debate before the vestry, he requested me to explain those words of our Lord, "Ye must be born again." My license was verbal. My Saviour was with me, and opened my way, although I was a little child. I rose up, and with freedom pointed out the necessity, nature, and effects of the new birth. Such was the occasion of my first sermon, and on finishing, the minister replied, Well, sir, and a very correct discourse you have committed to memory, &c. The vestry was dismissed, and we retired.

I met Mr. Rodda at Joseph Dallams, and told him that I had an appointment, and requested him to attend it, which he did. After sermon, I begged the society to stop, and told him there was a people prepared for him, and if he would take charge of them, I should be thankful; to which he assented, and I formally committed them to his care. I dearly loved the Methodists, but was afraid to join them, for I greatly dreaded becoming an itinerant minister. I can only give a brief sketch of what I passed through during the following eight or nine months. I retired with my Bible, as my companion. I suffered many privations and sore conflicts, which I afterwards saw were owing to my not cordially acquiescing in the designs and providences of God. What I endured can be known only to God and my own heart.

In May 1776, a conference was to be held in Baltimore, and with humble resignation to what I believed to be the will of God, I repaired to the place, made an offering of myself and of my services to the itinerant cause, passed through an examination before the little conference, was accepted, received a license from Mr. Rankin, and was sent out on the Frederick circuit.

This year there were five American preachers, who acted as assistants, and four of the English preachers, besides a number of probationers, who served as helpers. We were humble, and lived near to the Lord, and he greatly prospered his work. Three or four months of this year, I spent in forming what was called Berkley circuit in Virginia.

In May 1777, though the revolutionary war occasioned great heat, we all assembled at the Deer creek chapel in Maryland, to hold our conference. The English preachers expected that this would be their last meeting with their American brethren, as they intended returning to their native country. At this time we were a religious society, and a supplement to the church to which we had formerly belonged. In conference the question was asked, I think by Mr. Rankin, Shall we administer the ordinances? The question was debated, and a decision was suspended until the next conference, which was appointed to be held the following May in Leesburg, Virginia. I shall never forget the parting prayer put up by that dear servant of God, George Shadford; for surely the place was shaken with the power of God. We parted, bathed in tears, to meet no more in this world. I wish I could depict to the present generation of preachers, the state of our young and prospering society. We had gospel simplicity, and our hearts were united to Jesus, and to each other. We were persecuted, and at times buffeted; but we took our lives in our hands, and went to our different appointments, weeping and sowing our precious seed, and the Lord owned and blessed his work. My lot, for the first six months, was cast in Brunswick circuit, Virginia; after which I went to North Carolina, where there was a blessed work of sanctification, and many of us caught the holy flame. From east, west, north, and south, I heard that the blessed work was progressing, and greatly prospering.

May 19, 1778, conference met according to appointment. All our English brethren were gone, except Mr. Asbury, and he had retired to Judge White's, in Delaware state, William Watters, the oldest American preacher, was chosen chairman: every thing went on well;—we were humble, simple, and affectionate; embracing each other with tears of joy. The question debated at the Deer-creek conference was resumed,—shall we administer the ordinances?—in amount, shall we become an independent church? It was again laid over till the next conference, which was appointed to be held at the Broken-Back Church, in Fluvanna county, Virginia. At this time there were two circuits in the peninsula, to one of which John Littlejohn and John Cooper were sent, and Joseph Hartley and myself were appointed to the other.

Political troubles were very great; the Methodists were a small and despised people; and the wicked, as a pretext for their base conduct, falsely branded them with the name of tories. John Cooper was sick, and unable to preach; Littlejohn, under persecution, returned to Virginia; and the court prohibited Hartley from preaching. However he went about, and prayed with the people, and some of them said he preached on his knees. I was advised to retire, which I did for two days; but I was pressed in spirit, and came out, determined, whether for life or death, to go forth in the name of the Lord. I formed a circuit, to comprehend as nearly as possible the whole work; and though buffeted and abused, the Lord was with me.

My field of labour for more than two years was in the peninsula, a tract of land lying between the Chesapeak and Delaware bays, including the state of Delaware, eight counties of Maryland, and two of Virginia; a fertile, rich, and thickly inhabited country, immersed in luxury and pride, and supported by the toil of slavery. For a time I stood very much alone, but I was young, inured to hardship, and able to travel from twenty to forty miles, and to preach from one to four sermons a day. I never expect to be in such a field of labour again, though I would gladly go many thousand miles to get into one like it; for sinners were crying for mercy on every hand, and large societies were formed.

I was pursued by the wicked, knocked down, and left almost dead on the highway; my face scarred and bleeding. This was humiliating to me, but it was loud preaching to the people. I did not court persecution, but I gloried in the cross of Christ my Lord. Towards the latter end of this year we began to have considerable assistance. Brother Asbury (whom I sometimes visited in his retirement) preached in the neighborhood to which he had been confined, and the Lord thrust out several labourers into his vineyard, among whom was Philip Cox, a zealous and useful preacher. Brother Hartley had his bands loosed, and the Lord was with him. Soon after his enemies caught him again, and cast him in Talbot jail, but did not confine him long; for they feared that if he continued in prison, he would convert the whole town and country, so amazingly did the people crowd around his prison; and even the magistrate who committed him, when he was taken very ill, sent for Mr. Hartley from the prison to pray for him, and sometime before he died, gave him a charge concerning his family, and requested his wife and children to embrace Methodism; "for," said he, "they are in the right way; and even when I put Mr. Hartley in jail, my conscience told me I was doing wrong." A little after this they imprisoned me in Cambridge, but after detaining me about sixteen days, they willingly released me; for I suppose my imprisonment was the means of my doing more good in those few days, than I otherwise should have done in treble the time. The whole country seemed ripe to the harvest. The people flocked from every quarter to hear the word. Good brother Pedicord came from the Western Shore to help us in Dorchester, and was met on the road by a Mr. _____, one of my adversaries, who, when he discovered him to be a Methodist preacher, beat him until the blood ran down his face. He went to the house of a friend, and while they were washing his stripes, the brother of the persecutor rode up, and understanding that the preacher had been wounded by his brother, he said, "I will go after him, and chastise him." So saying, he galloped away, overtook and beat him, until he promised never to meddle with another Methodist preacher.

My manner was, when the circuits could be supplied, to go out and form new ones; and amidst the clash of war, God in a glorious manner prospered his work in the awakening and converting thousands of souls; so that in process of time the peninsula became comparatively as the garden of Eden, and the Lord thrust out many faithful, zealous, and useful young men. There was a blessed work among the African slaves; and in no part of my labours have I had more precious seasons, than I had in preaching to them. But they have been injured by being induced to become independent of us; and I think if I was now young, I should labour hard to bring them into the place which they once occupied; for I am convinced that those of them who have kept under the old itinerant system of doctrines and discipline, prosper more than those who have gone to themselves.

May 1779, the regular conference was held, according to appointment, in the Broken-Back Church, Fluvanna county, Virginia. The same question was asked, Shall we administer the ordinances? It was answered in the affirmative; and they set apart some of their oldest preachers to administer the sacraments. The troubles were such, that we to the north did not attend.

The next conference was appointed to be held at Manican town, Virginia, May 1780. Prior to this conference, we northern preachers thought it expedient, for our own convenience, to hold one in Baltimore; and we appointed F. Asbury, W. Watters, and F. Garrettson, as delegates to the Virginia conference, to bring them back if possible to our original usages. The proposition we made, was for them to suspend the administration of the ordinances for one year; in the mean while we would consult Mr. Wesley, and on the following May we would have a union conference in Baltimore, and abide by his judgment. To this proposal they unanimously agreed; and a circumstantial letter (indited by brother J. Dickens) was sent to Mr. Wesley.

May 1781, according to appointment we met, and received Mr. Wesley's answer; which was to continue on the old plan until farther direction. We unanimously agreed to follow his counsel, and went on harmoniously. I do not think that Mr. Drew in several particulars did justice to our *American* brethren; for he represents them as very refractory, and suppose that Mr. Asbury had a great deal of trouble with them; when the fact was that they were going forth in the power of the Spirit, disseminating gospel truth, and suffering much persecution, and many privations, while Mr. Asbury had a quiet retreat at Judge White's, in the state of Delaware, and that, during the hotest time of our conflict. It is true, our southern brethren (to satisfy the people and their own consciences) did administer the ordinances, and that, as they thought, in an extreme case. The leading members of the Fluvanna Conference were our good brothers Dickens, Gatch, Yeargan, Poytress, Ellis, Tatum, &c, &c; all faithful, pious, zealous men of God, who would do credit to any connection; and I admired their goodness in cordially agreeing to consult Mr. Wesley, and follow his judgment, and till that time to suspend the administration of the ordinances. If I am prolix on this part of the subject, it is to show that our Virginia brethren were undeservedly accused of schism.

Union is sweet, and we were now united under the direction of Mr. Wesley, and received Mr. Asbury as his general assistant. My conference appointment this year was in Sussex circuit: however it was so ordered, that I travelled at large, by special direction, in Virginia and North Carolina until the spring, when Mr. Asbury unexpectedly came to Virginia, and I gave up my charge to him, and formed one new circuit before conference.

Cornwallis was very troublesome in his marches through Virginia and Carolina; but in the midst of war, commotion, and persecution, we had great peace and prosperity in the church, and we thought not even our lives dear, so we could accomplish the great work of spreading the gospel through every part of the continent; and, blessed be God, he was with us, and the word ran through many parts, like fire in a dry stubble. The Carolinas, Virginia, Maryland, Pennsylvania, New Jersey, and some parts of New-York, shared in the blessed work; for while we were traversing the wilds of our afflicted country, mingling our tears with the gospel word, thousands were brought to taste the sweets of religion.

In the year 1784 the joyful news of peace saluted our ears; and in the autumn I had the pleasure of meeting our European brethren at Dover, in Delaware. Dear Mr. Wesley had an eye for good on his American children, and availed himself of the earliest opportunity to send us Dr. Coke, Richard Whatcoat, and Thomas Vasey, clothed with ecclesiastical powers, to constitute the American Methodists an independent episcopal church. We sent out heralds, and summoned the preachers from every direction to meet in Baltimore; and this we called our *Christmas conference*; at which time the organization of our church took place. Many of our oldest preachers were ordained, and Mr. Asbury was set apart a joint superintendent with Dr. Coke; and their names so appeared on the minutes of conference, according to the order and appointment of Mr. Wesley.

From this conference my lot was cast in Nova Scotia; and about the 10th of February, 1785, I landed in Halifax, accompanied by James Cromwell. After obtaining a small establishment in the city, I began to visit the towns, and to traverse the mountains and valleys, frequently on foot, with my knapsack at my back, up and down Indian paths in the wilderness, when it was not expedient to take a horse; and I had often to wade through morasses, half leg deep in mud and water, and frequently had to satisfy my hunger with a piece of bread and pork from my knapsack, to quench my thirst from a brook, and rest my weary limbs on the leaves of trees. This was indeed going forth weeping; but thanks be to God he compensated me for all my toil, for many precious souls were awakened and converted to God. John and James Mann, William Black, and another young preacher, united with us; we formed a little conference, and our hearts were sweetly joined. I expected only to have remained one year in this country, but I staid double that period, and my attachment was such, that the time did not seem to hang heavy on my hands. However for certain reasons Mr. Wesley requested me to repair to the Baltimore conference; so I bid my friends farewell, leaving about five or six hundred in society, and when I came to the States I was happy to find the work prospering gloriously.

The above mentioned conference began about the 10th of May. Dr. Coke had just arrived from England, with directions of considerable importance from Mr. Wesley; which caused much agitation in our conference. The business was, Mr. Wesley had appointed R. Whatcoat and F. Garrettson to be consecrated for the superintendency; the former as joint superintendent with Mr. Asbury in the States; the latter to have charge of the societies in the British dominions in America. The fears arising in the minds of many of the members of this conference, lest Mr. Wesley should recall Mr. Asbury, was the cause of R. Whatcoat's appointment being rejected. Jesse Lee, in his History of the Methodists, has given a detail of this matter; but as it respects my case he was incorrect; and therefore I think it my duty to give a fair and candid statement of it in this place. My appointment was brought before the conference, and was unanimously sanctioned. Dr. Coke, as Mr. Wesley's delegate and representative, asked me if I would accept the appointment? I asked the liberty of deferring my answer until the next day. I think on the next day the doctor came to my room, and asked me if I had made up my mind to accept the appointment? I told him I had upon certain conditions. I observed to him, that I was willing to go on a tour, and visit those parts to which I was appointed, for one year, and if there was a cordiality in the appointment with those to whom I was sent to serve, I would return to the next conference, and receive ordination for the office of superintendent. His reply was, "I am perfectly satisfied;" and he gave me a recommendatory letter to the brethren in the West India islands, &c. I had intended, as soon as conference rose, to pursue my voyage to the West India islands; to visit Newfoundland and Nova Scotia, and in the spring to return. What transpired in the conference during my absence, I know not; but I was astonished when the appointments were read, to hear my name mentioned to preside in the peninsula. Among many agreeable things, which happened at this conference, there were some things very disagreeable. I am not worthy to class myself with such a great and good man as Dr. Coke. I knew his value; and at this conference we mingled the tears of joy and of sorrow; for the rejection of Mr. Wesley's appointments, and the loss of his name from our minutes, gave us great pain. After Dr. Coke returned to England, I received a letter from dear Mr. Wesley, in which he spoke his mind freely. Mr. Wesley was dissatisfied with three things; first, the rejection of his appointments; secondly, our substituting the word Bishop for superintendent; and, thirdly, dropping his name from our minutes.

I went to my appointment, in some sense, I may say, with a sorrowful heart; but it was in a part of the country where I had spent many of my younger days in sowing the first seeds of Methodism; where I had suffered beating and imprisonment; but now all was peace and tranquillity, and we were now in more danger from the caresses of the people, than formerly from their stripes. I spent about twelve months in the peninsula, during which time I visited every circuit, and almost every congregation in it, and we had glorious times indeed; but I received a letter from Mr. Asbury, informing me that a suitable person must take my place, and I must go as soon as possible to Boston and its vicinity, and begin to sow some good seed in New England. A suitable person presented, to whom I gave my place, and as soon as possible I sat out, and came to New-York, where I found W. Hickson, a fine young man who was stationed there, at the point of death, and brother Dickens, the other stationed preacher, in ill health. I was solicited to go no farther till after conference, but to stay, and take charge of the society, which I consented to do.

Conference commenced—many petitions for preachers were sent in from new places; and it had pleased the Lord to thrust out an unusual number of young men in the New-York conference, more than we had regular places for; and our venerable father Asbury requested me to take charge of them, and to do the best I could. I was very uneasy in my mind, being unacquainted with the country, and an entire stranger to its inhabitants, there being no Methodist society higher than West Chester; but I gave myself to earnest prayer for direction. I know that the Lord was with me. In the night season, in a dream, it seemed as if the whole country up the North River, as far as Lake Champlain, east and west, was open to my view.

After the conference rose, I requested the young men to meet me; and light seemed so reflected on my path, that I gave them directions where to begin, and which way to form their circuits. I also appointed the time for each quarterly meeting, requested them to make a collection at every place where they preached, and told them that I should go up the North River to the extreme parts of the work, visiting the towns and cities on my way, and in my return I should visit them all, and hold their quarterly meetings; and I felt no doubt but that the Lord would do wonders, for the young men were pious, zealous, and laborious.

Accordingly on my return I found my expectation fully answered; for the Lord was with them, and began a good work in every place. Their little salaries were nearly made up the first quarter, and before winter they all had comfortable circuits. One circumstance I shall not soon forget:—as I passed down, a gentleman overtook me, and after the usual salutation, asked if I had heard the news?—"I understand," said he, "that the king of England has sent over to this country a great many ministers, to disaffect the people; he intends to bring on another war, and I fear it is too true," said he, "for as I have come down from Lake Champlain, I hear of them every where, preaching night and day, and I hear they have many followers." I told him that I could explain that subject to him;—that I was one of the men, &c, &c. After some conversation, he seemed satisfied, and much affected.

We mingled many tears with our precious seed in the formation of the New-York Conference, and I may say we laboured faithfully night and day, and blessed be God, we saw the rising glory of the church. In one of my tours to Boston, Rhode Island, and part of Connecticut, I was greatly rejoiced to meet my old friend Jesse Lee, who had come up to the help of the Lord. We travelled some time together, and it was agreed on that he should take charge of the eastern States. I used to call him the apostle of New England. Although the preachers in the eastern States had many deep rooted prejudices to contend with, the Lord opened their way. Great good was done; and I should not be surprised if New England should become the richest soil in the Union for Methodism.

While we to the north and east were forming circuits, districts, and conferences, our brethren to the west, and far to the south, likewise were sowing their precious seed. Oh who would not toil and labour in so glorious a cause. But we must enter on the second part of our subject.

II. We shall come again with rejoicing, bringing our sheaves with us.

When all the faithful ministers and their spiritual children are brought home to heaven, what a time of rejoicing there will be! Friends will meet to part no more, and all sorrow and tears will be for ever wiped away. I am reminded of a pleasing occurrence. —As I was passing by a cottage, a woman came out, and asked me if I knew her. I answered in the negative. "I am the woman," said she, "whose child you baptized at such a time, and you laid me under a promise to keep the covenant. I went home under deep conviction, and rested not till I found peace to my soul, and now I am happy in the Lord." Many of our precious sheaves will be brought home, with whom we were not acquainted on earth; and this should encourage us to a faithful discharge of our duty knowing that we shall no more lose our reward, than does a laborious husbandman, who after hard toiling, has in the time of harvest a copious crop to gather into his garner; and a wise husbandman will use every prudent precaution to secure his crop against the depredations of enemies.

I am free to say that we have prospects of a glorious harvest; and I am persuaded in my own mind, that if the Methodists should not continue in union and prosperity, it will be owing to a want of one or all of three things;—genuine piety, wisdom, and fidelity. It was predicted in England, that after the death of Mr. Wesley his people would divide and crumble away. This might have been the case without piety to support the Christian and ministerial character, wisdom in laying just and equal plans for the present and future generations of the church, and fidelity in the exercise or execution of those just and wholesome regulations.

The inquiry both in England and America was, who will be Mr. Wesley's successor? and on this subject various conjectures were formed. Under God Wesley was the father of the people called Methodists, and if any man on earth could claim the power he exercised, he certainly was the only one. He had a deeply rooted piety, and an unshaken faith; which in the midst of his great prosperity, kept him at the feet of Jesus: and he had the wisdom to devise a plan of settlement on one hundred of the veteran ministers who were to stand in his place, after it should please the Lord to call his servant home; and that number were to be perpetuated as the Methodist conference; and he had the firmness to prosecute the excellent plan. It is a blessed thing to build with good materials on a sure foundation.

We will now inquire into the use his European sons made of the treasure he bequeathed them in his last will and testament. Did they divide and crumble away, as was predicted? No:—What did they do? They met as brethren on the floor of conference, with equal rights and power, except the deference which age and merit called for. A president or chairman, and a secretary were elected, and they began their business like a band of brothers.

In looking over the minutes of their conference, I was pleased to see that there have been very few re-elected to the chair; and not more than one instance of the same person being re-elected more than thrice, in the course of more than thirty years. I saw, or at least I thought I saw, that they were brethren not aspiring after the upper seat, and that they were not at a loss for suitable men to fill that high office.

It may not be necessary for me, in this discourse, to give a particular account of the government formed by our transatlantic brethren, since the death of our venerable founder, as ample information on that subject can be had from Crowther's Portraiture of Methodism, and the Minutes of the English conferences. However, suffice it for me to say, that it appears evident that they have laid their plans in wisdom and piety, and have been going on ever since his death with increasing prosperity, in spreading the conquests of the gospel, and gathering many precious sheaves to the garner of God.

I bless God for an impartial and strong attachment to the cause of religion on both shores of the Atlantic; for we are one in sentiment and design; and it has been my sincere desire, that we should be so closely united, as to have a change of ministers, as I supposed the advantage would be reciprocal. We are not only one in religion, but we are also one in language; and I doubt not but that our heavenly Father designs still to carry on a great work through our instrumentality. Europe, Asia, Africa, America, and the isles of the sea, are before the harbingers of grace. Oh that there may be a blessed union in gathering in the great harvest of our Lord.

Our charge in America is very great: we have seventeen annual conferences, and a delegated general conference once in four years: we have in connection six or seven thousand ministers and preachers, local and itinerant, and nearly four hundred thousand in membership. To preserve such a body in union and spiritual prosperity, will require all the graces and gifts which we can possibly attain, and we need more than human wisdom. If we want to have the pleasure of gathering in millions of sheaves to the garner of God, in the present, and in future generations, our plans must be laid with wisdom and piety, which will centre in union and prosperity. We have been gathered into church fellowship from associations of various descriptions of people, who all possessed their own modes, sentiments, and prejudices; but these should be tested by the sacred truths of God's word, to which they should implicitly yield.

With regard to the usages of the church, St. Paul has given us most excellent directions. "Whereunto ye have already attained, let us walk by the same rule, let us mind the same thing." It is necessary that a church should have standards or way-marks, and that we should in this way transmit our doctrines and usages of the generations following. It appears to me, that if an attempt were made to remove or alter any of them, there would be an immediate whisper, "Stop! put off your shoes, you are on holy ground."

With regard to the Lord's prayer, and all our sacramental and other established forms, to be consistent with ourselves, we should make a regular use of them in all our churches and congregations; and I am happy to find that in many places there is an increasing attention to those sacred usages.

But I have been astonished to see some of our brethren in the ministry, especially the young, laying aside such beautiful and expressive compositions, and marrying, baptizing, and even administering the Lord's supper, extemporaneously. I am sorry to lose a single sentence or even word of our sacramental forms. To be a lovely people, a prosperous people, a united people, a people gathering in an abundant harvest, we must be a holy, inoffensive people, following all the usages of the church, as transmitted to us by the venerable Mr. Wesley. I say Mr. Wesley; for we all know that the Bible was his standard.

The world is good in its place, and riches are good when made a good use of. Formerly in this country we had but few churches, and our preachers were generally single men, who required but little; and it was not an uncommon occurrence in those days for the preachers to say in their zeal, "We have come for your souls, and do not want your money." But the case is greatly altered; for now we have many churches, and we want many more. We have many ministers, and many of them have large families. They cannot take proper care of the Lord's vineyard, and labour with their own hands to support their wives and children. Observe, it is one thing for a minister to preach for money, and make that his object; and it is another thing for him to receive a sufficiency, to enable him to go forth, and preach for souls. The ministers of Christ, those whom he has called and sent, should be decently supported, or their hands will hang down, the work will be retarded, and they will not, as otherwise they would, return with rejoicing, bringing their sheaves with them. Indeed the want of a competent support has been the pretext for many locations. I say again, if the ministers of Jesus Christ are not supported, and if on that account the work of God should be retarded, a very heavy responsibility will lie some where; and as it is a matter of considerable magnitude, it must be inquire

I think our venerable friend, Richard Reece, told me, that he thought the Methodists in this country were, in the aggregate, nearly as wealthy as those in the old connection; and records show that we are the most numerous. Why then cannot we support our ministers as amply as they do? The answer would be, We either have less religion, or our system is not as well digested as theirs. Their yearly collection for conference contingencies, including the book room revenue, is not less than $60,000. Besides this, they support Kingswood and Wood-House Grove schools, in which the preachers' children are educated; and raise annually nearly $200,000 for missionary purposes. They have, it seems, an ample supply for every necessary case.

Many years ago there was a proposal among us, to get up a chartered fund. One of our oldest ministers was opposed to it, as he thought he could suggest a plan which would be abundantly more productive, viz. a yearly subscription through all the societies, with an offer to every member. However the rejection of his plan did not prevent him from entering his name among the highest subscribers to the fund; for it was always his mind, for peace sake, calmly to submit to the order and suffrage of the body, and to labour to do good according to the openings of Providence.

For instance, suppose we have 300,000 members in our society, who would be able to contribute something, say a cent a week, here you have at once $150,000 a year, which will average about 8 or $9000 to each annual conference. This would set us perfectly afloat, and we should have money in hand to assist in extreme cases. Our chartered fund does not produce annually much more than one dollar apiece for the travelling preachers. Now you have the best of it—the worst will follow. I myself, as well as others, have heard conversations about this fund. One gentleman said, "How are the Methodist clergy supported?" "Oh," replied another, standing by, "they have an immense fund, and when they go to conference they draw their salaries from it." Even some of our own people do not know much better; and I have supposed such an idea has, in some measure, lessened the quarterly and yearly collections, at least in some places.

This plan is practicable. Even those who go out to service could do it in this country without injury to themselves; yea, even a slave who has a good master could do it; and if all the members did not comply, others would double and treble it. This recalls to my recollection two things:—Mr. Wesley wanted to raise some money on some emergency in London, and one of his friends proposed that each member should give a penny a week; "and," said he, put twelve of the poorest members with me, and what they cannot do, I will do for them."

Dear Mr. Asbury used to carry a mite subscription paper, and at the house of one of his old friends he presented the paper. The friend handed him a bill. "I do not," said Mr. Asbury, "take more than one dollar from any one person." Said the brother, "If that is your rule, I will give you as many names as there are dollars." Every person who has a spark of love for the cause of God, whether he be a church member or not, should give something towards supporting that cause; even those who are maintained by charity, should give something out of that charity. I have been astonished to see some of our constant hearers, and people, too, that appear clever and friendly, who seldom, if ever, reach out a helping hand. If I could not labour in the harvest field myself, I would render assistance to those who can, and are labouring hard night and day in gathering in the sheaves; especially if I had the smallest desire to profit by their labour. I should always wish to see the church of God as neat and as well finished as my own parlour, and her ministers provided for. Never hold the ministers of Christ in the light of beggars, while it is written, "The labourer is worthy of his (reward) hire;" and "Thou shalt not muzzle the mouth of the ox that treadeth out the corn." A minister of Christ is as much entitled to a living as any man.

I must touch on another particular, which I conceive to be allied to my subject; and that is, the employing labourers in this great harvest. Comparatively there are few who in every sense are qualified for the work; but thanks be to God, weak and unworthy as we have been, and still are, God has owned our feeble endeavours, and we will, God being our helper, strive to do better. Among the ministers of Christ there are various descriptions of men; some of them are very learned, and others not very learned. Some of them are sons of consolation, with systematic discourses, a pleasant cadence, and a musical voice: and others are sons of thunder, as a Bunyan, an Abbot, and an Everett. There is a perfect variety in the creation; and no two preachers are precisely alike in gift and manner; and I have seen the wisdom of God in such a diversity of gifts, especially among us, where there is such a continual changing, for all may be suited and profited. We sometimes say, he is the greatest preacher who does the most good, and this will not be fully known before the harvest is all gathered home.

A great point is gained in the proper selection of labourers for our Lord's harvest. When our blessed Lord was choosing his disciples, he did not take them from among the doctors and lawyers, and yet I have no doubt but that he chose men of a sound, intelligent mind; men of integrity and of diligence; men who bore a good character among those without. He called and qualified them for the great work. No graceless or unregenerated man is fit for the ministry; and not every religious man; nay, you may add learning to his piety, and yet find him destitute of the necessary requisitions. Pious men may suppose they are called to preach, and may be mistaken; and should they, under such circumstances, undertake the work of the ministry, in all probability they would do no good. If God were to call a man to the sacred office, and he were to reject the call, he would hardly get to heaven.

Do you begin to think it a difficult task to select labourers for this *great* harvest? Ministers are called ambassadors, and they receive their commission from above. There is a ministerial baptism. The Lord Jesus Christ "breathed on his disciples, and said, Receive ye the Holy Ghost," &c. "Go ye into all the world, and preach my gospel to every creature." God said to Isaiah, "Who will go for us?" Then said Isaiah, "Here am I, send me." The mantle of Elijah was cast over Elisha—Stephen was full of faith and of the Holy Ghost. When God called Jeremiah to the work of the ministry, he felt the burden of the Lord upon him, and said, "Ah! Lord God! I cannot speak, for I am a child." The answer of the Lord was, "Say not that thou art a child, for thou shalt go," &c.

I shall give you some leading features of the usages among the primitive Methodists, when a person offered himself as a candidate for the ministry;—Does he give satisfactory evidence that he is born of God? Does he evidence it by his life and conversation? Has he any distinguishing marks, that God designs him for that high calling, in love, zeal, gifts, knowledge of the Scripture, and deadness to the world, and the things of the world? Is he willing (if sent) to go to the ends of the earth, to call after poor sinners? Has he had a deep travail of soul for the work, and has he received an evidence from God, that he is commissioned as an ambassador? Are sinners awakened and converted, and does the church cordially receive him? I do not ask how many languages he understands, or whether he can solve the problems of Euclid. Bunyan and Abbot had very little learning; but the power of God accompanied them. It is true the ministry is a profession, and a learned profession too; but it never was designed as a step either to worldly honour, ease, or riches. You ask, what I mean by a learned profession? I mean this—the person who has an assurance from God that he is designed for that great work, whether he has a larger or smaller share of literary attainments, must turn his whole attention to his new calling. Knowing how to navigate a ship, or to solve the most difficult question in algebra, has very little to do with the cure of souls. Let him first look into his own heart, and learn the devices of Satan; let him study the nature of the fallen race, of those to whom he is sent. Let him study the holy Scriptures, the nature of redemption, salvation by faith, and its effects. Let him ask God for a knowledge of the best methods to bring souls to Christ. He should be deep and fervent in prayer. He may pay attention to elocution, and he must be sure to let no impure word or sentence proceed from his lips. The pulpit is the place for purity. The candidates in divinity may innocently and usefully aspire after every species of knowledge which is allied to the ministry, from the first rudiments of his native language, to other languages and the sciences; but at the same time he should value most of all, a holy, heavenly walk with God; and to have that holy anointing, and to maintain his commission, and to become instrumental in bringing many souls to Christ, he should consider as the essential parts of his work.

If a minister is faithful to God, to himself, and to the people, he will have very little time for unprofitable conversation or amusement. My inquiry is, Has God set the young man apart for this work? Is he faithful in the work, and that without any sinister motive? If so, he will assuredly be blessed of God, and will have many precious sheaves to bring with him to glory. I am speaking of the Methodists. Let other denominations look to their own concerns—my business is principally with ourselves. I fear we are not as attentive to this part of our duty as we should be; I mean in the selection of suitable labourers in our Lord's harvest. When we were a poor despised people; a people almost unknown in the world, we were not in much danger of imposition, but now we are spreading far and wide; and although in the aggregate we are not overburdened with riches, worldly influence, or ministerial emolument, yet there are grades in society who might think themselves greatly advanced, especially since there always has been a great passion among Christians, as well as among Jews and pagans, to wear the sacerdotal garment. Even king Henry VIII was not satisfied until he was accounted head of the church. Therefore I think great care should be taken with regard to the admission of persons to so high a station in the church; for one unsanctified minister might do more hurt than the good done by two sanctified ones could counterbalance.

Once more:—to be a real minister of Jesus Christ, is among the greatest honours that can be conferred on man this side eternity. What! to have an embassy from heaven committed to him! What! to be commissioned from God to say to the fallen race of Adam, "I pray you in Christ's stead, be ye reconciled to God." Oh how weighty the charge; how great the responsibility! We should as much as possible lay aside all worldly care and business, and give ourselves wholly to the work of the ministry; and in order thereto, the people ought to be attentive in making an ample provision for their ministerial servants and their families. In this blessed work there should be a pleasing reciprocity. Should his congregation be negligent, the pastor should bring himself to a strict examination;—have I been remiss in any part of my duty? Have I done every thing in my power for the good of the church, and have I been diligent in forming the young mind for God? It is said that the pastors of the primitive church knew where every member of their charge lived, and could call each by name, even to the most menial domestic.

How can a shepherd leave his flock for weeks together on trivial occasions? Should we neglect our charge, we need not think it strange if they neglect us.

We are too remiss in our visitations. I do not mean going to dinner, or tea parties, for these are widely different from pastoral visits. Formerly in these visitations, we called the family together, spoke to each person, and put up suitable prayers for their prosperity; and we seldom left a house at any time without prayer, and without giving the hand to each person, both white and coloured, with a parting exhortation. But to be acceptable and blessed, we ourselves must not only be zealous, but holy, humble, and heavenly minded, feeling what we say.

Can we answer to God for our conduct towards the rising generation? We baptize thousands of little children, and what becomes of them? The primitive ministers and Christians held them as members of Christ's mystical body, saluted them with the church's kiss of peace, gave them the eucharist, and had great patience with their childish inadvertencies, giving them instructions and admonitions, as their tender minds could bear it; and many, very many of them, were drawn, and enlightened, and enabled to take hold of Christ in the promises, and actually to feel themselves put into possession of their promised inheritance, by a living, active faith in the Son of God. When any of them proved stubborn and rebellious, refusing to accept their covenanted blessings, the bread that did not prove salutary, was withheld under suspension; or after long forbearance, when necessity compelled, they were excommunicated. Till thus prohibited, as far as they were capable, they were entitled to all the immunities of the Christian church. Our children should be put in classes, and as soon as they are able to receive religious instruction, they should be met weekly by the minister, or some other suitable person appointed for the occasion. I am well satisfied, that if parents, or guardians, and the church generally, were to take due pains in training the rising generation, instead of running wild, and fashioning themselves after the world as they grow up, their minds would be drawn to God, and most of them would embrace religion.

I have been astonished to see the children of pious parents careless and inattentive in places of worship; and even in time of family prayer, while their parents and others were on their knees, they would sit, or stand, as if they were brought up with no sense of religion, and even without the common civilities of life. The wise man saith, and he saith truly, "Train up a child in the way he should go, and when he is old he will not depart from it." In families, where from their earliest years proper pains have been taken with the children, I have found them in general to be amiable in their tempers, loving and friendly in their deportment, and respectful to religion and religious people. But I have been pained to witness the reverse of this: the children rough, rude, shy, and with very little respect for the religion of their parents, or the church in which they were baptized. Be ye well assured, my brethren, under God much depends on the pious, wise, and heavenly walk and deportment of parents and adult Christians. These are the lambs of the flock, which you must endeavour to gather in. I trust we shall have millions of these little sheaves to bring with us! Oh that parents and ministers may earnestly pray for it, and use every prudential means to accomplish it.

Once more:—I have, in many instances, discovered a deficiency in the distribution of the word.

I have heard sermons in which the *essentials* of the gospel were scarcely touched. Should the preacher have a propensity to display his oratory, and be anxious to turn his periods handsomely, at least his application should be pungent, pointed, and to the purpose. The design of preaching is to awaken sinners, and to bring them to Christ;— to urge believers to the attainment of holiness of heart and life;—to show sinners the turpitude of their hearts and sinfulness of their practice, and to bring them to the foot of the cross, stripped of self and of all self dependence;—to press the old Methodistical doctrines of justification by faith; the direct evidence from God, through faith in the merits of Christ, of the forgiveness of sin; and the adoption into his family. Nor are we to be ashamed of that unfashionable doctrine, Christian perfection:—but we should point out clearly a travail of soul, not only for justification, but for sanctification, and the evidence of it. The holier we are, the more fit we shall be both for this world and that reward which awaits us hereafter.

It is not uncommon for the servants of God to fear that they do but little good, and on that account to weep in secret places. We must not be satisfied with a mere round of duty, or perform duty as a task; but our whole souls must be in the work, and then we shall be happy, and bless God that ever gave us so high a calling. When the Lord calls a man to this work, he calls him for life. We may look round, and see private Christians, as well as other men, flourishing in business, and gaining their tens of thousands, while we are labouring hard, with but a small allowance for our families; and we may have a powerful temptation to locate. Ah! brother touch not! There may be "death in the pot." Remember that you are working in the Lord's harvest field, and that every soul you bring home to glory, will be a star in your crown eternally. The world is fading, and as a shadow will soon flee away. "But we shall wear ourselves out, and what will become of our families?" I have known the widows of Methodist preachers, and their children to the third and fourth generations, and I have admired the good hand of God towards them. The first eighteen or twenty years of my labours were mostly spent in what we call breaking up new ground, where there was very little to be had; during which time I suppose I travelled nearly one hundred thousand miles, and spent the greater part of my little patrimony; yet I never distrusted my blessed Lord, and he provided for my comfort and happiness in old age. And will such a man as you give up the word for fear of wanting a piece of bread? I hope we shall in future lay our plans in wisdom, and execute them with fidelity, that our prospects may brighten more and more. Were I called back fifty years, I would cheerfully retrace them in so glorious a cause, in preference to sitting on a splendid earthly throne. If the love of Christ sweetens toil, how amply will an eternal weight of glory compensate for our little suffering here, when we shall come again with rejoicing, bringing our sheaves with us.

I love Zion, for she is my chief joy.—I pray for the militant church wherever scattered, or of whatever sect; but I engaged to confine myself to the people with whom I have lived, and for whom I have spent the prime of my life.

The Wesleys lived to see a numerous family raised up in England and America; but they have long since gone to rest from their labours. How pleasing the prospect, could they be permitted to visit this earth, and behold the hundreds of thousands who have been gathered into the fold since their departure. I would make honourable mention of Fletcher and Perronet, Coke and Benson; holy and eminent ministers of Christ. They are safe housed with their heavenly Father, where they will sorrow no more. The worth of these venerable fathers in the church cannot easily be estimated:—Coke was the great friend of the missionary cause. Many thousands of the Africans in the West India islands will eternally bless God for his arduous and pious labours, and probably some thousands of them have met him in glory. Shall I mention Walsh, Nelson, Olivers, Pawson, and Mather? I might repeat the names of deceased worthies, until we should have a cloud of witnesses—men laborious and eminently useful in our Lord's great harvest field. They are gathered home, as shocks ripe for their Master's use.

Suppose these heaven-gained spirits were permitted to visit that connection, for whose prosperity they laboured so many years, what would they behold? They would see in England alone more than a thousand Wesleyan chapels, and on the Lord's day more than a million of peaceable people comfortably seated, and hearing the word of life. They might see scores of missionaries going to the four quarters of the globe, to preach the everlasting gospel, and supported by the friends of the Wesleyan cause in England. Suppose likewise that these heralds of the cross were permitted to make some communications of what is passing in their blood-bought world, how pleasing to hear of thousands of ripe sheaves gathered into the garner of God, and that others are daily ripening, and coming home, and that the armies of heaven receive them with acclamations of joy.

Francis Asbury has gone from his hard toil, and reposes with the blessed in Abraham's bosom. He was often afflicted, especially when far advanced in life, and frequently travelled and laboured, when he could scarcely put one foot before the other. A more indefatigable preacher I never knew. Few men have a greater knowledge of human nature than he had. My intimacy with him was of about forty years standing, and I can truly say, that his deportment called for respect wherever he went. He was, I believe, perfectly free from the love of the world. The powers of his mind were strong, and he was great in prayer.

Richard Whatcoat, joint superintendent with Mr. Asbury, was among the very best of men;—a man of a meek and quiet spirit: and he died as he lived, holy and happy.

John Dickens began to travel in 1777. He laboured long in the work, and died of the yellow fever in Philadelphia. He was a wise and a good man, a great and a useful preacher. He commenced our Book Concern, by printing one small hymn book, and that he printed principally with his own private funds. The Book Concern, which he managed with integrity and dignity, before his death acquired a considerable degree of magnitude. He compiled that most excellent Scripture Catechism, which has been so long and so very useful in the church. In his piety he was ardent, in his reproofs pointed, in his discipline rigid; but he was more rigid towards himself than towards others. He was one of my very intimate friends. He left a widow, who is still living, and has experienced much of the care and good providence of God to her and her children.

John Tunnel was a man of slender habit, who in early life wore himself out in the work, and went home to glory. He was a preacher much beloved, and much blest; a sweet singer in Israel; had a soft, clear voice, and his demeanour was humble, meek, and gentle. He was a son of consolation and of affliction; but, blessed be God, we doubt not he has reached the shore of eternal deliverance.

Henry Willis was a light in the church for many years. At a very early period of the work I met him in Virginia, took him by the hand, and thought he would be an acquisition to the church, and so he proved. His habit was slender, though he travelled a number of years; but want of health induced him to take a supernumerary station. After which he married, and located; but his zeal, and his love for the cause, continued to the day of his death, and rendered him a blessing to the people in his neighbourhood. What I have said of brother Willis would be very descriptive of my brother, Richard Garrettson, who entered the ministry about the same time. These have gone as ripe grain to the garner of the Lord, where we also hope to meet them.

William Gill was a man of a remarkably strong mind; and although called from the tailor's board, before he had travelled eight years he might be accounted a learned man, and especially he had improved himself in theology and in philosophy. He entered the travelling connection in 1777. He was great in prayer; his petitions seemed to wing their way to heaven. In his sermons he was deep and spiritual; and had he possessed the voice and utterance of some men, his celebrity would have been great. He was about the middle size, paid very little attention to his dress, and at first sight was rather diminutive in his appearance; but his good sense, usefulness, and piety, called for great respect from those who knew him; and he displayed so much wisdom, and such a profusion of excellent matter in his discourses, as greatly surprised those who had judged of him merely from personal appearance.

I must mention the name of dear Caleb B. Pedicord; for he was an affectionate, good, and useful preacher, and was instrumental in bringing many souls to God. When afflicted with hypochondria, to which he was subject, his mind would be in a state of great dejection; his usefulness would be hid from him; he would doubt his call to preach, and think of returning home. I remember a speech he made in a love feast during the sitting of the conference in Baltimore, which moved the whole assembly. He arose, bathed in tears, and said, "My friends, I have laboured under heavy trials during the past year. I was afraid that I was doing no good, and that I was not called to preach; but a little before I left my circuit, I went to a house, where I met an old negro woman, who told me that what I had said to her when I was there on a former occasion, had been a means of awakening her, and of bringing her to God. 'I bless God,' said she, 'that ever I saw you, for I am now happy in religion.' Oh!" said he, "how greatly did this encourage me; for I thought it was better to gain one soul for Christ, than to gain all the riches in the world; and now," said he "I am greatly encouraged to go forward in the good work, and God being my helper, I will spend the remainder of my days wholly in his service." After this he served the church several years, and then went home to glory.

Shall I mention a Ruff, a Watters, a Boyer, a Mair, an Ellis, a Bruce, a Poytress, a Baxter, a Tatum, a Hartley, &c. These were early in the field of labour; and although I had the honour of entering it a little before them, they have been gathered home long before me.

In looking over our Magazine, I saw a sweet account of our worthy brother Beauchamp, which reminds me of a paragraph in my Journal, which relates to his family. It may not be unsuitable to transcribe it here. "In the year 1778, when I was forming what was called Dover circuit, in the state of Delaware, Mr. Smethers, a respectable old gentleman, came out to hear the word, got his heart touched, and invited me to come to Dover, and preach in the academy, which I promised to do on sabbath afternoon. When, accompanied by three or four young converts, I came to the place, a large concourse of people had assembled, and I was surrounded by a mob, who swore they would put me in prison; for I was, they said, a tory. The magistrate of the town, with a Mr. Prior, a gentleman of influence, fearing there would be trouble, ran to my assistance, pressed through the crowd, took me by the hand, led me to a table, set without the door for me to stand on, and said, "I am the mayor of this town; preach, and I will stand by you." I chose for my subject the parable of the barren fig tree. God was with me; his power arrested the people, for there seemed to be but few dry eyes in the assembly; and the jailer's wife, who sat at her window more than a quarter of a mile off, was awakened, shortly after found peace, and became a heavenly minded woman. Even the mob wept, and expressed their sorrow for their behaviour. I soon joined a large society in the place, and this was the beginning of a great work in and about Dover.

"Some time after this, Mrs. Beauchamp (William Beauchamp's grandmother) invited me to preach at her house. I think she had nine children, eight of whom were married, and all of them, with their husbands and wives, staid to dinner. A large table was spread, at which, I think, nineteen of us sat down. The old lady sat at the head of her table weeping: "Here," said she, "are all my children;—they are happy in religion, and going to heaven; while I am a poor hard hearted, self righteous sinner." She was a true mourner, and it seemed as if the power of grace in this revival had reached the whole family. William Beauchamp, the subject of the memoir, at this time was about six or seven years old, and probably dates his first religious impressions as early as that period.

How shall we sufficiently praise God for the many, many thousands, who within the last eighty or ninety years have been brought into gospel liberty, either directly or indirectly, by the instrumentality of John Wesley. In looking over the minutes of our annual conferences, I should conjecture, that more than a thousand names, which have appeared on them since mine was first placed there, no longer appear there. What has become of them? Thank God, a goodly number wore themselves out in the good cause, ripened, and were gathered in. There are now more than ten thousand preachers, travelling and local, in the Wesleyan connection, in Europe, Asia, Africa, and America, and in the islands of the seas, and more than half a million in membership; and how many, can we reasonably conjecture, have been ripened by grace, and called home, since Mr. Wesley first began to preach salvation by faith, and a direct witness of the Spirit of the forgiveness of sins? Would you say two millions?—or suppose but one million—would not even this be a sufficient inducement to encourage us in the great work, especially when we view one soul as of more value than all the wealth and honour that this world can afford? The little treasure which, I trust, I have laid up in heaven, I would not part with for the riches of a thousand such worlds as this.

I must step without the particular pale of my own church, to speak of that numerous body of Christians who were marshalled under Mr. Whitefield and Lady Huntington. To these in their commencement Mr. Wesley bore the interesting relation of father. We likewise view with pleasure that body of men, who are called the evangelical clergy of the national church. We hear with joy of their preaching salvation by faith, and of their zeal in the promotion of Bible, missionary, and Sunday school societies. When did this change take place? Will not even prejudice allow, that the religious excitement, which has been spreading more and more, and awakening the energies of labourers in different sections of the Lord's vineyard, began through the instrumentality of the Wesleys? We see them taking the lead, and then you may observe an Ingham, a Hervey, a White-field, a Morgan, a Perronet, a Fletcher, a Coke, and several others, all ministers of the established church, making a powerful stand against the powers of darkness. We should not think it strange to find many hundreds of evangelical ministers in that establishment. My dear brethren, let the work spread to the ends of the earth, and let hundreds of millions be brought into gospel light and liberty.

Have we done no good in America but among our own people? I have heard it said, and that by those who were not very friendly to us, that we drive more to other churches than we draw to our own. Well, if in the order of God, let it be so: if they are safe housed; if they ripen, and get safe to heaven, there will be but one fold there, and one Shepherd; and though we could not perfectly harmonize on earth, there will be no discord in that sweet world of peace and joy.

CORRESPONDENCE RELATING TO GARRETTSON'S
IMPRISONMENT AND RELEASE

Feb. 19, 1780 (Thomas White Kent Co. Delaware State Deposition)

I hereby certify to whom it may Concern that I am well acquainted with Mr. Fr. Garrettson and that he has been an Inhabitant of this State for near Eighteen month Last past during which time he has supported an unblemished character and Generally supposed to be a man of Great Piety, and I believe has Complied with the Laws of the State in Every Instance so far as related to a Preacher of the Gospel.

Feb. 29, 1780 James Shaw to Governor and Council.

I hereby Certify that on the 26 Instant a Certain Person who calls himself by the name of Freeborn Garrettson (was brought before me the subscriber one of the Justices assigned to keep the Peace for Dorchester County) as a Fugitive Disaffected Person, from the State of Delaware, on Examination, he Acknowledged he had not taken the oath of Fidelity to his State, or either of the United States, and also refused to take the oath Prescribed by the General Assembly of the State of Maryland, in an Act entitled an Act for the better Security of the Government. I therefore Committed him to the Jail of Dorchester County, which Jail he is now Confined in.

Mar. 8 (Deposition of Thomas Hill Airey before Allen Quynn)

I hereby certify that I was in the Dellaware State some time last fall and having heared Mr. F. Garrettson Preach a Sermon was much pleas'd with it, on conversing with him afterwards he informed me he was born in the State of Maryland and that he had been a Preacher of the Gospel in this and the adjoining States for near Nine years last past that the usual places he preach'd at when I saw him were in Somerset, the head of Dorsett, and Talbot Counties in this State and some part of Dellaware State, that his residence was in the Dellaware State generally.

On being thus informed knowing that the Gospel was more wanted in my Neighbour-hood than any place I knew, I requested he would come and Visset our part of the County, on his coming he was much approved of, after he had preached, enquiry was made and it appeared he had not taken the Oath to this State but he produced good authority that he had complied with everything required by the State he belonged to. I really believe him to be a true friend of this County although he appears to have some scruples to take the Oath prescribed by this State.

Thurs. 9 Mar. 1780. Present as on Yesterday.

By a Certificate transmitted to this Board by James Shaw one of the Justices of the Peace of Dorchester County in the State of Maryland, it appears that F. Garrettson was carried before him as a Disaffected Fugitive from the State of Delaware, who on Examination by him acknowledged he had not taken the Oath of Fidelity to his State or either of the United States and refused to take the Oath prescribed by the Act of the General Assembly of Maryland entitled an Act for the better Security of the Government, Where upon he committed him to the Gaol of Dorchester County. Ordered that the said Freeborn Garrettson be released from his Confinement on his entering into a Bond in the Penalty of 20,000 with good and sufficient Security for his Personal Appearance before the Executive Council of the State of Delaware within 20 days from the Date of the Bond and also to return a Certificate from the said Executive Council of his having made his Personal Appearance before them within 30 days from the Date of the said Bond.

Council to James Woolford 3rd, Esquire Sheriff of Dorchester Co. Sir It appears to this Board by the Certificate of James Shaw that a certain Freeborn Garrettson has been apprehended as a disaffected Fugitive from the State of Delaware and committed to the Jail of Dorchester County . . . We have determined to release the prisoner, on his giving Bond with good and sufficient Surety in the sum of 20 thousand pounds, to make his personal appearance before the Executive of the State of Delaware within 20 days after the Date of such Bond; and on complying with the Terms specified in the Bond herewith sent, the Blanks of which Bond we request you have filled up and legally executed previous to giving a Discharge and transmitted to this Board.

Mar. 13, 1780 Freeborn Garrettson's Bond to the State of Maryland.

Know all Men by these Presents that We Freeborn Garrettson of the State of Delaware and Thomas Hill Airey of the State of Maryland are held and firmly bound unto the State of Maryland in the sum of Twenty thousand Pounds common Money to be paid to the said State of Maryland. To the which Payment well and truly to be made and done We bind ourselves and each of us, our and each of our Heirs Executors and Administrators jointly and severally firmly by these Presents Sealed with our Seals and Dated this thirteenth day of March Seventeen hundred and Eighty.

Whereas the above bound Freeborn Garrettson an Inhabitant of the State of Delaware has taken shelter in Dorchester County Within this State and for not complying with the Act of the said State for the better Security of the Government was by James Shaw one of the Justices of Dorchester County, committed to the Gaol of the said County.

Now the Condition of the above Obligation is such that if the above bound Freeborn Garrettson shall within Twenty Days from the Date hereof depart this State, and make his Personal Appearance before the Executive Council of the State of Delaware at what place soever they may be sitting within Twenty Days from the Date hereof and also cause to be returned to the Governor and Council of the State of Maryland aforesaid of his Personal Appearance before them as aforesaid within Thirty Days from the Date hereof, then the above Obligation to be void else to remain in full force and virtue in Law.

Frebn. Garrettson Tho Hill Airey

Mar. 20, 1780 Cesar Rodney, Dover, Delaware State Certificate

It is hereby certified, That agreeable to the Tenour of a Bond entered into by Freeborn Garrettson in compliance with an order of the Honourable Council in the State of Maryland, enjoining his Personal Appearance within a limited term, before the Executive Power of the State of Delaware; the said Freeborn Garrettson a Preacher among the People called Methodists, who hath a considerable time past resided chiefly in this state, and under its Protection; did upon the Day of the date hereof, appear in Person before me.

Apr. 5, 1780

It appears from a Certificate of the President of the State of Delaware of the 20th of March last Deposited with this Board, that Freeborn Garrettson who hath given Bond for his Personal Appearance before the Executive Council of the said State of Delaware, that the Tennor of the said Bond is complyed with. It is therefore Ordered that the same be Cancelled.

Source: Steiner, B. C., editor *Archives of Maryland—Journal and Correspondence of the State Council of Maryland (1779-1780)*. Baltimore, Maryland Historical Society, 1924 Vol. XLIII, pp. 103-104; 130; 430; 439; 444-445.

APPENDIX TWO

Garrettson in both his printed Journal as well as the Manuscript Journal has made occasional errors in the date. By using a perpetual calendar the correct date has been entered in brackets after the Garrettson date.

PRINTED JOURNAL
September 12 [13], 1778
Monday, September 13 [14]
19th [20] of September, 1778
Monday, September 20 [21]
Monday, September 25 [28]
Sunday, June 7 [6] 1779
Monday, June 8 [7]
Tuesday, June 9 [8]
Wednesday, June 10 [9]
Thursday, June 11 [10]
Sunday, June 14 [13]
Sunday, June 21 [20]
Sunday, June 28 [27]
Ms. JOURNAL NOTE
Monday, June 15 [14] 1779
June 16 [15]
June 17 [16]
June 18 [17]
June 20 [19]
Ms. JOURNAL NOTE
Monday, June 22 [21] 1779
June 23 [22]
June 24 [23]
June 25 [24]
June 26 [25]
June 27 [26]
June 29 [28]
Tuesday, June [29]
Wednesday June [30]
Friday [July 2, 1779]
Wednesday 8 [July 7]
June 10 [9]
June 11 [10]
PRINTED JOURNAL
Sunday, July 5 [4] 1779
July 6 [5]
July 8 [7]
July 12 [11]

Ms. JOURNAL NOTE
Monday, June 22 [21] 1779
June 23 [22]
June 24 [23]
June 25 [24]
June 26 [25]
June 27 [26]
June 29 [28]
Tuesday, June [29]
Wednesday, June [30]
Friday [July 2, 1779]
Wednesday 8 [July 7]
July 10 [9]
July 11 [10]
PRINTED JOURNAL
Sunday, July 5 [4] 1779
July 6 [5]
July 8 [7]
July 12 [11]
Ms. JOURNAL NOTE
Tuesday 4 [3] August 1779
August 5 [4]
Ms. JOURNAL NOTE
Sunday, October 2 [3]
October 3 [4]
October 4 [5]
October 5 [6]
October 10 [11]
October 11 [12]
October 13 [14]
October 14 [15]
October 16 [17]
Ms. JOURNAL NOTE
Wednesday, March 1 (1780]
Ms. JOURNAL NOTE
Monday June 22 [21] 1779
June 23 [22]
June 24 [23]
June 25 [24]

June 26 [25]
June 27 [26]
June 29 [28]
Tuesday, June [29]
Wednesday, June [30]
Friday [July 2, 1779]
Wednesday 8 [July 7]
July 10 [9]
July 11 [10]
PRINTED JOURNAL
Sunday, July 5 [4] 1779
July 6 [5]
July 8 [7]
July 12 [11]
Ms. JOURNAL NOTE
Tuesday 4 [3] August 1779
Ms. JOURNAL NOTE 5 [4]
Sunday, October 2 [3]
October 3 [4]
October 4 [5]
October 5 [6]
October 10 [11]
October 13 [14]
October 16 [17]
Ms. JOURNAL NOTE
Wednesday, March 1 [1780]
Ms. JOURNAL NOTE
Wednesday 15 [March 1780]
Ms. JOURNAL NOTE
Sunday 1 [2] 1780
April, Monday 2 [3] 1780
Wednesday 12
PRINTED JOURNAL
Sunday, June 3 [4] 1780
Tuesday, June 5 [6]
Ms. JOURNAL NOTE
Friday 8 [9] June 1780
June 9 [10]
PRINTED JOURNAL
Sunday, June 17 [18]
Thursday, June 21 [22]
Sunday, June 24 [25]
Ms. JOURNAL NOTE
Tuesday 12 [13] June 1780

Thursday 14 [15]
Saturday 16 [17]
Ms. JOURNAL NOTE
Wednesday, June 20 [21]
Ms. JOURNAL NOTE
Tuesday 27 [28] June
Friday 30 [29]
Ms. JOURNAL NOTE
Sunday 9 [July 1780]
Ms. JOURNAL NOTE
Monday 24 [July 1780]
PRINTED JOURNAL
Tuesday August 2 [1] 1780
Ms. JOURNAL NOTE
Thursday, November 1 [2] 1780
November 2 [3]
November 3 [4]
November 5 [6]
November 7 [8]
November 9 [10]
November 10 [11]
November 11 [12]
November 12 [13]
November 13 [14]
November 14 [15]
November 17 [18]
November 18 [19]
November 20 [26]
November 30 [uncertain date]
Monday, December 4 [1780]
PRINTED JOURNAL
24th [22] January 1781
Tuesday 25th [23]
26th [24]
Ms. JOURNAL NOTE
Friday 27 [26]
Tuesday 31 [30] 1781
Saturday 25 [24] February 1781
February 26 [25]
February 27 [26]
Wednesday 28 [Tuesday 27th Feb.?]
Friday 30 [Wednesday 28th Feb.?]
PRINTED JOURNAL
Wednesday 15 [14] [Feb. 1781]

Wednesday 22 [21]
Friday 24 [23]
February 26 [25]
Tuesday, March 1 [Thursday
    May 1, 1781]
Saturday, March 20 [Tuesday]
Sunday 21 [Wednesday]
Monday 22 [Thursday]
Ms. JOURNAL NOTE
Wednesday, March 15, 1781
    [March 14]
Thursday 16 [15]
Friday 17 [16]
Monday 20 [19]
Wednesday 22 [21]
Thursday 23 [22]
Friday 24 [23]
Tuesday April 23 [24]
Wednesday April 24 [25]
Sunday May 5 [6] 1781
May 6 [7]
May 7 [8]
May 12 [11]
May 13 [12]
May 15 [14]
May 16 [15]
May 22 [21]
Sunday 20 [appears to be out of
    sequence]
PRINTED JOURNAL
Saturday and Sunday [1781]
    August 12 [11] & 13 [12]
Friday 25 [24]
Ms. Journal NOTE
July 1st [1781]
Tuesday [Wednesday] 4 July
Wednesday [Thursday] 5 July
Friday July 7 [6]
July 8 [7]
July 9 [8]
July 10 [9]
July 11 [10]
July 12 [11]
July 13 [12]

July 14 [13]
July 15 [14]
July 16 [15]
July 16 [15]
July 17 [16]
July 18 [17]
July 19 [18]
July 20 [19]
July 21 [20]
July 22 [21]
July 23 [22]
July 24 [23]
July 25 [24]
July 26 [25]
July 28 [27]
July 29 [28]
Tuesday August 1 [July 31]
Wednesday August 2 [1] [1781]
August 4 [3]
August 5 [4]
August 6 [5]
August 5 [4]
August 6 [5]
August 9 [8]
August 10 [9]
August 11 [10]
August 12 [11]
August 13 [12]
August 14 [13]
August 16 [15]
August 17 [16]
August 19 [18]
August 20 [19]
August 21 [20]
August 22 [21]
August 23 [22]
August 24 [23]
August 25 [24]
August 26 [25]
August 27 [26]
August 28 [27]
August 29 [28]
August 30 [29]
September 3 [1781]

PRINTED JOURNAL
January 29 [1782]
Ms. JOURNAL NOTE
Monday 31 [October 1, 1781]
Tuesday, October 1 [2]
Thursday 10 [11]
October 11 [12]
October 12 [13]
October 13 [14]
October 14 [15]
Tuesday 15 [16]
October 16 [17]
October 18 [19]
October 19 [20]
October 21 [22]
October 22 [23]
October 23 [24]
October 25 [26]
October 28 [29]
October 29 [30]
October 30 [31]
Thursday, November 1 [1781]
Sunday 26 [27] [January 1782]
Saturday & Sunday [Feb. 2, 3, 1782]
Sunday, March 3 [1782]
PRINTED JOURNAL
Sunday 5 [May 1782]
Ms. JOURNAL NOTE
March 1782—*heading*
Friday May 3 [1782]
Saturday, June 1 [1782]
Ms. JOURNAL NOTE
Sunday, February 1 [1784]
Friday [February 6]
Saturday [7]
Sunday [8]
Monday [9]
Monday, March 1 [1784]
Tuesday 4th of May [1784]
Monday 18 [May 17]
Tuesday 19 [18]
Wednesday [19]
Tuesday, May 26 [25, 1784]
Tuesday, June 1 [1784]

Sunday, July 4 [1784]
Sunday, August 1 [1784]
PRINTED JOURNAL
February [1785]
Ms. JOURNAL NOTE
Tuesday [May 31]
Wednesday [June 1, 1785]
PRINTED JOURNAL
Sunday, April 16 [April 15, 1787]
Monday 24 [April 23]
Sunday, May 14 [13]
Friday 19 [18]
Saturday 20 [19]
Sunday May 28 [27] 1787
Tuesday 30 [29]
Ms. JOURNAL NOTE
1787
Sunday, 14 May [13]
May 17 [16]
May 18 [17]
May 19 [18]
June 1, 1787 [May 30]
June 2 [1] 1787
June 5 [4]
June 6 [5]
June 13 [12]
June 18 [17]
July 2 [1787]
PRINTED JOURNAL
Wednesday 31 [30] 1787
June 3 [2] 1787
June 4 [3]
June 11 [10]
Ms. JOURNAL NOTE
Wednesday [July 10, 1787]
July 12 [11]
July 15 [14]
July 16 [15]
July 17 [16]
July 18 [17]
July 19 [18]
July 20 [19]
July 21 [20] 1787
July 22 [21] & 23 [22]

July 24 [23]
Ms. JOURNAL NOTE
Sunday, June 14 [1789]
July 1 [1789]
Monday 17 [August 1789]
Sunday, October 3 [4] 1789
Monday October 4 [5]
October 5 [6]
October 6 [7]
October 7 [8]
October 10 [11]
October 11 [12]

October 18 [19]
October 19 [20]
October 20 [21]
October 24 [25]
October 25 [26]
October 27 [28]
October 28 [29]
December 4 [1789]
PRINTED JOURNAL
Wednesday [July 1, 1789]
Wednesday, August 19, [1789]
Thursday, November 19, [1789]

APPENDIX THREE
A RECORD OF THE CONFERENCE APPOINTMENTS
OF
FREEBORN GARRETTSON

1776, Frederick circuit, Maryland, with M. Rodda.

1777, Brunswick cir., Virginia, with Wm. Watters and John Tunnel; also, Roanoke Circuit.

1778, Kent cir., on the Peninsula, with Joseph Hartley, John Littlejohn, and John Cooper.

1779, State of Delaware cir., with Francis Asbury, Caleb B. Peddicord, Lewis Alfrey, M. Debruler.

1780, Baltimore cir., Md., with Daniel Ruff and Joshua Dudley.

1781, Sussex cir., Va., with James Morris.

1782, Somerset cir., Md., with James Magary.

1783-84, Talbot cir., with John Major and William Thomas.

1785, (ordained deacon and elder) Shelburne, Nova Scotia.

1786, associate "elder" in Nova Scotia with James O. Cromwell.

1787, "elder" of a district on the Md. Peninsula, and a few months previous to the conference in October, 1788, in New York with John Dickins and Woolman Hickson.

1788, "elder," Hudson River and Lake Champlain District.

1789, New York District, Long Island to Lake Champlain.

1790-92, Hudson River District

1793, "elder," Philadelphia District, and pastor Philadelphia station.

1794, New York District.

1795, "elder" Western Mass. and Eastern New York.

1796-97, New London, Pittsfield, and New York District, with Sylvester Hutchinson, associate.

1798, Albany District.

1799, New Jersey District.

1800-03, New York District.

1804, Rhinebeck.

1805, New York, with N. Snethen, A. Hunt, John Wilson.

1806, New York, with T. Bishop, S. Crowell, John Wilson.

1807, Conference Missionary.

1808, Rhinebeck.

1809-10, Conference Missionary.

1811-14, New York District.

1815, without appointment.

1816, Conference Missionary.

1817, Bridgeport cir., with A. Hunt.

1818-20, supernumerary, without appointment.

1821-27, Conference Missionary.

Source: Compiled from Minutes, Journals, and other sources.

MANUSCRIPT SOURCES

I. THE JOURNALS OF FREEBORN GARRETTSON

The Journals extend from 1752 to June 6, 1826. From 1752 until the Spring of 1791 the account is fairly complete for the Journals for these years were published in 1791 at the request of John Wesley. They appeared under the title: *The Experiences and Travels of the Rev. Freeborn Garrettson.* Excerpts from this publication were reprinted in *The Arminian Magazine.* London, G. Paramore, 1794. Vol. XVII, pp. 3-9; 57-62; 113-119; 169-175; 225-231; 281-287; 337-343; 393-398; 449-454; 505-511. The printed Journal, however, is a much more polished production than the MS Journals indicating that Garrettson edited and rewrote his Journal for publication. One MS available entitled *Journal till '79* seems to be a fragment of the MS submitted to the publisher. There is also one item entitled *Notes to the Printed Journal* which were, obviously, Garrettson's addenda to be included if the Journal was ever revised for publication. John Dickins offered two printings in 1791. This was the first truly American item on the book lists of early Methodism.

Of the period from 1752-91 only two years are unaccounted, 1786, and 1788. 1786 represented part of the time spent in the Nova Scotian mission and 1788 the initial year of his pioneer effort up the Hudson River Valley.

After 1791 the MS Journals become fragmentary. There is no reason for believing that they have been lost, but rather that Garrettson became more irregular in keeping his personal record.

The Journals for 1792-93 are fairly complete, but from 1793 until 1809 there is no account of Garrettson's work. Very brief notes are available for 1805 and 1807, the latter appearing in the Journal for 1790-91. There is a partial record for 1809 and nothing for the years between or after until 1817. From 1817 until 1821 there is record of his chief work. There is no record for 1822-23. From March, 1824 to June 6, 1826 the Journal was kept, but with more emphasis upon special interests than upon day-by-day happenings. There is no Journal for the period from June 6, 1826 until his death September 26, 1827.

The Journals provide abundant material relative to Garrettson's personal and ministerial life, and offer great help for understanding the development of early American Methodism.

A CHRONOLOGICAL LISTING OF THE MS JOURNALS

 I. Journal for 1752-1777.
 II. Journal till '79. Possible fragment of the MS from which the 1791 Journal was published.
 III. Journal for 1778-1779.
 IV. Journal for 1779 (May-June).
 V. Journal for 1779-1780 (Sept. 29-July 25).
 VI. Journal for 1780-1781 (Jul. 27-Oct. 23).
 VII. Journal for 1781-1782 (Nov. thru Oct.).
 VIII. Journal for 1782-1783 (Oct. thru Dec.).
 IX. Journal for 1784-1785 (Jan. thru June 19).
 X. Journal for 1787 (Apr. 10-Jul. 24).
 XI. Journal for 1789-1790 (May 26-Jan. 20).
 XII. Journal for 1790 (June-Sept.).
 XII. Journal for 1791 (May-Dec.).
 XIV. Notes to the Printed Journal.
 XV. Journal for 1792-1793 (Dec.-Feb.).
 XVI. Journal for 1793 (Feb.-May).
 XVII. Journal for 1805 (Mar.-Apr.).
 XVIII. Journal for 1807 (Apr.-Jul.) to be found in Journal for 1791.
 XIX. Journal for 1809 (Jul.-Aug.).
 XX. Journal for 1817-1821 (Jul.-Feb.).
 XXI. Journal for 1824-1826 (Mar.-June).

BIBLIOGRAPHY

PUBLISHED WORKS

Garrettson, Freeborn. *A Dialogue Between Do-Justice and Professing Christian.*
Wilmington: Peter Brynberg, 1820.
Garrettson on Slavery.

—— *A Letter to the Rev. Lyman Beecher containing Strictures and Animadversions
on the pamphlet entitled 'An Address of the Charitable Society for the
Education of Indigent Pious Young Men for the Ministry of the Gospel.'*
New York: J. C. Totten, 1816.

—— *The Experiences and Travels of Mr. Freeborn Garrettson, Minister of the
Methodist Episcopal Church in North America.* Philadelphia: Parry
Hall, 1791.
Part of Garrettson's Journals published at John Wesley's request
Excerpts of this were reprinted in *The Arminian Magazine*, London:
G. Paramore, 1794. Vol. XVII, pp. 3-9; 57-62; 113-119; 169-175;
225-231; 281-287; 337-343; 393-398; 449-454; 505-511.

The Methodist Magazine. Vol. 8, No. 6. New York: N. Bangs and J. Emory.
June and July, 1825.
Two issues print one of Garrettson sermons.

BIOGRAPHY

Bangs, Nathan. *The Life of the Rev. Freeborn Garrettson.* New York. J. Emory
and B. Waugh, 1832.
Garrettson journals woven together.

Garrettson, Catherine. "Memoir of the Rev. Freeborn Garrettson." *The
Methodist Magazine.* Vol. XI, No. 3, pp. 93-99. New York: N. Bangs and
J. Emory. March, 1828.

Simpson, Robert Drew. *Freeborn Garrettson: American Methodist Pioneer.*
Diss. Drew University, 1954.

Smith, George G. "Freeborn Garrettson," *The Methodist Review.* Vol.
XLI, No. 1, pp. 37-43. Mar.-Apr. 1895.

Tipple, Ezra S. *Freeborn Garrettson.* New York: Eaton and Mains, 1910.

CONTEMPORARY SOURCE MATERIAL

Asbury, Francis. *Journal of Rev. Francis Asbury.* New York: Lane and
Scott, 1852. Vols. II, III.

Christian Advocate and Journal, Vol. II, No. 5. New York: N. Bangs and J.
Emory. Oct. 5, 1827.
Freeborn Garrettson's Obituary.

Coke, Thomas. *Extract of the Journals of the Rev. Thomas Coke.* London:
G. Whitfield, 1793.

Hibbard, B. *Memoirs of the Life and Travels of B. Hibbard.* New York:
Piercy and Reed, 1843.

414

Lee, Jesse. *A Short History of the Methodists in the United States of America.* Baltimore: Magill and Clime, 1810.

The Methodist Magazine. Vol. 2, pp. 299, 300. New York: J. Soule and T. Mason. August, 1819.
> Freeborn Garrettson noted as one of the founders of Wesleyan Seminary in New York City.

The Methodist Magazine and Quarterly Review. Vol. 12, No. 3, pp. 341-360, New York: J. Emory and B. Waugh, July, 1830.
> Review of Nathan Bang's biography of Freeborn Garrettson.

Minutes of the Annual Conferences, etc. *(1773-1828).* New York: T. Mason and G. Lane, 1840. Vol. I.

Minutes of the General Conference, etc. *(1790-1836).* New York: Carlton and Phillips, 1855. Vol. I.

Richey, Matthew. *A Memoir of the Late Rev. William Black.* Halifax, Nova Scotia: William Cunnabell, 1839.

Steiner, B. C. Editor, *Archives of Maryland—Journal and Correspondence of the State Council of Maryland 1779-1780.* Baltimore: Maryland Historical Society, 1924. Vol. XLIII.

Stevens, Abel. *Sketches From the Study of a Superannuated Itinerant.* New York: Carlton and Phillips, 1853.

Wesley, John. *Wesley's Works.* London: Wesleyan Conference Office, 1872. Vol. VI; XIII, pp. 69-74.

SECONDARY MATERIALS

Barclay, Wade Crawford. *Early American Methodism,* New York: The Board of Missions and Church Extension of the Methodist Church. 1949. Vol. I.

Barker, C. A. *The Background of the Revolution in Maryland.* New Haven: Yale University Press, 1940.

Broune, N. M. *A Historical Sketch of the Methodist Episcopal Church in Somerset County from 1778-1878.* Salisbury, Md.: Advertiser Book and Job Office, 1878.

Buckley, James. *A History of Methodists in the United States.* New York: The Christian Literature Co. 1896.

Buckman, David Lear. *Old Steamboat Days on the Hudson River.* New York: The Grafton Press. 1907.

Cassell, Rev. Leonard. *Rise and Progress of Methodism on Sam's and Pipe Creeks.* Baltimore: Methodist Printery, 1895.

Collection of the Dutchess County Historical Society. ed. Helen W. Reynolds, Poughkeepsie: F. B. Howard. 1930.

Faulkner, Harold V. *American Political and Social History.* New York: F. S. Crofts and Co. 1944.

(Garrettson, Mary R.) *A Winter At Wood Lawn,* New York: Carlton and Porter, 1857.

(Garrettson, Mary R.)   *Little Mabel and Her Sunlit Home.* New York: Carlton and Porter, 1860.

Greene, E. B.   *The Revolutionary Generation 1764-1790.* New York: The Mac-Millan Co. 1943. Vol. IV. *A History of American Life* series.

Gewehr, Wesley M.   *The Great Awakening in Virginia, 1740-1790.* Durham, N.C.: Duke University Press. 1930.

Historical Sketch of the Wethersfield M. E. Church. Published for the Society, 1882.

Hunting, I.   *Eearly Methodism in North Dutchess and Pine Plains.* (no publisher; no date.)

Hurst, John Fletcher.   *The History of Methodism.* New York: Eaton and Mains, 1933. Vol. IV.

Ketcham, W. C.   *Pages of Methodism.* Mt. Kisco, New York: 1882.

Kitchen, W. C.   *Centenary History of the First M. E. Church, Schenectady, N. Y.* Schenectady: Published by the Official Board of the Church, 1907.

Larrabee, William C.   *Asbury and His Coadjutors.* Cincinnati: Swormstedt and Poet, 1853. Vol. II, pp. 121-173.

Manual and Directory of M. E. Church in Sheffield and Ashley Falls, Mass. (no publisher).

Manual of the M. E. Church of Pittsfield, Mass. Troy, New York: A. W. Scribner, 1864.

Morse, Howard H.   *Historic Old Rhinebeck.* Rhinebeck: Pecantico Printery, 1908.

North, Louise M.   *The Story of the North Branch of the Women's Foreign Missionary Society.* New York: The N. Y. Branch, 1926.

Peck, George.   *Early Methodism Within the Bounds of the Old Genesee Conference.* N. Y.: Carlton and Porter, 1860. Book II.

Raybold, Rev. G. A.   *Reminiscences of Methodism in West Jersey.* New York: Lane and Scott, 1849.

The Rhinebeck Gazette, July 6, 1950.

Reid, J. M.   *Missions and Missionary Society of the Methodist Episcopal Church.* New York: Eaton and Mains, 1895. Vol. I.

Sabine, Lorenzo.   *The American Loyalists.* Boston: Chas. Little and Jas. Brown, 1864. Vol. I. pp. 463, 464.

Seaman, Samuel.   *Annals of New York Methodism.* New York: Hunt and Eaton, 1892.

Shaffer, J. N.   *Methodism in Newburgh, N. Y.* New York: Phillips and Hunt, 1885.

Smith, Philip H.   *General History of Dutchess County.* Pawling: Published by the author, 1877.

Smith, T. Watson.   *History of the Methodist Church in Eastern British America.* Halifax, N. S.: Methodist Book Room, 1877. Vol. I.

Warriner, Edwin.   *Old Sands Street Methodist Episcopal Church of Brooklyn, N. Y.* Phillips and Hunt, 1885.

INDEX

Abbot, Benjamin, 397, 398
Abbottstown, Pa., 184
Aberdeen, Md., 23, 148, 176
Aberdeen Proving Grounds, Md., 1, 145, 148
Abingdon, Md., 22, 146, 255, 303, 314, 324, 326, 328, 339, 340, 349, 350
Abolition Societies, 25
Academy Church, Philadelphia, Pa., 303, 323, 328, 337, 338, 371
Academy, Rhinebeck, N. Y. area, 364
Adams, Brother, 175, 186, 213
Adams, Mass., 282
Africa, 388, 395, 402
African Methodist Church, Philadelphia, Pa., 338
Africans, 231, 268, 303, 327, 391, 400
Airey, Thomas Hill, 95, 96, 97, 100, 155, 170, 171, 174, 178, 220, 237, 239, 256, 404, 405
Airey, Mrs. Thomas, 95, 100, 170, 171, 174
Albany Circuit (N. Y.), 13, 380
Albany, N. Y., 11, 36, 137, 138, 142, 143, 258, 259, 263, 271, 274, 275, 276, 279, 280, 284, 285, 287, 293, 294, 296, 297, 299, 308, 352, 354, 380, 381, 388, 411
Albany, N. Y.: Pearl and Orange Sts., 380
Aldersgate, 2
Alfrey, Lewis, 160, 411
Allegany County (Md.), 148
Allegheny Mountains, 243
Allein. See Alleine.
Alleine, Joseph, 40, 146
Allen, 246
Allen, Mr., 314, 315
Allen Street Church, N. Y. City, 354
Allin, Brother, 190
Allin, Brother, 344
Amelia, Va., 186, 196
Amenia, N. Y., 329
America(n), 3, 4, 6, 7, 12, 17, 23, 36, 43, 75, 104, 122, 145, 146, 147, 148, 150, 158, 246, 247, 249, 251, 252, 334, 351, 381, 382, 386, 388, 389, 390, 391, 392, 393, 394, 395, 400, 402, 403, 412
American Bible Society, 29, 360, 382
American cause, 43, 68
American colonies, viii
American Methodist Society(ies), 4, 5, 6, 7, 21-22

American Revolution, viii, 4, 6, 10, 46, 147, 148, 248, 252, 380, 390, 391, 392
American Society for Colonizing the Free People of Colour of the United States, 26
Ames, Brother, 330
Anabaptist, 203, 212, 213, 230, 256, 258, 259, 261
Anderson, Dr., 320
Angel, Mr., 280
Angus, 235
Annapolis, Md., 145, 233, 340
Annapolis, Nova Scotia, 8, 126, 128, 243, 244, 250, 253
Annual Conference, 16, 28
Antigua, B. W. I., 9, 248
Antinomian, 40, 139, 142, 192, 199, 200, 248, 253, 254, 259
Apostle to New England, 12
Apostle to the North, 132
"the Appeal," 14
Arlington, N. Y., 297
Arminian, 128, 129, 130, 137, 139, 268, 296, 387
Armstrong, General, 14, 321
Arnol, Brother, 193
Asbury, Francis, viii, ix, 3, 4, 5, 6, 7, 9, 11-12, 13, 15, 16, 17, 20-21, 23, 24, 28, 29, 40-41, 68, 69, 73, 76, 94, 98, 103, 104, 108, 118, 119, 120, 122, 124, 135, 136, 146, 147, 148, 150, 151, 155, 157, 158, 159, 160, 167, 169, 170, 171, 172, 173, 174, 175, 176, 188, 189, 196, 201, 203, 205, 222, 230, 232, 240, 243, 246, 249, 250, 257, 264, 265, 275, 276, 328, 356, 380, 381, 382, 383, 388, 390, 391, 392, 393, 397, 400-401, 411
Asbury Church, Wilmington, Del., 324
Ash Grove, N. Y., 138, 258, 264, 283, 381
Asia, 388, 395, 402
Askin, Mrs., 178, 180
Aswell, 271
Atheism, 47
Atlantic Ocean, 28, 352, 395
Avery. See Airey

Baker, Brother, 199
Baker, Dr., 348
Baker, Major, 194
Baker, Mr. and Mrs., 264

417